Essays on Hume, Smith and the Scottish Enlightenment

Edinburgh Studies in Scottish Philosophy

Series Editor: Gordon Graham
Center for the Study of Scottish Philosophy, Princeton Theological Seminary

Scottish Philosophy Through the Ages

This new series will cover the full range of Scottish philosophy over five centuries – from the medieval period through the Reformation and Enlightenment periods, to the nineteenth and early twentieth centuries.

The series will publish innovative studies on major figures and themes. It also aims to stimulate new work in less intensively studied areas, by a new generation of philosophers and intellectual historians. The books will combine historical sensitivity and philosophical substance which will serve to cast new light on the rich intellectual inheritance of Scottish philosophy.

Editorial Advisory Board

Angela Coventry, University of Portland, Oregon
Fonna Forman, University of San Diego
Alison McIntyre, Wellesley College
Alexander Broadie, University of Glasgow
Remy Debes, University of Memphis
John Haldane, University of St Andrews and Baylor University, Texas

Books available

Hume's Sceptical Enlightenment by Ryu Susato
Adam Smith and Rousseau: Ethics, Politics, Economics edited by Maria Pia
  Paganelli, Dennis C. Rasmussen and Craig Smith
Thomas Reid and the Problem of Secondary Qualities by Christopher A. Shrock
Imagination in Hume's Philosophy: The Canvas of the Mind by Timothy
  M. Costelloe
Essays on Hume, Smith and the Scottish Enlightenment by Christopher Berry

Books forthcoming

*Adam Ferguson and the Idea of Civil Society: Moral Science in the Scottish
  Enlightenment* by Craig Smith
Eighteenth-Century Scottish Aesthetics: Not Just a Matter of Taste by Rachel
  Zuckert

www.edinburghuniversitypress.com/series/essp

Essays on Hume, Smith and the Scottish Enlightenment

Christopher J. Berry

EDINBURGH
University Press

Edinburgh University Press is one of the leading university presses in the UK. We publish academic books and journals in our selected subject areas across the humanities and social sciences, combining cutting-edge scholarship with high editorial and production values to produce academic works of lasting importance. For more information visit our website: edinburghuniversitypress. com

Edinburgh University Press Ltd
The Tun - Holyrood Road
12(2f) Jackson's Entry
Edinburgh EH8 8PJ

Typeset in 11/13 Adobe Sabon by
Servis Filmsetting Ltd, Stockport, Cheshire,
and printed and bound in Great Britain.

A CIP record for this book is available from the British Library

ISBN 978 1 4744 1501 9 (hardback)
ISBN 978 1 4744 1502 6 (webready PDF)
ISBN 978 1 4744 1503 3 (epub)

Contents

To Emma, Lucy and Zelda
in the hope that one day they may wonder what their
Grandad got up to

Acknowledgements

I am grateful to the following for permission to reprint material. To the editorial board of *Il Pensiero Politico* to reprint 'James Dunbar and Ideas of Sociality in Eighteenth-Century Scotland' 6 (1973: pp. 188–201) [Chapter 2]; to the University of Texas Press to reprint '"Climate" in the Eighteenth Century: James Dunbar and the Scottish Case' in *Texas Studies in Language and Literature* vol. 16, issue 2, pp. 281–92, © 1974 all rights reserved [Chapter 4]; to the Syndics of Cambridge University Press to reprint with permission 'Sociality and Socialisation' from the *Cambridge Companion to the Scottish Enlightenment* (2003: pp. 243–57) [Chapter 5] and 'Smith and Science' from *The Cambridge Companion to Adam Smith* (2006: pp. 112–35) [Chapter 17]; to the University of Rochester Press to reprint 'Rude Religion: The Psychology of Polytheism in the Scottish Enlightenment', in *New Essays on the Scottish Enlightenment* (2000: pp. 315–34) [Chapter 6]; to Pickering & Chatto, via UK Book Permissions, *Adam Ferguson: Philosophy, Politics and Society* (2009: pp. 143–53, 214–17) [Chapter 7]; to Wiley Global Permissions to reprint 'Hume on Rationality in History and Social Life', *History and Theory* 21 (1982: pp. 234–47) [Chapter 9]; to Imprint Academic for permission to reprint 'Lusty Women and Loose Imagination: Hume's Philosophical Anthropology of Chastity', *History of Political Thought* 24 (2003: pp. 415–32) [Chapter 10]; to Duke University Press, all rights reserved for permission to reprint (2006b) 'Hume and the Customary Causes of Industry, Knowledge and Commerce', *History of Political Economy* 38/2 (2006: pp. 291–317) [Chapter 11] and 'Adam Smith's Science of Human Nature'. *History of Political Economy*, 44/3 (2012: pp. 471–92) [Chapter 20]; to Taylor & Francis via UK Book Permissions to reprint 'Hume and Superfluous Value (or the Problem with Epictetus' Slippers)', in

David Hume's Political Economy (2008: pp. 49–64) [Chapter 13];
to Sage Permissions to reprint 'Science and Superstition: Hume
and Conservatism'. *European Journal of Political Theory* 10/2
(2011: pp. 141–55) [Chapter 14]; to University of Pennsylvania
Press for permission (copyright 1974) to reprint 'Adam Smith's
'"Considerations" on Language', *Journal of the History of Ideas*
35/1 (1974: pp. 130–8) [Chapter 16]; to Edinburgh University
Press for permission to reprint 'Adam Smith: Commerce, Liberty
and Modernity', in *Philosophers of the Enlightenment* (1989:
pp. 113–32) [Chapter 18].

I should also like to express my gratitude to Carol Macdonald
of EUP. It is largely thanks to her support and encouragement that
what began as a casual aside grew into the present work.

Preface

The essays in this volume represent a selection of my work on the
Scottish Enlightenment, written over a period of more than forty
years. My principles for selection were to make available some
early pieces, which were often published in outlets not usually
associated with the Scots, and to collect together more recent
pieces that have appeared in various places. There were, in addition, a couple of negative considerations. I wanted to avoid excessive duplication (though I hope some complementary overlap will
still be detected) and also to exclude some pieces that I judged
(often on balance) as peripheral; that is, I wanted this volume to
have some coherence rather than comprise a more or less random
collection of writings. I also chose to omit some pieces that were
more fully worked up in my books (1997, 2009, 2013). This last
point partly explains some slight unevenness in the contents. The
briefest of the three parts into which this volume is divided is
devoted to Smith and the explanation for that is that he figures
prominently in my 2013 book *The Idea of Commercial Society
in the Scottish Enlightenment*. This further explains that, of the
three new pieces that I include, two (both of them unpublished
lectures) are on Smith; the other is on Hume. In addition to these
three, I have written an opening chapter on the general study
of the Scottish Enlightenment over the period covered by these
essays, related to my own intellectual biography. Also added are
postscripts to each chapter that comment on the provenance of
the essay and refer to some subsequent commentary on them and
more generally on work done subsequently on the subject.

Throughout this book I have standardised the references, in
particular inserting into the original texts and notes a uniform
set of abbreviations. I have also inserted cross references to other
chapters in this volume and to my other writings. On occasion

(especially in Chapters 11 and 12) I have made some excisions to eliminate obvious reiteration. There are some silent corrections of citation locations, style and grammar. Those aside, I have decided to leave the previously published pieces 'as is' (the postscripts attend to where I would or should have said something different).

Series Editor's Introduction

It is widely acknowledged that the Scottish Enlightenment of the eighteenth century was one of the most fertile periods in British intellectual history, and that philosophy was the jewel in its crown. Yet, vibrant though this period was, it occurred within a long history that began with the creation of the Scottish universities in the fifteenth century. It also stretched into the nineteenth and twentieth centuries, as those universities continued to be a culturally distinctive and socially connected system of education and inquiry.

While the Scottish Enlightenment remains fertile ground for philosophical and historical investigation, these other four centuries of philosophy also warrant intellectual exploration. The purpose of this series is to maintain outstanding scholarly study of great thinkers like David Hume, Adam Smith and Thomas Reid, alongside sustained exploration of the less familiar figures who preceded them and the impressive company of Scottish philosophers, once celebrated, now neglected, who followed them.

Gordon Graham

Abbreviations Used in This Book

For full bibliographical details, see the references in the Bibliography.

James Dunbar

EHM   *Essays on the History of Mankind in Rude and Cultivated Ages*, 2nd edn, 1781. Cited by page.

Adam Ferguson

APMP   *Analysis of Pneumatics and Moral Philosophy*. Cited by page.

ECS   *An Essay on the History of Civil Society*, ed. D. Forbes. Cited by page.

IMP   *Institutes of Moral Philosophy*, 3rd edn reprint. Cited by page.

MSS   *The Manuscripts of Adam Ferguson*, ed. V. Merolle (London: Pickering & Chatto).

PMPS   *Principles of Moral and Political Science*, 2 vols (reprinted 1999). Cited by volume, page.

Reflections   *Reflections Previous to the Establishment of a Militia.* Cited by page.

Remarks   *Remarks on a Pamphlet Lately Published by Dr Price.* Cited by page.

Rom   *The History of the Progress and Termination of the Roman Republic*, 5 vols, new edn 1813. Cited by volume, page.

David Hume

DNR	*Dialogues concerning Natural Religion*, ed. N. Kemp Smith. Cited by page.
DP	*A Dissertation on the Passions*, ed. T. Beauchamp. Cited by page.
E	*Essays: Moral, Political and Literary*, ed. E. Miller. Essays in this edition are individually identified and cited by page as follows:
E-AS	'Of the Rise and Progress of the Arts and Sciences'
E-Avarice	'Of Avarice'
E-BG	'Whether the British Government Inclines More to Absolute Monarchy or to a Republic'
E-BT	'Of the Balance of Trade'
E-CL	'Of Civil Liberty'
E-Com	'Of Commerce'
E-CP	'Of the Coalition of Parties'
E-DM	'Of the Dignity or Meanness of Human Nature'
E-El	'Of Eloquence'
E-EW	'Of Essay Writing'
E-FPG	'Of the First Principles of Government'
E-Int	'Of Interest'
E-IP	'Of the Independency of Parliament'
E-IPC	'Idea of a Perfect Commonwealth'
E-JT	'Of the Jealousy of Trade'
E-Life	'My Own Life'
E-LP	'Of the Liberty of the Press'
E-Mon	'Of Money'
E-NC	'Of National Characters'
E-OC	'Of the Original Contract'
E-OG	'Of the Origin of Government'
E-PAN	'Of the Populousness of Ancient Nations'
E-PC	'Of Public Credit'
E-PD	'Of Polygamy and Divorces'
E-PG	'Of Parties in General'
E-PGB	'Of the Parties of Great Britain'
E-PO	'Of Passive Obedience'
E-PrS	'Of the Protestant Succession'
E-PSc	'That Politics may be Reduced to a Science'
E-RA	'Of Refinement in the Arts'
E-RC	'Of some Remarkable Customs'

E-SE	'Of Superstition and Enthusiasm'
E-ST	'Of the Standard of Taste'
E-Sui	'Of Suicide'
E-Tax	'Of Taxes'
E-v	Variants collected at the end of E.
HE	*History of England*, 3 vols (final edn). Cited by volume, page.
Letters	*The Letters of David Hume*, 2 vols, ed. J. Greig. Cited by volume, page.
M	*An Enquiry Concerning the Principles of Morals*, ed. T. Beauchamp. Known as the second *Enquiry*. Cited by chapter, paragraph.
Ab	*An Abstract of a Treatise of Human Nature*, in *T*. Cited by paragraph, page.
NHR	*The Natural History of Religion*, ed. T Beauchamp. Cited by chapter, paragraph/page.
SBNA	*An Abstract of a Treatise of Human Nature*, ed. L. Selby-Bigge and P. Nidditch. Cited by page.
SBNM	*An Enquiry Concerning the Principles of Morals*, ed. L. Selby-Bigge and P. Nidditch. Known as the second *Enquiry*. Cited by page.
SBNT	*A Treatise of Human Nature*, rev. edn, ed. L. Selby-Bigge and P. Nidditch. Cited by page.
SBNU	*An Enquiry Concerning Human Understanding*, ed. L. Selby-Bigge and P. Nidditch. Known as the first *Enquiry*. Cited by page.
T	*A Treatise of Human Nature*, ed. D. and M. Norton. Cited by book-part-chapter, paragraph.
U	*An Enquiry Concerning Human Understanding*, ed. T. Beauchamp. Known as the first *Enquiry*. Cited by chapter, paragraph.

Francis Hutcheson

PW	*Philosophical Writings*, ed. R. Downie, 1994. Cited by page.
SIMP	*A Short Introduction to Moral Philosophy*, Liberty Press reprint. Cited by page.
SMP	*A System of Moral Philosophy*, 2 vols. Continuum reprint. Cited by volume, page.

Henry Home Lord Kames

ELS   *Elucidations respecting the Common and Statute Law of Scotland*. Cited by page.

HLT   *Historical Law Tracts*, 2nd edn. Cited by page.

PMNR   *Essays on the Principles of Morality and Natural Religion*, 3rd edn, Liberty press reprint. Cited by page.

SHM   *Sketches on the History of Man*, 3rd edn, 2 vols. Cited by volume, page.

John Millar

HV   *An Historical View of the English Government*, 4 vols. Cited by volume, chapter /page reference to one-volume Liberty Press reprint.

OR   *The Origin of the Distinction of Ranks*, 3rd edn, ed. W. Lehmann. Cited by page.

William Robertson

HAm   *The History of America,* ed. D. Stewart. Cited by page to *Works* (in one volume).

VP   *A View of the Progress of Society in Europe*, ed. D. Stewart. Cited by page to *Works* (in one volume).

Adam Smith

CL   'Considerations Concerning the First Formation of Languages' in LRBL. Cited by paragraph/page.

Corr   *The Correspondence of Adam Smith*, ed. E. C. Mossner and I. Ross, Liberty Press edn. Cited by letter number/page.

ED   *Early Draft* of part of *The Wealth of Nations*. Cited by paragraph/page.

EPS   *Essays on Philosophical Subjects,* ed. W. Wightman, J. Bryce, I. Ross, Liberty Press edition.

HA   'The Principles which Lead and Direct Philosophical Enquiries, Illustrated by the History of Astronomy', in *EPS*. Cited by section, paragraph/page.

Letter   *'Letter to the Edinburgh Review'*. In *EPS*. Cited by paragraph/page.

Life	*Account of the Life and Writings of Adam Smith* by Dugald Stewart, 1793. In *EPS*. Cited by section, paragraph/page.
LJA	*Lectures on Jurisprudence 1762/3*, Liberty Press edn. Cited by lecture, paragraph/page.
LJB	*Lectures on Jurisprudence 1766*, ed. R. Meek, D. Raphael and P. Stein, Liberty Press edn. Cited by paragraph/page.
LRBL	*Lectures on Rhetoric and Belles-Lettres*, ed. J. Bryce, Liberty Press edn. Cited by lecture, paragraph/page.
TMS	*The Theory of Moral Sentiments*, ed. A. MacFie and D. Raphael, Liberty Press edn. Cited by book part, chapter, paragraph/page.
WN	*An Inquiry into the Nature and Causes of the Wealth of Nations*, ed. R. Campbell and A. Skinner, Liberty Press edn. Cited by book, part, chapter, paragraph/page.

James Steuart

PPE	*An Inquiry into the Principles of Political Economy*, 2 vols, ed. A. Skinner. Cited by volume, page.

Gilbert Stuart

HD	*An Historical Dissertation Concerning the Antiquity of the English Constitution*. Cited by page.
OPL	*Observations Concerning the Public Law and the Constitutional History of Scotland*. Cited by page.
VSE	*A View of Society in Europe in its Progress from Rudeness to Refinement* (1792), 2nd edn. Thoemmes reprint. Cited by page.

George Turnbull

PMP	*The Principles of Moral Philosophy*, ed. A. Broadie, Liberty Press edn. Cited by page.

Robert Wallace

CGB   *Characteristics of the Present Political State of Great Britain*, Kelley Reprints (1961). Cited by page.

DNM   *Dissertation on the Numbers of Mankind in Antient and Modern Times*, 2nd enlarged edn, Kelley Reprints (1969). Cited by page.

Prospects *Various Prospects of Mankind, Nature, and Providence.* Cited by page.

The Study of the Scottish Enlightenment: An Autobiographical Journey

I have told the story of how I came to work on the Scottish Enlightenment so many times that it has been honed in the retelling to the extent that the story is my recollection of events rather than perhaps the events as they actually happened. Maybe this shows, indeed, as Benedetto Croce (1955: 17) paradoxically argued, that all history is contemporary history.

The story goes as follows. Contrary to expectation, I am not Scottish. I was born and educated in south Lancashire in northern England. A 'grammar school boy' at an establishment with limited ambition for its pupils, in 1964 I matriculated at the University of Nottingham, on the non-academic grounds that they guaranteed two years on campus in a hall of residence. There I studied Politics, Philosophy and Sociology – dropping the last two in my third (final) year. In Philosophy, Jonathan Harrison taught me the moral philosophy of Plato, Hume, Kant and Mill. Harrison was something of an eccentric, who would sometimes switch off in mid-sentence as some 'thought' occurred to him. After I had graduated, he did write two books on Hume and his study of Hume on justice remains the most extensive examination of the subject. I was reasonably successful in Philosophy, but far less so in Sociology owing to my indolence. I was, however, lectured on the Classics by Julius Gould – a fact that was to stand me in good stead.

My experience as a student of Politics (my major) was a mixed affair. I chose the subject because, from my late schoolboy days, 'ideas' were what fascinated. However, two years of the 'history of political thought' almost killed that fascination. The class lacked any excitement and, according to the lecturer (who must have been close to retirement), the final word in the study of politics was to found in Bernard Bosanquet's *The Philosophical Theory of the*

State [1889] (1958). Fortunately, in my final year a young lecturer, J. S. ('Mac') McClelland, rekindled my enthusiasm for the subject. Mac was a charismatic figure who taught a specialist and exciting paper on 'Irrationalism in Modern Political Thought' – covering thinkers like Sorel, Nietzsche and Freud. His book *The Crowd and the Mob* (1989) drew on this with a common root in his PhD. His was the only 'theory' course I took – the syllabus was limited – and my optional dissertation was on local politics.

About halfway through my final year, I decided that graduate work was probably all I was suited for. Since in those days taught Masters were not common and I did not want to replicate the experience of Finals – the unseen examinations that alone determined the class of degree – this left applying for a PhD. The British system, which in its essentials persists, is that the student has to come up with a topic and then see if anyone is sufficiently interested/intrigued to want to supervise it. I came up with the 'Scottish Enlightenment'. This was by default. Complementing my classes with Harrison, my studies had covered the Enlightenment and Hume (also a component of my other philosophy course, following Locke and Berkeley in the standard trio). He was, in addition, a brief starting point for Mac's course. I just wondered whether there was a Scottish version of the Enlightenment. The only touchstone I had was that the university library had a copy of W. C. Lehmann's edition of John Millar's *The Origin of the Distinction of Ranks* and, judging from the bibliography, I surmised there might indeed be a possible subject. (I met Lehmann once, very briefly, in the late 1960s in my supervisor's study.)

With a rough topic in mind, I now needed to find a supervisor. Mac, who had a Cambridge PhD, said that Duncan Forbes was 'the man' but he advised against going there, on the grounds that Forbes would tell me to go away and read for a number of years before I was ready. My head of department (R. H. 'Dick' Pear), who had recently arrived from the London School of Economics, said he would write to a former colleague, Donald MacRae, for advice. MacRae in his reply mentioned Forbes plus George Shepperson at Edinburgh and also said he would be willing to take me on. The vagaries of scholarship funding meant I could not apply to both Edinburgh and LSE, since they were funded by two different research councils. By the time that bureaucratic process was untangled I had missed the deadline for Edinburgh and so I went to the LSE on a state scholarship, in the autumn of 1967.

My first year was eventful. The year 1968 is now 'famous' for *les évènements* in Paris, the 'Prague spring', Grosvenor Square anti-Vietnam War protests in London and general student unrest. LSE was at the centre of this. Even before 1968 an incident at 'the School' (as it was then known to those in the know) resulted in the indirect death of a porter. That this febrile atmosphere was not tempered by the actions of the governors meant, for example, that for a time the university library was closed (with my notes and books in a locker inside).

Aside from these noises off, my academic progress was rocky. When I arrived I was told MacRae was on leave in California for the year and that Ken Minogue would be my supervisor. Ken knew next to nothing about the Scottish Enlightenment – which made two of us! I was casting around for a topic, writing regular short pieces that were criticised more for style than content. In retrospect, that was salutary: I learnt the difference between being a quick-witted undergraduate and being a scholar. Over the years, until his death in 2013, I kept in touch with Ken. The one big benefit from that first year was that I attended (as an observer) Michael Oakeshott's graduate seminar. Aside from visiting speakers and papers from LSE colleagues like Maurice Cranston, Oakeshott himself gave some presentations. These I subsequently realised were drafts of what was to become *On Human Conduct* (1975). Slight in build but firm in manner, Oakeshott would swat away comments from the graduate students, and I cannot say that this exposure left any enduring impact on my work. Perhaps – and this may be as much Minogue as Oakeshott himself – I became alert to 'theory' as, in line with its etymology, being properly not at the service of 'practice'. In later years, when I gave undergraduate seminars on 'conservatism', Oakeshott was the main text and I used his arguments as articulated in *Rationalism in Politics* (1962) as a foil in a couple of my own writings (Berry 1983; also in Chapter 14 here).

Things looked up from the summer of 1968. Above all, I got married. My wife Chris(tine) got a job as primary school teacher and her small salary and my grant just about gave us enough to live on. MacRae returned and took over the supervision. He was the Professor of Sociology, with a background that turned out to be significant, in that he was a graduate of Glasgow, whence he went to Balliol (though not via Smith's route of a Snell Exhibition but another scholarship). He was an erudite man and his Scottish roots gave him a particular interest in Scottish intellectual history. He never published much but he did write a short piece on Adam Ferguson as a 'founding father' for a weekly magazine that was subsequently published (1969) in a volume that collected the series (including Gould on Comte). MacRae was very much a hands-off supervisor, who let me get on with things. I submitted a draft chapter and then after an interval and by appointment we had a conversation about it. The decisive event was his endorsement of my suggestion that the thesis could be written on James Dunbar.

My reasons for choosing Dunbar were not particularly edifying. Negatively, I wanted to steer clear of the two big names (Hume and Smith) and Dunbar had the great advantage of being a 'one-book man' and thus ideal doctorate fodder. The thesis, when it finally took shape, was not just on Dunbar but, because his book – *Essays on the History of Mankind in Rude and Cultivated Ages* – was a relatively late publication (1780), it served as a 'way in' to the thought of the Scottish Enlightenment more generally. In the autumn of 1969 I applied (after some hesitation – should I wait until the thesis was finished?) for a job at University of Glasgow. I was called along with five others for interview. When I learnt that one of these was already tutoring and, additionally, that a current member of the Politics and Sociology Department (as it then was) was completing a book on Smith, I was not optimistic. The Smith book in question was Tom Campbell's pioneering *Adam Smith's Science of Morals* (1971). Tom had followed Smith's itinerary of Glasgow–Snell/Balliol–Glasgow and his book was based on his Glasgow PhD supervised by David Raphael. Raphael was the chief interviewer, along with W. J. M. (Bill) Mackenzie – the doyen of British political scientists. To my surprise, I was on the day offered the job of Assistant Lecturer in Social and Political Philosophy. I was 23, had not published anything and had a minimum of teaching experience as a tutor at LSE (all of which in subsequent years would have ruled me out as a serious candidate, let alone appointee). I can only assume I was successful because MacRae gave me a good reference (his Glasgow background maybe helping) and I had a First Class Honours degree with some Sociology as well as Philosophy. In those days Firsts were rare; I was the only recipient in my subject in the three years of my undergraduate career.

I was offered the choice of starting in January or waiting until the October. On my return to London, I asked MacRae's advice and he thought the earlier start (with for me the incentive of a

jump-start in income) was feasible. I started as a Glasgow academic in January 1970 but in the meantime Raphael left Glasgow.
Although I thus never had the privilege of working with him as
(very junior) colleague, I remain ever grateful that he saw enough
potential in me to make me worth appointing. I was given a light
teaching load, submitted my thesis and was 'viva-ed' in December.
My examiner turned out to be Duncan Forbes. Again, the process
was very informal and with the caveat that it could not be published 'as is', I was recommended for the award of a doctorate.

I am in retrospect pleased that my thesis was not published and
(thankfully) it has been little read, Roger Emerson and Nicholas
Phillipson being among the very few. I did use it to produce some
earlier publications (some included here: Chapters 2, 3 and 4) and
a couple of spin-offs (Chapter 16 and Berry 1973b). The thesis,
however, did set a template for future work. As a full bibliography of my work (that is, including work outside the Scottish
Enlightenment) would testify, my focus has always been on 'ideas'.
My one bit of archival research was to discover Dunbar's date of
birth (published in 1974b and repeated in Berry 1995), although
the new edition of the *Dictionary of National Biography* continues
to state that his dates are unknown. My thesis tried to make something of Dunbar as an Aberdonian and the Enlightenment there
as distinctive. This has become now accepted but my account was
very circumstantial. Real research by Roger Emerson (1992) and
Paul Wood (1993) has now established the reality and contours
of the Aberdeen Enlightenment (see also Carter and Pittock (eds),
1987, in which I feature – reprinted as Chapter 3). Principally I
read as many of Dunbar's compatriots as possible, though not,
as I have already confessed, Smith and Hume with any great
assiduity. This meant that, for example, I read all six volumes
of Monboddo's *Origin and Progress of Language* and *Antient
Metaphysics*, as well as many of Dunbar's Aberdeen colleagues
like Ogilvie, Beattie, Gerard and Campbell, and their predecessors like Reid, Blackwell and Turnbull, but the main players in
my work were Ferguson, Millar, Robertson, Kames and Gilbert
Stuart, with walk-on parts by John Gregory, James Steuart and
Robert Wallace. That cast list has remained pretty much the same,
with Wallace and Steuart looming a little larger while Reid and
'common sense' have never been centre stage.

The Study of the Scottish Enlightenment in the 1960s

It is difficult, from our present vantage point with its extensive richness of scholarship, to imagine how sparse the material was during the 1960s. As a touchstone for that 'state of play', the bibliography in my thesis can serve as a starting point. This, of course, comes with the caveat that my focus meant there was no extensive reference therein to the scholarship on Hume as evidenced by, for example, the absence of Stewart (1963) or Ardal (1966) and the only monograph on Smith I actually cited was Cropsey (2001 reprint).

Of the monographs I did read, pride of place has to go to Gladys Bryson's *Man and Society: The Scottish Inquiry of the Eighteenth Century*. Published in 1945 by Princeton, it had not only no precedent but also no successor. (I perhaps immodestly said of my book *Social Theory of the Scottish Enlightenment* (1997) that it was attempting to be a 'new Bryson' – that is, a volume covering the range of the literati.) A professor at Smith College, Bryson wrote the book at Berkeley under the (probable) supervision of Frederick Teggart. Its biggest influence was A. O. Lovejoy and his notion of the 'idea-complex' that constituted 'the rationalism of the Enlightenment' (Bryson 1945, pp. 13–14). His work and his salience had put Monboddo on the map as a comparator to Rousseau (he also stimulated a flurry of studies in 'Scottish primitivism', which I read) and he is a frequent reference in her book. Her theme was that the Scots were endeavouring to establish an empirical basis for the study of man and society. I cannot say that her work deeply influenced me in any particular – I cited it infrequently – but it served as a set of indicative signposts. Lovejoy, of course, has fallen dramatically out of fashion but, shorn of that scaffolding, I think Bryson is still worth reading (the book was reissued by Kelley reprints in 1968); her general reading of the Scots as empirical ethicists and proto-social scientists I now realise is akin to the interpretation I have unfolded.

Bryson's work was noted by Louis Schneider (1967), who produced a selection of the Scots in a series 'The Heritage of Sociology', but he acknowledges that it was Hayek's work that inspired it. The selection is somewhat idiosyncratic – eight passages from Smith (including from *HA*) and Hume, four Ferguson plus some Reid, Stewart and Kames and one from Monboddo but no Millar. In a lengthy introduction (70 pages plus), Schneider notes the range of their sociological concerns and anticipations of functionalism. Until Jane Rendall's (1978) collection of brief extracts and a more substantial one, if still limited in scope, produced by Philip Flynn (1992) and then Alexander Broadie's (1997) much more comprehensive reader, this was the only compendium available but there is little evidence that it was put to much use.[1] That is almost certainly indicative of the fact that it had little pedagogic utility, since the 'Scottish Enlightenment' was not on the curriculum.

The other book of particular note was David Kettler's 1965 study of Ferguson. Lehmann had published a volume in 1930 picking up the notion of Ferguson as a sociologist; Kettler examined him in the context of his social position and environment. He emphasised his role as an intellectual alongside his compatriots in what he tended to call the Scottish Renaissance. His heavy emphasis on 'virtue', has in retrospect (that is, before J. G. A. Pocock's *Machiavellian Moment* – see below), mitigated its impact. What initially steered my early research was Lehmann's edition of Millar, already mentioned, especially for his fifty-plus pages on the 'chiefly theoretical background', as he called it (this had been trailed in Lehmann (1952)). To this should be added Duncan Forbes' forty-page introduction to Edinburgh University Press's beautiful edition of Ferguson's *Essay on the History of Civil Society* (1966). I have remained faithful to this edition ever since.

This paucity of monographs meant that most of the interpretative work was to be found in scholarly articles. Forbes, once more, was a prominent presence. His *Cambridge Journal* (1954) study of Millar and Smith not only put the term 'scientific Whiggism' into academic discourse ('Dunbar's Whiggism' was the title of the final chapter of my thesis) but also the pervasive presence of what he termed 'the heterogeneity of ends' (what Schneider called 'unintended social outcomes' with Hayek, though not he alone, cited). What made a particular, and enduring, impression on my own thinking was Forbes' distinction between Scottish and French views of reason and progress. Given the provenance of this article, I now have the suspicion that he was influenced by Oakeshott – long-time editor of the *Cambridge Journal* and in the pages of which he had first essayed his famous articles on rationalism (collected in Oakeshott 1962).

Forbes frequently referred to German scholarship in his article, and in a footnote cited an article by Roy Pascal, which Forbes judged had been prompted by Werner Sombart. Sombart was no Marxist, but Pascal was and his article appearing in 1938 in the first volume of *The Modern Quarterly* has retained its place as the first interpretation of what he called the 'The Scottish School'. As Pascal read them, this School adopted a 'materialistic and scientific' approach, albeit weakened by their middle-class social position and their (consequential) inability to recognise the 'dialectics of social progress'. Pascal's most notable successor was Ronald Meek, whose 1954 essay 'The Scottish Contribution to Marxist Sociology' was, as he acknowledged, considerably indebted to Pascal. One of Meek's pupils at Glasgow University – and subsequently his successor – was Andrew Skinner. Skinner published two articles in 1965 and 1967 on the 'Scottish School' with the common theme of the link between economic and social organisation, noting 'obvious if limited parallels' to Marx (1965: 2). (For more on this interpretative history, see Chapter 6 and, generally on Marxist readings, Berry 1997: Ch. 8.) Skinner in his notes acknowledged the work of A. L MacFie, Adam Smith Professor of Political Economy at Glasgow. MacFie succeeded W. R. Scott (another notable Smith scholar) as the incumbent of that Chair, and one that Skinner himself would subsequently occupy. Now best known as the co-editor with David Raphael of the Glasgow edition of Smith's *Moral Sentiments*, in 1967 MacFie had published a slim volume of essays on Smith, outlining the Stoic reading so evident in the Introduction to *Moral Sentiments*. Given that the book's focus is Smith (though there was a chapter in Millar), I did not make much use of it in my own work, in which I deliberately sidestepped Smith.

I did discuss Smith's views on the division of labour, however, because Dunbar also did. The more particular focus was the discussion in *The Wealth of Nations* Book 5, with its broader interpretative context. By the late 1960s the Marxism represented by Pascal and Meek had lost its salience (not, of course, on purely academic grounds), to be replaced by work on the recently 'discovered' concept of alienation in the unpublished work of the 'young Marx'. E. G. West (1969) had drawn a comparison between Smith and Marx, but concluded that it was limited. His work sparked a debate in which West continued to participate, but this was more fully expressed in the early 1970s when the work on the 'young Marx' really took off. However, in 1967, Douglas Young, the editor of a slim book of essays (originally radio talks on the BBC), *Edinburgh in the Age of Reason,* commented in the Introduction that alienation, as shaped by Smith and Ferguson, was 'perhaps one of the most important contributions of the Scottish intellect to European consciousness' (1967: 13). Young here was echoing, if more fulsomely, a point made by Duncan Forbes (1967) himself in his essay in that volume. I was not persuaded, saying in my thesis that this was unnecessary distortion and, though I was remiss in not acknowledging him, MacRae had in print already doubted its utility in an interpretation of Ferguson. I have ever since held to my view that any notion of 'alienation' (*Entfremdung/Entäusserung*), in its Hegel/Feuerbach/ Marx sense, is misapplied to Smith and the other Scots.

I tried to take seriously the wider literature on the Enlightenment, without its ever becoming a major focus. Perhaps not unexpect- edly, the launchpad was Montesquieu. I should – I now appreciate – have spent more time on Rousseau; one of the weaknesses in the thesis (and the early published work) was that the influence of the *Second Discourse* on Dunbar was underplayed (see my postscript to Chapter 2). Of general books on the Enlightenment, what impressed me most was Peter Gay's two-volume work (1967, 1970). For all the criticisms subsequently levelled at it, I still think it has stood the test of time. As a PhD student, I derived more benefit from it than from Cassirer (1955) or Hampson (1968), although I did read, with passing profit, on my daily commute to the School from Stanmore, Hazard's (1964, 1965) two paperbacks.

Not trained as a historian, I tried to pick up, rather fitfully, information on the Scottish background. I managed to purchase second hand two books by Henry Graham (1901, 1906), which – though dated even then – still, from my negligible base, were useful. I read a number of books on the history of Aberdeen and its University and William Ferguson's recently published (1968) modern (post-1689) history of Scotland. I purchased Henry Hamilton's (1963) fact-filled *Economic History of Scotland in the Eighteenth Century* and fell upon T. C. Smout's (1969) seminal volume on its publication just as I left London.

Lecturer at Glasgow and Pittsburgh

Thanks to my academic trajectory, my knowledge base was thin, so I spent the early 1970s educating myself. I was greatly helped by being forced to write a whole lecture course, from Plato to Rawls, as a visiting professor at the University of Pittsburgh in the academic year 1973/4. I taught the courses delivered by John Chapman who was on leave. He remained in Pittsburgh, however, and held weekly gatherings in his home for his PhD students, to which I was invited. Also, through his good offices, I got to meet some of the members of the redoubtable Philosophy Department at Pitt (including, briefly, Annette Baier, whose husband Kurt was a professor). Chapman was a scholar of very firm views and was by all accounts a rather difficult colleague but he and his wife Janet were extremely generous to my wife and me. Indeed, as a joint editor of *Nomos,* he later invited me to submit to the Yearbook (Berry 1980, 1992, 1993). It was during my time at Pittsburgh that I began a serious engagement with Hume and began to work on Hegel. The latter became a focus partly because I taught Marx (something I did for well over thirty years) and partly because he was a challenge. It was while I was in the US that my first publications appeared (see Chapter 9 and an article in *JHI* (Berry 1977b)) and eventually my first book, *Hume, Hegel and Human Nature* (Berry 1982a).

In the mid-1970s at Glasgow there was change in academic organisation. This enabled me to put on an elective specialist Honours (final-year undergraduate) paper on the Scottish Enlightenment and thus return to the subject. I taught it for the next thirty-five years and it was the basis for my 1997 book. This return meant that I engaged anew with the scholarly literature.

The Study of the Scottish Enlightenment in the 1970s

Work on the Scottish Enlightenment began to develop some momentum during the 1970s. What follows is a post-facto estimate of the work that seems to me to have shaped the study of the subject. To give some structure I will deal in turn with the Scottish Enlightenment in general and studies of particular scholars, except work on Hume and Smith, which I will cover separately. I do not claim to be either exhaustive or definitive and, of course, my own interests and the inevitably contingent nature of what crossed my desk have governed the selection.

In the first year of the decade Nicholas Phillipson and Rosalind Mitchison (1970) edited a collection of chiefly historical essays that contained an influential chapter by Ian Clark on the Moderate clergy. It was at a launch party for the book that I first met Nick Phillipson. I continued contact, via attending some seminars that Nick organised and where I gave a paper on Dunbar. Also attending that session was Hans Medick, as was Roger Emerson who was in Edinburgh that year and whose subsequent article on the Select Society (1973) was a harbinger of work on the Scots' network in clubs and universities that was in later years to produce the definitive work on patronage (2008). In the early 1970s Nick produced a series of complex papers (such as 1973a, 1973b) that put forward an arresting interpretation of the Scottish Enlightenment as an intellectual, predominantly Edinburgh-based, elite response to the 1707 Union in terms of an identity crisis (I discuss his reading in 1997 Ch. 8; now also see Kidd (2014)).

There were three single-authored monographs. Anand Chitnis (1976) wrote a book subtitled 'A Social History', which dealt with the key institutions in a chapter on 'The Study of Social Man'. A different sort of historical treatment (though not one confined to the Scottish Enlightenment) was provided by Medick (1973), who continued the Marxist reading, interpreting Smith as an ideologist of the petty bourgeoisie. This was not done crassly, but neither of these books made much impact (in the latter case perhaps because of the heavily Anglophonic nature of the commentary).[2] This cannot be said of the third monograph, by Ronald Meek (1976). By then, Meek's Marxism had become etiolated but his account of the 'four stages' has become a classic source and continues to be cited (I criticised it in Berry 2013). The book is a valuable compendium of views that helpfully does not treat the Scots in isolation from what he regards as similar arguments in France and beyond.

Meek aside, the most significant other books were two studies of Kames by Lehmann (1971) and Ian Ross (1972). Both contain a wealth of information, Lehmann making more effort to engage with Kames' protean and voluminous publications. Only in 2015 has Kames' thought received a serious book-length treatment (Rahmatian 2015). There is still no extended, rounded commentary/analysis of Millar or of Robertson – though in Robertson's case commentary is increasing and Jeffrey Smitten (2017) has produced a biography. Of academic articles, MacRae's student Alan Swingewood published a piece on the Scots and the origins of sociology but the most influential was Harro Höpfl's (1978) critique of the materialist reading of the Scots of the Pascal/Meek persuasion. This article, written from what could be called an

Oakeshottian perspective (Höpfl had been a student at the LSE), remains one of the most succinct critiques. Hugh Trevor-Roper reiterated (1977, 1967) his controversial view of the Scottish Enlightenment as a reaction to Scotland's backwardness stimulated by the Union (for an assessment, see Kidd 2005).

It is when we turn to Smith and Hume that we see the launch-pads for the work that was to take off in later decades. Pride of place goes to the now definitive Glasgow edition of Smith. While its version of *The Wealth of Nations* replaced the standard Cannan (1961) edition, it was the other volumes that were catalytic. There had never been a scholarly English edition of *Moral Sentiments*; indeed, the previously available edition had been produced in the Bohn Library in 1892 (there was a scholarly annotated German translation with a lengthy seventy-page introduction that put paid to the internally generated German debate over 'Das Adam Smith Problem' (Eckstein 1926)). Tom Campbell's dedicated treatment of Smith as a moral philosopher-cum-social scientist gave an initial fillip to the study of Smith outside the confines of *WN* that the appearance of the Glasgow edition consolidated and which would in due course produce a wealth of serious scholarship. While the presence of Smith's *Essays on Philosophical Subjects* stimulated interest in his *History of England* and a fuller version of *Lectures on Rhetoric and Belles-Lettres* replacing Lothian's (1963) earlier version, it was the publication of *Lectures on Jurisprudence* that was really exciting. Only previously available in a limited form (Cannan (ed.) 1896), scholars were now able to appreciate not only Smith the pedagogue but also Smith the historian, the legal theorist and the proto-economist.

The first book to take advantage of the availability of the range of Smith's work was Donald Winch's 1978 book on Smith's politics. Lindgren (1973) and Reisman (1976, on which I wrote a booknote for the now defunct *British Book News*) were limited in comparison. Winch's book was a deliberately polemical work that sought to rescue 'Smith' from anachronistic interpretations as some sort of harbinger of the 'Chicago School'. Methodologically, Winch was influenced by the contextualist Cambridge School of Quentin Skinner and John Pocock (see below). His aim to embed Smith in eighteenth-century debates has become to a significant extent orthodox.

Prior to Winch, a large volume of essays on Smith was published (Skinner and Wilson 1975) as a companion to the *Works*, which for the first time used them as the common reference and established the citing notation that is now standard. While half the contributions dealt with *WN*, notably it was only half. It also included essays by Campbell and Raphael on Smith's moral thought, Howell on his rhetoric, and Andrew Skinner and Forbes on history.

While Glasgow held a big conference in 1976 to mark the bicentenary of *WN*, Edinburgh held a big conference to mark the bicentenary of Hume's death. This was marked with a stellar list of speakers – including Forbes (again), Raphael, Mossner, Isaiah Berlin, Passmore and Davie (collected in Morrice 1977).[3] In addition to the plenaries there was a series of short-paper panels and I participated in one, with a paper on 'Hume, Property and Causation', which, though never published, was incorporated into my 1982 book and earlier in *Nomos* (Berry 1980).

Forbes' Edinburgh lecture essentially rehearsed the theme of his 1975 book. From my perspective – and for once I was not being idiosyncratic – this was the most significant publication on Hume in that decade. At that time, Humean philosophical scholarship was still largely preoccupied with the problems in the *Treatise* Book I and the is/ought issue generated out of an overinterpreted passage in Book III Part 1, Chapter 2. The latter has faded and, while Humean exegesis is still occupied with the former issues, there has been a shift away from the narrowness of that focus. It is on this wider front that Forbes made his mark. His reading of Hume as laying the foundation for the new Hanoverian regime, as giving the hitherto neglected *History of England* a central role, produced a perspective that has remained pertinent. While I think his view of Hume as a (sort of) natural lawyer needs to be qualified, his careful attention to the shifts and tenor of Hume's argumentation has remained a benchmark.

There are two especially influential works, which, though not specifically about the Scottish Enlightenment, established a per- spective that informed a lot of subsequent work on the Scots. I bought both Albert Hirschman's (1977) and J. G. A. Pocock's (1975) books on their appearance – the former chiefly out of curi- osity. I knew of Hirschman's work but not that he had an interest in the history of ideas. The purchase turned out to be serendipitous since the book quickly gained a reputational salience. Its impact stemmed from its suggestiveness rather than definitive exposition but this meant it stimulated further exploration. For my own part, it was less his use of the predictability of 'interest' – an argument already made by Joyce Appleby (1978) in a work Hirschman does not cite – than his exploitation of Montesquieu's idea of *doux commerce*, which he illustrated with a quotation from Robertson's *View of Society*.

The '*doux*' here is a link to Pocock (a work Hirschman acknowledges as dealing with related themes to his but which he had not been able to utilise). Whereas, as befits a slim volume, Hirschman's work was exploratory, Pocock's was a complex, reflexive account of (to use a Pocockian expression) 'paradigms' or interpretative languages within which, and by means of which, historical actors understood themselves. He was already a well-known intellectual historian (1957) and, as noted above, a pioneer, with Quentin Skinner (1969), of the contextualist approach to the history of ideas, with an emphasis on historicity (an approach with which I 'experimented' in the very different context of a Christian idea of progress (Berry 1977a)). Although only about a dozen pages (out of 550) touched on the Scots, Pocock's book set an agenda that has powerfully resonated through the study of the Scottish Enlightenment. This resonance was abetted by his more explicit engagements with the Scots in some later work (especially 1983 and 1999).

What Pocock did was resurrect the vocabulary of virtue, corruption and republicanism and in so doing recast (away from a neo- or sub-Marxist) the account of commerce. The applicability of this vocabulary and this recasting has inspired interpretations of the Scottish Enlightenment ever since. Hence, for example, Ferguson is treated less as an anticipator of alienation than as a citizen worried about commercial passivity; or discussions of Smith's warnings about the effects of the division of labour on pin makers now pick up on his use of virtue language (especially the enigmatic reference to 'martial virtue'). It will become apparent in the following chapters, and from my discussion of what I call the 'Pocock problematic', that, while a firm admirer of his work, I adopt a lukewarm attitude to the problematic itself.

William & Mary, Glasgow and Other Work

In early 1980 an opportunity arose for me to spend another academic year in the US, and so I spent 1980–81 teaching at the College of William & Mary in Williamsburg. Compared to the year in Pittsburgh, extra-academic activities were constrained for both financial and familial reasons (our sons were born in 1976 and 1979). Academically, I did not teach the Scots but I did give a paper on Hume at the South Western Political Science Association in Dallas in 1981. This appeared in print a couple of years later and a version of it constitutes Chapter 9 below. I was part of a panel and my discussant was John Danford, who himself subsequently wrote a good book on Hume (Danford 1990). My own book on Hegel and Hume appeared in 1982. It was generally well received, although its impact was chiefly among Hume scholars (Chapter 12 represents a republication of my 2007 partial response to some of it).

In Glasgow, aside from continuing to teach my Honours option on the Scots – alongside a detailed text-based course on the *Philosophy of Right* and Marx's *Early Writings,* which produced an article (Berry 1987b) – and the publication of three pieces on the Scots (Berry 1986b, 1987a [Chapter 3], 1989a [Chapter 18]), my major efforts were two books (Berry 1986a, 1989b) in political philosophy. Towards the end of the decade I received a personal grant from the National Funding Council to embark on a study of luxury, which bore eventual fruit in the most successful (in sales and citations) and most broadly influential of all my writings: *The Idea of Luxury* (1994). That book contained a long chapter on the eighteenth century, wherein Hume and Smith featured prominently (Smith was also a considerable presence elsewhere in the volume). That, along with my teaching, meant that I kept my 'hand in' with respect to the now swelling commentary on the Scots.

The Study of the Scottish Enlightenment in the 1980s

The developing momentum of the 1970s produced a 'lift off' in the 1980s. Knud Haakonssen (1981) published a study of Smith's jurisprudence that was the first work fully to exploit the Glasgow edition of the *Lectures on Jurisprudence*. His stress on the natural law background (and of Hume's influence on Smith) became influential and constituted an interpretative line that he has continued to pursue (see, for example, his work collected in Haakonssen (1996)). What added to its subsequent impact was that it came to be seen as representing a non-Pocockian strand.

One marker of a subject's maturity is the appearance of volume of essays. Two such appeared in close temporal proximity – Hont and Ignatieff (1983) and Campbell and Skinner (1982). I wrote a lengthy review article covering both volumes (Berry 1986b). The latter, which contained contributions from Chitnis, T. Campbell, Forbes and Haakonssen, was a more general mix of social and intellectual history. The former has turned out to be more influential, partly because it was more focused on the 'shaping of political economy', as its subtitle states, though strictly that does not apply to all the chapters. The long opening chapter by the editors, which, along with Pocock's essay (see above) and an individual piece by Hont on the rich country–poor country debate, have chiefly contributed to this volume's subsequent salience (it also included contributions from Phillipson, Winch and John Robertson). But this collection was also a harbinger of the debate between the virtue/corruption and jurisprudentialist reading of the Scottish Enlightenment. This is neatly encapsulated in Ignatieff's chapter on Millar, whose thought, he judges (and the same applies to Smith), exhibits 'deep tensions' between (and he employs a Pocockian idiom) the 'language of corruption' and the 'language of markets and interests' (1983: 341).

Those two discourses do not exhaust the ways of reading the Scots. A number of scholars, notably Roger Emerson and Paul Wood, have long argued that the study of the Scottish Enlightenment has been distorted by neglecting the role of 'science' broadly conceived. Another 1980s collection (Jones ed. 1988) including a contribution from Wood, but in which Emerson is identified by a number of others as a key figure, addressed this, at least in part. Emerson himself pursued this interpretative line in a series of articles (1986, 1988a, 1988b). One of the other contributors in Jones's collection was Arthur Donovan, who had published a book on 'philosophical chemistry' in 1975 but which remained sidelined as 'history of science' – a prejudice Wood and Emerson were concerned to combat. It is worth noting that Jones, and Campbell and Skinner, were published by John Donald, a small press that, over a number of years, sustained and made available a wide range of work on the Scottish Enlightenment. This was both a cause and an effect of the growing interest in the period: this publisher was responsible for John Robertson's (1985) book on the militia question and John Dwyer's (1987) *Virtuous Discourse*. In their very different ways, these books reflect or react to what I call the 'Pocockian problematic'. Nor should it be thought that scholarship was confined to that. What we might call traditional critical/expository work continued to be produced, as for example in another collection edited by Peter Jones (1989), with chapters by two authors – Livingston and Baier - to whom I will return.

Donald also published books on Scottish eighteenth-century history (for example by Shaw (1983) and Murdoch (1980)) but it was the other, more established, outlet, Edinburgh University Press, that published the stand-out 'history' book by Sher (1985). His 'cultural interpretation' centred on Edinburgh and the Moderate regime in the Scottish Enlightenment, which, while inevitably subject in due course to criticism, marked out the territory on and from which subsequent discussion proceeds. Sher also inaugurated (1987) an annual newsletter of the Eighteenth-Century Scottish Studies Society, which has become (under the title *Eighteenth-Century Scotland*) a valuable resource tracking the developing scholarship.

On more obviously intellectual history territory there were two other brief publications of note, which in their own way exemplify two further lines of enquiry. George Davie (1981) published a pamphlet – later reprinted (Davie 1994) – that stressed the Scottishness of the issues that confronted intelligent Scots in the eighteenth century. Davie was well known as the author of *The Democratic Intellect* (1961), a work revered as a totemic nationalist tome. And although he never published much, he was an influential and exceptionally well-informed presence in Edinburgh University, and the subject of a *Festshrift* (Hope 1984). I met him at Phillipson's seminars in the 1970s but our paths rarely crossed. Without the nationalist slant, the view that the Scottish Enlightenment had roots in Scottish history and thought that predate the Union with Scotland has become a (disputed) motif (I discuss this in Berry 1997 Ch. 8).

The other publication by Hamowy (1987; reviewed by me in *Political Studies* 1988) deals with the 'theory of spontaneous order'. This revives the Hayekian theme that Schneider had introduced and which Hayek himself in a series of later publications reinforced (see 1967, 1978). In part owing to the intellectual profile that Hayek obtained, with the rise of anti-Keynesian (free-market) economics, this has become another interpretative theme, even if Hamowy's extremely slim volume did little of itself to advance it. Among the notable later utilisations are Otteson (2002, which I reviewed in the *Journal of Scottish Philosophy* 2003) and Craig Smith (2006) whose Glasgow thesis I supervised.

When it comes to treatments of the 'big two', what I call the critical/expository approach dominates. Significant works on Hume include Norton (1982; reviewed briefly by me in *Political Studies*), Livingston (1984: which I also reviewed in *Political Studies* 1986) and Whelan (1985). While Livingston developed a sophisticated argument, and I have engaged more overtly with his argument (see Chapter 14), I think Whelan's book has been unduly neglected. Part of the reason for this lower profile is that much of the Hume commentary is more ostensibly 'philosophical', so that Whelan's politics-oriented book has had comparatively less exposure, an outcome abetted by the fact that Hume is not a 'big player' in the history of political thought, certainly when compared with his contemporary Rousseau, Hobbes and Locke before him, and Burke after him. David Miller (1981), in the first overview of Hume's political thinking since Stewart (1963), did not change the pedagogic or intellectual landscape. At the end of the decade Philipson (1989) wrote a slim book on Hume as a historian, which (as it turned out) portended a serious scholarly interest in that important aspect of Hume's work.

Aside from Haakonssen, not much of significance was published on Smith that caught my attention. David Raphael (1985) wrote a typically sharp little primer. While not confined to Smith, a number of works included him prominently in more general discussions. Dwyer, already mentioned, picked up a theme in the scholarship that has endured, namely the extent to which the final 1790 edition of *Moral Sentiments* signalled a significant departure. Lawrence Dickey (1986) had given this an airing and, again, the Pocockian problematic is a factor, since it served to highlight the new chapter on 'corruption'. Of these other works, one that made an impression was by Richard Teichgraeber III (1986), who looked at Smith via a discussion of Hutcheson and Hume.

The 1990s: Consolidation

During this decade I finally became Professor and then head (Chair) of the department, an office that continued into the next millennium. It also marked the beginning of a serious involvement in university administration/management that persisted, more or less, until I retired in 2012. After the publication of *The Idea of Luxury* (and several invited follow-ups (1999a, 2005, for example)), my own academic endeavours were chiefly devoted to the Scots (1992), through various encyclopedia entries and an introduction to the Thoemmes reprint edition of Dunbar (1995). I did publish some (Humean-inspired) pieces on what I call the philosophical anthropology of politics, publishing one article at the end of decade (and a couple more a little later: Berry 1999b, 2000a, 2006c) as well as contemporary political theory (for example, Berry 1993).

The scholarship on the Scots was now firmly embedded. More collections of essays appeared (Stewart 1990, Dwyer and Sher 1993, Hook and Sher 1995). The last of these on the Glasgow Enlightenment – published by Tuckwell, a successor of John Donald – alongside Paul Wood's book on the Aberdeen Enlightenment represented recognition that Edinburgh and the Scottish Enlightenment were not synonymous. The Stewart volume included a contribution from Wood that presaged his book on Aberdeen. It also contained essays by such well-established scholars as Emerson, Sher and Haakonssen, as well as a particularly influential essay by Michael Barfoot on Hume and the 'culture of science'.

The interpretative lines already laid down continued to be pursued. Colin Kidd (1993) made the case for the 1707 Union as setting problems for the Scottish thinkers. His framing is not that of Davie but reflects a provenance stemming from (though far from reducible to) Hugh Trevor-Roper. David Allan (1993: reviewed by me in *Utilitas* 1994) gave a different emphasis: for him, the Union occasioned no break in Scottish intellectual life in the seventeenth century. Allan also deliberately set out – like Kidd – to widen the area of discussion beyond the usual established names. As will become apparent in the following chapters, my own emphasis on the Scottish thinkers' self-conscious modernity means I am not inclined to attach any great weight to such continuity. Individual thinkers began to be the subject of dedicated publications: hence Brown (ed. 1997) on Robertson (and his presence in O'Brien 1997), Zachs (1992) on Gilbert Stuart, and a flurry of papers on Ferguson and civil society (see Chapter 8).

Of works on the two biggest names, John Stewart returned with another book on Hume (Stewart 1992). This pugnaciously confronts the view of Hume as some sort of conservative and I echo this in Chapter 14, as well as in my book on Hume (2009) despite its presence in a series 'Conservative and Libertarian Thinkers'. The other notable book on Hume was Annette Baier's (1991).

Baier, having previously written a number of important articles, in this volume devoted to the *Treatise* she made the case that the book is a whole. In this argument she establishes herself as a leading interpreter of the developing view that to focus on Book I is to misrepresent Hume's intentions and ambitions. Ian Ross's (1995, 2nd edn 2010) biography of Smith appeared, although there were already full-length studies by, for example, Patricia Werhane (1991) and Athol Fitzgibbons (1995), who, like MacFie, stressed the Stoic aspects of Smith's thought. The view of Smith as Stoic has remained strong (see, for example, Force (2003), the subject of long review article (Berry 2004)) – an interpretation I do not share. Vivienne Brown (1994) also highlighted the Stoic presence in Smith, but her book is noteworthy for other reasons.

Brown, without heavy-handedness, adopted (or at least utilised) the perspective of Derrida and others, that authorial intentions are not authoritative, and thus more or less implicitly criticised Winch's 'Cambridge-inflected' approach and the whole Pocockian problematic. What is striking is that work on the Scots has not been strongly colonised by strong perspectives that have flourished in other arenas. The crux of Brown's interpretation was to treat Smith's works as 'discourse' and it can be identified, diffusely, as having affinity with a Foucaultian/post-modernist line. Before Brown, Gilles Deleuze (1953 but only translated 1991) wrote a book on Hume. It is fair to say that this has engaged students of his thought rather than of Hume's, which is unfortunate because his interpretation (not overburdened with his later 'critique' of 'philosophy') is often insightful. Jerome Christensen (1987) approaches Hume through a broad post-modern prism, including, as well as Deleuze, Baudrillard and Foucault.

For Foucault (tr. 1970) himself, Smith is swept up in his self-proclaimed 'archaeology of the human sciences'; he is important as a hiatus in the fundamental discontinuity that Foucault is outlining but is scarcely a subject of any special attention. The subterranean presence of Foucault on economic discourse can (perhaps) be detected, even if via Keith Tribe (1978), in Margaret Schabas's (2005) argument that the concept of an 'economy' is post-Enlightenment. Thomas Markus (1982) wrote a more overtly Foucault-inspired piece on Scottish architecture 1780–1820, criticising standard interpretations for their shallowness in not seeing the basic institutions (concrete as well as ideological) as 'control mechanisms'. However, its apparently narrow focus has resulted in it making no significant impression on subsequent work. Foucault is utilised by Fonna Forman-Barzilai (2013) and is a clear presence in Michael Shapiro (1992), but his opening sentence that his book 'is not about Adam Smith in the usual sense' perhaps explains why relatively few subsequent scholars have picked him up. An exception is Mike Hill and Warren Montag (2015: reviewed by me in the *Journal History of Economic Thought*, 2016) who commend Shapiro's 'uniquely critical direction' while criticising him for too narrow a focus. Hill and Montag, for their part, have an eclectic approach, a mix of neo-Marxism and Foucault that obscures as much as it throws any light.

If the post-modernist perspective has not a large presence (cf. Dunyach and Thomson, 2015: 16), feminist scholarship has had more impact, despite the fact that, for radical feminism in its various forms, if any Scots figure at all they are typically exemplars of phallocratic thought, intellectual deafness or systemically rendering women invisible. A good reason why the Scots do figure in feminist (or feminist-inspired) scholarship is because, compared to Foucaultian (or, indeed, Habermasian)[4] approaches, the Scots' own thought more easily invites 'historical' investigation, a fact made all the more amenable since the Scots themselves do refer to the changing role of women in their various stadial histories (I discuss these briefly in Berry 1997: 109–13). Although most overviews/surveys do not include the Scots, scholars like Jane Rendall (for example 1987), Chris Nyland (for example 2003), Henry Clarke (for example 1993), Catherine Moran (2003) and Maureen Harkin (2013), among others, have examined Smith and others. Hume is the subject of a volume in the series 'Feminist Interpretations' (Jacobson ed. 2000) which includes one of Baier's influential essays (see also Chapter 10 where I discuss Hume on chastity). Discussions of the Scots more generally are fewer, but see Mary Moran (2013), Jane Rendall (1999) again, and Silvia Sebastiani (2013) as part of a wider sweep also encompassing race, and Rosalind Carr (2013), who draws on feminist (post-structuralist gender) theory, including that critical of Habermas.

Studies from 2000 onwards

By the millennium, studies of the Scottish Enlightenment were flourishing. *The Cambridge Companion to the Scottish Enlightenment*, edited by Alexander Broadie, was published in 2003, with a second edition planned. My own (amended) contribution is reprinted as Chapter 5 and the book is filled by well-established scholars like Emerson, M. A. Stewart, Wood, Haakonssen, Fleischacker, Andrew Skinner and Broadie himself, who had previously (Broadie 2001) written an overview. Particularly notable is an upsurge in studies of *TMS*, prefaced by Charles Griswold (1999), the first comprehensive examination since Campbell.

The sheer volume of the literature makes it unwieldy to identify particular texts; it would quickly degenerate into an idiosyncratic and circumstantial reading list. I refer to some of these in the chapters that follow, not only those published since 2000 but also in the postscripts to the earlier work. Here I shall comment on approaches to the study of the Scots and then make a few observations regarding my own 'take'.

One feature of recent work that is unaligned to some grand interpretative perspective is the presence of a number of comparative studies. There has been a long-standing recognition of the links between the Scots and the American colonies (John Clive and Bernard Bailyn (1954) was an early exploration). The extensive scholarship on these links has tended to concentrate on the influence of the Scots, with Caroline Robbins (1954) and especially Douglas Adair (1957) setting a kind of (now inevitably contested) template. The wider comparative tempo picked up after 2000 – for example Emma Rothschild (2002) on Smith and Condorcet and John Robertson (2005) – produced a genuinely comparative examination of Scotland and Naples in the early Enlightenment. Deirdre Dawson and Pierre Morère (2004) edited a volume of comparative studies of Scotland and France and Jean-François Dunyach and Ann Thomson (2015) edited a wider-ranging volume. Michael Frazer (2010), focusing on moral sentiments, compared not only Smith and Hume but also Kant and Herder and in so doing provided a refreshing antidote to the more Kantian readings of Smith, especially, that have burgeoned. Broadie published a collection of essays on Scottish/French 'connections' (2012). More recently, Dennis Rasmussen (2015: reviewed by me in *Adam Smith Review* 2017) wrote a thematic comparison of Hume and Smith with Montesquieu and Voltaire. The relation between Rousseau and Smith has generated considerable attention: see, among others, Rasmussen (2008, 2013), Hanley (2008a and b), Griswold (2010 and 2017) and Hont (2015).

The Berry Line?

The question mark here is not merely a matter of diffidence (though it is also that) but an acknowledgement that I have not self-consciously provided or developed some unifying, overarching 'big idea'. If I were to identify my motivation, it would be some initial curiosity and then a willingness to go where the 'evidence' leads me. Of course, it would be disingenuous to claim that I start each enquiry with a blank sheet; rather, the slate has been inscripted with some (pre)dispositions. Some of these are the product of my intellectual history. I am not a historian, nor am I a philosopher in the way that practitioners of those disciplines would obviously recognise. My self-chosen academic label 'professor of political theory' captures at least some of the indeterminacy or catholic eclecticism that has marked the full range of my published work (indeed, my book *The Idea of Luxury* encapsulates the hybridity of my work as a whole). Yet some of those dispositions are more substantive and, as will be apparent in the following chapters, some motifs regularly recur which might pass as themes in the Scottish Enlightenment à la Berry. What follows is necessarily partial and terse – the chapters that follow provide what substantiation there is. I am only too well aware that any summation of this sort rides roughshod over nuance and discrimination (hopefully those qualities, too, will be discerned in the subsequent chapters).

For all their divergences on particular (which is not the same as 'minor') points, the group[s] of thinkers – the literati – working in Scotland from about 1730 to 1790 covered a range of concerns, from art, science, history, medicine, morality, religion and philosophy. That breadth is neither incidental nor accidental and establishes that there is a Scottish Enlightenment.

The geographical qualifier is precisely that. They were genuine members of the Enlightenment. The Scots were not parochial. They were open to ideas from Dutch/Continental Law (Grotius, Pufendorf, Heineccius), from French literature (Bayle, Montesquieu, Voltaire, Rousseau) and English science (Newton, Boyle). They also exhibited some commonly shared characteristics of Enlightenment thinking. There was a firm commitment to 'light' against the 'darkness' of superstition and ignorance; to the explanation of order, in particular the expansion from physical to what Hume called 'moral subjects' and to 'improvement', encompassing both fertilisation and civilisation.

Notwithstanding these shared characteristics, there are some more distinctive traits or points of emphasis. These are only to be expected. Few have subscribed to the notion of the Enlightenment as a monolithic body of ideas (I remember a lecture given by Peter Gay in Pittsburgh, where he ruminated that the definite article in the title of his two-volume work may have been unfortunate). To claim further, as Pocock (2008), for example, has done, that we should properly refer only to 'Enlightenments' or develop systemic qualifiers like Jonathan Israel's (2001) 'radical' becomes a matter of taste. That the Scottish literati have some shared characteristics and emphases does not, it seems to me, warrant some grand interpretative perspective along those lines. Among these distinctive Scottish characteristics are their recognition of the role of habit/ custom; seeing institutions as 'sticky' so that they change slowly and are not readily susceptible to a 'rational' quick fix; and their alertness, in Ferguson's phrase, to 'action not design'.

In these aspects I see manifestations of what a 'Berry line' might be. Calling this a 'line' means, to reiterate, that I am self-consciously aware that this is a particular perspective. I am not committed to any monolithic definition of *the* 'Scottish Enlightenment' but nor do I think that it is bereft of 'identity'.

From the perspective of my interests, I see the Scots as social scientists. They are 'scientists' in the spirit of Bacon and Newton. From the former they take the position, along with the rest of the Enlightenment, that knowledge of causes is power and the purpose of that power is to make a positive difference in the social world. The touchstone of this 'difference' is whether it improves, in Hume's phrase (co-opted by Smith), 'common life'. This includes both material betterment in the form of diet, clothing and shelter and attitudinal progress in the form of tolerance and civility. From Newton they take the view that causal knowledge needs to be systematised; a good and thus useful explanation is one that uses few causes to account for many effects. Given their touchstone, their focus is the social world of 'moral subjects'. While disinterestedness is not alien, those who we might today label 'scientists' – such as Cullen, Black or Hutton – saw their work as helping to make common life better. In that way I see them as engaged in the same 'project' as those writers who have been my major focus. As, therefore, a matter of relative emphasis, not categorical separation, I detect at the heart of their concerns a non-discrete intermingling of law, ethics, commerce and history, with history typically the 'history of man(kind)'.[5] They develop a concept of 'society' as a set of interlocking institutions, which, while more or less internally coherent, are subject to change over time. As I have expressed it (Berry 2013), the Scots adopt a twin-pronged diachronic and synchronic approach.

They are social scientists but they are not positivists. Their Baconian agenda is also a moral but (with inevitable exceptions) not an overtly moralising one. They are committed to amelioration and to the judgement that the basic institutions of their own society are an improvement on what has gone before; some ways of life are better than others (see my more developed exposition of this in Chapter 8). The criteria that warrant that judgement are implicit (using Smith's recorded phrase, of which I make much use in the following chapters) in the joint achievement of opulence and freedom. Underpinning this – and in line with their science – is their reasoned conviction that the universality and uniformity of human nature provide a solid base. Of all my propositions, first essayed in my 1982 book, this has perhaps been the most contested. This contestation it seems to me often stems from a reluctance to read the Scots as holding positions that now seem untenable or from a subscription to the tenets of debatable anthropology/historicism.

There are two further corollaries. One is that the Scots are resolutely modernist. This is not to say they are intellectual iconoclasts but they do judge that their Baconian enterprise can do its work without the structural assistance of classical and neoclassical thought and, especially, without theology. This is not down to ignorance: as Hume said, they were in their infancy infused with classical texts (cf. E-RA 275) and brought up in a more or less rigorous Presbyterian culture. Second, what integrates these various judgements and commitments is an intellectual engagement with their own commercial society. While they were predominantly university professors, in eighteenth-century Scotland universities were not ivory towers. The classroom and the laboratory sought to equip students with the intellectual tools to make their way in the world (often, indeed, away from Scotland). The literati were members of the key social institutions, both formal and informal, and they engaged reflexively with the role, meaning and justification of those same institutions.

Within the context of their society, the Scottish thinkers gave their support to economic 'improvement' and modernity, especially liberty under the impersonal rule of law. In their thought they stressed that humans were social beings who, as a matter of historical fact, have lived in a variety of settings. This made them aware that their own society was but one variant and they wished to understand what made it distinctive (and to establish its superiority to its predecessors). Their contribution to the history of social sciences, we can say, is twofold. It lies in understanding society in general as an interrelated set of institutions and behaviours that varies over time. It also lies, more particularly, in their recognition that commercial society represented something new. While, of course, they did not anticipate capitalism, they did appreciate that a society where every man was in some measure a merchant marked a qualitative difference in the way societies, and the individuals within them, operated.

When this volume and several other pieces currently in the pipeline are published, it is doubtful I will make much further contribution to future study. My journey in that sense will come to a conclusion but the road along which I travelled stretches on. The selection of my work collected here, and in my books, is but a way station. On a valedictory note, fifty years on from my doctorate I feel confident that the study of the Scottish Enlightenment is well established. Aside from dedicated works on Hume and Smith, of which there seem no end, scholarship on other Scots and on the Scottish Enlightenment itself will flourish. The geographical diffusion of interest and subsequent scholarship augurs well, especially since there remain significant lacunae. John Millar is seriously under-studied (Miller 2017 has just appeared and is hopefully a harbinger). There is no proper biography and his extensive lecture notes have not yet been collated. An intellectual biography of Hutcheson would fill a serious gap. The 'educational' theory and writings thereon have not been systematically examined. Relatively minor writers like Gregory, Blair and Wallace would benefit from more intensive scrutiny. These all reflect my own preoccupations but the work of economic, social, cultural, scientific/medical and agricultural historians will proceed apace to add depth and breadth to the study of the Scottish Enlightenment. More and more journeys will be taken.

Notes

1. Slotkin (1965) produced an extensive selection of 'early anthropology', which included sections on the 'Scotch School' with brief

non-continuous extracts from the main players but also including Monboddo, Gregory and, indeed, Dunbar.

2. The same can be said of Italian – where there is a long tradition of scholarship, especially on Hume – and French works. Japanese work has become better known as they have begun to publish in English, pioneered by the doyen of the study of the Scottish Enlightenment Hiroshi Mizuta (see, for example, 1975), the collection of essays edited by Sakamoto and Tanaka (2003) and the work of younger scholars like Susato (2015), Nohara and Mori. Somewhat similarly, Spanish (and Latin American), Finnish and Greek work has also begun to appear in English but Polish, Turkish and (burgeoning) Chinese scholarship less so.

3. A similar gathering was held at McGill in Montreal and its proceedings, too, were published (Norton et al., eds 1979). This included an important piece by James Moore (1979), who in a series of articles over a number of years built up a significant body of interpretative work, in particular 1977 but also, for example, 2009. Also contributing were Livingston, giving an early outing for his interpretation (see below), Pocock and Davie once more (for Davie, see also text above).

4. Despite an influential early work on 'civil society' (1962 tr. 1989) and the take-up of that theme by some scholars of Ferguson pre-eminently (see Chapter 8), Habermas's concern with an 'emancipatory' in contrast to a 'technical' interest has not been put to significant use. The only work I am aware of that does something along those lines is Strasser as far back as 1976. However, see Dunyach and Thomson (2015: 14) for references to work on 'the reading public' as manifestations of a 'Habermasian public sphere'.

5. That term is used in titles by Dunbar (*EHM*) and Kames (*SHM* and *HLT*) and is employed by Hume (for example *U* 3, 9), Smith (for example *WN* IV.vii.c.80/626), Ferguson (for example *ECS* 3) and Millar (for example *OR* 180). While Robertson's Histories have area-specific titles, they are animated by 'philosophical' reach and ambition (especially *VS* and *HAm*, which contains the phrase 'history of the human mind' (Bk 4) 811).

Part I

The Scottish Enlightenment

Introduction to Part I

The seven chapters in this first part of the book here reproduce material that is not explicitly devoted to either Smith or Hume. To some extent that is misleading. I have written extensively on the Scottish Enlightenment across a wide range of thinkers and topics but that discussion is found in my two synoptic volumes (Berry 1997, 2013). The consequence is that this part does not deal in depth with, for example, Millar and Kames (though Kames is more than a passing presence in Chapter 6). The thinker who does figure prominently in Part I is James Dunbar, for the reasons outlined in Chapter 1. The essays here cover a range of subjects but they complement, and provide some intellectual background, for themes in Parts II and III, such as Hume on climate and Smith on language. In addition, the acceptance of human sociality as a major premise in Hume and Smith is foregrounded in a couple of these essays. A new essay (Chapter 8) does discuss Hume and Smith at some length, but aims to place their argument into the more general context of a recurrent theme in this volume as a whole, namely the shift in Scottish thought away from a focus on 'the political'.

I have never written an essay that seeks to encapsulate my considered overview of the Scottish Enlightenment. In the conclusion to Chapter 1, I put forward what I there identified as the 'Berry line' and this gestures to such a reflective overview. I am content to let those paragraphs, along with the collected essays across this volume and my books, serve as an interpretation of the Scottish Enlightenment.

2

James Dunbar and Ideas of Sociality and Language in Eighteenth-Century Scotland

Attention has been drawn to the writers of the Scottish Enlightenment as beginning the systematic treatment of society – as being the first sociologists.[1] The intention of this essay is twofold: one, to place one seemingly crucial aspect of this claim, namely the belief in the social nature of man, under closer scrutiny; and, two, to conduct this scrutiny by way of an examination of the theory of James Dunbar on this point. Dunbar is a suitable subject for this exercise because his theory of sociality is distinctive and interesting in its own right but has not been closely examined. Furthermore, besides having a positive theory of his own, he also indulges in a critique of alternative theories – a critique that not only helps to characterise the broad approach of the Scottish Enlightenment on this question of sociality but also indicates the presence of differences within it.

As a preliminary to examining Dunbar's theory of sociality, we have to take heed of a more general element in his thought, namely his theory of development. This theory is best appreciated in the light of the Aristotelian Theory of Substance. Dunbar's direct reference to Aristotle in this context is found in his opening essay, where he writes: 'The celebrated distinction of Aristotle ($E\nu\acute{\epsilon}\rho\gamma\epsilon\iota\alpha$ and $\Delta\acute{\upsilon}\nu\alpha\mu\iota\varsigma$) will then appear to have ample foundation in nature' (*EHM* 4). That is, there is in 'nature' the distinction between latent capacity and manifest energy and a development or actualisation from the latent to the manifest. This is not to suggest that Dunbar is an Aristotelian in any strong sense; rather, he simply utilises, and acknowledges the source of, a widely received notion. Indeed, this notion of development underpins Dunbar's argument on several occasions but here we shall only consider its utilisation in his theory of sociality.

Thus, referring specifically to the human faculties (though averring that the progress of nations and men 'though not exactly parallel is found in several respects to correspond'), he states:

> we may remark this gradual opening ... First of all, those of sense appear, grow up spontaneously or require but little culture. Next in order, the propensities of the heart display their force; a fellow-feeling with others unfolds itself gradually on the appearance of proper objects, for man becomes sociable long before he is a rational being. Last in the train, the powers of the intellect begin to blossom, are reared up by culture, and demand an intercourse of minds. (*EHM* 16)

The underlying development theory can be evidenced here in the phrase 'unfolds itself gradually on the appearance of proper objects' and its significance will become apparent below. All the principles of these stages – 'senses', 'propensities of the heart' and 'powers of the intellect' – are faculties in the psyche. They are, as such, original (natural) endowments, but endowments that are only manifested gradually. Furthermore, pertinently, this quotation enables us to identify the source of man's sociality for Dunbar, that is, in a 'fellow-feeling' in the second and not in the first sensual or third rational stages. These two other stages or principles are, in fact, the basis of two alternative theories of sociality and Dunbar thus rejects them both.

To take, first, his rejection of the view that men are sociable through their utilisation of their reason, here Dunbar is in the mainstream of the Scottish Enlightenment. All the Scots rejected the notions of a 'state of nature' and a 'social contract', both characteristic of the 'rational' theory. These notions were employed by Natural Lawyers (and Hobbes) in the seventeenth century to help to give an account of the motives that made society, and more particularly government, a rational choice for man.[2] These institutions were deducible from the dictates of Natural Law and in conformity with man's nature, of which the 'chief adornment' was his reason. These notions of a state of nature and a social contract were employed only and explicitly as heuristic devices,[3] their existential character being denied; yet the Scots took these ideas as possessing such a character. Then they declared them to be fanciful because no evidence could be found to indicate the existence of such a state or the enunciation of such a contract.[4] This empiricism is, of course, the chief factor separating the eighteenth-century Scots from the deductions of the seventeenth-century jurists. This open and combative use of empiricism did not prevent the Scots from using the traditional method of introspection based on the axiom that human nature was uniform. Accordingly, the Scots came up with their own answer to the source of man's social existence, namely that it was instinctive or appetitive.[5]

Though this answer is scarcely distinctive (it was, for example, common to all the Natural Lawyers) it is, nevertheless, part of a wider animus held by the Scots against reason. Reason was regarded as being a 'weak principle in man'[6] and its operations fallible. In consequence, it was believed, all the important issues relative to man's life were decided by infallible instinct and not by capricious reason. Thus, just as the propagation of the species and self-preservation were the product of instinct, so was man's existence within society and, accordingly, this existence could not be correctly attributed to man's use of his reason.

We have seen that Dunbar, like his contemporaries, regards man's sociality as a natural endowment; yet, as indicated above, we have also seen that he opposes a sensual theory of the origin of this social nature. In other words, Dunbar argues against one form of instinctive sociality. This form is that man's sociality is analogous to that of other animals. In a revealing passage, at the beginning of Essay 1, Dunbar outlines another development theory, essentially complementary to the one quoted above, of the human species:

> First, man may have subsisted in some sort like other animals in a separate and individual state, before the date of language or the commencement of regular intercourse. Secondly, he may be contemplated in a higher stage; a proficient in language, and a member of that artless community which consists with equality, with freedom and independence. Last of all, by slow and imperceptible transitions, he subsists and flourishes under the protection and discipline of civil government. (EHM 2–3; for further discussion of this passage, see Chapter 3)

Here we see that Dunbar is implicitly rejecting the animalistic thesis – that as an animal, man is solitary. However, Dunbar also rejects the argument explicitly, but before we can appreciate this rejection we need to expand upon Dunbar's own theory of sociality, that of fellow feeling.

It seems from what was said above about the Scottish rejection of the 'state of nature' that Dunbar's location of sociality in the second of his three stages poses two problems. Firstly, it implies that man is not sociable in the first stage of his development. Is this first stage, then, Dunbar's equivalent of the state of nature?

The answer to this question is that Dunbar seems not to regard the man of his 'first stage' as distinctively a man. Man as a creature of the senses, is indeed, as we have just seen, more properly regarded as an animal. It is only in the second stage when sociality is manifest that man can be said to be a man in any proper meaning of the word: 'every effort beyond what is merely animal has reference to a community' (*EHM* 5). If man is properly understood in this manner, then for him there is therefore no state of nature. This leads on to the second, related, problem because the presence of the social appetite as an original endowment should mean that it is impossible for even a man qua animal to be solitary.

We can rephrase this second problem in the form of the following question. Given that man has a social appetite and that this is natural, as are the senses, why then does Dunbar not locate this appetite in the first (sensual or animal) stage? The answer to this question is to be found in Dunbar's theory of development. The social appetite is latent within man and it does, therefore, like all other latent attributes, require the appearance of proper objects. Dunbar thus seems to believe that the appropriate 'proper object' does not exist *ab initio* and only with its appearance does the first stage come to an end. Nevertheless, because the social appetite is an original endowment, man still is, for Dunbar, as with the other Scots, naturally sociable.

This notion of 'proper objects' is obviously of key importance.[7] We have already seen what Dunbar conceives to be associated with the appearance of the proper object in this context, namely the actualisation of sociality, or fellow feeling. It is this fellow feeling that is the cornerstone of Dunbar's social theory; yet we must elaborate on the association between it and its appropriate proper object: why does it operate when it does? What are the mechanics of this operation? Dunbar does consider questions such as these.

This fellow feeling exhibited in the second stage of development is the source of society, but it is society itself which is 'the theatre on which our genius expands with freedom. It is essential to the origin of all our ideas of natural and moral beauty, it is the prime mover of all our inventive powers' (*EHM* 5). There is an appearance of circularity here, since Dunbar seems to be saying that society is necessary for the sociable feelings to manifest themselves while these feelings are themselves supposedly the source of society. This circularity is, however, only an appearance and Dunbar helps to clarify his position by explaining why and how the fellow feeling exhibits itself.

After asserting that men are more or less identical (the axiom of uniform human nature), Dunbar declares that men's needs and wants are also identical. These men, it must be stressed, have yet to exhibit sociability and are thus only men qua animals. This identity of the needs of these men means, in practice, that there will be a tendency for them to meet at, to give one of Dunbar's own examples, 'riverbanks' (*EHM* 24). These meetings 'ripen' the social appetite and as it ripens it needs, like other appetites, to be satisfied. Society is the agency of this satisfaction. The organic analogy is instructive since it underlines the centrality of Dunbar's theory of development. It is this theory that acquits him of the charge of circularity: meetings originally of a contingent character generate sociability, which establishes in time a permanency of contact, that is, society. Dunbar's social theory thus takes the form of a unilinear unfolding of potential principles in man. A corollary of Dunbar's theory, which is, as we shall see, an important element, is that the theory presupposes that the fellow feeling is unrestricted.

Now that we have, in outline, Dunbar's own theory, we can now turn to his critique of the alternative theory mentioned above – that man is instinctively sociable in an analogous manner to animals. Dunbar himself neatly enumerates views contrary to his own, as well as reaffirming his own position, when he writes: 'Society is held together by the tie of affection or conscious delight more than by fear, or mutual wants or any necessary call of nature' (*EHM* 13)[8]. Here we have Dunbar's own position of 'tie of affection', or what we have previously identified as fellow feeling, and three opposed positions. The inclusion of fear as one such position is, of course, an allusion to Hobbes' theory, which is rejected for the 'anti- rational' reasons given above, as well as for Hobbes' own explicit denial of natural sociality. The position of 'mutual wants' will be considered later; here it is the rejection of the 'argument from necessity' that concerns us. This rejection is the basis of Dunbar's dismissal of the animalistic account of sociality. Such an account was upheld by Kames.

Kames was scarcely being exceptional when he undertook to

regard man as an animal,[9] but he hoped that 'the social laws by which such animals are governed might open views into the social nature of man' (*SHM* I, 377). Kames proceeds by, firstly, classifying animals. Into one group go such animals as are not sociable. These are the animals of prey. Into another group Kames places the herding animals. He identifies two causes of herding: 'we find that the appetite for society is withheld from no species to which it is necessary whether for defence or food' (*SHM* I, 380).[10] There is, however, still another category. Some animals – Kames' example is horses[11] – are found in society without need for defence or subsistence and Kames holds that their sociality is 'derived from pleasure of living in society' (*SHM* I, 380). But this last cause of sociality Kames, significantly, regards as 'an imperfect kind of society, and far from being so intimate, as where it is provided by nature for defence, or for procuring food' (*SHM* I, 381). Kames then applies these findings to man and believes that this application makes it 'evident . . . that to no animal is society more *necessary* than to man for food or for subsistence' (*SHM* I, 387; my emphasis).

Kames' position has two aspects. Firstly, herding is seen as the product of instinct. But, in addition, Kames has endeavoured to discern the 'final cause' for this instinct. His answer is that it is only in the herd, by mutual cooperation, that the particular animal can seek food in safety. In fact, what Kames has done is analyse the herding appetite into another, and thereby more basic, appetite or instinct, namely preservation.

By contrast, Dunbar, it will be recalled, maintains that society is not held together by 'any necessary call of nature'. By this he evidently means, from the context, instinct. To understand why Dunbar rejects this position, we have to examine his strictures on the utility of the man/brute analogy along the lines employed by Kames.

Dunbar admits that animals crowd together in danger but he does not regard such herding as significant, since these animals disperse at the 'approach of a more rapacious beast' and 'rarely attempt to supply their weakness by collective strength', so that the animals, in fact, 'derive no security from mutual aid' (*EHM* 7–8). The analogy here breaks down since 'Man almost alone becomes considerable by the combination of his species' (ibid. 7–8). Kames, as we saw, has another motive for herding, common to man and the brutes, namely care for subsistence. But, Dunbar declares: 'I am not ignorant that (animals) are gregarious from *necessity* . . .

and require joint labour for their subsistence or accommodation' (*EHM* 9; my emphasis). Here Dunbar is stating what Kames had discerned – that the herding instinct is reducible to the instinct of preservation and the thrust of Dunbar's argument is against the necessitarian character of instinct.

Dunbar maintains that, through anthropomorphism, the role of instinct in animals has been misinterpreted:

> An opinion of intercourse in the lower ranks is often suggested or favoured by a propensity there is in man to confer on every creature a portion of his own nature. Suitable to this propensity, in observing a concourse of animals, however fortuitous, he magnifies every appearance in favour of the social principle and presumes a concert and government where none in reality subsist. (*EHM* 11)

In fact, more briefly, Dunbar believes 'interested intercourse in the animal oeconomy is greater in appearance than in reality' (*EHM* 12–13). The upshot of this is that once again the validity of the man/brute analogy is greatly suspect.[12] Thus, although the 'brute creation' may be held together and generally subsists by instinct, the same is not necessarily the case for man.

Aside from his doubts on the interpretation of instinct, Dunbar regards the man/brute analogy as invalid because of the essential difference of man's moral nature. Dunbar asks, whence the superiority of man over the brutes? As one possible answer to this question, he rejects the idea that this superiority can be evidenced in the senses because, simply, the senses of many animals are more acute than man's. Dunbar also dismisses as a possible answer the fact that men act jointly because animals can often do singularly acts similar to those upon which men cooperate. It must be admitted that Dunbar does not specify what these acts might be. Instead of these, Dunbar locates man's superiority in 'some inward consciousness, some decisive mark of superiority in every condition' (*EHM* 14). The relevance of this mark of superiority to the present context is clearly expressed by Dunbar himself: 'But in this his (man's) preeminence consists, that being as *independent* as they (animals) in all corporeal functions, impelled by *no necessity* but by generous passions, he rises to improvements which flow from the union of his kind' (ibid.; my emphasis).

We can now draw together the various threads of Dunbar's argument hitherto. He believes that there is a natural affection (see below) common to both man and animals, hence the fact that the 'tie of affection encompasses the whole circle of being'. Man, however, does differ from animals and the most important source of this difference,[13] this moral element, makes the argument from analogy that man is sociable from necessity invalid. Man's sociality is not the instinctive reaction of brutes. Instead, it is a *conscious* delight'; man is moved by 'generous passions'. This is a truly social appetite. By definition, it encompasses others and is irreducible to a necessarily selfish instinct of self-preservation. Dunbar, moreover, reinforces his critique of the view that man is sociable from instinctive necessity by maintaining that such a necessitarian view disparages man's moral nature.[14]

But Dunbar's theory of sociality is of wider import. His theory entails – besides a rejection of rational and instinctive sociality – a rejection of three other associated theories, namely coeval animosity, partial affection in general and partial affection in the particular guise of the family. We take these in turn.

As said above, Dunbar's theory of fellow feeling supposes that it is at first unrestricted and such a view clearly presents Dunbar with the problem of accounting for antisocial behaviour. Aside from Hobbes' straightforward assertion of man as the enemy of every man (at least potentially) ([1651] 1991: Ch. 13), an assertion that was almost universally rejected, it was, nevertheless, a common position to hold that man had both antisocial and social passions.[15] With respect to the former of these, Adam Ferguson believed that 'men appear to have in their minds the seeds of animosity' (*ECS* 20). True to his avowal of empiricism, Ferguson followed this up by remarking that no evidence demonstrates men living together in any large numbers in complete amity. But in all those situations alike, they were broken into cantons and affected a distinction of name and community (*ECS* 21). Ferguson, indeed, proceeds to draw from this a number of prosocial consequences whereby he reconciles the presence in man of both a social appetite and a disposition to animosity, since, in the final analysis, this disposition contributes to both the individual's own and society's well-being.[16]

Dunbar cannot – indeed, does not – deny the presence of antisocial behaviour, so how does he explain it while still upholding his theory of sociality from an unrestricted fellow feeling? The key to Dunbar's explanation of this behaviour is seen in the following phrase: 'the principles of union are in the order of things prior to those of hostility' (*EHM* 26). Dunbar thus does not deny the existence of hostility but, crucially, he makes them posterior to the factors responsible for union. It follows from this that Dunbar believes there was a time when only the principles of union were operant 'at a time when no discordant interests or various pursuits, had diversified the scene, a small community might be kept together by the tie of sociability and reciprocal love' (*EHM* 25). This is a 'time' of great significance in Dunbar's thought as a whole since, while no primitivist (man flourishes 'under civil government' – see above), he looks wistfully at certain aspects of society at this time and uses this as a yardstick to criticise certain features of his own society. Dunbar, moreover, true to his own declaration of empiricism, gives examples of such communities, namely the Soldurii and 'some of the South Sea isles' (*EHM* 26).[17]

Dunbar has thus indicated that there is a succession from the principles of union to those of hostility and he does provide some elaboration on this point. The relationship between these two principles is not merely one of priority: it is also causal, 'but the former (union) are in truth productive of the latter (hostility)' (*EHM* 26). This is explained as follows:

> The affections of the heart are of limited exertion and that mutual love which is confined within a narrow sphere triumphs as it were over the sentiment which gave it birth and creates in a competition of interests, such fierce animosity among contending tribes. (*EHM* 26)

As an example of this change, Dunbar gives 'Even pride, the passion which divides mankind, was originally a principle of union. It was a sense of the dignity of the species, not an opinion of superiority among individuals' (*EHM* 26).[18] Further, society itself, through, for example, the division of labour,[19] generates circumstances detrimental to the social passions. This point Dunbar shares with a number of his compatriots and it has also been used to indicate their claim to be sociologists.[20]

Again, we see that it is Dunbar's theory of development that enables him to afford a reconciliation between the two 'facts' of sociality and antisociality. Both are equally natural, in that both are original endowments but the appropriate proper object for their unfolding occurred at different times. Thus, we can say that, because of his position that union is prior to and causal of hostility, for Dunbar it is the dynamic of social interaction and density that generates conflict. This means society is already established *before* the appearance of animosity so, it follows, this animosity cannot be coeval with the principle of union, fellow feeling.

To expand on this, it seems that Dunbar's conception of the relationship between 'arts and dependence' is crucial. As quoted above, the social stage (that is, prior to the manifestation of hostility and and characterised by unrestricted fellow feeling) is noted for being 'artless' and 'independent'. Dunbar declares that 'arts and dependence grow together' (*EHM* 17) but again, and importantly, the relation is causal. It is 'the arts of life, which by enervating our corporeal powers and multiplying the objects of desire, have annihilated independence' (*EHM* 6–7; cf. Rousseau 1962). This development of arts, together with a growth in population, resulted in the development of 'mutual alliances and mutual support' (*EHM* 6) and since, once again, society itself has generated these characteristics or – in terms more consonant with the development theory – has actualised this potential, to explain society by these 'mutual wants' is to commit the fallacy of post hoc ergo propter hoc and hence, too, we can now see, Dunbar's rationale for rejecting (as quoted above) sociality from this source.[21]

As said above, a common position was to hold that man possessed both social and anti- or dis-social passions. In some writers this position manifested itself in a theory of partial affection, which is the remaining theory of sociality rejected by Dunbar. As an instance of a theory of partial affection, we can once again cite Kames.

As we illustrated above, Kames believes that the analogy with animals can help enlighten some aspects of human behaviour and his review of the 'animal kingdom' brings him to the conclusion that no animal has an appetite for association with the whole species. That is, the herding instinct is naturally limited. When these findings are applied to man, the same conclusion is reached: 'we find now after accurate scrutiny that the social appetite in man comprehends not the whole species but a part only' (SHM I, 388; my emphasis). A variation of this argument, not based on instinct but on the proximity and frequency of association, was propounded. Here, developing the point that man possesses selfish passions, Smith, for example, declares that affection extends outwards from the individual to his family, to his friends, etc., with decreasing fervour (*TMS* VI.2.1/219; cf. Hume *T* 3.2.2.8/ *SBNT* 488). These beliefs in a partial social instinct or affection are clearly contrary to Dunbar's belief in an initially unrestricted fellow feeling.

Dunbar, as we have seen, is not disposed to accept the Kamesian argument from analogy but, aside from his strictures on this point, he has a general argument against the claim that sociality is partial. Again, this argument is couched in terms of his developmental theory so that the force of opposition is directed at the origin of society, which is in this first essay his major concern.[22] Dunbar's argument is that the tie of affection is not at first restricted since it is not possible to 'explain the combinations of tribes and moral harmony among nations from the operation of partial instincts' (*EHM* 30). That is, the actual existence of society is, to Dunbar, evidence that there is some wider principle than partial instinct responsible for it. Instead, like conflict, partial affections are the product of society. Man has first to be in concourse with his fellows before he can discriminate between them as a relative, friend or stranger. If this discrimination were inherent, then the initial intercourse at those riverbanks (see above) would never have acted as a 'proper object'. That is Dunbar's answer in general terms to the argument of sociality from partial principles but he also rejects, as mentioned above, this argument in the particular terms of the family.

The argument that society is to be understood as the growth of families, whether from Adam and Eve or from the institution of pacts between fathers, was, of course, well established. Nevertheless, to Dunbar such an argument is inadequate because, once again, such partial principles could not be responsible for society: 'It is not then such partial principles which could have formed or embodied the larger communities of mankind. It is not a parent, a child or a brother but the species itself that is the object embraced by humanity (*EHM* 23; my emphasis). [23] Dunbar is arguing that without some other principle, namely fellow feeling, the posited interfamilial intercourse as the germ of society could not have occurred. But still, the argument that man belongs by nature to a family would, unless refuted, undermine Dunbar's position and, accordingly, we find Dunbar pursuing this point.

He is aware of the part the family plays.[24] Indeed, he produces the common argument that the 'period of pregnancy . . . were by far too short to dispense, in the human species, with the parental cares' (*EHM* 18).[25] But now Dunbar subjects this common argument to further scrutiny. Dunbar's own theory is, to repeat, concerned with the very origin of society, that is, for him, with the pre-familial situation. Hence, he asks, 'Is love then *at first* devoted to a single object?' and replies with the statement that 'the supposition ... is irreconcileable with the history of ruder ages' (*EHM* 20; my emphasis).

Although Dunbar concedes that parents are attached to their offspring for a longer period in the human than in the animal world, this does not mean that the family can be rightfully regarded as the source of society, since he maintains that this not truly a family relationship. He cites in substantiation of this thesis that the paternal instinct is 'of precarious exertion' and then he conjectures whether the maternal instinct might not also have been equally transient 'at an aera further back' (*EHM* 23). If, therefore, the parent–child relationship were originally fluid and because men are naturally initially sociable to all, it follows, for Dunbar, that the family unit cannot be considered the source of society. The family as *now* conceived is a consequence of the 'improvements of social life' and Dunbar explains that to see it as the source of society is another instance where 'certain appearances in the civil aera have been transferred, in imagination, to all preceding times' (*EHM* 6).

Although the structure of Dunbar's argument against the family theorists is distinctively his own, he does nevertheless share his antipathy to this theory with most of his compatriots.[26] For example, Ferguson declares that 'Families may be considered as the elementary forms of society' but then goes on to state that 'Before the force of the first family affection is spent, relations multiply and instinctive attachments grow into habit' (*PMPS* I.27 30). The other Scots similarly place little emphasis on the family, in this context, because their own theories stress instead the group: 'Mankind are to be taken in groupes as they have always subsisted' (Ferguson *ECS* and almost identically *IMP* 262).

In conclusion, we can see that the crux of Dunbar's theory of sociality is his conviction that this must be found in an unambiguously social, other-regarding, principle. Thus, we have seen, he rejects a theory that can look upon man's social existence as, in his own words, the 'production of an aspiring understanding' (*EHM* 17). Here, like his compatriots, he, in contrast, stakes his claim on man's social nature – he is a creature of society. It is here where the eighteenth-century Scots are noteworthy, whether as sociologists or not, since, breaking away from the subsumption of this claim in a wider deductive system with its attendant individualism, they spell out some of its consequences and implications. They, probably more than anyone else in their century (including even their mentor Montesquieu), make society their focus of analysis.

Dunbar, by pressing further his analysis as to what sort of social creature man is, not only expounds his own distinctive theory but also usefully makes it possible to identify, among his contemporaries, a number of different approaches within their broad stance, thereby bringing into it a finer appreciation. In addition, we have seen that Dunbar develops his own theory of social dynamics. By incorporating into his theory a greater timescale, he endeavours to explain those human attributes, which his contemporaries take as given, as natural, such as parental affection, friendship and dislike of neighbours. Moreover, through his theory of development, he is still able to regard these attributes as natural but can also provide an explanation of them in social terms: that they are socially induced. There is, as it were, in Dunbar a dialectic. The action of society generates new circumstances and conditions from which man is not unaffected but, rather, his inherent propensities are actualised and these in turn interact anew with social conditions. So, despite its undoubtedly sketchy nature, Dunbar does, in developing his theory of sociality, and criticising opposed accounts, outline a radical theory of social causation.

Postscript

This was the first academic article I had published, in 1973. Largely through my inexperience but also partly because of the obscure subject matter, it took time to find a home. I fastened on to *Il Pensiero Politico* on the grounds that Pocock had published in it. I think the argument stands up but it suffers, as intimated in Chapter 1, from not appreciating the impact of the ideas in Rousseau's *Second Discourse* (we know this work was discussed in the Aberdeen Wise Club, although before Dunbar himself joined it (Ulman 1990: 62)). Like the thesis from which it was derived, a central aim of the article was to use Dunbar's distinctive account to highlight the wider Scottish discussion of sociality. (Chapter 5 represents a follow-up; and see its postscript.)

Despite his view of the 'social nature of man' constituting the opening selection in Adams' (1789) compendium, this did little to disseminate Dunbar's argument. In a backhanded fashion this is substantiated by David Irving (1804: 168) who, having placed Dunbar in the company of Robertson, Kames, Millar and Stuart, says the *Essays* with their 'eloquence and energy . . . entitle them to a more ample share of the public attention than they seem to have received'. I do think Dunbar's discussion is more worthwhile and intellectually interesting than Lehmann's uniformly hostile account in his book on Ferguson (1930: 213–14). An early account, not cited here but which I had read, that picks up on Dunbar's particular stadial version is Pearce (1945) who, influenced by Lovejoy, puts him in a 'primitivist' frame (see Chapter 1). Spadafora (1990: 272n, 314n, 275n, 301, etc.), not entirely reliably, places Dunbar's argument in a developmental framework but with limited references to the opening essay. Miller (2017: 104–6) discusses Dunbar's view of family and marriage, helpfully comparing his account to Robertson and Millar. Like Adams' opinion of Dunbar, I cannot claim that this article (aside from my passing use of it in Berry 1997), judged by the relatively few citations to it (Paul Wood is one (1993: 216)), has made academic ripples.

Notes

1. Cf. Swingewood (1970), Schneider (1967) and, more specifically, Lehmann (1930; 1952), MacRae (1969) and Bryson (1945).
2. Cf. Pufendorf (1934: Bk 7, Ch. 2, *passim*).
3. Cf. Pufendorf (1934: Bk 7, Ch. 2, para 4.)
4. Cf. Ferguson (*ECS* 6): 'If there was a time in which he (man) had his acquaintance with his own species to make . . . it is a time of which we have no record.' Hume's critique is of course well known; see *T* 3.2.2.14/*SBNT* 493.
5. Cf. inter alia Ferguson (*ECS* 11), Kames (*SHM* I, 387) and Stewart (1854: VI 137 *passim*).
6. Gregory (1788: 14).
7. He writes (*EHM* 3): 'There is one general observation strongly applicable, in all ages, to human nature: the appearance of proper objects is essential to the exertion of its powers.'
8. Cf. the very similar passage: 'nor is it perhaps so much the call of necessity or mutual wants as a certain delight in their kind, congenial with all natures, which constitutes the fundamental principles of association and harmony throughout the whole circle of being' (*EHM* 7).

9. Dunbar himself upholds this, as we have seen, and cf. Ferguson: 'Man it must be confessed . . . is an animal in the full extent of that designation' (*ECS* 46). The point is, of course, a commonplace going back at least as far as Aristotle.

10. For a similar classification, see Ferguson (*IMP* 23–4, *PMPS* I, 20–1). Cf. Stewart (1854: VI, 136).

11. Cf. Ferguson: 'He is in short a man in every condition; and *we* can learn nothing of his nature from the analogy of other animals' (*ECS* 6), but see n4 *supra*.

12. Language is also cited as a differential and developed by Dunbar in later essays (see Chapter 3). This was a commonplace – which is why Monboddo is so egregious and utilised as such by Kames (*SHM* Preliminary Discourse).

13. Not, of course, that this is denied by Kames, although an earlier work, *Principles of Morals and Natural Religion* (1751) was attacked for its denial of free will. See Lehmann (1971: 29 f.).

14. Cf. inter alia Kames (*SHM* I, 403), Hutcheson (*SMP* Bk 1, Ch. 1) and Smith, who distinguishes social from antisocial from selfish passions (*TMS* 1.ii.3–5/34–43).

15. For example, 'the sense of common danger and the assaults of an enemy, have been frequently useful to nations by uniting their members more firmly together' and on the individual's plane, conflict 'often furnish(es) a scene for the exercise of our greatest abilities' (*ECS* 22, 23–4). That Gumplowicz called Ferguson the 'Father of modern sociology' as the result of his 'conflict' theory has been duly noted by commentators – Forbes (1966: xviii), Lehmann (1930: 98) and Bryson (1945: 257).

16. Cf. Monboddo, who seems to accept that there was a time before antisocial traits were evident. His account is physiological as well as psychological because he believes that men were originally 'frugivores' but 'as soon as he became a hunter the wild beast which is part of his composition became predominant (*OPL* I, 259–60).

17. Cf. here (and generally) Rousseau's distinction between *amour de soi* and *amour-propre* (1962: 118).

18. See, for example, 'that the sub-division of arts, which is so conducive to their perfection, degrades the character of the common artisan is a proposition consonant to the uniform experience of civilised nations' and this degradation is manifest in 'a torpor of intellect' and a tendency to 'debilitate the body and to engender disease' (*EHM* 402, 404). Adam Smith's influence is evident: not only does Dunbar refer to pin manufacture but his phraseology is strikingly similar. See, for

example, where Smith refers to 'the torpor of his (man who performs a few simple operations) mind' (*WN* V.i.f.50/782).

19. Cf. Swingewood (1970), MacRae (1969, though with a caveat) and Forbes (1967). See also West (1969) on comparing Smith and Marx, though Marx's own absorption of the German Idealist tradition, together with the Scots' own concerns with man's moral well-being, make a comparison of limited significance.

20. An example of a theorist from 'mutual wants' would be Turnbull ([1742] 2003: 94, 119).

21. This is explicit: 'It is the design of this Essay to enquire into the principles which either superseded the first (that is the animal) or hastened the second (that is the social) stage' (*EHM* 3).

22. See also 'Yet the attempt were in vain to refer the origin of large communities to domestic relation and ties of blood' (*EHM* 18).

23. That 'natural affection' (see above) common to man and animals is, in fact, Στοργη. This term refers specifically to the relationship between parent and progeny and is employed by many of the Scots, such as Ferguson (*PMPS* I, 31).

24. Cf. J. Locke (1965), paras 79–80, whence its popularity.

25. Monboddo, again, is an exception: 'the whole history of mankind is nothing but a narrative of the growth of families into nations, of small nations into great, of great nations into mighty empires' (*OPL* I, 245). See similarly his *Ancient Metaphysics,* vol. 4 (1795), Bk 2, Ch. 8. Hume sees the family tie as the origin of society, if not of its natural growth (T 3.2.2.4/SBNT 486). For Hume and the family, see Chapter 10.

3

James Dunbar and the Enlightenment Debate on Language

James Dunbar was regent at King's College, Aberdeen from 1765 to 1794 and published in 1780 a volume entitled *Essays on the History of Mankind in Rude and Cultivated Ages*.[1] As the title indicates, this work took the form of a number of more or less discrete disquisitions on universal history. This was a favourite Enlightenment theme with Scottish writers. Dunbar's book may thus be compared with Ferguson's *History of Civil Society* (1767), Millar's *Observations Concerning the Distinction of Ranks* (1771) and Kames's *Sketches on the History of Man* (1774). Like these and many other works, Dunbar's *Essays* exhibit methodologically the two key features of what Dugald Stewart called theoretical or conjectural history, namely that when direct factual evidence is unavailable then it is necessary to conjecture how men are 'likely to have proceeded from the principles of their nature and the circumstances of their external situation' (*Life* II, 46/293). The immediate context of these remarks was Adam Smith's *Considerations Concerning the First Formation of Languages* (1761) and one of the special features of Dunbar's own conjectural history of mankind is the attention he pays to language. The object of this chapter is to present Dunbar's account not only for its own sake but also for the ways in which it exemplifies certain broader Enlightenment assumptions about human nature, history and society.

Dunbar's own version differs from that of his compatriots by adopting a different periodisation. He identifies three eras in the history of the species:

> First, Man may have subsisted, in some sort, like other animals, in a separate and individual state, before the date of language, or the commencement of any regular intercourse. Secondly, He may be con-

templated in a higher stage; a proficient in language, and a member of that artless community which consists with equality, with freedom and independence. Last of all, by slow and imperceptible transitions, he subsists and flourishes under the protection and discipline of civil government. (*EHM* 2–3)

Whereas most Scots, with the exception of Monboddo, are chiefly concerned with the changes within the third of Dunbar's eras (the so-called four-stages theory),[2] Dunbar is concerned in his opening essay with the change from the first to the second era, and in his second essay with the fact that the possession of language is one of the specific differences between the two eras. In addition, Dunbar's own periodisation, as his terminology reveals, is indebted to Rousseau's conjectural history as found in the *Discourse on Inequality* (1755).

To see the history of mankind as in some sense developmental was, of course, an Enlightenment commonplace. This development was underwritten by the attribution to human nature of a principle of progress or improvement (what Rousseau, for example, called man's *perfectibilité*). While most writers were content with this simple attribution, Dunbar provides also a periodisation of development of human nature. He is here exploiting, though with an explicit acknowledgement that the parallels are not exact, a long-standing analogy between the individual human being and the species at large. Hence we find that the three eras of the history of the species have as a complement the following periodisation:

First of all, those of sense appear, grow up spontaneously, or require but little culture. Next in order, the propensities of the heart display their force; a fellow-feeling with others unfolds itself gradually on the appearance of proper objects; for man becomes sociable long before he is a rational being. Last in the train, the powers of intellect begin to blossom, are reared up by culture, and demand an intercourse of minds. (*EHM* 16)

One of the distinctive characteristics of Dunbar's thought is that he makes it explicit that the principle underlying this capacity to develop is of Aristotelian provenance. Mankind possesses latent powers, which, upon the appearance of those above-mentioned 'proper objects', open and expand. Dunbar puts this schema to various uses throughout his book, but here we will examine how he applies it in the particular case of language. (See Chapter 2 for further discussion.)

First, it is worth bringing out the significance of what we have already established. We know from the way that Dunbar has set up the question that he postulates a time when man was without language. This approach enables him to achieve two objectives: one, it permits the origin of language to be conceptually identified and, two, it permits him to clarify the difference between man and animals. This latter objective had considerable topicality due to Monboddo's publication of the first volume of his *Origin and Progress of Language* in 1773. It was Monboddo's belief that language was not natural to man and, in his argument to prove that it was rather merely an acquired habit, he cited the behaviour of orang-utangs. According to Monboddo, the orang was really a species of *Homo sapiens* since, although devoid of language, it nevertheless practised such other human habits as living communally, building homes, possessing a sense of decorum, using weapons and so on (*OPL* vol.1, Bk 1, Ch. 14; Bk 2, Chs 8, 9; *Antient Metaphysics,* vol. 3, Bk 2, Ch. 1, etc.).

Dunbar noted the apparent similarity in the possession of vocal cords (*EHM* 67), but later referred to the work of Camper because he had shown, in opposition to Monboddo, that the orang was organically incapable of speech (*EHM* 203).[3] The former of the two above objectives betrays the Enlightenment approach. Overwhelmingly, Enlightenment thinkers located the origin of language naturalistically, that is to say in human nature, so that from that locus they were able to conjecture how language developed alongside man's own development. There is a clear connection between the two objectives. The conceptual search for the origin of language was simultaneously a search for the special capacity of humans that differentiated them from the brutes.

Openly acknowledging that there is no evidence concerning the 'opening scene of man' (*EHM* 2), Dunbar provides a conjectural description of the psychology of man at that time. These conjectures are underwritten by the belief in the uniformity of human nature (perhaps the key premise of Enlightenment thought)[4] and the similarity of the individual and the species. This permits Dunbar in typical fashion to draw on the evidence of children.[5] And since 'savages' are the children of the human species, then, where available, their practices can be used as corroborative evidence. Dunbar provides a striking illustration of this. He declares that the 'South Sea Isles' enable us 'to glance at society in some of its earliest forms' (*EHM* 26), and then later remarks that Omiah (the celebrated Tahitian) is as 'circumscribed as a child in the number of his ideas' (*EHM* 110).

Dunbar depicts this primitive psychology as follows: 'Man, we may observe, is at first possessed of few ideas, and of still fewer desires . . . he seldom indulges any train of reflection on the past, and cares not, by anxious anticipation, to antedate futurity' (*EHM* 68). Significantly, as we shall see, this also means that man 'uses the resources of instinct, rather than the lights of the understanding; is scarce capable of abstraction, and a stranger to all the combinations and connections of systematic thought' (*EHM* 69). The immediate inference Dunbar draws from this picture is that at this time 'there is no need for the details of language'. There is silent communication as the 'feelings of the heart break forth in visible form'. Coeval with this, and equally 'independently of art', there is a 'mechanical connection between the feelings of the soul and the enunciation of sound' which declares 'the purposes of man to man' and it is these 'accents and exclamations [that] compose the first elements of a rising language' (*EHM* 70).

This notion that the origin of language is to be found in natural exclamations or cries was common. Thus, views similar to Dunbar's can be found throughout the contemporary literature.[6] An indication of the character of this natural speech is provided by interjections, for they have retained 'its primeval character' (*EHM* 71). The language of early man, it can thus be conjectured, was unarticulated or monosyllabic and exempt from arbitrary rules. Similarly, to Priestley (1762: 65), interjections were unarticulated cries of passion; to Blair (1848: 64), they represent as passionate exclamations the 'first elements of speech'; to Harris (1751: 290) they are 'adventitious sounds which arise spontaneously in the human soul' and for Monboddo (*OPL* II, 181) the interjection 'may be considered as remains of the most antient language among men, that by which they expressed their feelings not their ideas'.

These natural cries are thus the first step in Dunbar's account of the development of language. The second step is imitation. Dunbar refers to man having an 'imitative faculty' (*EHM* 78). (The question of 'faculties' will concern us later.) He argues that man is not alone in possessing a talent for imitation because it is also found in animals; but man alone can imitate all other animals while none can imitate him. More significantly, in man imitation is performed from 'a love of the effect' and it may 'be justly called the first intellectual amusement congenial with our being' (*EHM* 76). That imitation plays a role in the development of language was also an idea found in many writers – in Monboddo (*OPL* I, 191 – where he uses the term 'imitative faculty'), Blair (1848: 65) and Condillac (1947/53: I, 61), to name but a few.

After the imitative faculty, Dunbar posits the development of another – the analogical faculty. This faculty in general 'has vast powers in binding the associations of thought in all mental arrangements' (*EHM* 79). In the more particular case of language, this 'power' is such that there is no object which the mind 'cannot assimilate to something antecedently in its possession. By consequence a term already appropriated, and in use, will, by no violent transition, be shaped and adjusted to the new idea' (*EHM* 80). We now witness a decisive move. These analogical connections 'supply the place of real resemblance' and now 'instinct borrows aid from the imagination' (*EHM* 79). This is decisive because it is here that the 'reign of invention' commences and it is also here that 'perhaps we should stop and draw the boundary of art and nature'. The consequence of this is that man and brutes can be decisively differentiated since it is the 'weakness of this principle [analogical faculty] which imposes the law of silence and excludes all possibility of improvement in the animal world'.

As his schema of the three eras of species-development testifies, there is a social counterpart to this. Dunbar is explicit that 'every effort beyond what is merely animal has reference to a community' (*EHM* 5). This communal life, attained in the second era, is the 'prime mover of our *inventive* powers' (*EHM*; my emphasis) and it is there that 'the springs of ingenuity are put into motion' so that 'the language of nature gradually participates of art' (*EHM* 31).

Dunbar's postulated analogical faculty provides a particularly clear exemplification of Aarsleff's (1974: 104–5) observation that the point behind the search for origins was to attempt to get down to basic principles in order to distinguish what was owing to nature and what to art. However, Dunbar puts this faculty to greater use. The vital role that Dunbar allots to the analogical faculty is to account for the development and generation of language and speech in all parts without recourse to powers of abstract reasoning. Such a recourse would be inconsistent with his conjecture that Man in the rudest ages was 'scarce capable of abstraction'. The question of abstraction arose because of the still-prevalent

conception of language in terms of its grammatical composition
– nouns, verbs, adjectives and so on – with the crucial corollary
that some of these 'parts', especially particles such as prepositions,
expressed abstract or metaphysical relations. Dunbar believes that
if language is thought of as invented then it means that these putative inventors 'must have resolved in imagination all the subtleties
of logic and entered far into the science of grammar, before its
objects had any existence. Profound abstraction and generalisation must have been constantly exercised' (*EHM* 93). But, thanks
to the postulated presence of the analogical faculty, the need for
this 'constant exercise' can be obviated.

We have already seen that this faculty operates by appropria-
tion and assimilation, and the cumulative effect of these processes
is that language develops through 'the laws of analogy [which]
by one gentle and uniform effect superseding and alleviating the
efforts of abstraction permit language to advance' (*EHM* 92).
Once again, the speech patterns of children are cited in corroboration (*EHM* 80). Since *ex hypothesi* children have not developed
their reasoning powers, to attribute the development of language
to abstraction is 'by no means compatible with the limited capacity of the human mind' (*EHM* 94).

This argument against abstraction was integral to a lively
Enlightenment debate on the evolution of the parts of speech.
While Dunbar does not himself engage in this debate to any great
extent, he explicitly follows Adam Smith's argument that verbs
have developed from impersonal to personal without supposing
any act of abstraction or metaphysics (*EHM* 113) (see also Chapter
16). Moreover, when Dunbar remarks in passing that 'though
every sound formed not a complete sentence as at the beginning'
(*EHM* 85), he reveals that he also shares with Smith, and many
others,[7] the conception that at the root of linguistic structure lie
primal or pre-syntactic utterances and that the development of
language is the breaking down of such utterances (sentences) into
their constituent logical parts.[8] Dunbar's point, to repeat, is that
the development of the parts of speech is not in itself an exercise of
logic or abstraction but the operation of the analogical faculty as it
moves 'from object to object in the *concrete*' (*EHM* 89; Dunbar's
emphasis).

Dunbar's governing assumption, derived ultimately, like all
standard Enlightenment accounts, from Locke, is that language
and the human mind develop concurrently. He states this key

point unequivocally when he observes that 'ideas and language' are 'uniformly in close conjunction' (*EHM* 94). While the conceptual and polemical thrust behind this point, and thence behind the postulated analogical faculty, lies in its implications for the *processes* of language, there are two further points we can make.

First, though the formal attention Dunbar pays to analogy is greater than that of his contemporaries,[9] the postulated presence of an analogical faculty is his version of the prevalent associationist psychology. This is apparent in his explicit avowal of the common link between association, imagination and invention, as seen for example in his fellow Aberdonian, Alexander Gerard (1774). It is because of this link that Dunbar is able to use this faculty to account for the development of the figurativeness of language, whereby, in orthodox fashion, corporeal or material ideas are by analogy taken to encompass 'qualities of the mind' (*EHM* 82) – not, he notes, citing D'Alembert, that the reverse is not possible in a 'cultivated language' (*EHM* 111). In a closely related vein, this faculty also serves as his explanation for the universally metaphorical quality of early speech (*EHM* 112). On this latter point Dunbar essentially shares the views of those who explain the ubiquity of metaphor in early language by the poverty or scarcity of words.[10]

The second point will enable us to relate Dunbar's treatment of language to his wider concerns. Given the conjunction between 'ideas' and 'language', then, according to Dunbar, in that 'artless community' with its equality, freedom and independence – that is, in the second of the three eras identified above – 'men were not only devoid of the inclination but unfurnished with the means of deceit' (*EHM* 70). It was only with the subsequent developments in social life that the 'powers of intellect begin to blossom' and, though this was indeed an improvement, yet it carried with it the consequence that 'feuds and animosities' were introduced into the world (*EHM* 32). The linguistic development that ran *pari passu* with this was that the indissoluble natural tie between sentiment and expression (*EHM* 72) was lost, so that, along with artificial language, equivocation in due course entered into the scene (compare *EHM* 397, 402). The wider import of this example is that it is indicative of the strategic use to which Dunbar puts his adaptation of Rousseau. He openly acknowledges that Rousseau's view that progress is corrupting is an exaggeration (*EHM* 154); nevertheless, one of the lynchpins of Dunbar's entire analysis is that the second of the three eras – a time of unrestricted fellow feeling, the depiction of which owes much to Rousseau – acts as a normative benchmark for the later period of dependency.

But we have not yet completed our exposition of Dunbar's theory of language because he postulates yet another faculty:

> On a more exact survey, the mind discriminates its objects, and breaks the system of analogy by attending to the minute differences of things. As therefore the analogical faculty enlarges the sense of words, the discriminating faculty augments them in number. It breaks speech into smaller divisions and bestows a copiousness on language by a more precise arrangement of the objects. (*EHM* 96–7)

Since Dunbar had earlier observed that it was 'easier for the mind to perceive resemblance than to specify the minute differences of things' (*EHM* 89), the operation of this discriminating faculty can be presumed to be a later development. In a subsequent essay Dunbar remarks that one of the advantages of a 'cultivated', in contrast to a 'rude', tongue is its 'copiousness of expression' (*EHM* 130) – though in keeping with his moderate Rousseauism the rude tongue is acknowledged to enjoy an advantage when it comes to vivacity.[11] Yet there is here also a clear indication of Dunbar's distance from Rousseau. Rousseau thought that the more primitive a language the more copious *(étendu)* is its dictionary, because it takes a long time before similarities rather than differences are perceived (1962: 54).

To Dunbar, therefore, language develops through four stages – from natural cries to imitation to the operation of the analogical faculty and, finally, to the exertions of the discriminating faculty. He is aware that this fourfold process is an oversimplification. He allows that the analogical faculty is 'allied' to the imitative and that it is 'often undistinguished in its operations' (*EHM* 79) and, towards the end of the second essay, he admits that in the development of language through its various stages 'the mind has no doubt exerted collectively at all times various powers' (*EHM* 99).

These admissions by Dunbar that his scheme is an oversimplification defuse in some measure the obvious criticism that this use of 'faculty psychology' misleadingly atomises human consciousness by implying that it has separate parts, of which only some are in operation at any one time.[12] However, Dunbar seems less exempt from other standard objections. His faculties would appear to be little better than occult agencies. The mind, for example, perceives an analogy; 'something', it is posited, must be responsible for this perception. The answer is a specific mental faculty, since of what else could the perceived analogy be an effect? A further weakness of faculty psychology, which this assumption of specific agencies engenders and of which Dunbar provides a clear example, is the tendency to multiply the number of faculties in order to accommodate any new process believed to exist.

Despite its inherent weaknesses, what this recourse to the terminology of faculties indicates is Dunbar's basic commitment to the proposition that the development of language is integral to mental development. We can, in conclusion, pursue a little further this idea of mental development and its bearing on the 'language question'.

Dunbar himself identifies three schools of thought on the origin of language: 'Is language, it may be asked, derived to us at first from the happy invention of a few, or to be regarded as an original accomplishment and investiture of nature or to be attributed to some succeeding effort of the human mind?' (*EHM* 63). With regard to the first of these arguments, Dunbar adopted the anti-individualism characteristic of the Scottish Enlightenment and we have seen that the whole thrust behind the idea of the analogical faculty was to explain the development of language without recourse to some imagined 'great projectors in an early age, balancing a regular plan for the conveyance of sentiment and the establishment of general intercourse' (*EHM* 93). In contrast, it seems undeniable that Dunbar considers language to be 'a succeeding effort of the human mind'. He is explicit that his account was designed to show 'the *gradations* of a simple institution referring to those faculties of the mind which appear principally concerned in conducting its *successive* improvements' (*EHM* 99; my emphasis).

There is, however, more to Dunbar's developmental theory than the above. This additional element derives from the Aristotelian nature of his theory – so that language, for Dunbar, is really the actualisation of the potential possessed by each individual. It follows from this that Dunbar, in addition to regarding language as a 'succeeding effort' (the third of his schools), could be said to believe it to be an 'original investiture' (the second of his schools). Indeed, at the end of the second essay, he pronounces that language has developed as a 'superstructure' constructed 'on the foundation of nature' (EHM 99). The natural bases of language comprise natural cries and imitation (common to both man and beast), and the operation of the analogical and discriminating faculties (where 'the boundary of art and nature' is drawn and which are therefore the prerogative of man alone) represent the superstructure of language.

To believe that language is natural to man is to acknowledge, with very few exceptions in the eighteenth century, that man has been given language – like everything else, from instincts to a sense of humour – by his Designer. In the case of language, on Dunbar's account, man has not been given it from 'without' but internally, by possessing it *in potentia*. Such a theory in fact runs contrary in its explanatory thrust to a theological explanation of the origin of language – a view still to be found in some of his contemporaries[13] – which invoked the 'super-natural' agency of divine inspiration. Dunbar, it may be said, believes that language is an 'original investiture' but not an 'original accomplishment'.

In fine, Dunbar's theory represents a characteristically Enlightenment attempt at explaining the development of language in terms of the concurrent evolution of man's mind: language is a distinctively human characteristic and an explanation of its possession must be in human terms and commensurate with human abilities. The entire enterprise is admitted to be conjectural but nevertheless is that which is 'most consonant to the probability of things, to the experience of early life, and to the genius and complexion of the ruder ages' (*EHM* 99).

Postscript

The paper on which this chapter is based was delivered in 1986 at a conference in the University of Aberdeen and was subsequently published in 1987 as part of the selected proceedings. As such, it develops some of the themes addressed in Chapter 16 (and see my postscript to that chapter for wider comment). In addition to complementing that discussion of Smith, this essay is, more clearly, a companion to the discussion in Chapter 2. This later publication enabled me to identify to some extent the debt Dunbar owes to Rousseau.

In spite of the considerable scholarship on Enlightenment debates on language, this remains the only dedicated account of Dunbar's version (Spadafora makes passing reference 1990:

354–5). We know from the records of the Aberdeen Wise Club, of which Dunbar was a member from 1765, that he delivered a discourse on the origin of language as early as 1768 (Ulman 1990, Appendix; he also cites this piece). Like the bulk of Dunbar's work, his treatment of language is a response to, or reflection upon, current issues but with a distinctive slant, which, I think, makes it worthwhile to disseminate.

Notes

1. For further information on Dunbar's life and career, see Berry (1974b).
2. This theory that societies passed successively from hunting to pastoral to agricultural and finally to commercial stages was seminally developed by Adam Smith and has been the subject of extensive commentary. For a recent overview of this, see Skinner (1982). (For a critical assessment of the commentary on this question, see Berry (2013: Ch. 2).)
3. Dunbar's relation to Monboddo is interesting because of the Aristotelian elements in their philosophies. Dunbar holds that the orangs need an enlargement of ideas, but he also believes that the ideas of animals are fixed and they have no potential to progress (*EHM* 68). Monboddo himself believes that what 'distinguishes human nature from that of the brute is not the actual possession of higher faculties but the greater capacity of acquiring them' (Letter to Harris, reprinted in Knight (1900: 73)). The crucial difference between the two is that Dunbar excludes the orang from the genus Man, whereas for Monboddo 'the large monkeys or baboons appear to me to stand in the same relation to us, that the ass does to the horse' (Letter to Pringle in Knight (1900: 85)). To Monboddo the orangs are related to man because they use sticks, desire human females and so on but are not identical since they do not possess language, yet since language is not natural to man then this absence cannot deny them the 'appellation of men' (*OPL* vol. 1, p. 176n). For discussion of the debates raised by the orang, see several writings by Wokler (1980, for example).
4. For further discussion, see Berry (1982: Ch. 1).
5. This heuristic device is used by writers as otherwise diverse as Vico, de Brosses, Priestley and Herder (for references, see Chapter 16). It played a crucial role in Condillac's (1947/53) *Essai sur l'origine des connaissances humaines* (1746: Pt 2, sect. 1), which Aarsleff (1974)

has argued is the key eighteenth-century text on the question of the origin of language.

6. See, inter alia, Turgot, 'Autres réflexions sur les langues' (1913: I, p. 351), Blackwell (1972: 37), Beauzée, articles 'Interjection' and 'Langue' in Diderot (ed. 1765: v VIII, IX), Rousseau (1962: 53), Mandeville (1988: II, 285ff.) and Condillac (1947–53: I, 61).

7. See inter alia Smith (*CL* 28/216), Rousseau (1962: 54), Monboddo (*OPL* I, 360, 395) and Blair (1848: 89), who explicitly follows Monboddo.

8. For an instructive analysis of Smith's position, see Land (1977 and 1976).

9. Turgot, in his article 'Etymologie' in the *Encyclopédie* (Diderot ed. 1765 VI: 100), referred in passing to '*les lois de l'analogie*'; Smith, who explicitly said (*Corr* 69/88) that he had received 'a good deal of entertainment' from the grammatical articles in the *Encyclopédie*, referred to the 'love of analogy' rather than any act of abstraction as the source of the rules of grammar (*CL* 16/211); finally, Condillac (whose work Smith possessed) mentions, in a discussion of '*le genie des langues*', '*les règles de l'analogie*' (1947/53: I, 101). In a later discussion Condillac made analogy the source of all methods of instruction and invention – 'Langue des Calculs' (1947/53).

10. For a full discussion of this point, see Berry (1973b).

11. Thomas Reid, in his *Inquiry* (1764), had pointed out the superior 'force and energy' of the savage tongue (1846: 118). The more general point that early speech had a distinctive tonal quality was widely made, and featured in debates concerning the origin and development of music as well as the relative priority of poetry or prose – see Berry (1973b) for further discussion.

12. Herder mounted a thoroughgoing contemporary assault on faculty psychology within, significantly, his own prizewinning discussion of language (1891: V, 29–30).

13. See, for example, Warburton (1765: III, 106), Beattie (1783: 304ff.), Beauzée, 'Langue', and H. Blair (1848: 63). Blair is prompted to invoke a divine original by Rousseau's conundrum (though he does not identify his source) that society needs language yet language needs society (1848: 64). Blair is not alone in this: for comment, see Aarsleff (1974: 131ff. on Süssmilch) and Droixhe (1976).

4

'Climate' in the Eighteenth Century: James Dunbar and the Scottish Case

Many writers in the eighteenth century had occasion at some time to refer to climate. It is essential at the outset to understand the meaning of climate as the term was used in the eighteenth century. It does not have its present meteorological denotation; instead, Samuel Johnson (1792) defines it as 'A space upon the surface of the earth, measured from the equator to the polar circles in each of which spaces the longest day is half-an-hour longer'.[1] These references occur in a variety of contexts but there is one predominant theme, namely its evocation as an explanatory factor. Thus, for example, it is used by Buffon (1812: III, 446) to account for racial differences, by Bullet (1754: I, 7) and Herder (1891: V, 125) for differences in pronunciation, by Dubos (1755: II, 500; and *passim* on climate and 'air,' esp. Chs. 14–19) for differences in stylistic sensibility, and, most renownedly of all, by Montesquieu (1961: esp. Bk 14, but see *infra*, hereafter cited as *Esprit*) to account for differences in laws. The purpose of this chapter is not to catalogue the different usages to which climate was put, but to examine one particular theory in some detail. This theory – that of James Dunbar – is not only one of the most thoughtful (and relatively neglected) pieces on climate but also, by its very nature, as will be illustrated, it helps to enlighten and clarify some of the issues raised in the literature, with particular reference to that of his fellow Scots.

The Scots' treatment of climate is of interest for two reasons. First, they have been regarded as being among the foremost thinkers in laying the groundwork for the social sciences.[2] Adam Smith's contribution to economics needs no justification; nor, increasingly, does the work of Adam Ferguson (in particular) or John Millar. Lord Kames and others need much advocacy to be regarded as important contributions to the development of sociology. In their writings, these thinkers emphasised the study of society rather than the state or the individual and, in so doing, they broke away from the prevailing tradition of rationalistic individualism. Instead of, for example, social development and institutions being seen as the results of the deliberate actions of individuals, the Scots (including Dunbar) realised that more remote factors such as the means of subsistence, the pattern of ownership and the size of the population were a positive influence in shaping society, in its broadest sense. Thus we find them attacking the legislator myth (still adhered to by many of their contemporaries),[3] stressing the circumscription of purposive action by habitual behaviour,[4] spelling out the impact of 'unintended consequences' of human actions,[5] and generally being aware of the impression of the 'state of property and manners' (Smith WN III.iv. 8/416)[6] on social life. Their usage of climate belongs in this general sociological context. It is another factor of social causation, another factor irreducible to the deliberate actions of individuals and, as such, utilisable, though not without considerable reservation, as we shall shortly see, as a factor helping to account for social diversity.

This usage of climate to account for diversity in general is indeed part of the reason for its continued popularity and importance in eighteenth-century literature as a whole. It now became a concomitant of that widespread and largely ill-defined adoption of an empiricist epistemology. Evidence of different races, tongues, tastes, and customs generally was becoming more and more available but the century, by and large, was not ready to welcome all this diversity per se. There are standards. The diversity is intelligible as the universe is intelligible, hence the search for explanatory factors (preferably of a 'Newtonian' character); and climate was one ready-made answer and progress or development became another. The latter, indeed, was the principle to which the Scots mainly resorted.[7]

To return more particularly to the Scots, aside from the general tie-up between climate and proto-sociology, pointed out above, the Scots' treatment of climate is more especially interesting for a further reason, namely their relationship with Montesquieu. They were among his greatest and most fulsome admirers,[8] and their writings are shot through and through with both obeisance to their 'Bacon'[9] and also with a shared similarity of subject matter and sympathy of method. But, when it came to the question of climate, their allegiance faltered. Here the impact of their compatriot David Hume is important.

Although some of Hume's views in epistemology and religion might be unpalatable, he was a close friend of all the Scottish literati. He was, in particular, a respected counsellor on style, and several of the books written by the Scots were first given to Hume that he might examine them for 'Scotticisms'.[10] More concretely, Hume, in his essay 'On Natural Characters', had produced an argument against climate or (see his definition below) 'physical causes' and instead proposed 'moral causes' as a more accurate and adequate explanation of such character. The significance of this short essay is heightened when Hume's personal popularity is borne in mind because, when this is juxtaposed with the respect in which Montesquieu was held, it meant that their apparently anti-thetical (as we shall see) positions on the question of climate made their disagreement all the more notable and the resulting debate all the more vital.[11] This is where Dunbar comes in. We find in his theory an attempted reconciliation of these two thinkers.

We shall approach Dunbar's own theory after briefly consider-ing first of all the positions of the principal antagonists, Hume and Montesquieu. Secondly, we shall see what some of Dunbar's compatriots made of these positions so that they can provide a context within which to place Dunbar's own particular argument.

As said above, Hume was a champion of moral causes, while Montesquieu was commonly held to be a champion of physical causes. Hume provides the necessary clarification by defining these two terms: 'By moral causes, I mean all circumstances which are fitted to work on the mind as motives or reasons, and which render a peculiar set of manners habitual to us' (E-NC 202). As examples of these circumstances, Hume gives the nature of government, the revolutions of public affairs, the plenty or penury in which people live, and the situation of the nation with regard to its neighbours. The other definition is as follows: 'By physical causes, I mean those qualities of the air and climate which are supposed to work insensibly on the temper, by altering the tone and habit of the body, and giving a particular complexion' (E-NC 203).[12] Between these two, Hume's preference is clear: 'As to physical causes I am inclined to doubt altogether of their operation in this particular; nor do I think that men owe anything of their temper or genius to the air, food or climate' (E-NC 205–6). He follows this declaration by an argument wherein he produces nine reasons for believing that moral, not physical, causes are responsible for shaping the 'national character'.

Montesquieu's alleged advocacy of the decisive effect of physical causes on social life is found essentially in Book 14 of the *Esprit*. There he argues that climate has a direct physiological effect on the individual:

> L'air froid resserre les extrémités des fibres extérieures de notre corps; cela augmente leur ressort, et favorise le retour du sang des extrémités vers le coeur ... L'air chaud, au contraire, relâche les extrémités des fibres, et les allonge; it diminue donc leur force et leur ressort. (*Esprit* I, 239)

These differences in physiology cause differences in 'sensibilité' so that, for example, '*Les peuples des pays chauds sont timides comme les vieillards le sont; ceux des pays froids sont courageux comme le sont les jeunes gens*' (*Esprit* I, 240). Quite simply, the difference in climate, by acting in different ways on the body, 'Enfin cela doit faire des caractères bien différents' (ibid.).

It should be noted that Montesquieu was 'alleged' to be an advocate of physical causes. Shackleton (1961: 302) remarks that Montesquieu's climate theory attracted more attention than any other aspect of the *Esprit*. It is a reasonable conjecture that such attention would cause Montesquieu's argument to be exaggerated, a tendency that would be accentuated in Scotland by Hume's exposition so that, in fact, their respective positions would tend to be polarised. Indeed, an analysis of the total of Montesquieu's writings does suggest that he allowed a much more influential role to moral causes than is apparent from Book 14.[13]

The Scots undoubtedly, however, did identify Montesquieu as a propounder of the thesis that climate had a direct physiological effect. Yet despite Shackleton's claim that this aspect of Montesquieu caused the greatest stir, such climatic theories were far from new, particularly in Scotland. Thomas Blackwell (an Aberdeen professor and correspondent of Montesquieu) in his *Enquiry into the Life of Homer* [1735] (1972: 5–6) propounded the direct physiological argument: 'In the division commonly made of Climates, the Rough and Cold are observed to produce the strongest Bodies, and most martial spirits; the hotter, lazy Bodies with cunning and obstinate Passions.' Blackwell cites as his chief authorities for this unremarkable statement Galen and

Hippocrates. Dedieu has illustrated just how much Hippocrates was in vogue in the 1730s, his *Treatise on Airs, Waters and Places* being translated into English, and Simson (Professor of Medicine at St Andrews University) did work on the effect of cold air on the human body. Most significantly, Dedieu argued that the work of John Arbuthnot (another Scotsman and holder of a degree in medicine from St Andrews) contains the germ of much of Montesquieu's Book 14 and that this, too, was a result of the interest shown in Hippocrates.[14] The upshot of this is that the Scots were familiar with climatic theories from sources other than Montesquieu and, as this suggests, climate, even in this context, was no novelty – hence again, indeed, its aforementioned 'ready-made' character in the explanation of diversity.

But now we must consider the actual interpretation placed on Montesquieu's work, in this context, by the Scots. John Millar (Professor of Law at the University of Glasgow) writes:

> It is pretended that great heat, by relaxing the fibres, and by extending the surface of the skin, where the action of the nerves is chiefly performed, occasions great sensibility to all external impressions; which is accompanied with proportionable vivacity of ideas and feelings ... The inhabitants of a cold region are said, on the other hand, to acquire an opposite complexion. (*OR* 179)

Although Montesquieu is not mentioned by name, the vocabulary makes it clear that it is his theory to which Millar is principally addressing himself. Kames is more explicit; he openly identifies Montesquieu. Kames treats as the gravamen of Montesquieu's position his belief that in hot climates men are timid like old men, while in cold climates they are as bold as young men (*SHM* I, 33).

How was this position evaluated? Kames has no doubt that Montesquieu's theory is false. He believes it to be wrong because, though Montesquieu's argument is ingenious, it is 'contradicted by stubborn facts' (*SHM* I, 34). These 'facts' take the form of an argument from 'exceptions' (the same approach that Hume had adopted). For example, Malays and Scandinavians are compared for being equally courageous yet living in 'opposite climates'. Kames, in fact, curtails his argument by remarking, 'I stop here; for to enter the lists against an antagonist of so great fame, gives me a feeling as if I were treading on forbidden ground' (*SHM* I, 34) – another testimony to the respect in which Montesquieu's work was held. Kames's overall conclusion is that 'It is my firm opinion, that neither temper nor talents have much dependence on climate' (ibid.). Yet, as we said above, the Scots, even with such reservations, do utilise climate and Kames is no exception. Thus he believes that the level of social development is directly related to climatic conditions, since in cold climates there is no progress beyond the 'herding' or shepherd stage, owing to the difficulties in cultivating corn through the hardness of the ground. The impact is more significant still in hot climates: 'In every step of progress the torrid zone differs. We have no evidence that either the hunter or shepherd state were ever known there; the inhabitants at present subsist upon vegetable food and probably did so from the beginning' (*SHM* I, 34).

Millar and Ferguson both believe that the direct effect of climate on the individual cannot, given existing physiological knowledge, be determined one way or the other. From this position of reservation Millar proceeds to argue by implication that, at least from the present evidence, Hume's is the more likely position. Millar, too, employs the familiar mode of argumentation. Thus he contrasts the 'mild' Chinese with the 'rough' Japanese, while both are alleged to enjoy the same climate. Or, again, Millar produces a more local example: 'How is it possible to explain those national peculiarities that have been remarked in the English, the Irish and the Scotch, from the different temperature of the weather under which they have lived?' (*OR* 180). Millar concludes with the general statement that:

> in the history of the world, we see no regular marks of that secret influence which has been ascribed to the air and climate, but, on the contrary, may commonly explain the great differences in the manners and customs of mankind from other causes. (*OR* 179–80)[15]

But again, even so, climate or physical cause is not omitted altogether, since

> In searching for the causes of those peculiar systems of law and government which have appeared in the world, we must undoubtedly resort, first of all, to the differences of situation, which have suggested different views and motives of action to the inhabitants of particular countries. (*OR* 175)

Ferguson, though, like Millar reserving final judgement, on occasions seems to place more weight, than Millar at least, on the direct effect of climate: 'The animal and rational temperament is comparatively phlegmatic and dull in cold climates; is more ardent and quick in warm climates' (*IMP* 17). Nor is this the only statement to this effect, since its import is echoed elsewhere,[16] even so far as to seem to contradict Hume.[17]

Having briefly seen the respective positions of some of Dunbar's contemporaries, we can now examine and appreciate the distinctiveness of his own contribution to the debate. Dunbar is conscious of the polarisation seen to exist between Hume and Montesquieu:

> A writer [Montesquieu] of the first rank, who illustrates and adorns the history of mankind with plausible and ingenious theory, has assigned to physical causes an almost unlimited empire. Another writer (Hume) no less illustrious, contracts into a point the sphere of their dominion. (*EHM* 296)

But, instead of accepting this polarisation, he establishes another relationship between them. The relationship which Dunbar holds to exist between moral and physical causes is expressed explicitly on two occasions: 'The series of events, once begun, is governed more perhaps by moral than by physical causes' (*EHM* 239)[18] and 'it deserves to be remembered that causes physical in their nature, are often moral only in their operation' (*EHM* 296). Therefore both moral and physical causes have their part to play in determining or shaping social life. These two causes are not mutually exclusive, which was of course Montesquieu's own true position, as we have seen; yet Dunbar goes further since he defines the relationship between the two.

But first Dunbar explains why this relationship has not previously been seen: 'Local circumstances are so blended in their operations with a variety of other causes, that it is difficult to define them with such precision' (*EHM* 295). These 'local circumstances' are the key to Dunbar's whole argument. Among examples of such circumstances, Dunbar supplies 'the division of a country by mountains, by lakes or rivers, the vicinity or distance of the sea, insular or continental situation, and the relative condition of the surrounding nations (*EHM* 257)[19] Although these circumstances are still 'physical causes,' awareness of them is a refinement on the simple hot, cold and temperate division. In the failure to take account of such circumstances, Dunbar sees the 'confusion' that has caused the whole debate as to the relative merits of physical and moral causes, because their unobtrusiveness has resulted in their being overlooked. Yet though these local circumstances are physical causes and indicative of climatic influence, they are nevertheless contrasted by Dunbar, with climate as a 'natural principle, acting with powerful energy, or with irresistible impulse, on the *fabric* of our being' (*EHM* 221–2; my emphasis). The significance of this contrast will become apparent below.

The importance of these local circumstances is that their influence on social life is not constant, and it is the recognition of this that distinguishes Dunbar's theory. The physical causes themselves remain static; it is their impact that fluctuates. For example, 'a people may be long incapable to avail themselves of external advantages, that circumstances ultimately beneficial, may have proved for a long while incommodious or destructive' (*EHM* 296), which means that 'the import of local station, far from being permanent, varies not only with the contingencies of the natural world, but with the course of political events and the *general state of human improvement*' (*EHM* 297; my emphasis). These quotations contain the essence of Dunbar's reconciliation between physical and moral causes. To support this, we can first examine one of the examples that Dunbar himself gives in his own elucidation of his position.

Thus, he writes, the fact that Britain is an island, though 'so fertile a source of national security, opulence and grandeur, rendered us long an uncultivated and sequestered people' (*EHM* 298). At one time being an island meant isolation for Britain from the rest of Europe and civilisation, but this insular circumstance in the 'aera of navigation' was a source of wealth and power and, furthermore, meant that Britain was able to avoid Continental wars and the consequent dissipation of wealth. Hence, the influence of the static physical cause (being an island) was not constant but varied with particular situations.

We are now in a position to begin to evaluate Dunbar's contribution to the debate on the relative merits of physical and moral causes. Above all, Dunbar argues that the positions of Hume and Montesquieu are not really antithetical once climatic influence is correctly understood in terms of local circumstances. Dunbar rejects the import of Montesquieu's argument that climate is a natural principle, that is, that it has a direct physiological effect:

'there is no need to recur to the positive and direct influences of the outward elements on the human *mind*' (*EHM* 239; my emphasis).[20] On the other hand, however, still in agreement with his compatriots, he asserts that 'geographical relation ... will always be, in some degree, instrumental in retarding or accelerating, in every country, the progress of civil life' (*EHM* 318).[21] It follows, and here is Dunbar's reconciliation, that physical causes influence society but only moral causes can dynamically affect the individual. The two sources of influence are not opposed because the individual cannot be separated from the society in which he lives. The two types of causes are, therefore, interrelated. This interrelation, distinctively for Dunbar, is based on his belief in the contingent nature of local circumstances.

To elucidate: this contingency arises from the conjuncture of the static physical with the fluctuating moral cause. A change in social conditions or knowledge (moral cause) can result in a change in the relationship with a particular environment. In other words, the influence of the environment or climate (physical cause) on society can change with an alteration in social conditions. The change can be baleful (for example, Britain's isolation from Roman civilisation) or beneficial (for example, Britain's isolation from continental wars), depending on the particular instance; but the new situation occasioned by this changed relationship can itself have some bearing on the influence of physical causes (for example, continental isolation leads to the development of the empire). This means that any beneficial or other effect of the cooperation of physical with moral causes is adventitious and unlikely to be permanent.

It is in this way, therefore, that climate influences society. But the nature of this influence is indirect and does not in any way diminish the significance of moral causes; yet the moral causes themselves are affected and thus alone cannot totally explain social phenomena. Hence, through his analysis, which is more precise than that of his compatriots, Dunbar endeavours to do justice to the positions of both Hume and Montesquieu.

There is, however, a further (final) aspect of Dunbar's theory. Although he demarcates a sphere of climatic influence, this, as we have seen with respect to the individual, is held to be indirect. He emphasises this in this final aspect of his theory because it constitutes an attack on a corollary of the idea that climate has a direct effect: 'But the various circumstances hitherto under review ought to be considered rather as occasions of prosperous or adverse fortune, than as direct causes of human perfection or debasement' and 'nor the local circumstances we have mentioned [be confounded] with that more mysterious influence which, reaching the principles of our nature, is supposed to produce original and constitutional differences in the human species' (*EHM* 319).

This 'mysterious influence' is the mind/body interaction. Though the body is subject to mechanical laws and thereby amenable to climatic influence, 'changes introduced into the former [body) by external impulse, will imply no corresponding changes in our *moral* frame' since man 'by his rank in the creation is more exempted from mechanical domination than the classes below him' (*EHM* 342; my emphasis).[22] In other words, man has a degree of freedom consonant with his possession of a mind. This freedom, and this is the relevant point, means that climate cannot be considered a deterministic principle. On the contrary, man's possession of free will enables him 'to become in some degree the arbiter of his own happiness and perfection' (*EHM* 347). Significantly, this 'degree' is increased as man and society develop: 'Upon the whole we may observe local advantages, which fluctuate in every age, and often owe their existence and duration to a train of independent events, to be of the least relative moment in the most flourishing stage of the arts and sciences' (*EHM* 317).

Thus, although man is susceptible to 'natural' and 'moral' ills – indeed, exemption from these is, to Dunbar, a divine attribute – man is free; he is 'neither chained down by necessity nor impelled by fate (*EHM* 353). Man's freedom, in this context, is freedom from the putative determinism of the direct effect of physical causes, since 'the action of the elements on his frame is not more conspicuous than his reciprocal action on those very elements which are permitted to annoy his being' (*EHM* 354). Though there are certain limitations (unspecified by Dunbar) to this reciprocity, 'soil and climate are subject to his [man's] dominion; and are indeed susceptible of improvement and variable, in a high degree, with the progress of civil arts' (*EHM* 360). That is, to reiterate, the impact of local circumstances, of physical causes, becomes less important as man progresses.[23]

To conclude: Dunbar's theory of climate is an expression of, at one and the same time, the general eighteenth-century interest in climate and the more particular Scottish treatment of the phenomenon. Dunbar, like many others, is endeavouring to order the chaos of the evidence of differing social experiences. Climate, indeed, is an important ordering principle, but to be really effective in this role its scope must be defined more clearly, and Dunbar, by pointing out the significance of seeing it (categorically) as a local circumstance, attempts this clarification. Along with most of his compatriots, he rejects the direct physiological aspect of climatic influence, but this now only makes all the more acute the question of precisely how and to what extent climate was influential. Dunbar's answer is that climate, in its broad eighteenth-century sense, establishes an initial set of circumstances (which are often 'local' in character), but man's relationship with these circumstances is not fixed but changes as man himself, and the society of which he is necessarily a part, develop. Thus Dunbar works together the two main eighteenth-century ordering principles, climate and development, in order to make sense of the increasingly complex panorama of social experience. Of course, he is not alone in this,[24] but his attempt is noteworthy both for its exemplification of a widespread aspect of eighteenth-century thought and for its own intrinsic argument.

Postscript

I chose *Texas Studies in Literature and Language* as a locus for this piece, published in 1974, because Ernest Mossner was one of the editors. In Berry 1997 I revisited Dunbar's treatment of climate but not to any revisionary extent, although I did talk up there, more than here, the parallel with Robertson. I also referred to the work of Cullen (1997: 83) and am inclined to think that the various medical debates are a significant backdrop and probably worth pursuing. For general background, see, for example, Vickers (2011) and Janovics (2010), who has one mention of Dunbar and references this article (160–1n).

Subsequent treatments of Dunbar and climate are few. However, when writing this paper I was unaware of Glacken (1967: Ch. 12); this is the best overview of the 'climate issue' and, moreover, discusses Dunbar. The fullest discussion of Dunbar is given by Sebastiani (2013), who includes his views in climate within her broader argument that he 'forged a radical version of the history of man in society'; the nub of this radicalism lying in his opposition to the 'naturalisation' of human differences (including a divergence from Robertson) (2013: 130, 126, 127). Sebastiani does not cite this article but makes use of my 1997 discussion (and even refers to my thesis); nor does she refer to more specific literature on climate.

Golinsky (2007) produces a general survey, wherein the Scots including Dunbar figure prominently (citing this paper in his notes). He notes the similarity with Robertson but sees Dunbar as more systematic (181) and, drawing on Paul Wood (1993), identifies him, like his university colleagues, as 'uniformly hostile to materialism, which they associated with Hume's skepticism' (ibid.). Wood is the best source of information on Dunbar's teaching. A transcription of his lecture notes (MS 3107/5/2/6 in Aberdeen University Library) from the end of his career (that is, post publication of *EHM*) was produced by Hiroshi Mizuta, who in a typical display of both kindness and scholarly collegiality, gave me a copy (Center for Historical Social Science Literature, Hitosubashi University, 1996). I confess my ignorance, and consequent scholarly deficiency, of this source material at the time of writing. In fact, 'climate' is referred to only in passing and he cross-references *EHM*; there are references 'to physical and moral causes'. Climate was the subject of one his Discourses (23 April 1771) to the Aberdeen 'Wise Club' (see Ulman 1990: 42). John Adams (1789) chose an extract on the influence of climate in his collection.

Dunbar on local circumstances is picked up in a passing discussion in Fielding (2008: 52–3, 41, 60), who cites this article but also makes some interesting observations on the link with language and reads him – implicitly contra Golinsky – as accepting a determinist view, though not in uniform way (2008: 52–3, 41, 60). Spadafora (1990: 311), as part of his general survey of the Scots, mentions in passing Dunbar and climate, again referencing this article for the discussion of climate and see also Mills' (2018) article on Falconer (an Edinburgh-trained physician and correspondent of Cullen), a far-reaching and valuable piece that takes in Dunbar *en passant*.

Notwithstanding this relative paucity, I remain of the opinion that the topic of 'climate' is an important organising principle when the Enlightenment set about explaining social diversity, and Dunbar's interpretation one of the more useful in his attempt to conceptualise the relation between space and time (history/ progress).

Notes

1. Cf. the 1771 *Encyclopaedia Britannica*: climate is a 'space upon the terrestrial globe'. 'Air' is the nearest eighteenth-century equivalent to present usage, though this is dependent on the above; for 'climate' as a category, see *infra*.
2. Cf. Bryson (1945), Schneider (1967) and Swingewood (1970).
3. See, for example, Ferguson (*ECS* 124, 136) and Millar (*OR* 177–78). Compare from the *Encyclopédie* (Diderot, 1765) Jaucourt ('Lacedaemon') and St Lambert ('Legislateurs'). Cf. Brumfitt (1958: 101), which is not to mention either Montesquieu or Rousseau.
4. See, for example, T. Reid: habit acts 'without will or intention' (1846: 550); Gregory (1788: 36); and Ferguson (*ECS* 76). (For the role of habit in Hume and further discussion, see Chapters 5 and 11.)
5. Smith's 'invisible hand' (*WN* IV.ii.9/456) is the best example but is not isolated, either in that book or in the work of others – for example Ferguson (*ECS* 122) or Dunbar himself (*EHM* 183).
6. Property was an important concept in the Scots' writings; see, though with some overemphasis, Pascal (1939: 167–79) and Meek (1954: Ch. 3).
7. Cf. Skinner (1967, 1965).
8. See, for example, Ferguson (*ECS* 65), 'When I recollect what the President Montesquieu has written I am at a loss to tell why I should treat of human affairs.'
9. So called by Millar (*HV* II, 404n).
10. See, for Hume's popularity, Mossner (1954 *passim*) and Graham (1901 *passim*). On Scotticisms, see Berry 1974 (Ch. 16).
11. Not, of course, that Hume and Montesquieu were open antagonists. Hume wrote his essay before the *Esprit* was published. A more likely target was Dubos, to whom he refers in other contemporary essays. (Chamley (1975) has subsequently argued that Hume had sight of an unpublished version. For my doubts on this, see Chapter 11.)
12. Throughout the literature, climate is the most important physical cause. Indeed, given its broad contemporary meaning (see n.2 above), the two are near synonyms; or at least other instances of physical causes are easily subsumable in climate, with the possible exception of what Wallace (*DNM* 12) calls more 'variable instances' – for example earthquakes. But even these, at best, merely constitute a subsection within a permissible categorisation.
13. For example, climate is only one cause among several in Montesquieu's summation of the 'esprit general' in Bk 19, Ch. 4; and even in the

next chapter moral causes are mentioned. Outside the *Esprit*, see particularly his 'Essai sur les causes' (1892 in 1955: III, 398–430), in which he makes the following statement: '*Les causes morales forment plus le caractère général d'une nation et décident plus de la qualité de son esprit que les causes physiques*' (p. 421).

14. Dedieu (1909: 206–11). The work of Arbuthnot's in question is *An Essay Concerning the Effects of Air on Human Bodies* (1733). For doubts on the importance of Arbuthnot's influence on Montesquieu compared to Chardin and Dubos, see Gates (1967). (For comment, see the postscript.)

15. Cf. W. Robertson, 'Moral and political causes as I have formerly observed affect the disposition and character of individuals as well as nations, still more powerfully than the influence of climate' (*HAm* 851).

16. See, for example, 'But under the extremes of heat or of cold the active range of the human soul appears to be limited . . . In the one extreme they are dull and slow . . . In the other they are feverish' (*ECS* 112,111).

17. He writes, 'The Hollander is laborious and industrious in Europe; he becomes more languid and slothful in India' (*ECS* 118). Hume had written, 'The Spanish, English, French and Dutch colonies are all distinguishable even between the tropics' (*E-NC* 210).

18. Cf. Fletcher (1939: 98–9) for the only other consideration of Dunbar's climatic theory.

19. Further examples are 'the comparative fertility of soils, the nature of their production and the position of the globe (*EHM* 257). Climate is explicitly referred to as a local circumstance (*EHM* 222). These examples, too, are without distortion categorisable under 'climate'.

20. In a passage added to the first edition (1780), Dunbar notes: 'Though it is of importance to ascertain the qualities of the atmospherical air, and the changes it undergoes, yet the air in general is good in all countries; and that small differences which in reality subsist are by no means so formidable as some people are apt to suppose' (*EHM* 376–7). This is possibly a reference to Dubos' theory of emanations (Dubos 1755: II, 221 ff.).

21. Cf. climate as a local circumstance 'will appear eminently to affect the progress of arts and government' (*EHM* 222).

22. Hence Dunbar's rejection, as mentioned above, of the import of Montesquieu's theory. Compare (*EHM* 221–2, 318).

23. Cf. Robertson, 'This powerful operation of climate is felt most sensibly by rude nations and produces greater effects than in societies

more improved' (*HAm* 850). The same sentiment is found in Montesquieu; see *Esprit,* Bk 19, Ch. 4, which is significant given his above-mentioned influence on the Scots.

24. Shackleton (1961: 319) claims this for Montesquieu but then states that it is only 'implicit' and certainly Montesquieu does not use development or progress as an ordering principle, as Durkheim (1965: 57ff.), among others, has noted.

5

Sociality and Socialisation

James Dunbar commented that humans are sociable long before they are rational (*EHM* 16).[1] The implications of that remark establish the leitmotif for this chapter. Positively, these extend to an understanding of the effects of sociality on the individual and also to an understanding of the principles that produce and sustain social coherence. As we shall see, these two aspects are importantly linked in the writings of the Scots and constitute one of the most salient and characteristic features of their thought. This particular priority has at least the further implication of displacing claims that have been made for the role of reason. The first (brief) part of this chapter will consider this negative implication, the second, more extensive, part the more positive implications.

I

The claim that humans are social before they are rational means that it is literally preposterous to explain human social living as the product of reason, understood here as the process of calculation. The Scots alleged that such an explanation had been been made by those thinkers who subscribed to the idea of an original or social contract. The Scots, however, were being somewhat, if not entirely, disingenuous in making this allegation. The contractarian argument dealt not with social living per se but more specifically with civic or political living, that is, with the establishment of government. Indeed, it was central to the argument of mainstream contractarians (that is, excluding Hobbes) that the pre-political condition was not asocial. What they were centrally interested in was the legitimacy of government: what gave a particular individual or group the right or authority to command others.

Once the principle of natural rulership was abandoned,

government or civil society could be conceptualised as an artificial construction, a product of deliberate choice. This choice, prompted by the 'inconveniences' (to use Locke's terminology) of the pre-political condition (the 'state of nature'), took the form of a contract. Typically, the terms of this contract were that I would agree to lay aside my natural right to govern myself and obey your rule, provided you protected me and did not interfere with my other natural rights. This is a cost–benefit analysis that makes the role, even the existence, of government a function of individualistic instrumental reasoning.

The Scots criticise this whole account. They dismiss the 'state of nature' as fantastical, as empirically unwarranted. Ferguson, for example, opens his *Essay on the History of Civil Society* with a chapter entitled 'Of the question relating to the State of Nature'. In that chapter he accuses those who talk of such a condition as deviating from the practice of the 'natural historian', who thinks 'facts' should be collected and general tenets derived from 'observations and experiments'. By contrast, contractarians (he clearly has Hobbes and Rousseau in mind) resort to 'hypothesis' or 'conjecture' or 'imagination' or 'poetry'. To these Ferguson juxtaposes, respectively, 'reality', 'facts', 'reason' and 'science' and it is the latter list that 'must be admitted as the foundation of all our reasoning relative to man' (*ECS* 2). We must, in other words, turn to evidence. This reveals that we have 'no record' of any pre-social state (*ECS* 6); all the evidence reveals that 'mankind are to be taken in groupes, as they always subsisted' (*ECS* 4; cf. 3, 16).

All the Scots rejected the idea of the 'state of nature' and its corollary, the idea of a original contract. Hume outlines a straightforward historical critique: that government originated in a contract is 'not justified by history or experience in any age or country of the world' (E-OC 471). If the contractarian account of origins is empirically invalid, it is even less tenable when it claims that the legitimacy of current government rests on consent (E-OC 469), since if 'these reasoners' were to examine actual practice and belief, they 'would meet with nothing that in the least corresponds to their ideas' (E-OC 470). Neither rulers nor subjects believe that their relationship is the effect of some prior pact. This is a damaging line of argument. The very core of contractarian doctrine is that it is some 'act of mind' (making a deliberate choice) that constitutes legitimacy, so that the fact that any such act is 'unknown to all of them' is fatal to the theory's cogency.

Hume's historical/empirical refutation was widely followed. Millar, for example, argues that merely obtaining some form of protection does not warrant the conclusion that this is the consequence of a promise (*HV* IV, 7/804). Ferguson regards the idea of men assembling together as equals and deciding their mode of government as 'visionary and unknown in nature' (*PMPS* I, 262). Stuart (*HD*: 151n) thinks there is no evidence and 'it is absurd to suppose that the original contract ever happened', while Smith picks up Hume's point that any contemporary obligation cannot stem from a past contract (*LJA* v.115/316).

It is within this negative descriptive rejection of the 'state of nature'/Original Contract that the seeds of the Scots' positive account are to be found. In the opening chapter of the *Essay*, Ferguson comments that 'all situations are equally natural' (see also Chapter 7). This means, as he goes on to illustrate, that the 'state of nature' is 'here and it matters not whether we are understood to speak in the island of Great Britain, at the Cape of Good Hope, or the Straits of Magellan' (*ECS* 8). It equally follows that it matters not whether it is eighteenth- or eighth-century Britain and so on. Since the 'natural condition' of humans is life in society, the premise from which norms are generated must also be social. It is, therefore, a category mistake to generate those norms from some extra-social or extra-temporal perspective. We cannot meaningfully assess the legitimacy of a government by invoking such a perspective, by, so to speak, stepping outside our social selves. The legitimacy has to be found within society. It is still possible to talk of 'natural rights', as Ferguson and other Scots do, but, given natural sociality, these rights are not divorced conceptually or normatively from actual social existence.

II

If humans are not social as a consequence of an act of reason, what, then, does account for human sociality? One common explanation of human sociality was that it was instinctive or appetitive. Kames declared that it has never been called into question that man has 'an appetite for society' (*SHM* I, 376).[2] There was, however, a marked reluctance to push this recourse to instinct too far. To a large extent, this stemmed from the desire to insist on qualitative differences between humans and animals and, of course, the possession of reason is just one such difference – the fact that human sociality cannot be attributed to rational decision does not mean that humans do not reason. What is vital is not the possession of reason nor that it is purposive or calculative in its operation, but its delayed employment. Whereas the infant antelope (say) is able within a few hours of birth to join and follow the herd, the human neonate is helpless.

By virtue of this dependence, humans require extensive nurture and Dunbar explicitly draws attention to the fact that, as a consequence, the parent–child bond is more durable than in animals (*EHM* 18). This durability results in family or kin ties extending beyond mere instinct and Ferguson fastens upon this to account for the family's minor role as an explanation of sociality (*PMPS* I, 27). The affection that children have for their parents does not disappear (as it does in animals) once physical independence has been reached; rather, it grows closer 'as it becomes mixed with esteem and the memory of its early effects' (*PMPS* I, 16). The affective basis here is what is important. Children do not esteem their parents because they are honouring their part of a bargain or contract, the parents having already fulfilled their part. Family life, and by extension social life, is not reducible to rationalistic or instrumentalist explanations.

Ferguson makes much of this point. For him, there was more to human sociality than either 'parental affection' or an appetitive 'propensity . . . to mix with the herd' (*ECS* 16). Once some durability has been established, the independent principles of friendship and loyalty come into play. In each case they represent a sphere of human conduct that is not reducible either to animal instinct or to self-interested rational calculation. Ferguson, indeed, declares that the bonds formed by these principles are the strongest of all and this is precisely because they transcend the self-centred quality of the other two. They are for that reason the most genuinely social. As supporting evidence, he offers the observation that 'men are so far from valuing society on account of its mere external conveniencies that they are commonly most attached where those conveniencies are least frequent' (*ECS* 19). Indeed, to lay down one's life for one's friend or country is not some mental aberration (as Hobbes would have it) but the very stuff of humans as social beings.[3]

In his argument that sociality is not reducible to the familial (a point also made by Dunbar),[4] Ferguson remarks that, as a further consequence of the durability of the child–parent relation, the instinctive attachments 'grow into habit'. This reference to habit is to a principle that plays a central role in the Scots' social theory. The very fact that humans are social creatures who require extended nurture means that they are exposed to the formative force of habit; they are, as Ferguson put it, 'withal in a very high degree susceptible of habits' (*ECS* 11; cf. *PMPS* I, 209).

Habits are repeated responses that are made possible by a stable set of circumstances. This repetitiveness leaves its mark. In a common but revealing phrase, habits become 'second nature'. As such, they share some of the key features of 'first nature' or instinct. Reid quite explicitly linked them. Both are 'mechanical principles' that 'operate without will or intention' (Reid 1846: 550). They can both in this way also be contrasted with rational action. In a straightforward sense rationality can be associated with maturity, whereas a baby's behaviour is largely instinctive. (Reid (1846: 545) prominently includes breathing, sucking and swallowing in his examples of instincts.) Picking up the earlier point that it is the delayed employment of reason that is vital, habits are especially potent in childhood; as Hume puts it, by 'operating on the tender minds of the children' they 'fashion them by degrees' for social life (*T* 3.2.2.4/*SBNT* 486). There is a consolidating dynamic work at here. Hume once again is instructive: 'whatever it be that forms the manners of one generation, the next must imbibe a deeper tincture of the same dye; men being more susceptible of all impressions during infancy, and retaining these impressions as long as they remain in the world' (*E-NC* 203). This is a crucial argument because it is central to the Scots' appreciation of the significance of the effects of sociality and their understanding of the factors underpinning social coherence – what I shall call institutional stickiness.

By stressing habit formation in childhood – what Turnbull (*PMP* 134) terms 'early accustomance'– the Scots are emphasising the importance of socialisation. Hume provides a good example of this process in operation in his positive alternative to the contractarian account of legitimation. He argues that if human generations (like silkworms) replaced themselves totally at one moment, then that might give credence to the contractarian theory, but the facts are different. Human societies are comprised of continually changing populations so that, to achieve any stability, it is necessary that 'the new brood should conform themselves to the established constitution and nearly follow the path which their fathers, treading in the footsteps of theirs, had marked out to them' (*E-OC* 476–7).

The 'brood' conforms not as a consequence of any deliberate (read, adult) decision but because there is a pre-existing path. This path they follow because that is the way of their world, the one into which they have been socialised and whose institutions are correspondingly sticky.

The implications of this stickiness are that habits or customary ways of behaving, and the institutions thus constituted, not only stabilise but also constrain. Ferguson remarks that habits 'fix the manners of men' (as instinct fixes the behaviour of animals) (*PMPS* I, 232). Echoing Hume's argument about stability, Ferguson goes on to observe that without that fixity 'human life would be a scene of inextricable confusion and uncertainty' (ibid.). This fixity constrains by circumscribing the range of effective or discernible options. What might appear a 'rational' solution runs up against the 'fact' that sociality precedes rationality, so that, as Kames observed, it is 'a sort of Herculean labour to eradicate notions that from infancy have been held fundamental' (1781: 282).[5] These 'notions' are the socialised/ habitual second nature and 'the force of habit', as Millar felicitously terms it, is the 'great controller and governor of our actions' (*HV* IV, 7/798). He cites as an example how the 'power of habit', as it 'becomes more considerable as it passes from one generation to another', explains hereditary authority (*OR* 250).

Hume's discussion of chastity reinforces this point. (For an extended discussion, see Chapter 10.) For Hume – though not for all his fellow Scots – since women are not naturally chaste, they must be taught to be so. This teaching is nothing other than a process of socialisation: 'education takes possession of the ductile minds of the fair sex in their infancy' (*T* 3.2.12.7/*SBNT* 572). As he says of the related case of 'sentiments of honour', by taking root in 'tender minds' they 'acquire such firmness and solidity that they may fall little short of those principles which are most essential to our natures and the most deeply radicated in our internal constitution' (*T* 3.2.2.26/ *SBNT* 501). It is the 'tenderness' or 'ductility' of the infant mind that makes 'custom and education' so powerful as they inculcate 'principles of probity' and 'observance of those rules by which society is maintain'd as worthy and honourable' (*T* 3.2.2.26/ *SBNT* 500). It is through families, and the societies within which they are embodied, that girls learn the value of chastity. This becomes so deeply 'radicated' that they will look upon extra- or premarital sex as conduct unbecoming a lady.

They will know (will have internalised) the social consequences of the 'smallest failure'; they know they will become 'cheap and vulgar', will lose 'rank', will be 'exposed to every insult'; they know, in short, that their 'character' will be 'blast[ed]' (*M* VI, 14/ *SBNM* 238–9). Chastity is a sticky institution; it is difficult for an individual to 'break free' and, even if one does defy convention, the obloquy that would follow is likely, in fact, to strengthen what has been defied.

III

This awareness of the 'stickiness' of institutions expresses itself in various ways in the Scots' writings. A significant case in point is their explanation of social change. Since customs are creatures of time, then time, that is, gradual alterations in the sentiments of people, is what changes them. In contrast to any glib confidence in 'progress' – the ever-increasing efficacy and transparency of reason – the Scots are more cautious (Forbes 1954). They do believe in improvement but it is not guaranteed and it is a gradual process.

It follows from this gradualism that it is not the case that social institutions, on being perceived as irrational, can then simply be changed overnight, as it were. Institutions are 'sticky'; they are the repository of socialised norms and values. Robertson, referring to trial by combat, observes that no custom 'how absurd soever it be' was 'ever abolished by the bare promulgation of laws and statutes'; rather, it fell into disuse with the development of 'science' and 'civility' (*VP* 325). Smith, in a well-known account, argues that feudal power was destroyed not by legal edict but 'gradually brought about' by the 'silent and insensible operation of foreign commerce and manufactures' or, more generally, by changes in the form of 'property and manners' (*WN* III, iv.8–10/415–18). 'Manners', in fact, have a salience precisely because as a 'mode of behaviour' (Kames *SHM* I, 181), as the socialised way of behaving, they are too complex for law (Kames 1781: 21). Millar puts this principle into effect when he uses the changing lot of women to illustrate the 'natural progress' from 'rude to civilised manners' (*OR* 176), thus adding an historical dimension to Hume's discussion of chastity.

This recognition that change takes time also restricts the scope for individual (rational) initiative. Much was made of this in the Scots' critique of the tradition of 'great legislators'. These legislators

(Brama, Solon, Romulus, Lycurgus and Alfred) were traditionally portrayed as the source of constitutions. But the role attributed to them is sociologically implausible. Millar comments that before any legislator could have the requisite authority 'he must probably have been educated and brought up in the knowledge of those natural manners and customs which for ages perhaps have prevailed among his countrymen' (OR 177). Ferguson argues that if today in an age of 'extensive reflection' we 'cannot break loose from the trammels of custom' then it is very unlikely that in the times of the legislators, when 'knowledge was less', individuals were more inclined to 'shake off the impressions of habit' (ECS 123).

The consequence of this 'entrammelling' is that, according to Millar, the legislators will 'be disposed to prefer the system already established'. From the effects of this socialisation it follows that it is 'extremely probable' that they will have been 'at great pains to accommodate their regulations to the spirit of the people' and 'confined themselves to moderate improvements' rather than 'violent reformation'. Millar thinks the case of Lycurgus bears this out, because his regulations appear 'agreeable to the primitive manners of the Spartans' (OR 178). Alfred, too, fits this picture. Millar notes that his interpositions have been identified as 'the engine' to explain the origin of various English institutions (HV I, 271), but this is to uproot him implausibly from his social environment. Hence, for example, the institution of juries rose from the 'general situation of the Gothic nations' (ibid.) and the military institutions were not the product of some 'political projector' (HV I, 6/98); rather, they stemmed 'imperceptibly' from 'the rude state of the country' (HV I, 6/97).[6]

Ferguson argues that the supposed legislator in fact 'only acted a superior part among numbers who were disposed to the same institutions' (ECS 124).[7] For Ferguson, the 'rise' of Roman and Spartan government came not from 'the projects of single men' but from 'the situation and genius of the people' (ibid.). Millar adopted the same line: 'the greater part of the political system' derived from the 'combined influence of the whole people' (OR 177). Dunbar allows, as Millar had, that some individuals have had some impact but institutions are 'more justly reputed the slow result of situations than of regular design' (EHM 61). In his account of language, for example, he regards it as a 'fundamental error' to refer to 'great projectors' in order to explain the development of the different parts of speech (EHM 93).

A sociological/institutional rather than rationalist/individualist explanation is being offered. The Scots criticise the latter as superficial and simplistic. When confronted with a particular institution or social practice, the 'simplest' explanation is to attribute it to some 'previous design', that is, to attribute it to some individual's will or purpose as the cause of the institution as an effect; as Stuart observes, 'it is easy' to talk of the deep projects of princes but it is 'more difficult to mark the slow operation of events' (*OPL* 108). Because individualistic explanations are simplistic, they are misleading. They remove individuals from their social context and, since humans are naturally social, this removal is a distortion. From the perspective of the history of social theory this is an important conclusion: social institutions are to be explained by social causes. Stuart neatly summarises this point when he remarks that the disorders between the king and the nobles which affected the whole of Europe in the high Middle Ages are 'not to be referred entirely to the rapacity and the administration of princes. There *must be a cause more comprehensive and general* to which they [the disorders] are chiefly to be ascribed' (*VSE* 71).[8] From the earlier discussion we can identify these general causes as 'situation and genius' (Ferguson), prevalent 'manners and customs' (Millar), the 'slow result of situations' (Dunbar) or the 'slow operation of events' (Stuart).

There is a juxtaposition here between the general (social) and the particular (rational individual). What can be clearly explained by recourse to the latter is of a markedly lesser extent than the former. Hume notes that from one roll of a biased die the outcome is 'chance' but from a 'great number' the bias will reveal itself as a 'determinate and known' cause (E-AS 112). (See also Chapter 11.) Millar adopts a similar image. He aptly applies the example of a die in his assault on the 'legislator theory'. In one or two rolls the results will be random, but over time (over many rolls) the results will be 'nearly equal'. The former case is like the impact of a legislator, the latter like 'the combined influence of the whole people', which provides a more certain (or 'fixed') causal explanation of a nation's 'political system' than any 'casual interposition' by a particular individual (*OR* 177).

As this last phrase suggests, Millar, Ferguson and the others obviously do not deny that humans are purposive but they nonetheless believe that individual deliberate action falls short of explanatory power when it comes to institutions. In perhaps the best-known expression of the point, Ferguson writes: 'nations stumble upon establishments which are indeed the result of human action, but not the execution of any human design' (*ECS* 122).[9] The insight was not his alone. Hume, for example, provides a good illustration of the point. He remarks that the first leader was an effective military commander and that in due course (through time and custom) this ad hoc position solidified into a monarchical form of government. Hume comments on this process that, though it 'may appear certain and inevitable', in fact government commenced casually because it 'cannot be expected that men should beforehand be able to discover them [principles of government and allegiance] or foresee their operation' (E-OG 39–40).

This recognition of the limitations of individual rationality and of the associated recalcitrance or stickiness of institutions to rational 'quick-fixes' is only to be expected from a group of thinkers who, as social theorists, take the 'social' seriously. Human experience is experience of social life. As products of socialisation, individuals are embedded within their societies. To speak generally, the Scots plotted societies on to a temporal grid (the four-stages theory is the most famous instance of this) and then this grid was 'read across' to discern the ways in which the different institutions cohered. This is central to how the Scots' social theory generated a concept of society as a set of interlocked institutions and behaviours. A society of hunter-gatherers will thus have little in the way of personal possessions, nothing to speak of in the form of governmental machinery, few status distinctions except the inferiority of women, and will live in a world populated with a multiplicity of gods. These savages would also respond to these events in a speech abounding in vivid and animated images and would likely bedaub themselves and/or indulge in self-mutilation (cf. Dunbar *EHM* 389; Kames *SHM* II, 437). They would have been socialised into accepting this conduct as normal. Millar acknowledges this clearly: 'individuals form their notions of propriety according to a general standard, and fashion their morals in conformity to the prevailing taste of the times' (*HV* IV, 6/777; cf. Robertson *HAm* 811). However, as moralists, the Scots did not merely accept the diversity of social experience and thence the diversity of moral beliefs. They had no doubts that life in a free and civilised society was a better life than all that had gone before. The way in which they avoid inconsistency is by treating as axiomatic the uniformity and universality of human nature and then attributing to it the capacity to improve or progress (*ECS* 8; *OR* 176, etc.).

IV

We can illustrate this point, in conclusion, with reference to Smith's moral theory. In a famous passage, he likens society to a mirror (*TMS* III, 1.4/110; cf. Hume *T* 2.2.5.21/*SBNT* 365). The force of this comparison is that moral judgements are generated by social interaction – learning how to behave through seeing how others react to our behaviour. To give one of Smith's own examples: 'if I see a grief-stricken stranger and am informed that he has just learnt of his father's death, then I, via sympathy, approve of his grief. What makes this possible is that I have learnt from experience that such misfortune excites such sorrow' (*TMS* I, i.3.4/18). The experience can only come from 'common life', from the fact that humans are social creatures. The importance and centrality of sociality is once again underwritten.

In line with the earlier argument, this now seems to imply that moral judgements are the socialised product of a particular society. Smith even seems not to exempt the principle of conscience from this process, since he declares that the authority possessed by conscience is the effect of 'habit and experience' (*TMS* III, 3.3/135). The fact that it is habitual, so that 'we are scarce sensible' that we do appeal to it, means that it, too, is a learnt resource. However, this does not mean that it – or moral judgement more generally – is a mere reflex of prevalent social norms.[10] His account of infanticide provides the concluding illustration.

While openly admitting that virtues differ between 'rude and barbarous nations' and 'ages of civility and politeness' (*TMS* V, 2.8/205), Smith nonetheless believes that 'the sentiments of moral approbation and disapprobation are founded on the strongest and most vigorous passions of human nature; and though they may be somewhat warpt, cannot be entirely perverted' (*TMS* V, 2.1/200). He illustrates this with the example of infanticide, which 'in the earliest period of society' was commonplace and the 'uniform continuance of the custom had hindered them [the practitioners] from perceiving its enormity' (*TMS* V, 2.15/210). He does allow the practice to be 'more pardonable' in the rudest and lowest state of society, where 'extreme indigence' obtains, but the practice was inexcusable 'among the polite and civilised Athenians'. Smith is adamant that just because something is commonly done does not mean it is condonable when the practice itself is 'unjust and unreasonable' (ibid.). (For further discussion of this passage in Smith, see Chapter 17.)

What this example underwrites is the fact that the writers of the Scottish Enlightenment combined a 'scientific' appreciation of the complexity of social life with an evaluative assessment of the relative worth of forms of social experience. On the one hand this combination makes them fully members of the Enlightenment family but, on the other, their insight into the limits of individual rational action, the stabilising yet constraining power of customs, and the stickiness of social institutions means they never subscribed to that aspect of Enlightenment thought which could confidently envisage the conquest of dark irrationality by the irresistible force of the light of reason.

Postscript

In 2000 I was invited to contribute to the essay collection *The Cambridge Companion to the Scottish Enlightenment* by the editor and Glasgow colleague Alexander Broadie, for which I am grateful. The circumstances of its writing were not ideal and due to vagaries in the production my original text was not published (it will, however, appear in 2018 in the planned second edition of the book). I have not made further changes, even though I now rather wish I had taken more time and done some more thinking. Nevertheless I chose it for this volume because it complements the comparative discussion of Dunbar in Chapter 2 and because it was the major location where I developed my notion of 'stickiness' when discussing institutions (see also Chapter 10). This has been picked up by, for example, Fonna Forman-Barzilai, although she is also critical of my argument on social norms (2010). I can reveal that I was the 'incisive anonymous referee' for her earlier pursuit of this theme (Forman-Barzilai 2007).

Gordon Graham (2014), while taking this essay as his starting point, duly takes me to task for not including within it a discussion of Hutcheson. Graham's discussion can be recommended for taking further, within its self-defined limited focus, the theme of sociability.

Notes

1. See, further, Berry (1997: 30). This chapter expands the point while drawing upon the earlier discussion. (See also Chapter 2.)
2. Cf. Kames (*PMNR* 54, 86, 88). Similar assertions are made by, for

example, Ferguson (*ECS* 11, 122, 182; *PMPS* I, 32), J. Gregory (1788: II 114), Turnbull (*PMP* 175) and Dunbar (*EHM* 24).

3. Ferguson's thoughts on this issue are closely connected to his worries about the tendency of contemporary commercial societies to increase the prevalence of calculative behaviour. Some commentators have made much of this: see, inter alia, Brewer (1986), Benton (1990) and Varty (1997).

4. Dunbar argues that even maternal instincts were fluctuating in earlier times (*EHM* 23). For more discussion of this point, now see Miller (2017: 104–6).

5. Elsewhere, Kames uses a different metaphor to the same end: 'the influence of custom in rivetting men to their local situation and manner of life' (*SHM* II, 87).

6. See also Hume, who comments that, as Alfred's institutions were similar to those found elsewhere, this counts against him being 'the sole author of this plan of government'; rather, 'like a wise man he contented himself with reforming, extending and executing the institutions which he found previously established' (*HE* I, 50, 53).

7. Stuart (*HD* 248) cites this argument and closely follows Ferguson's terminology.

8. Cf. Millar, who argues that it was the 'improvement of arts and the consequent diffusion of knowledge' leading to dispelling superstition and 'inspiring sentiments of liberty' that 'is to be regarded as the *general cause* of the reformation' (*HV* II, 10/407; my emphasis). (For the importance of 'general causes', see Berry 2015.)

9. See for comment, inter alia, Hamowy (1987) and Hayek (1967).

10. See for comment, inter alia, Raphael (1975: 90), Hope (1989: 105) and Berry (2006a; Chapter 17).

6

Rude Religion: The Psychology of Polytheism in the Scottish Enlightenment

The idea that human society passes through the 'four stages' of hunting, herding, farming and commerce is generally regarded as one of the major contributions of the Scottish Enlightenment. This general regard has not, however, meant any unanimity as to the precise character and significance of that idea. Indeed, a distinct history of interpretation has developed.

The initial emphasis was on the proto-Marxian character of the stadial theme. While Ronald L. Meek is chiefly identified with this emphasis, the ground was broken in English by Roy Pascal, who characterised the 'Scottish Historical School' by its 'materialistic and scientific approach'.[1] In an essay openly indebted to Pascal entitled 'The Scottish Contribution to Marxist Sociology', first published in 1954, Meek likewise identified the Scots as proponents of 'a materialist conception of history'.[2] Although Meek did qualify his initial formulations in subsequent writings, he nevertheless explicitly said about his earlier account that he did not think he was 'all that wrong in describing this theoretical system [that is, the four stages] as *a* if not *the* materialist conception of history' (1977: 19; Meek italics). A third exponent[3] of this interpretation was Andrew Skinner. Skinner also employed the Marx-derived terminology of 'productive forces' (1965: 21) and talked explicitly of an 'almost Marxian reliance' in Smith's account upon economic forces (1975: 175). Skinner, however, later wrote an explicit critique of Meek (using the same title as Meek's original 1954 essay but adding a question mark), wherein he stated that Smith was a neither a determinist nor a materialist.[4]

Between Skinner's essays of 1975 and 1982 a shift away from the materialist interpretation occurred. Explanations for such shifts are elusive but it would seem that, on an academic front, Donald Winch's *Adam Smith's Politics* (1978) had an impact.

Winch (1996) restated his views: he was concerned to argue against those interpretations of Smith that read him backwards from the nineteenth century; this included not only Marxists but also 'Manchester liberals'. Winch combined together three strands. From Quentin Skinner (1969) he took up the emphasis on the need to focus on the historicity of an author's intentions, from John Pocock (1975) he incorporated the significance of the discourse on virtue and corruption, and from Duncan Forbes he adopted the distinction between 'vulgar' and 'sceptical Whiggism' (1975a, 1975b, 1954). The effect of this synthesis was to alert scholars to the pitfalls of anachronism and of the need to heed eighteenth-century preoccupations. One consequence of this was to shift the centre of intepretative focus away from the four stages.

This shift can be seen explicitly in Knud Haakonssen. He denied that Smith's theory of motivation was materialistic and drew attention to the way Smith admitted non-economic factors, such as geography and religion as well as pure chance, into his account of social change.[5] Before Haakonssen, Harro Höpfl had openly challenged Meek's idea that the Scots operated with a base/superstructure distinction. For Höpfl, the conjectural history written by the Scots gave no particular motive or interest automatic priority and the notion that material agencies were the real explanans of social change, while political and other ideational institutions were epiphenomenal, was 'quite alien to the Scots' (1978: 35). Roger L. Emerson took this argument one step further. He argued that the Scots were committed to 'complex usually idealistic theories of social change' and observed that all institutions are susceptible to a conjectural history – religion, language, government, taste and science (Emerson 1984: 65, 82, 89nn, 89, 90).

I want here to pursue that observation with reference to the first of these. More specifically, I wish to explore the reasoning behind the Scots' identification of polytheism as the first form of religion. This exploration will focus on the psychology that the Scots assume to be operant. I have elsewhere argued that this psychology underwrites generally the four-stages theory itself[6] and this paper aims to consolidate that argument and lend weight to Emerson's claim that the 'four stages' is only a specific case of a more general historical approach.

I

The opening sentence of the first chapter of Hume's *Natural History of Religion* reads, 'It appears to me, that, if we consider the improvement of human society, from rude beginnings to a state of greater perfection, polytheism or idolatry was and necessarily must have been the first and most ancient religion of mankind' (*NHR* 1, 1/34). In an appropriately liturgical sense, this sentence will be the 'text' for this paper. It contains two points of note: the context is that of 'improvement' from rude religion to greater perfection and, secondly, that rude religion is polytheistic.

On both these counts Hume's position is unexceptional; we find them reiterated by many of his compatriots.[7] The conjunction of these points produces the proposition that polytheism is the 'early' experience of humankind. In other words, the evidence is assimilated to an explanatory 'model' that accounts for the differences in human experience by imparting to it a temporal structure: some societies (forms of human experience) are more developed or improved than others.

It is this commitment to temporality that explains why the social theory of the Scottish Enlightenment characteristically took the form of writing 'history'. This history was not a descriptive list of dates and battles or 'singular events', as Lord Kames (*HLT* iv) terms them; rather it was to be, in John Millar's formulation (*OR* 180), the 'natural history of mankind'. Millar proceeded to characterise this as the enterprise of 'pointing out the more obvious and common improvements which gradually arise in the state of society and by showing the influence of these upon the manners, the laws and the government of a people'.[8]

To Millar's list can be added religion. This addition is supported by Hume's choice of 'Natural History' as the title of his essay.[9] We can utilise our 'text', taken from that essay, to develop the argument. Most particularly, I want to fasten on to Hume's use of the term 'necessarily' when claiming that polytheism was the first religion of mankind. That term plays two roles in Hume's and the others' accounts of religion. The first of these alludes to the *type* of history Hume and the others were practising, the second to the shape or structure that they see this history embodying. As we will see, this second role is integral to the context of 'improvement' within which the Scots situate their discussions. I take up these two roles in turn in the next two sections.

II

Hume published his *The Natural History of Religion* in 1757. Since Dugald Stewart had used the term 'natural history' as a synonym for 'theoretical or conjectural history' and had cited Hume, along with Kames and Millar, as an exponent, we can reasonably expect this essay to exhibit the characteristic traits of that genre. Prompted by Smith's 'Considerations' on language, Stewart's discussion has the character of a retrospective summation.[10] From that perspective he regards it as an 'interesting question' in the 'history of mankind' to discern by what 'gradual steps' the transition from the 'simple efforts of uncultivated nature' to a 'complicated' state has been made. (*Life* 292) He also remarks that little information can be gleaned, especially in the earliest ages, from 'the casual observations of travellers'. The consequence is that:

> In this want of direct evidence, we are under a necessity of supplying the place of fact by conjecture; and when we are unable to ascertain how men have actually conducted themselves upon particular occasions, of considering in what manner they are likely to have proceeded, from the principles of their nature, and the circumstances of their external situation. (*Life* II, 46/293)

Theoretical or conjectural history thus rests on two pillars: the principles of human nature and external circumstances. The first of these is decisive since they are supposed to prevent conjecture degenerating into mere idle fancy (as when Ferguson accuses advocates of a 'state of nature', like Hobbes or Rousseau, of indulging in 'conjecture' (*ECS* 1)). In order for the 'principles' to do the work required, they must have the property of constancy or uniformity. These, of course, are the traits of human nature that Hume identifies in the *First Enquiry*. He confidently asserts that 'it is universally acknowledged that there is a great uniformity among the actions of men, in all nations and ages, and that human nature remains still the same in its principles and operations', so that it now follows that

> history informs us of nothing new or strange in this particular. Its chief use is only to discover the constant and universal principles of human nature by showing men in all varieties of circumstances and

situations and furnishing us with materials from which we may form
our observations and become acquainted with the regular springs of
human action and behaviour. (U 8, 7/SBNU 83)[11]

If we ask what these 'principles' are, they are the 'regular
springs' of human behaviour. If we further ask what these 'springs'
are, the general answer is the passions. In the first *Enquiry* Hume
lists ambition, avarice, self-love, vanity, friendship, generosity and
public spirit (U 8, 7/SBNU 83). In the *Natural History* the passions include anxiety (about future happiness), dread (of future
misery), terror (of death), appetite (for food) and, more generically, hope and (especially) fear, which 'actuate the human mind'
(NHR 2, 5/39).

It is in these latter two generic passions that Hume locates the
source of religion. This means he dismisses the argument upheld by
Kames, for example, that 'the image of the Deity must be stamped
upon the mind of every human being'. In a directly analogous
fashion to the moral sense, there is in humans an 'internal sense,
which may be termed the sense of Deity' (SHM II, 283; cf. Gregory
1788: II, 241). This sense, for Kames, was the only explanation for
the universality of religious belief.[12] Hume admits that the belief
in an 'invisible intelligent power' has been 'very generally diffused'
but thinks it has not been so universal that there are no exceptions
(NHR Intro, 1/33). Moreover, where such a belief is found it is
rarely the same across the places and ages. It is this lack of both
universality and convergence that prompts Hume to conclude that
religion, unlike 'self-love, affection between the sexes' and the like,
is not the product of an 'original instinct or primary impression of
nature' but is, rather, a 'secondary' principle' (NHR Intro, 1/33).

Its origin lies in the passions or 'ordinary affections of human
life'. More precisely, the 'first obscure traces of divinity' emerge
from the hopes and, most especially, from the fears of 'barbarians' (NHR 2, 5/39). Whereas Kames dismissed fear's universality because it was dependent on intermittent localised events like
eclipses and earthquakes (SHM II, 380), Hume is able to assert
universality by fastening on to the everyday fears and anxieties of
human life. As we will see later, these fears are especially potent
in primitives. Though they differ, Kames and Hume do agree in
tracing religion back to human nature. Both the 'difference' and
the 'agreement' are significant. Whereas Kames' source implicates
Divinity so that a semblance of orthodoxy can be retained, Hume's

source looked 'human-all-too-human'. Yet, since human nature is constant and uniform, this not only provides the 'ingredients' for a 'scientific' causal account but also forms the premise from which a natural history can be written.

This brings us back to Stewart. As he proceeds to develop the characterisation of 'natural history', he says that 'in examining the history of mankind' when 'we cannot trace the process by which an event *has been* produced, it is often of importance to be able to show how it *may have been* produced by natural causes' (*Life* II, 47/293; original emphasis). Natural history deals with natural causes, not with the 'supernatural' for, as Stewart continues, to show how language (in this case) might have arisen from the 'known principles of human nature' is to check that 'indolent philosophy which refers to a miracle' whatever it cannot explain. To locate these causes and, as Kames said, to 'join all in one regular chain' is to give an explanation (*HLT* 25). To seek causes in order to explain is to undertake a scientific inquiry; to refrain from such a search is to remain with the vulgar in a state of ignorance. This contrast between science and ignorance, or between the philosopher and the vulgar, is basic to Hume's quest for a science of man. This is borne out by his explicit aim in the essay on natural religion; it is, he says, an enquiry into the origin of religion in human nature (*NHR* Intro, 1/33).

Both Hume and Kames think that to enquire into origins is to search for causes. Human nature as constant and uniform in its operations has the stability to establish causal relations; to invoke it is thus to deny that religious belief can be put down to 'chance' (*SHM* II, 378; Ferguson agrees that it cannot be attributed to 'peculiar circumstances' (*IMP* 120)). Hume had elaborated on the distinction between chance and cause in the opening paragraphs of his essay 'Of the Rise and Progress of the Arts and Sciences' (*E-AS* 111). (See also Chapter 11.) If an event is put down to chance then it precludes all further enquiry. This leaves everybody (including the enquirer) in a 'state of ignorance'. However, when an event is 'supposed to proceed from certain and stable causes', this advances the enquiry and, by means of this advance, it uncovers 'what escapes the vulgar and the ignorant'.

Hume illustrates the distinction between chance and cause ('certain and stable') but it is not a distinction in kind. He illustrates it with the performance of a biased die. In a few throws the bias will not reveal itself but it 'will certainly prevail in a great number'

(E-AS 112). Millar uses a very similar example. He supposes that in one or two throws of a die very different numbers will be produced, but 'in a multitude of dice thrown together at random the result will be nearly equal' (OR 177). There is a link here with the project of natural history. Just as Kames had said that 'singular events' were not the province of the reader of 'solid judgement' (but of the vulgar), so Stewart remarked that the theoretical historian deals, apparently paradoxically, not with the 'real progress' but with what is 'most natural' because the former may be determined by 'particular accidents' (Life II, 56/296). The natural historian, on this basis, is concerned with many rolls of the die, not with just one.

This is a quantitative difference between one roll (chance) and many rolls (stable cause), not a qualitative one. Hume implies this when, in this same essay, he twice refers to 'chance, or secret and unknown causes' (E-AS 112, 114).[13] The same language is also to be found in the Natural History. In a passage that neatly ties matters together, he states that 'secret and unknown causes ... become the constant object of our hope and fear' (NHR 3, 1/40). Given what we already know, we can infer that polytheists are vulgar (NHR 5, 1/51) and in a state of causal ignorance and that they live, therefore, in a more or less constant state of anxiety. The significance of that inference will become apparent.

The first role played by Hume's use of 'necessarily' is thus to signal that the search for the origins of religion is capable of scientific analysis. The religious beliefs held are not a matter of chance but follow naturally or predictably, that is necessarily, from the operation of the constant principles of human nature in the circumstances of savage life. We will consider those circumstances later but first we need to consider the second role played by the term 'necessarily'.

III

Kames divides the development of religious belief into six stages. After polytheism is a stage – like that of the Greeks – where there is a mix of gods, some superior, others inferior, and that is followed by the same mix but now the gods are conceived as invisible powers. The fourth stage is a belief in one supreme benevolent deity with several inferior ones; the fifth differs in having only one inferior. Finally, 'through a long maze of errors men arrive at true religion, acknowledging but one Being supreme in power, intelligence and benevolence' (*SHM* II, 404). While this is the most elaborate scheme, all the Scots acepted the underlying structure of a development from polytheism to monotheism.

What underlies this common structure is the shared acceptance of Lockean psychology. This psychology provides the developmental framework not only for the Scots' account of 'improvement' but also for the entire enterprise of natural history. For Locke, in his *Essay Concerning Human Understanding*, all our ideas come either from sensation or reflection, that is, either from 'sensible objects without' or from 'what we feel within ourselves from the inward workings of our own spirits' (1854: 3.1.5/II, 3). While considerable effort was expended in the Enlightenment in developing and amending Locke's account (especially concerning the status of ideas of reflection), what is important for our current purposes is a feature of Locke's own way of arguing. In the context of language, he developed a genetic or historical argument. According to Locke, our words stem from common, sensible ideas, and even words that refer to notions 'removed from sense' nevertheless 'have their rise from thence'. For example, the source of the word 'spirit' is 'breath' (1854: 3.1.5/II, 2).

Revealingly, Locke refers frequently to the experience of children. Their first words – he mentions 'nurse' and 'mamma' – are always particular, since their ideas are only particular (1854: 3.3.7/II, 11). Children's ideas as particulars are predominantly sense-derived and it is only later, as they mature, that their mind by degrees advances to exercise its faculties of enlarging, compounding and abstracting ideas (1854: 2.1.22/I, 222). But Locke does not confine this childlike condition to children because he goes on to remark that 'children, idiots, savages and illiterate people' all function without any capacity to refer to general maxims and universal principles (1854: 1.2.27; cf. 1.2.12/I, 152, I, 140). Both children and savages are confined to the world of immediate sensation, which means that they are unacquainted with all universal or abstract ideas.

This model of cognitive development, with its analogy between children and savages, explains the Scots' habit of referring to the savage as living in the 'infancy of society'. The following passage from William Robertson encapsulates what is at stake:

> As the individual advances from the ignorance and imbecility of the infant state to vigour and maturity of understanding, something

similar to this may be observed in the progress of the species. With respect to it, too, there is a period of infancy, during which several powers of the mind are not unfolded, and all are feeble and defective in their operation. In the early ages of society, while the condition of man is simple and rude, his reason is but little exercised, and his desires move within a very narrow sphere. Hence arise two remarkable characteristics of the human mind in this state. Its intellectual powers are extremely limited; its emotions and efforts are few and languid. Both these distinctions are conspicuous among the rudest and most unimproved of the American tribes . . . (HAm 819)

The Lockean provenance of this picture is underscored when Robertson then remarks that 'the first ideas of every human being must be such as he receives by the senses' and, he immediately continues, 'while in the savage state there seem to be hardly any ideas but what enter by this avenue'. The savage indeed employs his reasoning powers 'merely on what is sensible' (HAm 819, 820). Millar echoes this. In the mind of the 'poor savage', he declares, there are 'few traces of thought beyond what arise from the few objects which impress his external senses' (Millar HV IV, 6/760; cf. II, 7/368). These savages live in a world of concrete immediacy, the 'here and now'. Because they prize things for present use or because they minister to present enjoyment, savages set no value on what is not immediately wanted; they act, as Kames (SHM I, 48) puts it, 'by sense not by foresight'. Similarly, Robertson refers to 'their inconsiderate thoughtlessness about futurity', which for him is the corollary of their limited understandings and inactive minds (HAm 819) And again, James Dunbar observes that man is 'at first possessed of few ideas and of still fewer desires. Absorbed in the present object of sense he seldom indulges any train of reflection on the past and cares not, by anxious anticipation, to antedate futurity' (EHM 68; cf.15).

Following the broad thrust of Locke's genetic argument, the confinement of savages to the world of immediate sensation means that they are unacquainted with all universal or abstract ideas. Robertson draws attention to the Amerind's inability to count beyond three and he explains this inability by the fact that 'savages have no property to estimate, no hoarded treasure to count, no variety of objects or multiplicity of ideas to enumerate' (HAm 819). Their experience to which their ideas conform provides no opportunity for the exercise of such capacities. Both Robertson

(*HAm* 819) and Kames (*SHM* II, 377n) also note the absence of terms for time, space and substance from American languages. Indeed, following Locke's lead, much of the speculation about cognitive development was conducted by means of an investigation of language;[14] it is thus no accident that Stewart's delineation of natural history is prompted by Smith's 'Considerations'. In that essay we find these themes repeated. For example, Smith says of 'number' that it is 'one of the most abstract and metaphysical ideas ... and consequently is not an idea which would readily occur to rude mortals who were just beginning to form a language'. In similar fashion, substantive nouns predate adjectives, impersonal verbs predate personal, while prepositions and pronouns 'expressing so very abstract and metaphysical an idea would not easily or readily occur to the first formers of language' (*CL* 22, 32/214, 219).

Since this is a basic psychological or cognitive structure, then, in conjunction with an account of the prevalent circumstances (of which more later), it is applicable to the full range of 'savage life'. This point can be taken to support Roger L. Emerson's argument quoted at the beginning of this chapter. That is to say, the 'four-stages theory' is only part of a general approach (and hence it is a distortion to privilege a putatively 'materialist' history of means of subsistence). This can be illustrated (no more) by the Scots' theory of property, which is the pivot of the 'four stages'. One of the standard features of that theory is that the hunter-gatherers of the 'first stage' are strangers to the idea of property. Why? Because the priority of the sensible to the thoughtful means that initially property and possession are not distinguished and that their later separation marks the 'maturation' of cognitive abilities. In his Glasgow Lectures, Smith remarks that 'among savages property begins and ends with possession and they seem scarce to have any idea of anything as their own which is not about their own bodies' (*LJB* 150 /460; cf. *LJA* I, 41/18). Kames says the same: 'independent of possession they [savages and barbarians] have no conception of property' (*ELS* 228). Kames also explains why: the 'conception' of 'property without possession' is, he maintains, 'too abstract for a savage' and the explanation for this, he further supposes, is that savages are 'involved in objects of sense' (*HLT* 91; cf. Stuart *HD* 26).

The Scots' account of religious belief mirrors this 'model' of structural development perfectly. The concrete immediate world of the here and now is a random and disjointed world. This lived reality of discrete multiplicity evokes a commensurate response. Since the world itself is perceived as multiply animated, so that the savage identifies a corresponding multiplicity of animating causes, then polytheism is the 'natural result'. It is only once it is possible to achieve some 'distance', to mediate this immediacy, that it becomes possible to see some unity 'behind' the multiplicity, some pattern, intelligibility or order. And commensurate with this developing (or 'improving') ability is the ability to recognise one rather than many gods.

This is the appropriate backcloth against which to discern the force and implications of Hume's reference to the 'natural progress of thought' as the 'mind rises gradually from inferior to superior; by abstracting from what is imperfect it forms an idea of perfection' (NHR 1, 5/34–5). Consistent with this, it 'must appear impossible', he affirms, that 'theism could from reasoning have been the primary religion of the human race, and have afterwards, by its corruption, given birth to polytheism' (NHR 1, 8/36). On a similar basis, 'the pure love of truth' is a motive 'too refined' and to enquire into 'the frame of nature' is a 'subject too large and comprehensive for the narrow capacities' or the 'narrow conception' of savages (NHR 2, 5, 3, 3/38, 41). Citing the 'barbarous and ignorant' Africans, Indians and Japanese, Hume says more specifically that they can 'form no extensive ideas of power and knowledge' (86). Beset as they are with anxieties, savages seek to allay them by ascribing 'malice and good-will to everything that hurts or pleases' (NHR 3, 2/40). Hume regards this anthropomorphism as a natural human propensity.[15] In fact, two propensities are later implicated: the first is to believe in 'invisible intelligent power in nature', the other, 'equally strong', is to rest attention on 'sensible, visible objects'. Polytheism is the consequence of their conjunction as it unites the invisible power with the visible object; hence the sun, moon, fountains, and animals all become sacred (NHR 5, 2; cf. 3, 2/51; cf. 40).

Other Scots give this same 'structural' explanation. For Kames, polytheism is 'embraced by the rudest savages' because 'they have neither the capacity nor the inclination to pierce deeper into the nature of things'. They lack any words except those for 'objects of external sense' and, knowing 'little of cause and effect', they treat every event as a singular occurrence that, if it exceeds human power, they 'without hesitation' ascribe to the action of a superior being. And, accustomed to a plurality of visible objects, they 'are naturally led to imagine a like plurality in things not visible' (*SHM* II, 389–980; cf. II, 377).

Two other Scottish accounts can be cited to back up this picture. Building explicitly on the child analogy, Smith (*HA* III, 2/49) remarks that:

> a savage whose notions are guided altogether by wild nature and passion waits for no other proof than that a thing is the proper object of any sentiment than that it excites it. The reverence and gratitude, with which some of the appearances of nature inspire him, convince him that ... [they] proceed from some intelligent beings, who take pleasure in the expressions of those sentiments.

This for Smith is the origin of polytheism. Nor is this a random remark because he repeats its essential thrust in another of his essays.[16]

Robertson, whose account of Amerindian/savage psychology has already figured prominently, did not omit religion from his account and it is of a piece with his overall depiction. He writes that 'in the early and most rude periods of savage life' the 'refined and intricate speculation which conducts to the knowledge of the principles of natural religion' is 'altogether unknown'. The mental faculties of these savages 'are so limited as not to have formed abstract or general ideas'; their language is barren of terms to distinguish anything not perceived by the senses and 'it is preposterous' to think they are capable of accurately tracing causal relations. Following Hume rather than Kames, Robertson even thinks that at the beginning they were so bereft of mental capacity that they had no idea of any superior power. But when they did marginally improve, they 'naturally' ascribed events via the imagination ('a more forward and ardent faculty of the mind') rather than the 'understanding' – especially events that filled them with dread – to the influence of invisible beings. They become, in effect, polytheists (*HAm* 840–1) – though Robertson does not use the term itself.[17]

We know enough now to appreciate how religious belief will develop (or 'ripen', as Kames puts it (*SHM* II, 404; cf. *PMNR* 340)). This development is not haphazard but orderly and structured. The second role played by Hume's use of the term 'necessarily' is thus recognition of this determined order. Religion moves from the particular and concrete to the general and abstract. Polytheism is a concrete religion and deism abstract. Whereas the former is a question of passions (hope and fears) or the initial faint promptings of a separate sense, and definitely not the fruit of speculation or reflection, the latter is built upon the 'scientific' base validated by Newton, that the Universe is an orderly, designed, law-governed system. Where does the difference between the two lie? To answer that question means returning to the two pillars of natural history.

IV

We recall that the second pillar of natural history was 'circumstances' and we now have to take them on board. Hume defines polytheism as the 'primitive religion of uninstructed mankind' (*NHR* 2, 1/37). That savages are ignorant is a point made again and again by Hume (*NHR* 3, 3/41; E-PG 61; E-RA 271; again, the point is a commonplace among his compatriots). It is because they are ignorant of the true connections between causes and effects that they call upon the immediate and discrete action of gods to explain phenomena (especially those that frighten them). This ignorance is attributable to their circumstances. Primitive man is a necessitous creature, pressed by 'numerous wants and passions' (*NHR* 1, 6/35). These pressing needs mean a lack of leisure and that shortcoming means no time to acquire instruction. The natural propensity to anthropomorphise will produce polytheism if it is not 'corrected by experience and reflection' (*NHR* 3, 2/40). What is crucial is having the opportunity to reflect. As Smith emphasises, 'free' time is required to enable humans to begin the process of tracing causal links (*HA* III, 3/50).[18] This now fits religious speculation into the broader schema of the development of civilisation. As humans become civilised, so 'science and literature' as the 'natural fruit of leisure, tranquillity and affluence' have grown (Millar *HV* III, 3/507; *OR* 176). Accordingly, in Smith's straightforward formulation in *Ancient Physics*, 'as ignorance begot superstition, science gave birth to the first theism' (*EPS* 9/114). Kames' (*SHM* II, 402, 404) more elaborate stadial theory generates the same associations as it plots how 'men improve in natural knowledge', becoming thereby 'skilful in tracing causes from effects' until they arrive at 'true religion'.[19]

By embedding the history of religious belief within the history of civilisation, it, too, can be plotted on the Lockean graph. But the relationship between these histories and the graph needs to be interpreted with care. Human nature is progressive, as many Scots affirmed, but this is a capacity that is part of human nature's constancy. The capacity is an ahistorical principle, since *all* humans are presumed to possess 'a principle of progression' (Ferguson *ECS* 8; Millar *OR* 176; and many others). This capacity (allegedly) explains why individuals in one generation endeavour (and, circumstances permitting, succeed) to improve what they inherit. The growth of civilisation is just such an improvement. Even Hume, who refrains from identifying any progressivist principle in human nature, is clear that civilisation is superior to barbarism. He explicitly identifies as the 'chief character' that distinguishes a 'civilised age from times of barbarity and ignorance' the former's humanity. This humanity is the product of the softening of their 'tempers' and is indissolubly linked to knowledge and industry (E-RA 274, 271). These are 'sociological' differences that relate only to the 'tempers' and, as he had made clear in the *Treatise*, differences in the 'tempers and complexions' of men are 'very inconsiderable' (*T* 2.1.3.4/SBNT 281). These remarks are echoed in the *Natural History*. Hume observes that human sacrifice has 'never prevailed very much in any civilised nation', yet, even so, as the case of Carthage testifies, this prevalence is not so 'deep' as to preclude exceptions (*NHR* 9, n51/62n).

Seeing the history of religious belief in this context serves to undermine the cogency of those views that seek to attribute a more thoroughgoing historicism to the Scots. In the case of Hume, Simon Evnine has made an attribution along these lines. Evnine can be taken as representative, inasmuch as his article also surveys the literature on this topic. While conceding that Hume's view is 'complex', and admitting that his article emphasises Hume's 'historicist aspects', he nonetheless declares, generalising from the discussion of polytheism (and from Hume's account of the social contract), that this constitutes 'some kind of developmental picture of the powers of the human mind' (Evnine 1994: 606).[20]

If the 'human mind' here refers not to individuals but, rather, to some societally or historically specific 'mind' (what is sometimes called the savage and civilised 'mind'), then this declaration is a misplaced anachronism. This judgement can be substantiated by noting the Scots' attitude towards the 'vulgar'. The vulgar and the ignorant are one and the same (E-AS 111; cf. Manuel 1959: 179).

Hence, for Hume, the polytheist is not only uninstructed but also 'vulgar' (*NHR* 5, 1; cf. 7, 1; 82/49; cf. 56, 59). The vulgar are those who go by first appearances and are to be contrasted with the 'wise' or 'philosophers' (*U* 8, 13/*SBNU* 86; *T* 1.3.13.12/*SBNT* 150). The crucial point is that the vulgar are not some historically removed group; they are also with us here and now. Kames is explicit. Immediately after having pronounced in good Lockean language that property without possession is too abstract a conception for a savage, he remarks: 'to this day the vulgar can form no distinct conception of property' (*HLT* 91). Robertson prefaces his discussion of rude religion with the remark that those in the 'inferior ranks even in the most enlightened and civilised nations' do not derive their system of belief from 'inquiry'. Then he writes:

> That numerous part of the human species, whose lot is labour, whose principal and almost sole occupation is to secure subsistence, views the arrangement and operations of nature with little reflection, and has neither leisure nor capacity for speculation which conducts to the knowledge of the principles of natural religion. (*HAm* 840)

From this perspective, Hume's remark that the 'vulgar *in nations which have embraced the doctrine of theism* still build it upon irrational and superstitious principles' (*NHR* 6, 4/53; my emphasis) makes perfect sense.[21] In short, there has been no change in human nature; in Hume's formulation already cited, in 'all nations and ages' it 'remains still the same in its principles and operations' (*U* 8, 7 /*SBNU* 83). The vulgar of today are akin to the savages in the past, in that both are relatively uninstructed. The decisive variable is sociological, not some historicist development of the human mind. This holds good for Robertson, Kames and the others just as much as for Hume. If Pascal could be criticised for seeing the Scots as proto-Marxists, then Evnine's representative argument can be criticised for turning the Scots into proto-Hegelians.

A further consequence of interpreting Hume's own argument 'sociologically' is that it provides a more satisfactory explanation of what would be from the historicist perspective a puzzling passage in the *Natural History*. The relevant passage is where Hume claims that there is a 'reflux' in the principles of religion such that the 'natural tendency' to rise to theism is matched by the same tendency to sink again. His explanation is that the vulgar, who quite explicitly are 'all mankind, a few excepted', are ignorant and uninstructed and thus still in the dark about causal relations. They are accordingly always prone, through their 'active imagination', to 'clothe' these (to them unknown) causes of pleasure and pain 'in shapes more suitable to [their] natural comprehension' (*NHR* 8, 1/58). They do seemingly apprehend theistic notions of 'unity, infinity, simplicity and spirituality' but they pay these mere lip service (*NHR* 8, 2; 7, 1/58; 56) and, as such, they are unstable precisely because such 'refined ideas' are 'disproportioned to vulgar comprehension' (*NHR* 8, 2/58). This very instability of the refinement is indicative of the fact that the human mind/nature has not, *pace* the historicist account, developed. It is thus more than stylistic preference that in our 'text' Hume refers to the 'improvement of human society' and not to human nature.

V

To conclude, we can return to our text. Polytheism is necessarily the religion of the savage because that is a finding of the science of man.[22] Hume is committed to tracing the source of polytheistic beliefs to their origin in human nature and to identifying their natural causes. In this commitment Hume is not exceptional. What lies behind this commonality is the broad acceptance of a Lockean-inspired psychology. While, as Locke had duly demonstrated, there were no innate ideas, there were, as he had also insisted, connatural 'principles' and 'powers' and these manifested themselves in a determinate or structured manner. It was this determinate course that underlay the individual/species analogy: just as the individual develops from childhood to adulthood, so, analogously, society can be seen to develop from infancy to maturity. In both cases the development is 'natural', in the sense that it is predictable and normal (rather than inevitable). This is a 'natural' progression and it is this that 'natural history' traces. What it traces generically is the 'natural progress' from (in Millar's version) 'ignorance to knowledge and from rude to civilised manners' (*OR* 176) or from 'the rude' to the 'cultivated' (the subtitle of Dunbar's *Essays on the History of Mankind*) or, again, as Stewart and Robertson both put it, the 'simple' to the 'complicated'. The natural history of religion is a specific version of this generic tale.

Given this natural blueprint (so to speak), a particular social institution can be diachronically located. It also makes possible reasonable conjecture as to the synchronous features of a particular society's institutions at the various stages of its development. This most reliably applies in the earliest ages where uniformity is greatest. Millar makes the point clearly. Echoing Hume's view of the relationship between variety and uniformity, he remarks that

> however such people [rude and barbarous] may happen to be distinguished by singular institutions and whimsical customs, they discover a wonderful uniformity in the general outline of their character and manners; an uniformity no less remarkable in different nations the most remote from each other. (*HV* IV, 8/832)[23]

Since 'the attention of a rude people is confined to a few objects' (*HV* III, Intro /438), their manners are 'simple'. The various improvements of humankind serve to diversify their circumstances and, as a consequence, complicate their manners. Diversification and complication are thus marks of progress and the correlative of knowledge and civilised manners, whereas uniformity and simplicity are the correlative of ignorance and rudeness.

What this means, in short, is that it is as certain a conclusion as it is possible to get that the religion of savages will naturally be polytheistic. This is as well established as the claim that the first of the four stages will take the form of 'catching and ensnaring wild animals or by gathering the spontaneous fruits of the earth' (Millar *OR* 176). It is, moreover, established on the same premise – the nature of savage psychology. If there is any determinism here, it is of a psychological rather than materialist sort. This also means that the correlates (rather than 'effects') of this 'infant' society of polytheistic hunter-gatherers will include a paucity of personal possessions, an effective absence of governmental machinery, the presence of few status distinctions except the inferiority of women, the decoration, even mutilation, of their bodies and a vivid and highly metaphorical nature of speech. By the same token, in the fourth commercial age property can take the abstract form of credit notes and religious beliefs will be formally montheistic and tend to deism, just as correlatively the rule of law will operate, the moral sense will be accurate and discerning and good taste will flourish. In such a world a 'rude religion' would be out of place for, as Hume says,

> We may as reasonably imagine, that men inhabited palaces before huts and cottages, or studied geometry before agriculture; as assert that

the the Deity appeared to them [the ignorant multitude] a pure spirit, omniscient, omnipotent and omnipresent, before he was apprehended to be a powerful, though limited being, with human passions and appetites, limbs and organs. (*NHR* 1, 5/35)

Hence it is that rude religion is polytheistic or, as our text averred, polytheism 'necessarily must have been the first and most ancient religion of mankind'.

Postscript

I wrote this essay at the invitation of Paul Wood, who edited the volume (2000), of which this is a chapter, to mark the contribution of Roger Emerson to the study of the Scottish Enlightenment. *The Natural History of Religion* is a neglected work; by far the most studies of Hume and religion are devoted to his posthumous *Dialogues*. An exception to this is Lorne Falkenstein (2003). I have attempted here to integrate this essay not only into the rest of Hume's output but also to demonstrate how it intersects with other works by his fellow Scots. In virtue of this second aim, I may have been guilty of underselling Hume's differences but not, I think, at the cost of undermining the basic argument.

If *NHR* has still not garnered extensive commentary, Kames' work on religion has now attracted attention. Aside from Ian Ross's (2000) contribution to this same Wood volume, Benjamin Crowe (2010) and Robin Mills (2016) have both written far-reaching essays that will set a benchmark (they both cite this paper). Andreas Rahmatian (2015), as part of his account of stadialism in Kames, covers religion in passing. Smith's views on religion have – even in his lifetime – been a subject of speculation. Paul Oslington (2011) has produced a slim volume that talks up his theism, while Gavin Kennedy (2013) gives a forthright statement of the opposite view; both can be consulted for additional references. Even so, it remains the case that what we can fairly call Smith's own natural history of religion has not been excavated from the passing references he makes in various works. A different account of Robertson than the one offered here, focusing on his sermon 'Situation of the World at the Time of Christ's Appearance' (1755), is offered by Joshua Ehrlich (2013).

Notes

1. Pascal (1938: 178). It is likely that Pascal was picking up on some remarks of Werner Sombart about Millar in his *Die Anfänge der Soziologie* (1923) that he was in effect a Marxist before Marx (cf. Medick and Leppert-Fögen 1974: 22).

2. R. Meek (1954: 92). The reference is to Millar but is applied more generally.

3. Other exponents include Reisman (1976: 296), Swingewood (1970), Pollard (1968), Bowles (1985) and Hirschman (1977).

4. A. Skinner (1982: 104). A reprint of his 1975 essay is modified in the light of this piece and omits the quoted reference to 'almost Marxian' (A. Skinner 1996: Ch. 4).

5. K. Haakonssen (1981: 185). Haakonssen acknowledges Winch and Forbes in the Foreword. As is the way with scholarly interpretations, Haakonssen and Winch have been criticised for their antimaterialism, while at the same time Pascal, Meek and Skinner are criticised for their 'determinism'; see Salter (1992).

6. See Berry 1997. I draw upon this discussion in what follows. (I have pursued the 'four stages' in more depth in Berry 2013: Ch. 2.)

7. Cf. inter alia Kames (*SHM* II p. 389f.), Smith (*HA* 49), Stuart (*VSE* 6) and Ferguson (*PMPS* I, 168).

8. Cf. Millar (*HV* IV, 7/795–6), where he talks of the 'natural history of legal establishments' in similar terms and refers to Kames and Smith (as well as Montesquieu) as practitioners.

9. Malherbe (1975: 272n) points out that the phrase 'natural history' does not appear in the essay itself. While acknowledging the 'polysemic' nature of the concept of 'natural history', Malherbe goes on to distance Hume's usage from an inductivist, classificatory one, labelling Hume's enterprise variously as philosophical or theoretical.

10. Wood (1989: 113) judges this summation misleading because in it Stewart conflates two distinct forms of enquiry: natural and conjectural history (he criticises Emerson (1984) for using the latter indiscriminately). Contrary to Malherbe's notion of 'polysemy', Wood wishes to confine the term 'natural history' to the practice of recording and classifying the creation, since this is, he argues, more accurately reflective of contemporary usage.

11. I have elaborated upon Hume's argument in Berry 1982 Ch. 4. This elaboration has been criticised by, for example, Dees (1992) and Evnine (1994). (I discuss Evnine below.) As this suggests, there is a debate in the literature. For a recent statement in the broad context

of Hume's treatment of religion, see Herdt (1997). (For further discussion, see Chapter 12.)

12. Ferguson is less definite. The universality may be the 'result of human nature' but it may also be the 'suggestion of circumstances that occur in every place and age' (*IMP* 120).

13. In the *Treatise* he had referred to 'what the vulgar call chance', as 'nothing but a secret and conceal'd cause' (*T* 1.3.12.1/*SBNT* 130). Cf. Kames (*PMNR* 195). (For a more extended discussion, see Chapter 11.)

14. One of Robertson's chief references here is La Condamine, who in his report on the South American Indians (1745) commented on the absence of abstract terms in their languages. La Condamine was also cited on precisely this point by Condillac in his directly Lockean-inspired treatise on human knowledge (see *Essai sur l'origine des connoissances humains* (1947–53: Pt 2 sect.1, Ch. 10/I, 87n). In this same chapter Condillac appositely quotes Locke's argument that the first names derive from sensible ideas. Condillac himself adopted the view that polytheism was the earliest form of human religion – see *Traité des Animaux* (1947–53: Pt 2, Ch. 6/I, 366).

15. Yandell (1990) stresses the role played by 'propensities' in Hume's account.

16. In his 'History of Ancient Physics' (*EPS* 9/112), Smith remarks on the incoherence of nature to those living in the 'first ages of the world' who, out of their ignorance, gave birth to 'superstition, which ascribes almost every unexpected event to the arbitrary will of some designing though invisible beings'.

17. Nicholas Phillipson (1997: 66) has argued that Robertson challenged Hume's claim that 'polytheism was the only natural form of religious belief' inasmuch as monotheistic beliefs could flourish in societies without priests or public worship. He does, I think, overstate his case. The one portion of the text that he cites does not bear the weight he puts upon it. Although Robertson does indeed refer to the belief in the 'Great Spirit', he also remarks, in the same passage, on both the corporeal nature of this conception and the belief of these same tribes in 'gods'; aptly, Robertson notes their 'childish credulity' (*HAm* 841).

18. The links between Smith's account and Hume's in the *Natural History* is stressed by Pack (1995).

19. *SHM* II, 402, 404.

20. In his survey Evnine omits Pompa (1990). Pompa, however, does not discuss the *Natural History*.

21. Just before that statement, Hume had observed that '*Even at this day, and in Europe,* ask any of the vulgar, why he believes in an omnipotent creator of the world; he will never mention the beauty of final causes of which he is wholly ignorant'. Why is he ignorant? Because 'as an invisible spiritual intelligence is an object too refined for vulgar apprehension, men naturally affix to some sensible representation' (*NHR* 6, 1; 5, 9/51; 52; my emphasis). To similar effect, he says elsewhere that the 'propensity of mankind toward the marvellous', though it may 'receive a check from sense and learning can never be thoroughly extirpated from human nature' (*U* 10, 20/ *SBNU* 119.

22. It is worth recalling that Hume explicitly refers to Natural Religion as one of those 'sciences' that depend on the science of man, and he singles it out as the one where most 'improvements' can be hoped for by the successful development of that science (*T* Intro 5/*SBNT* xix).

23. Cf. Robertson in the context of Amerindian religion: 'Were we to trace back the ideas of other nations to that rude state in which history first presents them to our view, we should discover a surprising resemblance in their tenets and practices; and should be convinced that, in similar circumstances, the faculties of the human mind hold nearly the same course in their progress and arrive at almost the same conclusions' (*HAm* 841).

7

'But Art itself is Natural to Man': Adam Ferguson and the Principle of Simultaneity

One of the central characteristics of the social thought of the group of thinkers who collectively constitute the Scottish Enlightenment is their adoption of a stadial account of social development. This is usually labelled the 'four-stages theory', although explicit avowals in published work are not as common as might be supposed (see Berry 2013: Ch. 2 for a thorough examination of this question). Typically it is associated with Adam Smith (pre-eminently) but other names, such as those of John Millar, William Robertson and Lord Kames, are usually invoked. David Hume is acknowledged not to have subscribed to it explicitly, although passages in his *Political Discourses* (1752), in particular, betray clear recognition of step-changes in the history of commerce and the refinement of arts. Adam Ferguson is another whose relation to this theory is not straightforward.

A preliminary step is to note that there are clear expressions in Ferguson's work of a stadial approach in its presumptively typical form. Two are worthy of note. One occurs in his *Essay on the History of Civil Society* where he appropriates, without acknowledgement, Baron de Montesquieu's division between savage and barbarian nations (*ECS* 82; Montesquieu [1961: Bk 18, Ch.11). Moreover, the difference between these 'nations' is made in terms of 'property'– savages are not acquainted with it while barbarians are albeit without formal legal form (*ECS* 82). In addition, in a manner typical of the four-stages version, savages are essentially hunter-gatherers, although some 'rude agriculture' may be practised (for Montesquieu, the distinction was explicitly between *chasseurs* and *pasteurs*). Both savage and barbarian socie-ties are labelled 'rude' and thus can be contrasted with 'civilised'.[1] This latter more generic contrast is also stadial. Indeed, in the same context that he distinguishes savage and barbarian, Ferguson remarks that 'property is a matter of progress' and he identifies as the 'principal distinction in the advanced state of mechanic and commercial arts' that there is a 'habit' formed of taking 'a view to distant objects'. What this signifies, typical of the underlying psychology of the four stages (Berry 1997: Ch. 5; and see Chapter 6 in this volume), is the necessity to separate property from possession to enable 'industry' to develop and overcome the disposition of the 'uncivilised' to live indolently always in the present (*ECS* 82). A second, more straightforward expression occurs in his *Institutes of Moral Philosophy*. Here Ferguson lists the arts that men 'practise for subsistence' such as fishing, hunting, pasturage and agriculture and (he goes on) progress of arts renders commerce 'expedient even necessary' (*IMP* 1.1.9/28, 32).

Nonetheless, there is something distinctive about Ferguson. What marks him out is not a rejection of the fundamental governing assumptions of the four-stages narrative (the progressiveness of man whose advance follows a natural, that is, predictable path) but, rather, a contestation of a typical application of those assumptions, namely that some aspects of human life (the modes of subsistence or 'commercial arts') can be prioritised temporally over others. This lack of priority I term 'the principle of simultaneity'. According to this principle, the three chief types of art that Ferguson identifies – the commercial, political and fine – are coeval. While politics does indeed have a salient place in Ferguson's thought, to attribute to it special significance, I argue, fails to take on board his subscription qua natural historian to those fundamental assumptions of a stadial account.

Artifice and the State of Nature

In the well-known opening chapter of his *Essay*, Ferguson criticises (without naming them) Thomas Hobbes' and Jean-Jacques Rousseau's accounts of the 'state of nature'. His criticism is in a related fashion both methodological and epistemological. Both Hobbes and Rousseau seek via the heuristic device of the 'state of nature' to isolate mankind's 'original qualities' and thus distinguish the 'limits between art and nature'. This, however, is an act of imagination, of poetry rather than reason and science. Ferguson here interprets the latter as a process of induction. In the narrow Baconian sense of 'natural history' (*ECS* 2), knowledge of human qualities can be attained only by collecting facts. These are to be found in both ethnography and history – 'the earliest and latest accounts collected from every quarter of the earth' (*ECS* 3) – and are supplemented by introspection. This cumulative evidence, collected in this way by the natural historian, establishes that mankind is always 'assembled in troops and companies' or groups (*ECS* 3–4).

This empirically underwritten sociality means, according to Ferguson, that the contractarian intent to distinguish what is natural from what is artificial is fundamentally misconceived; rather, in the phrase that gives the title to this chapter, 'art itself is natural to man' (*ECS* 6; see also *MSS* 243–7; *APMP* 12). In these opening pages of the *Essay* the gloss that Ferguson puts on this is to indicate that man has 'in himself a principle of progression' (*ECS* 8), a principle that manifests itself in omnipresent activity to improve his condition. It is for Ferguson a postulate of human nature that 'man is not made for repose' (*ECS* 210): indeed, 'to advance . . . is the state of nature relative to him' (*PMPS* I, 199; cf. 193). This inherent drive to be active means that it is as applicable to the 'streets of the populous city' as it is to 'the wilds of the forest' (*ECS* 6). Accordingly he answers his own question, 'where is the state of nature?' by stating that it is 'here', whether that be Britain, the Cape of Good Hope or the Straits of Magellan, for 'all situations are equally natural' (*ECS* 8). The savage and the 'citizen' both practise art; hence arboreal lodgements, cottages and palaces, for example, are, for Ferguson, all equally natural and artificial. Moreover, the 'refinements of political and moral apprehension are not more artificial in their kind than the first operations of sentiment and reason' (*ECS* 8). While the polemical aspect is prominent here, the implications of this understanding of the nature/art relation go to the heart of a distinctive ingredient in Ferguson's philosophy. It is that distinctiveness I here seek to investigate.

The Principle of Simultaneity

This investigation will focus on Ferguson's more extensive discussion of 'arts' in the *Principles*. The key passage for this purpose is this:

> The wants of men, indeed, are of different kinds, and may be unequally urgent; but the movements, performed for the supply of very different

wants, appear to be simultaneous and bring at once into practice the rudiments of every art, without any such order as we might suppose to arise from their comparative degrees of importance or the urgency of occasions on which they are practised. (*PMPS* I, 239–40)

The crux here is the 'principle of simultaneity' (my term of art), with its explicit denial that some arts are only evident after others. It is not the case that urgent wants call forth some arts prior to those that meet supposedly less urgent wants. This reveals something significant about both Ferguson's philosophical anthropology and his sociology.

For Ferguson, one of the most significant ways that humans are distinctive is that they are exposed to greater hardships than any other species (*PMPS* I, 239; cf. II, 37). Human wants or needs (Ferguson does not make a conceptual distinction) are more numerous and the supply of the means to meet them sparser than is the case for any other animal (*PMPS* I, 242).[2] The 'arts' originate as the human way of supplying the means to deal with the gap between exigency and exiguousness. However, as we have seen, Ferguson does not draw the conclusion that in this supply 'consideration of necessity must have operated prior to that convenience and both prior to the love of mere decoration and ornament' (*PMPS* I, 239). Rather, the convenient, the ornamental and the necessary 'arts' are coeval. As here indicated, Ferguson operates with a tripartite division of commercial, political and fine (or intellectual) arts and, before proceeding to discuss them, he articulates again the principle of simultaneity by denying that 'the pursuits of external accommodation or the rudiments of commercial arts had a priority in time to those of political institution or mental attainment' (*PMPS* I, 240). Following his lead, we can investigate in turn the characteristics of the three types.

Commercial arts 'originate in the wants and necessities of animal life' (*PMPS* I, 242, II, 325) or 'exigencies of mere animal nature' and their object is the 'supplies of necessity, accommodation or pleasure' (*PMPS* I, 205). 'Commercial arts' is the general title for all the various ways of effecting that 'supply' and it is, perhaps, worth observing that, despite some undoubted ambiguity, it follows that commercial arts are not the prerogative of supposedly stadially advanced 'commercial societies'. More significant, however, is that these arts do not exhaust what engages 'the attention of man'. This 'attention' is not restricted to 'mere supply of necessities' in the form of 'subsistence or safety' because man's 'views extend to decoration and ornament' to which, in a restatement of the principle of simultaneity, Ferguson adds 'nor is ornament less an original want of his nature than either shelter or food' (*PMPS* I, 243). In all humans – the savage no less than 'the polished citizen' – the 'double purpose of ornament and use is evident in the fashion of his dress, in the architecture of his dwelling, and in the form of his equipage, or furniture of every sort' (*ECS* 286; *PMPS* I, 59). Humans do indeed have basic needs but these cannot be co-extensively identified as those that minister to subsistence; man truly, for Ferguson, does not live by bread alone.

The commercial arts have their source in human skill and labour or industry as they compensate (Hume's phrase) for the meagreness of the means to meet human needs (*PMPS* I, 242). But humans do not labour simply to meet some putatively prior material needs because labour is 'its own reward' (*PMPS* II, 13); indeed, it is 'a source of enjoyment' (*PMPS* I, 175). One consequence of this is that 'the trader continues to labour, even after his necessities are provided for and after his wants might have suffered him to rest' (*PMPS* I, 245). The trader's motives here are symptomatic of the dynamic whereby the rich affect a superiority of wealth and the poor aspire to it. While this dynamic contributes to the 'progress of arts', it also has injurious side effects in the form of the unequal cultivation of the mental faculties that accompanies the division of labour (*PMPS* I, 251). That is, Ferguson is able to reiterate his concerns (*ECS* 181–2; cf. *MSS* 143–52) while echoing Adam Smith's critique of the deleterious effect on the intellectual, social and martial virtues of the simple operative in Book 5 of *The Wealth of Nations* (*WN* V, i.f.50/782).

However, from the perspective of the principle of simultaneity, a further aspect of this familiar Fergusonian stance is revealed. Though individuals in commercial societies evidently enjoy greater material well-being, they are in fact no more satisfied with their condition than savages are with theirs (*PMPS* I, 247–8). More pointedly, despite the advantages of commerce, which Ferguson does not deny, our judgement is distorted if we dismiss the savage life as valueless (*PMPS* I, 251). The individual savage in several respects is superior to the 'mere labourer' in commercial society and it is in non-commercial societies that the virtues of loyalty, courage and patriotism flourish with greater vigour than in the commercial. These virtues are all forms of our political existence with its corresponding arts. The necessity for the practice of these political arts is as deeply rooted as the need for the commercial in the human condition.

The origin of the political arts is located in 'the wants and defects of instinctive society' (*PMPS* I, 256). Echoing passages in the *Essay*, Ferguson draws attention, once more, to human distinctiveness. It is true that (like the beehive) humans instinctively assemble in 'troops and companies' with a 'species of government' (*PMPS* I, 257) in line with natural hierarchies of age, gender and personal qualities like courage. Nonetheless, because humans are distinctively progressive, their political arts are not confined 'to the first suggestions of nature' (*PMPS* I, 257). Furthermore, because 'art is natural', then just as society 'is the natural state of man', so 'political society is the natural result of his experience in that society to which he is born' (*PMPS* II, 268). The political arts thus 'relate to the order of society or the relations of men acting in collective bodies' (*PMPS* II, 325). These arts are employed to establish neither society nor subordination (as might be supposed by contractarian thought or by the recourse to 'celebrated law givers' (*PMPS* I, 264; cf. *ECS* 123)).

Although Ferguson does claim that these arts serve to perfect or correct abuses (*PMPS* I, 262) so that they might thus appear responsive, this is no different from the others. While the commercial arts are a response to the environment, necessitated by humans being less well provided 'naturally' with the means to satisfy their wants such that, as we have seen, they have to labour to cultivate the ground and erect habitation, the political arts respond to the 'extreme disorder' of society 'prior to any manner of political establishment' and are produced by the 'spur of necessity' with no less urgency than the commercial (and fine) arts (*PMPS* I, 236; see also II, 414). Moreover, the thrust of simultaneity is retained because Ferguson is not claiming that politics was a reaction to past abuses or disorder that arose as a result of the development of economic (commercial) activity. It can be a response, for example, to 'casual coalitions or force' (*IMP* 41) or have 'no other foundation than custom' (*PMPS* II, 286).

The granting of coeval status to the political comports with a defining feature of Ferguson's thought. He does think, and this is the truth in the reading of him as a 'republican', that active participation in public affairs (*rei publicae*) is an authentic expression of human nature. As is well known, this is a major polemical component of the *Essay* and I do not wish here to contend the point. However, I do wish to link this to the principle of simultaneity and in so doing put it into perspective or temper some of the claims made on behalf of his 'political' emphasis or republicanism.[3] For Ferguson, the 'political genius of man' (*PMPS* I, 262) manifests itself in the exercise of the political arts because it presupposes not tensions in material life (the commercial arts) but simply the established fact that humans live in troops that are marked by casual subordinations of various sorts (*PMPS* I, 261; cf. *ECS* 133). Hence, just as the development of the commercial arts are the fruit of human industry and ingenuity, so too, equally, are the political, as both work on the 'materials' that have been providentially provided (*PMPS* I, 263). The attainment of a 'just political order' is 'an occasion on which the principal steps of man's progress are made' and gives scope for him 'to improve his faculties' (*PMPS* I, 265). This is a self-standing, self-generating process. The political is coeval with the commercial; it is not explained as an effect of economic causes but, as coeval, it is 'an occasion' – and not the sole or only aspect of human progress. In similar vein, in accord with the principle of simultaneity, Ferguson also treats as on a par human actions 'to supply his occasions' both for subsistence and ornament (*PMPS* I, 122).

As we have noted, for Ferguson, mankind – in the course of meeting animal necessities and obtaining political knowledge – is 'also disposed to invent and to fabricate' works that 'give scope to his faculties' and enable the enjoyment of 'the fruits of his ingenuity' (*PMPS* I, 285). Mere functionality is never the sole object – the necessary is adorned and there is 'an original disposition' to fabricate 'on the models of beauty presented in nature'. These adornments and fabrications – in the form of poetry, painting, sculpture and music – constitute the fine arts (*PMPS* I, 286). In line with the principle of simultaneity, they 'spring from the stock of society' and, while they do 'adorn its prosperity', they also 'actually contribute to the growth and vigour of the plant' (*PMPS* I, 269). In his unpublished *Manuscripts* we can also see an expression of the principle, when he remarks that in 'the charms of History, of Poetry & Painting' man 'proceeds on the Law of His Nature' (*MSS* 244). The fine arts are, thus, not add-ons but integral to human experience, for 'men in all ages are fond of decoration; they combine ornament with the means of subsistence and accommodation' (*IMP* 31); indeed, 'man is formed for an artist' (*PMPS* I, 299; cf. I, 200).

This conception of the place of the fine arts helps throw light on why Ferguson includes a chapter on the history of literature in his *Essay*.[4] He begins the chapter by affirming that what he calls the literary or liberal arts and the mechanical or commercial arts are both 'a natural produce of the human mind'. While the claim that they are contemporaneous is not here explicitly addressed, it would not be unreasonable, given their common source, to regard them as in harmony with the principle of simultaneity. Ferguson elaborates by claiming that the commercial or mechanical arts are 'encouraged by the prospects of safety and gain', while the literary or liberal 'took their rise from the understanding, the fancy and the heart' (*ECS* 171). In line with a familiar strain in eighteenth-century linguistic speculation (see Berry 1973b), he declares that the language of the savage reveals that 'man is a poet by nature' (*ECS* 172). It is integral to the natural human condition of sociality that all three types or categories of 'art' are 'natural' expressions of humanity. A 'history of civil society' might, as its title principally suggests, concentrate on the political arts but the interrelatedness of human artfulness means that it is appropriate to incorporate within that 'history' chapters on commercial arts (like 'population and wealth' (*ECS* Pt 4, sect. 3)) as well on the fine arts, in the form of a treatment of the history of literature.

It is true that, in line with his earlier reference to 'intellectual arts' and mental attainment', Ferguson also regards 'the fine arts' more capaciously than how we might now understand that term. It is, he affirms, the case that the human pursuit of knowledge is 'no less an exigency of the mind than the means of subsistence and accommodation are an exigency of mere animal life' (*PMPS* I, 206). Accordingly, exercises of intelligence are manifest in science and moral improvement as well as in elegant design. This capacious conception explains why Ferguson's chapter in the *Principles* on the 'fine arts' of poetry, sculpture and so on occurs in the middle of chapters devoted to the 'pursuits and attainments of science', 'the progress of moral apprehension', and concludes with a discussion 'of a future state'. As societies develop, so too do the forms of literary expression grow more complex, as historical, moral, scientific and philosophical modes are exhibited in line with the character of societies.

Of course, all three types of arts suppose the distinguishing mark of human intelligence and this itself underpins the definitive trait of human progressiveness. Ferguson links progressiveness and intelligence by identifying within humans a striving for more, or the 'desire of something better than is possessed at present'. This desire he labels 'ambition' (*PMPS* I, 2067; cf. I, 56; II, 94, 423). In this generic sense it is this desire or ambition that operates 'in the concerns of mere animal life, in the provision of subsistence, of accommodation and ornament; in the progress of society and in the choice of its institutions' (*PMPS* I, 235). In short, it underlies, respectively, human artfulness in its commercial, fine and political forms.

Betterment and the History of Man

We are now in a position to bring back the discussion to the opening remarks about the four stages, because it is the context of ambition that Ferguson also declares that 'every person, in one sense or another, is earnest to better himself' (*PMPS* I, 200). There are clear echoes here of Smith's observation that 'the desire of bettering our condition . . . comes with us from the womb and never leaves till we go into the grave' (*WN* II, iii 28/341). While Smith never explicitly links this desire to the four stages, John Millar does. In his introduction to the third edition of *The Origin of the Distinction of Ranks,* he prefaces one of the clearest of all published expressions of the four stages with this statement: 'there is, however, in man a disposition and capacity for improving his condition, by the exertion of which he is carried on from degree of advancement to another . . .' (*OR* 176).

Ferguson's articulation of the principle of simultaneity means that he does not adopt the same reading of this 'advance'. This difference is most simply grasped by noting the direction and explanatory thrust of Millar's argument. This argument unfolds as follows. Savages 'feel the want of almost everything requisite for the support of life' and 'their first efforts are naturally calculated to increase the means of subsistence'. This they achieve by hunting and gathering. It is the 'experience' thus acquired that 'is apt successively to point out the methods of taming and rearing cattle and of cultivating the ground'. Success in these 'improvements' results in less difficulty in meeting 'bare necessaries' and a correspondent gradual enlarging of human 'prospects' as 'their appetites and desires are more and more awakened and called forth in pursuit of the several conveniencies of life'. This awakening introduces manufacture and 'science and literature, the natural offspring of ease and affluence'. These advances in making life 'more comfortable' produce the 'most important alterations' in the 'state and condition of a people'. Millar identifies these 'alterations' as increase in population, the cultivation of humanity, the establishment of property and associated legal rights, along with government and 'suitable variations in their taste and sentiments' (*OR* 176).

An unforced reading of this argument reveals that Millar does not articulate the principle of simultaneity. Whereas Ferguson questions the sequence of necessity, convenience, decoration/ornament (*PMPS* I, 239),[5] Millar effectively subscribes to it. He prioritises meeting necessities over pursuing conveniences and he, similarly, regards literature and science as subsequent to the attainment of leisure and affluence. In terms of Ferguson's typology, for Millar the commercial does predate the fine arts. Millar also in this argument identifies government and laws as emerging from the systemic need to regulate the complexities generated by the passions of 'a large and opulent community'. While this echoes the responsiveness with which Ferguson had associated the political arts, Millar, even in his later treatment (*OR* Ch. 3), never treats these arts as coeval with the 'commercial' but a temporally subsequent expedient.

All this said, their differences should not be overplayed: both Ferguson and Millar subscribe to the enterprise of delineating a 'history of man' (a phrase they both employ on numerous occasions throughout their writings). Accordingly, they both accept a developmental model with a similar motif, the move from ignorance to knowledge, and a similar structure, the progress from concrete to abstract (Berry 1997: Ch. 5). For Millar, implicitly dormant desires 'awaken', while for Ferguson, 'nothing that the human species ever attained in the latest period of its progress was altogether without a germ or principle from which it is derived in the earliest or more ancient state of mankind' (*PMPS* I, 196; cf. I, 44). Nevertheless, difference there is and the principle of simultaneity lies at its heart. In addition, I suggest that this role played by the principle throws light on the moralism often attributed to Ferguson's thought.

Uneven Development and Critique

While Ferguson admittedly does not commit himself explicitly to the point, the implicit thrust of his argument is that the simultaneity of the arts, because they are equally natural, can underwrite judgements about their differential societal expression – that some societies can develop one of the arts more than others.[6] This unevenness provides him with some needed critical space, since it signals a distortion of the different, yet equally rooted (and providentially endorsed), expressions of human endeavour. Hence, to occlude the fine arts is damaging and to neglect the political is injurious. It is the latter, of course, that looms largest in Ferguson's work but it needs to be put in context.

Although Ferguson's commitment to 'progress' means that he is no fundamental critic of 'modern' politics, we can discern at work a more subtle critique of commercial society than that proffered by Rousseau and other civic republicans. What the principle of simultaneity enables him to do is develop a critique of commercialism, while recognising it as an important, ineradicable component of human life. We can recall that for him the 'commercial arts' have their source in the exigencies of human material life. He accepts a major thrust of the Smith–Humean defence of commerce.[7] Even in the *Essay*, he notes that when the 'merchant forgets his own interest to lay plans for the country . . . the solid basis of commerce is withdrawn (*ECS* 144), so that his later high praise for *The Wealth of Nations* represents no volte-face. Additionally, as we have noted, he recognises that 'industry' is a proper outlet for the natural human proclivity to improve. His argument here thus means that he does not indulge in the Rousseau-like critiques of, for example, John Brown's *Estimate of the Manners and Principles of the Times* (1758), John Gregory's *Comparative View*, Robert Wallace's *Dissertation on the Numbers of Mankind* and, indeed, Kames's *Sketches on the History of Man*; he recognises that their jeremiads are both intellectually and morally misplaced. Nonetheless, because he does not privilege the commercial, he is able to address the 'corruptions' that attend wealth (the product of commerce) and that so exercised Kames and the others, by drawing upon the equally exigent demands of human collective life that the political arts are developed to meet. The real danger in commerce is its 'privatisation', diverting humans away from, and thus undermining, the public sphere (see, for example, *ECS* 250, 255–6, 258, 263). Relatedly, it is a danger in the 'intellectual arts' that 'too much abstraction tends to disqualify men for affairs' (*IMP* 65; see also Smith 2006b).

Yet for all Ferguson's commitment to the political arts and his polemic against concentration on the commercial, the latter should not be repressed. Despite his admiration for Sparta (*ECS* 156–61), Ferguson does not in the end endorse their efforts (or those of the 'ancient Romans' (*ECS* 93) to forbid commerce (*ECS* 245; *PMPS* I, 252)). This proscription not only runs against human ambition for betterment but it also necessarily has to attempt to impose equality. However, it can do so only by making a sharp qualitative distinction between citizens and slaves (*PMPS* II, 402, 422). Ferguson never countenances the injustice of the Spartan or Roman practice of slavery; indeed, slavery is a 'violation of the law of nature' (*PMPS* II, 505). Nor does he deny a connection between its presence and the absence of commerce (*ECS* 185; *PMPS* II, 472). Notwithstanding the weight he attaches to the martial virtues, he does not demur from Montesquieu's *doux commerce* argument.[8] Moreover, even if this is more emphatic in his later writings, liberty 'consists in the communication of safety to all, nothing could be more repugnant to it than the violation of right in any part in order to level the whole' (*PMPS* II, 463).[9] And this basic liberty is available, given proper political arrangements, in a society where the commercial arts are practised.

In the same vein, and of equal moment, is his argument that because the fine arts are coeval with politics in human endeavour then the Roman and Spartan policy toward those is also not endorsed. These polities may have reprobated the fine arts, or even in Sparta's case with regard to decoration excluded them, but these policies did not 'secure the foundations of private or public felicity' (*PMPS* I, 294). The policy is injurious because, in line with the principle of simultaneity, the fine arts are as fundamental as the political and, as such, of equal worth. The common source of this worth, as always in Ferguson, is Providential Design. It is this that underlies his declaration that so deeply rooted is the disposition to decorate, invent and imitate that the 'fine arts will ever make a part of the unrestrained progress of human nature' (*PMPS* I, 296). He elaborates by means of an instructive metaphor: 'the monuments of art produced in one age remain with the ages that follow; and serve as a kind of ladder by which the human faculties … [arrive] at those heights of ingenious discernment and elegant choice' (*PMPS* I, 299).

By in this way linking the fabrication of the fine arts to the generic human capacity to progress, he is able, further, to identify the incipient danger to which they are prone. Given the common source of all arts, the danger is the same. Just as tranquillity is a threat to political liberty (*ECS* 270) and lassitude or enervation undermines the efforts to further commercial betterment (*PMPS* I, 251, 254), so it is only when humans 'acquiesce in the enjoyment of what is supplied' that their (fine) artistic improvement falters (*PMPS* I, 298). In all the arts it is the 'enjoyment' of fruits without the expenditure of effort to attain them that runs foul of the active genius of mankind (Smith 2007).

Conclusion

To summarise, Ferguson postulates the value-laden presence in human nature of a universal generic principle of progressiveness. He also holds that it follows that 'art' as the application or expression of that principle is thus 'natural'. The consequence Ferguson draws from this is that the three chief types of art he identifies – the commercial, the political and the fine – are coeval. Given their common source and its postulated normativity, if developments in one of these arts seem to inhibit the expression of another then it can be criticised. This enables Ferguson to criticise Sparta for privileging the political over the fine and criticise commercial societies for emasculating the political. As a pervasive feature of the whole of his thought, the latter argument is made more noisily or vehemently than the former.[10] What is less commonly noted is that this criticism does not mean that he conceptually privileges the political. He is, indeed, alarmed by developments in the commercial arts that seem to him to sideline it but, unlike Rousseau, say, this is not because commerce per se is corrupting. Rather, in virtue of his 'principle of simultaneity', the political and the commercial are on the same footing: both are arts that are natural to humans.[11]

Postscript

The two-volume book of essays in which this chapter first appeared – *Adam Ferguson: Philosophy, Politics and Society* (ed. Heath and Merolle 2008, 2009) – marked an important step forward in serious study of Ferguson. I wrote this essay at the invitation of the editors and I was prompted to pursue this theme by a long-standing query as to why Ferguson included a section on the history of literature in *ECS*. This led me to a desire to counter an emphasis in Ferguson scholarship on *ECS* (to the relative neglect of *PMPS*) and, with that, a Pocock-inspired reading of Ferguson as a 'Machiavellian' (Pocock 1975: 499). Jack Hill (2017: xxii; cf. 146–7) declares himself to be in 'subtle disagreement' with my notion of 'simultaneity'. In addition to Hill's book, the Heath and Merolle collection of essays has been augmented by McDaniel's (2013) study (principally) of the history of Rome.

Notes

1. Ferguson was explicit in his lectures that 'ages are said to be savage, barbarian or polished' (*APMP* 11). For a discussion of stadialism in Ferguson, see Hill (2006: 64–9) and Wences Simon (2006: 143–6).

2. Compare Hume's similar account of the mismatch in humans between 'numberless wants' and 'slender means' to satisfy them (*T* 3.2.2.2/*SBNT* 484).

3. See, inter alia, F. Oz-Salzburger (2001), Varty (1997), Kettler (1977), G. McDowell (1983), Geuna (2002), Finlay (2006) and H. Medick and A. Leppert-Fögen (1988). (See also Broadie 2012: Ch. 6.) I don't exempt myself from this; see Berry (2003c). (See also Chapter 8.)

4. In *APMP* (p. 11) Ferguson's consistent tripartite division was 'commercial, literary and political arts'.

5. But see *PMPS* II, 39 for one occasion where Ferguson's subscription to the principle seemingly slips.

6. This is given a chronological dimension in *APMP* 11.

7. David Kettler (1965: 236) judges that 'in the final analysis . . . Ferguson's position eventuated in a vindication of commercial society'. See also Merolle (1994: 79–80) and, for general context, Berry (1994: Ch. 6).

8. Montesquieu (1961: Bk 20, Chs. 1, 2). Even in his history of Rome, Ferguson, while comparing commercial Carthage unfavourably with Rome's public virtue, still says their commercial interests 'should have inculcated the desire of peace' (*Rom* I, 110).

9. The link between civil liberty and security is the central theme of his polemic against Richard Price; see *Remarks* (1776). Yet even in his earlier most 'republican' pamphlet on militias, Ferguson refers, among the circumstances to 'boast of', to 'the Perfection to which our Arts are arrived; the Extent of our Commerce . . .' (*Reflections* 11).

10. This is perhaps signalled by his choice of 'ambition' to capture the

generic desire to improve, since that term had long had a political resonance and is how, indeed, he employs it in *IMP* 78.

11. Thanks to Craig Smith for Fergusonian conversation over many years and his comment on an early draft of this essay, and to the editors for their subsequent observations. (Craig's book on Ferguson will appear in the same series from EUP as this volume.)

8

Finding Space for Civil Society in the Scottish Enlightenment

One of the themes in this volume and in my books has been that the Scots were 'social' theorists. In this chapter I explore an aspect or corollary of that theme. More exactly, I develop an argument that the Scots established what I call a conceptual space that becomes in later thought termed civil society. I do not claim to provide either a definitive or an exhaustive exploration; rather, I suggest or intimate how some aspects of the Scots' thinking can be interpreted to map the contours of that space. That this is not an altogether fanciful or idiosyncratic enterprise is borne out by a raft of commentary that makes links between the Scots and civil society.[1] I do not directly engage with this literature so much as take its presence as a pretext for my own independent cartography.

I

To comment briefly on the term itself, the notion of 'civil society' is both ancient and modern. In modern times it came to particular public notice during the transitional events in Eastern Europe, especially in Czechoslovakia and Poland, before and after 1989 and, more recently, in and around the notion of the 'Arab Spring' and whether affected countries could experience a successful transformation to 'democracy'. This stimulated academic discussion about the term's meaning and provenance. It is fair to say that specific agreement on its meaning is lacking but there is a rough consensus, which is sufficient for my purpose here. Regarding its provenance or history, this has been traced back by Antony Black (1984), though not I think very securely, to at least the Middle Ages, although there was an extensive debate on the relationship between *societas civilis perfecta* and *imperfecta*.[2] Nevertheless, there is consensus that the contribution of Hegel was decisive. This is partly (though by no means entirely) attributable to two contingent factors. First, Hegel influenced Marx who, in his early writings particularly, contested Hegel's conception of civil society. Second, the East European debates took place in regimes where Marxism remained the official state ideology. It would take this discussion too far afield to analyse Hegel's argument, with its heavy philosophical baggage, so instead I shall for expository/contextual reasons utilise Manfred Riedel's (1962) influential analysis of Hegel's idea of civil society within his *Philosophie des Rechtes*.

Riedel argued that Hegel transformed an older concept. As I gloss it, his argument is as follows. Whether in its classical Aristotelian guise or in its 'modern' natural law form, the terms *societas civilis* and *koinonia politike* were treated as identical to, respectively, *civitas* and *polis*. That is, in general terms, civil society was synonymous with the state. As additional support for this reading is the first translation of Aristotle's *Politics* by William of Moerbeke (*c.*1250), where *polis* is rendered as *civitas*. These synonyms stand in contrast to the *societas domestica* or *oikos*. Hegel's structural or conceptual transformation (*Strukturwandeln*) was to turn this dichotomy (state/civil society or household) into a trichotomy (family, civil society, state). On this conception, the family, from being defined as an economic household, became a sentimental institution based on love, its previous economic role displaced into what Hegel (1955) terms *bürgerliche Gesellschaft*. 'Civil society' is the accepted translation of this term. Etymologically it is linked to the English 'burgher' or 'burgess' (compare the French *bourgeois*). Burghers were the inhabitants of fortified towns (burgs). Towns or cities (whence 'civic' and 'civil') were the locus of markets and trading. Hence Hegel situated market transactions in 'civil society', in what he calls a 'system of needs' orientated around the activity of labour, and as the sphere of particularistic socio-legal relationships and institutions such as the administration of justice and 'police' (*Polizei*), together with the development of trade associations (*Stände*). Crucially for Hegel, civil society is now non-political and thus conceptually distinguishable from *der Staat*, which retains the original political focus on the public or the universal good, as actualised in a constitution.

In sustaining this interpretation, Riedel acknowledges that the term 'civil society' was freely used in the eighteenth century and, despite going through a gradual process of change, remained a synonym for the 'state'. In his account, he declares in passing that

Adam Ferguson still adopted the traditional political understanding of the term; at best, he thought, the traditional concept possessed a faded (*abgeblaßter*) form (Riedel 1962: 220). Although Riedel does not discuss Ferguson, other scholars have viewed his book as a contribution to the eventual articulation of an idea of civil society,[3] largely, one suspects, because of the title of his best-known work, *An Essay on the History of Civil Society* (1767). That this is liable to lead by giving Ferguson an undue salience can be crudely illustrated through his terminology. He uses the terms 'society' and 'state', with their range of meanings, pretty much as we now do. However, we do not find him using the terms 'society' or 'state' as a counterpoint to each other; certainly, 'state' is never juxtaposed against 'civil society'. He is not exceptional in that respect: in the few times that Smith and Hume, for example, use the phrase 'civil society', it is in the broad Lockean sense as a synonym for civil government.

If we look at the term 'civil society' itself, we find that it occurs infrequently in the *Essay*. However, two of these references raise, as I will argue, significant issues. The first of these is when Ferguson seems to echo Locke's distinction between a civil, political or legitimate and an absolute government (1965: §90). The second is when he plots civil society on a temporal graph, giving the sense that 'the history of civil society' is a history of a full range of institutions – of civilisation in a general sense. That granted, in the discussion that follows Ferguson will play a relatively subordinate role in comparison to Hume and Smith.

The transformation Riedel attributes to Hegel provides, in my terms, a conceptual space that the Scots may be judged to have prefigured, but without the philosophical self-conscious intent found in the German philosopher – and so much the better for that. Hegel's own schema distinguishing civil society from the state is hierarchical, in that the former is dialectically transcended (*aufgehoben*), while in the latter civil society is conceptually dependent on the idea of the state. In the Scots' prefigurement of the distinction, it is functional.

II

While this prefigurement is ideational and my main focus, it can be reasonably suggested that the Scots were able to draw on their own societal experience. After the crushing defeat of the Jacobites in 1745, Scotland was firmly committed to the Hanoverian constitution; yet, thanks to the 1707 Treaty of Union, it also retained important spheres of life – the law, universities, the Church – informally separate from the 'state'. This institutional structure and its members existed alongside and mingled with a shifting network of clubs and associations, accompanying a lively print culture of pamphlets, journals and magazines, such as the *Caledonian Mercury* and *The Scots Magazine*. These various interconnections centred on the three major urban centres – Edinburgh, Glasgow and Aberdeen.

While it is not fanciful to see this interweaving mix of formal non-state institutions, informal societies and civic consciousness as a manifestation of many of the features that have come to characterise a 'civil society', caution needs to be exercised. The 'idea' of a 'civil society' (a notion that, as now comprehended, was unknown to the Scots) is not some 'effect' that can be directly read off their social environment. To deny that is not, of course, to claim that 'ideas' occupy some realm immune to the circumstances of their articulation. Thinkers exist in a context – and that includes ideas as well as institutions – but do so dynamically: they do not start from nowhere but neither do they remain passive or static in their location.

The Scots developed a social theory wherein a society was held to comprise an interlocking set of institutions, behaviours and values. This integration is as true of the tribes of the Americas, the nomadic Tartars, the patchwork of territorial lordships of feudal Europe and the city-states of the ancient and Renaissance world as it is of commercial societies. Of course, these interlocking sets differ. Accordingly, the world of commerce, as now (partially) represented in Scotland, has its own distinctive set and this distinctiveness is the work of history. I note two corollaries of this integration. First, political institutions do not have a privileged position; they are part of the mix. In effect, the Scots may be thought to de-emphasise 'politics', but by the same token this demotion is not the same as a dismissal or an omission. Secondly, because 'values' are an integral part of the Scots' social theory, societies are not to be understood as value-free zones (see Chapters 12 and 19). Accordingly, their label 'commercial' as societal descriptor, while incorporating and recognising the place of economic transactions between individual agents, is not reducible to those. Social individuals are moral agents all the way down. Not for nothing did

Smith, on the title page of *The Wealth of Nations*, identify himself as 'formerly professor of moral philosophy at the University of Glasgow'.

Exploiting Riedel's reading of Hegel and accepting the pivotal significance of civil society as non-political, my task here is to explore how, with their idea of society as a set of interlocking institutions and values, the Scots can be interpreted as finding conceptual space for civil society. Alternatively put, I investigate whether there are resources within the Scots' pre-Hegelian social theory to approximate elements of the modern post-Hegelian consensus.

III

I commence my spatial mapping, in line with that metaphor, through a process of 'triangulation'. This process will mark out by exclusion or negatively a space within which a relationship between the 'state/political' institutions and the non-state ones (potentially identifiable as 'civil society') can be located. The first point of this triangle is the opposition shared by all the Scots[4] to contractarian language and assumptions. Ferguson famously opens his *Essay* with an assault on the idea of the 'state of nature'. Since 'art itself is natural to man' (*ECS* 6), it follows, he argues, that there is no meaningful contrast between the 'natural condition of mankind' (the state of nature) and their artificial (made by a contract) civil, political existence (see also Chapter 6). Hume, of course, is renowned for subjecting the entire individualistic Lockean/contractarian mode of thinking to a devastating and influential[5] attack in his essay 'Of the Original Contract' (1748), which itself built, at least partially, on the *Treatise*'s declaration that the 'state of nature' is be 'regarded as mere philosophical fiction' (*T* 3.2.2.14/*SBNT* 493).

By dismissing the cogency of contractarian thinking, the Scots are undermining one powerful and pervasive feature in the thought of post-Reformation Europe and the 'wars of religion' that followed. What this turmoil brought to the fore was the legitimacy of rule. In articulating arguments that sought to identify the grounds for legitimacy, contractarian language was prominent. For example, for Mornay (1924: 175) – or whoever was the author of *Vindiciae contra Tyrannos* (1579 – kings are created by the people on the basis of a *pactum* and, for Buchanan (1579:

100), there is a mutual pact between king and subjects.[6] This salience developed *pari passu* with a focus on the 'the state' as the site of the rule to be legitimated, which eventually grew out of the Roman notion of *imperium* and the legal principle of *plenitudo potestas*, the recognition of 'state sovereignty'. However, with the establishment of sovereignty also came an anti-contractarian argument for 'absolute' rule, as most fully articulated by Jean Bodin in his *Les Six Livres de la République* (1576). For Bodin, without sovereign power there is no true 'republic' or common-wealth and the key *marque* of the sovereign is the right to give and to annul (*casser*) law without the consent of either a superior or (tellingly in this context) an inferior (1993: 101). This intellectual contestation continued through the bloody civil wars that infected Europe, producing eventually, as well as Grotius's *De Jure Belli ac Pacis* [1625] (2002), two other 'classics' of political philosophy – Hobbes' *Leviathan* [1651] (1991) and Locke's *Treatises* [1689] (1965). Hobbes attempted, through his notions of personation and authorisation, to derive absolutism from the individualistic premises of covenants, while Locke – who as we have seen was the explicit target of Hume's anti-contractarianism – wrote his *Two Treatises of Government* (published in 1690 but written almost a decade earlier) to combat absolutism.

The second point of the triangle is that the Scots are fundamentally opposed to absolutism. They have no truck with Hobbes and thus agree with the principles of Locke's critique of absolutism while, as we have seen, disagreeing with his individualistic premises. We can thus identify in the Scots an opposition to both contract thinking and the claims for absolute rule. This twin opposition begins to open some initial conceptual space for 'civil society' to occupy but there remains the third point of the triangle to complete the mapping.

When the Scots contested contractarianism and absolutism, this did not mean that they subscribed to another, more venerable, political strand. They are not Aristotelians in either its communitarian or its republican guise. Regarding the former, while the Scots shared its anti-individualistic stance, their assumptions are very different. This difference is captured in their divergence over rationalism. The Scots demote not only the calculative means–end rationalism within contractarian thought but also the privileged, authoritative role played by reason in the teleology of Aristotle and his Thomistic heirs. This is perhaps most evident in their moral theory, which, being rooted in 'sentiment', gives no judgemental role to 'reason', despite the Christianised Stoicism of Ferguson and most of his compatriots (excepting, as ever, Hume – and Smith, too, in my judgement).

Regarding the latter, the Scots have no significant allegiance to the tenets of classical (or neo-classical) republicanism. Of course, echoes can be heard, louder in some – like Ferguson in the *Essay* or Wallace – than others. And even when issues like luxury or the role of militias were debated, it is hard to see in those opposed to the former and in favour of the latter any deeply principled commitment like that expressed by, say, Algernon Sidney or Andrew Fletcher. I cannot claim to be neutral here (as other chapters in this volume will testify) but, more especially in this context, my argument that the Scots de-emphasise the 'political' commits me to downplaying republican elements.

IV

We need now to take stock of this triangulation. The empty (negative) space thus identified needs to be filled. In summary, the Scots occupy this space as historical institutionalists. A corollary of this occupation is that, in principle, they can accommodate a non-political arena that – and this is important – is not peopled with monadic individuals but indicative of something subsequently labelled 'civil society'. It is a basic proposition in the Scots as social theorists that, while of course humans are rational, the basic institutions of society are not deliberate or planned but rather the unanticipated product of, variously, immediate problem-solving (Magna Carta was prompted by the depredations of King John and was not intended as a foundational statement of liberty (see Millar *HV* II, 228) or, as with socio-political sites of authority, established and legitimated opinion or habit, not deep principle (see, for example, Hume E-OG 33, E-OC 474–5) or the cumulative unintended effect of particular decisions (see Ferguson's well-known comment that 'nations stumble upon establishments which are indeed the result of human action but not human design' (*ECS* 122)).

Contractarianism, Aristotelianism and absolutism, as the last of these developed in the doctrine of the Divine Right of Kings, are in principle ahistorical. For Hobbes and Locke natural rights are by definition atemporal; for Aristotle the normativity of political life is established *kata phusin* and not subject to temporal transience; and for Filmer civil power is divinely instituted (1949: 57, 96) and thus not subject to any human or temporal amendment. By contrast, the Scots are committed to understanding society and its institutions diachronically. This is inherent, in particular, in the basic distinction they draw (in Millar's terms (*OR* 176)) between 'rude and civilised manners'. I will come back to 'manners' but here pick up on 'civilisation'. While that term is not subject to any intense self-conscious investigation by the Scots, Hume does in one place provide a helpful analysis, which also, as we shall see, throws further light on the opposition to a non-Lockean, non-civic republican resistance to absolutism. Rejecting this categorical opposition, Hume observes that 'civilised monarchies', like 'republics, are a government of laws not men' (E-CL 94). He identifies three components that serve collectively as the criterion of 'civilised', namely the security of property, the encouragement of industry and the flourishing of the arts. Three inferences can be drawn from this observation.[7]

The first is that, because the weight falls on the qualifier 'civilised' rather than the substantive 'monarchy', it enables constitutional form to be historicised. This is clear in Smith. He contrasts contemporary 'civilised' to 'ancient monarchies' (*WN* V.ii.a.16/822). The latter were martial states and in them the administration of justice (on which more below) was paid for; it was a source of revenue not expense. In the former, revenue is collected by tax. The degree of civilisation is the key criterion rather than outward constitutional form when it comes to assessing whether the 'general principles' of government are adhered to.

The second inference is that, by employing 'civilised' as his criterion, Hume, like Smith, has displaced constitutions from their central role of classifying difference in regimes (cf. Castiglione 2000: 60). At least since Aristotle, the way to identify difference between regimes was by the constitution (as the adopted early-modern usage suggests they were constitutive), whether this is the sextet of monarchy, tyranny, aristocracy, oligarchy, or polity and democracy. There was a more simplified categorisation that distinguished monarchy/empire from a republic and it is clear that Hume is adapting that. That puts us on our guard that there are no clean ruptures here.

The third inference from Hume's analysis does, however, portend a significant difference. Within this political framework, yet crucially independent of it, commerce (industry, arts, property) will develop. A civilised monarchy is conducive to its development but it is inhibited in the uncivilised species. An alternative label to the latter is 'absolute' or despotic monarchy. Ferguson, following Montesquieu, treats despotism as a corrupted (that is, uncivilised) monarchy (*ECS* 71) but – I can interpolate – for all their indebtedness to him, the edge the Scots have over Montesquieu is their historicisation of institutions; time or moral causes, not space or physical causes, carries explanatory clout. Hume famously contested Montesquieu's account of climate in the *Esprit* (see Chapter 4) but here it is his claim, more systematic than anything to be found in Montesquieu, that an absolute monarchy is 'hurtful to commerce' which is of moment. Under the 'government of laws', commerce, he argues, is able to develop its own independent dynamic. Hume treats as a definitive characteristic of what he terms 'refined and luxurious ages' the presence of an 'indissoluble chain' that links together 'industry, knowledge and humanity' (see Chapter 11 for extensive discussion of this). The more civilised or refined a people become, the more economically productive, more informed and more sociable they become. This sociability is a product of the increased density of population as they 'flock into cities', where they indulge 'their taste in conversation' as 'particular clubs and societies are everywhere formed' (E-RA 271). (This is one place where we can see a link between the Scots' thought and their contemporary society, the awareness of urbanisation and the endeavour to identify and cultivate urbanity.) Richard Boyd has emphasised the more than merely etymological connection between the emergence of civility and the idea of a civil society (2013: 450).

Smith also develops an argument (itself indebted to Hume – see discussion and references in Chapter 11) that recognises that changes in political form or constitutions are not decisive or, alternatively put, this argument can be seen to establish the importance, and autonomy, of non-political institutions. The argument of Smith's in question is his well-known account of the decline of feudal, including ecclesiastical, nobility (*WN* III.iv.4–18/ 412–22, V.i.g.25/803 – see Chapter 16 for an outline discussion).[8] In the current context Smith's account has two significant aspects.

Firstly, it sees an autonomous dynamic in what can defensibly be called the 'social'. There are forces at work – systems of ownership (property) and ways of behaving (manners) – that operate independently of political decisions. Moreover, these 'forces' are institutional rather than individual. Of course, individual land-lords and merchants interacted but neither had the 'least intention to serve the publick' nor did they have 'knowledge or foresight of that revolution'. Social change (from the agriculture/feudal to the commercial age) is explicable by social causes (see Berry 2015).

Secondly, this self-same 'revolution' also explains the emergence of the 'state' – it, too, is the work of this change in 'property and manners'. The only place in *The Wealth of Nations* (V.i.i/ 689–708) where Smith exploited the so-called 'four-stages theory' that he (like Millar) had professed in his Glasgow lectures concerned changes in military organisation and thence how the duties of the sovereign are executed.[9] Extrapolating from his text, the following historical process is identified. In the first stage of hunter-gatherers, rule is personal/dynastic in the form of strong men, in the second stage of herders the rules are personified in khans, in the agricul-tural stage individual feudal landowners have power and this is replaced in the fourth commercial stage by the impersonal rule of law and the strict administration of justice (one of the three duties of government in a commercial society – the other two are defence and the provision of 'public goods' (*WN* IV.ix.51/687)).

This is a recognisably 'modern' state in two respects. This state is constituted by rules and offices. Moreover, it is not crucially dependent on the exercise of specific political 'virtues' by political leaders or adult citizens of specific political/republican 'virtues' or on the particular talents of a monarch, when, that is, the monarchy is of the 'civilised' species. Rather, given that one of its chief tasks, as we have just seen in Smith, is the administration of justice, then the political class are administrators (Hegel's *'allgemeine Stände* or universal class'). Their chief function as administrators is to provide a stable framework within which individuals (and groups) can function and they for their part are required to respect the law, without any requirement for more active political participation (see also Chapter 18).[10]

In addition to Smith, the primacy of justice and the rule of law is emphasised not only by, among others, Hume (*T* 3.2.2.22/ *SBNT* 497) but also by Kames (*PMNR* 65), Millar (*HV* IV, 787) and Ferguson (*PMPS* II 476–7). As befits the modernity of the state, the operation of justice is itself historicised. Smith concludes his *Theory of Moral Sentiments* by contrasting the circumstances where the 'rudeness and barbarism of the people' make the system of justice irregular with those in a 'more civilised nations' where the 'natural sentiments of justice' arrive at 'accuracy and precision' (*TMS* VII.iv.36/341). The state, and 'politics', has come to occupy an enabling background condition. The focus shifts to the sort of society that is thus enabled. Famously, Smith characterises this as a commercial society, wherein 'every man lives by exchanging or becomes in some measure a merchant' (*WN* I.iv.1/37). It is in the articulation of this sort of 'society' that we can see another crucial component in the conceptual space we are mapping.

This now links to the second respect that the state is modern. It has emerged as a disengagement from the entangled feudal circumstances where political/judicial authority was bound up with localised power. While this disentanglement can, as we saw above, result in absolutism it can also, as most gloriously for the British (and French admirers), result in the rule of law, to which the sovereign/government is as subject as much as any other individual or organisation. As a matter of conceptual cartography, there cannot be a 'civil society' unless there exists a strong, non-local (national) rule-bound 'state' that in the Weberian formulation monopolises legitimate coercion to which it can be counterposed.[11] The constituents of this counterposed component, it also follows, will be non-political. This comports or fits with the Hegelian picture that has supposedly led the way to what has become the standard picture of 'civil society'. Though Smith's presence in Hegel's *Philosophy of Right* is largely implicit – he is merely name-checked – in his so-called Jena writings (1922: 239) the references are explicit, discussing, for example, the famous example of pin makers as he continued to do fifteen years later in his Heidelberg lectures (1995: 175–6) that became, in an amended form, the *Philosophy of Right*. But what matters is not any 'anticipatory' Smithian intimations but that Smith's 'commercial society' is indeed a form of society in which the 'political' of course figures but its enabling role is not to be confused with any privileged primacy. A commercial society, like the other forms, is, to repeat, an interlocking set of institutions, behaviours and values.

As a next step, we need to investigate in what sense or on what basis this interlocking occurs. This investigation takes us back to the question of absolutism.[12] Locke's critique of Robert Filmer's patriarchalism having proved decisive, this question took on a new focus in the shape of French pretensions, infamously embodied in Louis XIV's alleged declaration '*L'état, c'est moi*'. Once again

Hume is a helpful starting point. With France in mind, he says it is a feature of that absolutist regime that there 'law, religion and custom concur' (E-LP 10).[13] Since absolutism, as we have seen, is inimical to commerce and commerce can only flourish under a free government (E-CL 92), it also inhibits the expression of what he explicitly calls 'a new plan of liberty' (*HE* II, 606; cf. *HE* II, 581n, *HE* I, 115, *HE* I, 175, etc.). This is akin to what Smith calls freedom 'in our present sense of the word' (*WN* III.iii.5/400) (see Chapter 21 for a detailed treatment), which, when generalised, expresses 'natural liberty, where everyman is left perfectly free to pursue his own interest his own way', as long as he 'does not violate the laws of justice' (*WN* IV.x. 51/687).

What is important is that there is an implicit pluralism here – I choose to become a butcher, you a baker, while someone else devotes themselves to sport or music and so on (and on). Vavlav Havel (1990: 21) commented that the most important thing about the 'Prague Spring' (1968) was a 'plurality of social associations from below'. And a clear link between pluralism and civil society is emphasised by Gellner (1966) and Shils (1997). This pluralism is more than individual: it is also – and crucially so – institutional. Hence it encompasses not only the 'economic' sphere of butchers and bakers and the cultural sphere of soccer and opera, but also that of education, law, manners (folkways, commonly accepted ways of behaving) and religion. Under the framework of general, abstract, publicly enforced rules (laws), a variety of (private) institutions and beliefs are, in line with natural liberty, properly permitted. If we return to Hume's characterisation of France, then law, custom and religion do/should not 'concur'.[14] That lack of concurrence is a principle that will in due course constitute a central ingredient in the idea of a civil society.

Historically identifying the proper place of religion was crucial. Elsewhere I have expanded on what the Scots' views were on this question and draw selectively on that treatment here (Berry 2016). One clear implication of linking religion with private freedom under law is that expressions of creedal conviction, provided they do not impinge on the beliefs of others, are a matter of choice, not compulsion. That is, the principle of tolerance is a hallmark of what we can label (adapting Michael Braddick (2000)) the 'de-confessionalisation' of politics and that, in its turn, facilitates the presence of civil society within a polity. Kames notes approvingly that 'in England [Britain] and Holland men are permitted to worship God their own way, provided they give no disturbance to society' (*SHM* II 516n). Hume dismisses religious persecution because, among other reasons, it seeks 'to settle an entire uniformity of opinion' (*HE* II 301). Instead he judges (with the historical record behind him) that, once sects have diffused themselves, then 'unlimited toleration' is a superior policy since it is the most effective way ('the true secret') of 'managing' religious conflict by relaxing mutual hate (*HE* II 302, II 336, II 580, III 625) (Siebert 1990: 115).

The argument for toleration had, of course, been worked through earlier. John Locke gave perhaps the definitive statement.[15] But the Scots, it can be argued, have, relevantly for the present context and as part of their incipient pluralism, moved the argument on. As we saw earlier, they reject Locke's contractarianism in favour of a non-individualistic, institutional 'society' approach. It is this same approach, together with the circumstances of their Hanoverian social environment, which contributes to the Scots making implicitly a link between religious tolerance and civil society.

With an allusion to the urbanisation that accompanies the commercialisation of society, Smith contrasts the circumstances 'in a country village' to those of a 'great city'. In the latter situation, Smith depicts a 'man of low condition' (say, the pin maker). This individual is liable to be 'sunk in obscurity and darkness' with the consequence that he is apt to 'abandon himself to every sort of low profligacy and vice' (*WN* V.i.g.12/795). Clearly influenced by Smith, Millar notes that these 'pin makers', when they are not actually working, will draw little improvement from the company of companions similarly afflicted and what interaction there is will take the form of 'drinking and dissipation' (*HV* IV 732). Kames, for his part, simply links together in the same phrase the ignorance and unsociableness of the 'operator' confined to 'a single object' (*SHM* II, 111).

Smith now observes that the only way this operator can gain attention is by joining a small religious sect. Here he finds companionship and his conduct becomes 'remarkably regular and orderly'. Yet seemingly despite this, there is a further consequence to which Smith draws attention. It is that these sects induce a commitment to austerity, which makes them a breeding ground for fanaticism, prone to instil socially disruptive zealotry. To alleviate the austerity, Smith judges that it is appropriate for the state to encourage 'publick diversions', such as drama, poetry, music, dancing and the like (not an uncontentious issue in a Calvinist country). By 'encourage', Smith means give 'entire liberty' to those who would 'for their own interest' put on these diversions, provided this was done 'without scandal or indecency' (WN V.i.g.15/796).[16] And to offset the tendency of these sects to zealotry, and here echoing Hume on diffusion, he believes this troublesome zeal is only serious when the sects are few in number and the magistrate is *parti pris*. Freed from political intervention and thus allowing every man to choose his own religion, the consequence would 'no doubt' be 'a great multitude' of sects.[17] The very diversity of these he holds would help mitigate the tendency to fanaticism. These twin remedial manifestations of 'toleration' follow from his normative espousal of natural liberty. They permit the conclusion that Smith is identifying, within the operation of a modern society, a proper place for religious institutional pluralism.

There is another consideration in this conceptual cartography. In his *Theory of Moral Sentiments,* Smith remarks that a state is divided into 'different orders and societies' with their own 'powers, privileges and immunities' which, within the security afforded by the state, they defend and contest (*TMS* VI.ii.2.8, 10/230–1). Of course, this contestation can become fanatical, as exhibited by these austere sects, but the 'idea' of a civil society does not mean unanimity; indeed, the opposite is true. The same extrapolation can be applied to Hume's recognition that social tranquillity is a false veneer in despotic regimes, because beneath the façade the powerful interests oppress the weak. For Hume, differences in interest (he mentions merchants, soldiers, nobles and people (E-PG 60)) cannot be extirpated and so the requirement is to accommodate them. And consistent with his argument, though going beyond it, this can be achieved by civil society's providing that accommodation while the state eliminates the oppression.

V

As I argue across this volume and in my two 'Scottish books' (Berry 1997, 2013), the Scots can justifiably be said to have recognised the 'social' as an object of study. Humans are social beings and their sociality expresses itself in a set of interlocking institutions that include the religious along with the economic, the familial, habits and customs and the political, with the last of these, importantly, given no automatic privilege. The Scots also brought to this concept of society an historical dimension. They wrote 'natural histories' of these institutions – property, government, manners and religion. The common thread in these various histories was the move in societal life from rude simplicity to civilised complexity. This combination of 'sociology' and 'history' allowed them to theorise about their contemporary society as distinctively 'commercial'. One of the implications of this theorisation is that it opens up a 'conceptual space'.

This space, we can say, was achieved by making two broad complementary arguments. First, negatively, they recalibrated the place of the state. While still giving it a decisive role in the maintenance of social order, they restricted its scope; the state was no longer the definitive differentiating principle between societies, nor had it direct responsibility for the internal conduct of society's institutions, especially not to enforce a view of the good society as if, in Smith's famous analogy, governing was like moving pieces on a chessboard, forgetting that in the 'chessboard of human society every single piece has a motion of its own, altogether different from that which the legislature might chuse to impress upon it' (TMS VI.ii.2.17/234). This second argument is of course explicitly normative but 'civil society' as now understood is equally so, even if typically this is more implicit.

What gives the Scots' development of this view of the state special significance is their second argument. Unlike the negativity of the first argument, this is positive; it centres round their articulation of a model of commercial society. Because this society was based on the interactions of socialised and, by the same token, moralised free individuals within a common established framework of law, it properly allowed a variety of institutions and value systems to co-exist. While 'the market' was a key example, the positive principle applied across the board; it would be a mistake to view their relative demotion of the political as promotion of the centrality of the economic. The Scots' position encompasses *in potentia* an idea of civil society as more than economic institutions (or a 'system of needs'). They are renowned for their insight into the 'law of unintended consequences' and their own relation to the idea of civil society might be thought to fall under that law.

On a more forthright and more obviously contestable note, what the above analysis prompts is the judgement that it is the affinity between pluralism and liberal institutionalism that is central to a functioning civil society. To use the language of this paper, it inhabits a space between an overemphatic libertarian concern with individual rights, a socialist or republican concentration on political agency, whether by the state or the citizens, and while it recognises communities it does so fluidly rather than as definitive of identity. It is, putatively, the creation of this space that I think can best sustain an argument that the Scots contributed to a conception of 'civil society' *avant la lettre*.

Postscript

This chapter is an amended version of a plenary lecture delivered in May 2016 at the International Society for Intellectual History in Crete. I am grateful to the organisers for the invitation and support and most especially to Spiros Tegos. The lecture was also presented to a seminar of graduate students at Georgetown University in November 2016 and my thanks go to Richard Boyd for that invitation. The chapter also represents a thorough reworking of earlier (relatively obscure) papers (Berry 2003c; 2010).

Notes

1. See, for example, Keane (1988: 39–44), Seligman (1992), Gellner (1994), Hall (ed. 1995), Varty (1997), Ehrenberg (1999), Oz-Salzburger (2001), Gautier on Hume (ed. 2001) and Livesey (2009).

2. See, for example, Marsilius of Padua (1956: I, 3). Cf. Gierke (1934) for wider references.

3. See, for example, Gellner (1994), Ehrenberg (1999), Keane (1988: 39–44), Oz-Salzburger (2001) and Varty (1997). It should be acknowledged that the Scots are not uniquely singled out in the literature.

4. As ever, there is room for qualification. Hutcheson (*SIMP* 237) and Reid (1990: Ch. 15) both attach some weight to contract. For the former it is as part of a critique of Hobbes, for the latter it is part of an analysis of the assumptions that govern the accepted idea that there is indeed a contract between ruler and people.

5. Smith follows him almost verbatim in his Glasgow lectures (*LJ* 317). See, among others, Millar (*HV* IV, 803), who employs the Humean argument that a promise adds 'but little' to the obligation to obey,

and Ferguson (*PMPS* I, 262), who regards the idea of men assembling together as equals and deciding their mode of government as 'visionary and unknown in nature'.

6. Buchanan (1579: 100): '*Mutua igitur regi cum civibus est pactio*'.

7. Ana Marta Gonzalez (2013: 63) at one point imputes 'una teoria de la civilizacion' to Hume. Her analysis of Hume as providing a normative theory of civil society is essentially based on the *Treatise* and she places Hume in the broadly Grotian tradition, which means that she is not concerned with the term 'civil society' outside that context. Christopher Finlay (2007: Ch. 8) does attribute a 'theory of civil society' to Hume but in a manner not dissimilar to my own (he cites Berry 2003c).

8. Compare Hume's account in *HE* II, 53–4, acknowledged by Smith.

9. On the four stages and the limited explicit references to them, see Berry (2013: Ch. 2).

10. This is emphasised by Jürgen Habermas (1992: 19 but throughout), who links the development of a civil society to the depersonalisation of public authority.

11. This was recognised by Marx (1975) in his early (1843) critique of Hegel, albeit he wished to reintegrate what Hegel had separated.

12. One explanation of the East European intellectuals' revival of the idea of civil society in their critique of 'totalitarianism' was their seeing a parallel to the general Enlightenment discourse that criticised 'absolutism'. See, for example, Taylor (1990: 115).

13. In a later retracted passage in his much-amended 'Essay of the Parties of Great Britain', Hume distinguishes between England and Scotland on the basis that in the latter 'political and religious division have been since the revolution regularly correspondent' and this explains Jacobitism, with its zealous partisanship for 'absolute monarchy' and willingness to 'sacrifice our liberties' (E-v 615).

14. For 'philosophical pluralism' in Hume, see Merrill (2015: 151)

15. In his *Letter Concerning Toleration* (1689) Locke defines a church as a 'free and voluntary society' (1948: 129) and argues that the 'magistrate has no power to enforce by law . . . the outward form and rites of worship' (1948: 142) and neither it is 'the business of the laws' to 'provide for the truth of opinions but for the safety and security of the commonwealth' (1948: 151).

16. Kames ([1762] 1817: II, 43) also makes the link between 'public spectacles' and support for the social affections. He believes that these spectacles and amusements, by being available to all ranks,

help to counteract the divisiveness of the 'separation of men into different classes by birth, office or occupation'.

17. See, further, Boyd (2004: 133–40) and Smith (2016). I touch on it in Berry (2016b).

Part II

David Hume

Introduction to Part II

The essays here exemplify two general characteristics of my reading of Hume. They take a robust view of his account of human nature. I take him at face value as a strong universalist and thus run counter to many other scholars who take a softer approach. I happen to think a universalist view is more right than wrong but that does not mean that Hume's view should be sanitised. His prejudices and cultural assumptions should not be wished away – *le bon* David would not, I surmise, be altogether welcome in contemporary polite society. The second characteristic, which is to a large extent related to the first, is the emphasis on his 'modernism'. This is less about his antipathy to 'old-time religion' – powerful a sentiment though that is – than, with the exception of its literature, his thoroughgoing disparagement of classical thought.

Largely as a consequence of these two characteristics, these essays pay relatively little attention to the *Treatise* (Chapter 10 is an exception, but even there the focus is on an aspect of the book that has not garnered extensive commentary). The major reason for this focus is that I covered Hume's account of justice in my book (Berry 2009b Ch. 2, partly reprised in Spanish in Berry 2009c) along with, more systematically, his view of sympathy. I have treated Hume's account of convention in another essay (Berry forthcoming b), which for contractual reasons preclude its conclusion in this collection. The one new essay (Chapter 15) reflects some cognate interests of mine but its argument is in line with the other components of this part of the book.

9

Hume on Rationality in History and Social Life

The chief aim of this chapter is to identify and illustrate the normative character of Hume's theory of human nature and society, although a second, albeit implicit, aim is to indicate his affinity with the *philosophes*. To assist the subsequent discussion, some introductory remarks and stipulations are needed.

It was widely accepted by thinkers of the Enlightenment that, though humans were social creatures, this sociality was not constitutive, so that, despite the differences between societies, human nature remained constant and uniform. This position was overturned (with the work of Herder being of particular significance) and this newly articulated contrary view – that sociality is specific and constitutive of human nature – is here termed contextualist. Although it is now something of a commonplace to hold that human nature is in some manner and to some extent contextual, the nature of the relationship between human nature and social experience (the nub of contextualism) is contentious. Is it possible to have an intelligible concept of human nature per se, or is its contextual character such that the very variety and multiplicity of societal forms deprives the concept of any general non-specific intelligibility?

Much of the debate can be, not unfairly, characterised as concerned with some form of compromise, in particular with the location of some defensible constants. Owing to the problems now recognised in cross-cultural comprehension, such constants tend to be formal in character. Perhaps the most frequently employed (although there are attempts to utilise some form of biological substratum) is the notion of minimal rationality, which is to say, the application of certain constitutive or presuppositional features of social intercourse itself that will pertain equally to (say) contemporary Britons, the Azande and Periclean Athenians. Three different positions can be discerned and I will distinguish these in the ensuing discussion by using certain stipulative terms. The view that the differences between societies are immaterial to a comprehension of human nature is termed a formal account of social life. The reverse of this – that the differences between societies do make a material difference to the comprehension of human nature – is termed a substantive account of social life.

The view that it is only by invoking nonmaterial presuppositional features of social intercourse that cross-cultural comparison and comprehension is possible is termed a formal account of rationality. The reverse of this, that cross-cultural comprehension – indeed, cross-cultural appraisal – is possible in terms of some concrete material criteria, is termed a substantive account of rationality. Thus, in these terms, while much 'modern' analysis typically provides a substantive account of social life and a formal account of rationality, Hume provides a formal account of social life but a substantive account of rationality. Hegel, by contrast, gives a substantive account of both social life and rationality. The meaning of these terms will now be established through an analysis of Hume's writings.

In his anonymous review of the *Treatise*, Hume states that the author 'proposes to anatomise human nature' (*Ab* 2/*SBNA* 646; cf. *T* 1.4.7.23 /*SBNT* 263; 3.3.6/620; *Letters* I, 32) and in the important introduction to the *Treatise* itself Hume declares, in a striking military metaphor, that the aim of the work is 'instead of taking now and then a castle or village on the frontier to march up directly to the capital, or centre of these sciences [logic, morals, criticism, politics] to human nature itself' (*T* Intro 6/*SBNT* xvi). This is to be accomplished, as the subtitle of the work indicates, by the experimental method, which means 'that we are unable to go beyond experience' and 'must therefore glean up our experiments in this science [of man] from a cautious observation of human life' (*T* Intro 10 /*SBNT* xix).

Thus human nature is (and remains) central to Hume's concern; but what does this term mean for him? This question can best be answered by focusing upon what is, given Hume's programme as outlined above, its most important characteristic – its constancy. Constancy plays a vital role in many aspects of Hume's thought, but it may be illustrated by his conception of history.

Hume wrote a short essay – 'Of the Study of History' – with the aim of recommending history to 'my female readers,' although the advantages he outlines that flow from its study are suited to 'everyone'. These advantages are threefold: 'as it amuses the fancy, as it improves the understanding, and as it strengthens virtue' (E-SH 565). Although Hume was later to declare that this essay was 'too frivolous' (*Letters* I, 168), and he did omit it from later editions of his *Essays,* nevertheless he here reflects a general eighteenth-century understanding of history.

History was a branch of literature and thus matters of 'interest' were at a premium. As Kames put it, 'the perfection of historical composition ... is a relation of interesting facts connected with their motives and consequences' (*SHM* I, 148)[1] and Hume himself admitted, of the first volume of his own *History,* that he had therein entered 'into no Detail of minute, uninteresting Facts' but rather had adopted his customary 'philosophical Spirit' (*Letters* I, 193).[2] A corollary of this was the derogative dismissal of annalists or chroniclers because of their indiscriminate preoccupation with facts. Bolingbroke (1870: 37), whose delineation of history was contemporaneously influential, put this point graphically:

> it is the business ... of others to separate the pure ore from the dross, to stamp it into coin, and to enrich and not encumber mankind. When there are none sufficient to this task, there may be antiquaries, and there may be journalists or annalists but there are no historians.

But, perhaps above its literary pretensions, history was seen to be an important vehicle for, in Hume's words, 'strengthening virtue'. This 'humanist' perspective (neatly encapsulated in perhaps the best known of Bolingbroke's remarks, that 'history is philosophy teaching by examples' (1870: 18)[3]) is the real import behind the deprecation of antiquarians. To study the past for its own sake is an inferior and less worthwhile pursuit than its utilisation apropos contemporary concerns.

Although Hume's remarks on the scope and function of history – 'the great mistress of wisdom' (*HE* III, 396) – are scattered throughout his *History,* his most famous or notorious pronouncements are of interest here, since it is in these that he exposes the assumption of a constant human nature. These pronouncements are to be found in the chapter on liberty and necessity in the first *Enquiry* (though the corresponding chapter in the *Treatise* contains the same argument). In this chapter Hume avers that 'it is universally acknowledged that there is a great uniformity among the actions of men, in all nations and ages, and that human nature remains still the same in its principles and operations' (*U* 8.7/ *SBNU* 83), so it now follows that:

> Mankind are so much the same, in all times and places, that history informs us of nothing new or strange in this particular. Its chief use is only to discover the constant and universal principles of human nature, by showing men in all varieties of circumstances and situations, and furnishing us with materials from which we may form our observations and become acquainted with the regular springs of human action and behaviour. (*U* 8.7/*SBNU* 83; cf. 8.15/88)[4]

While Flew (1961: 145) is correct to draw attention to the 'classical' reference in this passage as a whole, the important point about these pronouncements is the general understanding of history and human nature thereby implied. In his second *Enquiry*, Hume gives an analogy which can be seen to be expressive of this understanding – 'men in different times and places frame their houses differently'; but because the 'purposes which they serve are everywhere exactly similar', then 'all houses have a roof and walls, windows and chimneys' (*M* 3.44/*SBNM* 202). This is an analogy (to the ubiquity of property laws) that permits a distinction between constants (roofs, etc.) and the contingencies of time and place of (say here) the size, shape and fabric of houses. This distinction is vital. There is no attempt to avoid the evidence of the variety of fabrics, etc., but, within all this variety, there are roofs. The fabric only constitutes a house, and can only be understood as such, because it is put to constant uses. The roofs are constant because they pertain to universals (exactly similar purposes). Similarly, without these constant universals – 'were there no uniformity in human actions' (*U* 8.7/*SBNU* 85) – then 'it were impossible to collect any general observations concerning mankind'; more particularly, 'what would become of history had we not a dependence on the veracity of historians according to the experience we have had of mankind' (*U* 8.18/*SBNU* 90; cf. *Ab* 13/ *SBNA* 651; 33/661). Crucially, 'we' are able to have this experience because the principles of human nature are, as such, common to all and operate in a constant and uniform manner, so that the 'pastness' of what these historians relate is no obstacle to its comprehension. Human nature is not historically defined.

The uniform presence of these principles and the constancy of their operation mean that there is 'necessity' in human action; it is causally explicable by reference to these principles. No matter what variety of 'circumstances and situations' history reveals, there still exists in human institutions and behaviour, by virtue of their being human, certain constitutive constancies that render them explicable – hence the centrality of the science of man. These constancies are revealed in the experience of everyday life. It is from this experience that historical knowledge is made possible. Since we are able to understand what writers about, and in, the past tell us (history tells us 'nothing new or strange' about human nature – it does not upset our continually reinforced habitual expectations), history can be used to confirm our scientific conclusions. This is explicit. Hume remarks that the study of history 'confirms the reasonings of true philosophy [the science of man]' when it shows the 'original qualities of human nature,' to wit here, that political controversies are of less moment than the interests of peace and liberty (T 3.2.10.15/SBNT 562). In a similar vein, in the key passage in the first *Enquiry*, Hume remarks that the historical record provides 'experiments' that enable the 'politician or moral philosopher' to fix the 'principles of his science' (U 8.7/ SBNU 84). There is, accordingly, nothing 'special' about history, and this helps to explain the somewhat dismissive tone of Hume's comments about its 'chief use' (it is perhaps this tone as much as anything else that has given these remarks their notoriety).

It is necessary now to examine this universal constant more closely. What, for Hume, constitutes this constant? There are a considerable number of references in his writings where 'human nature' is synonymous with the human race, mankind or, explicitly in one place, 'man in general' (T 3.2.1.12/SBNT 481). It is seemingly in such a sense that we must interpret statements like 'The Roman Emperors ... were the most frightful tyrants that ever disgraced human nature' (E-LP 12) or 'enormous monarchies are probably destructive of human nature in their progress' (E-BP 341). But such usages do not, by any means, exhaust Hume's employment of the phrase.

Indeed, allowing some latitude by including the phrase 'human mind' (his discussion is clearly not simply dealing with physiological factors),[5] Hume uses the following terms in this connection: faculty, property, principle, quality, disposition, propensity, inclination, structure and capacity. Although some of these terms are technical,[6] it is improbable, in the face of such an array, that

Hume was using them stipulatively. Nevertheless, some observations can be made. As just noted, Hume does subscribe to a faculty psychology or 'mental geography' – to an 'obvious' division of the mind into imagination, will, understanding and passions (*U* 1.13/*SBNU* 13) – which has the consequence that 'the faculties of the mind are supposed to be naturally alike in every individual' (*U* 8.1/*SBNU* 80). True to his anatomical intent, Hume does, in the *Treatise*, break down the passions into direct and indirect. This distinction, when further analysed (*T* 2.1.1.4/*SBNT* 276–7), produces the following: desire, aversion, grief, hope, joy, fear, despair, security, pride, humility, ambition, vanity, love, hatred, envy, pity, malice and generosity. All men are supposed to be susceptible to these feelings and, as such, they are constant constituents of human nature. This can be substantiated by noting what Hume has to say about just two of these: 'Can we imagine it possible, that while human nature remains the same, men will ever become entirely indifferent to their power, riches, beauty or personal merit, and that their pride and vanity will not be affected by these advantages?' (*T* 2.1.3.4/*SBNT* 281).

Since this pertains to human nature as such, it means that it holds good independent of specific societal context. Indeed, this independence is so marked that a traveller's report that did describe men as bereft of avarice and ambition would immediately be detected as a 'falsehood' (*U* 8.8/*SBNU* 84; cf.10.17/117; *T* 2.3.1.10/*SBNT* 402). Of course, differences exist between men (and societies); but, significantly, Hume immediately follows his remark that 'in all nations and ages the same objects still give rise to pride and humility' (*T* 2.1.3.4/*SBNT* 281) with the comment that any variation 'proceeds from nothing but a difference in the tempers and complexions of men and is, besides very inconsiderable.' He repeats the point later: 'There are also characters peculiar to different nations and particular persons, as well as common to mankind. The knowledge of these characters is founded on the observation of a uniformity in the actions that flow from them' (*T* 2.3.1.10/*SBNT* 403; cf. *U* 8.7/*SBNU* 83). Thus, and this is an important point, the comprehension of these peculiar or variable 'characters' is still founded on knowledge of constant uniformity. This is the 'essence' of the necessity inherent in human behaviour. All human behaviour, even if it has a peculiar or local character, is comprehensible and explicable because, as human behaviour, it is constituted by 'regular springs' and 'constant and universal principles' which have uniform effects. It is here, in accounting for these variable characters, that the principle of habituation plays a crucial role: 'Are the manners of men different in different ages and countries? We learn thence the great force of custom and education, which mould the human mind from its infancy and form it into a fixed and established character' (U 8.11/SBNU 86). The different manners of men in different ages and places (variables) are accordingly the habituation (constant principle) of particular contingencies. Uniformity is presupposed in variety.[7]

We must now, however, return to our question, because we have not exhausted our examination of what, according to Hume, is a constant constituent of human nature. A reading produces the following universal attributions: sympathy and humanity (T 2.1.11.5/SBNT 318; 3.3.1.10/577; 3.3.6.1/618; M 9.5/ SBNM 272, etc.); fortification through unanimity (E-PG 60); an assumption of resemblance between the experienced and inexperienced (U 10.16/ SBNU 117); dissatisfaction with a falling short of a standard (T 2.2.8.2/SBNT 372); benevolence and resentment, love of life and kindness to children (T 2.3.3.8/SBNT 417; cf. NHR 33); arrogance and presumptuousness (E-AS 126); a delight in liberty yet a submission to necessity (E-PD 188); a craving for employment (E-Int 300); credulity (T 1.3.9.12 /SBNT 112); a need for society (T 2.2.5.15/SBNT 363; 2.3.1.8 /402); personification (T 1.4.311/SBNT 224; NHR 40); a diminution of aversion through familiarisation (T, 355); a despising of that to which one is accustomed (T 2.1.6.4/SBNT 291); stimulation in the face of mild opposition (T 2.3.8.4/SBNT 433); curiosity (T 2.3.10.11/ SBNT 453); unpleasantness at too sudden a change (T 2.3.10.5/ SBNT 453); a preference for the contiguous over the remote (T 3.2.7.3/SBNT 535); an addiction to general rules (T 3.2.9.3/ SBNT 551); blaming the present and admiring the past (E-PAN, 464; HE, 238); selfishness (T 3.3.1.17/SBNT 583; M 5.1/SBNM 214); principles of taste (E-ST 243); a sense of morals (T 3.3.6.3/ SBNT 619); a disapproval of barbarity and treachery (M Appx. 1.16/SBNM, 293); a tenacity of memory (U 10.5/SBNU 112); an inclination to truth (T 2.3.10.1/SBNT 448; U 10.5/SBNU 112); shame in the detection of committing a falsehood (U10.5/SBNU 112); imitativeness (E-NC 202); a propensity to the marvellous (U 10.20/SBNU 119), to self-overvaluation (M 8.9/SBNM 264), to adulation (NHR 77), to fame (M 9.10/SBNM 276), to divide into factions (E-PG 56), to believe what is to the disadvantage rather than to the advantage of government (E-v 604), to believe in an intelligent and invisible power (*NHR* 97); and the contraction of habits (*U* 5.5/*SBNU* 43; *T* 1.3.126/*SBNT* 133; 1.3.16.9/179; 2.3.5.1/422–3; E-OG 39).

This list is not exhaustive: Hume also invokes a number of mental processes, especially in the *Treatise*. Nevertheless, it gives an indication of what Hume regards as constituents of human nature, which, though distinguishable from 'original instincts,' are yet 'general attendants of human nature' (*NHR* 86) and, as they are inseparable, can be justifiably regarded as 'natural' (cf. *T* 3.2.1.19/*SBNT* 484). Thus, while habitual action is not instinctive, human nature is such that men form habits so that this propensity is truly a constant, universal constituent.[8]

From these constant, universal, and necessary principles it is possible to come to far-reaching conclusions. For example:

> The different stations of life influence the whole fabric, external and internal; and these stations arise necessarily, because uniformly, from the necessary and uniform principles of human nature. Men cannot live without society and cannot be associated without government. Government makes a distinction of property and establishes the different ranks of men. This produces industry, traffic, manufactures, law-suits, war, leagues, alliances, voyages, travels, cities, fleets, ports and all those other actions and objects which cause such a diversity and at the same time maintain such an uniformity in human life. (*T* 2.3.1.9/*SBNT* 402)

Hence, Hume's conception of human nature is that it possesses certain constant and universal principles, 'regular springs,' the operation of which are, as such, unaffected by history; or, more generally – for here space and time are co-relative – by different sociocultural contexts. These contexts do provide evidence of diversity and variety but, decisively, they are not constitutive or definitive of human nature.

Although Hume is far from indifferent to the impact of these contingencies of time and place, he does not regard them as relevant to an adequate comprehension of human nature; for, despite these variations, 'mankind are so much the same in all times and places' so that knowledge of the Greeks and Romans can be attained from study of the French and the English (*U* 8.7/ *SBNU* 83). Here is a point of cardinal importance. Hume has a non-contextualist theory of human nature; man as the fit subject for science is not a local phenomenon, only to be comprehended parochially, but a universal exhibiting necessary uniformities and constancies. It would be contrary to the Newtonian canon of economy (Rule 1) if these variations were not explicable by a few simple causes (cf. *T* Intro 8/*SBNT* xvii; 2.1.3.7/282; *Ab* 1/*SBNA* 646) but had to be accounted for in their own various and specific non-subsumable constitutive terms (as is upheld by those contemporary philosophers who reject the adequacy or appropriateness of the 'covering-law' method of explanation in history). The fact that Hume's theory of human nature does not regard the diverse forms of social life as constitutive entails that this universality is, in Hegelian terms, abstract.

This point should not be misunderstood. It is here that the introductory stipulations can assist. In those terms Hume (to repeat) provides a formal account of social life with a substantive theory of rationality. The formality of Hume's account of social life stems from its non-constitutive character with respect to human nature. The behaviour of men, though it takes place in diverse settings, can be understood and explained independently of these settings because it instantiates universals. But this very independence means that human nature is not historically or societally defined. Though man cannot be understood outside society, he can be understood without reference to the specific society in which he is found. Such specificity is irrelevant to the science of man. It is this relationship between human nature and society that makes formal the account of social life that Hume proffers.

There is, however, a further dimension. Although these principles, operations and springs (the passions; cf. *U* 8.7/*SBNU* 83) in human nature are abstract, in the sense of pertaining regardless of specific context, this does not mean that what Hume, in fact, regards as constant is devoid of content. Rather, as the list just supplied indicates, Hume's delineation of the content, of what is constant in human nature, is extensive and reveals that human nature for him is no mere residual cipher (although such an ascription is implied by those recent commentators who wish to correct the common interpretation of Hume's theory of human nature as naively uniformitarian).[9]

Again, due caution should be exercised. Hume's examples are often those of an eighteenth-century gentleman; and although these often read as universal propositions – for example, 'Our forefathers being regarded as our nearest relations; everyone naturally affects to be of a good family, and to be descended from a long succession of rich and honourable ancestors' (*DP* 12) – it is important to note that they are only examples. Hume is concerned to explain individual and social behaviour by universal properties of human nature (in the above example, by the operation of the principles of association); and as such – in line with the formality of his account of social life – these properties could, in principle, equally well illustrate Amerindian customs. Furthermore, it is a plausible conjecture, given the contemporary lack of awareness that there was any 'problem' to be associated with the comprehension of 'exotica', that the persuasiveness of Hume's argument would be enhanced by making the familiar (to his readers) conform to his system.

Hume's awareness of diversity, which is considerable, is too acute for him directly to universalise the prejudices of the eighteenth century. Yet the inclusion in the list of contents of 'taste', 'craving for employment', 'arrogance' and so on suggests that human nature is no mere neutral residuum. This is not simply his parochiality coming through (although it is undeniably present) because, more interestingly and significantly, it is a basic ingredient of his thought that human nature functions as a normative principle. (It is here, if anywhere, that Hume himself derives an 'ought' from an 'is'.) It is because the specificity of societal location is irrelevant to the comprehension of human nature or to the findings of the 'science of man' that Hume is able to evaluate social practices by an 'external' standard. This is Hume's substantive theory of rationality: some social practices are more rational or more 'in tune' with human nature than others.

Lastly, to focus on this final point, Hume distinguishes in the *Treatise* between two sorts of general rules. First, there are imaginative, customary, general rules or 'prejudices', such as the view that 'an Irishman cannot have wit and a Frenchman cannot have solidity' (*T* 1.3.13.8/*SBNT* 146). According to Hume, 'human nature' is 'very subject to errors of this kind' (*T* 1.3.13.8/*SBNT* 147) because, owing to the 'nature of custom,' it associates those similar in some degree – all those born in Ireland, for example. Against this first sort of general rule, which prevails among the 'vulgar,' Hume sets the second sort, which are 'form'd on the nature of our understanding and on our experience of its operations in the judgements we form concerning objects' (*T* 1.3.13.9/

SBNT 149). It is these latter rules (themselves, of course, the product of habit and experience) by which 'wise men' (*T* 1.3.13.12/ *SBNT* 150) are guided, and by which 'we learn to distinguish the accidental circumstances from the efficacious causes' (*T* 1.3.13.11/ *SBNT* 149).

The principle behind this distinction here – between the rules of the wise and those of the vulgar – is an important one in Hume's thought, because, besides being an explanation of the role of the 'scientist' ('moral' as well as 'natural'), it throws considerable light on the meaning and significance of this theory of human nature. Crucially, it enables Hume to pass judgement on habitual practice; in particular, as we shall see in more detail below, to designate superstitions for what they are, to wit 'false opinion' and a 'pestilent distemper' (E-Sui 579–80) – inferior beliefs produced by ignorance and barbarism. There is no suggestion that they might be the expression of a distinct self-authenticating way of life; instead, they are not merely 'frivolous, useless and burdensome' (*M* 3.38/ *SBNM* 199) but also injurious to morality itself (*DNR* 222). [10]

Again, what is at issue here is the relationship between a formal account of social life and a substantive account of rationality. For Hume, habit forming is part of human nature; it is a constant uniform principle and so everybody contracts habits. Habit must be a constant principle because of the 'work' it has to do in explaining the world's evidentially apparent orderliness. This applies to the social as well as to the natural world. Amid the variety of particular social habits is the uniformity of habituation, which, owing to the uniformity of human nature and the inescapable relative scarcity of resources in all societies, is responsible for the rules of justice. This line of argument, since it yields all the requisite information about social life, permits Hume to regard as unimportant the question of how having particular habits affects an individual. In other words, Hume's non-contextualism separates the habituating from the particular habits habituated. It is a contingent variable that one group of people has one particular set of habits – for example, worshipping their ancestors – while another group has another set. The particularity of the society and the beliefs of its members make no difference to the operation of the 'regular springs' of human behaviour, or to the operation of 'the constant and uniform principles of human nature'.[11] This is why history (and anthropology) can 'give us a clue' (*U* 8.9/*SBNU* 85) or 'furnish us with materials' as to their operation – materials that can be gleaned without prejudice from the reported experience of the ancient Germans, the contemporary tribes of the Americas and the observation of eighteenth-century Scotsmen.

The 'science of man' has no parochial subject matter. Indeed, like the other sciences, it is able to penetrate beneath the 'pretexts and appearances' (*U* 8.9/*SBNU* 85) that deceive the vulgar and reveal the causes at work – the uniform principles of human nature. It is this general indifference to specific social location, when seeking a comprehension of human nature, that supports the claim that Hume's account of social life can be denominated formal, and it is his conviction that the 'science of man' can reveal the true springs of human nature that justify the attribution to Hume of a substantive theory of rationality.

Both of these are involved in Hume's labelling of particular habits as superstitions. Hume has no compunction about labelling savages stupid (DNR 155, 129; cf. NHR 52) and ignorant (NHR 35, 37, 42, 52; E-SE 74; E-RA 273; E-PG 61, 62; U 10.20/SBNU 119; HE, 425, etc.) and directly associates these with superstitiousness – 'from the grossness of its superstitions we may infer the ignorance of the age' (HE III, 113).[12] Moreover, his explanation of polytheism, in the *Natural History of Religion*, in no way entails his attributing to its practitioners their own 'rationality' or standard of authenticity; rather, he explains this practice as the constant properties of human nature. These properties are the causes that the 'science of man' can elicit and the fact that practitioners might not heed these is (*pace* Winch and modern analysis) irrelevant. Neither human nature nor (it follows) any study of it based on observation is societally specific.

Once such specificity is accepted, when a substantive account of social life is proffered, the question of 'understanding a primitive society' becomes problematic; for if particular practices and their intrinsically attached meanings are societally specific, how is it possible for a member of another society (an anthropologist or historian, say, since the 'past is another place') to appreciate its 'meaning-impregnated' practices? It is in the answers to this question, in terms such as 'fundamental notions', that all human life is involved or in which, by holding to the presence of distinctions like that between the real and the unreal necessitated by the very concept of a language,[13] we can discern a formal theory of rationality.

For Hume, the specificity of the practices is unimportant, owing to the basic constancy and uniformity of human actions and motives; and this constancy does, in his eyes, permit understanding (as we have seen, it makes history possible). But, of course, the fact that the 'science of man' has elicited the proper basis of human nature means that Hume possesses a benchmark (what the 'wise' habituate) that enables him to evaluate the social practices evident to experience.[14] Accordingly, Hume is able to dismiss derogatively 'a considerable ingredient in almost all religions' (E-SE 75) as superstitions. Indeed, priests, instead of 'correcting these *depraved* ideas of mankind, have often been found ready to foster and encourage them' (*NHR* 84; my emphasis; cf. E-NC 200n). Conversely, superstition is exposed by the 'scrutiny of sense and science' (*M* 3.37/*SBNM* 198) and only philosophy can conquer the fear upon which it is based (E-SE 75). In all superstitious practices a proper (universalist) scientific study of human nature reveals that the practitioners have a false picture of the world. These are not different pictures, self-validating 'forms of life,' but false ones that can be legitimately so judged. Thus, for example, the Koran is labelled 'a wild and absurd performance' and 'uncivilised,' since not only does it commend inhumanity but also its bigotry means that 'no steady rule of right seems there to be attended to' (E-ST 229), whereas the rule of law and liberty is 'the perfection of civil society' (E-OG 41). For Hume, 'civilised' Europe enjoys 'great superiority' over 'barbarous Indians' (*M* 3.19/*SBNM* 191) and progress is evident in the development away from superstition to the normatively superior order of liberty and humanity.

Hume does have in this manner a general theory of cultivation, or the advance of civilisation; but it is a corollary of his theories of rationality and social life, as here depicted, that human nature itself does not change along with society. The 'chief characteristic' that distinguishes civilisation from barbarism is the 'indissoluble chain' of industry, humanity and knowledge (E-RA 271; see Chapter 11); but this correlates positively with a sociological variable (namely, the amount of leisure enjoyed in society) and, moreover, pertains to the 'tempers' of men, which means that it produces merely a 'very inconsiderable' variation (*T* 2.1.3.5/*SBNT* 281; v. *supra*). That is to say, Hume does not tie together the degree of social development with a distinctive societally inclusive 'intellect'. It follows from this that the savage 'character,' with its ignorance and superstition, does not belong exclusively to some faraway (in either time or space) society but is also characteristic of a considerable portion of eighteenth-century British society (the vulgar or the rabble).[15] Since Hume has a non-contextualist theory of human nature, then those who lack leisure in any culture can exhibit 'savage' behaviour.

One final corollary worth observing is that Hume's distinction between the constant and variable in human nature is static, in that man does not have 'attributes' that develop. The variable element (character, temper, manners, habits, etc.) is a local contingency explicable by the 'science of man'; the diversity is simultaneously evidence of uniformity. Although people do behave differently in different circumstances, there is no need, in order to explain these differences, to have recourse to Aristotelian[16] or evolutionary[17] perspectives. For Hume, the development of liberty and humanity is merely metaphorically organic. They are the offspring of knowledge and refinement, but although more is now known in 'enlightened' and 'polished' societies, the men who comprise these societies are the same as those of an earlier epoch. Thus, in his attack on the grounds of belief in miracles, Hume remarks that the accounts of miracles chiefly 'abound among ignorant and barbarous nations', but

> In proportion as we advance nearer the enlightened ages, we soon learn that there is nothing mysterious or supernatural in the case but that all proceeds from the usual propensity of mankind toward the marvellous and that, although this inclination may at intervals receive a check from sense and learning, it can never be thoroughly extirpated from human nature. (*U* 10.20/*SBNU* 119)

In fine, though he is resigned to the fact that customs are too deep-rooted to be eradicated (*écrasés*), Hume's theories of rationality and social life permit him to identify and censure superstition (*l'infâme*). *Le bon David* is, indeed, a man of the Enlightenment.

Postscript

As indicated in Chapter 1, I gave a version of this paper at a conference in Dallas in 1981 and it introduced an argument and a terminology that informed my 1982 book. It does stand alone, however, and it represents an initial post-thesis re-engagement with the Scots. The treatment of Hume has generated some comment and debate and my later paper (here reprinted as Chapter 12, the postscript to which can serve the same function for this) is in part a restatement and defence of my position.

Notes

1. Cf. similarly, Voltaire's opening comments to his 1756 *Essai sur les Moeurs* (2001).
2. Cf. from the *History* itself: 'History also, being a collection of facts which are multiplying without end, is obliged to adopt such arts of abridgement, to retain the more material events, and to drop all the minute circumstances which are only interesting during the time, or to the persons engaged in the transactions ... What mortal could have the patience to write or read a long detail of such frivolous events as those with which it is filled, or attend to a tedious narrative which would follow through a series of fifty-six years, the caprices and weaknesses of so mean a prince as Henry [III]?' (*HE* I, 338).
3. Cf. H. Blair, 'The general idea of History is a record of truth for the instruction of mankind' (1838: 482), or Hume himself: 'The object of ... history [is] to instruct' (E-ST 240).
4. Hume's practice conformed to this principle: 'This crisis [Reformation] was now visibly approaching in Scotland; and whoever considers merely the transactions resulting from it, will be inclined to throw the blame equally on both parties; whoever enlarges his view and reflects on the situation will remark the *necessary* progress of human affairs and the operation of those principles which are inherent in human nature' (*HE* II, 336; my emphasis).
5. Cf. R. F. Anderson (1966: 23), who takes 'human nature' to be the same as the human mind or the self, and T. E. Jessop (1966: 42), who takes 'human nature' to be 'beliefs, emotions and reactions and the introspectively evident processes'.
6. Cf. Kemp Smith (1964: 55), who writes that Hume uses the term 'principle' 'frequently' in the Newtonian sense of an ultimate.
7. This is missed by G. Vlachos (1955: 115ff., 149, 232), since it is a prominent motif in his account that Hume's thought contains two contradictory methods: the one analytic and psychological, emphasising the uniformity of human nature, the other concrete and sociological, emphasising the variety of human nature. G. Giarrizzo (1962: 18, 29, 77) also sees the tension between uniformity and variety dominating Hume's thought.
8. Cf. T. Reid (1846: 550), who, while distinguishing habit from instinct (the former being 'acquired' rather than 'natural'), neverthe-

less remarks: 'I conceive it [habit] to be part of our constitution, that what we have been accustomed to do, we acquire not only a facility but a proneness to do on like occasions.' Before Hume, Bishop Butler (1907: Bk 1 Ch. 5, paras 15–16) – whose opinion of the *Treatise* the young Hume was eager to solicit – had stressed the capacity of human nature to 'finish' itself through acquiring habits.

9. Thus S. K. Wertz (1975) maintains (correctly) that constancy of human nature for Hume is a 'methodological principle'; and he criticises J. B. Black (1926) for not distinguishing between methodological and substantial uniformity. Similarly, Forbes (1975: 119) maintains (also correctly) that the universal principles of human nature for Hume are abstractions from concrete variety. Nevertheless, Hume did operate with a normatively loaded view of human nature and cannot be entirely excused from parochiality (but see *infra*).

10. See also a passage from the first edition, where Hume writes: 'Like all other species of superstition, it [Catholicism] rouses the vain fears of unhappy mortals . . . sometimes at the expense of morals'. This is included in Forbes's edition (1970: 99), which was quoted in the text in the original version of this essay.

11. Cf. Voltaire, 'Letter to Frederick the Great' 1737 (1969: IV 383): '[Savages] make war from anger and passion: the same crimes are committed everywhere: to eat your enemies is an extra ceremonial'; and Montesquieu (1951: 335): 'For as men have had at all times the same passions, the occasions that produce great changes are different but the causes are always the same' (my translation).

12. This connection between superstition and ignorance is a well-established 'classical' sentiment – see, for example, Plutarch's essay *On Superstition* (2014) or Cicero's *de Divinatione* (1923). (Hume explicitly refers to Cicero in this regard (E-Sui 579).) More recently, in the Deist movement in England it had been a prominent motif to decry superstition; again, the same sources were drawn upon – Toland planned a book, 'Superstition Unmasked', of which the first part would be a commentary on Plutarch's 'admirable treatise' (cf. Redwood (1976: 142); Trenchard wrote *The Natural History of Superstition* (1709) whose title and content suggest to Manuel (1959: 72) that Hume 'probably perused' it.

13. Cf. P. Winch (1971: 78–111). Even modern critics of Winch still outline what can be fairly labelled a formal theory; see, for example, S. Lukes's contribution to the same volume (1971: 194–213 or 1973: 237–40).

14. Kemp Smith, indeed, sees Hume here using 'experience' in a normative

sense (1964: 384). Cf. the argument of Noxon (1973: Pt 5 *passim*), who, though not using these terms, appears to be making a similar point in his interpretation of Hume's 'belief' as 'philosophical', in that it provides an evaluative criterion, and in the close connection he sees between this and Hume's antipathy to religion.

15. Cf. Manuel (1959: 129), who comments that Hume's conclusion (also that of Bayle) was that 'the vulgar and the primitive mind' were the same.'

16. Thus, by implication, J. B. Stewart (1963: 291–2), when he interprets Hume as holding that 'the potentialities of human nature always are the same, but in the beginning they are not realised, so that civilisation may be described as the development of man's attributes'.

17. Thus Giarrizzo, who attributes to Hume the notion of a politico-social organism that has an evolutionary capacity towards *perfettibilita* (1962: 121). However, to Giarrizzo this notion belongs only to Hume's 'liberal phase', for it is a leading theme of Giarrizzo's interpretation that Hume becomes increasingly conservative (and relativist), a movement that is put down to his *paura della perfezione* (1962: 48). Cf. Freidrich Meinecke (1946: 211–12), who sees the *Natural History* opening the door to a developmental history of the human mind, although Hume's psychological theory is held to have prevented him from proceeding further.

10

Lusty Women and Loose Imagination: Hume's Philosophical Anthropology of Chastity

Hume's account of what John Rawls labels the 'circumstances of justice' is well known, not least because of Rawls's (1972: 127) description of it as 'especially perspicuous'. Rawls divides these 'circumstances' (not without some blurring at the edges) into objective and subjective. In the guise of the dynamics of sex and reproduction, it is an aspect of the former, chiefly, that is the subject of this chapter. However, this aspect is not discussed by Rawls and, on the implications of this, Susan Moller Okin (1989: 27), for one, has taken him to task; he merely assumes that the family is just.[1] Okin also, and more forcefully, extends this critique to Hume. She claims that, according to him, the circumstances of family life are such that justice is not the appropriate standard to apply to them. In support of her thesis she quotes a passage from Hume where he remarks that 'between married persons the cement of friendship is by the laws supposed so strong as to abolish all division of possessions and has often, in reality, the force ascribed to it'. However, she then points out this was an idealisation because, in practice, he was justifying 'coverture', the legal fiction whereby married women were non-persons (Okin 1989: 30; quoting *M* 3.7/*SBNM* 185).[2]

My concern here is with sexual regulation, and its necessity in the light of the dynamics of sex and reproduction, in Hume's philosophy. The focus is on his treatment of chastity.[3] I will endeavour in my analysis to uncover some more general anthropological assumptions and their bearing on 'circumstances of justice'.

I

There is one aspect of Hume's account that has not attracted much comment. At the beginning of his discussion, Hume compares the situation of humans to that of animals:

> Of all the animals . . . there is none towards whom nature seems at first
> sight to have exercis'd more cruelty than towards man, in the number-
> less wants and necessities with which she has loaded him and in the
> slender means which she affords to the relieving of these necessities. In
> other creatures these two particulars generally compensate each other.
> (T 3–2–2.2/SBNT 484–5)

He then elaborates on this 'compensation' with references to lions,
sheep and oxen and, in contrast, he reaffirms that an individual
human experiences 'in its greatest perfection' an 'unnatural conjunction of infirmity and necessity' (T 3–2–2.2/SBNT 485). To deal
with this conjunction, humans need society. The root of this need
('the first and original principle of human society') is 'the natural
appetite between the sexes' (T 3–2–2.4/SBNT 486). Clearly, there
is nothing uniquely human about the possession of this 'appetite'
but, for Hume, in implicit contrast to the natural facts about
sheep and other animals, the 'circumstances of human nature', in
particular the selfishness in 'our natural temper', make its operation insufficient. This is compounded by the incommodiousness of
'outward circumstances', with the consequence that human social/
group life is naturally unstable. Now follows the oft-told Humean
story whereby the only remedy is an artificially or conventionally
induced stability, with justice given the pivotal role.

If, instead of telling the unfolding tale, we pause to turn back
the pages, then it seems that a crucial step is the place allotted
to sex in the human psychical economy. The differing modes of
(non-human) animal social life (say, the pride of lions or the flock
of sheep) are able to accommodate the sexual appetite as part of
the same naturally regulated system. Rams may well seasonally
compete for ewes but that competition remains an integral part
of the natural regulation. The impact of sex on humans is specifically distinct; it has consequences that are absent in other animals.
It is true that this point does not loom large in Hume's ongoing
argument, but it does resurface in the shape of a discussion of
chastity. While this discussion has the appearance of a tidying-up
afterthought, it can be seen to have a significant bearing on the
initial question of why humans have to develop conventions.

Given that Hume in his *Treatise* is explicit that the virtues of
modesty and chastity are instances of his more general argument
(T 3–2–12.1/SBNT 570), we need to analyse his discussion in some
detail. Beyond any narrow exegetical worth that such an analysis

might possess, Hume's discussion bears careful scrutiny because, more broadly, it contains (albeit suggestively, not demonstratively) an intimation of why the conventional regulation of sexual relations is both a universal in human experience and one that exhibits variety. In doing this it also signals that these relations, and their consequences, are properly a constituent of the 'background conditions' that establish the circumstances of justice.

II

Hume briefly discusses chastity, which, along with modesty, is explicitly labelled a female virtue, in both the *Treatise* and *The Principles of Morals*. He declares it obvious that 'exterior modesty' in the dress and behaviour of the 'fair sex' (as he typically dubs women) has no 'foundation in nature'. Instead, these virtues are said to arise 'from education, from voluntary conventions of men and from the interest of society' (*T* 3–2–12.2/*SBNT* 570), while in *Morals* their source is put down more simply to utility (*M* 4/5/ *SBNM* 207).

Natural Foundations

What is striking is that in both these texts, after shifting the source of these virtues from nature to convention, Hume does not take this to mean that all recourse to nature is misplaced. On the contrary, he immediately seeks a naturalistic foundation to account for their perceived utility (cf. Baier 1988: 769f.).

Nonetheless, the source of this foundation still needs to be carefully identified. As we have just seen, Hume does *not* evoke any pertinent natural disposition possessed by women. Even Mandeville, whose account is close to Hume's in many respects,[4] refers to women as 'more or less in their own Nature Chaste'.[5] While, as befits his medical background, Mandeville's comments were physiologically based, Hume's account is a direct dismissal of the 'naturalism' most typical of his contemporaries, that is, of some divine or deistic underpinning of the natural order of things. For example, in *Emile*, Rousseau declares that God has given women modesty (*la pudeur*) (1863: II, 150/1991: 359). Here the 'natural' is already saturated with moral significance and the appropriate human response is to act accordingly. To run counter to this predesignated response is 'unnatural'. Conventions are thus to be judged by their compliance to the providential scheme. Fidelity is so 'natural' that, for women, it is a duty that is also their propensity or inclination (*le penchant*) (1864a: II, 174/1991: 389).[6]

Hume's own identification of the natural foundations to the convention of chastity has two components. First, 'both sexes naturally' have a concern 'for their offspring'[7] and, second, this concern is bound up with the natural fact of the 'length and feebleness of human infancy' (*T* 3–2–12.3/*SBNT* 570). These two presuppose a third, namely, as we have already noted, that there is 'natural appetite betwixt the sexes' (*T* 3–2–2.4/*SBNT* 486), a 'passion evidently implanted in human nature' (*T* 3–2–1.12/*SBNT* 481).

These three appear uncontentious, although the reference to 'both sexes' in the first component is worth noting. That fathers love their children naturally is indeed an important ingredient in Hume's account but, as we shall see, the critical issue is the problematic character of the possessive 'their' as the object of the love. The intricacy and value of Hume's account of sexual conventions in general, and of chastity in particular, can be seen to lie in the relations between these three components.

Starting with the first, the 'natural concern' or 'affection' of parent towards child (*T* 3–2–2.4/*SBNT* 486; cf. E-DM 85) is cited by Hume in his essay 'Of the Original Contract' as an example of moral duty, to the performance of which 'men [sic] are impelled by a natural instinct or immediate propensity' (E-OC 479). They are not, and this is Hume's point here, impelled by any sense of the good social consequences that flow from 'such humane instincts'. That we do indeed label the love of children 'virtuous' is the effect of reflection on these consequences, but the affection itself is not prompted by any opinion that it is the morally right thing to do. In this same essay Hume identifies 'fidelity' as a different sort of moral duty. Like 'justice' and 'allegiance', fidelity is a duty the performance of which is consequent to 'reflection and experience'. These duties check or 'restrain' 'original inclination(s)' because it has been learnt that unless these are reined in the 'total dissolution of society . . . must ensue' (E-OC 480).

Since chastity is defined as 'fidelity to the marriage bed' (*M* 4.5/ *SBNM* 207), then it belongs to the second category of duties: it is an instance of what in the *Treatise* Hume calls 'artificial virtues'.[8] This means that it is the (conventional) product of 'reflection and experience' and serves to restrain (natural) 'original inclinations'. This restraint is needed because it must be presumed that, if left unchecked, sexual appetite will threaten to dissolve social life.

Sex, it now seems, is a two-edged factor in human life. On the one hand, we recall that Hume had declared that the 'first and original principle of human society' is the natural sexual appetite between the sexes. The supporting reason for this declaration was that this appetite 'unites them together'. By 'unites' here he means more than physical congress, because he adds 'and preserves their union' (T 3–2–2.4/SBNT 486). On the other hand, as we have just observed, sex is presumed to threaten the social bond. This Janus-like duality is perhaps a case of the 'contrariety of passions' (T 3–2–2.7/SBNT 487) and can be exemplified by the distinction between love and lust, in that the former selflessly bonds while the latter selfishly threatens. Hume himself implicitly makes that distinction.

In Book II of the *Treatise*, in seeking to identify the sentiment of love, Hume placed it in 'a just medium' between the 'appetite to generation' and 'kindness and esteem'. Nonetheless, this placement means explicitly that at 'one extreme' are those who are 'inflam'd with lust' and who feel a kindness that is only 'momentary' (T 2–2–11.4/SBNT 395). Hume has thus recognised the distinction between a temporary (selfish) act of copulation and an enduring emotional attachment. In the light of this recognition, he should have said more accurately in Book III that it is 'love' that preserves the union (a statement he does make in a later essay) (E-AS 131). Of course, whatever it is that preserves it obtains support (it is augmented by a 'new tye' (T 3–2–2.4/SBNT 486)) from parental 'concern for their common offspring', that is, the first component in the three natural foundations. But it is precisely here that the need for conventional restraint re-emerges. Lust, as Book II allowed, is indeed separate from love, and children, though the natural object of the latter, are also a natural product of the former. There is nothing in the 'nature' of human life to ensure that these two potentially distinct natural facts coincide; it is another case of 'unnatural conjunction'. As we saw, it is that conjunction which generically produces the need for conventions. It is in that context, as we shall see, that Hume locates chastity and, while he may indeed unwarrantedly concentrate on that particular sexual convention, the need for particular conventions in this area at all has been identified by this account.

To pursue this further, we need to return to the presumption that unregulated sex is a threat to social life. What is it about sex (lust) that requires it to be restrained? The crux of the answer is that humans like it a lot. It is a basic tenet of the Humean 'science of man' that humans will seek pleasure and will always be tempted to attain it. In his chapter on chastity Hume is unequivocal. 'Nature', he says, 'has inspire'd ... a propensity' to the pleasures of sex. Moreover, this is 'strong' because ''tis absolutely necessary in the end to comply with for the support of the species' (*T* 3–2–12.6/ *SBNT* 572). This compliance is not irksome. The 'appetite of generation', when not overused, is 'pleasant' and 'has a strong connexion with all the agreeable emotions' (*T* 2–2–11.2/*SBNT* 394).[9] Since humans always seek pleasure, then, in order for human society to subsist, these temptations need to be 'policed' – hence the necessity for the artifices of justice and the rest. In this way chastity is to be understood as a convention to limit the outlets of sexual pleasure; it does not extirpate the pleasure.

This raises the next question: how is the restraint to be effected or how is this pleasure to be policed? Hume's short answer to this question is: by education. However, the full force of that answer can be best appreciated after answering a further question: who is to be restrained? Since the sexual appetite is common to both sexes, they both require restraint. Hume acknowledges the point but he holds (or perhaps finds) that the restraint is more rigorously imposed upon women than upon men. Hume accepts or assumes a 'double standard'. In the *Treatise* he openly states that chastity (and modesty) are duties 'which belong to the fair sex' (*T* 3–2–12.1/*SBNT* 570), although in *Morals* he acknowledges that the 'laws of chastity' (*M* 4, 6/*SBNM* 207) apply to both sexes, albeit more strictly to women. His supporting argument, however, is more than prejudice (though it is also that) and it throws more than incidental light on sexual regulation in general.

The Double Standard

There are (at least) two dimensions to Hume's account of the double standard.[10] He maintains that a woman's standing is so intimately bound up with her chaste fidelity that any deviation results in irreparable damage to her character. There are seemingly no redemptive conventions open to her. This is not an idiosyncratic observation: Mandeville stresses it, while the self-inflicted fate of Richardson's Clarissa or Laclos' Mme de Tourvel bear further eloquent fictional witness to the structure and force of the contemporary conventions. Indeed, the finality of the loss of this virtue appears to be a distinguishing characteristic. By contrast, Hume affirms, in line with tradition, that the quintessential male (*vir, aner/ andra*) virtue of courage (*virtus, andrei*) is capable of reinstating the good character of a man who was previously a coward (M 6, 14/*SBNM* 239). In this way this set of social conventions privileges the male; the 'cowardly warrior', unlike the 'fallen woman', may be conventionally redeemed.

The second, and more significant, dimension of Hume's account of the double standard lies in his claim that infidelity is 'much more pernicious in women than men' (M 4, 6/*SBNM* 207). Lusty women apparently pose more of a threat to the social fabric than do lusty men, with the consequence that in the male case the 'social interest' in restraint is weaker, so therefore the obligation is weaker. Why? There seem to be two reasons. First, men do not apply the same restraint on themselves because they assume 'modesty and decency have a regard to generation' (*T* 3–2–12.7/ *SBNT* 573) and that 'regard' applies with less force in their case. As Hume puts it, the 'trivial and anatomical observation' that 'the principle of generation goes from the man to the woman' means that there is no possibility of error in the case of the latter: a woman, that is, always knows she is pregnant, a mother-to-be, but a man cannot be as sure that he is the father-to-be (*T* 3–2–12.3, 3–2–12.7/*SBNT* 571, 573). Though 'trivial', this difference has far-reaching consequences.[11]

This epistemological divide between male and female[12] is only decisive because of two natural facts: in contrast to the way that bleeding follows a cut, birth does not immediately follow fertilisation, and fertilisation does not necessarily follow from each act of copulation. It is the quality of sheer ineluctability of these two facts, of the inescapability of the way the world just happens to be, that makes precise paternity naturally uncertain. Certainty can, however, be contrived artificially. Chastity (for Hume) is that artifice and it serves to, or helps to, close the epistemological divide.

Given that love of one's children is a fatherly (*T* 3–2–2.5; 3–2–5.6/*SBNT* 487, 518) as well as a motherly trait, female chastity makes it more certain, from the man's point of view, that he is loving his own children. This certitude can, however, never be absolute. The inescapability of the two natural facts mentioned above means that the male may indeed have been cuckolded, so that he is loving a child that shares none of his genetic history. For the woman's part, she, too, if she has broken the 'laws of chastity', may be uncertain who the father of her child is but she is, nonetheless, secure in the knowledge that her genetic history is present. It does not follow, though, that a mother's love is necessarily greater than a father's. Recall that on Hume's account parental concern or love is 'natural', that is, the belief that one is the father does not generate an artificial sentiment. Chastity is not a sentiment; it is an artifice. This broaches the second reason why males are less restrained than females.

Hume baldly states that 'those who have an interest in the fidelity of women, naturally disapprove of their infidelity and all the approaches to it' (T 3–2–12.7/$SBNT$ 572). The possessors of this 'interest' are unspecified but are presumably males (but see later). In *Morals* male complicity seems clear when Hume remarks that 'a female has so many opportunities of secretly indulging these [sexual] appetites that nothing can give *us* security but her absolute modesty and reserve' (M 6, 14/$SBNM$ 239; my emphasis).[13] Aside from any complicity, two issues are raised by this remark. First, there exist 'opportunities' in the first place only because women have in some cultures a degree of freedom. In other cultures the 'end' of chastity is met by conventions that restrict these opportunities, such as harems guarded by eunuchs, infibulation and domestic confinement or claustration. Second, regardless of the particular convention, why should such 'security' be so important? That is, we have seen how chastity might help close the epistemological divide but not why the divide itself should be thought to matter; why, in other words, it is a concern of males that a particular female is bearing in her womb an egg fertilised by his sperm. Conceivably it could be that if men know they will, as a natural fact about themselves as human, love a child, and want consequently to commit resources to nurture it, in the belief that (biologically) it is theirs, then they will want to be secure in this belief. While 'love' is genuine (natural), they might also know enough to know that if they do not believe the child is theirs – if their affection is 'directed to a wrong object' (T 3–2–12.3/$SBNT$ 570) – then they may not love it. (Wicked step-parents are a staple of fiction and a phenomenon that has some support in fact.[14]) There is thus an 'interest' in secure beliefs.

We can attribute some contextual plausibility to this if we see it in the light of contemporary patriarchal assumptions. From that perspective, the most obvious sense of 'security' in which males have an interest would be the preservation and transmission of property (resources). Here lies the source of the presumed greater threat posed by 'lusty' women. The male in a patriarchal society (*T* 2–1–9.13/*SBNT* 308; *DP* II, 27/12) is presumed to desire a clear line of succession, since bastards bring confusion (Vogel 1991: 241). To that extent Hume follows the jurisprudential tradition[15] and much of what he says about property is couched in jurisprudential language.[16] However, he is no mere follower and it is one of the key features of his own account of property that it (as opposed to 'possession') is a product of the rules of justice. In particular, and here is the tie-in, property rules function to stabilise or secure the belief that an object is 'mine' (*T* 3–2–2.9/*SBNT* 489).

We shall pick up a further aspect of this shortly, but, as we noted, males are not entirely exempt from restraint. The 'double standard', as the version in *Morals* acknowledges, pertains to the differential degree of restraint, not to its presence and absence. It is in the 'interest of civil society' that (lusty) males should be restrained, that they should not have 'an *entire* liberty of indulging their appetite in venereal enjoyment' (*T* 3–2–12.9/*SBNT* 573; Hume's emphasis). As we will see, the most plausible source of this 'interest' is the second component in Hume's natural foundation, the fact of the prolonged dependency of the human infant.

Education

We can now return to our postponed question: how chastity restrains. As an artificial virtue it is the product of 'reflection and experience'. It is a pervasive feature of Hume's social theory that he gives a vital role to custom and habit, and it is their operation that best explains what Hume means by 'reflection and experience'.

In the context of giving an experiential account of how rulers emerged, he remarks that 'habit soon consolidates what *other* principles of human nature had imperfectly founded and men once accustomed to obedience never think of departing from that path in which they and their ancestors have constantly trod' (E-OC 39; my emphasis). Given, from this, both the solidity and efficacy of habit in shaping human behaviour and values, it is no surprise to find that education, broadly defined, or what today we might call socialisation, afforded a critical role. Without specifying its content, in the chapter on chastity in the *Treatise*, Hume announces that 'education takes possession of the ductile minds of the fair sex in their infancy' (*T* 3–2–12.7/*SBNT* 572). As he says of the related case of 'sentiments of honour', by taking root in 'tender minds' they 'acquire such firmness and solidity that they may fall little short of those principles which are most essential to our natures and the most deeply radicated in our internal constitution' (*T* 3–2–2.26/*SBNT* 501).[17] It is the 'tenderness' or 'ductility' of the infant mind that makes 'custom and education' so powerful, as they inculcate 'principles of probity' and 'observance of those rules by which society is maintain'd as worthy and honourable' (*T* 3–2–2.26/*SBNT* 500).

These rules operate through 'habit and experience' (*T* 1–3–13.8/ *SBNT* 147) and, given the power of habit, they are capable of not merely 'influencing' but also 'restraining' such 'common principles of human nature' as 'avidity and partiality' (*T* 3–2–6.9/*SBNT* 532). This last phrase re-invokes the 'circumstances of justice'. 'Partiality' reflects both the objective and subjective aspects. Objectively, sexual relations (broadly speaking) are competitive and possessive[18] and, subjectively, they reflect a bias such that some particular person (partner/child) is viewed preferentially; this is 'simply', as Rawls puts it, 'part of man's natural situation'.[19] 'Avidity' reinforces this. It reasonably describes the natural/ pleasurable sexual appetites that are part of the 'general course of nature' such that 'two young savages of different sexes will copulate' (*T* 2–3–1.8/*SBNT* 402). While this may indeed improve ('civilised' young men and women are more likely to be restrained than 'savages'),[20] the avidity will, as a 'course of nature', ever remain, as will the need for some restraint.

For Hume, chastity is the restraint; it serves to regulate (for women especially) the outlets for sexual pleasure. But, as we have also seen, in their case, adherence to these rules is the product of deep socialisation. The consequence is that chastity is so much part of a woman's 'make-up', is so 'deeply radicated', that women will look upon extra- or premarital sex as conduct unbecoming a lady. They will possess a 'preceding backwardness or dread . . . a repugnance to all expressions, and postures and liberties, that have an immediate relation to that [sexual] enjoyment' (*T* 3–2–12.5/ *SBNT* 572).

They will know (will have internalised as 'second nature') the social consequences of the 'smallest failure' from fidelity. They know they will become 'cheap and vulgar', lose 'rank' and be 'exposed to every insult'; they know, in short, that their 'character' will be 'blast[ed]' (M 6.14/SBNM 123) since, once they are associated with lack of virtue, 'society' will see to it (remember there are no redemptive conventions) that this stain will be constantly conjoined to their name (the 'punishment of bad fame or reputation . . . has a mighty influence on the human mind' (T 3–2–12.4/SBNT 571)). Of course, necessarily this is imperfect. Not only is the very need for the artifice premised on the presence of the avid natural pleasure of sexual enjoyment, so it is ever prone to erupt, but also the very existence of a double standard implies that there are some women who are 'available' – for without their existence, how can there even exist the 'debauch'd' bachelors to whom Hume refers (T 3–2–12.7/SBNT 572)?

These bachelors are, nonetheless, said by Hume to be shocked by lewdness in women. This, for him, is testament to the fact that all women are expected to be modest. He realises, however, that this is problematic for his account, because its focus on rules surrounding procreation appears to leave post-menopausal ('post-lusty?') women out of the reckoning. While it is for him a theoretical possibility that such women might be exempted from the conventional constraints of chastity, the practice, as gleaned from 'cautious observation' (T Intro 10/SBNT xix), tells otherwise. Hume formally explains this by pulling out of the hat another finding from his science of man. The general rule of fidelity is, he affirms, like other such rules, 'apt' to be extended 'beyond those principles from which it first arose' (T 3–2–12.7/SBNT/M 4.7, 207). However, in effect, this is merely a restatement of the role of habit/education. It is because women have been socialised since infancy into the character-defining virtuousness of chastity and modesty that these norms cannot be psychologically sloughed off once the menopause is reached.

While applied to women, the operant assumption in this entire argument is not sex-specific – *all* children are ductile. Accordingly, it was open to Hume to hold that boys could be so inculcated with a principle of honour (see *Treatise*, n17 quoted above) such that, in manhood, cuckoldry or marital infidelity would not cross their minds. Moreover, since Hume does accept the power of 'moral causes' to render 'a peculiar set of manners habitual' (E-NC 198), then, in the presence of appropriate socialisation, there are grounds for an individual male to generalise his own fidelity to his fellows, thus rendering his wife 'safe' when out of his sight. Charitably, Hume's failure to address this possibility might be put down to his 'experimentalism'; the evidence from 'men's behaviour in company, in affairs and in their pleasures' (*T* Intro 10/ *SBNT* xix) is that this possibility has never been actualised.

The Human Predicament

Whether the laws of chastity ought to apply equally to both sexes or not, what these laws indicate is the perceived universal need for sexual regulation in human cultures; as Rom Harré says categorically, 'there are no promiscuous systems'.[21] If fidelity were 'natural', that is, part of the 'compensatory' regime enjoyed by other animals (*T* 3-2-2.2/*SBNT* 485), there would be no call for regulation in the first place. This universal need is why, indeed, sex and reproduction are properly components of the circumstances of justice. Underlying this is a philosophical anthropology. A clue to this is found initially in the difference between humans and other animals. The 'other' is important here. Hume includes a discussion of animals at several points in his writings and the general thrust throughout these discussions is an assimilation of human and animal behaviour and processes.[22] Of course, there are limits to this assimilation; there are differences. Hume identifies two general areas of difference: animals have less imagination (*T* 2-2-12.3, 8/*SBNT* 397, 398) and inferior reasoning abilities (*T* 3-3-4.5/*SBNT* 610; *U* 9, 5/*SBNU* 106; E-PD 183).

In both cases the difference is of degree, not kind. Hume reinforces this point in the second case by pointing out that, by the same token, some men are more prudent and sagacious than others. That said, this general human superiority is most decisively manifest in the fact that 'all the advantages of art are owing to human reason' (*T* 3-3-4.5/*SBNT* 610). Animals do not possess these advantages; they do not establish conventions or artifices.[23] (Animals can no more act justly, keep promises or own property than they can be chaste.) This is because they do not need to; their needs and the means of satisfying them are, as noted above, in compensatory balance. Although Hume refers here only to food, we can reasonably include procreation as one of these needs.

In his essay 'Of Polygamy and Divorces', he remarks that 'among the inferior creatures, nature herself, being the supreme legislator, prescribes all the laws which regulate their marriages', but in humans nature has not 'so exactly regulated every article' of the marriage contract (E-PD 183). This seemingly follows from humans' being 'endowed with reason' so that they may adjust their marital arrangements according to prudence and circumstances. These adjustments take the form of municipal laws that, like all conventions or artifices, restrain natural liberty. Given that scope, and consequent upon the inexactness of nature's regulation, these laws may differ from place to place (such that polygamy may be allowed), although all are 'equally conformable to the principles of nature' (E-PD 183).[24]

Not being provided by nature with ready-made solutions, humans have had to come up with their own answers in order to make social life possible (T 3–2–6.1/SBNT 526). While there is no 'natural law' that lays down a normative pattern to guide human intercourse authoritatively, nature does, in the form of human passions, provide the raw material out of which humans construct (diversely) the solution to their predicament. The crux of this construction is the establishment of social cooperation by means of 'art' or conventions.

Hume's account of how this construction takes place is schematic and theoretically undernourished. His argument appears to be that humans establish the 'pattern' of restraining their passions (their original inclinations) to guide their intercourse by artfully creating conventions that are themselves the invention of their passions (T 3–2–2.9, 3–2–6.1/SBNT 489, 526). It is a homeopathic remedy: passion restrains passion. Hence the artifice of property establishes the stability of possession by restraining 'the heedless and impetuous movement' (T 3.2.2.9/SBNT 489) of the passion to acquire goods for ourselves (our family and friends) but is, itself, the 'alteration' of the 'direction' of that passion. Experience makes it 'evident' that the 'passion is much better satisfy'd by its restraint than by its liberty' (T 3–2–2.13/SBNT 492).

How does this apply in the case of chastity? Annette Baier doubts its applicability[25] but, with some licence, two answers seem possible. The first would take the homeopathic process broadly so as to incorporate passions generally rather than confine its operation narrowly, or 'internally', to just the one passion. On these grounds it is the passions involved in the first and third of the natural foundations that can be invoked. It is the 'passions of lust' (T 3–2–2.5/SBNT 486) that need restraining and it is the related, though separate, passion of natural affection for children that seemingly provides the motive to restrain.[26] If promiscuous venery were the order of the day, the randomly produced offspring would not be guaranteed survival, let alone socialisation. While it takes very little 'experience' to bring home the message that this is undesirable, the crucial underpinning is the fact that offspring are not objects of indifference, but naturally objects of love. It is this passion that prompts the regulation of sex/promiscuity. And, due to their anatomical sexual differences, Hume believes the centrepiece of this regulation is the imposition upon women of the artificial duty of chastity.

The second possible answer relies on Hume's own later, more general, account. In discussing the origin of government, Hume declares it to be a 'quality of human nature' to prefer the contiguous to the remote (T 3–2–7.4/SBNT 535). This is a 'dangerous' quality because it makes humans prefer trivial 'present advantage' to the more distant maintenance of justice. However, this dangerous 'infirmity of human nature becomes a remedy to itself' (T 3–2–7.5/SBNT 536) (that is, homeopathically) as humans create the artificial institution of magistracy. By the means of this artifice, the observance of justice is made the 'immediate interest' of a few who 'inforce the dictates of equity thro' the whole society' (T 3–2–7.6/SBNT 537). This 'dangerous quality' reappears in Hume's discussion of chastity. Women, like 'all human creatures', though they especially, are 'apt to overlook remote motives in favour of any present temptation'. We have already seen how the pleasures of sex make this temptation 'the strongest imaginable' (T 3–2–12.5/SBNT 571). Chastity is the invented remedy, which, supposedly through the artifice of education, gives women 'what they really (that is, remotely) want', namely, the pleasures of sex and a good name. Just as Hume blandly identifies the few who are magistrates with those 'satisfied with their present condition' so that they have 'no interest' in injustice, so he blandly assumes the double standard, so that the immediate enjoyment of males is less in need of artificial restraint than that of females.

All conventions or artifices are inventions and it is thus no mere incidental attribute that mankind is an 'inventive species' (T 3–2–1.19/SBNT 484). For Hume, following an eighteenth-century commonplace, invention is an act of the imagination,[27] the second area where humans are held to differ by degree from animals. In the present context, the power of the imagination (humans 'are mightily govern'd' by it (T 3–2–7.2/SBNT 534) gives an important twist.

The lack of natural regulation of sex in humans, when compared to other animals, is exacerbated by their greater reflective powers and imaginative capacity. Hume remarks that 'reflecting' on sex 'suffices to excite the appetite' (*T* 2–2–11.6/*SBNT* 396). The 'very thought of you' can be sexually arousing and 'you', thanks to the imagination, may be anybody. The artificial virtue of chastity is thus a way of policing or regulating 'acting on the thought' promiscuously. The regulation attempts to ensure that it is an authorised 'somebody' and not just 'anybody' who is the sex object. Just as possession needs affixing to an owner through the conventions of justice so that it becomes his 'property', so a particular woman needs affixing through convention to a particular man so that she becomes his wife and any offspring theirs. Although this is a further underwriting of the double standard, women, too, are imaginative creatures (Mandeville (1973: 44) was explicit on that point). Lusty women we might presume, with Hume, to be prone (like Emma Bovary?) to let their imaginations run away with them.

We can now appreciate that Hume's discussion of chastity is not some egregious component in his social philosophy but of a piece with his treatment of justice, obligation and other conventions, since, like them, it acts as an antisolvent, a socially cohesive agent. And in so doing, equally like them, it imposes a stability and predictability that is naturally absent from human affairs. In its turn this stability makes entering into future commitments viable, which redounds to the overall benefit of civil society.[28]

This 'benefit' is clearly in the interest of the man, because he can imagine that any child is not his but contains the genetic history of another male. Here a woman does, of course, differ; she knows the child is hers. This male imaginative 'looseness' needs stabilising. Males can be more certain of the actuality of their paternity if 'society'[29] instils in the ductile minds of girls the virtue of chastity. The more a woman's sexual second nature overlays her first, the more men will be assured of their paternity. Indeed, it might be interpolated that this is likely to be a more efficient – while of course necessarily imperfect – mechanism than claustration or eunuch-guarded seraglios. This assurance is, for Hume, straightforwardly in the male interest. Men need to be confident that the 'fatigue and expences' they undergo to support mother and child are for the sake of 'their own' and not another's (*T* 3–2–2.5/ *SBNT* 487). This 'confidence' is, of course, another expression of the background conditions that give rise to the circumstances of justice – as Rawls (1972: 126) puts it, 'men [sic] are not indifferent' to the distribution of collaborative benefits.

That males do supply that support is in the interest of the mother and child and in this way civil society generally benefits (an argument still made, of course). The second of the three natural foundations now comes into play. The frailty and length of human infancy 'requires the combination of parents for the subsistence of the young' (M 4, 5/SBNM 206). This combination is also necessary precisely because humans are cultural animals. Male and female (husband and wife) are needed 'for the education of the young' and this must be of a 'considerable duration' (T 3–2–12.3/SBNT 570). A vital element of this education, the work of 'every parent' (T 3–2–2.14, 3–2–2.26, 3–2–6.11/SBNT 493, 500, 534), will be to instil the artificial virtue of justice and, as we have seen, to impress more particularly the virtue of chastity on their daughters.

III

Hume's account of chastity and its implicit philosophical anthropology exemplifies, in outline, a particular way of conceptualising the relation between the natural facts of sexual reproduction and the possible human responses to those data of experience. In contrast to the then-dominant approach that holds that chastity comes directly from following some Providential ordering, Hume's naturalism dispenses with this metaphysical baggage.

Shorn of that teleological load, Hume's account is closer to the naturalism of contemporary biology.[30] This proximity can be discerned in the way that his naturalism serves to anchor human sexual conventions. The particular evolutionary niche occupied by humans is such that they experience, in Hume's formulation, an 'unnatural conjunction'. The consequence of this is that they have to establish conventions in order to achieve the orderly group life that in other group-living animals is achieved through nature alone. Sex is a major case in point. In a specifically distinctive way, it is naturally both a bond (a source of cooperation) and a solvent (a matter of competition).

In Rawlsian terms, that humans cooperate but also compete is the hallmark of the circumstances of justice. Hume's philosophical anthropology serves to locate 'sex' among those 'circumstances'. What makes his account so 'perspicuous' is that it establishes that the resolution of this duality is not provided immediately by nature itself, but mediately by humans themselves, by convention. Moreover, it establishes that this resolution is at once universal and diverse. Sex is always regulated but, because humans are naturally inventive and imaginative creatures, these regulations (the mediated resolutions that they contrive) are also various. While, therefore, Hume's own anchorage is confined to an articulation of the rationale of chastity, it is, in principle, extendable to the range of conventional regulations of sex.

What this indicates is that, given that humans are group animals, sexual regulation is going to be an integral aspect of the circumstances of justice. Human society, though natural, is not naturally cohesive like that of other group-livers. Here is a vindication, if it were needed, of the argument that the 'sexual is the political'. 'Politics', no matter how more precisely identified or defined, presupposes that some form of 'regulation' is required in order for humans to sustain their natural existence in groups. And a necessary ingredient in that regulation is a response to the natural facts of reproduction and nurturance. This characterises all human societies but, as imaginative creatures, humans have dealt, and still deal, with the causes and consequences of these facts in a variety of ways. There is no choice but to frame conventions: in classical terms, humans are jointly creatures of *phusis* and *nomos*.

Postscript

I was prompted to write this essay in 2003 by a separate exercise in what I called 'the philosophical anthropology of politics' (see Berry 2000a). In that particular version of the enterprise I used Hume's notion of 'convention' as one of my motifs and, since I was interested more generally in the possible links between sexual regulation and the establishment of political authority, Hume and chastity became a topic in its own right and this chapter is the result – some of the references reveal its intellectual provenance. I was, accordingly, not led into this discussion by the various writings of Annette Baier, though it was clearly her work that – in conjunction with some broader feminist concerns – put the topic on the agenda. It has to be said that it still remains an issue of minor interest to Hume scholars.

Notes

1. Compare G. A. Cohen (2000: Ch. 9), who uses the case of familial relations to deliver a more radical critique of Rawls.

2. Hume's position is rather less straightforward than Okin allows; he does hold that justice pertains to intra-familial relations (T 3–2–2.14, 3–2–2.26/*SBNT* 493, 500; M 3, 16/*SBNM* 190).

3. While Brian Barry (1989: 153n) thinks the extension of Hume's argument about justice, beyond the narrow confines of property rules, would require 'substantial modification' before it would apply to chastity, my focus is the 'wider' case. I do, however, indicate how Hume's argument accommodates both virtues within its scope.

4. See Yeazell (1991: 20), who thinks Hume had Mandeville in mind when he declared that it was obvious there was no natural foundation in the fair sex.

5. Mandeville (1973: 42). Despite this, Mandeville also refers, in a strikingly Humean phrase, to 'artificial Chastity' (ibid.). In the *Fable of the Bees* (1988: I, p. 72) he stressed that the difference between male and female modesty was 'altogether owing to early Instruction'. Hume, of course, cited Mandeville as one who had begun to put the science of man on a new footing (see T Intro/*SBNT* xvii, n1). He does, however, dissent from Mandeville's view that there is no sense of virtue in mankind, that it is solely the 'artifice of politicians' (T 3–2–2.25/*SBNT* 500; 3–3–1.11/*SBNT* 574).

6. See also J.-J. Rousseau in *Lettre à M d'Alembert*: '*toute femme sans pudeur est coupable et dépravée, parce qu'elle foule aux pieds un sentiment naturel à son sexe*'. (1858: I, 235/Bloom 1960: 85). If Rousseau's typicality can be questioned, the remarks of Thomas Reid can serve to represent that here Rousseau echoes the mainstream. Reid (1990: 220) stated, 'Women are under a strong natural Obligation to chastity . . . [and] Nature has aided this Obligation to Chastity in the fair Sex by a Sense of Honour, a Natural Modesty and consciousness of Worth.'

7. See T 2–2–4.2/*SBNT* 352, 'love of parents to their children' is the 'strongest tie the mind is capable of'. Also to 'kill one's own child is shocking to nature' (E-PAN 400).

8. See Baier (1979: 11), who argues that 'chastity' is not all square with 'fidelity' as an artificial virtue. While Baier astutely stresses the atypicality of chastity, it must not be regarded as *sui generis* but, as I hope to show, is best regarded in the more general context of the need of humans to regulate their sexual relations. See also Levey (1998).

9. See also Hume (*DP* I, 20/6): 'A virgin on her bridal night goes to bed full of fear and apprehensions though she expects nothing but pleasure'. There is never any question in Hume that women might not enjoy sex.

10. See, for example, Burns (1976) and Lacoste, where the latter agrees with the former that the 'Humean female' is an expression of male chauvinism (1976: 425). Battersby (1981) gives a good analysis of Hume's defence of the double standard. More recent scholarship has sought a 'feminist recuperation' – see Jacobson (ed.) (2000). As Jacobson says in her introduction, Baier's work has been particularly influential (the book reprints her 1993 essay (see n. 12 below)); Nancy Hirschman employs the phrase 'feminist recuperation' in her contribution (2000: 175).

11. See O'Brien (1981) for a thoughtful feminist exploration.

12. Baier (1989: 38) refers to the 'male epistemological predicament' in this context. She makes much of 'chastity' rather than 'obedience' as the artificial female virtue – see Baier (1988: 774). Indeed, Baier (1989: 45) is able to detect in Hume 'radical feminist ideals' and a 'radically anti-patriarchal stand' (Baier 1993: 47).

13. This is not the only place where Hume's language betrays a male perspective; see also for example *T* 2–2–11.4/*SBNT* 395, where 'one' who is 'inflamed with lust . . . fancies her more beautiful'.

14. See the literature cited in Daly and Wilson (1992). Hrdy (1999: Ch. 10) puts the phenomenon into a wider context. Hume for his own part juxtaposes 'the care of a step-mother' to 'the fond attention and concern of a parent' (E-PD 188).

15. Baier (1989: 52), in making her point that Hume disavows 'obedience' as the female virtue, quotes both Grotius (2002: I-v-8) and Pufendorf (1991: II-2/121) for the avowal.

16. For a good account of Hume's relationship to natural jurisprudence, see Buckle (1991).

17. See also *T* 3–2–2.4/*SBNT* 486, 'custom and habit operating on the tender minds of the children makes them sensible of the advantages which they may reap from society, as well as fashions them by degrees for it, by rubbing off those rough corners and untoward affections, which prevent their coalition'. Also *T* 1–3–9.17/*SBNT* 116, 'All those opinions and notions of things, to which we have been accustom'd from our infancy, take such deep root, that 'tis impossible for us, by all the powers of reason and experience, to eradicate them.'

18. This is now a staple of evolutionary psychology, according to which

the sexes follow different 'investment strategies'; males are presumed to compete to maximise (quantitatively) the diffusion of their genes and women to maximise (qualitatively) the survival of their genes in their children. There is no need to subscribe to this particular doctrine (which is, of course, far more sophisticated than this) to recognise both the power and disruptiveness of sexual passion.

19. Rawls (1972: 127). It is not obvious why this 'natural situation' is not an 'objective' circumstance.

20. One mark of 'civilisation' is the treatment of women. In 'barbarous nations' men exhibit their superiority by 'reducing their females to the most abject slavery; by confining them, by beating them, by selling them, by killing them' (E-AS 133; see also *M* 3, 19/*SBNM* 191). In a 'polished age' the sexes 'meet in an easy and sociable manner' (E-RA 271). This account was echoed by many of Hume's compatriots, who developed more systematically the implicit 'historicisation' of sexual conventions here implied. See especially John Millar (*OR*, Ch. 1). For a discussion of Hume on chastity in this context, see Berry (1997: 111–13).

21. Harré (1993: 17). Compare Daly and Wilson: 'In no human society are all sexual relations casual and impersonal' (1978: 266).

22. Contrast with Rousseau, who seemingly categorically disavows any utility in comparing humans and beasts (1864b: I, 236 /1960: 86).

23. Cf. Pitson (1993) for a more general argument concerning the difference between humans and animals as moral agents.

24. This also demonstrates that even in Hume's own writings his analysis of sexual conventions is not confined to chastity. See Whelan (1985: 279, 225 *et passim*), who stresses how variation or diversity is important evidence of artificiality.

25. Baier (1979: 12) argues that the sexual appetite is not self-correcting but is corrected by independent motives that focus on the need for paternal recognition and inheritance.

26. In fact, Hume's account itself is often very general – it is the abstract 'interested affection' (*T* 3–2–2.13/*SBNT* 492) that restrains itself and it is conceivable that its concrete application requires, for example, that the (avid) passion for those goods that belong to another is restrained by the (avid) passion to avoid the punishment inflicted by the magistrate (see text below). Moreover, if children were a matter of emotional indifference it would be difficult to see why 'my' property and 'my' children should go together.

27. This was especially common in literary theory. See, for a discussion of Hume in this context, Kallich (1970: 84ff.).

28. The public utility of chastity and modesty is emphasised by Andrea Levey, who points out that it is in the interests of all that there is an orderly means for raising children; indeed, it is the latter, not 'the control of women', that is 'the end of chastity' (Levey 1998: 222–3, 218).

29. See *T* 3–2–6.11/*SBNT* 533–4, 'the public instructions of politicians, and the private education of parents, contribute to the giving us a sense of honour and duty . . .'

30. Cf. Mackie (1980: 157, 161), who cites the work of Richard Dawkins on the 'selfish gene', Baier (1988: 777), who comments on the 'biological or sociobiological tenor of Hume's social theory', and Bernard Williams (1995: 106), who draws an explicit parallel between Symons's (1979) work on the evolution of sexual double standards and Hume's account of chastity. In a similar context, I have invoked Hume (see Berry 2000a).

Hume and the Customary Causes of Industry, Knowledge and Humanity

David Hume employs the phrase 'industry, knowledge and human-ity' in his essay 'Of Refinement in the Arts' and, conjoined with that employment, are two claims. First, the links that connect these three are said to comprise an 'indissoluble chain'; and second, these links are said to be 'peculiar to the more polished, and, what are commonly denominated, the more luxurious ages' (E-RA 271). I will say little about the first of these claims, about how this linkage characterises synchronically a commercial society. My focus, rather, is on an implication of the diachronic second claim. From this latter perspective, if this passage represents a *terminus ad quem*, then the *terminus a quo* is encapsulated in the phrase 'ignorance, sloth and barbarism' that Hume employs in the slightly later essay 'Of the Jealousy of Trade' (E-JT 328). If we juxtapose the two-word trios, we can discern a transition from ignorance to knowledge, from sloth to industry and from barbarism to human-ity. These transitions can be expressed generically as going from a rude condition to a polished one, or from a savage, barbarous society to a civilised, luxurious one.

Clearly, for Hume, this transition represents an improvement. But what is it that improves? The answer is not human nature, but customs and manners. A single chapter precludes any lengthy dis-cussion of the former negative point;[1] accordingly, I here concen-trate on the latter positive one. The aim, therefore, is to examine Hume's account of the history of civilisation, which he presents as a history of customs and manners. Aside from his 'theory of money' (understood generically), which has dominated the discus-sion of his work, the other context within which Hume is treated in the 'history of economics' is as an exemplar of a 'historical' perspective.[2] It is this latter context that this discussion explores. More precisely, and given that Hume believes that the subject matter of 'economics' is amenable to scientific analysis, I focus on his employment of causal analysis. Hence my aim is directed at the basic or underlying principles of Hume's invocation of customs as causes that account for social change.[3] In pursuing this objective, I will dwell mostly on Hume's *Essays*, although I will also draw upon the *History of England* (especially) and the *Treatise of Human Nature* for elaboration.[4]

Hume's essay 'Of Refinement in the Arts' appeared first in the 1752 *Political Discourses*, where it was entitled 'Of Luxury.' His first essay in that collection ('Of Commerce') makes a few general defensive methodological points. He wants to justify the role of 'abstruse thinkers' who, because they indulge in 'extraordinary refinement', practise 'general reasoning' with respect to commerce, money, interest and other 'economic' topics. Unlike the preoccupation with particulars that characterise 'coffee-house conversation', philosophers are able to take an 'enlarged' view and encompass the 'infinite number of individuals' in 'universal propositions'; they can even, indeed, capture a 'whole science in a single theorem'.[5]

In his essays that follow, Hume endeavours to 'philosophise' in this manner.[6] For example, in both 'Of Money' and 'Of Interest' he detects the fallacy of taking a collateral effect for a cause.[7] In both locations, scarcity of money is falsely given a causally explanatory role, when the cause is rather ('really arises from' or 'is really owing to') 'the manners and customs of the people' and the prevalent 'habits and manners' (E-Mon 290, 294) or 'the habits and way of living of the people' (E- Int 298). While Hume's account of the 'quantity theory' and species-flow mechanism is perhaps the most celebrated (certainly the most commented upon) aspect of his economics,[8] here I will concentrate instead on the 'true' cause, namely, customs and manners. (In line with Hume's own usage, I treat the terms customs, manners, habits and way of living as effective synonyms.) Here the relevant, causally effective difference when it comes to explaining changes in the rate of interest is the difference between commercial and pre-commercial ways of living.

The initial message I want to draw from this is twofold. Firstly, the indissoluble chain of industry, knowledge and humanity is to be understood as a 'way of living' or pattern of habit and manners and associated institutions. Secondly, these three ingredients can be understood as the effects of the emergence of commerce, or what Hume (*HE* III, 58) calls that 'great revolution in manners'.

Since the manners themselves embody a way of living, then they are able, in their turn, to function as causes. (For example, in 'Of Refinement in the Arts,' Hume (E-RA 272) says that manners render government great and individuals happy.) While I will return illustratively to the *History*'s account of this particular 'revolution' at the end of this chapter, my primary aim here, to repeat, is to investigate the basic principles that enable manners, customs and habits to function as causes.

In his articulation of the importance of general reasoning in those opening paragraphs in 'Of Commerce', Hume contrasts the activities of domestic government – where the public good (the supposed object of that governance) depends on a 'multitude of causes' – with foreign politics, where the activities depend on 'accidents and chances, and the caprices of a few persons.' As Eugene Rotwein (1970: xxx–xxxi) noted, Hume had made this distinction some ten years earlier in his essay 'Of the Rise and Progress of the Arts and Sciences'. This essay, too, opens with some methodological considerations. Employing here the term 'nicety' rather than 'refinement', he says this is needed to distinguish 'exactly' between what is 'owing to chance and what proceeds from causes' (E-AS 111). Hume proceeds to proffer a general rule (with built-in qualifications) to help make that distinction – 'What depends upon a few persons is, in a great measure, to be ascribed to chance, or secret and unknown causes: What arises from a great number, may often be accounted for by determinate and known causes' (E-AS 112). As the wording reveals, this is a quantitative not a qualitative difference. Indeed this is to be expected, for as he says in the *First Enquiry* (U 6.1; cf. U 8, 5/SBNU 56, 82), there is 'no such thing as chance in the world'. The characterisation of chance as secret cause had been articulated in the *Treatise* (T 1–3–12.1/ SBNT 130) and was repeated in the *Natural History of Religion* (NHR 3, 1/40). In each of these contexts there is significant similarity of association. In 'Arts and Sciences', to ascribe an event to 'chance' is said to preclude further enquiry, but to discern 'certain and stable causes' is to go beyond 'what escapes the vulgar and ignorant' (E-AS 111). In the *Treatise*, 'chance' is what the vulgar call 'secret and conceal'd causes,' and in the *Natural History of Religion* the 'ignorant multitude' has a confused conception of unknown or secret causes.

Hume proceeds, in 'Arts and Sciences', to offer two explanations for this difference between chance/caprice and determinate/stable causation (E-AS 112). First, as with a biased die, the bias will only reveal itself after several rolls, so when any 'causes beget a particular inclination or passions at a certain time and among certain people', the multitude will be 'seized by the common affection'. This 'affection', moreover, is no mere surface phenomenon: Hume says the multitude is 'governed by it in all their actions'. This is not to deny – and perfectly in tune with Hume's circumspection on this topic – that some particular individuals may 'escape the contagion and be ruled by passions peculiar to themselves'. The second explanation seemingly elaborates on the first, since Hume identifies the causes that operate on the multitude as being 'always of a grosser and more stubborn nature' and thus (presumptively) being 'less subject to accidents and less influenced by whim and private fancy than those which operate on a few only'. In a contemporaneous essay, Hume (E-El 97) declared that civil history, where the 'stubborn and intractable nature' of the passions of interest and ambition (and others) are the 'prime movers', is more uniform than the history of learning and science. In 'Arts and Sciences' he gives two instances of this distinction.

The first reiterates the difference between domestic (stable causes) and foreign (capricious chance) politics and is illustrated by the difference between the rise of the commons in England and the comparative strengths of the French and Spanish monarchies after the death of Charles V. The second, echoing 'Of Eloquence', contrasts the rise of commerce with the rise of learning and the refined arts (the subject of the essay). Since the difference is of degree not kind, causal explanations are in principle always available. Of course, care must be taken neither to 'assign causes which never existed' nor to 'reduce what is merely contingent to stable and universal principles' (E-AS 113). Nonetheless, and this is an important point as we shall see, the reason why arts and sciences arise is a general one that can be 'accounted for, in some measure, by general causes and principles' (E-AS 114). The contingent will remain, so that to seek to explain why a particular poet, say, Homer, existed when and where he did is to pursue a chimera. But even when dealing with the seemingly quintessential individuality of a poet, there remain causally relevant general considerations that a scientific or philosophic account can elicit. Hence Hume claims that these individuals nevertheless share the 'same spirit and genius' that is 'antecedently diffused throughout the whole people'. In a typical Enlightenment, pre-Romantic sense, spirit and genius are thus not the prerogative of exceptional individuals, and the important point (for reasons to be elaborated) about 'antecedence' is elaborated by means of a metaphor: the poet's inspirational fire burns brightest where 'the materials are best prepared'.

There is an implicit causality here because Hume maintains that this social spirit serves 'to produce, form and cultivate' from 'earliest infancy' the 'taste and judgement' of the poet (E-AS 114). What is implied here is a model (so to speak) of social causation to which we shall return. Because this is 'social,' that is, 'general' or stubbornly intractable, it is diffused throughout the whole; and further, because it is not localised or contingent on 'particulars', it is open to philosophical or scientific analysis. It is this model that Hume's evocation of manners and customs as causes relies upon.

There are two key issues to be considered: how manners and customs function as causes, and how in so doing they, as social phenomena, have an impact upon individuals. The place where Hume most explicitly addresses these issues is his essay 'Of National Characters'. This essay, published in 1748 – midway between 'Of Arts and Sciences' and the *Political Discourses* – is essentially a polemic. Its argumentative thrust is that moral causes are the effective explanation for national character, while physical causes fail in that task. The latter he defines as

> those qualities of the air and climate, which are supposed to work insensibly on the temper, by altering the tone of the body and giving a particular complexion, which, though reflection and reason may sometimes overcome it, will yet prevail among the generality of mankind, and have an influence on their manners. (E-NC 198)

He defines moral causes as 'all circumstances which are fitted to work on the mind as motives or reasons, and which render a peculiar set of manners habitual to us' (E-NC 198). 'Moral' here thus means pertaining to mores or customs.

If we compare the definitions, we can identify where the crucial difference lies. Physical causes work 'insensibly on the temper' by way of the 'body'; hence in a later essay, 'Of the Populousness of Ancient Nations', Hume (E-PAN 378–9) can also call physiological ageing and disease physical causes. Moral causes work on the 'mind' as a 'motive' by making a set of manners 'habitual'. Though the difference is crucial it is, again, one of degree, not kind. This difference I have expressed elsewhere as that between hard and soft determinism (Berry 1997: Ch. 4). The former is most famously associated with Montesquieu's analysis in Book 14 of *De l'esprit des lois*. But Montesquieu is not alone and Hume, despite the conjectures of Paul Chamley (1975),[9] is likely for chronological reasons to have in his sights Abbé Dubos [1719] (1755) or William Temple (1680). Physical causation operates directly on the body as a mere automatic reflex, as when, in Montesquieu's experiment, the fibres on a sheep's tongue contract in response to being frozen. This is then supposed to determine 'sensibility', such that physical punishment regimes have to be harsher in cold than in warm climes or even, further, that the same opera is differently received in England and Italy (Montesquieu 1961: Bk 14, Ch. 2).

Hume's support for moral causes is an expression of 'soft' determinism, because it operates through the 'mind' and allows for a flexible response. But it is still deterministic, because the way the various circumstances that constitute moral causes operate is to establish a set of motives or reasons that 'render a peculiar set of manners habitual'. In other words, as he continues in 'Of National Characters', 'the manners of individuals are frequently *determined* by these [moral] causes' (E-NC 198; my emphasis).[10] This last point should not be misunderstood. Hume's differentiation between the general and the particular (read: individual) does not impart to the former any ontological status. He is unambiguous in 'Of National Characters' that 'a nation is nothing but a collection of individuals'. This has two significant consequences. First, individuals have a dual aspect: they both possess a national character and transmit it. Second, this does not mean that the explanation for social change – like the rise of the commons or of that indissoluble trio of industry, knowledge and humanity – is the effect of the causal impact of particular individuals. Of course, any particular individual can escape the general contagion or in some aspect of their behaviour act idiosyncratically or be 'exceptional' (as Homer was). But Hume allows for such particularities when he inserts the adverb 'frequently' before 'determined' in the quotation above.[11] But precisely because there is such a phenomenon as 'national character', that case cannot be generalised; 'exceptions' must by definition be deviations from some norm, there must be (to restate the point) an antecedent 'spirit and genius'.

What are these moral causes that form national character? Hume has the following list: 'nature of government, the revolutions of public affairs, the plenty or penury in which the people live, the situation of the nation with regard to its neighbours' (E-NC 198). If we look at which moral causes Hume actually invokes, we find 'government' to be the most common.[12] Generally, differences of manners track differences in government and, more particularly, for example – and here echoing the causality identified in 'Arts and Sciences'[13] – it is an oppressive government that explains the absence of liberal arts. The second most common factor is close communication, with Jews given as an example (E-NC 205) – an illustration that incidentally rules out national character from having a nationalistic meaning. Hume also supports this point when he notes that neighbouring nations who – through policy, travelling or commerce – have 'very close communication' acquire 'similitude of manners' (E-NC 206). He also alludes to rarity to account for the fondness of liquor in northern climates (E-NC 213), and to how poverty and hard labour 'debase the mind' so that individuals subject to them are unfit for science (E-NC 198). The two commonest factors (government and communication) are in fact closely allied. One of the reasons why government is so causally effective is that when people are politically united, their intercourse, over matters such as government itself, defence and commerce, is frequent. This frequency or repetitiveness, abetted by the same language, means a people 'must acquire a resemblance in their manners' (E-NC 203).

We can now move directly to the primary aim of this chapter, which is to examine how customs can function as causes or what underlying principles give moral causes their efficacy. Three inter-related ones can be identified. The first is associationism. In Hume's conception, the principle of the association of ideas accounts for the coherence within imaginatively generated complex ideas. Imagination can separate and reunify simple ideas, but this does not result in random incoherence because there is a 'gentle force which commonly prevails' such that there is 'a bond of union' whereby the same simple ideas fall regularly into complex ones. This 'force' or 'bond' is association. Of Hume's three universal principles of association – resemblance, contiguity of time and place, and cause and effect – the third is, of course, the most significant (T 1–1–4.1/SBNT 11). While, in principle, anything may be the cause of anything, this is not how the world appears; it is experienced as regular, not random. And the root of the regularity is the habit-forming propensity of human nature (T 1–3–16.9/

SBNT 179; *U* 5.5/*SNTU* 43). Hence we only suppose the future is conformable to the past because the constant conjunction in the past of (say) heat with a flame has established a habitual association in the mind to that effect (so to speak). Since the universe is in this way experientially cemented together, then should we wish to obtain heat we can reliably or predictably get it from a flame.

Central to his endeavour to establish a science of man, Hume regards the causal association between heat and flame, or the motion of billiard balls one upon another, as applicable to human affairs. This principle surfaces in 'Of National Characters'. Government and the rest are moral causes because, as we will note later, their modus operandi conforms to the criteria of causal association. (This is why, in the *Treatise* (*T* Intro 5/*SBNT* xv) and in the *First Enquiry* (*U* 8.18/*SBNU* 90), Hume can say politics is a science.) Hence in 'Of National Characters' the national characteristic of politeness among the Athenians is attributable to the habitual associations of life under their government, while the rusticity of the neighbouring Thebans is attributable to the set of associations under their government (E-NC 204).

This is not an empty principle. Hume is clear that some customs are inferior to others, as indeed in this case, where the contrast between politeness and rusticity is not neutral – it would be self-defeating to the enterprise of a science of man if such judgements could not be made. This example is of a synchronous difference, but perhaps the most significant difference between physical and moral causation is that the latter can also account for diachronic difference. Hence, in another triadic set of contrasting pairings, Hume draws attention to the 'ignorance, barbarity and grossness' of the Gauls, as described by Caesar, and the 'civility, humanity and knowledge of the modern inhabitants of that country' (E-NC 206). This example of change in manners, like that which produces industry, knowledge and humanity, reveals the second of our three principles – temporality.

This principle appears trite, almost banal, for at least two reasons. First, the causal relation incorporates into its Humean meaning precedence or temporal priority. Second, recalling that the definition of a moral cause referred to manners being habitual, then a custom is necessarily a creature of time. It is meaningless to talk of acquiring a habit overnight; an uneliminable gradualness is built into the process (*T* 3–2–10.4/*SBNT* 490). But what helps rescue this principle from banality is that its operation is more than merely formal. This is apparent when, for example, in the context of his anti-contractarianism Hume affirms that 'Time, by degrees ... accustoms the nation' to regard as lawful those princes who were initially thought usurpers (E-OC 474–5). This claim echoes the argument put forward in Book III of the *Treatise*. In that work he had noted already that the 'first origin of every nation' is scarcely ever anything other than usurpation and rebellion, and he had observed that it is 'time alone' that 'gives solidity' to the right of rulers to govern (*T* 3–2–10.4/*SBNT* 556). A few pages later he repeated the observation with a significant refinement: 'time *and custom* give authority to all forms of government and all successions of princes; and that power which at first was founded only on injury and violence becomes in time legal and obligatory' (*T* 3–2–10.19/*SBNT* 566: my emphasis).

This is a startlingly radical argument of some consequence. In an association that is typically identified with Edmund Burke, Hume is here exploiting the link between title and time made by the established principle of prescription. I say 'exploit' deliberately because, although this principle is a standard component in the formal jurisprudential and more informal common-law account of property, Hume's use of it is non-standard, hence his radicalism.[14] In his discussion of property in the *Treatise*, Hume had defined prescription or long possession as conveying title 'to any object' (*T* 3–2–3.9/ *SBNT* 508). In 'Of the Original Contract' he used this principle in his rebuttal of the contractarian account of government when, in developing his generalisation that this account is 'not justified by history or experience', he observes that subjects originally obeyed a ruler not out of some predetermined contractual arrangement but out of 'fear and necessity' (E-OC 471). Yet, independently of that origin, subjects come, over time, to consent willingly 'because they think that from long possession he has acquired a title' (E-NC 475).[15] In this way the principle of prescription provided Hume with a means to show how what matters is current belief (right), not any set of facts about what happened 'originally' in the past (might). I will return briefly to Hume's use of prescription, but it is evident that the principle of temporality is integral to it. But for Hume, just like the title to an heirloom, the ruler's title is the product of time. But since time produces nothing 'real', to talk of property, or title to it, as the effect of time can only mean that each is, as he says in the *Treatise*, the 'offspring of the sentiments on which time alone is found to have any influence' (*T* 3–2–3.9/*SBNT* 509).

How does time influence sentiments? Despite Hume's use of the causal language of 'influence', time is better understood as the medium, so to speak, through which custom or habit operates; 'nothing', he says, 'causes any sentiment to have greater influence upon us than custom' (*T* 3–2–10.4/*SBNT* 556). The context of this remark is again political authority. In his essay 'First Principles of Government', in developing his argument that all government is founded on 'opinion only', he observes, more particularly, that 'antiquity begets the opinion of right' (E-FPG 32–3). This imparts to philosophical history the presumption that it is concerned with the 'history of opinion', the history of what Hume himself calls the 'the minds of men' (*HE* III, 2).[16] 'First Principles of Government' was published only a year after Book III of *The Treatise of Human Nature*, wherein Hume had already remarked that time 'alone' gives 'solidity to title' because working 'gradually on the minds of men,' in the form of habitual obedience, it instils the moral senti-ment of obligation.

We have yet to explain how this happens, what the causal mechanism is by which customs and manners instil sentiments, and more generally, how they form both national and individual char-acter. This task is performed by the third principle. This principle comes in two guises, sympathy and education, where the former is more explicit and specific than the latter, which is correspondingly implicit and general. Contagion or sympathy is identified as the explicit mechanism in 'Of National Characters'. It is there held to be integral to the propensity to company (E-NC 203). Manners are contagious (E-NC 201 n. 204). Significantly, we have already met the metaphor of 'contagion' in 'Arts and Sciences'. There (we recall), though individuals may escape the contagion and be ruled by 'passions peculiar to themselves', the 'multitude' is seized by 'common affection' and is 'governed by it in all their actions'. The contagion is the product of the facility or propensity humans have to be imitative and 'enter deeply into each other's sentiments' (E-AS 202). Similarly, in the second *Enquiry* 'sentiment' is caught by 'contagion or natural sympathy' (*M* 7, 2/*SBNM* 251), while in the *Treatise* passions are said to be so 'contagious that they pass with the greatest facility from one person to another' (*T* 3–3–3.5/ *SBNT* 605). This is said in Book III as part of his elaboration of the sympathetic process that he had introduced in Book II (*T* 2–1–11.3/*SBNT* 317). Looked at substantively, Hume declares, sympathy is a powerful process (cf. *T* 3–3–1.10/*SBNT* 577); even, he observes, 'men of the greatest judgement and understanding' find it hard to follow their own reason when it is opposed to that of 'their friends and daily companions' (*T* 2–1–11.2/*SBNT* 317; cf. *DP* 2, 33/14). Moreover, and in anticipation of the argument in 'National Characters' (and, incidentally, throwing further doubt on Paul Chamley's (1975) argument that Hume was directly rebutting Montesquieu in that essay), he claims that sympathy is a better explanation for the 'great uniformity in the humours and turns of thinking of those of the same nation' than 'any influence of soil or climate' (*T* 2–2–11.2/*SBNT* 317).[17]

Hume provides another revealing illustration in this context. Echoing here a point made by Hutcheson (*SMP* I, 20),[18] he observes that the principle of sympathy is 'conspicuous in children' since 'they implicitly embrace every opinion propos'd to them' (*T* 2–1–11.2/*SBNT* 316). What is revealing here is that this reference to children broaches the second, more general mechanism – education in the wider sense of the process of socialisation (cf. Whelan 1985: 124). It is this process that lies at the heart of moral causation. It is possible that underlying this is a Malebranchian argument that habits are acquired with more facility by children than by adults because their brain fibres are soft, flexible and delicate (n.d: 3: 187–8, Bk 2, Ch. 6, para 2]).[19] Despite recurring references to 'animal spirits', Hume by and large foregoes, as he puts it, imaginary dissections of the brain; but when he does, somewhat apologetically, embark on such an exercise, his language is evocative of Malebranche (*T* 1–2–5.20/*SBNT* 60) (Wright 1983: Ch. 5). In his more basic intention to be abstemious, Hume is closer to Locke, who in his chapter on the association of ideas in the *Essay Concerning Human Understanding* also links customs and animal spirits, but also pulls back from further investigation. Locke (1854: 1, 535, Bk 2, Ch. 33, sect. 6) does, though, employ without acknowledgement Malebranche's (nd: 3, 185) example of learning a musical instrument, to declare that 'custom settles habits of thinking in the understanding, as well as of determining in the will, and of motions in the body'. However, while both Malebranche and Locke use this line of argument to locate sources of error, Hume's account of what I have called socialisation is more far-reaching.

In 'National Characters,' Hume (E-NC 203) employs the conceit of the 'infancy of society' to draw out the impact of moral causation or socialisation:

Whatever it be that forms the manners of one generation, the next must imbibe a deeper tincture of the same dye; men being more susceptible of all impressions during infancy, and retaining these impressions as long as they remain in the world.

According to Hume's assumption of associationism, with its denial of innate ideas, and his philosophical physiology, the minds of children are 'tender' so that 'customs and habits' are able to 'fashion them by degrees' for social life (*T* 3–2–2.4/*SBNT* 486).

This implicitly fits Hume's model of causation (at least the *Treatise* version). First, there is 'priority', in that knowledge both expressly and – perhaps more important – tacitly is conveyed by knowers to non-knowers (children), and not vice versa. Recall, again, the importance of the 'antecedence' of spirit and genius 'to produce, form and cultivate' from 'earliest infancy' the 'taste and judgement' of the poet. Second, there is contiguity in that there has to be contact. The children have to be in a society to be socialised; that is, after all, how different national characters are formed – it is because Athenians are exposed to the civic culture or manners of Athens that they are indeed Athenians and not Thebans. That it is the manners that are decisive Hume illustrates in his polemic against physical causes when he observes that 'manners follow the nation' and therefore the Spanish, English, French and Dutch colonies are distinguishable 'even between the tropics' (E-NC 205): that is, their direct physical exposure to uniform climatic elements has not made them indistinguishable from each other. Third, this is not a one-off lesson but is constantly repeated, reinforced, underwritten and so on; to be told, to learn, that this is the 'way we live here' is to establish through constant conjunction the way we live here.

Hume (*T* 1–3–9.16, 1–3–9.19/*SBNT* 80, 81) emphasises the impact of repetition; his implicit model of 'artificial' education in the *Treatise* is seemingly rote learning. Given continually changing populations, these socialised habits supply a needed continuity, something social contract theory, for example, is unable to provide. As he says in 'Of the Original Contract', what is required to achieve stability is that 'the new brood should conform themselves to the established constitution and nearly follow the path which their fathers, treading in the footsteps of theirs, had marked out to them' (E-OC 476–7). The 'brood' conforms not as a consequence of any deliberate (read: adult) decision, but because there is a pre-existent path. This path the children follow because that is the way of their world, the one into which they have been socialised or habituated, for 'men are guided more by custom than by reason [to] follow, without inquiry, the manners which are prevalent in their own time' (*HE* I, 395; cf. III, 116).

According to Hume, custom induces a facility in doing an action (practice makes perfect, as the proverb has it) and thence an inclination or tendency to do it (*T* 2–3–5.1/*SBNT* 422; cf. *U* 5.5/*SBNU* 43). It is perhaps here in the *Treatise* where we can best appreciate his use of prescription as a source of temporal normativeness. Property for Hume (*T* 2–1–10.1/*SBNT* 309) at its most general is a relation between a person and an object. Indeed, it is a species of causation (cf. *T* 3–2–3.7/*SBNT* 506; *DP* 2, 9n./13n.). This is in a Pufendorfian sense a moral, not a physical, relation (*T* 3–2–3.7/*SBNT* 507); otherwise property could not be distinguished from possession. While as a moral relation it depends on the recognition of other people, it also has a profound psychological dimension. We allude to that in the idea of an object possessing 'sentimental value', a value at odds with its insurable replacement cost. Indeed, in many cases it is irreplaceable because it is its associations that matter. Prescriptive title partakes of that associationism. Hume remarks that it is 'an effect of custom' that it 'gives us an affection' for something we have long enjoyed. This affection informs our preferences. We prefer to retain possession of a familiar object than to possess one that is more valuable but unknown (cf. *T* 2–2–4.8/*SBNT* 355). I will not swap my sentimentally valued ring for one with more and bigger diamonds. The converse of this is also true since, according to Hume, we can 'easily live without possessions' that we are 'not accustom'd to' (*T* 3–2–3.4/*SBNT* 503).

Implicit here is that humans routinise their behaviour. It is not that they are incapable of novelty or will not rise to challenges; they can break from custom and disturb the psychological cosiness that comes from doing what is habitually done. But even this break – if persisted with – can in turn lead to a new comforting pattern of behaviour; it is part of the power of custom that it can turn pain into pleasure (*T* 2–3.5.1/*SBNT* 422). A low-key example would be broadening one's range of gustatory experience; perhaps sake or whisky is an acquired taste (as the phrase revealingly has it). Aside from such individualistic cases, habits and customs are so powerful in society because they are mutually reinforcing; the human mind 'is wonderfully fortified by an unanimity of sentiments' (E-PG 60). Put a group of humans together and, if they converse often enough, they will acquire a 'similarity of manners' (E-NC 202). This is part of the force of the metaphor of contagion abetted by human proclivity to imitate. Indeed, Hume (E-PG 61–2n) refers to the imitation of 'Roman manners' by the conquered Gauls as weaning the Gauls (over about a century) from their 'ancient prejudices'.

There is another aspect to the power of habits and customs in society. Of their very nature, they circumscribe the range of putatively 'free' actions. For most of the people for most of the time (even poets when not being creatively poetic), their 'reasons' for acting are habitual, a product of their pre-reflective child-hood. Habits are repeated responses that are made possible by a stable set of circumstances, the very stability of which is at least partly constituted by the prevalent system of habitual manners. This repetitiveness leaves its mark. In a common but revealing phrase, habits become 'second nature'. As such, they share some of the key features of 'first nature', or instinct; they not only stabilise, they constrain, they 'infix' ideas, as Hume puts it in the *Treatise* (T 1–3–5.6, 1–3–9.17/*SBNT* 86, 116). In a Veblen-like manner, social habits constitute institutions.[20] Hence, with respect to government, for example, Hume says that 'habit consolidates' as 'men once accustomed to obedience never think of departing from that path' (E-OC 469). This means that it is an uneliminable characteristic of institutions that they are cor-respondingly 'sticky'.

Sticky institutions such as, for example, chastity (see Chapter 10) make it difficult for an individual to 'break free', and even if one does defy convention, the obloquy that would follow is likely, in fact, to strengthen what has been defied. Yet a habit is not instinct; it determines soft-ly, not hard-ly. The set of circum-stances necessary for habit formation may become unsettled or destabilised. This is the other side of the principle of prescription. Ownership can be lost if association is not persistent; indeed, much of the legal literature turned on this point. In Kames's (*ELS* 230) psychological account, which arguably had some influence on Hume's argument, the property relation is dissolved when the 'subject has been long lost and no remembrance of it remaining' (which in Scots law turned out to be forty years).[21] If there were not this temporally conditioned, soft determinism, then moral causes would not have the capacity to account for social changes.

One such change is in the treatment of women. Part of the meaning of 'humanity' in that indissoluble chain of 'industry, knowledge and humanity' reflects this (hence the relevance of the discussion of chastity). A commercial society is civilised, and a significant indicator of this is that its citizens no longer live at distances from one another (a characteristic peculiar to 'ignorant and barbarous nations'), but flock into cities. Therein both sexes meet in an 'easy and sociable manner' as temper and behaviour become more refined (E-RA 271).[22] This is a far cry from the earlier depiction where the 'abject slavery' to which 'their females' is reduced is a hallmark of 'barbarous nations' (E-AS 133). Hume (1875: 4, 417), indeed, treats as evidence against the authenticity of Ossian's poetry that in it women are depicted with 'extreme delicacy', when such treatment is 'contrary to the manners of the barbarians'.

This difference between barbarity and civilisation is a difference in customs and manners. What accounts for this change? The answer lies in Hume's basic understanding of the relation between human nature and history. As he says in the first *Enquiry*, history uncovers 'the constant and universal principles' of human nature, so that most of what animates the Greeks can be gleaned from a study of the English (*U* 8.7/SBNU 83). This is not to deny difference between the two cultures, but to presuppose the uniformity of manners within each one. If the 'manners of men differ in different ages and countries', then, in line with the principles we have already adduced, the difference is causally attributable to 'the great force of custom and education which mould the human mind from its infancy and form it into a fixed established character' (*U* 8.11/SBNU 86).

Customs are causes because individuals are born into an ongoing community, which we recall is a collection of individuals and which necessarily reproduces itself through acculturating, socialising or softly determining its members into a particular 'way of living' (as it was called in 'Of Interest'). This is necessary because, unlike other animals (even 'social' ones), humans 'naturally' lack self-sufficiency (*T* 3–2–2.1/SBNT 485). They have to learn conventionally or artificially how to coexist (they impose rules – pre-eminently those of justice – upon themselves). This is made feasible because the great dependency of human infants is itself a consequence of their immaturity (relative to other animals) at birth and the associated physiological fact of their ductility. Parents might be the immediate agents of instruction, but they themselves are patients and, as such, are 'softly' determined by the prevailing mores to pass on their way of life.

A 'way of life' means the general mode of behaviour, the social customs and the consonant set of institutions (government, law, property, family and so on) thereby constituted. Hence, to explain the generality or what affects the 'multitude', what it is that establishes a recognisable way of life, it is necessary to turn to a commensurately general cause. This principle of 'fit' between cause and effect Hume states concisely in 'Of Interest': 'an effect always holds proportion with its cause' (E-Int 296; cf. U 10.12, 13/SBNU 115–16, E-PSc 24). This is a statement that Eric Schliesser (2008) has called Hume's ninth rule of reasoning. When the effect is a way of living, then generically social customs (manners, institutions) are the proportionately appropriate cause; to identify some particular event in history or some particular individual (even the aptly labelled 'great' Alfred)[23] as causally decisive is to fall into the way of the vulgar coffee house. Social change is properly conceived as a change in customs. This may occur simply through 'the inconstancy to which all human affairs are subject' (E-NC 206; cf. M Dialogue 50/SBNM 340) – what the ancients and their heirs from Machiavelli onwards tended to call *fortuna* – and change may be exogenously generated, as when the Romans conquered the Gauls. But in either case the actual change in manners was the endogenous work of time and custom. If we properly, as scientists of man, look upon the commercial way of life (encapsulated in the linked presence of industry, knowledge and humanity) as an effect in need of explanation, then we have to undertake a causally informed social history, the task of which is to identify and trace the links in the chain of cause and effect to account, thereby, for the changes in prevalent customs (see U 3.9).[24] Hume throws out hints of this in his *Political Discourses* but it is one of the principal motifs of his *History of England*. Thus, revealingly in the light of the earlier discussion, he remarks that the development of the burgesses, the 'true commons', was not 'an affair of chance', since it 'became customary' for them to seek redress for grievances, in return for granting Edward I funds (HE I, 414, 412).

In conclusion, Hume's 'great revolution in manners' was a change that in Carl Wennerlind's (2002: 267 n. 18) terms 'initiated the modernisation process'. I wish to examine this 'revolution' as a particular episode of customary change and in so doing pull together some of the threads of this chapter. In the *History of*

England – in his treatment of the growth of the Crown's authority, which began in the reign of Henry VII but stretched into the reign of Elizabeth – Hume (*HE* II, 602), after referring to a number of 'peculiar causes' of this growth, then claims that the 'manners of the age were a general cause'. The outline of the story is that the 'habits of luxury' dissipated the fortunes of the great barons, cities increased, the 'middle rank of men' began to grow rich, and eventually the 'farther progress of the same causes begat a new plan of liberty', although in the interim the sovereign took advantage to assume an 'authority almost absolute'.

We can discern in this treatment that the decisive change in this 'secret revolution of government' is the subversion of the power of the barons, and it is of this that Hume repeats his explicit declaration that 'the change of manners was the chief cause' of that subversion (*HE* II, 603). Pivotal in this process was the barons' acquisition of 'habits of luxury' (and this whole discussion evokes that given in 'Of Refinement in the Arts' – originally, of course, entitled 'Of Luxury' – and is echoed closely and not coincidentally by Smith in Book III of *The Wealth of Nations*).[25] The medieval barons expended their surplus on 'ancient hospitality' and maintained many retainers, which historically resulted in 'vice, disorder, sedition and idleness' (*HE* II, 601). However, 'by degrees' the nobility acquired a 'taste for elegant luxury' in housing and apparel. Hume here neither accounts for the source of this luxury[26] nor identifies the hidden motivating passion(s) among the 'constant and universal springs of human nature', which, from the list of 'regular springs' supplied in the *First Enquiry*, are likely to be avarice, self-love and vanity (*U* 8.7/SBNU 83).[27] What mattered in practice was that the limited availability of these luxury items restricted their acquisition to those few who could supposedly afford them. However, their desirability, which was as much a matter of peer-group emulation as of their inherent quality (E-RA 276) (see Berry 2006 Ch. 13), was such that they appealed to the generality of the nobility (and later, by imitation, to the lesser gentry (*HE* III, 99)). This taste, once acquired, in line with the habit-forming capacity of human nature (and the underlying assumptions of associationism, temporality and socialisation) itself became habitual, and to feed this habit the nobles retrenched on their hospitality and reduced the number of their retainers. Having fewer dependent retainers, the barons were less able to resist the execution of laws – thus inadvertently, in due course, advancing the rule of law and its entailed consequence, the security of private property. Moreover, by spending money on goods, they 'promoted arts and industry' (*HE* II, 601) and 'gave subsistence to mechanics and merchants who lived in an independent manner on the fruits of their own industry' (*HE* II, 602).

If we are to explain this growth in sovereign authority, this 'revolution in government', then it is inadequate to look to legislation passed (recall that Hume refers to this as a 'secret' revolution).[28] What matters is not passing laws but whether doing so makes a difference; what needs to be explained is how law comes to be effective in the first place. Thus Hume remarks on the ineffectiveness of Elizabeth's attempts to restrain luxury by proclamation (*HE* II, 602), just as earlier attempts (including three by Henry VIII) at sumptuary legislation had been to no avail (*HE* II, 231; cf. 1: 595 on Edward III's attempt).[29] These 'failed' because they were out of step with the temper of the times – the state of 'property and manners' in Smith's Humean-influenced phrase (*WN* 3.4.8/416). While particular pieces of legislation are by definition 'individual' or 'peculiar', law/government is a social institution requiring appropriate and commensurate social causes to account for changes (revolution) in it. And, as we have already pointed out, Hume explicitly identifies 'the change of manners' as 'the chief cause' of this revolution. To gloss this, we can say that the institution of the rule of law arose causally from a two-stage change in manners.

First (and the source is again the *History of England*), the cause of the emergence of 'general and regular execution of laws' was the loss by the barons of their localised power bases (the erosion of the habit of obedience to their rule by those dependent on them), thus removing the key obstacle to central authority (*HE* II, 603). This loss itself was the effect of the barons' pursuit of personalised luxury, since that pursuit caused them to release their now useless retainers. Second, this 'regular execution of laws' became entrenched just as the discretion of the central authority in its turn began to be curtailed. The cause of this subsequent curtailment was the rise of the commons, composed of the middle rank whose numbers had been increased by those retainers released by the barons and whose power increased *pari passu* with the growth of commerce, thus forcing the crown to accede to the new 'plan of liberty'. For Hume, the 'middling rank of men' (tradesmen and merchants) is the 'best and firmest basis of public liberty' because they 'covet equal laws', since without the security that comes from the consistent and predictable (regular) operation of law, 'markets' will not function (E-RA 277–8).[30] In other words, the habits and manners – such as law-abidingness and frugality – of the commercial way of life brought about by the barons' loss of power and prodigality themselves serve as a customary cause of the maintenance of the rule of law (E-Int 302).[31]

The nature of government and revolutions in public affairs, we recall, were the major types of moral causation, and this story from the *History* is given potted expression in 'Of Commerce' and 'Of Refinement in the Arts', where 'progress in the arts' (and industry, their 'inseparable attendant') is depicted as favourable to liberty and the establishment of the rule of law (E-RA 274, 277). Since industry is indissolubly linked to knowledge and humanity, then they must all be implicated in this change. Hence 'industry is much promoted by the knowledge inseparable from ages of art and refinement' and 'laws, order, police, discipline' can never reach 'any degree of perfection before human reason has refined itself by exercise and by an application to the more vulgar arts, at least, of commerce and manufacture' (E-RA 272–3).[32] Moreover, industry and 'refinements in the mechanical arts' go along with 'refinements in the liberal' (E-RA 270) – so 'we cannot reasonably expect that a piece of woollen cloth will be wrought to perfection in a nation which is ignorant of astronomy or where ethics are neglected' (E-RA 270–1). This same nation will become civilised and urbane as its citizens 'flock into cities'. Such proximity encourages conversation, which, as we have seen, advances the status of women, and which, together with the 'improvements' in knowledge and the liberal arts, makes it 'impossible but they [both sexes] must feel an encrease of humanity' (E-RA 271).

These are not 'chance' events or interrelations. The *History* reveals that a change in a set of manners, through the causal mechanism of gradual changes in the socialised pattern of customs and habits, will produce a different set as an effect (*HE* I, 127). Hume summarises the 'manners of the Anglo-Saxons' as those of a 'rude, uncultivated people, ignorant of letters, unskilled in mechanical arts, untamed to submission under law and government, addicted to intemperance, riot and disorder', who exhibited a 'want of humanity' throughout their whole history. The story of how England got from that state of manners to that implicitly depicted in 'Of Refinement in the Arts' is the story of the customary causes of industry, knowledge and humanity.

Postscript

This chapter is a version of an invited lecture I gave at the Hume Studies Conference, Tokyo, in August 2004. I am grateful to the committee (especially Tatsuya Sakamoto) for the invitation and to the participants for comments, and to Carl Wennerlind in particular. It is a companion piece to Chapter 13; see the postscript there for general comment.

Notes

1. There is an extensive literature on this point. Some writers have detected in Hume historicist (or relativist) principles; see, for example, Forbes (1975: Ch. 2), Capaldi (1978), Farr (1978), Livingston (1984), Dees (1992), Evnine (1993), Herdt (1997), Meyer (1958), Burke (1978), Schmidt (2003) and A. Cohen (2000). I argued to the contrary in Berry 1982a and have replied to some more recent accounts in Berry 2007 (reprinted as Chapter 12). In the context of Hume's economic writings, Hutchison (1988: 201, 214) has detected 'historical relativism' in his work, but Davis (2003: 280) has seen that Hume's concept of human nature 'sets severe limits to the variability of individual behaviour across periods of social and cultural change'.

2. Andrew Skinner (1993: 248), for example, has linked Hume's historical approach to the German historical school and American institutionalists. Without being anachronistic, this paper can be read in that vein.

3. In one of the very few references to this (there is, for example, no discussion in Redman 1997), John Berdell (1996:117), in his account of Hume's treatment of technological change, notes 'Hume's rich analysis of the origin and diffusion of customs' but does not explore the governing assumptions (my aim here) of that analysis.

4. I do not engage here with possible changes in Hume's position. Tatsuya Sakamoto (2003), for example, traces changes within Hume's essays, and Constant Stockton (1976) draws contrasts between the economics in the *Essays* and in the *History of England*. However, my major concern is with Hume's underlying principles, and there is no convincing evidence that these changed.

5. This is echoed in the *History*: 'Most sciences, in proportion as they increase and improve, invent methods by which they facilitate their reasonings, and employing general theorems, are enabled to comprehend in a few propositions, a great number of inferences and invent invent methods by which they facilitate their reasonings; and are able to comprehend ... a great number of inferences and conclusions. History also, being a collection of facts which are multiplying without end, is obliged to adopt such arts of abridgement' (*HE* I, 338). Later in the same paragraph, Hume refers to 'general causes' to account for the activities of the Catholic Church in the reign of Henry III. The significance of that reference will become apparent.

6. Contemporary philosophers have paid scant attention to Hume's 'economic' writings; they largely remain enthralled by Book I of the *Treatise* and some selected passages from books II and III. 'Political' philosophers have been more willing to consider Hume's 'economics' as a significant component in his thought. See, for example, Danford (1990), Stewart (1992) and Whelan (1985). There has been some (but not extensive) counterweight attention to Hume's broader philosophy from historians of economics. See, for example, Rotwein (1970: Intro), Teichgraeber (1986: Ch. 3) and Wennerlind (2001, 2002).

7. Hume regards the avoiding of such mistakes as important. Nothing, he says in 'Of Interest', can be of 'more use' than to improve the 'method of reasoning,' especially when dealing with political and economic issues, since they are 'commonly treated in the loosest and most careless manner' (E-Int 304). That is to say, we need to identify causes carefully, because only in so doing will these issues be correctly understood and any action based on them be effective. These were practical, live issues in post-'45 Scotland. For some discussion in this connection, see Caffentzis (2001).

8. The salience attached to this in extensive discussions of Hume does not signal any particular agreement about his actual position. See, for example, Duke (1979) and Gatch (1996). For an up-to-date survey of the literature and debate, and an argument that Hume has been persistently misread, see Wennerlind (2005).

9. An earlier, more tentative version was proposed by Roger Oake (1941).

10. Compare the following from the *Treatise*, which says that 'there is but one kind of necessity, as there is but one kind of cause, and ... the common distinction betwixt moral and physical necessity is without any foundation in nature' (*T* 1–3–14.33/*SBNT* 171).

11. As the quotation in the text reveals, Hume also, typically, qualifies

physical causation. He says that it supposedly prevails among the 'generality of mankind', though 'reflection and reason may sometimes overcome it' (E-NC 198).

12. Compare E-PSc 16, where Hume says that the great force of 'particular forms of government' is a certainty comparable to 'any which the mathematical sciences affords us'.

13. In E-AS 115, the first general cause of the rise of knowledge of the arts and sciences is identified as free government.

14. Hume is aware that his usage was contrary to the standard understanding, according to which prescription did not have that morally transformative power. Aquinas (1932, pt 3, supp., Q. 55, art. 9) exemplified standard usage when he said, 'No prescription can legitimate that which cannot be done without sin.' Equally among civilians and 'modern' natural lawyers – for example, Pufendorf (1991: 89, Bk 1, Ch. 12, para 15) – it was accepted that prescriptive title to property presupposed that it was obtained in 'good faith'. The nearest to Hume's position is perhaps Sir Matthew Hale (1971: 54), who in his *History of the Common Law of England* (published nearly forty years after his 1676 death), in the context of a discussion of the relation between conquerors and the conquered (with 1066 pre-eminently in mind), declared that 'by long Prescription, Usage and Custom, the Laws and Rights of the conquered People were in a Manner settled'. Even in Hale the transformation is rather implied, and he articulates in general the common-law argument that long usage indicates consent. Edmund Burke knew his Hume, but a possibly significant intermediate is William Paley (1845: 100, Bk 2, Ch. 6), who closely follows Hume to the extent of appropriating his language. Paley, like Burke (and indeed Hume in moods), uses this terminology to blunt political radicalism.

15. Hume also uses the phrase in the politically charged context of the Hanoverian succession: 'long possession ... must ere this time, in the apprehension of a great part of the nation, have begotten a title ... independent of their present possession' (E-PrS 511).

16. Later, in the *History*, Hume (*HE* III, 395) reiterates his position that government is 'always founded on opinion not force' but he adds the moral that therefore it is 'dangerous to weaken by these speculations [about the doctrine of resistance] the reverence which the multitude owe to authority'. See Pocock (1999: 203) and Phillips (2000: 50). (I comment on this latter passage in Chapter 14.)

17. See also E-AS 122: 'China is one vast empire, speaking one language, governed by one law and sympathising in the same manners.'

18. Hutcheson, too, uses the metaphor of contagion (*SMP* I, 20), which Hume had used earlier (E-AS 112). See also Hutcheson (SIMP 33/ Bk 1, Ch. 1, sect. 9).

19. Malebranche (n.d: 3, 278, Bk 2, Ch. 3, para 1) also refers to '*la communication contagieuse*', principally from those with '*les imaginations fortes*' to those with weaker ones.

20. Veblen (1909: 628) writes that 'institutions are an outgrowth of habit. The growth of culture is a cumulative sequence of habituation, and the ways and means of it are the habitual response of human nature to exigencies that vary incontinently . . . the underlying traits of human nature . . . remain substantially unchanged'. That whole essay resounds with (post-Darwinian) Humean echoes for those who want to hear them.

21. Kames here repeats the argument from his earlier *Essays upon Several Subjects in Law* (1732). How 'lengthy' the possession has to be before it achieves the status of 'title' Hume (*T* 3-2-3, n. 71/SBNT 504n) would regard as determined by the 'imagination or the more frivolous properties of our thought'. (Compare *M* 3, 33/SBNM 96.)

22. See also E-NC, where politeness is said to be commonly dependent on 'free intercourse' between the sexes.

23. Compare, from the *History,* it is 'the similarity of these institutions to the customs of the ancient Germans, to the practice of the northern conquerors and to the Saxon laws during the heptarchy [that] prevents us from seeing Alfred as the sole author of this plan of government' (*HE* I: 53).

24. This paragraph was omitted in later editions, so is absent from *SBNU*.

25. For a comment on the relation between Hume and Smith here, and for critical observations on the coherence of Hume's account, see Brewer 1988. A more positive version of Hume's account of development is offered by Macfarlane (2001: 86), who refers to Hume's articulation of a 'virtuous circle' whereby trade and manufactures stimulate productivity that becomes self-sustaining.

26. Hume (E-Com 263) refers to foreign trade giving birth to domestic luxury, and in the *History of England* gives the example of the importation from Germany of pocket watches in Elizabeth's reign (*HE* II, 599). For wider discussions of Hume on luxury, see Berry (1994: 42–52) (see also Chapter 13).

27. Smith (*WN* III.4.10/418) in his account makes the premise overt when he remarks of the 'great proprietors' releasing their retainers 'for a pair of diamond buckles' that 'all for ourselves, and nothing

for other people, seems in every age of the world to have been the vile maxim of the masters of mankind'.

28. Compare Smith's (*WN* III.4.10/418) reference in the same context to the 'silent and insensible' operation of foreign commerce.

29. Compare (E-Com 260) sovereigns cannot in practice 'pretend to introduce any violent change' because they have to take 'mankind as they find them' with the 'long course of time, with a variety of accidents and circumstances are requisite to produce ... great revolutions.'

30. Compare 'There is something hurtful to commerce inherent in the very nature of absolute government' (E-CL 92). (I discuss this passage further in Chapter 8.)

31. When, however, Hume looks at the causes of the growth of public debts, he refers to 'a strange supineness' that 'from long custom' has crept into all ranks (E-PC 360).

32. Sakamoto (2003: 94) has stressed the primary role of knowledge in Hume's account of 'technological and industrial progress'.

12

Hume's Universalism: The Science of Man and the Anthropological Point of View

My focus in this chapter is Hume's advertised attempt to establish foundationally a science of man. Though it is not his sole motivation, central to this effort is his intention to undermine the credibility of superstitious, supernatural accounts of what makes humans and their social life function. My argument is that attempts to downplay Hume's universalism and, in virtue of his recognition of diversity, to identify him as subscribing to some form of historicism or relativism, are mistaken or at best fail to apprehend the centrality of his assault on unscientific accounts of human nature.

I divide the argument into five sections. In the first I outline, chiefly via a brief exposition of the work of Clifford Geertz as its representative, what I will call the anthropological point of view. It is such a view, I contend, that is imputed to Hume by those commentators who identify him as a (sort of) historicist or relativist. My aim here is not to analyse Geertz's position but to employ it in order to throw into relief the interpretation of those Humean commentators with whom I am taking issue. The second section gives an exposition of Hume's universalism, while the third outlines his account of the process of socialisation as the strongest evidence of his supposed principled acceptance of the non-universality of behaviour/values/ manners. In section IV I elaborate a Humean account to illustrate how he is able to accommodate a recognition of diversity while still sustaining his commitment to universalism. In the final section I distinguish Hume's position from the anthropological on two fronts – the first stresses how the decisive variable in Hume's account of historical change is institutional, not human nature, and the second indicates (no more) how Hume's universalism functions evaluatively, with the consequent implication that not all ways of living are on a normative par.

I

Underlying the subscription to Hume of historicism or relativism, or what sustains it at an unexplicated level, is a pervasive understanding of 'culture', especially as expressed in (cultural) anthropology. Using the work of Clifford Geertz, I aim to illuminate this understanding and thereby the interpretation put forward by (among others) Livingston (1988), Capaldi (1978) and Schmidt (2003) (for further examples, see n. 5). While there is no suggestion that Geertz dismisses neo-Darwinism, what he does maintain is that human evolution occurred within a 'cultural setting'. As he puts it, humans are 'unfinished animals' who complete themselves through culture (1975: 49) Culture is not properly considered an add-on to biological evolution but, rather, an intrinsic ingredient; humans are 'cultural artefacts' (1975: 51). We become human by becoming individual but we only become individual under the guidance of cultural systems of meaning, which are 'not general but specific' so that 'to be human here is thus not to be Everyman; it is to be a particular kind of man and of course men differ' (1975: 52–3). Geertz does not deny that there are universals, such as, for example, some conception of what a human individual is (as opposed to a rock or an animal).[1] Nonetheless, while there are indeed universal 'existential problems', their solutions are 'unique' (1975: 363). The inference Geertz draws from this is that 'we all begin with the natural equipment to live a thousand kinds of life but end in the end having lived only one' (1975: 45).

One way of interpreting the central Geertzian claim is that it denies that Balinese conduct (say) is comparable with conduct A from culture z and with conduct B from culture y and that all are instances of the general rule R. Different cultural practices, that is to say, are not just particular examples of some general metacultural condition, a 'consensus gentium that does not in fact exist' (1975: 40).[2] Rather, each practice is distinctive and specific. If that is the case, then it follows that to explain a practice it is pointless to appeal to some external metacultural factors, 'bloodless universals' as he typifies them (1975: 43).[3] Instead, the explanation must be sought internally within the practice.

An 'internalist' perspective was propagated by Peter Winch (1958; cf. 1970) in a now classic exposition. To Winch, a Humean 'externalist' account of causality cannot explain, for example, the belief in witches. For Hume, witchcraft was a superstition and its persecution an act of fanaticism (*HE* II 366, III 416). Both superstition and fanaticism are for Hume the consequences of ignorance and the 'science of man' will account for them. An increase in knowledge will produce – as a causal regularity – a decrease in inhumanity (such as burning witches). Moreover, since this is a causal regularity, it holds good regardless of cultural differences. Winch, on the contrary, argues that in order to explain why a certain society acted in a certain way towards witches, such actions must be placed in the specific context of that society's way of life, its beliefs and so on. On this view the internal nature of beliefs makes them useless for any general or trans-societal explanation; their explanatory power is confined to their own society. It may, however, be fairly imputed to Hume that this is tantamount to giving up on explanation altogether; all that it provides is 'thick description' (a term Geertz was instrumental in diffusing). This is unacceptable because – and this is a point of some significance, as we shall see – it has the perverse consequence of affirming superstition as an inherently valuable way of life.

Hume, in fact, used the expression 'way of living' in his essay 'Of Interest'. This essay was one of the 1752 *Political Discourses*. As a preface to the opening essay ('Of Commerce'), he made some justificatory methodological observations. He states that it is his aim to develop some general propositions, beyond the particulars with which coffee-house conversation concerns itself. He identifies this ability to 'regard the general course of things' as the 'chief business of philosophers' who are able to take an 'enlarged' view and encompass the 'infinite number of individuals' in 'universal propositions'; they can even capture a 'whole science in a single theorem' (E-Com 253/4). While this particular wording here may be a rhetorical flourish, the science of man is indeed an 'endeavour to render all our principles as universal as possible' and this must encompass a way of living, since it evidently has a 'close and intimate' connection to human nature (*T* Intro 8, 5/*SBNT* xvi, xv).

II

The *locus classicus* for Hume's account of the relation between human nature and 'culture' occurs in his remarks about history in the first *Enquiry*. Although this is not the only source, nothing Hume says elsewhere fundamentally contradicts that account. It is there that he most unequivocally puts his case for the constancy and uniformity of human nature. Its location is in the chapter on liberty and necessity and that, too, is where similar expressions in the *Treatise* correspondingly occur. The location is significant because it places the discussion within Hume's attempt to treat human nature scientifically, as susceptible to causal regularity or necessity, as 'natural' and 'moral evidence' link together to 'form only one chain of argument' (*EHU* 8.19/SBNU 90).

In a well-known passage, Hume confidently asserts that 'it is universally acknowledged that there is a great uniformity among the actions of men, in all nations and ages, and that human nature remains still the same in its principles and operations', so that it now follows that

> history informs us of nothing new or strange in this particular. Its chief use is only to discover the constant and universal principles of human nature by showing men in all varieties of circumstances and situations and furnishing us with materials from which we may form our observations and become acquainted with the regular springs of human action and behaviour. (*U* 8.7/SBNU 83)

Hume is quite explicit that these 'materials' provided by the historical record are 'collections of experiments' that enable the 'moral philosopher' to fix 'the principles of his science' just as 'the natural philosopher becomes acquainted with the nature of plants [etc.] ... by the experiments which he forms concerning them'. If we ask what these 'principles' are, they are the 'regular springs' of human behaviour.

If we further ask what these 'springs' are, the general answer is the passions and he here lists ambition, avarice, self-love, vanity, friendship, generosity and public spirit. These operate regardless of the social context. If you want to know the Greeks and Romans then, he advises, you can pretty much study the French and the English. This independence of the principles of human nature from their particular social context – what I elsewhere have labelled a 'non-contextualist' theory (Berry 1982, 1986) – gives them authority. Hume supposes that a traveller's report which described a society of humans without avarice or ambition would immediately be detected a falsehood and the traveller a liar, just as he would be if he reported the presence of centaurs and dragons (*U* 8.8/SBNU 84).

Of course, there are differences and variations in what he here labels 'characters, prejudices and opinions' (*U* 8.10/*SBNU* 85), but the comprehension of these is still founded on knowledge of constant uniformity. In a metaphor employed in 'A Dialogue', included within the second *Enquiry,* he says that the difference in the courses of the Rhine and Rhone rivers is caused by the different inclinations of the ground but both rivers have their source in the same mountains and their current is actuated by the same principle of gravity (*M* Dialogue 26/*SBNM* 333). By the same token, all human behaviour, even if it has a 'local' character, is explicable because it is governed by regular springs that have uniform effects. Thanks to Hume's non-contextualism, 'man' is a fit subject for a 'science' because his behaviour necessarily exhibits certain uniformities. Man is not some locally defined phenomenon that can only be understood parochially. It would be contrary to the first Newtonian rule of philosophising if these local phenomena could not be subsumed under and explained by a few simple causes but had, rather, to be accounted for in their own strictly non-comparable terms, where (as he puts it) 'every experiment' was 'irregular and anonymous' (*U* 8.9/*SBNU* 85). We would, in effect, remain in the coffee house.

The scientific credentials that Hume bestows on his view give to it more than a merely formal or methodological status (cf. Wertz 1975, Forbes 1975: 119). That is to say, for Hume the constancy of human nature is not just a methodological rule of thumb or necessary presupposition to make any historical knowledge possible (cf. Walsh 1975, Pompa 1990); it is also a normative or judgemental yardstick. That dimension was implicit in the authoritative dismissal of the traveller's report and, as we will bring out in due course, it can be seen to be at the centre of his conception of the purpose or utility of the science of man.

Never far away from Hume's campaign for this science is his view of religion. In this broad context the *Natural History of Religion* is a key document (and one strangely marginalised in these debates). Its remit is to investigate the origins of religion in human nature. (For a fuller discussion, see Chapter 6/Berry 2000b.) To that end he produces another list of passions: anxiety (about future happiness), dread (of future misery), terror (of death), appetite (for food) and, more generically, hope and (especially) fear, which 'actuate the human mind' (*NHR* 2.4). It is in these latter two generic passions that Hume locates the source of religion. He admits that belief in an 'invisible intelligent power' has been 'very generally diffused' but he thinks it has not been so universal that there are no exceptions (*NHR* Intro). He also admits that where such a belief is found it is rarely the same across places and ages. It is this lack of both universality and convergence that prompts Hume to conclude that religion, unlike 'self-love, affection between the sexes' and the like, is not the product of an 'original instinct or primary impression of nature' but, rather, a 'secondary' principle – that is, one that may be '*perverted* by various causes and accidents' and 'by an extraordinary concurrence of circumstances be altogether *prevented*' (*NHR* Intro; my emphases).

Though Hume does not develop it, this distinction between primary and secondary principles signals something important about his conception of the science of man. It needs to be sustained if Hume's account is to maintain its alignment of science and uniformity and not succumb to the anthropological point of view, where there is no conceptual room for perverse accidents or preventable extraordinary concurrences. However, without putting it in those terms, a number of Humean scholars have assimilated his argument to that point of view or, more exactly, to its historicist corollary ('the past is another country').[4] With varying degrees of emphasis or nuance, and with varying views as to its implicit or explicit character, these scholars impute to Hume the position that he adopts a historically relativist perspective.

III

Hume's account of diversity seemingly underpins the anthropological point of view or historicist interpretation. In particular I want to pick up his answer to his own rhetorical question on history in the first *Enquiry*. He asks, 'Are the manners of men different in different ages and countries?' and replies, 'We learn thence the great force of custom and education which mould the human mind from its infancy and form it into a fixed and established character' (*U* 8.11/*SBNU* 86). What we have here is a clear and strong recognition of the process of socialisation. Hume makes much of this process and its power throughout his writings.[5] Indeed, so powerful does he seem to make it that it appears to take on Geertzian proportions; Nicholas Capaldi (1978: 99), for example, has attributed to Hume the view that he sees man as a 'cultural product'. Given this, it is necessary to show that for Hume the process of socialisation, as an explanation of difference, does not underwrite the conclusion that man is solely a Geertzian cultural artefact or product.

Hume's most extended discussion of socialisation is in his essay 'Of National Characters', where he observes that, 'whatever it be that forms the manners of one generation, the next must imbibe a deeper tincture of the same dye; men being more susceptible of all impressions during infancy, and retaining these impressions as long as they remain in the world' (E-NC 203). Underpinning this is his associationism, with its denial of innate ideas, and his (Malebranchian) philosophical physiology, according to which the minds of children are 'tender'; so that 'customs and habits' are able to 'fashion them by degrees' for social life (*T* 3–2–2.4/*SBNT* 486).

In 'Of National Characters' this is elaborated in his argument that moral rather than physical causes determine national character. He defines moral causes as 'all circumstances which are fitted to work on the mind as motives or reasons, and which render a peculiar set of manners habitual to us' (E-NC 198). What are the circumstances that form national character? Hume has the following list: 'nature of government, the revolutions of public affairs, the plenty or penury in which the people live, the situation of the nation with regard to its neighbours' (E-NC 198). His most cited moral cause is 'government'. For example, because 'manners follow the nation', the Spanish, English, French and Dutch colonies are distinguishable 'even between the tropics' (E-NC 205). Rather than these colonies adopting similar manners because of their physical exposure to the same climate, the children of English parents in the tropics possess an English rather than a Dutch character because they are socialised into the civic culture or manners of the English, not the Dutch. This socialisation, or 'fashioning', establishes through a process of moral causation different national characters.

Hume emphasises the impact of repetition and imitation. Given continually changing populations, these socialised habits supply a needed continuity – something social contract theory, for example, is unable to provide. What is required to achieve social stability is that 'the new brood should conform themselves to the established constitution and nearly follow the path which their fathers, treading in the footsteps of theirs, had marked out to them' (E-OC 476–7). The 'brood' conforms not as a consequence of any deliberate (read, adult) decision but because there is a pre-existent path.

This path they follow because that is the way of their world, the one into which they have been socialised or habituated, for 'men are guided more by custom than by reason [to] follow, without inquiry, the manners which are prevalent in their own time' (*HE* I, 395; cf. III, 116).

Manners as a way of living constitute institutions. Because habits are repeated responses that are made possible by a stable set of circumstances, which are themselves at least partly constituted by the prevalent system of habitual manners, then this repetitiveness leaves its mark. Habits and customs not only stabilise; they also constrain. They are so powerful in society because they are mutually reinforcing; the human mind 'is wonderfully fortified by an unanimity of sentiments' (E-PG 60). Put a group of humans together and, if they converse often enough, they will acquire a 'similarity of manners' (E-NC 202).

Institutions established in this way are correspondingly sticky. Yet no matter how sticky, a habit is not instinct or primary principle. The stability of circumstances necessary for habit formation may be disrupted. Indeed, one of the key reasons why moral causes are more explanatory than physical is because they accommodate social change – customs are chronologically constituted. One such change is the treatment of women. A commercial society is civilised, which means, inter alia and literally, that its citizens congregate in cities and no long live distantly (an aspect peculiar to 'ignorant and barbarous nations'). In an urban setting urbanity reigns, so that both sexes meet in an 'easy and sociable manner' as temper and behaviour became more refined (E-RA 271). This is a far cry from the depiction in 'Of the Rise and Progress of the Arts and Sciences', where the 'abject slavery' to which 'their females' is reduced is a hallmark of 'barbarous nations' (E-AS 133). Hume, indeed, treats it as evidence against the authenticity of Ossian's poetry that in it women are depicted with 'extreme delicacy', when such treatment is 'contrary to the manners of the barbarians' (1875: IV, 417). Yet none of this amounts to recognition of what Donald Livingston (1984: 225) refers to as 'each age . . . governed by its own laws and principles'.

IV

While it is clear from this exposition of Hume's account of socialisation and social change that he is acutely aware of social or cultural difference, this is not an expression of an anthropological or historicist account of human nature. To explain why, I want to pursue an implication of the account of chastity. Chastity is a particular way that some societies organise sexual and parental relations. Some such organisation is necessary if any way of life is to be sustained and that maintenance requires, as we have seen, that a society/culture reproduces itself through socialisation. This is necessary because, unlike other animals (even 'social' ones), humans lack self-sufficiency (T 3–2–2.2/SBNT 485). They have to learn how to co-exist. This is made feasible by the great dependency of the human infant, itself a consequence of their immaturity (relative to other animals) at birth, and by the associated physiological fact of their ductility.

In his essay 'Of Polygamy and Divorces', Hume remarks that 'among the inferior creatures, nature herself, being the supreme legislator, prescribes all the laws which regulate their marriages'. There is, he continues, a precisely attuned adjustment so that where the newborn animal is independent then 'the present embrace terminates the marriage' and where there is a period of dependency (where, for example, food is more difficult to obtain) then 'the marriage continues for one season', that is, until the offspring can fend for itself, whereupon the 'union immediately dissolves'. In humans, however, nature has not 'so exactly regulated every article' of the marriage contract; they have to adjust their marital arrangements according to prudence and circumstances. These adjustments take the form of municipal laws, which, although they may differ from place to place (such that polygamy may be allowed), are yet 'equally conformable to the principles of nature' (E-PD 183). Importantly, these universal principles are not effaced by the diversity of the regulation but serve to explain its presence in the first place. From that perspective, Hume can be read as here drawing attention to a distinctive quality of being human. I now limn a Humean argument about this distinctiveness.

What distinguishes humans is how they contrive diversely to cope with the uniformly universal imperatives of reproduction and nurture. These uniform imperatives in other animals are met in a species-specific uniform way by natural regulation. As Hume puts it in the *Treatise*, their wants and necessities 'compensate each other' (T 3–2–2.1/SBNT 484). By contrast, for humans there is a shortfall (there is an 'unnatural conjunction of infirmity and necessity'). This is especially acute because 'men cannot live without society' (*T* 2–3–1.9/*SBNT* 402), so that there is a need on their part to make their social or group life possible. This they achieve by creating rules to regulate their relations. The rules are 'human contrivances' (*T* 3–3–1.9/*SBNT* 577); they are not conjured from thin air but constructed from natural materials. In other words, being human requires naturally framing conventions to deal with the circumstances within which humans naturally find themselves.

These rules or conventions comprise *nomoi*; they are not behavioural/natural responses like (say) shivering when cold. However, humans have to form conventions; convention forming is not itself a matter of convention – it may even be said to be *kata phusin*. Hence Hume's remark that the artificial rules of justice may not improperly be called laws of nature, where 'nature' means what is common to or inseparable from any species (*T* 3–2–1.19/*SBNT* 484). As the case of chastity (as well as polygamy) testifies, sex is an unavoidable aspect of human social existence where humans necessarily have to regulate themselves through conventions. (Recall that in the *Natural History* Hume cites 'affection between the sexes' as an instance of a primary principle.)

Sex is not the only area where there is a shortfall. We can add, as Hume does, sustenance, shelter and clothing (*T* 3–2–2.2/*SBNT* 485). In each of these cases, groups of humans have fashioned a response to some ineluctable features of their existence. The ineluctability of these features means that no group fails to fashion a particular response to sustenance, sex, shelter and apparel and (we might care to include) to intimations of mortality. The form of the response is the establishment of conventional rules of conduct. Human life is made 'orderly' by these rules. Order is made or contrived in the sense that it cannot be read off directly or immediately from 'natural' promptings. Humans in Hume's philosophical anthropology are naturally inventive and imaginative creatures, so these mediated resolutions that they contrive are various. And it is by imposing these mediated rules (diversely) upon themselves that humans establish what are usually termed 'cultures'.

V

This universalist Humean argument can explain both why institutions recur ubiquitously and why they differ. However, this recognition of cultural difference is distinct from the position adopted by the anthropologist (and historicist). This distinctiveness reveals itself in two basic ways.

First, for Hume, cultural differences are questions of manners and customs (which are a form of what I referred to as mediated conventions) but these do not constitute human nature. It is a Geertzian presumption to think otherwise – a presumption that is contrary to Hume's conception of a science of man. If we ask 'what distinguishes a "savage culture"?' Hume's uniformly reiterated answer is that it is ignorance (*NHR* 1.3, 2.1, 3.3; *U* 10.20/ *SBNU* 119, etc.). And constantly conjoined with ignorance is superstition: 'from the grossness of its superstitions we may infer the ignorance of the age' (*HE* III, 113). The *Natural History* is again instructive. For example, it is because they are ignorant of the true connections between causes and effects that savages call upon the immediate and discrete action of gods to explain phenomena (especially those that frighten them). This ignorance is attributable to their circumstances. A savage is a necessitous creature, pressed by 'numerous wants and passions' (*NHR* 1.6). These pressing needs mean a lack of leisure and that shortcoming means no time to acquire instruction. The natural propensity to anthropomorphise will produce polytheism if it is not 'corrected by experience and reflection' (*NHR* 3.2). What is crucial is the relative breadth of experience and the opportunity to reflect. This now fits religious speculation into the broader schema of the development of civilisation and, more generally, it is worth recalling that Hume explicitly refers to natural religion as one of those 'sciences' that depend on the science of man; indeed, it is singled out as the one where most 'improvements' can be hoped for by the successful development of that science (*T* Intro 4, 5/*SBNT* xv).

A causal consequence, and one that holds independently of 'context', of being rude and untaught is the narrowness of intellectual capacities (*NHR* 3.3, 6.4, 6.5, 7.1). This argument is not confined to the *Natural History*. Still in the context of religion, Hume in the first *Enquiry* remarks that the illiterate form 'an idea of religion' that is 'suitable to their weak apprehension' and 'speculative dogmas' could not be 'conceived or admitted' by them (*U* 11.3/*SBNU* 133). In the second *Enquiry* he, more generally, remarks that savages have 'but faint conceptions of a general rule or system' (unlike 'us' who are accustomed to 'enlarged reflections') (*M* 9.8n57/*SBNM* 274n). This inability to generalise is echoed elsewhere, notably in the essay 'Of the Original Contract', where the idea of a compact for general submission is beyond the 'comprehension of savages' (E-OC 468). Although it is a Lockean truth that thinking in terms of concrete particulars precedes abstract generalisation, that epistemological point is true of the human mind as such – of children as well as savages – and it does not map on to a historicist account of unfolding rationality. Despite Claudia Schmidt's (2003: 421, 416ff., 379–84, 210–17)[6] attempt to establish common ground between them, Hume is not a contextualist Hegelian.

From his totally different premises, Hume is as clear as Hegel that civilisation is superior to barbarism. In his essay 'Of Refinement in the Arts', he explicitly identifies the former's humanity as the 'chief character' that distinguishes a 'civilised age from times of barbarity and ignorance'. This humanity is the product of the softening of their 'tempers' and is indissolubly linked with knowledge and industry (E-RA 274, 271). These are 'institutional' differences and relate only to the 'tempers' and, as he had made clear in the *Treatise*, differences in the 'tempers and complexions' of men are 'very inconsiderable' (T 2–1–3.4/SBNT 281). These remarks are echoed in the *Natural History*. Hume observes that human sacrifice has 'never prevailed very much in any civilised nation'; yet, even so, as the case of Carthage testifies, this prevalence is not so 'deep' as to preclude exceptions (NHR 9, n51).

Seeing the history of religious belief in this context serves to undermine the cogency of those views that seek to attribute a more thoroughgoing historicism to the Hume that, in the words of Simon Evnine (1993: 606), has 'some kind of developmental picture of the powers of the human mind'.[7] If the 'human mind' here refers not to individuals but, rather, to some anthropologically or historically specific 'mind', then this reference is a misplaced anachronism. The Humean savage is vulgar and ignorant (NHR 5.1–2, 7.1, 8.2). The vulgar are those who go by first appearances and are to be contrasted with the 'wise' or 'philosophers' (U 8.13/ SBNU 86, T 1–3–13.12/SBNT 150). But, crucially, the vulgar are always with us; they are on good Lockean grounds with us here and now. From this perspective, Hume's remark that the 'vulgar *in nations which have embraced the doctrine of theism* still build it upon irrational and superstitious principles' (NHR 6.4; my emphasis) makes perfect sense.[8] In short, there has been no change in human nature; in Hume's formulation already cited, in 'all nations and ages' it 'remains still the same in its principles and operations'. The vulgar of today are akin to the savage in the past in that both are relatively uninstructed. The decisive variable is institutional, the stickiness of which Hume can accommodate and consistent with which some 'progress', albeit neither guaranteed nor irreversible, can be made. But this 'progress' is not some historicist development of the human mind, nor do any of the putative stages into which it may be divided constitute anthropological, internally self-referential ways of life.

Hume's position is distinct in a second way, although a full account of its assumptions and implications cannot be developed here. Because Hume's argument does not regard ways of life as self-authenticating, it means that their diverse institutional expression is open to external evaluation. Just because polygamy is explicable as a naturally human contrived institution does not mean, Hume believes, that it cannot be appraised as to its comparative utility and, indeed, pronounced as barbaric and 'odious' (E-PD 183, 185). The universalism of human nature allows a scientist of man (a 'philosopher') to judge between true (better) and false (worse) institutional expressions (something beyond the 'vulgar').[9] Hence, by Hume's lights, the science of man can, for example, properly judge the Koran to be a 'wild and absurd performance' (E-ST 229) or, again, can decry, as we have seen, the barbarous treatment of women and, throughout, can denounce superstition. To label these judgements as mere reflections of 'anticlerical prejudice' (Hursthouse 1999: 75) or, as the anthropological view would have it, to regard them as resting on an unfounded universalism, is to miss their centrality in his philosophy. Within the limits of this paper I can only provide an indicative justification of this argument.

In the second *Enquiry* Hume deliberately notes how easy it is to ridicule vulgar superstition but then proceeds to demonstrate that more is at stake. He seeks a ground for the distinction between two seemingly similar cases: the reason, on the one hand, 'why another articulating certain sounds, implying consent, should change the nature of my actions with regard to a particular object' and, on the other, 'why the reciting of a liturgy by a priest, in a certain habit and posture, should dedicate a heap of brick and timber, and render it, thenceforth and for ever, sacred' (M 3.38/SBNM 199). The difference lies in the fact that the former is 'absolutely requisite to the well-being of mankind and existence of society', while the latter is 'frivolous'. If we ask on what grounds that distinction is sustained, the answer is the universality of human nature as elicited by the science of man. Accordingly, 'how great so ever the variety of municipal laws . . . their chief outlines pretty regularly concur; because the purposes to which they tend are everywhere exactly similar' (*M* 3.45/*SBNM* 202). Justice is 'the habit that takes place in all societies', although it is not 'without some scrutiny that we are able to ascertain its true origin' (*M* 3.47/*SBNM* 203). That 'scrutiny' is of the essence and it is executed by the science of man. This signifies that trans-societally, and trans-temporally, science is able to discern utility as the true source of justice. Further, and in accord with 'Newton's chief rule of philosophising', it is able to account for the comprehensiveness of its reach (*M* 3.48/*SBNM* 204). In this way we are authorised by scientifically grounded scrutiny to pronounce particular social practices 'frivolous, useless and burdensome' (*M* 3.38/*SBNM* 199) or false, like all forms of superstition. Hume can, for example, thus condemn modern convents as 'bad institutions . . . as nurseries of superstition, burthensome to the public and oppressive to the poor prisoners, male as well as female' (E-PAN 398).[10]

Underpinning and informing this condemnation is the fact that what the scrutiny of scientists/philosophers uncovers more generally is that humans have universally felt the same about the same kinds of things. In his conclusion to the second *Enquiry* Hume spells this out. The 'notion of morals' itself implies a sentiment 'so universal and comprehensive as to extend to all mankind' (*M* 9.5/*SBNM* 272). Indeed, 'the humanity of one man is the humanity of every one; and the same object touches this passion in all human creatures' (*M* 9.6/*SBNM* 273). Hence, illustratively, it is the universal 'structure of human nature' that 'unavoidably' makes everyone condemn, that is, express the 'sentiment of disapprobation' towards, treachery and barbarity (*M* Appx 1 6/*SBNM* 293). This is what humans do; they so judge because it is (the scientifically warranted) characteristic of human nature that, when analysed, what they approve of is 'every quality which is useful or agreeable to ourselves or others' (*M* 9.3/*SBNM* 270).

That universal ground of approbation may, however, be overlaid with the 'delusive glosses of superstition and false religion' (ibid.). These are overlays. Hume's very language indicates that they cannot be taken to represent equally valid alternative expressions. They are local deviations from the evidentially supported universalism that is the (human) natural source of all moral distinctions and value-laden forms of life. There can be no other credible locus. Morality is not miraculous and nor are social practices/institutions normatively *sui generis*. Witchcraft, and its associated beliefs, is subject to evaluation; it embodies empirically confoundable error and rests on a (externally explicable) lack of humanity or sympathy, that is, a deficiency in natural sentiments, the only sustainable basis for moral judgement.

This evaluative capacity goes to the heart of Hume's enterprise. Beyond a cognitive commitment, there is an animus at its core.[11] This is indicatively encapsulated at the beginning of the first *Enquiry,* when he declares that philosophers should not leave superstition 'in possession of her retreat' but rather 'draw an opposite conclusion and perceive the necessity of carrying the war into the most secret recesses of the enemy' (*U* 1.12/SBNU 12). A similar militaristic image had been offered in the Introduction to the *Treatise* (*T* Intro 6/SBNT xvi). The science of man as the 'only solid foundation' for the other sciences, including explicitly that of morals, and, itself resting solidly on 'experience and observation', is 'much superior in utility' to any other form of human comprehension (*T* Intro 7, 10/SBNT xvi, xix). This utility should not be underplayed. Hume's science of man is programmatic and since that rests on, and supports, the universality of human nature then it can serve as a benchmark. One key central manifestation of this utility is its ability to discount, as well as those reposing on philosophical abstractly rational bases, all supernatural accounts of morality and to replace them with a naturalistic account.

This replacement is not a neutral activity. While, as he famously says, philosophical errors are ridiculous, those of religion are dangerous (*T* 1-4-7.13/SBNT 272). And, as he spells out in the following paragraph, it is the science of man that can disarm the latter by correcting the former, by establishing a 'set of opinions . . . satisfactory to the human mind' (*T* 1-4-7.14/SBNT 273), for we 'ought to prefer that which is safest and most agreeable' (*T* 1-4-7.13/ SBNT 271). Without any scruple, philosophy is preferable to 'superstition of every kind or denomination' (ibid.). In other words, in its most modest expression, the universalism of human nature that the science of man reflexively supports can be legitimately employed – indeed, it is its essential point here – to evaluate different ways of living.

This brings us back to those interpreters of Hume, who would have him implicitly disavowing such evaluations and acknowledging what Livingston terms 'incommensurable . . . forms of human flourishing' (1998: 390). Pace Livingston, 'A Dialogue' contends against incommensurability for, as Hume explicitly states, 'the original principles of censure or blame are uniform'. Moreover and crucially, and also here echoing the *Natural History*, he continues that 'erroneous conclusions can be corrected by sounder reasoning and larger experience' (*M* Dialogue.36/*SBNM* 336). But their own arguments enjoin both the historicists and anthropologists to eschew such 'corrections' and their consequent interpretation of Hume disarms his animosity and renders the science of man a toothless enterprise. Reflecting perhaps a lack of confidence in evaluations resting on claims of human nature, or a supposed greater sensitivity to 'difference', they impose on Hume an alien agenda; he himself has been 'decontextualised'.

In fine, Hume's universalist account of human nature does not disregard cultural differences but neither does his recognition of those equate to a Geertzian anthropological or neo-Hegelian historicist perspective. Hume's science of man is authentically, yet distinctively, Enlightened.

Postscript

This chapter is an abbreviated version of a paper I delivered at the Hume Studies in Britain conference held in Oxford, September 2004. I am grateful to participants for helpful comments and, especially, to James Harris, its organiser, for his follow-up.

A useful complement (not, I think, a corrective) to my discussion is Jennifer Herdt (2013), who has followed up her book with an essay of which a key theme is that Hume, on the one hand, adopts a sympathetic understanding of historical difference while, on the other, recognising limits to that enterprise. Jacqueline Taylor argues somewhat similarly but is clear that Hume is no relativist and that 'he takes sides' (2015: 184). Claudia Schmidt (2013), in the same volume as Herdt, repeats the argument from her book that Hume is a 'contextualist'. For a full-blown restatement of the 'contextualist' case, see Gregoriev (2015). A more nuanced view that takes an explicitly differing view to mine is Dennis Rasmussen (2014 – see my long review in *Adam Smith Review* (2017, 10). One writer who acknowledges this article and also interprets Hume as a universalist is Marko Tolonen (2015).

Notes

1. Geertz (1983: 59). He immediately goes on to declare that the Western concept of a 'person' is a 'rather peculiar idea within the context of the world's cultures'.

2. The term 'metaculture' is used by John Tooby and Leda Cosmides (1992: 91) in their critique of what they call the Standard Social Science Model (they identify Geertz as an exponent).

3. For example, discussing 'art', he argues that the question is not whether it is 'universal' but 'whether one can talk about West African carving, New Guinea palm-leaf painting, quattrocento picture making and Moroccan versifying in such a way as to cause them to shed some sort of light on one another' (Geertz 1983: 11).

4. Although I am admittedly painting with a broad brush, my argument is not ad hominem but with an interpretative perspective, for representatives of which, in addition to Capaldi, Livingston and Schmidt (see text above), see Farr (1978), Dees (1992: 227, n. 25), Evnine (1993), Herdt (1970), Meyer (1958), Burke Jr (1978) and A. Cohen (2000). (See also postscript.)

5. For an elaboration of the principles underlying this, see Chapter 11 (Berry 2006).

6. Berry (1982) is an identified target, along with Pompa (1990).

7. See also A. Cohen (2000: 120): 'Hume advances the thesis about the historical progress of the human mind to demonstrate that savages cannot attain the truth in advance of civilised man.' But that chronological priority does not require a thesis about the 'human mind'. Similarly, although it appears without gloss, Livingston (1998: 175) characterises Hume's account of civilisation as 'the story of the development and cultivation of the human mind'.

8. Just before that statement, Hume had observed, *'Even at this day, and in Europe*, ask any of the vulgar, why he believes in an omnipotent creator of the world; he will never mention the beauty of final causes of which he is wholly ignorant.' He is ignorant because 'as an invisible spiritual intelligence is an object too refined for vulgar apprehension, men naturally affix to some sensible representation' (*NHR* 6.1, 5.9; my emphasis). To similar effect, he says elsewhere that the 'propensity of mankind toward the marvellous', though it may 'receive a check from sense and learning, it can never be thoroughly extirpated from human nature' (*U* 10.20/*SBNU* 119).

9. The force of this contrast had been noted by Kemp Smith (1941: 382).

10. Hume goes on to give an explanation for the occurrence of these convents and compares them to the ancient practice of infanticide. Here, too, he essays an explanation but *tout comprendre* is definitely not *tout pardonner* (as deeply consistent historicists might be thought to endorse) because he criticises classical authors for not speaking of this practice with the 'horror it deserves' (E-PAN 398).

11. Garrett (1997: 7) notes that Hume saw his age as 'a battleground' between philosophy and superstition (p. 7); and goes so far as to identify the avoidance of superstition as 'the principal goal of the entire *Enquiry*' (1997: 240; cf. 161).

13

Hume and Superfluous Value (or the Problem with Epictetus' Slippers)

Hume opens his essay 'Of Refinement in the Arts' by stating that 'luxury' is a word of 'uncertain signification' (E-RA 287). He knows full well the position of, on the one hand, those 'severe moralists' (as he calls them – Sallust is named as an example) who berate 'luxury' as a vice and, on the other, those men of 'libertine principles' (Mandeville is his unnamed exemplar) who treat luxury as advantageous even when 'vicious'. As is his wont, Hume states that this essay is designed to correct these opposed extremes. It is, however, clear, if only from the relative attention paid to it, that it is the former position that is principally in his sights. That focus is unsurprising because it is central to a particular animus within his political economy. It is this animus – his engagement with a distinctive but well-established and still well-entrenched moral stance – that concerns us here. While to look upon Hume from this perspective is not novel, its ramifications are more extensive than might be supposed. I here give an indication of this extent and limit the discussion to a key central argument. This argument I seek to capture in the notion (or conceit) of 'superfluous value'.[1]

I

The late Stoic slave/philosopher Epictetus is recorded as saying that the measure for a slipper or sandal is the foot. 'Measure' (*metron)* here means not merely size 8 feet for size 8 slippers but, more significantly, that a slipper is for the purpose of foot protection. Once that appropriate measure is forsaken, there are no limits; there is nothing inappropriate about, successively, a gilded, a purple and an embroidered slipper (Epictetus 1928: para 39). The clear message is that these are superfluous refinements that should be eschewed. It follows, moreover, that there is no poverty in possessing 'merely' an unadorned sandal; indeed, the reverse is true.

The meaning of 'poverty' here needs unfolding. There is a long-standing discourse within which poverty has a positive moral connotation. Within this discourse two emphases can be identified. The first of these is exemplified by Epictetus' Stoicism but is equally manifest in the ascetic tradition in Christianity. Here, like its contextual close relations, 'simplicity' and 'austerity' as well as 'severity', 'poverty' refers to the estimable practice of temperance and continence. To be severe in this sense is to be in control of oneself and thus of one's actions; it is to know the true and proper value of things and be in a position of forswearing temptations, that is, things of illusory value or luxurious superfluities like embroidered slippers. The second emphasis is more civic and is embodied in Sparta and 'ancient Rome'. Of the latter, Hume explicitly says that (according to the severe moralists) it combined its 'poverty and rusticity' with 'virtue and public liberty' (E-RA 275). This virtue is undermined once luxury goods for private consumption (like embroidered slippers) are available; in the words of the seventeenth-century civic moralist Algernon Sidney, poverty is 'the mother and nurse of . . . virtue' (1990: 254).[2] Hume reflects this duality of emphasis when he states that he will consider the 'effects of refinement both on private and on public life' (E- RA 269). One consequence, common to both emphases, of situating poverty in this lexicon is that it is a product of choice or will or reason. This understood, it is possible to draw a conceptual distinction between poverty and being impoverished (or necessitous, that is, having no choice). As we shall see, this distinction is a significant ingredient in Hume's political economy.

There is an accompanying philosophical anthropology to this moralised use of poverty. This can be expressed variously but at its core is the hierarchical division between reason and desire. In its paradigmatic Aristotelean form, the *enkratic* man acts from choice, not from 'desire' (*epithumia*) (Aristotle 1894: 1111, b15). All humans properly aim at (*hairetos*) eudaimonia, which is a 'perfect and self-sufficient end' (Aristotle 1894: 1097, b15–20). Those who attain eudaimonia are living life as it should be led; it is a complete life and, as such, one without 'desire'. (Epictetus has no 'craving' for a slipper beyond what is necessary to protect his feet.) There are, it is true, 'natural desires' (*phusikais epithumiais*) but these are naturally (*kata phusin*) limited (Aristotle 1894: 1118b,

15–18) and it is a hallmark of the *akratic* that they pursue bodily pleasures excessively and *para . . . orthon logon* (Aristotle 1894: 1151a, 10–12).[3]

In line with this anthropology the individual expresses the virtue of poverty by, in the light of a rational apprehension of the natural order, controlling his desires so that indulgence is forsworn. Just as Epictetus appreciates the appropriate measure of slippers, so the Stoic sage will drink but not get drunk and one informed with Patristic teaching will forgo sex with (or as) a pregnant woman. Similarly, in the civic emphasis, the virtuous citizens of Rome's early years were portrayed as forgoing indulging themselves with the spoils of victory, such as by banqueting sumptuously and building magnificent villas, and, instead, as dedicating the resources to public monuments.[4] These examples underwrite the fact that this anthropology has a particular focus on the body. Of course, the body has needs that must be satisfied but there is also a natural or rational limit to this satisfaction – hence only drink when thirsty and only have sex for the sake of conception and only wear on one's feet what is functionally needed.

Here in the meeting of functional needs, we have classically the place of economics – it deals literally with order or rule of the household. Once again, Aristotle lays down the basic model (see also Chapter 19). The household is geared to the meeting of 'everyday needs' (Aristotle 1944: 1252b) and what makes them quotidian is their reference to the recurring somatic satisfactions – food, clothing and shelter for warmth, protection and nurture. The activity of meeting these needs is for Aristotle a finite task, that is, though they ceaselessly recur there is an inherent, natural (*kata phusin*) limit that identifies proper satiation (Aristotle 1944: 1256b). In this context exchange can take place but this, too, is properly finite. Hence a shoe may be exchanged for food but only so long as the recipients use each of them for their proper ends – meeting the need for foot protection and hunger. What is not permissible is to produce the shoe for the sake of exchange (rather than need) (Aristotle 1944: 1257a). Aristotle is particularly exercised that those (*hoi kapeloi*) who spend their time exchanging will come to regard moneymaking (*chrēmatistikē*) as an end in itself rather than an instrumental activity. For Aristotle this inversion of means/end is a perversion, or corruption, and one marker of this is that once the natural/rational limit of need satisfaction is overstepped then the unnatural/subrational limitlessness of desire can take over.

Those who are taken over – who become 'slaves' to desire, to bodily pleasures (see Epictetus 1923: para. 1; Sidney 1990: 254) – no longer live the simple, natural life of virtuous poverty; instead, they are prone to a life of luxury. Epictetus' embroidered slippers would qualify as an item of luxury. It would be consistent for the 'corrupted' owner of gilded purple slippers to feel poor when she (the gender is not incidental) sees an embroidered pair. This is a matter of 'feeling'; it is certainly not a matter of rational judgement. Once the rationally determined natural limit is transgressed there is no resting place and, viewed from that perspective, life will always appear too short. Those who see matters in this light will become 'soft through a life of luxury' and, accordingly, afraid of death (Seneca 1932: no. 78). Such fear is unmanly and it is here that we can discern the long-running association between luxury and softness and effeminacy. On an individual level, men who live a life of luxury become effeminate. That is to say they become 'soft', unable to endure hardship and to act courageously in the etymologically definitive masculine fashion.[5] Accordingly, to live luxuriously is to the detriment of both the resolve of individuals and the strength of their *patria*.

It follows that such a life is to be morally censured. Within this discourse, poverty/luxury exist as categoric opposites – as virtue and vice. However, it will follow that if the former term is displaced then the latter, too, is uprooted. If, that is, poverty is understood not as virtuous austerity but as necessitousness, then luxury can lose its moralised (categorical) meaning. This reconfiguration is Hume's radical agenda, his animus.

Implicit in this reconfiguration is a double shift. First, Hume associates poverty with a pre-existing sense of destitution,[6] linked traditionally to the plight of orphans, widows, the aged and so on, who were the proper recipients of alms. This is a compassionate, not a severe, morality.[7] Secondly, he associates the necessity of labour (the traditional, specific lot of the poor) with the universal virtue of industry. In Hume, this virtue is one of those qualities the purpose of which is to make mankind cheerful and happy and which are, as such, opposed to the severe or austere demands exacted by reason in order to control appetites, as enjoined by 'the perpetual cant of the Stoics and Cynics' (M 6.21/SBNM 125).[8] Luxury/commerce, as we shall see, increases industry and thus both reduces destitution and augments the resources available for amelioration.

The reason why this can be an 'agenda' for Hume is (sweepingly) because 'luxury' had come again to the fore of debate in the later seventeenth and throughout the eighteenth century. The (short-hand) explanation for this recrudescence is that its longevity gave to it a ready-made quality that enabled it to encapsulate the range of disquiet that had been generated by the pace of social change – by the emergence of a commercial society of private market relations as well as of public credit and national debt.[9] To debate 'luxury' was to debate this emergence. The worries about commerce intensified – as is evident from the scale of the literature. The popularity of John Brown's *Estimate*, which went through six editions in its year of publication (1757) and which sums up the 'character of the times' as manifesting 'a vain, luxurious and selfish effeminacy', is merely an indicative case (Brown 1758: I, 29, 67, 129). A similar avalanche of literature is evident in France.[10] It is not that the articulation of these worries was particularly profound – there was a predictable sameness about them with the moralised fate of Rome being a favourite *topos*. Though this might comprise a 'tired litany' (Hont 1983: 309), it, nonetheless, had sufficient energy to warrant Hume taking issue.[11]

In an attempt to bring out (an aspect of) Hume's own agenda within his 'economic' essays, I employ as a term of art the idea of 'superfluous value'. What for Epictetus, and those severe as well as civic moralists who share his perspective on poverty, would be an oxymoron is, rather, for Hume, an expression of his rejection of that outlook. He rejects the philosophical anthropology that privileges reason and he displaces the ethic of poverty. For Hume, to be poor is to be necessitous – it is to lack the basics. What commerce holds out is the way to improve that condition and integral to that improvement is giving value to the production of luxury goods such as exquisitely embroidered slippers. There are two aspects to giving a positive evaluation of that footwear. Firstly, they represent a source of pleasure or enjoyment that is intrinsically valuable in its own right – consumption is a good. Secondly, as consumption goods, their production and participation in a system of commerce has instrumental benefits that redound generally. I examine these in turn.

II

This examination commences with a return to the beginning. In 'Of Refinement in the Arts', having declared 'luxury' to have an uncertain signification, Hume gives his own definition: luxury is 'great refinement in the gratification of senses' (E-RA 268). This is not to be read censoriously as an endorsement of the moralists, because he goes on declare, as a generalisation, that 'ages of refinement' are 'both the happiest and most virtuous' (E-RA 269). In a clear break, therefore, from the moralist tradition, Hume is coupling luxury/ refinement with happiness/virtue – not opposing them.

Hume can now put forward arguments that would be anathema to the severe moralists. For current purposes, we can focus on how Hume is able to give a positive gloss to the 'superfluous' – why there is no inherent fault/vice in those embroidered slippers. Such slippers would qualify as one of those 'commodities which serve to the ornament and pleasure of life'; they represent 'innocent gratification' (E-RA 272). Hume, indeed, scarcely bothers to argue for this innocence. He affirms that it would not occur to anyone that 'indulging of any delicacy in meat, drink or apparel' is of itself a vice; unless, that is, they were 'disordered by the frenzies of enthusiasm' (E-RA 268). A little later, Hume reasserts the point by remarking that 'refinement on the pleasures and conveniencies of life has no natural tendency to beget venality and corruption' (E-RA 276). The fact that Hume is so disdainful reflects his animus, that his chief target is the moralised poverty/luxury pairing.

Underpinning this disdain is his rejection of the philosophical anthropology that underlies that moralism. The 'modern' view, to which Hume subscribes, rejects the idea that desires can be limited to some fixed end. As Hobbes pointed out, the only way to be 'free' of desire is to be dead. Desire, or 'uneasiness of the mind' (Locke 1854: II.21.31), is the spring or spur of action as humans move towards what they imagine pleases and away from what they imagine will occasion pain. For Aristotle, such mutability was characteristic of normative imperfection. It was this judgement that established the basic classical/ Christian distinction between, on the one hand, the tranquil/ascetic life, devoted to the contemplation of the immutable First Cause or the eternal perfection of God, and, on the other, the mundane life which is unceasingly at the beck and call of the demands of bodily desires.

According to Hume, the 'arts of luxury' add to the 'happiness of the state *since* they afford to *many* the opportunity of receiving enjoyments with which they would otherwise have been unacquainted' (E-Com 256; my emphases). Humans, he goes on, are roused to activity or industry by the presence of 'objects of luxury' and by, consequently, a 'desire of a more splendid way of life than what their ancestors enjoyed' (E-Com 264).[12] Hume does not specify the content of this splendour but we know from his definition that it encompasses sensual gratification and it is thus reasonable to suppose that it refers to those same sorts of goods that were deprecated by the moralists – fine homes, fine food and fine apparel like embroidered slippers. In addition, there is dynamism to this desire – my ancestors may have thought gilded slippers the very acme of luxury; I know that hand-embroidered ones are far more desirable. Hume reinforces the anthropological fact that desire moves humans, and signals further his dismissal of the moralised perspective when he also refers to 'men's luxury' making them 'covet' commodities (E-Com 261) and, perhaps most strikingly of all, when he then enumerates as effective human motivations 'avarice and industry, art and luxury' (E-Com 263). Since the civic and severe moralists uniformly condemned 'avarice',[13] this statement alone effectively signals the switch in evaluations that has occurred. It is, moreover, not 'alone'. Elsewhere avarice is depicted as a 'constant and insatiable' 'craving' (E-Int 149), as being thus 'universal', operating 'at all times on all persons' (E-AS 113) and as, accordingly, an 'obstinate passion', it is 'the spur of industry' (E-CL 93). As we will develop later, this spur is central to the benefits that flow from the recognition of superfluous value. When industry abounds then individuals will be not only opulent but happy as they 'reap the benefit of . . . commodities so far as they gratify the senses and appetite' (E-Com 263).

Against the backcloth of Epictetus' slippers, it is worth underlining the import of this remark. Sensual gratification is a source of happiness; to indulge one's appetites by delighting in a pair of embroidered slippers is not something to be severely censured. Furthermore, the inhabitants of opulent nations will 'desire to have every commodity in the utmost perfection' (E-JT 329; cf. E-Com 264). Epictetus' downward spiral of gilded, purple and embroidered slippers is rather the upward thrust for more and better. And because this is comparative, and rooted in the anthropology of infinite desire (cf. E-Com 264), then this 'utmost perfection' is ever evanescent. One implication of this is the recognition of qualitative differences. The Epictetean view treats all these 'departures' from functionality as superfluous. For Hume they are the essence of refinement. He aptly compares the gluttonous Tartars, who feast on dead horses, to the 'refinements of cookery' experienced in the contemporary courts of Europe (E-RA 272). To develop refinement – as manifest both in the presence of qualitatively differentiated goods and in the ability to appreciate both the skill and the beauty of a fine meal or splendid slippers – is not to indulge in excess. Excess, as exhibited by the Tartars, is mere quantitative increase beyond some fixed sum but, as such, it is conceptually distinct from qualitative refinement. To recognise that goods possess superfluous value is to recognise and endorse that distinction.[14]

To own an elegant (refined) pair of slippers, with their 'superfluous' stitchery, is not only satisfying but also makes a 'statement'; their possession is an object of pleasurable pride. In an image that Smith adopts (*TMS* IV, I-10/110), Hume refers to men's minds as 'mirrors' in which the owner of the slippers will see reflected the esteem of others and which, in its turn, supplies him with further satisfaction (*T* 2–2–5.21/*SBNT* 365). This recognition of deep sociality that Hume, along with his compatriots, regards as a foundation of the science of man (see Berry 2003, Chapter 5), affords another reason to dismiss the Epictetean perspective. The essence of the austere poverty prescribed by Epictetus was to be self-sufficient, not dependent on the views of others. It is the same outlook that sustains Christian asceticism and makes the hermit 'saintly'. For Hume these are 'monkish virtues', which for him means they are really not virtues at all: recall that ages of refinement are the 'most virtuous'.[15]

Once it is acknowledged that real human beings live in society and when, as in a commercial society, there is both more sociability (as they 'flock into cities' E-RA 271 – recall ancient Rome's 'rusticity') and a variety of differentially refined goods, so that their consumption takes place under the gaze of others, there is, once more, a dynamic imparted to such societies. These 'others', seeing how the owner of splendid slippers enjoys both the slippers and the social esteem that goes with their ownership, will seek to desire them also. This desire (though this is implicit in Hume – Smith makes it explicit) becomes one of the 'passions' causing labour and thus increases both the quantity and quality of consumables (cf. E-Com 261). In consequence, as we will show in the next section, those who live in non-opulent states will be less 'happy'; they will consume fewer and inferior commodities and they will be poor in the sense of being impoverished.

This recognition of the social context means that it would be misleading to think that Hume was crudely Epicurean. In his 'economic' essays he treats happiness as more than passive (hedonistic) consumption. In 'Of Refinement in the Arts' he analyses happiness into three interrelated components: repose, pleasure and action (E-RA 269–70). Of these, the last is given most weight. Repose or indolence is agreeable only in the short term, as a necessary recuperative interlude, but if prolonged it subsides into lethargy and, in fact, 'destroys all enjoyment'. Pleasure, Hume thinks, is attained as much from the activity itself as it is from the enjoyment of its fruits. There is, he affirms, 'no craving or demand of the human mind more constant and insatiable than that for exercise and employment'; this 'desire' seems, as a result, to be the 'foundation of most of our passions and pursuits' (E-Int 300). Action, industry and employment or labour enlarge mental powers and faculties and, crucially, produce great social benefits.

III

Both political and economic benefits ensue from the recognition and acceptance of superfluous value. As we have seen, an opulent nation is also a happy and industrious one. However, while that might be accepted, there was a long-standing argument that such opulence represented the weakness of the nation – that a commercial nation given over to luxury would be soft (cf. Hirschman 1977: 64).

Hume takes it upon himself to rebut this. A key part of his strategy is to develop a contrast between the civilised or refined on the one hand and the barbarous or rude on the other. (This contrast we have already met in the form of that between Tartars and the European courts as well as between the rustic and the urban(e).) He declares that it is 'peculiar' to 'polished or . . . luxurious ages' that 'industry, knowledge and humanity are linked together by an indissoluble chain' (E-RA 271). The converse, as neatly expressed in a later essay, is that rude states 'are buried in ignorance, sloth and barbarism' (E-JT 328) and, by extension, from what we ascertained in the previous section, its inhabitants will be unhappy and impoverished – unappreciative of 'the pleasures of the mind as well as those of the body' (E-RA 271). Nonetheless, this positive argument in favour of 'civilisation' might still fall foul of the severe moralist's claim that 'hardiness' is vital to national greatness, as measured by military strength. It is, accordingly, important to the argumentative success of Hume's ('political') defence of a commercial society that this view of 'greatness' and its associated virtues is undermined.

It is a mark of the growth in 'humanity' within civilised states that the 'tempers' of men are 'softened'; and one manifestation of this softening of manners is that wars are less cruel and the aftermath more humane (ERA 274). Despite this, Hume denies (here echoing Mandeville (1988: I, 122–3)) that this softening has enervated 'the martial spirit'. The supposed causal link between luxury and military weakness is undermined by the cases of France and England, that is, of the two most powerful *and* most polished and commercial societies (E-RA 275; cf. *HE* II, 598–9).

Hume elaborates on this latter causal link. It is, for him, 'according to the most natural course of things' that 'industry and arts and trade encrease the power of the sovereign' and that they do so without impoverishing the people (E-Com 260). This combination is made possible by the very 'superfluity' that industry, in the pursuit of luxury, has created. In times of peace this superfluity goes to the maintenance of manufactures and the 'improvers of liberal arts' (hallmarks of civilisation) but when an army is needed the sovereign levies a tax the effect of which is to reduce expenditure on luxuries, thus freeing up, for the military, manpower previously employed in luxury-good production (E-Com 261). In both 'Of Commerce' (E-Com: 262) and 'Of Refinement in the Arts' (E-RA 272), Hume declares that the more labour is employed beyond 'mere necessaries' the more powerful is the state due to the ease with which that labour (as a sort of 'storehouse') may be converted to the 'public service'. Nor does it follow that these will be inferior troops. On the contrary, recalling the 'indissoluble chain', these fighters will benefit not only from the technology that a civilised society can command but also from the overall higher level of intellectual competence.[16] All that the 'ignorant and unskilful' soldiers of rude nations can achieve are 'sudden and violent conquests' (E-Com 261 cf. *HE* I, 627). As Culloden recently testified, they are ineffective against trained troops armed with sophisticated weaponry.[17] It is a further consequence of this that the quintessentially male virtue of courage is now passé. The fact that Hume calls luxurious ages 'most virtuous' signifies that he sees no loss – rather a gain – in the fact that this virtue is largely absent. In its place is put equity and justice.[18]

Incidentally, this argument also enables Hume to dispel, in

effect, the classical prejudice against *hoi kapeloi*. Once the military virtues are downgraded, the accusations of effeminacy and commitment to their own private – rather than the common public – good levelled at merchants can be dismissed as untenable. This opens the way for an endorsement of their role. Hume thus unambiguously declares that 'merchants are one of the most useful races of men'. They 'beget industry' and, in contrast to the landed gentry and peasantry, they accumulate capital that can be lent (competitively) at a rate to stimulate further commerce and consumption (E-Int 300–3). What is equally (if not more) significant about this vindication of merchants is its link with the virtues of a commercial society.

Merchants, as the 'middling rank of men', are 'the best and firmest basis of public liberty' (E-RA 277).[19] In essence, this is because they 'covet equal laws'. This linkage between liberty and equality under law (what he calls 'true liberty' (*HE* I, 115; cf. I, 175; I, 320; II, 602)) is a prerogative of commercial states – 'progress in arts is rather favourable to liberty and has a natural tendency to preserve ... free government' (E-RA 277). It is, accordingly, a background condition of the happiness enjoyed by the citizens of such states that they are 'free'. But this is a (private) liberty to receive securely what their art or industry has produced. There is a polemical bifocality to Hume's argument. We have already seen how he contrasts the rule-governed liberty of a commercial society (government of laws) with the licentious anarchy of pre-commercial eras (government of men) but Hume is also here, more subtly, subverting the 'republican' or civic case for free government, where public liberty is conceived of as embodying, and sustained by, active civic virtues.

In 'Of Civil Liberty' he comments that ('notwithstanding the French') 'there is something hurtful to commerce inherent in the very nature of absolute government' (E-CL 92). Although in this essay Hume puts this down to the lack of 'honour' socially attributed to it, he is aware of the more common argument that absolutism breeds insecurity and is thus harmful to commerce. Hume does address this latter argument in 'Of Taxes', where he identifies the most 'pernicious' taxes as 'arbitrary'; a sovereign can easily convert these (such as a poll tax) to 'punishments on industry', so that they become 'oppressive and intolerable' (E-Tax 345/6). It is a 'natural if not an infallible effect of absolute government' that the 'common people' are 'in poverty' (E-Com 265). For Hume, the connection between liberty and opulence is a definitive characteristic of a civilised (where industry, knowledge and humanity cohere) nation. Moreover, 'honour' itself 'acquires a fresh vigour' with the advance of knowledge and good education and one effect of this is to 'restrain' the 'love of money' (E-RA 274, 276).[20] It is, accordingly, not the case that refinement has a 'natural tendency' to venality; once again, excess characterises rude rather than civilised societies. This is reinforced by his notion of a civilised monarchy (E-CL 94; cf. E-AS 125; *HE* II, 15). Civilisation, not regime type, is decisive. It brings free government and does so without any recourse to the possession of civic virtues.

The prime embodiments of such virtues were Sparta and the Roman republic. Though beloved of the moralists (whom 'we peruse in our infancy' (E-RA 275)), they are unworthy of emulation. Their much-vaunted poverty, supposedly the basis of their civic virtue and military prowess, rested on slavery and slavery, if nothing else, is 'disadvantageous' to 'happiness' (E-PAN 396).[21] Slaves are impoverished. Note here how Hume's reconfiguration has shifted the argument. Once the moralistic perspective, with its 'idealised' advocacy of poverty as the transcendence of bodily desire, is displaced, then a more 'realistic' assessment of the actual 'experience' of being poor is possible. From that latter perspective, slavery, not liberty, is the more likely outcome; peasants, he says explicitly, submit to slavery 'from poverty' (E-RA 277). From that same realistic perspective, Spartan policy goes against the 'natural bent of the mind' (E-Com 263), so that to govern along Spartan lines would require a 'miraculous transformation of mankind' (E-RA 280).[22] Government, however, is not in the business of miracles; it must deal with the world and human nature as it is. ('Politics' was announced in the introduction to the *Treatise* as a subject properly a concern of the 'science of man' [*T* Intro 5/*SBNT* xvi].) All it can do is channel the passions so that their effects minimise social disharmony. This is (in grand simplifier mode) in contrast to the classical framework and its influential early-modern embodiment in the neo-Stoicism of Lipsius for example, where the proper response to unruly bodily passions was the cultivation and application of reason.[23] Rather, for Hume, the 'magistrate' can 'very often' only cure one vice by encouraging another, where the latter's effects are less damaging. It makes no sense to criticise the magistrate for not imposing in line with 'classical' principles some objective, rational doctrine of the 'good life'. Instead, the appropriate judgement is: does this policy promote the material well-being of those individuals subject to it?

This is the crux of the 'benefits' argument for superfluous value. It is a form of utilitarianism – 'Le superflu chose très nécessaire' (Voltaire 2003: I, 22).[24] Understood in this way, luxury can be justly cultivated because it is superior to sloth. The stimulus for such cultivation is initially external, since foreign trade has 'given birth to domestic luxury' (E-Com 263/4). This has the effect of acquainting men with both the 'pleasures of luxury' and the 'profits of commerce'. The latter are attained by exporting what is 'superfluous at home' to nations where that commodity is in short supply. The appreciation of such 'great profits' stimulates more merchants to set up in competition. Domestic manufacturers replicate this dynamic as they seek to 'emulate the foreign in their improvements'. Industry is thus advanced to the benefit of all. But 'delicacy' is also stimulated by the pleasures of luxury and, as we have seen, desires for a more splendid way of living ensue. Delicacy and industry come together, as noted above, to work up commodities to 'utmost perfection'. The result is the happiness of those who live in refined societies, able to wear elegant ('the last word' in) slippers.

This defence of luxury still enables Hume to allow that it can be 'vicious' as well as innocent (virtuous). What Hume means by 'vicious' is non-beneficial or without advantage to the public (E-RA 269, 278).[25] His argument is exiguous and little more than a jibe at Mandeville's supposed casuistry – Hume sees no need to deny that pernicious luxury is poisonous (E-RA 279).[26] However, this brevity is to be expected once it is appreciated that Hume's animus is directed at the moralist critique of luxury. In effect, 'vicious luxury' for Hume is when obligations cannot be met. He is able to take this line precisely because he has already displaced the ethic of poverty and its counterpart deprecation of luxury. Once poverty becomes thought of as necessitousness or impoverishment, then luxury, as its counterpart, is so only contingently rather than categorically. That is, we could criticise expenditure on embroidered slippers ahead of the purchase of staples but that criticism is a judgement about misallocation of priorities.

But that is a relative (contingent) and not an absolute (categorical) judgement in at least two respects. Firstly, what counts as 'staple' is not necessarily fixed (poverty, as we would now say, is 'relative'). This recognises, as contemporaries said explicitly, that one-time luxuries have become necessities,[27] which implies that the relation between them is (temporally) contingent. Secondly, 'value' is not intrinsic but relative. Hume himself says the 'value which all men put upon any particular pleasure depends on comparison and experience' (E-RA 276; cf. *T* 2–1–6.2/*SBNT* 291) (recall the inadequacy with which a pair of 'merely' gilded slippers is now viewed). It is at least feasible that I might 'set my heart upon' owning such slippers to the extent that I deliberately skew my expenditures to afford them. You might think I am foolish but for me it is a sacrifice worth making; the slippers truly have superfluous value. Regardless, what Hume is at pains to reaffirm is that though luxury 'when excessive' can generate both private and public ills, nevertheless it is still better to accept it than attempt vainly to eradicate it (E-RA 279–80). It is a 'trade-off'. Without the spur to industry that luxury supplies, individuals (and thence their society) would fall into sloth and idleness. The social and individual cost of those outweighs any benefits that might conceivably accrue from a proscription on 'luxury' – a circumstance that the historical record bears out.[28]

In other words, once luxury is detached from its moralistic anchorage it can be viewed 'positively'. Of course, the evolution of ideas is not smooth and 'luxury' as the prerogative of the 'idle rich' continued (and perhaps continues) to be criticised, though even here it is Hume's bugbear of 'sloth' rather than luxury itself that is the real target. Rather more symptomatic is that, once luxury was detached from a moralistic context and 'economics' developed as a discipline, 'luxury' came to attain a technical neutral meaning as high-income elasticity of demand.

The shift away from moralism that Hume's account exemplifies means that luxury can be understood as the (contingent) opposite of necessity. It can be assessed by the extent to which it promotes employment, industry, population and all-round national strength (and by the opportunity-costs of its absence). And central to this enhancement is its improvement of the conditions of the 'poor'. As we noted above, Hume is explicit that in ages of refinement 'many' can now 'enjoy' the 'finer arts'; they are not the prerogative of the (few) rich. The more people who are employed in the 'mechanical arts' the more the appropriate equality, where every person 'ought to enjoy the fruits of his labour, in full possession of all the necessaries and many of the conveniencies of life', will obtain (E-Com 265). This enjoyment adds more to the happiness of the poor than it diminishes that of the rich. Moreover, this 'equality' inhibits the rich from increasing burdens 'on the poor' and oppressing them still further (E-Com 265; cf. M 3.25/SNBM 91). A life confined to 'necessity' now signifies not the austere life of poverty but an impoverished one, a life of misery. There is nothing ennobling or redemptive about *this* poverty. This is spelt out unambiguously in an earlier essay, where he exclaims that 'poverty and hard labour debase the minds of the common people' (E-NC 198).[29]

This rejection of the virtue of poverty exemplifies Hume's rejection of the mercantilist/Mandevillean advocacy of 'low wages'.[30] In order for the manufacture of slippers, beyond Epictetus' severe criterion, to act as a 'spur' to industry, sufficient 'spending power' has to be present in the economy. While this rejection of the 'utility of poverty' (Furniss 1920: Ch. 6) is 'economic', it also reveals a (loosely construed) utilitarian ethic – to be poor is to be unhappy and that 'painful' state is 'bad'. Again, just as the degree of 'civilisation' is more decisive than political form when it comes to liberty, so the 'poverty' that accompanies the absence of industry obtains, whether the government be republican or monarchical (E-Com 267).

IV

From the perspective of the simple/poor life, any alteration to Epictetus' functional slipper is unwarranted for, as noted earlier, the mutable is the imperfect. There is seemingly no place for change or innovation; a slipper simply does what a slipper does – keep feet warm indoors. This fixity is a corollary of the categorical opposition between poverty and luxury. But once poverty becomes impoverishment, the relation with luxury becomes contingent and potentially dynamic.

One of the striking things about the moral critique of poverty is that very often in practice it served to underwrite a hierarchical status quo. Politically Hume is no egalitarian but his recognition of superfluous value does imply a rejection of the precommercial world, where, for example, sumptuary laws operated. This legislation sought to preserve the pecking order, to attempt through display to maintain 'distance'[31] and thus to confine the incidence of a good and prevent its diffusion. Luxury – 'new' wealth – always threatened to overturn this. Those in the lower ranks of these societies may well have wanted some of those privileged goods, like embroidered slippers, but that 'wanting' was a mark of their unworthiness. The animus that Hume's view contains is a rebuttal of that disparagement. This egalitarianism should not be misinterpreted – Hume is no more an 'economic' egalitarian than he is a political one. Rather, what his view represents is closer to what Werner Sombart called *Versachlichung*, the wish to enjoy the tangible reality of magnificent clothes and comfortable homes (Sombart 1913: 112).[32] It is the enjoyment of such goods (intrinsically), and the motivating desire to attain them (instrumentally), that gives 'value' to the 'superfluous'. And since the presence of that enjoyment and that motivation in an age of refinement makes us at once happy and virtuous, then the desire on the part of the 'have-nots' to those goods currently possessed by the 'haves' is legitimate; indeed, it is part of human nature, realistically, that is materialistically understood.[33]

To offer a generalising conclusion: one consequence of rejecting the normative superiority of the eternally immutable was the acceptance of the worth of the mundanely mutable, of what has been called 'the affirmation of ordinary life' (Taylor 1989: Pt 3). Life, self-preservation, from being for Epictetus a 'thing indifferent' or for civic moralists being nobly sacrificeable (*dulce et decorum est pro patria mori*), became valued for its own sake. Politically this means that desires are to be accommodated, not proscribed, as the sovereign's interest lies not in the specific content of desires but only in the likelihood of their peaceful co-existence. This is the view that comes to be called liberalism. In effect, liberalism valorises the mundane. When seen against this, admittedly very broadly drawn, backcloth, Hume's recognition of what has here been called 'superfluous value' is an endorsement of that valorisation and a key ingredient of his political economy.

Postscript

This chapter was originally a paper delivered in 2003 at a conference on Hume's political economy at Barnard College, New York. I am grateful to Carl Wennerlind and Margaret Schabas for the invitation. It subsequently appeared in a volume of the proceedings (Wennerlind and Schabas 2008). That collection remains the best source for Hume's economics (Wennerlind and Schabas 2011), in addition to which the editors have followed up in a jointly authored manuscript that, when published, will set a benchmark.

This is all the more the case since Hume's economics continues to be understudied. He features in some histories of Scottish economics (ed. Dow and Dow (2006) in a contribution from Wennerlind) and more recently Rutherford, who cites my HOPE article (2012) (see Chapter 11). Willie Henderson (2010 – reviewed by me in the online *Erasmus Journal for Philosophy and Economics*) is narrowly construed and not as helpful as it could have been.

Notes

1. I used this term (without specific reference to Hume) in passing in Berry (1999a). This paper develops some points made therein.
2. Cf. Livy (1934), who in the preface to his *History*, remarks that no *res publica* was greater than Rome when poverty was there highly esteemed (a condition lost once riches and wantonness were introduced).
3. Aristotle links incontinence (*akrasia*) with softness and luxury (*malakia, truphē*), where the latter is sometimes revealingly translated as 'effeminacy' (Aristotle 1894: 1145, a35).
4. Cf. Sallust (1921: para 9). Of course this is a rhetorical ploy but that presupposes established judgements. For commentary on the practice of public endowment ('evergetism'), see Veyne (1976).
5. The pagan/classical roots of this were exploited by early Christians. Tertullian (1951: II, 13), for example, talked of *fidei virtus* being rendered effeminate (*effeminari potest*) by the softening of luxury (*deliciae*).
6. Cf. his characterisation, 'when a poor man appears, the disagreeable images of want, penury, hard labour, dirty furniture, coarse or ragged cloathes, nauseous meats and distasteful liquor, immediately strike our fancy' (M 6.33/SBNM 129). The references to apparel, furnishing and food recall the focus on bodily needs.
7. In one of his few explicit references to Epictetus, Hume remarks that 'he scarcely ever mentioned the sentiment of humanity and compassion but in order to put his disciples on their guard against it' (M Appx 4.14/SBNM 181).
8. The critique of 'austere pretenders' who talk of 'useless austerities and rigours, suffering and self-denial' is a recurrent theme (see M 9.15/SBNM 153).
9. There is now an extensive literature on the growth of 'luxury trade/ goods' and patterns of consumption. A recent collection that reviews (and adds to) that literature is Berg and Eger (eds) (2003).

10. Cf. Ross (1976), Maza (1997), Roche (1993: 507–20), Labriolle-Rutherford (1963) and Shovlin (2000).

11. I forgo discussion/speculation as to his motives, but see Emerson (2008a) and Hont (2008).

12. See Chapter 15, 'Hume on Happiness', where I also finesse this particular passage by more closely attending to the precise context.

13. Cf. Sallust's remark that public *mores* had been corrupted by luxury and avarice, as poverty became a disgrace rather than a virtue and *corpus animumque virilem effeminat* (1921: paras 5, 11, 12).

14. Hume does on occasion employ the term 'refinement' less positively (see, for example, his early essay 'Of Simplicity and Refinement in Writing', but it recurs at E-Com 254 where he comments, apropos modes of thinking, that 'an extraordinary refinement affords a strong presumption of falsehood'). I am grateful to Eric Schliesser for drawing my attention to this more negative usage. (I discuss this essay more fully in Chapter 15.)

15. It is not merely circumstantial that Hume, at the very start of E-RA, chooses a monk to exemplify someone who is disordered by the frenzies of enthusiasm as he covenanted with himself never to look out of his cell window on to the 'noble prospect'. Cf. M 9.3/SBNM 146.

16. In his *History* Hume implicitly connects the development of artillery with humanity (the third link on the chain) when he observes that though 'contrived for the destruction of mankind' it has 'rendered battles less bloody' (*HE* I, 498).

17. Not that Hume was starry-eyed about the competence of contemporary military conduct. He witnessed first-hand the disastrous campaign in Brittany of St Clair (Mossner 1980: Ch. 15).

18. Cf. Hume (M 7.15/SBNM 135): 'it is indeed observable that among all uncultivated nations who have not as yet had full experience of the advantages attending beneficence, justice and the social virtues, courage is the predominant excellence'. (A little later the 'social virtues' are identified as 'humanity, clemency, order, tranquillity'.) A particular case is sixteenth-century Scotland when 'arms' prevailed over 'laws' so that 'courage preferably to equity or justice was the virtue most valued and respected' (*HE* II, 82; similarly the Anglo-Saxons, *HE* I, 10, 115).

19. But see Forbes (1975: 176ff.) for further (complicating) comment.

20. It is true that Hume remarks that 'it is an infallible consequence of all industrious professions, to beget frugality, and make the love of gain prevail over the love of pleasure' (E-Int 301). But two comments

are in order. First, this itself expresses the differentiation of a commercial society since Hume uses 'industrious' in a narrow sense to refer to merchants in distinction from lawyers and physicians as well as the landed gentry. Second, these frugal merchants are nonetheless beneficial because they use their wealth to stimulate industry through investment.

21. Hume makes a telling ad hominem critique of Seneca, who is quoted as complaining about the beating of servants not as an example of cruelty but of the disorders attendant upon luxury (E-PAN 386).

22. For an examination of Hume's treatment of Sparta, see Berry 1994: 142–52.

23. Lipsius (1583: Bk 1 Ch. 5) distinguishes *ratio* – from obedience to which flows command of all lusts (*cupidines*) – from *opinio* – through which, as the offspring of the body, the vices rule.

24. Voltaire, *Le Mondain* (2003: l.22). There is here detectable a critique of Fénelon (1962: 453–4), the most influential critic of luxury in early eighteenth-century France, who had contrasted *les arts superflus* to *les vrais besoins* imposed by Nature (Cf. Bonolas 1987). Voltaire was directly influenced by Melon and indirectly (probably) by Mandeville. Hume knew Melon's 1734 *Essai politique sur le commerce* (1842) and cites him in 'Of Commerce and Of Money'. For discussions of Hume's reception in France, see the papers by Charles (2008), Hont (2008) and Shovlin (2008).

25. Hume had called luxury (along with prodigality, irresolution and uncertainty) 'vicious' in the *Treatise*, the fault being that these characteristics 'incapacitate us for business and action' (*T* 3.3.4.7/SBNT 611). In line with Hume's later account in E-RA, this fault is consequential, not intrinsic. I am grateful to Carl Wennerlind for drawing my attention to this passage.

26. Sallust (1930; para. 11) had declared avarice a *venenis malis*.

27. Melon (1842: 742), for example, *'ce qui était luxe pour nos pères est à présent commun, et ce qui l'est pour nous ne le sera pas pour nos neveux'*. See also Mandeville (1988: I. 169–72).

28. Cf. his account of England under Elizabeth when the 'nobility were by degrees acquiring a taste for elegant luxury' and though this led to the decay of 'glorious hospitality' yet it is 'more reasonable to think that this new turn of expense promoted the arts and industry; while the ancient hospitality was the source of vice, disorder, sedition and idleness' (*HE* II, 601).

29. He is similarly explicit when he depicts the era of the Normans as one where the 'languishing state of commerce kept the inhabitants

poor and contemptible; and the political institutions were calculated to render that poverty perpetual' (*HE* I, 320; cf. I, 2; I, 127).

30. There has been some debate over this. The text most quoted as indicating that Hume was an advocate of low wages is his report that ''tis always observed in years of scarcity, if it be not extreme, that the poor labour more and really live better than in years of great plenty' (E-Tax 635). This is cited by Johnson who treats Hume as 'partially' accepting low wages as incentive (1937: 287), by Himmelfarb (1984: 51) and by Furniss (1920: 122). However, Furniss later identifies Hume as urging the utility of increasing real wages so that the stand-ard of living might rise (p. 189). According to Coats (1958), Hume presents both sides but the main weight of his case was against restrictions on the expansion of labourer's wants and improvement of their living standards. (Coats (1992: I, 90) elsewhere is more emphatic in aligning Hume with the view that a rising standard of living was a good for all. The passage from 'Of Taxes' was omitted from the 1768 and subsequent editions of the *Essays* (note also the conditional clause) but see *HE* II, 259, where 'necessity' is cited as required to shake people from 'habits of indolence'. (For an expansion of this note, see Berry 2013: 88–9n.)

31. Cf. Bourdieu (1979: 58), '*le pouvoir économique est d'abord un pouvoir de mettre la nécessité économique à distance; c'est pourquoi il s'affirme universellement par le destruction de richesses, le dépense ostentoire, le gaspillage et toutes les formes de luxe gratuit*'. Compare Hume's comment on the process historically, 'High pride then [in the reign of James I] prevailed; and it was by a dignity and stateliness of behaviour, that the gentry and the nobility distinguished themselves from the common people. Great riches acquired by commerce were more rare and had not yet been able to confound all ranks of men and render money the chief foundation of distinction. Much ceremony took place in the common intercourse of life and little familiarity was indulged in by the great. The advantages which result from opulence are so solid and real, that those who are possessed of them need not dread the near approach of their inferiors. The distinctions of birth and title, being more empty and imaginary, soon vanish upon familiar access and acquaintance' (*HE* III, 97). In his usual forthright manner Hume called the sumptuary legislation of Edward III 'ridiculous' (*HE* II, 259).

32. This coincides with the decline in luxury as 'display', especially by rulers to signify their 'majesty', a function necessarily undermined by the diffusion of such 'signifiers'. Hume himself remarks on how

the nobility moved from vying with each other over the number of retainers to 'a more civilised species of emulation, and endeavoured to excel in the splendour and elegance of their equipage, houses and tables' (*HE* II, 53).

33. Cf. E. Hundert (1974: 139–43), who refers to Hume's 'psychological egalitarianism', his conviction that 'the lower orders' were 'the psychic equals of all men'.

14

Science and Superstition: Hume and Conservatism

It is convenient, probably inevitable, to affix shorthand characterising labels to major thinkers. Sometimes these are simply a
reflection of the thinker's own self-identification, so that Marx is
a 'communist' and Jefferson a 'republican'. But in other cases the
labelling is an attribution, so Locke is a 'liberal' and Machiavelli
a 'realist'. In this second category Hume is a 'conservative'. These
attributive labels are gross-grained summary judgements and they
can thus be qualified, or indeed rejected, by a finer-grained analysis. Hence Locke's supposed liberalism can look less secure when
his view of toleration, for example, is subject to closer scrutiny;
and Machiavelli's supposed 'realism' can be seen as distortion
when viewed in the context of his 'virtuous' republicanism.

Here I want to argue that Hume as a conservative is similarly a
shorthand label that is at least insecure and at most a distortion. I
do not want to claim that the label is fanciful or without justification, but to raise questions as to its accuracy once it is subjected to
further inspection and, consequently, to doubt its aptness or utility
in capturing what is a key characteristic of Hume's socio-political
thought. This argument is constituted as follows. After some preliminary refinement of the topic, I then, in order to establish that
the paper is not attacking a 'straw man', identify in Part I those
aspects of Hume's thought that most securely underwrite attributing the conservative label. In Part II I construct an argument
to render insecure the conservative label and, also in so doing,
suggest or intimate grounds for the further claim that, when his
commitment to 'science' and his polemics against superstition and
other 'chimerical' practices and principles are taken on board, the
stronger case that the label is a distortion can be judged to have
substance.

Firstly, though, I am excluding from consideration that line of interpretation that reads Hume as becoming conservative (or more conservative) as he grew older. Even if this is true, and the evidence is not decisive, it itself implicitly recognises the 'insecurity' of Hume's conservatism and thus removes the rationale for this chapter. The variant of this view that, in the Hegelian trope, 'wisdom comes at dusk', such that the 'late' Hume is the 'true' Hume, I leave uncontested because it begs too many hermeneutical issues.

The second preliminary is a refinement of the scope of this discussion. Historically, religion, whether as an institution, a practice or a theology, has played a prominent role in the articulation of conservatism. Given Hume's antipathy to religion – his effective dismissal of tenable belief in miracles, his demolition in his posthumous *Dialogues* of the meaningfulness of regarding this world as embodying some special design and his critique of all forms of superstition – he can be assigned no role in the formulation of a religion-based conservatism. However, it is reasonable to say that this dimension is now less salient, while not altogether absent. This relative de-emphasis has opened some 'space' for the identification of a Humean 'contribution' to contemporary conservative thinking. Sheldon Wolin (1954: 1015) marked this by characterising Hume's conservatism 'analytical' rather than 'metaphysical', while Jerry Muller (1997: 24) declares Hume's thought a 'watershed' in the development of a secular conservative doctrine.[1] It is this secular aspect that I want to consider.

I

We can identify the following four interrelated aspects of conservative thinking without endowing them with any strong criterial properties.[2] As a heuristic benchmark we can use perhaps the most significant Anglophonic secular conservative thinker of the twentieth century, Michael Oakeshott (see Berry 2009: Ch. 4 for an earlier articulation).

A Critique of Rationalism

The first aspect is a critique of rationalism or recognition of the limitations of reason. Oakeshott identified a 'rationalist' disposition that consisted of enmity towards authority, prejudice and the 'merely traditional, customary or habitual', so that 'to form a habit' is thought be a failure (Oakeshott 1991: 6, 7). This Oakeshottian rationalist utilises 'technical' knowledge, which is characterised by formulation into rules, as – to give one of his favourite examples – the technique of cookery is contained in the cookery book. Oakeshott is allusive as a writer but it is possible to glean from his discussions that he sees Descartes as standing at the fount of this interpretation of rationalism and regards as its embodiments, inter alia, Bentham, advocates of progress in the manner of Helvetius or Godwin and, above all, socialist ideology. Oakeshott does acknowledge Hume as one of those writers from whom one can learn about what, in contrast to the rationalist, he calls the conservative disposition (Oakeshott 1991: 435).

Certainly, Hume is not a Cartesian rationalist. For him, reason 'is the discovery of truth and falsehood' (T 3–1–1.9/SBNT 458) and for that alone is it equipped. This limitation means that it does not apply to 'actions', which are the work of the passions; famously or notoriously, Hume considers reason inert (T 2–3–3.4/ SBNT 415). This makes him critical of rationalist philosophers who extend reason's role, who believe it is possible to arrive at demonstrative conclusions in the operation of common life. His target is a type of moral philosopher who affirms that 'virtue is nothing but a conformity to reason; that there are eternal fitnesses and unfitnesses of things which are the same to every rational being that considers them' (T 3–1–1.4/SBNT 456).

Hume's rather narrow critique of rationalism might be thought to contribute little distinctive to a conservative case, but there might appear to be more affinity from the fact that against the demonstrativeness of reason Hume upholds a sceptical stance. Almost invariably when analysts of conservatism invoke Hume (as they invariably do), they cite his scepticism as a justification of the invocation, with Frederick Whelan's (1985: Ch. 5) account the most nuanced and sophisticated. Scepticism, it is frequently claimed, corrodes the certainty that sustains those who wish not to conserve the status quo but replace it by (in their eyes) some-thing better. This scepticism then leads to something approaching Oakeshott's conservative disposition, 'to prefer the familiar to the unknown, to prefer the tried to the untried, fact to mystery, the actual to the possible, the limited to the unbounded, the near to the distant, the sufficient to the superabundant, the convenient to the perfect, present laughter to utopian bliss' (1991: 408).

Certainly, as we shall see, there are passages in Hume that

express alarm at radical change and exhibit distaste for political zeal. But Hume called himself an exponent of 'mitigated scepticism'. He does indeed think this approach can instil a 'modesty and reserve' into those ('the greater part of mankind') who exhibit a dogmatic one-sidedness in their views (U 12.24/$SBNU$ 161). It can also wean our minds 'from all those prejudices which we may have imbibed from education or rash opinion' (U 12.4/$SBNU$ 150). But, and this is crucial, there is an intimation here that Hume does not utilise his scepticism passively, as inducing acquiescence. As we will argue below, he considers it a central role of the science of man to challenge and overturn prejudice, notably in the form of superstition, and his conviction of the possibility of a science of politics indicates that his scepticism is not pressed into conservative political service.[3] Indeed, Hume distinguishes his scepticism from its extreme form (which he calls Pyrrhonian) because that would undermine the intelligibility of a science of man and thus of his attempt to put 'a compleat system of the sciences' on an 'almost entirely new' foundation (T Intro 6/$SBNT$ xvi). That this reposes on probability (T 1–4–1.4 /$SBNT$ 181), not demonstration, does not, in a wider or non-technical sense, amount to a derogation of 'reason'.[4] Indeed, he recurrently defends the 'philosopher' or 'abstruse' reasoner against vulgar and shallow thinkers (for example, E-Com 254; U 8.13/$SBNU$ 86; T 1–3–13.12/$SBNT$ 150).

Philosophically, Hume's 'disposition' is anything but 'conservative'. Donald Livingston (1995: 156), however, does hold that Hume's thought expresses 'the philosophical core of the conservative intellectual tradition'.[5] Livingston's broad argument is that Hume's conservatism rests on a radical critique of (false) philosophy and a rejection of what Livingston (1984: 23) calls 'the autonomy principle', of which (once again) the Cartesian method is the prime example. But he does observe that this critique is only an intimation of a later (post French Revolution) structure of thought (Livingston 1995: 152). What Livingston does regard as central to this intimation is an interpretation of common life as 'custom'. Although Livingston never cites him, this allies his argument with Oakeshott's alternative to rationalist technique.

Before turning to the place of custom, there is one final aspect of conservative anti-rationalism to broach. This aspect is the recognition that the limits of reason establish the unattainability of 'perfection.' There is no blank sheet on which humans can write and which script can, if 'irrational' obstacles are removed, be put into effect; rather, we operate and think (reason) in an inherited, complex, concrete context. Leaving aside Hume's technical use of 'reason', his recognition of these limits can be detected in, for example, his view that edicts to restrict consumption behaviour were ineffective (*HE* I, 535), that a Spartan regime was contrary to the grain of human nature (E-Com 259), as well as the crucial role he sees habit playing in social life. 'Human nature', he says, has 'incurable' weakness (E-OG 38). This sensitivity to imperfection is why commentators such as Noel O'Sullivan and Anthony Quinton, who pick up Oakeshott's argument, enlist Hume in the conservative camp and, more dramatically, it is Hume's *'paura della perfezione'* that for Guiseppe Giarrizzo (1962: 48) gives the particular hue to his conservatism.

Custom or Habit

I use Hume's references to custom or habit, along with the associated traits of a commitment to continuity and gradualism, to develop my second aspect of conservatism. While this is undoubtedly a recurrent motif in Hume's thought, some care is needed. He does declare (in his own *Abstract* of the *Treatise* [*Ab* 35/*SBNT* 662]) that habit is the cement of the universe but that declaration reflects his analysis of causality and the centrality he apportions to it. However, as an expression of his commitment to the association of ideas, this is, as he claims, so universal in its scope (*T* 1–1–4.1/ *SBNT* 10) that it cannot at this level support any one particular application over another. It is, for example, habit that makes equally the prisoner and the designer of prisons causally associate secure incarceration with stone, not paper, walls. Accordingly, in the context of 'conservatism', the operant idea of custom/habit is its expression in human conventions and institutions – or what Oakeshott (1975: 75) calls a 'practice'.

As an example of this expression, Hume writes that the 'wise magistrate' will be aware that 'habits more than reason' are 'in everything . . . the governing principle of mankind' (*HE* III, 116). And, in a strong passage that does reflect on his part a downplaying of human autonomy in its rationalistic individualist guise, he remarks that human societies comprise continually changing populations, so that to achieve any stability it is necessary that 'the new brood should conform themselves to the established constitution and nearly follow the path which their fathers, treading in the footsteps of theirs, had marked out to them' (E-OC 476–7). The 'brood' conforms not as a consequence of any deliberate (or as we might say with the metaphor, 'adult') decision but because there is a pre-existent path. This path they follow because they neither know no other route nor even consider the possibility of there being one. As he puts it in another related essay, 'habit soon consolidates what other principles of human nature had imperfectly founded and men once accustomed to obedience never think of departing from that path in which they and their ancestors have constantly trod' (E-OG 39). Oakeshott (1975: 100) echoes this metaphor, characterising practices as 'footprints left behind by agents responding to their emergent situations'.

Socialisation plays a key role in Hume. No individual is ever in position to 'stand outside' their time and place; they are born into communities that embody values and norms of conduct, which, like children following in their parents' footsteps, they necessarily assimilate. As he says appositely in his critique of contract theory, that argument supposes humans are like 'silk-worms and butterflies' whereby one generation goes 'off the stage at once, and another succeed' (E-OC 476). For Hume, the key social convention of justice that serves to stabilise possession arose 'gradually' and acquired 'force by slow progression' by means of the 'repeated experience of the inconveniences of transgressing it'. This same process is also how languages are 'gradually established' and how 'gold and silver become the common measure of exchange' (T 3–2–2.10/SBNT 490).

Conservatives do not reject change but they are resolutely opposed to radical, revolutionary or violent change. This opposition rests on the contention that revolution dangerously upsets an order established over time. The conservative will advise circumspection – any change should go with the grain of both human nature and the established institutional framework. This is undeniably a central plank in Hume's social theory. His narrative of the growth of liberty, outlined in the History (HE II, 601–3), is a clear example, while his Essays refer frequently to the power of habit, as when it consolidates the chieftain's power (see E-OG 39). To equal and consequential effect, Hume thinks that to attempt to short-cut or accelerate this gradual process is to court disaster; 'violent innovations' are 'dangerous' as 'more ill than good' is to expected from them (E-OC 472, 477). The danger is that, because of their lack of gradualism, these violent innovators imperil the stability of the social order. But Hume, as ever, is non-dogmatic. This is a rule that has exceptions (as with Henry VIII's break with Catholicism). Less dramatically, Hume admits that innovations do have a place, though when the magistrate attempts some public improvements he will wisely 'adjust his innovations, as much as possible to the ancient fabric and preserve entire the chief pillars and supports of the constitution' (E-IPC 513).

Functionality

The longevity or persistence of current institutions and norms warrants the presumption that they are extant because they function – that is, perform a useful task. This functionality is the third aspect of conservative thought that I have chosen to select. The survival of these institutions, ways of living, systems of value and the like means that they have been tested and thus, the conservative claims, are to be valued. In Hume this is central to the necessity of justice in the maintenance of systemic social stability. It is the function of property rules to sustain, through their inflexibility, expectations and confidence in future regularity. We know from experience that this redounds to 'public utility'; if the 'distinction and separation of possessions [were] entirely useless' then that convention would never have arisen (M 3.47/SBNM 203). For Oakeshott (1991: 421), routines are all the more useful the more familiar they are, as they serve to 'establish and satisfy expectations'. Characteristically, perhaps, in Oakeshott the force of this is negative; it is 'obvious folly' not to be disposed conservatively toward a fixed routine – the familiar, whatever it is, has value because it is too disruptive to amend (see Knowles (2000), Brennan and Hamlin (2004)). I will return to this last point because it will constitute a point of departure to examine why labelling Hume a conservative is at best insecure and at worse a distortion.

Concreteness

I identify the fourth aspect of conservative thinking as 'concreteness'. I employ this term of art to pick out the conservative sensitivity to actual situations, and the response of specific groups of humans to them, as well as a distrust of hypothetical abstraction. This appreciation of the concrete leads to a tendency towards particularism in conservative thought (and thus in some guise to an affinity with nationalism). I will also return to this in Part II, because, on this specific point, Hume is an uncertain fellow traveller. He has no time for any valorisation of local superstitions when set against the findings of the science of man. But, more generally, it can be allowed that Hume does recognise that humans act in concrete circumstances. We can again illustrate this recognition by his account of the accretion of power by a chieftain. The contractarian account that there was an original compact that was 'expressly formed for general submission' (something 'beyond the comprehension of savages') is unsustainable in the face of the experiential observation that 'each exertion of authority in the chieftain must have been particular; and called forth by the present exigencies of the case' (E-OC 468–9). Moreover, he chides contractarians for being 'reasoners' who have not looked 'abroad in the world' but who have, instead, articulated a 'refined and philosophical system' to which 'nothing in the least corresponds' for the idea of an original contract is contrary to 'history and experience' (E-OC 470–1). And Oakeshott's 'conservative' will have 'nothing to do with innovations designed to meet merely hypothetical situations' and when there is an innovation, one that is a 'response to some specific defect' is more desirable than one designed generally to improve the human condition (Oakeshott 1991: 470, 431, 411–12).

II

I now turn to the 'case' that Hume's thought is not accurately characterised as conservative. I noted above, when discussing functionality, Oakeshott's view that the familiar of itself has value. This is where, notwithstanding all the above, we can see Hume's divergence. This is most tellingly present in his treatment of superstition. While, as we have seen, Hume clearly appreciates the conservative power of custom, he also recognises that customs can be bad as well as good, though in either case they are capable of enduring for a considerable period. It is here where Hume's scientific agenda comes into play, since the major example of a 'bad' custom is a 'superstition'. The judgement as to whether Hume-as-conservative is an insecure or distorting label will crucially depend on how much weight is given to this dimension of his thinking. That is to say, a Humean conservative would presumptively acquiesce in an institution (say, fasting) if it was a well-established custom and would counsel against an 'external', or rational, assessment of its operant functionality by some ideal of good conduct. Hume the scientist qua natural historian of religion would neither so acquiesce nor so counsel; for him it is 'odious and burthensome', possessing all the hallmarks of a superstition (*NHR* 14.5).[6]

In an early essay he identifies 'weakness, fear, melancholy together with ignorance' as true sources of superstition (E-SE 74). Though his focus here is on a contrast between superstition and enthusiasm as species of 'false religion', he sustains his critique of superstition throughout his work and what is increasingly salient is the link with ignorance. Hence, when characterising 'savage life', the feature that Hume uniformly identifies is that they are ignorant (*NHR* 1.6; U 10.20/*SBNU* 119, etc.); it is 'from the grossness of its superstitions we may infer the ignorance of the age' (*HE* III, 113; *HE* I, 148).

A crucial consequence of this assessment of savages as ignorant and superstitious is that Hume does not regard their 'way of life' as self-authenticating; rather it is open to external evaluation (see Berry 2007; Chapter 12). Just because polygamy, for example, is explicable as a naturally human contrived institution does not mean, Hume believes, that it cannot be appraised as to its comparative utility and, indeed, pronounced as barbaric and 'odious' (E-PD 183, 185). The universalism of human nature allows a scientist of man to judge between true (better) and false (worse) institutional expressions. Hence, by Hume's lights, the science of man can, for example, properly judge the Koran to be a 'wild and absurd performance' (E-ST 229) or, again, can condemn modern convents as 'bad institutions . . . as nurseries of superstition, burthensome to the public and oppressive to the poor prisoners, male as well as female' (E-PAN 398–9).

Underpinning and informing these judgements is the fact that what the scrutiny of scientists/philosophers uncovers more generally is that humans have universally felt the same about the same kinds of things. In the conclusion to the second *Enquiry* Hume spells this out. The 'notion of morals' itself implies a sentiment 'so universal and comprehensive as to extend to all mankind' (*M* 9.5/*SBNM*). Indeed, 'the humanity of one man is the humanity of every one; and the same object touches this passion in all human creatures' (*M* 9.6/*SBNM*). Hence, illustratively, it is the universal 'structure of human nature' that 'unavoidably' makes everyone condemn treachery and barbarity (*M* Appx 1 16/*SBNM* 293).

That universal ground of approbation may, however, be overlaid with the 'delusive glosses of superstition and false religion' (M 9.3/ SBNM 270). As Hume's very language here indicates, superstitions cannot be taken to represent equally valid ways of living. They are local deviations from the evidentially supported universalism that is the (human) natural source of all moral distinctions and value-laden forms of life. There can be no other credible locus. All supernatural accounts of morality are to be discounted and replaced with a naturalistic account.[7] Morality is not miraculous and nor are social practices/institutions normatively *sui generis*. Superstitions fall clearly under this rubric. Hume judges that it fits men for slavery and is thus an enemy to civil liberty (in that respect enthusiasm fares better) (E-SE 78).

This evaluative capacity goes to the heart of Hume's enterprise (cf. Garrett 1997: 240). It is indicatively encapsulated at the beginning of the first *Enquiry* when he declares that philosophers should not leave superstition 'in possession of her retreat' but, echoing the militaristic imagery in the Introduction to the *Treatise* (T Intro 6 SBNT xvi), rather 'draw an opposite conclusion and perceive the necessity of carrying the war into the most secret recesses of the enemy' (U 1.12 /SBNU 12). It is Hume's conviction that the science of man, as the 'only solid foundation,' is 'much superior in utility' to any other form of human enquiry (T Intro 6, 7, 10/ SBNT xvi–vii, xviii). This utility should not be underplayed and central to it is the capacity of the science of man to evaluate different ways of living. And since these 'ways' comprise fundamentally customs and habits then it means he is seeking to replace one set of customs by another 'better' set.[8] Hence, for all the 'conservatism' that comes from recognising the intractability of customs, and from acknowledging that 'revolutions' are dangerous and inapt, Hume does not think this provides a 'normative trump' to conserve indifferently a set of current customs. 'Erroneous' moral conclusions, he judges, can be 'corrected by sound reasoning and larger experience' (M Dialogue 36/SBNM 336).

The commitment to the science of man that underlies this external assessment of superstition also underlies Hume's positive agenda. His philosophy embraces his understanding of the findings and implications of modern science.[9] Moreover, his conviction that philosophy consequently has to be put on 'new footing' results in a critique of traditional understandings of morals, economics and politics as well as religion. Inasmuch as a new conception of freedom is a central ingredient in that critique then, if, with all the caveats about their utility and aptness still in place, a label is to be attached to his thought, then he is in a significant way a 'liberal', albeit as we will acknowledge that qualifications need to be made.

A central feature of this new conception of freedom is a defence of the world of commerce – of industry, knowledge and humanity (E-RA 271) – and since for Hume commerce 'can never flourish but in a free government' (E-CL 92) then this defence is also a defence of liberty. Hume declares that 'progress in the arts' is favourable to liberty and the establishment of the rule of law (E-RA 277). This itself is a 'modern' view of liberty. Liberty, he declares, is 'the perfection of civil society' but this is necessarily connected to the operation of the rule of law, 'to act by general and equitable laws that are previously known to all the members and to all their subjects' (E-OG 40–1).

Importantly, this liberty, which he characterises as 'true or regular liberty', is enjoyed by all. This inclusiveness demarcates it sharply from 'ancient liberty'. Ancient liberty was exclusive. It was enjoyed by those who had leisure and that was made possible, as Hume pointed out, with a 'dig' at 'republicans' (or 'zealous partisans of civil liberty' (E-PAN 385)), by the presence of a class of slaves (E-Com 257; E-PAN 383). The abolition of slavery was part of the civilising process brought on by the emergence of the commercial way of life – its customs and habits (cf. HE I, 702). If superstition is a form of bad habit then commerce is a good habit or 'way of living' (E-Int 298). The realisation and maintenance of this liberty 'requires such improvement in knowledge and morals as can only be the result of reflection and experience and must grow to perfection during several ages of settled and established government' (HE I, 175). This exemplifies the general maxim that 'all advances towards reason and good sense are slow and gradual' (HE I, 249). Although this is a clear espousal of gradualism, its talk of 'improvement' (and, indeed, of 'perfection') gives it a definite progressivist hue. Admittedly, Hume is far less committed to 'progress' than his (particularly French) contemporaries, just as his defence of commerce is not without some reservations.

Nonetheless, it is testament to his commitment to commerce that he supported positive action to remove hindrances to the exercise of economic liberty in order to foster good and to counteract bad habits. Certainly Hume believes social change occurs at the level of 'ways of living' (Berry 2006; Chapter 11). But while this affects the pace of change, and thus implicitly counsels against short cuts, nevertheless this 'gradualism' is integrally directional; there is a commitment to improvement. Ireland is a recurrent example (but the contemporary Scottish Highland economy would also qualify, even if Hume is less explicit). Regarding the Irish, Hume clearly commends, for example, James I's 'civilising' policy. In practice, this meant reconciling the Irish to 'laws and industry', thus making their subjection 'durable and useful to the crown of England'. To achieve that end, it was necessary to 'abolish Irish customs which supplied the place of laws and which were calculated to keep that people for ever in a state of barbarism and disorder' and, in particular, to replace those customs that hindered 'the enjoyment of fixed property in land' (without which there is no incentive 'to enclose, to cultivate, to improve') (*HE* III, 33, 34).

His writings are littered with other expressions of his support for 'economic liberty.' Hence he is opposed to restrictions ('absurd limitations') on industry such as the erection of corporations (*HE* II, 56–7); to usury laws ('unreasonable and iniquitous laws') because they damaged trade by prohibiting profits of exchange (*HE* II, 55); to fixing wages by statute (*HE* II, 231); to prohibiting (an 'absurd law') cloth manufacture until a seven-year apprenticeship had been served (*HE* II, 323); to the 'pernicious' consequences of granting of patent monopolies (*HE* II, 573; cf. II, 595; III, 83–4n); to the passing of 'ridiculous' sumptuary legislation (*HE* I, 535; cf. *HE* II 231; *HE* II 602). In the same vein, he advocated consistent, non-arbitrary taxation (E-Tax 345) and free trade, arguing forcefully against the 'narrow and malignant' policies of prohibition (E-JT 328; cf. E-BT).

With respect to toleration, another key 'liberal' principle, Hume's view is clearly inferable from his scathing comments on religious persecution for heresy and his remark that toleration is the most effective way ('the true secret') of 'managing religious factions' (*HE* II, 580; cf. II 302; II 336; III 625). On occasion he expresses a more explicitly principled view, as when he calls toleration 'so reasonable a doctrine' (*HE* II, 320) or, again, when he refers to Elizabeth I's persecution of papist and puritans as 'extremely contrary to the genius of freedom' (*HE* I, 589) and declares 'laudable' a 1681 bill repealing her persecuting statute (*HE* III, 677). Finally, we can note, in his endorsement of the Protestant Succession, his hope, expressed in language far removed from that typically voiced by a conservative, that 'the progress of reason will, by degrees, abate the acrimony of opposite religions all over Europe' (E-PrS 510).

Of course, there are places in Hume's writings where he qualifies these endorsements of 'liberty'. One example, less to mitigate than to contextualise Hume's argument, is the implication of his frequently expressed view of the role of opinion (see E-FPG). In the *History*, after reiterating his position that government is 'always founded on opinion not force', he adds a particular gloss. The context for this is the execution of Charles I. Precisely because government relies on opinion, it is 'dangerous to weaken . . . the reverence which the multitude owe to authority.' He explicitly locates the source of that danger in the 'speculative' reasoning about the doctrine of resistance. From this he draws the conditional conclusion, 'if ever, on any occasion, it were laudable to conceal truth from the populace it must be confessed that the doctrine of resistance affords such an example' (*HE* III, 395). A little later, and in the same approximate context, he says that if a choice has to be made then 'utility' should be preferred to 'truth in public institutions' (*HE* III 605). Should that concealment be impractical, which, given the 'licence of human disquisition', is likely, then 'the doctrine of obedience ought alone to be inculcated' and any rare exceptions 'ought seldom or never to be mentioned in popular reasonings' (*HE* III, 395).

But even in these, arguably conservative, remarks, the particular context needs to be recalled. It is the 'dethroning' of a 'prince' that it is worrisome, not 'resisting' him. True, Hume does in this passage come out with a remark very reminiscent of Burke (1987: 67) when he says that the 'illusion, if it be an illusion' that makes us 'pay a sacred regard' to the persons of princes is 'salutary'. That said, however, Hume dismisses the argument of 'tracing up government to the Deity' so that it is 'sacred and inviolate' with its consequence that, no matter how tyrannical a government was, it would be 'sacrilege' to 'touch or invade it in the smallest article (E-OC 466). Similarly, the doctrine of passive obedience cannot stand without exception. Despite the 'maxims of resistance' being destructively pernicious, nevertheless, this is so only 'in general' and resistance can, if only in 'extraordinary emergencies', be 'lawful and commendable' (E-PO 475–6).

What does emerge when Hume's views on liberty are examined as a whole is that he never deviates from the view that 'order' is necessary (Giarrizzo 1962: 121). However, whether this, when allied to arguments about the limitations of reason, the importance of customs, the presumption in favour of the function and the recognition of the concreteness of human life that were covered in Part I, amounts to an espousal of conservatism brings us back to the starting point about the aptness of 'labels'.

III

I do not want to deny what might be called a Humean contribution to the development of conservative thinking. I do, however, want to maintain that this is distinct from an interpretation of his thought as conservative. Labels, as I have said, are a shorthand and, in many circumstances, little of substance rests on their employment. From that perspective, the debates outlined in this chapter can be thought to be 'much ado about nothing'. However, once the seeming inevitability of the employment of labels is granted, then this is not to say they can be used arbitrarily or whimsically. Hence, if Hume's thought is indeed to be summarily characterised, there is enough evidence of his commitment to its basic ideas to warrant the label 'liberal' to be affixed to his thought. The effect of that warranted characterisation is such as to render the alternative label 'conservative' insecure. In this chapter I have also intimated that a stronger argument could be mounted, namely it is a distortion to call Hume a conservative. I want to conclude by briefly elaborating upon this latter argument. I do not claim this is anything more than a 'case for discussion'.

It is patently the case that writing before and after the 1789 French Revolution makes a significant difference to how conservative thought developed, a point borne out by the universal recognition of Burke as the key formative thinker. While there are similarities between Hume and Burke, it would be a mistake to read back these into Hume so that he too becomes conservative. Hume's religious scepticism makes him chary of giving to history or tradition a Providentialist cast or regarding man as a 'religious animal' who consecrates the state (Burke 1987: 80). Indeed, the principle underlying Hume's account of artifice is the naturalist principle: that for all the limitations on individual reason it is humans themselves who, without any need of divine aid or other supernatural guidance, have constructed extra-familial social life.

Establishing that distinction is at the heart of Hume's philosophical achievement. He is centrally concerned to distinguish between unwarranted and justified imaginative constructions (see, for example, *M* 3.38/*SBNM* 199). Into the former category fall the original contract of the Whig and the Tory doctrine of passive obedience, as well as superstitions, like worshipping trees, but also believing that bread is transformed by the uttering of certain words by a certain person in a certain place. In the latter category are the utterances that constitute promises and all the other artifices like justice, property and chastity that have been contrived to enable humans to live together. While these latter conventions pass the methodological/scientific test outlined in the Introduction to the *Treatise*, the former on that same basis can be shown to be 'chimerical'.

Of course, these basic human constructions need robust attention and if individuals arrogantly forget their limitations then they can damage the fabric. On a pragmatic or prudential front, acting habitually can be the most appropriate course of action but there are 'habits' and 'habits'; for Hume, civilised habits are patently superior to superstitions. It is an intellectual challenge to explain how civilisation emerges but we can now, with the science of man, rise to that challenge. Accordingly, even if humans most of the time act in a conservative manner, and do so necessarily and beneficially, this is a naturalistic scientific conclusion, not some extra or supernatural revelation. Nor is that conclusion an endorsement of the established way of things. That conservative reading distorts Hume's enterprise. For him, science/philosophy is being derelict if it does not identify 'bad habits' and point the way to their dissolution – for example, introducing commerce with its good habits to remove the inertial obstacles of traditional ways of living. In sum, his commitment to science and his antipathy to superstition make Hume genuinely a thinker of the Enlightenment and not a harbinger of the conservative 'reaction' to it.

Postscript

This essay is cognate to the discussions in Chapters 9 and 12 in its argument that Hume is a 'universalist' with a robust evaluative notion of human nature. It also is an offshoot of my book on Hume (2009b) in the series 'Major Conservative and Libertarian Thinkers', in which the opening sentence of Chapter 2 declares 'Hume is not a conservative'. I had discussed conservatism in a much earlier piece (Berry 1983) which was well received and where, again, Oakeshott loomed large. This essay deliberately sidesteps an old debate about Hume as a Tory but, as the literature here cited testifies, his work continues to be viewed through the prism of his supposed conservatism. However, recent books by (for example) Sabl (2012), Merrill (2015) and Susato (2015) do not take that line. It is one of the recurrent themes in James Harris's intellectual biography that Hume self-consciously strove (against the current at the time) to be impartial. As Harris reads him, the 'late' Hume betrays pessimism rather than (I here interpolate) deep conservatism (Harris 2015: 375, 438).

Earlier versions of this paper were given at Glasgow to my colleagues in the HINT group, at the University of Kyoto and (partially) at an ECSSS Session at the University of St Andrews. I am grateful to all for their comments.

Notes

1. See also David Miller (1981: 118; cf. 204), who describes Hume's conservatism as 'wholly secular'.

2. I here add my contribution to the large literature that seeks to identify, variously, 'constellations' (Muller 1997), 'canons' (Russell Kirk 1960), 'principles' (F. Hearnshaw 1933) or a 'configuration' (Allen (1981), while others, again, treat it as an ideology (Huntingdon 1957 and Mannheim 1953) or characterise it definitively in terms of 'imperfection' (O'Sullivan 1976 and Quinton 1978).

3. McArthur (2007: 117), while insightfully contesting readings of Hume as a conservative, does characterise him as a 'precautionary conservative' (2007: 120–30).

4. There is a large literature on Hume's view of reason – covering not only his epistemology, his account of causation and his scepticism but also his moral theory. Recent expositions include Norton (1982), Owen (1999), Beauchamp and Rosenberg (1981), Danford (1990) and Cohon (2008). It is, however, I think, fair to state that interpreters of Hume as a conservative do not invest much energy in the details of his philosophy (Snare 1991 is an exception). I follow their abjuration.

5. I select Livingston (rather than Snare 1991), partly for the salience his views have attained but also because he is concerned (as this quotation exemplifies) with conservatism more generally. Snare outlines what he calls a 'deep' reading (based on Hume's account of natural virtues and the imagination) that I think neglects Hume's wider polemical project (see text below).

6. Hume's context for that judgement is 'the Rhamadan of the Turks', together with the 'four Lents of the Muscovites and the austerities of some Roman Catholics'. For a wider exploration of Hume's 'natural history', see Berry 2000 (Chapter 6).

7. For a recent vigorous statement of Hume's naturalism, see Hardin (2007: 25), who judges it a misreading of Hume to present him as a purveyor of conservatism rather than as an explainer of social order.

8. Compare Laursen (1992: 166). That Hume's claims for 'science' are a masquerade for an ideology reflective of the prejudices of the Hanoverian ruling elite is put forward by MacIntyre (1985: 231).

9. I share Stewart's reading of Hume as a confident reformer (1992: 13). McArthur (2007:13) acknowledges his debt to Stewart.

15

Hume on Happiness

In a well-known passage at the conclusion of Book I of the *Treatise*, Hume confesses that his argument to that point has led him into a state of 'philosophical melancholy and delirium'. Yet, in the same sentence, he admits that this condition is unsustainable. He proceeds to remark that this melancholy is alleviated by the 'lively impression of his senses'. Continuing in first-person mode, he then, as examples of this liveliness, writes, 'I dine, I play a game of backgammon, I converse and am merry with my friends' so that, after 'three or four hours' amusement', that mentally destabilising argument now appears 'ridiculous' (*T* 1-4-7.9/*SBNT* 269). He has shifted from being sad and melancholic to being merry and amused. It would seem unproblematic to associate merriment and amusement with happiness but, though the association is not false, it is incomplete, as Hume elsewhere appreciates. I here examine Hume's understanding of happiness, what it is and its role or significance. To help illuminate this last point, this examination will lead to a brief exploration of the relationship of Hume's views to an aspect of the relatively recent upsurge in 'happiness studies'. This can be fairly described as an 'upsurge' because, of course, there is nothing novel about a philosophical interest in happiness.

I

From the perspective of intellectual history/philosophy, a distinction is often made between two senses of happiness: the eudaimonic and the hedonic. Each of these has its paradigmatic representative – Aristotle in the first sense and Bentham in the second. For Bentham, there is a 'felicific calculus'; happiness is when the sum of pleasures is greater than sum of pains and it is the 'fundamental axiom' that the 'greatest happiness of the greatest number' is 'the measure of right and wrong' (Bentham 1948: 120; cf. 3, 127, 147). For Aristotle, happiness (*eudaimonia*) is a virtuous activity of the soul [and] . . . demands not only complete goodness but a complete life'[1] and the good life of virtue is one lived for its own sake; it is an entelechic fulfilment not a calculable contingency. To treat pleasure (*hedone*) as the end of activity is beneath true humanity. It is the masses (*hoi polloi*) or slaves who prefer a life of merely bodily pleasures (*somatikon hedonon*); a preference that exemplifies their quasi-animality (*EN* 1177a8/328).

By contrast, Bentham, in his opening sentence of the *Principles*, declares, 'Nature has placed mankind under the governance of two sovereign masters, pain and pleasure' (1948: 125) and he denies that the term 'virtuous' is applicable to anything other than what increases happiness, itself a composite of positive pleasure and exemption from pain (Bentham 1983: 119, 122, 342). Far from dismissing some humans as quasi-animals, Bentham famously says that the time may come when animals themselves have rights, the key question being not can animals reason or talk but can they suffer (Bentham 1948: 412n).

There is a clear gap between these two senses of happiness but the advocates of the modern view (or some of them, at least) implicitly claim to bridge it. For example, Richard Layard (2006: 7), a leading exponent (but far from the only one)[2] of what he calls the 'new science of happiness' holds both a positivist and a normative position. On the one hand, after Bentham, he thinks that it is now possible, thanks to developments in neuroscience/cognitive psychology, to measure, in a statistically relevant manner, happiness as an objective dimension of experience (Layard 2006: 224). On the other, with Aristotle, he judges that society (especially a modern one), if it is to be happy, needs a concept of the common good and 'should teach the principles of morality . . . as established truths . . . essential for a meaningful life' (Layard 2006: 5, 225, 234).

I want to situate Hume's account around these three positions, together with a fourth in the form of Stoicism, which, unlike the others, is one that Hume himself addresses. But to be clear, rather than making systematic comparisons, I will draw upon these other approaches in a pragmatic fashion to help further the main aim of this chapter – an investigation of Hume's account of happiness and its implications.

II

Hume's most succinct yet explicit analysis of happiness is in his essay 'Of Refinement in the Arts' (E-RA).[3] The context of his analysis is the debate over luxury (hence the essay's original 1752 title 'Of Luxury'). I have covered this debate extensively elsewhere as well as in Chapter 13 in this volume and will thus not expatiate further. Within E-RA he links virtue with happiness (as he also does elsewhere – see E-PG 5, M 9.15/SBNM 279). That of itself says little. We have already seen that Bentham thinks 'felicity coincides with virtue', that Aristotle makes virtue fundamental and that virtue is also prominent in Stoicism, as seen for example in Seneca.

Early in E-RA, Hume makes the bold – and, for this argument, key – declaration that 'ages of refinement' are 'both the happiest and most virtuous' (E-RA 269). Hume's use of the term 'refinement' is not without ambiguity, although consistently it is the binary antipode to simplicity. In his early (1742) essay 'Of Simplicity and Refinement in Writing' he deals, as the title informs us, with the well-worn issue of literary style. After the manner of Aristotle's doctrine that virtue lies actively in the mean state (*meson*) (*EN* 1106b/101), he observes that a 'just medium' between the excesses of each is typically favoured. While he counsels against precisely fixing this medium, he maintains that excessive refinement poses a greater danger to good style and taste than excessive simplicity (E-SR 193,196). However, in the very different context of the 1752 *Political Discourses*, the advantages lie with refinement. Whereas in the 1742 work 'refinement' is a disfiguring ornamentation (E-SR 192), in 1752 commodities that increasingly serve to the 'ornament and pleasure of life' are socially advantageous (E-RA 272). Refinement now is an aspect of improvement (E-RA 271), whereas 'simplicity' comes to be linked with an unimproved state of rusticity or uncultivated rudeness.

In line with his working definition of luxury as 'great refinement in the gratification of the senses' (E-RA 268), Hume contrasts the gluttony of Tartars, as they feast on dead horses, to European courtiers 'with all their refinements of cookery'. Similarly, drunkenness is rare in 'ages of refinement' or, as they are here termed, 'polite ages' (E-RA 272). Refinement now counters excess. Implicit here is a scheme of social progress away from the rude or barbarous simplicity of Tartar life towards not merely refinement and politeness but also, as he had boldly declared, towards happiness and virtue. But considerably more is involved than more elaborately prepared food. What that particular elaboration exemplifies is the general refinement in the mechanical arts and they, in their turn, 'commonly produce some refinements in the liberal'. This exemplifies what he calls the 'spirit of the age' such that, he claims, in refined, polite societies great philosophers and poets live alongside skilful weavers and ship-carpenters (or chefs) (E-RA 270) (for the implied causality here see Chapter 11). In a well-known passage, the upshot is that 'industry, knowledge and humanity are linked together by an indissoluble chain and are found, from experience as well as reason, to be peculiar to the more polished and ... luxurious ages' (E-RA 271).

Refined ages are thus the happiest and most virtuous, as well as distinctively (it is 'peculiar' to them) exhibiting industry, knowledge and humanity. From this it follows both that this trio are, at the very least, consonant with happiness and virtue and also that this consonance is missing from earlier ages. These earlier times encompass two types of society and Hume moves, as his argument suits, between them. The nomadic Tartar tribes represent one type, ancient Rome the other. Of these two, the latter case is especially telling in our context. The 'severe moralists', as Hume labels them, lauded that era because it conjoined poverty with rusticity as well as virtue with public spirit (E-RA 275). Hume mentions Sallust as one such moralist but it was typical of Stoicism.

Thus far, 'happiness' is indeterminately formal but Hume proceeds to give it substance. He identifies three components: indolence, pleasure and action (E-RA 269–70). While it is important that all three have their part to play, the place of the first component needs clarifying because, as we shall see, Hume is generally critical of indolent behaviour; indeed, he treats it as counter to the virtue of industry. Here, however, as a component of happiness, it appears in the more particular sense of rest or repose and thus as a dependent or derivative component. We need 'intervals of repose' because the 'weakness of human nature' means a period of recuperation is necessary. These intervals are 'agreeable for a moment' – think of a game of backgammon – but if prolonged they induce the negative state of lethargy.

The other two components require more consideration. Pleasure links with happiness on broadly Benthamite lines.[4] As tersely put in the second *Enquiry*, it is 'inseparable from our make and constitution' that 'appearance of happiness' gives pleasure (*M* 6.3/ *SBNM* 120n). It is a finding of the science of man that pleasure, along with pain, is the 'chief spring or actuating principle of the human mind' and in their absence we are incapable of action or desire (aversion) and incapable of joy (grief) (*T* 3–3–1.2/*SBNT* 574). In this way Hume explains the implicitly commonplace view that 'all men . . . are equally desirous of happiness' (*M* 6.15/*SBNM* 239).

What is it they wish for when they desire happiness? Hume never gives a definitive answer, although we already know that being 'active' and enjoying a relaxing game of backgammon, for example, are components. Beyond those, he associates being happy with enjoying the pleasures of sensory gratification, partaking of 'commodities and conveniencies' such as 'a cheerful house, elegant furniture, ready service and whatever is desirable in meat, drink or apparel' (*M* 6.33/*SBNM* 247). All of these are eligible to be refinements that define luxury and, to the degree that they meet that definition, they are typically enjoyed by the rich. But Hume, in a passage that Smith must have taken on board, also says that, in addition to the happiness conveyed by these possessions, the rich also get enjoyment from the disinterested esteem of others, who as spectators themselves enjoy the images of happiness and gratification of every appetite exhibited by the rich (hence the reference to the 'appearance' of happiness above) (*M* 6.22, 30/*SBNM* 244, 246).[5] One consequence of this is that the non-rich have an incentive to convert their vicarious enjoyment into the 'real thing'; they want to possess the sort of goods enjoyed by the rich (as well as the esteem that comes with their possession). I will come back to this argument.

But Hume's argument is subtler. We need to recall that these ages are also the most virtuous and Hume distances his argument from the view that there is tight link between being wealthy and being esteemed. He claims that the link between fortune and happiness is looser than is 'vulgarly imagined' and someone who, from 'experience and philosophy', appreciates that looseness will, accordingly, base an evaluation of others on 'personal character' rather than the 'capricious favours of fortune' (*M* 6.34/*SBNM* 248).[6] More precisely, it is the 'mental quality in ourselves or others' that is the source of the satisfaction that attends virtue. An action is virtuous (or vicious) solely as 'a sign of some quality or character' evocative of 'durable principles of the mind which extend over the whole conduct and enter into personal character' (*T* 3.3.1–4/*SBNT* 575). There is an apparent Aristotelian flavour to this which I will pick up. But before that, with the aim of clarifying what Hume takes happiness substantively to be, I address the argument of the Stoics.

Despite a particular passage that I will consider at the end of this chapter, Hume's argument is far removed from that of the Stoics. He has, for example, a very different understanding of happiness from that put forward by Seneca .The full extent of this difference will become apparent later but we can note here their treatment of riches. In contrast to what he calls the 'perpetual cant of Stoics and Cynics' (*M* 6.21/*SBNM* 242), for Hume, riches are desired because they are 'valuable at all times and to all men because they always purchase pleasures' (E-RA 276), and pleasure, as we have seen, is a constitutive component of happiness (*M* Appx 1.21/ *SBNM* 294). For Seneca, a happy man is someone who elevates himself above pleasure (*voluptatem*) (and pain). This elevation or superiority is the 'gift of reason' (*beneficio rationis*) that frees the happy man from desire [*cupit*] (and fear) as he judges 'the fleeting sensations of the wretched body' to be 'paltry and trivial'.[7] This rational overcoming of desire constitutes virtue and that is the foundation of '*vera felicitas*' (*DVB* xvi.1); joy, indeed, is its very nature (*gaudere laetarique proprium et naturale virtutis est*).[8] Seneca somewhat defensively (he was a very rich man) allows that the *sapiens* would rather be rich than poor (*DVB* xxi.4). That judgement is in line with Aristotle (*EN* 1119b22ff./142ff.), since material resources provide more scope for virtuous action such as liberality. Yet Seneca insists that the *sapiens* grants no importance to his riches (*DVB* xxvi.1). Indeed, he is explicit that possessing the 'trappings of luxury' (*delicato apparatu*) makes one no happier than living without them (*DVB* xxv.2). More strongly, he affirms that living simply (*frugalitas*) is a virtue.[9]

I will return to this notion of simple living when I consider some modern assessments of happiness, but here note that this affirmation aligns Seneca with the more austere or severe Stoics like Epictetus. It was basic to Stoicism, across its expressions, that to place value in the goods of fortune (health, wealth, even life) is an error. These goods can be lost; they are by definition inconstant. Only the rational life of virtue is constant; living that life is the only true source of happiness (hence the paradox, and one to which Seneca subscribes, that one can be happy on the rack).[10] All this is contrary to Hume. Even apart from the radically different interpretation of the role of reason (notoriously it is the slave of the passions [*T* 2–3–3.4/*SBNT* 415]), he is explicit that to treat happiness as 'entirely independent of every thing external' is a 'degree of perfection impossible to be attained' (E-DT 5). Seneca and the Stoics sever what Hume links together – his claim that a life of luxury and refinement can be both happy and virtuous.

III

I now turn to the component of 'action' in Hume's delineation of happiness. As an initial step, I want, as promised, to pick up the Aristotelian argument. We have already seen that Aristotle defines happiness as a virtuous activity of the soul (*psuche*). Happiness, on Aristotle's analysis, is self-sufficient; it is the end to which action is directed and which is chosen for its own sake and not as a means to something else (*EN* 1097b2–5/73–4). This self-sufficient or complete goodness consists in fulfilling what distinguishes humans, what exhibits their distinctive function (*ergon*) (*EN* 1098a13/76). Aristotle identifies this function as a life that is spent in virtuous conduct; I leave to one side for the moment the place of contemplation (*EN* 1100b/83).[11] The moral virtues comprise not only the cardinal quartet of wisdom, justice, temperance and courage but also a host of others such as liberality, magnanimity, amiability and modesty. The exercise of these virtues is learned through habit (*ethimos*) but the ability to form habits is natural (*EN* 1103a20/91).

This training enables the mean to be identified and acted upon, so courage, for example, is the mean between rashness and cowardice (*EN* 1107b34/104). For Aristotle, we learn by doing. Happiness is thus not enjoying or being in a particular circumstance or condition (*EN* 1176a33/326) such that, for example, being wealthy is a 'state' of happiness. Rather, it would depend, in this case, on what was done with the wealth – what virtuous activity, like liberality, it might occasion (Annas 1993: 45). However, this exercise is not occasional because, as the result of habituation, it establishes a disposition or engrained character (*hexis*).[12] This is the apparent 'Aristotelian flavour' (as I called it) to Hume's notion of character.[13]

In Aristotle, dispositions are part of the soul (*EN* 1105b20/98) and, given their link with virtue, happiness is a matter of the soul rather than the body (*EN* 1102a17/87).[14] This does not mean that 'pleasure' has no place; rather, virtuous actions are pleasurable in themselves, indeed 'happiness is the best, the finest, the most pleasurable (*hediston*) thing of all' (EN 1099a14/79). This is not Benthamite, at least as judged by J. S. Mill's citation from 'somewhere' in Bentham that imputes to him the view that bodily pleasure (pushpin) is as good as virtuous pleasure (poetry) (Mill 1971: 95).[15] But neither is it Humean.

While Hume, somewhat after the manner of Mill,[16] clearly does regard some activities as more rewarding than others (especially those that call forth the exercise of cultivated taste – Milton is superior to Ogilby (E-ST 230)[17] – he does not deny that playing backgammon, conversing or enjoying wine is a real source of pleasure, enjoyable by all. Hence, even if the delights of repose are dependent on a break from prior exertion (action), they are, as he made explicit, a genuine component of happiness.[18] In other words, Hume's 'repose' as derivative rests on a very different foundation from Aristotle's teleological distinction between 'leisure' (*skolē*) as an activity undertaken for its own sake and 'rest' (*anapausis*) (EN 1179b/329, 1176b/327; cf. Aristotle 1944: 1334b35) as an instrumental recuperative passing of the time. This difference between Hume and Aristotle remains, even though they are both antipathetical to the Stoic's principled asceticism, to their strategy of negatively curtailing desires.[19]

Another difference between Hume and Aristotle, and one more consequentially significant for this discussion, returns us to the question of 'action'. Aristotle always links virtue with fulfilment, with the complete life as the expression of the human *ergon*. Famously, one manifestation of this is political participation, for the *anthropos* is by nature a being of the polis (1944: 1253a3–4). In contrast to the above difference between Aristotle and Stoics, there is here a narrowing of the space, bridged originally by Panaetius and Posidonius, between Aristotle and the Roman Stoics or at least those who write in a Stoic-inflected mode.

The Romans, almost by definition, linked *virtus* with involvement in public or political-cum-military life and, as in Sallust, fulminated against its corruption by luxury and avarice.[20] Cicero, in his characteristically eclectic manner, while acknowledging the Stoic injunction to be free from disturbances of the soul (*animi perturbatione*), proclaimed the merits or virtues of *negotiis publicis* devoted *ad rem publicam et ad magnas res*.[21] For his part, Seneca frequently held up Cato the Younger, who took his own life rather than compromise his republican principles, as an exemplar; indeed, he even said that Cato had 'reached the pinnacle of happiness (*felictatem*)'.[22] As we will now show, this is not where Hume puts his stress on the happiness occasioned by action.

IV

Given that Hume thinks activity is a component of happiness, in what way is this the case? It centres on energy. Hume in E-RA uses a number of expressions to convey this: 'quick march of the spirits'; through being 'occupied' the 'mind acquires new vigour' and its 'powers and faculties' are enlarged. This exercise is enjoyable of itself, in addition to the pleasures that are derived from its fruits. It is crucial to Hume's argument that these positive aspects characterise circumstances where 'industry and the arts flourish'; that is to say, they are inherent features of ages of refinement and absent in Tartary and ancient Rome. Industry we have already met, alongside knowledge and humanity, as a link in that indissoluble chain in polished, luxurious ages and since these ages are 'the most virtuous' as well as happy, it follows that the trio embody virtue.

I will take the three links in the chain in reverse order. Humanity is a universal human attribute and, as such, in the second *Enquiry* it is declared to be 'alone the foundation of morals' (M 9.6/SBNM 273).[23] To say it is foundational is not to say its expression is immutable. Although it is not absent in classical thought – Seneca, for example, links it with kindness (*EM* 83.30) – in Hume (and others of course) this takes on a distinctively modern hue (cf. M 7.18/ SBNM 257). Humanity is one of the 'social virtues', alongside clemency, gentleness, beneficence and affability (M 9.15/SBNM 279). Hume emphasises its modernity: it is 'the chief characteristic that distinguishes a civilised age from times of barbarity and ignorance' and as one manifestation of this wars are less cruel (E-RA 274). This temporality fuels once more Hume's antagonism to 'austere pretenders'. It is the Stoics, those severe moralists who talk of 'suffering and self-denial' (M 9.15/SBNM 279), whom he explicitly has in mind. Epictetus he claims 'scarcely ever mentioned the sentiment of humanity and compassion but in order to put his disciples on their guard against it' (M Appx 4.14/SBNM 319). Contrary to locating it in self-denial, the 'sole purpose of virtue', properly understood, is to make 'all mankind' in 'every instance of their existence, if possible, cheerful and happy' (M 9.15/SBNM 279).

It is worth pausing to draw attention to three features of this quotation. There is the clear linkage it makes between virtue and cheerful happiness (he had earlier in that same paragraph referred to the 'dismal dress' with which 'many divines' had covered virtue). Second, virtue is comprehensive; it is not limited to only some instances of human activity/life. Finally, there is the open avowal of universalism (see also Chapter 12). In contrast to the restrictiveness of Aristotle and the Stoics, everyone, no matter their gender or status, can enjoy happiness and be virtuous. In addition, humanity is sociable: modern society is urban and, within that setting with its clubs and coffee houses, sociability and conversation flourish and melancholy is counteracted. In a pointed contrast to the rusticity of ancient Rome, vaunted by the moralists, this sociability, by refining manners and behaviour, including that between the sexes, enhances humanity (E-RA 271). (For Smith's account of humanity, see Chapter 19.) The modernity of humanity, with its softening of manners, reflects the distance from the harsh cruelty and endemic warfare of both Romans and barbarians. As Hume points out, in that militaristic environment the virtue of courage has a prominent place (see, for example, *M* 7.13/*SBNM* 254 on the Romans, *HE* I, 155 on the Anglo-Saxons). As courage loses its prominence so humanity gains a salience in the catalogue of virtues.

The same processes that produce an emphasis on humanity also account for the growth in knowledge, the second link in the chain. In refined ages 'profound ignorance is totally banished' (E-RA 271). There is nothing commendable about ignorance. It is the ever-present companion to superstition, as manifest, for example, in 'monkish virtues' (like celibacy, fasting, mortification), which are, rather, to be accounted vices (*M* 9.3/*SBNM* 270). These practices are not too far removed from the austere virtues of the Stoics. Seneca, for example, says that to enjoy food for its own sake, to relish fresh ingredients and tasty dishes, is to let the body rule the mind and, accordingly, to fall away from virtue (*EM* 119.3). For Hume it is the advances in knowledge, those very developments in the mechanical and liberal arts, that enable men to 'enjoy the privilege of rational creatures to act and think to cultivate the pleasures of the mind as well as those of the body' (E-RA 271).

Here, again, Hume's universalism is evident. There is no indication in Hume that the dissemination of knowledge should be restricted; its virtuousness is not limited. This differentiates him

from Mandeville (1988: I, 288) but even more notably from classical thought (including Aristotle) in general. For those thinkers, the
'privilege' of rationality is denied to large sections of society – the
vulgar or *hoi polloi* in addition to women and slaves.[24] It might
be true that the Stoics were 'cosmopolitans' so that, in principle,
'virtue closes the door to no man; it is open to all, admits all, the
freeborn and the freedman (*ingenuos et libertinos*), the slave and
the king'.[25] The obverse of that, in practice, is that it diminishes
the significance of the 'common course of the world', the evidence
of human 'behaviour in company, in affairs and in their pleasures'
(*T* Intro 10/*SBNT* xix). In other words, it is what can be gleaned
from actual human experience. As Rachel Cohon (2008: 162)
observes, it is for Hume a 'matter for empirical investigation'
whether a virtuous person is happy. When Hume links virtue and
happiness, what is centrally at stake is not the 'life of reason' but
the unrestricted access to material goods and the enjoyment they
bring; an access and thus enjoyment that slaves cannot experience.
Hume was alert to slavery as a basic institution in classical societies. He judges that it is detrimental to both population and the
happiness of mankind. In the same essay he explains the inferior
happiness experienced in these societies, especially when viewed
across the populace as a whole, as a consequence of their lack of
trade, manufacture and industry (E-PAN 396, 416).

Industry, the final link in the chain is, for the argument of
this chapter, the most significant. As a virtue it has the sense of
industriousness and stands in contrast to indolence and lethargy. It
is the key expression of 'action' – they are coupled as virtual synonyms (*M* 6.1/*SBNM* 233) – and thus at the heart of what makes
us happy (cf. *M* 9.12/*SBNM* 276). Individuals are happy when
they are busy. Busy, industrious individuals produce flourishing
societies, the crucial mark of which, as we have already noted,
is the 'encrease and consumption of all the commodities which
serve to the ornament and pleasure of life' (E-RA 272). Rather
than this being a development to be excoriated, this increase in
commodities that 'gratify the senses and the appetites' (E-Com
263) is overwhelmingly positive. Echoing the de-privileging of the
Aristotelian/Stoic perspective, 'the arts of luxury . . . add to the
happiness of the state; since they afford to *many* the opportunity
of receiving enjoyments with which they would otherwise have
been unacquainted' (E-Com 256; my emphasis).

In contrast to Epictetus' admonitions about desiring superfluities, Hume says (in effect) that without the demand for the purple, embroidered slippers censured by Epictetus (see Chapter 13) 'men would sink into indolence and lose all enjoyment of life' (E-RA 272). Those slippers emblematically incentivise; people want to enjoy them as well as enjoy them being worn by the rich. This process of incentivisation is central to Hume's defence of commerce. Originally prompted by imported luxuries, the 'gayer and more opulent part' of a nation is roused to activity or industry by a 'desire of a more splendid way of life than what their ancestors enjoyed' (E-Com 264).[26] These imported goods are imitated by domestic manufacture and the desire for a generationally enhanced splendid way of living is diffused. More precisely, humans are stimulated by 'avarice and industry, art and luxury' (E-Com 263). The fact that 'avarice' was uniformly condemned by the severe moralists (it looms large in Sallust, for example)[27] is another clear signal of Hume's deliberate, and polemical, divergence from their perspective.[28]

But, further, consequentially if the simplicity advocated by these moralists was implemented it would leave the state poorer and thus weaker (E-Mon 293). As we have already observed, Hume is explicit that the slave-based 'ancient nations' are inferior in happiness to modern ones, where 'trade, manufactures, industry' flourish (E-PAN 416). A flourishing state of industriously happy individuals who consume imported goods benefits the 'public'. Security is enhanced because there are more resources available to devote to fleets and armies (E-RA 272) but so, too, is liberty entrenched because with commerce come merchants and middling ranks, whose occupations make them 'covet equal laws' and establish them as 'the best and firmest basis of public liberty' (E-RA 277–8). This 'new' liberty (cf. HE II, 603), it follows from all the discussion hitherto, is a feature of refined societies where luxuries are enjoyed.

This luxury enjoyed by individuals serves to 'diminish the force and check the ambition of the sovereign', while, conversely, the sovereign's ambition 'must entrench on the luxury of individuals' (E-Com 257). Hume is not specific here but a few pages later (E-Com 263), with Sparta in mind (E-Com 259), he had said that to banish luxury would 'convert a city into a kind of fortified camp'. Since it is 'the natural bent of the mind' to desire the happiness that comes with consuming goods that gratify their senses (such as luxuries), then it is inferable that such a conversion would be coercive.

This also applies to the more obvious antithesis to modern liberty – absolute government. It is 'a natural if not infallible' effect of absolute monarchy that the people are in poverty (E-Com 265). This is not the honorific or virtuous poverty advocated by Seneca (*EM* 17.5) and others,[29] but the condition of someone who is penurious, who endures 'hard labour', possesses 'coarse or ragged cloaths' and consumes 'nauseous meat and distasteful liquor' (*M* 6.33/SBNM 129). Industry, manufacture and trade (activity) are the way to ameliorate these circumstances and thus increase the sum of happiness. No such remedy is forthcoming from Stoic tranquillity or Aristotelian political action. Furthermore, an additional effect of industry is to diffuse wealth and the burden of taxation – a diffusion that adds more to 'the happiness' of the poor than it diminishes that of the rich. As noted, this has the consequential utility in strengthening the state but Hume adds a further dimension. Although, in an industrious society like England, the high price of labour might have disadvantages for foreign trade, that downside is 'not to be put in competition with the happiness of so many millions' (E-Com 265). There is a kind of felicific calculus in play.

Hume's argument linking happiness with commerce and industry separates him, yet again, from the classical moralists. For these moralists, commerce and its cognates were subordinate, even base, pursuits, because they were concerned merely with life and material satisfactions. They laid out alternative paths. One adopted by (say) Epictetus or Aristotle (*EN* Book X), was to locate happiness in tranquillity or the intellectually self-sufficient life, the *bios theoretikos*. The other adopted by (say) Aristotle in the *Politics* or Cicero, was to ground happiness in participation in intrinsically worthwhile action on the public stage. Hume has little time for the former but his approach to the latter takes us back to our starting point.

V

In summary, Hume's position is that individuals are happy when they are pursuing goods the consumption of which they anticipate they will enjoy, both directly and via the response of others. That pursuit itself starts from a rising base of a material well-being (comfortable homes, ample quality sustenance, warm and stylish apparel, etc.). Societies are, of course, happy when they contain happy individuals but also when their trade is extensive, when their industry is efficient and productive and when they are secure. Indeed, in his early essay 'Of Parties in General', Hume explicitly links happiness with 'peace and security' (rather than simple quantity) of the 'commodities and enjoyments of life' (E-PG 55).

It is a characteristic feature of some modern/contemporary discussions of happiness that they take issue with the assumptions and consequences of that summary.[30] Hume's articulation, as I have sought to bring out, is animated by a rejection of the severe moralists' understanding of happiness, as well as the entire Aristotelian teleological framework (he observes in passing that his fame has 'utterly decayed' (U 1.4/SBNU 7).[31] However, within this contemporary discussion, there is at times an explicit as well as implicit endeavour to recover and restate that classical understanding or at least some key elements of it. To capture that motivation, I have elsewhere employed the term 're-moralisation' (Berry 2016a – I draw on this discussion in the following paragraphs) and it was chosen to echo the term 'de-moralisation' that I coined in my book *The Idea of Luxury* (1994) and since widely adopted. In that context it referred to the overturning of the classical moralist critique of luxury. Seneca is an unambiguous representative of this view, just as Hume is of the de-moralising argument (see also Berry 1999a).

For the contemporary re-moralisers, Hume's position has damaging or deleterious effects. These effects are twofold. The Humean argument is damaging because of its endorsement, even celebration, of consumption and, secondly, because its assumptions are too restrictive, since they neglect, even undermine, the role of other motivations. At the heart of this critique is the judgement that while we might be materially richer we are no happier, a critique that goes to the root of Hume's assumption that refinements (such as enjoying fine cooking rather than being forced to guzzle horsemeat), by giving pleasure, make people happy.

There are, of course, a number of ways to gauge this mismatch between widespread materiality and happiness. There is a raft of empirical research.[32] The iterated finding of this research is, first, that having possessions in countries with a low GDP does indeed make people happier but, secondly, that after a certain point – certainly that now enjoyed by the citizens of the so-called 'developed' world – having more does not make you happier. The question is one of relativity. The poorer are always relatively unhappier than the wealthier within the same country, but when different countries are compared, those with lower GDP can produce more reported happiness or subjective well-being than in those with a higher GDP. This is the paradox (as it is sometimes labelled) of the happy peasant/miserable millionaire phenomenon (Graham 2011).

At the heart of this paradox lies the idea of the 'hedonic treadmill'. The evaluative connotations are apparent. According to its initial formulation by Brickman and Campbell, this 'condemns' us 'to seek new levels of stimulation merely to maintain old levels of subjective pleasure, to never achieve any kind of permanent happiness or satisfaction' (1971: 289). While there have been more neutral formulations[33] where it is, in effect, a process of adaptation so that while subjective well-being rises directly with income it varies inversely with material aspirations, the re-moralisers paint this in negative colours.

The treadmill is picked up by both Richard Layard and Robert Lane. In common with most 're-moralisers', they criticise advertising for increasing dissatisfaction, by 'creating wants' and fostering illusions, so that with the purchase of this watch or this car or this technological gizmo, life will be better. This leads Lane to declare that there is an 'aching void' that neither materialism nor post-materialism can seemingly fill (Lane 2000: 158, 174, 79, 335; cf. Layard 2006: 48, 160). Underlying this is a critique that mirrors Hume's twofold positive assessment in E-RA of the desire for luxuries, and consumption goods more generally. This desire is bad both for individuals and societies.

On the former front this desire is indicted for encouraging self-indulgence and for undermining self-discipline; it looks like a symptom of a malaise ('affluenza' or 'luxury fever' if you will), not some innocent pleasure; it is a merely fleeting source of happiness. So when Brendan Sheehan (2010: 78–9) identifies a 'morality of indulgence' as the consequence of 'the propaganda disseminated by the institution of marketing' then he is harking back to the strictures of a Seneca or an Epictetus. The recurrent finding that having more makes one dissatisfied which, in turn, stimulates the desire for more is a common refrain in Stoics (and other classic moralists). It is, for example, captured exactly in the Roman poet Horace's satirical jibe (*Odes* III, 16; 1961: 74), *semper avarus eget* or, as Robert Frank puts it, 'the more we have the more we seem to feel we need' (2000: 74).

The fact that Stoic disparagement of desires for material or bodily satisfactions provided the conceptual underpinnings for Roman sumptuary laws indicates that a societal critique is never far removed from that critical of individual behaviour. Robert and Edward Skidelsky, though critical of 'happiness economics', none-theless, adopt an explicitly Aristotelian approach, with *eudaimonia* at the heart of an objectivist version of the good life that they use to propose 'a new rationale for sumptuary legislation' (2013: 205). They identify Hume as 'a pioneer of the new approach' that redefined virtue/vice into utility/disutility (citing E-RA in support). The Skidelskys judge that a society 'devoid of the religious impulse' would be unlikely to pursue the common good. Not unexpectedly, perhaps, David Cloutier (2012), in his explicitly Christian analysis of luxury, follows suit but so, too, does Layard (the butt of the Skidelskys' critique), while Lane places great stress on companionship as the key source for happier individuals and thence society (Layard 2006: 5, 225, 234; Lane 2000: 160, 187, 192, 321, 334).

Implicit in these alternatives is the accusation that a Humean society driven to consume instils to deleterious effect individualism, atomism, egocentrism and so on, while also at the same time fuelling a neglect of the public sphere. This negative impact is captured in Gandhi's remark that 'the earth provides enough to satisfy every man's need but not every man's greed'. This is quoted by E. F. Schumacher (1973: 29), whose own re-moralisation involves advocating Buddhist economics. While not an explicit concern, that advocacy, without undue distortion, resonates with the severe moralism of Seneca or Epictetus and their abjuration of desires and their inherent limitlessness. Schumacher remarks in his one explicit reference to happiness that it, along with intelligence, serenity and peacefulness, is destroyed by 'greed and envy' (1973: x). And with an implicit counter to Hume, he goes on to refer to the 'predatory attitude which rejoices in the fact that 'what were luxuries for our fathers have become necessities for us' (1973: 28–9).

Schumacher linked that attitude to the adoption of unlimited growth as a societal goal and in this he proved influential in stimulating the ecological critique of consumer-driven societies. Many of these critics implicitly invoke the presence of the 'classical' Stoic link between self-control, reason and freedom and are thus proponents of 're-moralisation' in my terminology. For example, William Ophuls (1996: 34, 42) argues that the 'teaching of ecology is limitation' and the unlimited drive to consume should, in face of the 'ecological crisis', be replaced by the imperative to 'govern our appetites' and in that way achieve 'real freedom'. In a similar idiom, Juliet Schor (1998: xiii, 136), in her book evocatively subtitled *Why We Want What We Don't Need*, implicitly invoking Seneca and Cicero, draws attention to those she calls 'simple livers' who, in response to 'ecological devastation', aspire to 'rein in desire' – an aspiration she believes should be adopted more widely.

VI

I want to conclude by assessing, albeit briefly, a Humean response to the central claims of this re-moralised account of happiness. The world of the classical moralists was severely hierarchical and within that context luxury, and 'new' wealth generally, was seen as a threat. In practical (political) terms the counter to the threat took various forms, but at the heart of an intellectual 'defence' was a deprecation of desires for bodily goods. By definition, these desires were limitless. To pursue or indulge in them was categorically not the way to a happy life. That life was defined by acknowledging that it could only be a life of virtue and that was synonymous – especially in Stoicism – with a natural simple life of reason. To deviate from this austere path is pathological, a harmful attribution of value to what is without value. This gave it an objective status: the good life could be identified with Aristotle's *eudaimonia* or Seneca's *felicitas*.

But central to the de-moralisation that Hume represents is a rejection of an objective good life, a discoverable definitive idea of happiness. Parallel to this is a rejection of the philosophical underpinnings of the hierarchy endorsed by the severe moralists. They were concerned to preserve a distinction between, on the one hand, those who exhibit rational and full virtue and live a humanly fulfilling life and, on the other, the *vulgus* or *hoi polloi*. Hume is not a political or economic egalitarian but he does not privilege a philosophical or political life over an economic one. Happiness is not the prerogative of the former. Being industrious, pursuing and enjoying material well-being is a genuine source of happiness. The wants and desires of those engaged in commerce (those folk disparaged by Cicero (see n.24; cf. Aristotle 1944: 1278a3)) are just as legitimate as those of their supposed 'betters'.

The recognition of this legitimacy is another way of expressing the process and impact of 'de-moralisation'.

As we know, Hume was not uncritical of aspects of his contemporary society and so in this artificial argumentative 're-creation' it does not follow that he would dismiss out of hand some aspects of the re-moralists' case. Yet his closing argument in E-RA, that to remove luxury is only likely to engender sloth and with that a 'mean uncultivated way of life . . . without society, without enjoyment' (E-RA 280), suggests that if the re-moralisers got their way, we would be less happy.

This, I judge, holds true despite one passage where Hume appears to approximate the Senecan view. In the second *Enquiry*, in a discussion of the 'sensible knave', he remarks that 'every honest man' recognises that 'inward piece of mind, consciousness of integrity, a satisfactory review of our own conduct' is 'very requisite to happiness'. Moreover, he observes, in a virtual paraphrase of Cicero, 'how little is needed to supply the necessities of nature'[34] and more 'pleasure' is to be had from 'conversation, society, study, even health and the common beauties of nature' than from the 'feverish, empty amusements of luxury' (M 9.23–5/SBNM 283–4). And yet, to treat these two heavily rhetorical and contextually specific paragraphs that conclude the main text of the *Enquiry* as if they outweigh the self-consciously philosophical (see E-Com 253–5) and sustained treatment in the *Political Discourses* is, to my mind, unpersuasive.[35] One certainly looks in vain, in Hume, for any discussion of needs, with an attribution of their normative superiority to desire. In addition, even that passage cannot reasonably be read as an endorsement of austerity, of *antiqua frugalitas*. It stretches interpretative charity too far to think Hume is a severe moralist.

At best, this passage serves to alert us to the fact that Hume is no simple or programmatic hedonist when it comes to happiness. Bentham may have thought a robust enough metric could be constructed to calculate what has been termed in our time Gross National Happiness, which is regarded by some as a better way of capturing the state of society rather than Gross Domestic Product. But, despite that passage in the *Enquiry*, nothing in Hume suggests that he would have countenanced such an argument. The state's fundamental task is to ensure justice (E-OG 37). By executing that function, it provides a stable predictable framework within which individuals can operate and, through such operations and the exercise of the virtue of industry, wealth will accrue and life will be better, will be happier. Moreover, these operations (actions) will include their pursuit of what they determine will bring them happiness. Happiness is not an affair of state, as either a calculable or a justifiable goal. Happiness is playing backgammon, is delighting in conversion with friends, is enjoying good food and in getting pleasure from being actively engaged in pursuits of one's choosing. All of these things are facilitated by living in a society where they can be enjoyed without prescription or proscription.

Postscript

The origins of this chapter lie in my work on luxury. The more recent interest in 'happiness' stems from a keynote lecture I gave in 2010 – a version now published (Berry 2016a) – abetted in the interim by a class I give regularly at Universitá Cattolica in Milan and an invited lecture at Trinity University, San Antonio, Texas (with thanks to Maria Pia Paganelli for the invitation). I gave an earlier version of this particular discussion to the HINT group at Glasgow (my thanks also to the participants for their input). The overall argument jells with the 'Berry line' (see Chapter 1) on the 'modernism' of Hume and other Scots, in particular with their defence (for the most part) of a commercial society.

Notes

1. Hereafter *EN*. I generally follow the translation of the Penguin edition (1977), supplying the pagination after the textual location, for which I use the Oxford Classical Text ed. Bywater (1894).
2. See, for example, Diener (2009) for a collection of his writings on the subject; he is perhaps the leading, certainly the most prolific, figure in this research. See Bok (2010: Ch. 5) for a judicious survey.
3. What (limited) discussion there is of Hume on this topic has tended to focus on what (somewhat misleadingly) has been called his 'four essays on happiness' – the Epicurean, The Stoic, The Platonist and the Sceptic (see Immerwahr (1989), Harris (2007) Heydt (2007) and Jost (2009)). Hume declares that his intention in this quartet is 'to deliver the sentiments of sects that naturally form themselves in the world and entertain different ideas of human life and happiness' (E-Ep 138n). In contrast to the statement in E-RA, these essays are elusive, as the various interpretations rather backhandedly bear out. Susato (2015: 116) makes some reference to the essays and

E-RA. McMahon (2006: 327–8) makes a brief passing reference beyond the 'four essays'.

4. 'Pleasure' for Hume is heterogeneous, incorporating listening to good music, enjoying good wine (as well as stimulating conversation and backgammon) (*T* 3–1–2.4 /*SBNT* 472). See Sutherland (1977) for a brief treatment of some interpretative problems in Hume's discussion of pleasure with reference to his moral philosophy.

5. Unlike Smith, Hume does not treat this appearance as 'deceptive'. Vicarious pleasure is still pleasure, even if it lacks the tangibility of direct consumption of commodities. (For Smith's own complex account, see Berry 1997: 44–6.)

6. Despite this last phrasing, 'fortune' in this context means wealth or riches, not luck – the two meanings were, of course, originally intertwined.

7. Seneca (1928: vol. 2), *De Vita Beata* iv.4–v.1. Hereafter DVB.

8. Seneca (1928: vol.1), *De Ira* II vi.2.

9. Seneca (1932), *Epistulae Morales* 5.5. Hereafter EM. For an extended discussion, see Berry (forthcoming a).

10. See, for example, Seneca (1928; vol.1), *De Constantia* v.5. Epictetus (1926: I.1.11) is typically forthright (extreme). For him, our body is not 'our own'; what is ours is *prohairesis*, the capacity to choose. For a discussion of Epictetus' notion of the 'self', see Russell (2012: Ch. 7).

11. For discussion of relation between moral and intellectual virtue, centring on *EN* Bk X, see for example Cooper (1975).

12. See Hutchinson (1986) for an extensive discussion.

13. For an account that this 'flavour' is strong, see Homiak (2000). Contrary to Aristotle (*EN* 1113a3/120), Hume denies any substantive, as opposed to verbal, distinction between moral virtues and 'natural abilities', since both are 'mental qualities', produce 'pleasure' and to are to a large extent involuntary (*T* 3–3–4.1–3/*SBNT* 606–8).) Homiak acknowledges this difference (2000: 235n). See Harris (2011) for a fuller discussion.

14. Again, the 'gap' between Hume and Aristotle is evident. For Hume, his virtuous character traits are motivational matters of sentiment or feeling, not the imperious exercise of reason.

15. See Rosen (2003: 175–6) for a discussion of the original citation in Bentham, together with an argument that Bentham in context is making a point about public funding, which should leave 'prejudice aside'.

16. Compare Mill's (1910: 9) well-known comment that it is better to be

'Socrates dissatisfied than a fool satisfied', since the latter is unable to compare their position with that of another, with Hume's identification of comparison as a criterion by which a critic can determine a true standard of taste (E-ST 238, 241).

17. In an early essay Hume observes that when in possession of 'delicacy of sentiment', 'a man is more happy by what pleases his taste than by what gratifies his appetite' (E-DT 5).

18. Harris (2007: 234) picks up the passage in 'The Sceptic' where Hume says 'a little miss dressed in a new gown for a dancing school ball, receives as compleat enjoyment as the greatest orator' (E-Sc 166] as part of his argument that Hume is debunking the view that 'philosophy' can lead humans to live morally better lives.

19. For Aristotle, see Hardie (1968: 25), and for the difference between Aristotle and the Stoics, see Russell (2012: Ch. 5), who distinguishes what he calls the Stoics' 'sufficiency thesis' (that is, virtue itself is sufficient for happiness) from Aristotle's recognition of the role played by other 'goods'. The Benthamite counterpoint to Aristotle's non-asceticism is here germane. Bentham explicitly attacked asceticism with, implicitly, the Stoics as exemplars of what he calls 'the philosophical party' in mind (1948: 133) and his reasoning is Humean. For Hume, at the heart of the 'perpetual cant' he ascribes to the Stoics is their 'disgust in mankind' (M 6.21/SBNM 242), while Bentham's 'philosophical party' is judged to 'have scarcely gone farther than to reprobate pleasure' (1948: 133). Symptomatic (to my mind) of their shared outlook is that they both cite Sparta negatively as an example, in effect, of asceticism (Hume E-Com 257–8; Bentham 1948: 134).

20. Sallust (1921), *De Coniuratione Catilinae* I, 5.8; 12.2. For discussion, see for example Earl (1961) on Sallust as well as, more generally, Earl (1967); helpful background material is in Edwards (1993).

21. Cicero (1913: I.20.69, 21.70); cf. Cicero (1927: III.2.3), Cicero (1928: I.2).

22. Seneca (1928: vol. 1), *De Providentia* 3,14. Cicero himself was a prominent politician, as indeed was Seneca, albeit at the service of the imperial rule of Nero. See Griffin (1966) and, more recently, Wilson (2014).

23. Jacqueline Taylor (2015: 100) has emphasised the place of humanity in Hume, calling it the 'key concept of his Enlightenment moral philosophy'.

24. See, for example, Cicero (1913: 1:42.150), '[the activities of] manual labourers ... those who buy from wholesale merchants to retail

immediately . . . mechanics engaged in vulgar trades . . . those trades which cater for sensual pleasure: fishmongers, butchers, cooks [etc.]' are unfitting for a gentleman [*liberales*].

25. Seneca (1928: vol. 3), *De Beneficiis* III, 2.

26. This reading finesses earlier interpretations of this passage, as in Chapter 13.

27. Sallust (1921: I, 5.8; 12.2); cf. Seneca (1928: vol. 3), *De Beneficiis* VII, 1–4 and many others.

28. This is notwithstanding that he wrote a self-consciously 'literary' essay 'Of Avarice' (1741 but withdrawn 1770), which does not dispute that it is a vice, while admitting that it is 'irreclaimable' (E-Avarice 555). For a brief discussion of that essay, see Berry (forthcoming a).

29. See, for example, the general formulation by Cicero (1913: 1.30) that it is dishonourable (*turpe*) to sink into luxury and to live a soft life but, in contrast, honourable (*honestum*) to live frugally, simply, soberly and with self-restraint (*parce, continenter, severe, sobrie*). This had its version later in the idea of holy or apostolic poverty (see the discussion in Berry 2013: Ch. 3 and Chapter 13 in this volume for Hume's recalibration of 'poverty' into 'impoverishment').

30. I avoid a discussion of how Hume's view might comport with the neuroscience that aims to map 'pleasurable experience' with localised brain activity. While there are grounds to speculate that Hume's 'science of man' would not be averse to such findings, that is, they would presumably not constitute chimerical 'ultimate principles' (*T* Intro 8/*SBNT* xvii) and although he does talk of the activity of the animal spirits, he is critical of 'imaginary dissection of the brain' (*T* 1–2–5.20/*SBNT* 60) (a probable allusion to Malebranche) and there is nothing to suggest that he was, or would ever be, tempted or persuaded by Hartley's 1749 physiological account of association (Hartley 1810). Crucially, however, it is Hume's concern with human behaviour 'in the common course of the world' (*T* Intro 10/ *SBNT* xix) that makes his relation to contemporary moral argument of potential interest.

31. This is in contrast to Stoicism, which, in a Christianised form, remained a dominant moral and social perspective (openly avowed by Adam Ferguson, for example). This goes a long way to explaining Hume's engagement with that approach and his neglect of Aristotle; it also provides extra justification for my discussion of the Stoics in this chapter.

32. To give one example, according to World Data of Happiness, when

UK residents were asked in 1979 'Are you happy as you live now?' the score was 4.34 (on a 5-point scale) but to the same question in 2006 the return was 3.33, even though materially the UK grew 'richer' in the intervening quarter of a century. Worlddatabaseofhappiness.eur. nl.

33. Notably by Easterlin (2001).

34. Compare Cicero (1927: V, 35): '[the case for poverty] is evident and Nature herself teaches us daily how few, how small her needs are, how cheaply satisfied'.

35. Lorenzo Greco (2017) has interpreted this passage as an example of Hume's recognition of self-reflection (citing *T* 3–3–6.6/*SBNT* 620), which he sees as consonant with Hume's sympathetic account of morals. While Greco's focus is on 'conscience' and Hume's distance from Butler, this interpretation can also serve to distance this passage in Hume from any Stoic reading. That is, I gloss, the source of the Humean self-reflection is the ineluctable participation in societal common life and not the transcendence achieved by the sage or the freedom granted by 'reason', available to the (still few) fortunates, to discipline the inherent unruliness of the passions. There is an extensive literature on the 'sensible knave'; Greco usefully supplies a guide.

Part III

Adam Smith

Introduction to Part III

The theme that runs through this third part of the book is Adam Smith as a self-conscious thinker of modernity. This reflects my view of his thought as engaging in the same sort of enterprise as that carried out by Hume. In particular, I see Smith, too, committed to a 'science of man' (see Chapters 17 and 20). This commitment runs across the whole of his thought (discernible in Chapter 16). Part III includes two previously unpublished essays. They elaborate on the argument of Chapter 18, a relatively early exposition.

As Smith made explicit in the subtitle added to the third edition, his *Theory of Moral Sentiments* is an 'analysis' of 'principles'. Despite the occasional lament, it is not a moralising tract. This helps to explain my recurrence to his essentially negative view of the Stoics. As with the Hume essays in Part II, these are selective. Smith is a major (if far from sole) presence in Berry 2013, so there is no discussion here, except by inference, of his economic and moral arguments (discussed in my forthcoming book *A Very Short Introduction to Adam Smith* (Oxford University Press), written for a non-academic audience).

16

Adam Smith's 'Considerations' on Language

Adam Smith's 'Considerations Concerning the First Formation of Languages' was first published as an appendix to the third edition (1767) of the *Theory of Moral Sentiments*, but it has not been reviewed in its own right at any length. This is so even though Smith himself, according to Dugald Stewart, 'set a high value upon it' (*Life* II, 44/292). Stewart's estimation was borne out with the discovery of the student notes of Smith's lectures on rhetoric and belles-lettres, delivered at Glasgow in 1762–3 (although these were an expansion of lectures given some ten years previously at Edinburgh), since it seems that the only one of these lectures Smith thought it worthwhile to both expand and publish was the one on the origin of language (*LRBL* 3, 9–13).[1]

It is not surprising that Smith lectured on this particular topic, for two main reasons. First, a distinctive feature of the Scottish Enlightenment was its preoccupation with style and rhetoric, and a general concern with language both written and spoken. The great fear of the Scots was that they would appear provincial alongside the more fashionable centres of London and Paris. There are numerous manifestations of this fear. It can be seen to be one of the motivations behind the establishment of the innumerable clubs that existed in eighteenth-century Scotland; indeed, one of the best known of these clubs, the Select (whose members included Kames, Hume, Blair and Smith himself)[2] established the Select Society for Promoting the Reading and Speaking of the English Language in Scotland (McElroy 1969: 58). There was, further, the curious incident of the importation from Ireland of Thomas Sheridan, in 1761, to give lectures in Edinburgh on elocution and the English tongue.[3] Perhaps the most characteristic feature of this preoccupation was the desire to eradicate 'Scotticisms'. For example, James Beattie published in 1787 (after the original pamphlet had proved so popular that all copies were accounted for) a little book, the title of which is instructive, *Scotticisms; Arranged in Alphabetical Order Designed to Correct Improprieties of Speech and Writing*. Its aim was 'to put young writers and speakers on their guard against some of those Scotch idioms, which, in this country, are liable to be mistaken for English'.[4]

It is against this particular background and preoccupation that we are to understand the great popularity not only of Smith's lectures on rhetoric[5] but also those of Stevenson (Professor of Logic, Edinburgh) and, preeminently, Hugh Blair, the first Regius Professor of Rhetoric and Belles-Lettres at Edinburgh (Schmitz 1948). Smith's lectures were not only popular but also influential, especially on Blair, who was in Smith's audience in the early Edinburgh lectures and who later borrowed part of Smith's manuscript for his own use (1838: 238n).

In addition to this contemporary concern, there is in Smith a pedagogic element. John Millar, in his account of Smith's logic class at Glasgow, notes that, after a general review of ancient logic, Smith 'dedicated all the rest of his time to the delivery of a system of rhetoric and belles-lettres' because he believed – apart from its being more suited to the youthfulness of his class – that

> The best method of explaining and illustrating the various powers of the human mind, the most useful part of metaphysics, arises from an examination of the several ways of communicating our thoughts by speech, and from an attention to the principles of those literary compositions which contribute to persuasion or entertainment. (Quoted in *Life* I, 17/274)

Yet, even allowing for this pedagogic factor, Smith's interest in language is of wider significance. This constitutes the second broad reason, mentioned above, for his treatment of this topic. Language was a genuine and legitimate concern for Smith qua philosopher. In this he was not exceptional, since the whole question of the origin of language was one that exercised many of the leading (and lesser) minds of the eighteenth century. Smith was certainly aware of this general debate, although the only source he cites in the 'Considerations' is Rousseau's *Essay on Inequality* (a book which Smith reviewed in a letter to the editors of the abortive *Edinburgh Review* of 1755/6, though on that occasion he neither commented upon nor translated the passages pertaining to language) in which, of course, Rousseau himself refers to the work of Condillac. However, in a letter to George Baird, Smith remarks, apropos of an abstract of William Ward's *Essay on Grammar* [1765] (1969), that it was Girard's *Les Vrais Principes de la Langue Françoise* (1747) 'which first set me thinking upon these subjects. I have received more instruction from it than from any other I have yet seen upon them [nouns Substantive]'. He also goes on to note that he received 'a good deal of entertainment' from the grammatical articles in the *Encyclopédie*.[6] Regardless of Smith's sources, the fact remains that this subject was popular in the eighteenth century. But, before examining Smith's own discussion it is necessary to be aware of the context in which the eighteenth century viewed language.

The context was distinctive. First, the theorists of the eighteenth century were unaware of the 'family' of languages; they wrote, by and large, before the discovery of Sanskrit. Instead, the eighteenth century still viewed grammar as a set of rules to be followed; it was, in Jespersen's (1922: 24) phrase, 'prescriptive' rather than 'descriptive.' Underlying this view is the conception of Latin grammar as the paradigm of all language and, indeed, the general understanding of language in terms of Aristotle's Categories (Robins 1967: Chs. 2 and 3). This is, as we shall see, of particular importance for Smith because it helps to explain his concern with the different parts of speech and the order in which they were developed. Secondly, the eighteenth century is distinctive because of the sway and dominance of Lockean epistemology, differentiating it from earlier speculation:

> Philosophical empiricism seems to open up a new approach to language for, in accordance with its fundamental tendency, it strives, not to relate the fact of language to a logical ideal, but rather to understand it in its sheer facticity, in its empirical origin and purpose . . . it seeks to know it solely in its psychological reality and function. (Cassirer 1953: I, 133)

Though the eighteenth-century speculation on language is thus distinctively characterised by post-Lockean philosophy and pre-familial linguistics, this speculation is not homogeneous. Four approximate 'schools' can be identified.[7] The first school we may term the Theological. Its main tenet was that language was a divine gift to Adam and thereby denied to the brute creation. A corollary of this view was that different languages were to be accounted for by the dispersion of mankind after Babel. This theological view was upheld by Beauzée in France,[8] Süssmilch in Germany and Beattie in Scotland.

The second school we may term the Rationalists. The theorists of this school did not accept the Lockean epistemology and, as a result, there are relatively few representatives in the second half of the eighteenth century. To the Rationalists, language was an instrument of logical analysis by which a correlation was, or ought to be, established between thought and speech. The origin of language was ascribed to human invention. Some representatives of this school were Harris in England, Monboddo in Scotland and the followers of Bullet in France (cf. LeFlamanc 1934: Ch. 4).

The third school we may term the Organic. This school postulated that language grew alongside the development of mankind and that it had its origin in natural cries. Among representatives of this school we can identify Priestley and Mandeville in England, Condillac and Rousseau in France and James Dunbar in Scotland. The final school, the Emotionalist, is really a subdivision of the Organic because of a different emphasis that can be distinguished in it. This emphasis was placed on the nature of the origin of language, in which they agreed with the Organic School, whereas the Organicists placed more emphasis on the development of language. Among members of the Emotionalist School were the Scotsmen Blackwell and Blair.

It must be stressed that these four schools are not completely exclusive because we find that certain individuals' theories exhibit traces of more than one school. For example, Blair has a theological element in his emotional theory, Condillac a rationalist component in his general organic position; and certain thinkers, for example Vico and, especially, Herder, stand apart from all the schools.

Thus, in the general context of eighteenth-century language theory and in our classification, we can place Smith squarely in the Organic school, while determining more precisely the particular sphere of his interests. To speak broadly, we can identify two general problems considered by the eighteenth century relative to the origin of language. The first is put succinctly by Rousseau (1962: 56): '*je laisse à qui voudra l'entreprendre la discussion de ce difficile problème, lequel a été le plus nécessaire, de la société déjà liée, à l'institution des langues, ou des langues déjà inventées, à l'établissement de la société.*' This was a question that Rousseau thought Condillac had begged, the answer to which Monboddo (*OPL* I, 197) explicitly directed himself. The second problem was how to account for the presence of the different parts of speech. As previously stated, it was this second problem that exercised Smith; he was not concerned with the first problem. Nor, unlike many other thinkers (both organicists and emotionalists), was he concerned about the actual origin of language in natural cries[9] or in the role of imitation in the development of language.[10]

Smith, therefore, set himself a comparatively limited task, but this limitation meant that his discussion of the particular question of the evolution of the parts of speech is comprehensive. Smith's general theme is to account for the evolution of these parts of speech while circumventing the need for abstraction. The presence of the abstract parts of speech was a problem for the eighteenth-century theorists, particularly the Rationalists. In the words of Dunbar, the alleged inventors most improbably 'must have resolved in imagination all the subtleties of logic and entered far into the science of grammar, before its objects had any existence. Profound abstraction and generalisation must have been constantly exercised' (*EHM* 93). In fact, to Dunbar language developed through 'the laws of analogy [which] by one gentle and uniform effect superseding or alleviating the effects of abstraction permit language to advance towards its perfection free of the embarrassments which seemed to obstruct its progress' (*EHM* 92). The greatest of these embarrassments was to account for the abstract parts of speech, such as prepositions, pronouns, particles and so on.

Smith set about accounting for the evolution of these abstractions or 'metaphysical' elements in a manner consistent with the alleged mental ability and state of primitive man (the 'savage'). He opens by declaring: 'The assignation of particular names to denote particular objects ... would probably be one of the first steps towards the formation of language' (*CL* 1/203). In time, 'those words ... would each of them insensibly become the common name of the multitude' (*CL* 1/204) and this seems 'to have given occasion to the formation of those classes and assortments (in language)' (*CL* 2/205), namely those seemingly metaphysical and abstract grammatical categories.

The next development in language is adjectives and prepositions, that is, words expressing 'quality' and 'relation'. Smith illustrates how 'quality' was conceived: 'The quality appears in nature as a modification of the substance, and as it is thus expressed in language, by a modification of the noun substantive' (*CL* 8/207). This correspondence between what is 'natural' and what occurs in the development of language forestalls the need for abstraction; that is, new adjectival words are not invented but, instead, the endings of existing noun substantives are changed. The question of 'relation' Smith believes to be even more abstract than that of 'quality' but, again, the same procedure operates so that, in practice, there is no need for abstraction. For example, the relation of possession is expressed by the development of the genitive case and it is only as man develops that abstract words such as 'of' develop. It is in this way that the absence of particles and prepositions in Latin and Greek is accounted for: they are older languages, which alter the endings of words in order to express the same meaning as prepositions and so on.

Though Smith declares noun substantives to be the first elements of speech, in parts he also states that 'verbs must necessarily have been coeval' (*CL* 27/215). Smith argues that the first verbs were impersonal, and that there has been a development from impersonal to personal verbs. The rule governing this development is that the verbs grow more general as the number of words for subjects increases; that is, the development of verbs is an integral part of the development of language as a whole. Just as nouns incorporated 'relation' and 'quality' by altering their endings, so verbs incorporate number, tense and mood in the same way. It is a later development in language that the verbs of existence and possession come to be used as auxiliaries. Smith summarises his theory of the development of language in a maxim: 'The more simple any language is in its composition the more complex it must be in its declensions and conjugations' – and vice versa (*CL* 236/221–2).

This, in outline, is the tenor of Smith's argument. This argument was influential, especially in Scotland where we can cite two examples, Monboddo and Dunbar (for more on Dunbar and language, see Chapter 2). Monboddo's general thesis that language is invented is opposed to Smith's, yet he explicitly agrees with Smith on a number of issues. Monboddo allows that Smith's theory is 'ingenious', as is Smith's conjecture that the names of objects were particular before becoming general (*OPL* I, 297). Monboddo further agrees that children name themselves instead of employing the pronoun 'I' (*OPL* II, 45; cf. *CL* 32/219) and does, indeed, refer to Smith on several occasions during his own account of the development of the parts of speech (*OPL* II, Bk 1 Chs. 8–10).

While Dunbar, our second example, does not elucidate the development of the parts of speech in as much detail as Smith, there are indications that he accepts Smith's broad argument. The most concrete instance of Smith's influence on Dunbar is a note on the subject of the development of verbs from impersonal to personal, in which Dunbar expresses his agreement with Smith's argument (*EHM* 113).[11] In the text Dunbar sketches out how he envisaged the development of verbs. He postulates that the lion and the serpent are, to the savage, the most hostile animals, so that 'a certain species of terror would be excited by the approach of one: a different modification of the same emotion would be excited by the approach of the other' (*EHM* 83). Given these emotions, and the fact that the other inhabitants of the forest have names, it is then, to Dunbar,

> abundantly natural for the savage to join the term, indicating the dread of the lion or serpent with a proper name in order to notify the approach of any other offensive creature. This term by an easy extension will be transferred from offensive to other creatures: and hence by gradual transition even to inanimate objects, till it is charged at length with a general affirmation and possesses all the power of a verb. (*EHM* 84)

That is essentially the Smithian argument – indeed, the example of the lion is taken straight from Smith (*CL* 29/216) – that verbs develop from the particular to the general.

To appreciate Smith's position more fully, we can now take up a number of points he makes and indulge in some short comparisons. First, as we have seen, Smith avows that verbs and nouns are coeval – though he does conjecture that possibly all the first words may have been impersonal verbs (*CL* 28/216) – but this question of the priorities of the parts of speech was the subject of much speculation. Some thinkers assigned very definite priorities. Vico (1948: 137) and Priestley (1762: 56) both regarded verbs as later developments. Condillac [1746] (1947/53 vol. I, pt 2, sect. 1, Chs 9–10) believed verbs were the third part of speech to develop: after nouns substantive, first (also Priestley's position (1762: 50)), and adjectives, second, but before pronouns, fourth. Herder, on the other hand, believed verbs to be the first part of speech to develop, a consequence of his belief that hearing is the *Lehrmeister* – that it constitutes the 'proper gateway to the mind' so that 'Verba developed into nomina but not from them. A child does not call the sheep a sheep but a bleating creature, and this changes the interjection into a verb'.[12]

This quotation leads on to a second general point raised by Smith's analysis, since it was a feature of eighteenth-century discussions of the origin of language, as testified to by Herder in that quotation, that attention was paid to the speech patterns and behaviour of children. Thus Vico (1948: 137) and Priestley (1762: 56) both support their position on the order of the development of the parts of speech by citing as evidence the fact that children tend to omit verbs when they speak. Smith, too, regards the experience of children to be relevant. We have already referred to this in the context of the pronoun 'I' but there is another instance. He substantiates his point that terms develop from specific reference to become 'the common name of a multitude' by the fact that 'A child that is just learning to speak, calls every person who comes to the house its papa, or its mama; and thus bestows upon the whole species those names which it had been taught to apply to two individuals' (CL 1/204). The experience and behaviour of children was, of course, used at length by Condillac to explain the generation of language.[13]

The significance of this recourse to children by the eighteenth-century theorists was the belief that the growth of language in children was thought to be analogous to its growth in mankind (hence the importance attached to imitation in many theories). Added to this was the further belief or presupposition that (extant) primitive peoples (Smith's 'savages') exhibit the same processes as children. Dunbar (*EHM* 99) states this clearly at the close of his discussion, where he justifies his own theory as being 'consonant to the probability of things, to the experience of early life, and to the genius and complexion of ruder ages'.

To take up another point in Smith's analysis: his argument that the simplification of the structure of language was occasioned by the growth of 'particulars' was given, in addition to the 'logical' argument, an historical expression.[14] That is, this process of increasing complexity in the composition of language was brought about 'in consequence of the mixture of several languages with one another, occasioned by the mixture of different nations' (CL

33/220).[15] Smith conjectures that, from the mixing of two languages, those ignorant of the intricacies of the other language would 'naturally' in the case of declensions, for example, supply prepositions instead, and so on (*CL* 33/220). Again, this part of Smith's argument was not lost on Dunbar (*EHM* 97) and, indeed, many writers[16] acknowledged the influence of one language upon another through either conquest or contiguity or both.

Yet another feature of Smith's theory that needs noting is his concluding argument. This argument is really a lament, since he believes the increasing simplification of languages only serves to render them less perfect. He produces three reasons for this imperfection: simplified language is prolix, constrained and monotonous (*CL* 43–5/224). The languages most at fault, it follows from Smith's earlier analysis, are the most modern, with English, because it is the most simplified (the most mixed), by implication the worst offender. This aspect of Smith's theory needs to be placed in its original context, that is, lectures on rhetoric (Funke 1934: 31). In these lectures, in fact, Smith continues by investigating the remedies for these defects in English (*LRBL* 5/21–4) and discoursing at length on the correctness of style. Of course, this concern related to the contemporary Scottish concern with 'correct' language, as mentioned above. On the more precise question of rhetoric, it was something of a commonplace that the 'moderns' could not compete with the great rhetoricians of the past, such as Demosthenes or Cicero, or, indeed, with their poets. This aspect of Smith's theory is in perfect accord with these sentiments: 'How much this power of transposing the order of their words must have facilitated the composition of the ancients, both in verse and prose, can hardly be imagined', since this power, which greatly enhances the quality of ancient or classical literature, is non-existent in English, where the words in the sentence are 'almost precisely determined' (*CL* 45/225, 226).

A final point about Smith's theory also relates to imperfection in language, but this time to both classical and modern languages. Smith points out this general imperfection when he remarks that 'Alexander walking' or 'Alexander ambulat' expresses one concept, and

> the division of this event, therefore, into two parts, is altogether artificial, and is the effect of the imperfection of language, which, upon this, as upon many occasions, supplies, by a number of words, the want

of one which could express at once the whole matter of fact that was meant to be affirmed. (*CL* 28/216)

This state of affairs contrasts with the earliest condition of language, that is, when impersonal verbs prevailed and which 'express in one word a complete event' (*CL* 28/216).[17] This was an opinion shared by many of the theorists, for example, Dunbar (*EHM* 85) in passing and, more explicitly, Rousseau (1962: 53), Blair (1838: 89n) and Monboddo (*OPL* I, 360). Smith, however, elaborates the point by saying that these verbs 'preserve in the expression that perfect simplicity and unity, which there always is in the object and in the idea ... [and] with which the mind conceives its nature' (*CL* 28/216). There is a degree of similarity here with a position adopted by Condillac. Condillac believed that in primitive languages every word stood for an idea, and that there was, accordingly, perfect communication between individuals. This is Condillac when most rationalistic (see above), that is, when he continues the Port-Royal tradition;[18] and it is a corollary of this view that he regards modern language as inferior, since this perfect communication between individuals is no longer realisable. In fact, this perfect language he believes is now only to be found in algebra: '*L'algèbre est une langue bien faite*'.[19]

Thus we have Adam Smith's theory of language as found in 'Considerations'. Though his treatment of the subject is comparatively short in length and limited in scope, it is nevertheless significant. In Scotland, in keeping with his general 'seminal importance' (Forbes 1954: 644), his theory was taken up by both Blair and Dunbar and, in part, by Monboddo. In the broader terms of the eighteenth century, Smith's theory is typical of what we have here designated the Organic School: language is seen as developing in step with man's own (and society's) development. The merits of this theory must be adjudged in eighteenth-century terms, since the total conception of language changed with the work of the Schlegels, Jones, Bopp and others at the turn of the century.[20] Perhaps the aspect of Smith's theory that is most characteristic of his age is his explanation in terms of what is 'natural'[21] – hence Stewart's dubbing of his essay as 'Natural' or 'Conjectural History' – an explanation that is at once the most economic in its operating principle, the human mind, and most catholic in what it explains: the growth and development of the character and form of language.

Postscript

This was the first of my writings (a thesis 'spin-off' but no replication of any text therein) to be accepted for publication, although not the first to appear in print. The *Journal of the History of Ideas* was chosen because (correctly as it turned out) the essay looked like a good fit. When it was published, in 1974, there had been negligible discussion of 'Considerations'. In that sense it was a pioneer (as a possible testament to that status the essay was reprinted in Haakonssen (1998)). Since its appearance, a considerable number of later discussions have been published. The best piece is Land (1977), which, though he kindly cites me, provides a different perspective, supplying an informed analytical treatment. Among other specific or focused discussions are Schreyer (1989), Plank (1992), which reference this piece, and Dascal (2006). On the general context of the study of language in the Enlightenment, the magisterial work is Aarsleff (1974) and, though it ranges beyond the eighteenth century, a useful collection is Struever (ed.). There are, of course, many studies that deal with Smith's contemporaries, especially Condillac, Rousseau and Herder. On the Scots there is much less – I deal with Dunbar in Chapter 3 and Monboddo is the subject of another good piece by Land (1976).

I have come to regard 'Considerations' as an important work for spelling out some key Smithian assumptions (see also Chapters 17 and 20 and forthcoming a). Otteson (2002) uses *CL* in his own interpretation of Smith and notes this article. I link it to a broadly Lockean schema (especially in Berry 1997) and on those grounds this essay should have made much more of Locke's analysis of language in the *Essay on Understanding* (the key source for Condillac).

I should like to thank Mr A. S. Skinner, University of Glasgow, for his comments and suggestions on an earlier draft of this chapter.

Notes

1. See Scott (1927: 52), who conjectures that Smith finally published 'Considerations' because he became aware that his work for *The Wealth of Nations* would absorb much of his time and hence make it difficult to expand the theme fully.
2. See list in Stewart's 'Life of Robertson' (Robertson 1840: xxxii–iii).
3. Lothian (1963: xxxii–iv), McElroy (1969: 56–7) and, for a full

analysis, Howell (1971: 214–43). For a contemporary comment, see Thomas Somerville (1861: 56).

4. Beattie (1787: 2). See Mossner (1954: *passim*) for further illustrations of this concern.

5. For the background and analysis of the lectures, see Bevilacqua (1965).

6. Quoted in Rae (1895: 160). Now see *Corr* 69/87–8. When I wrote this piece I had not looked at Ward's book. It puts forward an argument very different from Smith's (there is no attention to 'development') and it is not surprising that he preferred the work of Girard and (presumably) Beauzée and Turgot.

7. Cf. the threefold divisions of Wellek (1941), 'Objective, Emotional, Organic'; Sapir (1907), 'Theological, Rational, Naturalist'; and Pascal (1953: Ch. 6), 'Theological, Ideological, Materialist'.

8. See his article 'Langue' (Beauzée 1765: IX, 241ff.). Cf. R. Hubert (1923: pt 2, Ch. 8). For doubts on Beauzée's authorship, see Juliard (1970: 23n.).

9. Inter alia Turgot (1913: I, 351), Blackwell (1735: 37), Blair (1838: 64), Priestley (1776: 237–8) and Condillac (1947–53: I, 60–2). For a discussion of an aspect of this feature, see Berry (1973).

10. Inter alia Blair (1838: 65), Monboddo (*OPL* I, 191) and Condillac (1947–53: I, 61).

11. Blair (1838: 101) also agrees with Smith on this point.

12. Herder (translation in Herder [1891: V, 52] 1969: 142). Cf. Turgot's argument that the names of animals in primitive (unmixed) languages are onomatopoeic in origin (1913: I, 353).

13. Condillac (1947–53: I, Pt 2, sect.1, Ch. 1). Also Blair (1838: 90), and especially de Brosses (1801: I, 200ff.).

14. Cf. Wellek (1941: 93), who accuses Smith of inconsistency on this point.

15. Note that the full title of the 'Considerations' is 'Considerations Concerning the First Formation of Languages and the Different Genius of Original and Compounded Languages'.

16. Priestley (1752: 220), Herder [1891: V, 126] (1969: 167), Turgot (1913: I, 358) and, especially, his article on 'Etymologie' in the *Encyclopédie* VI, 98–111 (Diderot ed. 1756).

17. Cf. the letter to Baird (1763), where Smith remarks that verbs are 'in my apprehension the original parts of speech, first invented to express in one word a compleat event' (*Corr* 69/88).

18. Knight (1968: Ch. 6). For Condillac's rationalism (his retention of Cartesian elements), see Frankel (1948: 51–5).

19. *Langue des Calculs* [1798] (1947/53 II, 420). For the significance and influence of this idea, see Acton (1959: 204ff.).
20. Muller (1875: I, 425ff.) treats Smith explicitly as a 'pre-scientific' theorist.
21. Cf. Girard (1747: I, 42): '*Persuadé de l'avantage qu'il y a à suivre le fil de la Nature dans toutes les choses dont elle est le principe*' – of which Smith thought so highly. See Campbell (1971: 55–60) for a discussion of Smith's use of the term 'nature'.

17

Smith and Science

There is a deliberate ambiguity about the title of this chapter. It refers at one and the same time to Smith as a commentator on and as a practitioner of 'science'. In the former role he explicitly addresses issues of method and implicitly reflects a pervasive Enlightenment commitment to the progressive agenda associated with science. In the latter role his actual investigations, if liberally interpreted, manifest both the method and the agenda.

The analysis that follows is divided into four parts. The first examines the 'Enlightenment commitment' – the high value placed on science – and notes what can be gleaned of Smith's own exposure to scientific thinking. Next, the focus is on Smith as a commentator, his specific account of science as the discovery of connecting principles. The third and longest part discusses 'Smith the scientist' – outlining and illustrating by means of a couple of case studies his commitment to causal explanation and to what I call 'soft determinism'. In the brief final part the point will be made that Smith does not divorce scientific 'findings' from moral significance.

I

The Enlightenment was a self-conscious movement of intellectuals who thought of themselves as *Aufklärer*, striving to make their age *un siècle des lumières*. This implied that earlier times were comparatively benighted. This idea is encapsulated in the contrast between science on the one hand and ignorance, prejudice and superstition on the other. Any institutions such as slavery, torture, witchcraft or religious persecution that still existed were to be opposed as relics of darker ages, which the light of scientific reason would clear away. This Baconian implication, that science is to be put to use for the good of humanity, meant a unity of theory and practice.

Nowhere is this unity better exemplified than in one of the Enlightenment's key products, the *Encyclopaedia or Rational Dictionary of Sciences, Arts and Professions* (a text that Smith was instrumental in purchasing for Glasgow University Library). In its *Preliminary Discourse* (1751), D'Alembert (1963: 80ff.), after commending Bacon's path-breaking role, attached particular weight to the work of Newton. This is typical: Newton is *the* hero of the Enlightenment. His perceived achievement was to have explained the full range of natural phenomena, celestial as well as terrestrial, by utilising only a few simple principles (laws of motion plus gravity). It became a challenge to emulate his work, to achieve for the moral or social sciences what he had done for natural science. Newton himself, in his *Optics*, had effectively thrown down the gauntlet when he remarked that if, through pursuit of his method, natural philosophy becomes perfected, so, in like fashion, 'the bounds of Moral Philosophy will be also enlarged'.[1]

The Scottish universities led the way in adopting Newton's framework. In a period of about half a century from 1660, Aristotle was replaced with Descartes, who was in turn superseded by Newton. Of the Scottish universities Glasgow was perhaps the slowest to adapt, although by 1712 Newton was on the curriculum (Shepherd 1982: 75). Newton's eventual dominance was facilitated by two factors – one particular, the other general. In particular, the adoption of Newton's system was aided by the establishment of designated subject 'chairs' to replace the regenting system (1727), where one individual had to teach a cohort of students the full run of subjects throughout the four years of their university career. More generally, Newton's system gradually became assimilated as a buttress to natural theology and, beyond that, to the established social order. In this process his work/name came to stand as a sort of cultural shorthand that, as such, paid little detailed attention to his own priorities and tended to subsume, more or less indiscriminately, the work of other experimental scientists within his. This is symptomatic of the interweaving of 'science' and 'society' that the term 'Newtonianism' came to represent. As we will see later, while Smith was a Newtonian, there are some grounds for questioning the extent of his subscription to Newtonianism.

When Smith entered Glasgow in 1737, 'natural philosophy' was the special responsibility of Professor Robert Dick (primus), while

Professor Robert Simson taught mathematics. There is indirect evidence that these two subjects were Smith's favourites.[2] Smith would have had lessons in mathematics in his 'semi' year (his own first but the third year in the usual progression). Simson, his teacher, was (or became) a leading authority on Euclid (Smith owned a copy of the second edition of his *Sectionum Conicorum*). Much later, Smith called him one of the two greatest mathematicians of his time (*TMS* III, 2.20/124); the other was the Edinburgh Professor Matthew Stewart (father of Dugald, Smith's first biographer) and a fellow student of Simson with Smith. In his final year Smith would have attended Dick's classes in experimental philosophy, using instruments that had been bought as part of a self-conscious 'modernising' drive (Emerson 1995: 29) in order to elucidate the 'doctrine of bodies' as 'improved by Sir Isaac Newton'.[3]

Smith himself compared his Glasgow education favourably with that on offer at Oxford, whither he went in 1740 as a Snell Exhibitioner. Commenting on the Oxford curriculum, his most recent biographer ventures that Smith 'must have been struck at Balliol ... by the lack of commitment to providing instruction in the New Philosophy and Science of Locke and Newton' (Ross 1995: 73). The justified presumption is that Smith spent his time at Oxford cultivating his linguistic skills and in developing the study of human nature in all its branches (*Life* I, 8/271). However, it does not seem that Smith's interest in natural philosophy atrophied. This is supported partly by the probable construction of his 'History of Astronomy' shortly after leaving Oxford and partly from some of his activities when he returned to Glasgow University in 1751. Aside from his pedagogic duties, Smith also occupied a variety of administrative posts. In the latter capacity he used his discretion to support scientific expenditure. On one occasion, against the objections of the Principal, he explicitly defended the outlay for a new chemical laboratory (Ross 1995: 150).

Undoubtedly Smith was sustained in this conviction by his friendship with William Cullen and Joseph Black, two of the leading chemists of the eighteenth century and successively professors of chemistry at Glasgow then Edinburgh. This friendship is symptomatic of a prominent strand in the Scottish Enlightenment – the clubbability of its members and the breadth of their interests. These features are embodied in the innumerable 'societies' that existed in all the major cities. Smith was a member of several, both in Glasgow and Edinburgh. From the extant evidence of their meetings it is clear that they were centrally engaged in fostering the Baconian association between science and 'improvement' (the appliance of science to agriculture in particular but also, as with Cullen's work on bleach for the linen industry (Guthrie, 1950: 62), increasingly, to wider aspects of the burgeoning economy). For example, the Glasgow Literary Society (which Smith helped to establish), despite what its name might suggest, included among its topics for discussion papers on chemistry, physics and medicine and it was at a gathering of that society that Black read a paper on latent heat (Sher 1995: 335ff.). (For more on the GLS, see Emerson 2015: Ch. 2). It is a significant feature of the period that 'science' did not exist in some separate intellectual compartment but permeated the polite and literary culture (Emerson 1988a).

Undue stress should not be placed on these snippets of biographical information. The principal evidence of Smith's scientific concerns has to be his writings. Nevertheless, there is clear evidence that he had a basic grounding in the principles of the paradigmatic physical sciences of his age and that, judged by the contents of his library, he had the means to keep himself abreast of the century's developments, including the ownership of twenty-one volumes of the *Philosophical Transactions of the Royal Society*.

II

Reflecting again the seamless nature of his personal and intellectual links, Smith appointed two of his close 'scientific' friends – Joseph Black and James Hutton – as his executors. He instructed them to destroy his manuscripts but allowed them, at their discretion, to publish a set of essays. This set appeared in 1795 with the title *Essays on Philosophical Subjects*. The most substantial component is his 'History of Astronomy'. This essay has occasioned much scholarship. In part this is due to the belief that anything a recognised 'great mind' or 'seminal thinker' wrote is bound to be of interest, but the 'Astronomy' does have intrinsic merits and these, not unexpectedly, bear on the theme of this chapter. The major point of interest in the scholarship, as it also is for us, is less Smith's impressive erudition than the 'methodological' views he appears to express. These are captured in the full title of the essay 'The Principles which Lead and Direct Philosophical Enquiries, Illustrated by the History of Astronomy'. Two other, shorter, essays also 'illustrate' these 'principles', namely 'Ancient Physics' and 'Ancient Logics and Metaphysics', but they scarcely live up to their billing, being for the most part expositions of, respectively, Empedoclean accounts of the four elements and Greek philosophy, with Plato prominent.

There is a body of circumstantial evidence as to when the 'Astronomy' was written. As noted in Part I, it is probable that Smith drafted its outlines after his departure from Oxford and he may have used parts of it in a series of lectures he gave in Edinburgh in 1748/50 (Ross 1995: 99). Smith himself called 'a history of Astronomical Systems ... down to the time of Des Cartes' a 'juvenile work' (*Corr* 137/168). In addition, the reference in the published text to the predicted appearance in 1758 of a (Halley's) comet (*HA* IV, 74/103) suggests that even the final Newtonian part was written before that date. Access to Smith's motives being unavailable, it is fruitless to speculate at any length on why Smith wrote the essay. Certainly it was not to add to an existing genre. He did own John Keill's *Introductio ad Veram Astronomiam* (1718), which is a printed version of his lectures at Oxford and would have been the source of the subject when Smith was at Balliol. Keill's work, however, is analytical rather than historical, devoted to expounding the Newtonian (the 'true') system.

Before addressing some of the issues raised by the 'Astronomy', it is necessary to outline synoptically the argument of the essay. Underlying the argument are a series of claims about the constituents and dynamics of human nature. These all betray an acceptance of an empirical, Lockean approach, especially, as we shall see, in its Humean guise. Thus his opening sentence declares humans to possess certain sentiments. He mentions three – wonder, surprise and admiration – which he maintains are distinct although they are often confounded. Without any supporting argument, he stipulates that wonder as a sentiment is excited by what is new and singular, surprise by what is unexpected and admiration by what is great and beautiful. Just as *The Wealth of Nations* was an inquiry into its 'nature and causes', so Smith says, at the end of the preliminary section of 'Astronomy', that the aim of the essay is to consider the 'nature and causes' of the three sentiments because their influence is greater than might be thought (*HA* Intro, 7/34). The next two sections deal with surprise and wonder, but admiration, rather unexpectedly, does not receive a separate treatment; instead, the third section is devoted to the question of the 'origin of philosophy'. The bulk of the essay's content is section four, which provides the illustrative 'history of astronomy'.

The key point made about surprise is that the opposition of contrasted sentiments heightens their vivacity, whereas resemblance renders them more languid (*HA* I, 9/37). This, Smith observes, accounts for the deadening effect of habit and custom (*HA* I, 10/37). The section on wonder contains more meat. The mind is declared to take pleasure in the observation of resemblances and it endeavours to sort or classify them (*HA* II, 1/38). This does not sit altogether happily with the earlier reference to their deadening effect and, while not inconsistent, the requisite conceptual tidying up is absent, as perhaps reflects the 'unfinished' nature of the manuscript. Smith illustrates the point about classification with an example drawn from language: 'animal' is a general name that classifies together all those things endowed with a power of self-motion. This example is not totally random and intimates Smith's typical Enlightenment concern with language, as represented by his 'Considerations concerning the First Formation of Languages' (see Chapter 16). Since the roots of that essay have been linked to his Edinburgh lectures, it gives some mild corroboration to the notion that the 'Astronomy' was composed at the same time. Smith proceeds to observe that the inclination to classify and subclassify develops along with the growth of knowledge and he makes, in effect, a distinction between the expert and the layperson. This has bearing later. Wonder properly occurs when something 'new or singular' occurs, when something defies classification, or when neither memory nor imagination is able to place it (*HA* II, 3/39). Since it is a postulated fact about human nature that the inability to classify induces 'uncertainty and anxious curiosity' then, given that it is another fact about the dynamics of human nature that anxiety or unease prompts remedial action, it follows that wonder is a psychological state to 'get rid of' (*HA* II, 4/40).

Wonder is generated not only by a singular event but also equally by an irregular succession. Here Smith, in his most conspicuously Humean passage (Raphael 1977), remarks that it is a break in the customary succession of two objects 'constantly' presenting themselves to the senses in a particular order that generates first surprise, then wonder. The languid, non-anxious, state occurs when the 'association of ideas' is so well established that the 'habit of imagination' passes from one to the other without any break or gap (*HA* II, 7/41). But if there is a gap, that is, when customary connection is interrupted, then

> the supposition of a chain of intermediate, though invisible, events, which succeed each other in a train similar to that in which the imagination has been accustomed to move, and which link together those two disjointed appearances, is the only means by which the imagination can fill up this interval, is the only bridge which, if one may say so, can smooth its passage from the one object to the other. (*HA* II,8/42)

Once this is achieved, wonder vanishes (*HA* II, 9/42). The emphasis on custom here reflects not only an endorsement of Humean empiricism but also non-reflective experience. The expert/lay distinction here re-emerges. Humans in general do not 'wonder' how the consumption of bread is converted into flesh and bones and, more particularly, artisans do not wonder about their craft, but philosophers are aware of gaps, and thus perceive a need for bridges, where others ('the bulk of mankind') experience no such break in their imagined associations (*HA* II, 11/45). Smith builds on this last point to characterise philosophy as the 'science of the connecting principles of nature' (*HA* II, 12/45). (He echoes this characterisation in 'Logics' in *EPS* 1/119.) Philosophy introduces order into chaos by 'representing the invisible chains' that bind together disjointed objects. In doing this it allays the 'tumult of the imagination' and restores it to tranquillity. Given this, then, philosophy can be 'regarded as one of those arts which address themselves to the imagination', a remark that has prompted several commentators to regard Smith's account of science as ultimately aesthetic.[4]

The third section changes tack by developing a sociological rather than a psychological argument (Moscovici 1956: 5). His concern here is to identify the circumstances originally conducive to philosophy. There is, he conjectures, a pre-philosophical age where, because subsistence is precarious, order and security are absent. As a consequence, the 'savage' has no curiosity about the seemingly disjointed appearances of nature, which are dealt with by invoking the favour or displeasure of gods – a response Smith identifies as the origin of polytheism (*HA* III, 1, 2/49) (see Berry 2000; Chapter 6). However, with the gradual establishment of order and security, there comes, for those of 'liberal fortune', sufficient leisure to enable them to attend to the world around them

(*HA* III, 3/50). These individuals now become 'embarrassed' by incoherences and are placed in the uneasy state of wonder. This they seek to allay not through the 'pusillanimous superstition' of the savage (*HA* III, 2/50; 'Physics' in *EPS* 9/114) but by the philosophical pursuit of the 'concealed connections that unite the various appearances of nature' (*HA* III, 3/51). This pursuit, Smith declares, is a disinterested affair; as befits the social status of its first practitioners, philosophy/science does not originate in any material need to extract advantage from its discoveries.

The first societies developed enough to practise philosophy were Greece and its colonies. The final section of the essay – the illustrative history of astronomy – now traces this practice. Smith's initial formulation, however, is unexpected. With no preparation, he reinvokes 'greatness and beauty', since these are the characteristics of the 'celestial appearances', but instead of linking them with admiration (as the opening section did), he says it made them the 'object of curiosity'. The link with admiration is duly made in the 'Physics' in *EPS* 9/114) but he gives a much more consistent explanation in *The Wealth of Nations*. There, Smith comments that (inter alia) the 'revolutions of the heavenly bodies . . . necessarily excite wonder so they naturally call forth the curiosity of mankind to enquire into their causes' (*WN* V, i.f. 24/767). In the 'Astronomy' itself, Smith charts its history from the system of concentric circles through Ptolemy to Copernicus, Galileo, Kepler, Descartes and finally Newton. In telling this story, Smith draws particular attention to the transition from one system to another and it is here, perhaps, that the chief interest, as well as the most debated aspects, lies.[5]

Much of the commentary on 'Astronomy' has an overblown air to it, inasmuch as it seeks to elicit Smith's 'philosophy of science' or, a shade less grandiosely, his 'history of the philosophy of science'. Smith, however, does not articulate anything so substantial. A common ploy is to explicate the various principles or criteria of scientific explanation within the text. Along these lines we find, for example, Cremaschi (1989: 86) identifying simplicity, familiarity, coherence and comprehensiveness, while both Lindgren (1969: 905) and Reisman (1976: 39) have the same first three but substitute beauty for the last. Christie (1987: 31) comes up with unity, simplicity and harmony; Brown with familiarity, uniformity, coherence and generality and Campbell (1971: 39) with coherence, simplicity and familiarity. Although all these identifications have textual support, the shades of difference between them indicate that nowhere is Smith himself explicit.

The imposition upon Smith of a philosophy of science has itself generated a debate about quite what that philosophy is. A prominent line of interpretation has been that Smith adopts a conventionalist or an 'anti-realist' posture.[6] There are seemingly two strands to this interpretation. The first, weaker, one is developed around the issue of the criteria whereby one system of astronomy is replaced by another. Skinner (1996: 35), for example, fastens on the development of the first system of concentric spheres, Brown (1988:37) on the acceptance of Copernicus's heliocentric theory, and Cremaschi (1989: 86) on the relation between Descartes and Newton. Because the stronger of the two strands in the anti-realist interpretation focuses upon Smith's wording in his discussion of Newton, it will be most apt to deal with the final case.

Smith had argued that after Galileo had removed the problem over the velocity of motion that had been associated with Copernicus' theory, and after Cassini's observations had established the accuracy of Kepler's laws, the only embarrassment suffered by the Copernican system was the gap between the ponderousness of the Earth and its rapid revolution (*HA* IV, 60/91). In accordance with his psychological theory, this 'gap' had to be bridged by some 'connecting chain'. Descartes attempted to identify this invisible chain with his theory of vortexes. This was successful inasmuch as it conceived of the planets as 'floating in an immense ocean of ether' (*HA* IV, 65/96), which was an idea or analogy familiar to the imagination so that 'mankind could no longer refuse themselves the pleasure of going along with so harmonious an account of things'.[7] Yet despite this, while Copernicus remains universally accepted, Smith observes that the Cartesian system is now almost universally rejected in favour of Newton's.

The advantages of the Newtonian system are that it explained all planetary irregularities (something Descartes failed to do), its predictions had proved accurate and it had linked into one system all celestial and terrestrial phenomena and had done so by utilising the principle of gravity which is 'so familiar a principle of connection' that it 'completely removed all the difficulties of the imagination' (*HA* IV, 67/98). In consequence, Smith declares, here echoing the standard Enlightenment judgement, it was 'the greatest and most admirable improvement that was ever made in philosophy' (ibid.) and Newton's principles 'have a degree of firmness and solidity that we should in vain look for in any other system' (*HA* IV, 76/105). Cremaschi (1989: 87), however, quotes Smith's remark that

> even we, while we have been endeavouring to represent all philosophical systems as mere inventions of the imagination, to connect together the otherwise disjointed and discordant phaenomena of nature, have insensibly been drawn in, to make use of language expressing the connecting principles of this one, as if they were the real chains which Nature makes use of to bind together her several operations. (*HA* IV, 76/105)

The consequence he draws from this passage is that for Smith we cannot suppose Newton's theory superior on the grounds that it is a 'better reproduction of reality', since every theory (Newton's included) is an invention of the imagination. This same passage, indeed, is quoted by most of those who subscribe to the stronger strand in the anti-realist interpretation.[8]

Such an interpretation is difficult to sustain. It needs to be recalled what Smith's aim is in the essay. The history of astronomy is meant to illustrate how philosophy is an activity that addresses itself to the imagination and Smith is explicit in this context that this is a 'particular point of view'. There is no implication that philosophy is nothing but an imaginative exercise. More pointedly, Smith continues that this particular perspective is distinct from any regard to the 'absurdity or probability' of the various systems of nature, of 'their agreement or inconsistency with truth and reality' (*HA* II, 12/46). Lindgren and the others seem guilty of overgeneralising the particular. There is, of course, a sophistication in Smith's account that has seemed to some reminiscent of T. S. Kuhn's account of the development of science as a series of paradigm shifts,[9] but that does not establish an anti-realist posture.

The actual argument of the text also serves to cast doubt on the accuracy of that posture as a portrayal of Smith's position. A case in point is the replacement of Cartesianism. Newton's triumph is inseparable (we recall) from two facts. First, Descartes' system could not account for the minute irregularities in the movement of the planets that Kepler had ascertained and which Cassini had established, while Newton's could (*HA* IV, 66, 67/97–8). Secondly, each predicted a different shape for the earth and this was resolved by actual measurements in Newton's favour (Smith possessed a copy of the English translation of Maupertuis' expedition to Lapland that undertook the measurements). What these two 'facts' indicate is that Smith (no more than Kuhn 1977) does not dissociate the history of astronomy from the accumulation of data. The imagination of scientists (experts) is disconcerted in the presence of wonder but it is the independent increase in data, accessible only to the expert and itself consequent upon the development of increasingly sophisticated equipment, that generates the 'gap' in the first place. In addition, elsewhere, in a different context, Smith describes Descartes' work as 'a fanciful, an ingenious and elegant, tho fallacious system' (*Corr* 5/244). In the light of these considerations, it seems a sounder interpretation of that oft-quoted passage (*HA* IV, 76) to treat it as a self-reprimand by Smith. He is chiding himself for transgressing his own announced particular perspective and, as such, this is not a positive endorsement of the view that Newton's system is only a 'more ingenious device' no better than that of his predecessors.[10]

Conceivably, there is in this disputed passage another, complementary, agenda. Almost from its inception, Newton's philosophy had been assimilated and appropriated. As noted in Part I, his authority was utilised to underwrite the providential foundations of the Hanoverian social order and to buttress natural theology. This latter role is clear in, for example, Keill's *True Astronomy* and in Colin Maclaurin's influential *General View of Sir Isaac Newton's Method* (1750).[11] Since eighteenth-century Newtonianism was more than a narrow methodology, it meant that to discriminate within it required a certain fastidiousness. It is at least arguable that Smith's relative reticence, like that of Hume,[12] in citing Newton in his major works betrays some such caution. If that is granted, then it allows that fastidiousness in the self-inflicted reprimand (as I have presented it) to be read as pertaining less to some abstract 'philosophy of science' than to a need to disentangle (say) MacLaurin's mastery of Newtonian mathematics (cf. *HA* IV, 58/90) from his Newtonian theology.[13]

What is indisputable is the high regard in which Smith held Newton. In his Rhetoric lectures he explicitly identified, within what he termed the didactical mode, a style of writing as the 'Newtonian method'. This method lays down 'certain principles known or proved in the beginning, from whence we account for the severall Phenomena, connecting altogether by the same chain' (*LRBL* II, 134/146). Such a procedure is the 'most philosophical', especially in contrast to its chief alternative – the Aristotelian method – where a different principle is given to every phenomenon. Because it is the most philosophical, in 'every science whether of Moralls or Naturall philosophy' there is presumptive reason to pursue it.

Some commentators have sought out Smith's Newtonianism. Hetherington (1983: 497), for example, thinks there are 'obvious similarities' between Smith's effort to discover general laws of economics and Newton's success in discovering natural laws of motion and Raphael (1979: 88) judges that 'Smith clearly regards sympathy as the gravitational force of social cohesion and social balance'. Others have been less confident that Smith himself carried out this project, though this is largely because of their more historically informed appreciation of what Newton's system in fact represented.[14] As Raphael acknowledges, and as we have already noted, Smith himself is not very helpful – there are, despite his emblematic status, minimal references to Newton in his two major works. Certainly, contemporaries drew parallels. For example, John Millar (pupil, then Glasgow colleague of Smith) declared him to be the 'Newton of political economy' because he had discovered the principles of commerce (*HV* II, 10/404n). Of Smith's more acute early critics, Governor Pownall opened his assessment of *The Wealth of Nations* by noting that Smith's treatise had fixed 'some first principles', becoming a '*principia* to the knowledge of politick operations' (*Corr* Appx A/337). The very prestige of Newton not only meant that to liken someone's work to his was to pay it the highest possible compliment but also that this was not very discriminatory, as when, for example, both Hume and George Turnbull claimed a Newtonian inspiration for their very different philosophies.[15] The prudent conclusion is that, while there is no reason to doubt the presence of that inspiration in Smith, it is better understood as a general orientation rather than a specific agenda. With that counsel in mind, we can now turn to Smith's own 'scientific' practice.

III

According to Newton (1953: 3), 'Nature is pleased with simplicity and affects not the pomp of superfluous causes', so that the first rule of reasoning in natural philosophy is: admit only such causes as are 'true and sufficient to explain appearances'. Here two familiar points are being made: the aim should be economy so that a lot is explained by a little and the explanation is achieved through the identification of causes. It is scarcely saying anything of moment to state that Smith adopts these two commonplaces. More informative is how this adoption is manifest.

While the issue of causal explanation does not figure prominently in the 'Astronomy', the role that Smith does allot to it conforms to the psychological account that he there outlines. The connecting principles that bridge the gap in the imagination are most satis-factorily grasped in the form of causes. In his Rhetoric lectures (in the context of historical composition) he again remarks that 'the very notion of a gap makes us uneasy' (*LRBL* II, 37/100) and it is the connection of cause and effect that best satisfies us (*LRBL* II, 32/98). This is not unexpected. The underlying argument, derived from Hume, was itself articulated in an account of causation and the imagery of invisible chains made in the 'Astronomy' harmo-nises with the standard image of explanation as the identification of a chain of causes and effects.

The fact that these last points have been drawn from Smith's discussion of history is more than coincidental. Along with his fellow Scots, Smith held that humans are naturally social and that this sociality expresses itself in institutions that differ over time. These facts are just as much a part of experience as apples falling to the ground. Though the latter fact might be classified as 'physical' or 'natural' and the former as 'moral', they cohabit the one experienced world. The natural aspect of that world has, since the Renaissance, been systematically investigated and causal explanations provided with great success. As we have already noted, the expectation throughout the Enlightenment was that a similar success, both theoretical and practical, beckoned for the moral aspect. Given that the moral and the physical are of the same species (a point to which we shall return), the way forward was to explain human institutions causally. Since to study society scientifically means tracing the chain of causes and effects, it builds into the study of a temporal or historical aspect: causes precede effects.

Sociality is true of all humans but it is evident to experience that its institutional expression is not uniform. Nevertheless, by seeking a causal explanation for these expressions, they can be revealed as non-random. Since the hallmark of successful natural science is the reduction of multiplicity to simplicity, then the hallmark of successful social science is the reduction of the diversity of institutions to some intelligible pattern. Smith's work bears this out. Perhaps its most celebrated manifestation is the 'four-stages theory' (see below) but that itself is only an expression of a more general approach that was labelled definitively by Dugald Stewart in his *Life of Smith* as natural or theoretical or conjectural history.

The lynchpin of this history is the relation between the principles of human nature and external circumstances. The 'principles' are fixed and constant. The 'circumstances' in any particular situation are, given the uniformity of nature, inferable from what is known generally to be the case. Between them they can, in the absence of direct evidence, license a 'theoretical' reconstruction with explanatory power. As Stewart (*Life* 293–5) puts it, 'in examining the history of mankind', when 'we cannot trace the process by which an event *has been* produced, it is often of importance to be able to show how it *may have been* produced by natural causes'. As examples of this approach, he cites, among others, the 'works of Mr Millar' as well as the pretext for this entire digression, Smith's 'Dissertation' on the origin of language (see Chapter 16).

Smith's account of language is worth briefly pursuing. The question of the origin and development of language was a hotly debated Enlightenment topic, notable in particular for its endeavour to treat the subject naturalistically. The argument of Smith's essay is that the various elements in language (verbs, nouns, adjectives, prepositions, etc.) develop *pari passu* with the maturing of human faculties. This developmentalism he believes will resolve Rousseau's puzzlement as to how linguistic categories like genera and species arose (*CL* 2/205). For Smith, words that were originally the proper names of individuals 'insensibly become the common name of a multitude' (*CL* 1/204). Echoing the account in the 'Astronomy', the 'mechanism' at work here is resemblance. Smith gives two telling instances of this process – a child when just learning to speak calls everyone who comes to the house its 'papa' or 'mama' (ibid.) and, secondly, a savage 'naturally bestows' on each new object the 'same name' that had previously been given to a similar object when it was first encountered (ibid.). This conjunction between the savage and the child is also echoed in the 'Astronomy', when Smith notes how while a child 'beats the stone that hurts it', the savage punishes the axe that had accidentally caused a death (*HA* III, 2/49).

This conjunction reveals once more the presence of an effectively Lockean model of human nature. Locke (1854: 1–2–27; cf. 1–2–12) himself remarked that 'children, idiots, savages and illiterate people' function without any capacity to refer to general maxims and universal principles. Savages thus represent, in a favourite phrase in the Enlightenment (and in Scotland especially), 'the infancy of mankind'. Both children and savages, it follows from this model of cognitive development, are confined to the world of immediate sensation, which means that they are unacquainted with all universal or abstract ideas.

If we now return to 'Considerations', we find these themes repeated. For example, he says of 'number' that it is 'one of the most abstract and metaphysical ideas . . . and consequently is not an idea which would readily occur to rude mortals who were just beginning to form a language' (CL 22/214). Similarly, substantive nouns predate adjectives, so the word 'tree' is developed before the word 'green', which itself precedes the word 'greenness'. And by the same token, impersonal verbs predate personal, while prepositions and pronouns 'expressing so very abstract and metaphysical an idea, would not easily or readily occur to the first formers of language' (CL 32/219).

Smith's adoption of this genetic/Lockean model of cognitive development pervades his thought and, in so doing, it establishes out of the diversity of social experience a coherent pattern or structure. This structure is that of a natural, that is, predictable, development from infancy to maturity, from the simple to the complex, from the concrete to the abstract. The four-stages theory is best understood against this backcloth. Though it may have been essayed in his Edinburgh lectures, Smith articulated this theory in his Glasgow lectures on jurisprudence in general and property rights in particular. The move from the first stage of the hunter-gatherer through to the fourth commercial age is thus marked by increasing abstraction. A telling case is his remark that 'among savages property begins and ends with possession and they seem scarce to have any idea of anything as their own which is not about their own bodies' (LJB 150/460). In contrast to this 'concreteness', by the time of the age of commerce property is not only conceptually distinguished from physical possession but itself assumes an increasingly 'abstract' form in, for example, the guise of credit and 'paper money' as promissory notes (WN II, ii.28/292).

The same story can be told using the growth in complexity as the index. The division of labour has developed from its rudimentary form in the first stage to one where the 'very trifling manufacture' of pins is divided into the labour of ten individuals. A society where tasks like pin making are minutely divided must necessarily be complex and its members deeply interdependent. The fact of interdependence means that each individual 'stands at all times in need of the co-operation and assistance of great multitudes' (WN I, ii.2/26) – a state of affairs illustrated by the fact that 'many thousands' are involved in the production of a coarse woollen coat (WN I, i.11/22)

Though, along these lines, Smith's reduction of the variety of historical experience to a simple structural model can be labelled 'scientific', this is too generalised to be of telling significance. In particular, the causal model remains unspecific. Before proceeding to a more precise treatment, an implication of the social scientific approach that Smith is apparently pursuing needs to be picked up. To say that the miserable poverty of savages (WN Intro 4/10) and the opulence experienced universally in a commercial society (WN I, i.10/22) are effects caused by the differential extent of the division of labour is to deny that the relations are accidental, just as eclipses are not random but caused by the orbits of the earth and the moon. This is a fraught issue. Some Smith scholars see his thought as implying a sharp division between natural and social sciences;[16] others hold that he places them on a similar footing.[17] While the latter are more nearly correct, a more precise account of Smith's position is needed.

Smith adopts what can be called a 'soft determinist' position (Berry 1997: Ch. 4). In eighteenth-century terminology, as spelt out by Hume, he is an advocate of 'moral', not 'physical', causes. Whereas physical causes 'work insensibly on the temper', moral causes are 'all circumstances which are fitted to work on the mind as motives or reasons and which render a peculiar set of manners habitual to us' (E-NC 198). Moral causes are a species of soft determinism because they operate through habituation or sociali-sation. These are still causes and are still deterministic but, unlike the hard determinism of physical causation, they can accommodate change or variation. The difference between the philosopher and the porter is not physical but moral, since it arises from 'habit, custom and education' (WN I, ii.4/29), yet neither is it random; there are real causes at work here, it is a predictable effect that different social experiences produce different characters.[18] This does not mean that human nature is a mere blank sheet; moral causation presupposes certain universal structures and dynamics in human nature, including necessarily a capacity to learn and to form habits.

To bring out the bearing of this upon Smith's social scientific practice, and attempt to move beyond the hitherto generalised discussion, I will consider two more particular cases - each chosen for its wider resonance.

Commerce and the Collapse of Feudal Power

In nomadic society, the second of the four stages, the leaders are those with the greatest herds and similarly in the third, agricultural, stage power lies with the landlords or, as Smith calls them, the 'great proprietors'. These individuals use their surplus in the same way as a Tartar chief (cf. WN V, i.b.7/712) did, namely to maintain a multitude of retainers and dependants who, in return for their keep, can offer only obedience (WN III, iv.5/413). Since the king was only another proprietor, the administration of justice lay in the (local) hands of those with the means to execute it (WN III, iv.7/415). At this point Smith observes that it is a mistake to see the origin of these 'territorial jurisdictions' in feudal law (WN III, iv.8/415). The source of this mistake is faulty social science, a misunderstanding of social causation. The cause of feudal power lies not in the deliberative and purposive decrees of law but in 'the state of property and manners' from which it 'necessarily flowed' (ibid.). For the properly informed expert (social scientist), this necessity is not a singular event causing wonder and surprise because it is duplicated in the histories of the French and English monarchies and exemplified by the case 'not thirty years ago' of Mr Cameron of Lochiel, 'a gentleman of Lochaber in Scotland' (ibid.). It is therefore a regularity amenable to scientific explanation; as Smith says explicitly, 'such effects must always flow from such causes' (ibid.).

Similarly, to explain the collapse of feudal power – both secular and ecclesiastical (WN V, i.g.25/803) – an appropriate social/moral cause has to be found. Once again, 'the feeble efforts of human reason' (WN V, i.g.24/803) lack sufficient explanatory power. Exemplifying Dugald Stewart's two lynchpins of theoretical history, Smith finds the requisite causal power in the conjunction of the principles of human nature and external circumstances. The former is represented by the selfish desire of those in power, the latter by 'the silent and insensible operation of foreign commerce'. Thanks to this commerce, the great proprietors – in exchange for a 'pair of diamond buckles' or similarly frivolous but privately consumable trinket – gradually bartered their whole power and authority (WN III, iv.10/419). As the 'effects' of a 'cause', there is an implicit 'regularity' here. The Tartar chief provides Smith with a counterfactual. The chief is able to maintain and control a 'thousand men' *because* there are no manufactured goods for which he can exchange his 'rude produce' (WN V, i.b.7/712). However, the presence of foreign commerce in the feudal era, by making available these baubles, resulted ultimately in the members of a commercial society being free of the thrall of personal dependency, since the proprietors 'were no longer capable of interrupting the regular execution of justice' (WN III, iv.15/421).

This process of social change is, for Smith, a general truth about social life. The truth it bespeaks is that social life is pervaded by unintended consequences or the operation of the 'invisible hand'. As Smith himself acknowledged in the one reference to the 'invisible hand' in The Wealth of Nations, the phenomenon applies in 'many other cases' (WN IV.ii.9/456). In this instance, the collapse of feudalism, which Smith calls a 'revolution of the greatest importance to the publick happiness', cannot be put down to any purposive individualistic explanation. Neither the proprietors nor the merchants had the 'least intention to serve the publick' and neither had 'knowledge or foresight of that great revolution' (WN III, iv.17/422). The public happiness, the general good, was not brought about by deliberate human policy. Smithian social science does not turn individuals into socially constructed ciphers; they do indeed have intentions (to obtain diamonds, for example) but these of themselves do not provide an adequate causal explanation of either social statics (institutions) or dynamics (change). To provide that, and presupposing a given model of human nature, moral causes have to be identified.

Moral Behaviour as an Effect of Socialisation

A pervasive theme in the Moral Sentiments is that morality is a learnt phenomenon. Hence, society would 'crumble into nothing' if 'by discipline, education and example' individuals were not impressed with a 'reverence' for rules of conduct (TMS III,

5.2–3/163) or it would 'crumble into atoms' (TMS II, ii.3.4/86) without the observance of justice, but the rules of justice may be taught to all (TMS III, 6.11/176). In these and other ways, moral behaviour is an effect of socialisation and thus exhibits the traits of soft determinism. Individuals internalise moral standards so that in practice the authority possessed by conscience is the effect of 'habit and experience' (TMS III, 3.2/135). The fact that it is habitual, so that 'we are scarce sensible' that we do appeal to it, means that, building on the given natural dynamics of human nature, it is a learnt resource.

The most graphic presentation of this theme is where Smith likens society to a mirror (TMS III, 1.3/10). Supposing 'a human creature could grow up to manhood in some solitary place, without any communication with his own species', then such a person 'could no more think of his own character, of the propriety or demerit of his own sentiment and conduct, of the beauty and deformity of his own mind, than of the beauty or deformity of his own face'. Society, however, acts as a mirror wherein it will be seen 'that mankind approve of some of them [passions] and are disgusted by others'. According to Smith's reading of human nature, in the former case 'he will be elevated' but 'cast down in the other'. The given universal dynamics of human nature are such that humans seek pleasure and shun pain (cf. TMS VII, iii.2.8/320), so that socially approved passions will be reproduced and disapproved ones shunned.

This emphasis on morality as learnt seems to entail a conflation of social conformity and ethical standards. Smith, however, denies that his account of morality precludes criticism or is, in effect, an endorsement of cultural and ethical relativism. He openly admits that virtues differ between 'rude and barbarous nations' and 'civilized nations' (TMS V, 2.8/205). Nonetheless, he believes that 'the sentiments of moral approbation and disapprobation are founded on the strongest and most vigorous passions of human nature; and though they may be somewhat warpt, cannot be entirely perverted' (TMS V, 2.1/200).

As an example he cites the practice of infanticide. He accounts for this by the fact that 'in the earliest period of society' infanticide was commonplace and the 'uniform continuance of the custom had hindered them [the practitioners] from perceiving its enormity' (TMS V, 2.15/210). Echoing the language of the 'Astronomy', Smith refers to 'we' not being in a state of 'wonder' or 'surprise' about this. The social scientist, armed with the notion of moral causation, is able to explain it. In the rudest and lowest state of society, where 'extreme indigence' obtains and human nature being what it is, an infant could be abandoned in order that the adult might live. But Smith does not subscribe to the maxim *tout comprehendre, tout pardonner*. He does allow that the practice in rude ages was/is 'more pardonable' than it was 'among the polite and civilized Athenians', where the practice was inexcusable. Smith is adamant that just because something is commonly done does not mean it is condonable when the practice itself is ''unjust and unreasonable' (ibid.). According to Smith, the Athenian practice of exposing their infants was the effect of a moral cause since, despite its own probable rude origins, the policy became accepted because 'the uniform continuance of the custom had hindered them afterwards from perceiving its enormity' (ibid.). So powerful is this, Smith implies, that even the most acute minds of the time, such as Plato and Aristotle, accepted it as normal.

IV

The normative tenor that Smith's treatment of infanticide exhibits runs throughout his writings. This does not, however, compromise his 'scientific' credentials; on the contrary, in his eyes, it underwrites them.

We noted above that Smith added a sociological thesis to his psychological account of philosophy/science. Those living in the concrete, simple, immature era of polytheism are prone to superstition, but with the growth of leisure philosophy becomes possible. In due course this produces the growth of genuine knowledge, so that those in the fourth stage know more. One consequence of that greater (scientific) knowledge is not only their greater opulence and improved material living standards but also, concurrently, their greater command of their environment. The 'natural progress of improvement' (WN V, i.a.43/708) brings about not only the superiority associated with gunpowder but also all that 'ennobles human life' as 'the whole face of the globe is changed' by turning 'the rude forests of nature into agreeable and fertile plains', making the 'trackless and barren ocean a new fund of subsistence and the great high road of communication to the different nations of the earth' (TMS IV, 1.10/).

Smith is here a fully paid-up member of the Enlightenment

'family'. One of the clearest expressions of his membership occurs in *The Wealth of Nations*. In the context of the public good of education, he remarks unequivocally that 'science is the great antidote to superstition' (*WN* V, i.g.14/796). He advocates making the 'middle ranks' study philosophy and science since, if they are immunised, then the spread of the poison to the 'inferior ranks' is liable to be countered. This policy prescription, as with all the others that *The Wealth of Nations* contains, is not breaking some supposed fact/value dichotomy but is, rather, what science is truly about. Although Smith may well have laid the foundations for the subsequent development of positivist, scientific economics this, as more historically nuanced commentators have long held, cannot be regarded as an accurate reflection of his own position.

Social life, in all its manifestations – economic, political, aesthetic, religious and moral – consists of data to be analysed, of causal relations to be uncovered. Moral philosophy or social science is that analytical causal enterprise as it pertains to the moral or social world. Smith essentially shares Hume's conviction that a 'science of man', or as he himself puts it, a 'science of human nature' (*TMS* VII, iii.2.5/319), is possible. This science demonstrates a universal fact about the constitution of human nature, that (for example) material well-being is better than miserable poverty, while the 'science of a legislator', operating from 'general principles' (*WN* IV, ii.39/468), will determine that this can be achieved by allowing the 'natural effort of every individual to better his condition . . . to exert itself with freedom and security' and by removing the 'impertinent obstructions with which the folly of human laws too often incumbers its operations' (*WN* IV, v.b.43/540). In sum, for Smith, science identifies folly and points out the road to enlightenment.

Postscript

Smith's essay on astronomy has continued to call forth commentary. While this chapter, first published in 2006, has not therefore put the issue to rest, it has been cited in the ongoing discussion. Without committing the fallacy of *post hoc ergo propter hoc*, most commentators adopt a version of my line and see Smith as some sort of 'realist'. See, for example, Kim (2012), Hanley (2010), Montes (2013) and Matson (2016 on line). The sketchily inadequate treatment here of Smith's own exposure to 'science' and its background needs supplementing with more detailed work from, for example, Emerson and Wood (2002), which I should have cited in this piece. My discussion of Smith's 'social science' (including his view of infanticide) is developed elsewhere in this volume (for example in Chapter 20).

I am grateful to Roger Emerson for running his (non-persuaded) eye over a draft of this paper and to Knud Haakonssen for editorial support.

Notes

1. *Optics* Question 31 in Newton (1953: 179).
2. Cf. D. Stewart, who cites the recollections of Archibald Maclaine, one of Smith's undergraduate contemporaries (*Life*, I, 7).
3. J. Chambelayne, quoted in Ross (1995: 55).
4. Cf. H. Thomson (1965: 219), Brown (1988: 47), Christie (1987: 301) and Reisman (1976: 45).
5. Smith characterises a 'system' as 'an imaginary machine invented to connect together in the fancy those different movements and effects which are already in reality performed' (IV, 19).
6. This is not a first-order debate. Like all other participants whose concern is with Smith, I also refrain from direct involvement in the disputes between realists and their opponents, who in fact articulate a variety of arguments.
7. Smith had earlier noted the significance of analogy: all individuals, philosophers included, explain phenomena strange to them in terms of those familiar to them and, in intellectual systems, what in some is an analogy that occasions a 'few ingenious similitudes' becomes in another the 'great hinge upon which every thing turned' (II, 12).
8. Cf. Raphael (1979: 90), Thomson (1965: 222), Reisman (1976: 41) and Brown (1988: 37).
9. Cf. Kuhn (1970). He is cited by Skinner (1974: 80) and Longuet-Higgins (1992: 91).
10. Cremaschi (1989: 103). Similarly, *pace* Christie (1987: 301), Smith does not explicitly disavow claims that the new chain of ideas that constitute scientific theories have a warrantable correspondence with the real world of external nature. Defenders (on various grounds) of a 'realist' reading include Olson (197: 123), Oswald (1995: 454f.), Becker (1961/2: 16) and Hetherington (1983: 502). The best and most sophisticated account of Smith as what he terms a 'modest realist' is given by Schliesser (2005).

11. In his opening pages MacLaurin comments, 'But natural philosophy is subservient to the purposes of a higher nature, and is chiefly to be valued as it lays a sure foundation for natural religion and moral philosophy; by leading us, in a satisfactory manner, to the knowledge of the Author and Governor of the Universe'. Quoted from extract in Broadie (1997: 782). Keill's book also opens with similar sentiments.

12. Cf. Forbes (1975: Ch. 2), who emphasises this point. See also Barfoot (1990: 162), who makes the point that 'Newtonian' became something of a 'catch-all' such that, for example, the views of Boyle were conflated with those of Newton.

13. Cf. Griswold (1999: 169), who identifies a deliberate scepticism in Smith with respect to certain metaphysical views about 'reality' or 'God' in this passage.

14. See, inter alia, D. Redman (1995), Hollander (1977), Griswold (1999: 72f.) and Campbell, although he differentiates between *TMS* and *WN* in this regard (1971: 31).

15. Hume subtitled his *Treatise of Human Nature* (1739/40) 'an attempt to introduce experimental reasoning into moral subjects'; Turnbull quoted Newton's statement in *Optics* Qn 31 (see n. 1) on the title page of his *Principles of Moral Philosophy* [1740] (2005).

16. For example, Lindgren (1969: 912–13), Skinner (1996: 41) and Redman (1995: 220).

17. For example, Brown (1988: 37), Thomson (165: 232), Campbell (1971: 41), Young (1997: 10) and Bitterman (1984: 196).

18. Cf. *WN* III, iv.3, where the 'different habits' of the merchant and the country gentleman 'affect the temper and disposition in every sort of business'. Hume distinguished the soldier and the priest similarly (E-NC 198–9).

18

Adam Smith: Commerce, Liberty and Modernity

Adam Smith, in his lectures at the University of Glasgow, is reported to have professed that 'opulence and freedom' were 'the two greatest blessings men can possess' (*LJA* iii.111/185). Smith here couples together what many have held asunder as contraries. One such thinker, with whose thought Smith was well acquainted, was Rousseau. He reviewed Rousseau's *Discourse on Inequality* for the second edition of the short-lived *Edinburgh Review* of 1755/6 and, as was characteristic of eighteenth-century reviews, Smith's account contained lengthy quotations. The first passage that Smith thought worthy of reproduction begins:

> while men contented themselves with their first rustic habitations; while their industry had no object, except to pin together the skins of wild beasts for their original cloathing, to adorn themselves with feathers and shells [etc.] . . . while they applied themselves to such works as a single person could execute, and to such arts as required not the concurrence of several hands; they lived free, healthful, humane and happy, as far as their nature would permit them, and continued to enjoy amongst themselves the sweets of an independent society . . .

The second passage contains the judgement that

> man, from being free and independent, became by a multitude of new necessities subjected in a manner, to all nature, and above all to his fellow creatures, whose slave he is in one sense even while he becomes their master; rich he has occasion for their services; poor he stands in need of their assistance; and even mediocrity does not enable him to live without them. He is obliged therefore to endeavour to interest them in his situation, and to make them find either in reality or in appearance, their advantage in labouring for his. (*Letter* 13–14/251–2)

Smith is aware that, despite the presence here of what he terms 'rhetoric', Rousseau represents a persistent and important strand in European political thinking. This strand, frequently referred to as civic humanism, linked the ideas of freedom and independence and identified threats to the latter as inimical to the former. The essence of civic humanism, as outlined by John Pocock[1] – the writer who has done most to bring out the presence of this tradition in European thought – lay in the link between virtue and the practice of citizenship as understood by the Greeks and Romans. This link entailed a civic equality and a moral disposition to maintain the public good, so that the (male) human personality was only fulfilled in the practice of active virtue in the *res publica*. Civic equality stemmed from proprietorship of a household, which gave independence; its function was not to promote the accrual of private profit or luxury but to permit the taking on of public tasks such as defence (warfare). This story was re-articulated by Machiavelli and other Florentines and was transported into seventeenth-century English republican thought by James Harrington and his associates. By the eighteenth century the threat to virtue was seen to lie in the growth of credit and commerce, whose fluidity and intangibility were judged to provide an insufficiently stable basis from which the citizen could engage in political action. The riposte to the challenge of commerce was, therefore, to reinvoke the image of the agrarian (thus solidly based) independent republican. It was claimed that without the presence of this foundation for virtuous activity, society, shorn of the bearings needed to direct it to the public good, would be cast adrift on the sea of contingency that an economy based on commerce and credit represents.

Against this backcloth, Smith's coupling of freedom and opulence can be seen as a vindication of modernity, and in that guise his thought is at the forefront of the Enlightenment.[2] The key to the modern world is that it is a world of commerce. It is a world where everyman 'becomes in some measure a merchant' (*WN* I, iv.1/37). We have in that statement and its implications the key to Smith's vindication. The pursuit of these implications can, therefore, provide a framework for a general overview of Smith's thought. More precisely, our pursuit will proceed by answering the question, 'what are the consequences of living in a society where everyman is a merchant?'

The first and most obvious consequence is that, where everyman lives by exchange, there is a network of interdependence. In a 'civilised and thriving country' (a description that is a significant synonym for a commercial society), the 'very meanest person' could not be provided with even his woollen coat without the 'joint labour of a great multitude of workmen' (*WN* I, 1.11/22–3). To appreciate the full significance of this interdependence, it is necessary to appreciate the alternatives.

Smith himself does this via an historical analysis, and here Rousseau's work is important. Smith agrees with Rousseau that the dependence of one individual on another is corrupting (*LJA* vi.6/333). He agrees further that, in the earliest forms of society, there was little if any dependence and that dependency was a subsequent social development. Although there are classical precedents, and Turgot contemporaneously enunciated a similar doctrine in France, Smith's account of this development – the so-called 'four-stages' theory[3] – was seminal and was echoed by many other members of the Scottish Enlightenment, notably John Millar (Professor of Law at Glasgow) in his *Origin of the Distinction of Ranks* (3rd edn 1779) and the lawyer Lord Kames in his *Historical Law Tracts* (1758). According to this theory, the 'lowest and rudest state of society' is the age of hunters (*WN* V, i.2/689), marked by its poverty, which in turn means 'there is scarce any property' and little or no inequality, subordination or dependency (*WN* V, i.b.2/709). In time, pressure of population makes the chase too precarious so that 'naturally' wild animals are tamed, thus initiating the second age (*LJA* i.27/14). In this age of shepherds there is great inequality, vast disparity in property, and great subordination and dependency:

> Tartar chief, the increase of whose herds and flocks is sufficient to maintain a thousand men, cannot well employ that increase in any other way than in maintaining a thousand men ... whom he thus maintains, depending entirely upon him for subsistence, must both obey his orders in war, and submit to his jurisdiction in peace. He is necessarily both their general and their judge, and his chieftainship is the necessary effect of the superiority of his fortune. (*WN* V, i.b.7/712)

Once more, population pressure leads 'naturally' to the cultivation of land and the establishment of the third age – the age of husbandmen or farmers. Here there is fixed settlement and a similar pattern of inequality and dependency. Just as the Tartar chief was such by virtue of his being the greatest shepherd, so the leaders in the third age are the greatest landlords (*WN* V, i.b.16/717). The fourth or commercial age sees a decisive change, which stems not from population pressure but directly from the natural human propensity to truck, barter and exchange. Rousseau sees in the commercial age only a deepening corruption but Smith, immediately after having proclaimed the link between dependence and corruption, remarks that 'commerce is one great preventive' of its occurrence (*LJA* v.6/333). Smith sees in the commercial age not only the re-emergence of independence but also its re-emergence in a form superior to that experienced by a nation of hunters. The explanation of this superiority lies precisely in the social condition that Rousseau abhors, namely opulence. This is because the conditions that make opulence possible also, in a mutually complementary fashion, make possible a superior form of freedom – that of liberty under law, the hallmark of civilisation.

How, according to Smith, does this conjunction of opulence and civilisation occur? In line with his basic schema, Smith provides an historical account; this account, Smith explicitly observes, is also to be found in Hume's *Essays* – especially 'Of the Rise and Progress of the Arts and Sciences' (1742), 'Of Commerce' (1752) and 'Of Refinement in the Arts' (1752) – and is again echoed in other Scots. The focus of this account is the collapse of the age of farmers, in the guise of feudal lords (see also Chapter 17). A great proprietor perforce uses his surplus to maintain large numbers of retainers and dependants whose only means of reciprocation is obedience (*WN* III, iv.5/413). These proprietors

> necessarily became the judges in peace, and the leaders in war, of all who dwelt upon their estates. They could maintain order and execute law within their respective demesnes, because each of them could there turn the whole force of all the inhabitants against the injustice of any one. No other person had sufficient authority to do this. (*WN* III, iv.7/415)

Since the king was no more than another proprietor, the administration of justice lay in the hands of those with the means to do it. At this point, Smith observes that it is a mistake to see the origin of these 'territorial jurisdictions' in feudal law. The law is a subsequent development and, if anything, is an attempt to moderate rather than to extend the authority of the 'allodial lords'. Instead, Smith declares that this authority 'flowed from the

state of property and manners' (*WN* III, iv.9/417). What makes
this statement important is the implicit understanding of social
causation that it embodies. The cause of feudal power lies not in
the deliberative and purposive decrees of law, but in 'property
and manners'. The former are subordinate to the latter. Smith sees
in this order of priority the regularity that characterises scientific
explanation, since it is duplicated in the histories of the French
and English monarchies and is instanced by the case 'not thirty
years ago' of Mr Cameron of Lochiel 'a gentleman of Lochaber
in Scotland' (*WN* III, iv.8/416). This priority, therefore, is not a
singular event causing wonder and surprise (cf. *HA* II, 37ff.) but a
scientifically expected state of affairs for, as Smith says here, 'such
effects must always flow from such causes' (*WN* III, iv.8/416).

The explanation for the collapse of feudal power – both secular
and ecclesiastical (*WN* V, i.g.25/803) – must have an appropriate
social cause. Smith identifies it as 'the silent and insensible operation of foreign commerce'. In a celebrated passage, Smith outlines
the effect of this commerce

Similarly, to explain the collapse of feudal power – both secular
and ecclesiastical (*WN* V, i.g.25/803) – an appropriate social/moral
cause has to be found. Once again, 'the feeble efforts of human
reason' (*WN* V, i.g.24/803) lack sufficient explanatory power.

> For a pair of diamond buckles perhaps, or for something as frivolous
> and useless, they [the great proprietors] exchanged the maintenance,
> or what is the same thing, the price of the maintenance of a thousand
> men for a year, and with it the whole weight and authority which it
> could give them. The buckles, however, were to be all their own and
> no other human creature was to have any share of them; whereas in
> the more antient method of expence they must have shared with at
> least a thousand people . . . and thus for the gratification of the most
> childish, the meanest and the most sordid of all vanities, they gradually
> bartered their whole power and authority. (*WN* III, iv.10/418–19)

As befits an instance in a scientific causal account, Smith elsewhere
observes that the sway of the Tartar chief stems from his using his
surplus to maintain a thousand men *because* 'the rude state of his
society does not afford him any manufactured produce, any trin-
kets and baubles of any kind for which he can exchange that part
of his rude produce which is over and above his own consumption'
(*WN* V, i.b.7/416).

However, the presence of these 'baubles' in the feudal era results ultimately in the members of a commercial society being free of the thrall of personal dependency:

> In the present state of Europe a man of ten thousand a year can spend his whole revenue, and he generally does so, without directly maintaining twenty people, or being able to command more than ten footmen not worth the commanding. Indirectly, perhaps, he maintains as great or even a greater number of people than he could have done by the antient method of expence . . . He generally contributes, however, but a very small proportion to that of each, to very few perhaps a tenth, to many not a hundredth, and to some not a thousandth, nor even a ten thousandth part of their whole annual maintenance. Though he contributes, therefore, to the maintenance of them all, they are all more or less independent of him, because generally they can all be maintained without him. (*WN* III, iv.11/419–20)

Once the tenants had attained their independence, the proprietors 'were no longer capable of interrupting the regular execution of justice'. This process of social change, which Smith calls 'a revolution of the greatest importance to the publick happiness', cannot be put down to any deliberative individualistic explanation. Neither proprietors nor merchants had 'the least intention to serve the publick' and neither had 'knowledge or foresight of that great revolution' (*WN* III, iv.17/422). The public happiness, the general good, was not brought about by human will. For Smith this is a general truth about social life, and it serves, as we shall note again, to expose the moralism of the civic humanists as unscientific.

As a consequence of this series of events, individuals in a commercial society enjoy a liberty from dependence on particular masters. They enjoy independence but, and this is what distinguishes commercial society, this independence is achieved through an interlocking social system (the market) so that these individuals (merchants) are truly interdependent. We now need to pursue how it is, for Smith, that opulence and freedom are consequences of this interdependence where every man is a merchant.

To take opulence first: the natural propensity to 'truck, barter and exchange one thing for another' produces slowly and gradually the division of labour (*WN* I.ii.1/25). The bigger the market for goods the greater is the specialisation, and the greater the specialisation, the more the productivity. Hence, in the famous example of pin manufacture, through the division of labour ten individuals could make 48,000 pins a day – equivalent to 4,800 each – whereas each working on their own could not have produced twenty a day. What this means in a developed market society is the presence of that 'universal opulence which extends itself to the lowest ranks of the people' (*WN* I, i.10/22). By contrast, those who best embody Rousseauan independence are 'miserably poor' and frequently resort to the policy of 'directly destroying, and sometimes of abandoning their infants, their old people, and those afflicted with lingering diseases, to perish with hunger, be devoured by wild beasts' (*WN* Intro 4/10). Indeed, Smith pitches the advantages of commercial society even higher. The presence of this universal opulence means that the accommodation of even the lowest 'exceeds that of many an African king, the absolute master of the lives and liberties of '10,000 naked savages' (*WN* I, i.11/24).[4] It is true that the abodes of the lowest rank in commercial society are far inferior to those of the rich but, though there is this inequality, there is also the second great human blessing of liberty.

This brings us to the next consequence of Smith's position: the character of the liberty enjoyed in commercial society. There are two related dimensions to this liberty. If those in the lowest rank partake in the universal opulence, it means that they are supplied 'abundantly' with what they have 'occasion for' (*WN* I, i10/22). This abundance gives them choice and discretion. Since individuals are not tied into relationships of dependence, they enjoy, for example, changing trades as often as they please (*WN* I.x.a.1/116). In this regard, Smith comments on the 'violent police' of Indostan and ancient Egypt in forcing a son to follow his father's occupation (*WN* I.vii.31/80). The freedom to change occupation, like the freedom to dispose of one's property by testament, is a private liberty not enjoyed in other ages. Indeed, the presence of these liberties makes individuals free 'in our present sense of the word Freedom' (*WN* III, iii.5/400). (See Chapter 21 for extensive commentary on this passage.) The maintenance of this freedom itself depends on the liberty that each man has to better his condition, because that liberty is the source of opulence (*WN* II, iii.31/343). More pointedly, this will be effective only as long as individuals are left free from political directives; it is the 'highest impertinence and presumption' of kings and ministers 'to watch over the economy of private people' (*WN* II, iii.36/346). Smith remarks that the 'private interests and passions of individuals naturally dispose them to turn their stock towards the employments which in ordinary cases are most advantageous to society'; crucially, this advantage will accrue 'without any intervention of law' (*WN* IV, vii.c.88/630). What Smith has done, therefore, is to yoke together the two great blessings of opulence and freedom with the private, self-interested life of economics. In so doing, he has also implicitly devalued the public or political life, with its goals of honour and glory, as the unique and privileged arena of human *Eudaimonia*.[5] Smith, however, by no means neglects politics, because the second dimension of the liberty enjoyed in commercial society is concerned precisely with that.

While the African chief is the 'absolute' master of his dependents, this superiority is not enjoyed by the rich in an interdependent commercial society. The reason for this is that commerce, as evidenced by Europe, has brought in its wake justice and the rule of law. Their presence is the hallmark of a 'well governed society', and constitutes the political liberty enjoyed by all in commercial society. One of the major distinguishing characteristics of absolute power is the possession in the same hands of judicial and executive power. The feudal lords, it will be recalled, controlled the jurisdiction in their lands. In that circumstance justice cannot be expected, because justice requires impartial administration and it is upon this impartiality that the 'liberty of every individual, the sense which he has of his own security' depends (*WN* V, i.c.25/722–3). The separation of judicial from executive (military) power is, Smith declares in another course of lectures, 'the great advantage which modern times have over ancient' and is a product of 'the increase of refinement and the growth of society' (*LRBL* ii.203/176). Commerce, having undermined the power of the feudal landlords, requires, if it is to flourish for any length of time, a 'regular administration of justice'. This is because only where there is such regularity do people 'feel themselves secure in the possession of their property' and have confidence in the 'faith of contracts' and the 'payment of debts' (*WN* V, iii.7/910).

The crux is the presence of confidence. Commerce depends on confidence, not only so that credit can be extended but also, more fundamentally, because the division of labour itself depends on confidence. To specialise is to commit oneself to the interdependence of market relationships. Put crudely, I will only specialise in making shoes in the expectation that others are specialising in other goods, so that I can take my surplus to market to exchange for theirs. This means acting *now* in expectation of future return, but without the stability that attends 'regular administration' this would be irrational. Where the future is uncertain, where the actions of others are not predictable, then it is better to be independent and self-sufficient and not rely on anyone. But, of course, that option means forgoing the blessing of the opulence that comes from interdependence.

It could be rejoined that Smith has missed the real thrust of Rousseau's indictment to the effect that commercial society has debased human relationships and, in the mainstream of civic humanism, that it has undermined virtue. The case against opulence or luxury was that as private goods they directed the citizen's attention away from the public weal. The roots of this argument lay in Aristotle's strictures against the acquisition of wealth for its own sake (accumulation), which perversely turned what should only be a means to the end of enjoying the good life into an end in itself (Aristotle 1944: 1258a). The good life is the political life of participation in the common affairs of the *polis,* which is genuinely an end in itself. To Aristotle, those who lived the political life were free men, since the *polis* itself is definable as an association of free men (Aristotle 1944: 1279a).

It should be clear how Smith's position repudiates this. In shorthand terms, he assigns a different meaning to 'liberty' by restricting its requirements while extending its application.[6] Smith's liberty under law is a liberty to be enjoyed by all but, as he points out, the Aristotelean political liberty was only enjoyed by a few and was only sustainable by the enslavement of a sizable proportion of the population (*LJA* iv.69/ 226). Slavery is not only morally objectionable (as Rousseau – though not all civic humanists[7] – would agree) but also economically unproductive (*WN* III, ii.9; IV.ix.47/387; 684). Wealth is increased by the 'liberal reward of labour', since where wages are high 'we shall always find the workmen more active, diligent and expeditious' (*WN* I, viii.44/99). Given further that 'servants, labourers and workmen' (*WN* I, viii.36/96) constitute the bulk of a society's population, then what improves their lot makes for a happy and flourishing society. It is, indeed, in the context of a discussion of slavery that Smith declares opulence and freedom to be mankind's greatest blessings.

Rousseau, however, might still regard this as begging the question. But the further consequences of Smith's identification of commercial society with everyman being a merchant relate to a new assessment of individual relationships. In a civilised (market) society, the individual 'stands at all times in need of the cooperation and assistance of great multitudes, while his whole life is scarce sufficient to gain the friendship of a few persons' (*WN* I, ii.2/26). This means that the individual in a market society deals preponderantly with other individuals who are strangers to him. In that circumstance, individuals must, as Rousseau had lamented, appeal to advantage. Hence it is that

> It is not from the benevolence of the butcher, the brewer, or the baker, that we expect our dinner, but from their regard to their own interest. We address ourselves, not to their humanity but to their self-love, and never talk to them of our own necessities but of their advantages. Nobody but a beggar chuses to depend chiefly upon the benevolence of his fellow-citizens. (*WN* I, ii.226–7)

This now commits Smith to upholding the position that commercial society does not rely on benevolence for its bedrock cohesiveness. Smith, of course, does not deny the virtuousness of benevolence, but society can subsist without it, though it will indeed be as a consequence 'less happy and agreeable' (*TMS* II, ii.3.2/86). What is necessary for social existence is not the positive virtue of beneficence, since a company of merchants can subsist without it (*TMS* II, ii.3.2/86), but the negative virtue of justice. This is because society cannot subsist at all among individuals who are ready to injure each other, that is, where injustice is prevalent. Justice, therefore, is 'the main pillar that upholds the whole edifice. If it is removed, the great, the immense fabric of human society . . . must in a moment crumble into atoms' (*TMS* II, ii.3.3/86). Justice is negative because it requires abstention from injuring others; indeed, 'we may often fulfil all the rules of justice by sitting still and doing nothing' (*TMS* II, ii.1.9/82).[8]

Contrary to both Rousseau and Aristotle, who stressed active participation, we can fulfil our public/political duties by doing nothing. In our conduct with others it is sufficient to follow rules in order to practise the virtue of justice. Furthermore, by making few demands in this way, the just life can be in the reach of all and need not be reserved to those with the resources necessary to underpin an active political life.

Since, for Smith, civilised societies enjoy liberty under law, he does not share the qualms of the civic humanists that rule following will be detrimental to the civic spirit. Indeed, Smith is sceptical of this spirit, resting as it does on an unjustified and overblown conception of the human will. As the collapse of feudalism testified, the public good (Rousseau's 'general will') does not depend upon being willed as such. Rather, the public good will be promoted through (in Rousseau's terms) particular wills. This, of course, is the force of Smith's evocation of the 'invisible hand': the individual 'intends only his own gain' but society does not suffer, because through pursuit of his own interest he 'frequently promotes that of the society more effectually than when he really intends to promote it'. Indeed, Smith goes on the offensive: 'I have never known much good done by those who affected to trade for the publick good' (WN IV, ii.9/456). Politicians, who exercise their will in directing others, are in fact a threat to the liberty enshrined in the rule of law. They will pursue policies that will affect their citizens differentially – as in the prohibition of wool exportation to promote manufactures – and which will, as such, be 'evidently contrary to the justice and equality of treatment which the sovereign owes to the different orders of his subjects' (WN IV, viii.30/654). In Smith's view, political will should confine itself to external defence, the maintenance of justice internally through 'regular administration', and the provision of 'certain publick works' (WN IV, ix.51/687–8). Once again, Smith's position here can be fruitfully interpreted as the product of his social science. The complexity and systematic interdependence of commercial society makes redundant the individualist, politically activist, approach of the civic humanists.

What sustains Smith's view that the just life is within reach of all is his sociological account of moral sentiments. Justice, as we have noted, consists in rule following and Smith, in one place, likens the rules of justice to the rules of grammar in their precision, accuracy and indispensability (TMS III, 6.11/175). This precision makes both grammar and justice susceptible to instruction; we 'may be taught to act justly'. This is important because the 'coarse clay of the bulk of mankind' means that ideal conduct is not to be expected, but

> there is scarce any man, however, who by discipline, education, and example, may not be so impressed with a regard to general rules, as to act upon almost every occasion with tolerable decency, and through

the whole of his life to avoid any considerable degree of blame. (*TMS* III, 5.2/163)

The very efficacy of this process in ensuring adherence to general rules means that it must be found in all ages, just as the very indispensability of justice means that all societies experience it. But, and this is the crucial point, rudeness and barbarism hinder the 'natural sentiments of justice from arriving at that accuracy and precision which in more civilised nations they naturally attain to' (*TMS* VII, iv.36/134).

The repetition of 'natural' here is no accident. 'Nature' for Smith frequently appears in a prescriptive role. It is central to the normative superiority of commercial society that it is also the most natural society. This identification stems from Smith's postulates that, firstly, it is a natural human propensity to truck, barter and exchange and, second, that in a commercial society everyman is in some measure a merchant, so that, when these are combined, it follows that it is only in commercial society that human nature is able to exhibit directly and centrally this propensity. Though exchange has always occurred (cf. *WN* I, ii.3/27) just as justice is ubiquitous, it is only in commercial society, the very rationale of which is to make things for exchange, that the propensity will be fully exercised. This provides crucial ammunition against 'unnatural' government interference, and sustains the basic rectitude of the system as 'the natural system of perfect liberty and justice' (*WN* IV, vii.c.44/606). It was, of course, this identification of commercial society and its values with the 'natural' society that led Marx, in particular, to accuse Smith of being a bourgeois apologist.

For Smith to be so confident about the rectitude of commercial society means that he must also be confident that general rules will be adhered to in a society where self-love is prevalent. The explanation of Smith's confidence takes us to the heart of his account of moral psychology, which is devoted to showing how social interaction humbles the arrogance of self-love (*TMS* II, ii.2.1/83). The lynchpin of this psychology is Smith's analysis of the principle of sympathy. Sympathy, in Smith's technical sense, is the human faculty of compassion or fellow feeling. By use of imagination, one individual sympathises with another and feels what the other feels (or should feel) (*TMS* I, i.1.4/10). What makes this feasible is the commonplace idea, but one particularly prominent in the Enlightenment, of the uniformity of human nature (cf. Berry 1982a: Ch. 1). Thus, upon hearing that someone's father has died, one is able to sympathise, even if the bereaved is a complete stranger (a significant point, as we shall see). The greatest consolation for the bereaved is to see others sympathise with him, 'to see the emotions of their hearts, in every respect, beat time to his own' (*TMS* I, i.4.8/22). There is, however, an inevitable shortfall between the two, since no compassion can ever match the original grief. The consequence of this is that (to continue this example) the bereaved learns to lower the pitch of his grief so that spectators can the more easily sympathise.

It is important that this is a learning exercise. Men learn from experience of life (through 'discipline, education and example') what is proper. In line with Smith's account of social causation, the social phenomenon of morality must have an appropriately social cause. In a key passage, with strong overtones of Rousseau, Smith remarks:

> were it possible that a human creature could grow up to manhood in some solitary place, without any communication with his own species, he could no more think of his own character, of the propriety or demerit of his own sentiments and conduct, of the beauty and deformity of his own mind, than of the beauty or deformity of his own face. Bring him into society and he is immediately provided with the mirror which he wanted before . . . and it is here that he first views the propriety and impropriety of his own passions. (*TMS* III, 1.3/110–11)

Morality thus becomes a matter of socialisation, of insensible 'habit and experience' (*TMS* III, 3.3/135). The effects of social intercourse teach the individual what behaviour is acceptable and, in due course, the individual internalises these social judgements as conscience, viewing his actions and motives as an 'impartial well-informed spectator' would (*TMS* III, 2.32/130). Through the dynamics of this social interaction, the emotions of the agent and the spectators can be harmonised. Although it is impossible that their emotions will ever be as one, yet there will be a concord that, significantly, is sufficient for 'the harmony of society' (*TMS* I, i.4.7/22).

The extent to which emotions will harmonise differs with the circumstances, and it is Smith's claim (though this is implicit rather than explicit) that the circumstances of commercial society are well suited to maintain harmony. It is this fit, so to speak, it explains Smith's confidence that the general rules of justice will be adhered to in a society where everyman is a merchant. As we have seen, the bulk of relationships in a commercial society take place between strangers. On Smith's account of the dynamics of sympathy, an agent can expect less sympathy from a stranger than from a friend. The effect of this is to make the agent moderate his emotions to a greater extent, so that more tranquillity is called forth in the presence of strangers than of friends (*TMS* I, i.4.9/23).

This ability on the part of the agent to tone down his emotions is the source for Smith of the virtue of self-command, the virtue from which 'all the other virtues seem to derive their principal lustre' (*TMS* VI, iii.11/241). A commercial society, where most men are strangers one to another, will call forth greater self-command than the more tribal or clannish character of earlier forms of society. Commercial society, for example, weakens family ties because the authority of law provides sufficient security, thus making the provision of mutual defence, which was the prime motive for keeping families together in earlier ages, redundant. It is, Smith declares, the case that 'regard for remote relations becomes in every country less and less according as this state of civilisation has been longer and more completely established' (*TMS* VI, ii.1.13/223). Nevertheless, though familial ties weaken and individuals mingle increasingly with those who are strangers to them, they remain, because of this necessary mingling, subject to its moralising constraints. Indeed, the 'pursuit of riches' itself is prompted chiefly by 'regard to the sentiments of mankind', to 'being the object of attention and approbation' (*TMS* I, iii.2.1/50).

Self-command, like all the virtues, is also a product of socialisation. The ubiquity of strangers in a commercial society will have the effect of strengthening the character, by making habitual the need to moderate one's emotions (cf. *TMS* III, 3.26/147). A stranger is more like the impartial spectator (cf. *TMS* III, 3.37/153–4), who corrects 'the natural misrepresentations of self-love' and who 'shows us the propriety of generosity and the deformity of injustice' (*TMS* III, 3.5/137). Moreover, commercial society need not go to the extremes of 'savages and barbarians' where self-denial is cultivated at the cost of humanity (*TMS* V, 2.9/205). Indeed, when self-denial expresses itself in suffering torture without any complaint whatsoever, the whole merit of self-command is taken away (*TMS* VI, 3.19/245).

There is thus a wide difference between the degrees of self-command required in 'civilized and barbarous nations'. The latter – as the case of the passive victim of torture exemplifies – 'necessarily acquire the habits of falsehood and dissimulation' and when they give way to anger their vengeance is 'always sanguinary and dreadful' (*TMS* IV, 2.11/208). The former, by contrast, become 'frank, open and sincere'. It is in the world of commerce that honesty is the norm. This point is made explicitly in the *Lectures*: 'when the greater part of the people are merchants they always bring probity and punctuality into fashion, and these therefore are the principal virtues of a commercial nation' (*LJB* 328/539). The very interdependence of that world contributes to the maintenance of such virtues because there is a preponderance of men 'in the middling and inferior stations of life', none of whom can ever be great enough to be above the law but are, rather, overawed into respect for 'the more important rules of justice'. Furthermore, in that condition personal success depends on the favour and good opinion of neighbours, and without that opinion 'a tolerably regular conduct' cannot be expected (*TMS* I, iii.3.5/63). Regularity, of course, is fundamental to a commercial society, where individuals must act in expectation of future return. The prime source of such regularity is, as we have already noted, adherence to the general rules of justice.

Justice, moreover, is self-supporting in commercial society. This is borne out in practice (Smith affirms) by

> that equal and impartial administration of justice which renders the rights of the meanest British subject respectable to the greatest, and which by securing to every man the fruits of his own industry, gives the greatest and most effectual encouragement to every sort of industry. (*WN* IV, vii.c.54/610)

It is also borne out in theory, because the 'reward' for acting justly, for keeping to the rules, is 'the confidence, the esteem and love of those we live with ... it is not in being rich that truth and justice would rejoice but in being trusted and believed' (*TMS* III, 5.8/166). To act justly, therefore, brings forth trust and confidence and they, in their turn, make it rational and feasible to specialise and thus create opulence. The fact, furthermore, that it is 'the gentler exertions' of self-command which find expression in commercial society means that it is there that both the 'amiable virtue of chastity' and the opulence-creating 'respectable virtues of industry and frugality' will be found (*TMS* VI, iii.13/242).

There is one final set of consequences of Smith's interpretation of commercial society as a society of merchants that needs mentioning. Despite Smith's confirmed support for the superiority of commercial society, he is not blind to its drawbacks, and in some much-discussed pages in *The Wealth of Nations* he draws attention to them. A consequence of specialisation is to confine some individuals to 'performing a few simple operations', the very simplicity of which makes them incapable of 'conceiving any generous, noble or tender sentiments and consequently of forming any just judgement concerning many even of the ordinary duties of private life' (*WN* V, i.f.50/782).[9] This is serious, given the importance that Smith attaches to private concerns. It is likely that the obligations of justice will suffer and that the pervasive 'torpor of the mind', and attendant ignorance, will enervate the self-command of these individuals and will fuel 'enthusiasm and superstition', a frequent source of 'dreadful disorders' (*WN* V, i.f.61/788).

Confronted with these consequences, while firmly accepting the desirability of their causes, Smith seeks to palliate their impact. He sees it, accordingly, as a legitimate task of government (one of its public works) in commercial society to finance the instruction of those 'in the lowest occupations' that they might acquire the 'most essential parts of education' ('read, write and account', together with some 'elementary parts of geometry and mechanicks'; (*WN* V, i.f.54, 55/785–6). The effect of such instruction, he believes, would be to instil self-respect and to promote thereby decency and order. This, in its turn, would further the stability of the entire society because that ultimately rests, as we have seen, on confidence. What lies behind this advocacy of education is Smith's subscription to one of the most characteristic of all Enlightenment tenets, namely, that encapsulated in Voltaire's slogan *écrasez l'infame*. Science, Smith declares in this definitive Enlightenment idiom, is 'the great antidote to the poison of enthusiasm and superstition'. Accordingly, Smith advocates the state making almost universal 'the study of science and philosophy' among the middling (and superior) ranks. Since this would make these ranks immune, then, thanks to their example, 'the inferior ranks', too, would be little exposed to the poison (*WN* V, g.14/796).

We can best draw to a close the threads of this deliberately synoptical and inevitably coarse-grained treatment by highlighting one of its themes. It is Smith's attempt (never realised in its entirety) to establish 'the general principles of law and government' (*TMS* VII, iv.27/342) by means of a social scientific approach that marks off his thought from that of Rousseau and the civic humanists.[10] The hallmark of scientific explanation is the discovery of regular connecting principles (cf. *HA* II, 12/45). For the Enlightenment, the paradigm of such explanation was provided by Newton, and the desire to emulate his achievement in the natural world by arriving at a few simple but general explanatory principles for the social world was common. For example, it was the animating force behind the great Encyclopedia project of Diderot, as is unambiguously apparent from d'Alembert's *Preliminary Discourse.* In Scotland, this desire is seen clearly in Hume's *Treatise of Human Nature,* which he subtitled 'An attempt to introduce the experimental method of reasoning into moral subjects'. This ambition – as with much else – Smith shared with Hume.[11]

As the full title of his major work – *An Inquiry into the Nature and Causes of the Wealth of Nations* – testifies, Smith's search for regular and general principles put a premium upon causal analysis (cf. Campbell 1971: Ch. 1). The evident constancy and cohesiveness of the social world must, being an effect, have an appropriately constant cause. Such constancy could not be found in isolated, individual human will or reason which, in itself, is both too weak and too fickle to provide the causal premiss for scientific generalisation. Instead, Smith locates the requisite solidity and generality in 'natural' facts and processes. Such natural facts (like population pressure on resources) 'necessarily' produce their outcomes (like changes in the mode of subsistence).

Thus the division of labour was not the effect of 'any human wisdom' but the necessary consequence of the uniform and universal human 'propensity' or 'natural disposition to truck, barter and exchange' (*WN* I, ii.2/25). Thus, also, government was not the product of any deliberate human will or agreement but was made 'absolutely necessary' by the effect of the 'natural progress' of private property (*LJA* iv.20/207). Similarly, being a political subject is not a product of choice – for no one chooses their place of birth – but the effect of being 'born and bred up under the authority of the magistrates', together with the 'natural modesty' of mankind which disinclines them to dispute the title of their superiors (*LJA* v.119/317–18). Finally, morality itself cannot be explained as the product of reason but rather 'it is by finding in a vast variety of instances that one tenor of conduct *constantly pleases* in a certain manner and that another *constantly displeases* the mind that we form the general rules of morality' (*TMS* VII, iii.2.7/320; my emphases). This experiential constancy coalesces insensibly into habits, so that the social phenomenon of morality is best understood as the habituated response to social circumstances.

In the trading circumstances of a commercial society, the operant morality was one of prudence and probity, although these same circumstances could also lead to 'mental mutilation'. But none of this was a matter of human will. No one decided to put great weight on honesty or to establish 'alienating' work conditions. These are both the natural effects of life in society, in the same way that the different characters of the philosopher and the porter arise gradually 'from habit, custom and education' (*WN* I, ii.4/29). The circumstances where human will might seem to have some moment – when there was room for heroes or Machiavellian princes suffused with *virtu* – no longer obtains.[12] Yet it is just such times that the civic humanists presuppose in their critique of credit or commerce. To this critique, Smith is able to rejoin that it is not only anachronistic but also unsoundly (unscientifically) based. It is true, in one sense, that Rousseau fares better because he realises that it is the very circumstances of the world of commerce that makes political will redundant. He aims to establish his virtuous republic among a people not yet moulded by customs, so that the values of economically independent smallholders can entrench themselves as the customary norm. But, and this brings us full circle, such an enterprise, aside from being mere wishful thinking (you cannot stop the world and get off at a destination of your own choosing), prevents mankind enjoying both of their greatest blessings – opulence and freedom. The modern world of commerce, even with its drawbacks, still offers the prospects of those twin delights.

Postscript

This chapter, written at the invitation of the editor Peter Gilmour, has benefited from comments from my Glasgow colleague, Professor Andrew Skinner. After my earlier piece on Smith on language (1974; and see Chapter 16), it was my next published work (1989) dedicated to Smith. This, along with a cognate article in *Nomos* (Berry 1992), laid down the foundations for most of my subsequent work on his thought (as will become apparent in the chapters that follow this as well as in Berry 1997, 2013: I have let some duplication stand).

I would now be less assertive about the prescriptiveness of Smith's use of 'natural' (cf. p. 337). The key notion, I think, is interdependency; it is that which transfigures the worry about dependency (and unfreedom) that is a central ingredient in the 'republican' vocabulary. It is because of that centrality I used Rousseau as a foil. The relation between Smith and Rousseau has become, as I noted in Chapter 1, a prominent theme in recent scholarship. Griswold (2010 and again in detail 2017) pursues it, as do Rasmussen (2008) and Hanley (2009), who cite this piece. Outside that context, it is picked up by Sher (1994), while Griswold (1999), Sen (2010) and McCloskey (2016), among others, refer to the cognate *Nomos* essay and Calkins and Werhane (1998) take me to task, though I believe they misrepresent my argument. For my own part, Michael Ignatieff's suggestive book (acknowledged in n.5) likely had a role in my initial framing.

Notes

1. Pocock (1975). More recent essays that continue to elaborate his argument and that concentrate on the eighteenth century are collected in Pocock (1985). One essay not included in the collection, and the one that bears most directly on the Scottish Enlightenment, is Pocock (1983). For comment on Pocock's account of the Scottish Enlightenment and the debate in which his essay engages, see Berry (1986b).
2. Cf. P. Gay (1966, 1969), who characterises the 'family' of the philosophers as engaged in 'The Pursuit of Modernity'.
3. Cf. Meek (1976, 1977) and Skinner (inter alia 1975, 1982).
4. Cf. *LJB* 211/489, 'when the nation is cultivated and labour divided a more liberal provision is allotted them; and it is on this account that a common day labourer in Brittain has more luxury in his way of living than an Indian sovereign'. That the poor in commercial societies enjoyed a better standard of living than in earlier ages was crucial to Smith's defence of the modern commercial world is well maintained by Hont and Ignatieff (1983).
5. According to Smith, what constitutes the 'real happiness of human life', namely 'ease of body and peace of mind', is enjoyable by all, regardless of rank. This statement occurs at the end of a long

paragraph that opens with a vivid description of how industry has 'entirely changed the whole face of the globe' (*TMS* IV, i.10/183–5). The editors point out how Smith's wording recalls that of Rousseau in a passage from the *Discours* that Smith translated in the *Edinburgh Review*. Cf. Ignatieff (1984) for a perceptive discussion of Smith's relationship to Rousseau.

6. Cf., inter alia, Haakonssen (1981: 140) and Robertson (1985: 12). The differing interpretations of liberty (as of property) are one of the benchmarks Pocock (1983) uses to distinguish the civic humanist and jurisprudential paradigms. Hexter (1977: 331) had picked up this point in his review essay of Pocock's *Machiavellian Moment*.

7. For example, Andrew Fletcher of Saltoun, in his *Second Discourse on the Affairs of Scotland* [1698] (1979: 48), advocated as part of his package of economic reforms that estates should directly employ vagabonds, who, if in local excess, should be sold to other estates where there was a lack. While Fletcher denies that he was thereby advocating slavery, he makes clear that this was the policy of the 'ancients'. Pocock (1975: 427–32) included Fletcher in his civic humanist camp. Davie (1981) and Phillipson (1981) have affirmed Fletcher's importance to the Scottish Enlightenment.

8. The inclusion of 'often' here indicates that Smith is not committed to any unqualified assertion of this principle and in the *Moral Sentiments* it is clear that he thinks 'bare observance' of rules without more positive acts of virtue is to lack certain feelings of humanity (*TMS* IV, i.10/82). But justice and benevolence are not inversely related; one who acts justly will also exhibit great humanity and benevolence (*TMS* VI, ii.intro.2/218), as well as being the recipient of esteem (see text below).

9. Although Smith does in this context use the term 'corruption', this does not mean he is thereby adopting the conceptual framework of civic humanism – not even as 'transforming' it, *pace* J. Robertson (1983). Those who are vulnerable are not those (that is, independent labourers) who would have qualified for citizenship and their 'corruption' affects not their economic independence but their ability to adhere to the requirements of propriety. Cf. E. Harpham (1984).

10. The weakness of Donald Winch's (1978) admirably conceived attempt to view Smith resolutely in eighteenth-century terms is that he says little about Smith's – impeccably 'enlightened' – scientific pretensions.

11. That *The Wealth of Nations* had succeeded in emulating Newton was a judgement passed by contemporaries. For example, John

Millar, Smith's former pupil, observed that 'The great Montesquieu pointed out the road. He was the Lord Bacon in this branch of Philosophy. Dr Smith is the Newton' (*HV* II, 10/404n); Governor Thomas Pownall opened his pamphlet on *The Wealth of Nations* by remarking how Smith had achieved the task of fixing 'first principles in the most important of sciences' so that his work 'might become *principia* to the knowledge of politick operations' ('A Letter from Governor Pownall to Adam Smith' affixed as Appendix A to *Corr* 337, cf. 354).

12. Cf. *TMS* 241–2, where Smith observes that 'the most intrepid valour may be employed in the cause of the greatest injustice'. Courage, while sometimes useful, is 'equally liable to be excessively pernicious' and will be called upon when law and justice are 'in a great measure impotent', that is, 'in times of great public disorder'.

19

Adam Smith and the Virtues of a Modern Economy

For Adam Smith, humans are both social and moral beings, with each quality integral to the other. Everyone is born into an existing community and the process of socialisation we necessarily undergo is simultaneously a moralisation. As we learn how to behave in the presence of others like ourselves, we learn how to act appropriately (with propriety). As I argue in Chapter 20, this is not the same as saying that humans are socially and morally determined so that, in its most radical guise, different societies produce different values that go 'all the way down'. Conversely, it is not the case that every society has identical values. It is one of the themes of this volume that the Scots (and Enlightenment thinkers more generally) are centrally involved with what John Millar calls 'amazing diversity' (*OR* 175); they seek to explain and understand the range of societal/moral differences. In Smith's terms this 'wonder' or amazement, as a source of uncertainty when confronted with novelty, is a crucial step in prompting scientific enquiry (see *HA* II, 5/40 and *HA* III, 1/48, where Smith himself uses the term 'amazement'). I discuss this, and the surrounding debate, in Chapter 17 (Berry 2006).

In this chapter I examine one particular manifestation of this differentiation: how and why the moral standards by which 'economics' was judged needed to be recalibrated for the modern world of commerce. By labelling this a 'recalibration', the implication is that when Smith displaces the dominant view of economic morality he replaces it with another; he does not, contrary to some interpretations by both friend and foe, situate economics in an ethics- free zone.

Classical Morality

Etymologically, the word 'economics' is derived from the Greek for *oikos*, or household, and *nomos*, or rule/order. As presented by Aristotle, the economic sphere of the household was distinct from the 'political' sphere within the *polis* as a whole. Here I draw on Aristotle's account in Book 1 of *The Politics*, in which his *oikos/polis* distinction, in line with his teleological philosophy, was determined by their respective functions or ends. The purpose of the household was the procurement and maintenance of what was necessary for everyday life: food, clothing and shelter. It was essentially (that is, this is its definitive nature) concerned with the instrumental business of mere living. The purpose of the *polis* is the realisation of the 'good life' (*eu zen*). This comprises not instrumental activity but what is intrinsically worthwhile. A key manifestation of this latter activity is the practice of politics by citizens (see Chapters 8 and 15 for further discussion). There is a clear hierarchy here. Instrumental actions, while partaking of the good and manifesting appropriate virtues, are subordinate to the end to which they are the means. With respect to the household/ *polis* distinction, the former is the realm of particularity, the latter generality. It is in the household that slaves and women have their proper place; it is in the *polis* where free men deliberate on what is for the common good (Aristotle 1944: 1279a23).

One relevantly significant consequence of this hierarchy is that the intrinsically worthwhile public task of politics should not be confused with the instrumental private purpose of the household and its governance. Ideally, the household's function of needs satisfaction should be accomplished through use of its own resources. Nonetheless, Aristotle allows that it is permissible, when meeting needs and thus still fulfilling its function, for the household to engage in exchange. A goat may be exchanged for some olives, as long as the recipient uses it for its proper or natural purpose (*kata phusin*), that is, the olives should not be produced for the sake of exchange (to get goats) but to be eaten or pressed, to meet the need for food and cooking (Aristotle 1944: 1257a12). While money can play a legitimate role in facilitating this process, this is a potential source of corruption. The danger is that this instrumental, facilitative role becomes perversely an end in itself; money making (*chrêmatistikê*) itself could become the dominant purpose and would thereby subvert the natural hierarchy. This exemplified a generic enduring threat or corruption, whereby private interests subvert the public good.

This established a moralised context for 'economics'. This moralisation rested on a conception of a worthwhile human (male) life that is debased if it is spent slavishly pursuing private ends. The marker of this debasement was that this pursuit was driven by desire, in particular by the desire for bodily satisfactions. Unlike meeting the needs of the household, which were finite, these desires were infinite. This valorised contrast between needs and desires became a staple of the 'classical' judgement of 'economic' activity. The corollary of this was that traders or merchants were superfluous intermediaries in the need-determined exchange of olives and goats; their purpose, rather, was to furnish and fuel these desires. Given the normative hierarchy, the actions and motives of merchants were thus morally suspect. Merchants are motivated by their private interest. Compared to a citizen in the full sense, that is, the independent male head of a household who dedicated his life to the public good, a merchant lived a less fulfilling, less humanly worthwhile, life.

This prejudice already present, for example, in Plato, for whom merchants (*hoi kapelloi*) were distinguished by their lack of *thumos*, the quality needed in soldiers (1902: 375a), and in Xenophon, who makes the same link between artisanal activities (*banausikia*) and weak, effeminate bodies with, in consequence, military incapacity (1923: IV, 2). Aristotle, for his part, holds that those who work for a living (*banausoi*) are not properly qualified for the duties of citizenship which require the capacity and will to bear arms and fight (1944: 1278a8). This disparagement persists into the Roman era. According to Cicero, for example, merchants do not exhibit *liberalitas* – the virtue of a 'gentleman', that is, someone of independent means (wealth); indeed, they have to tell lies to make a living (Cicero 1913: I, 150). In summary, from the 'classical' view it was not that men could not adopt the commercial life but that such a life was unworthy; it was (as Cicero, Seneca and others had observed) the inferior, sub-human/sub-masculine, concern of animals, slaves and women. By contrast, in Smith we can summarily say that 'economics' is the natural business of humanity.

Prudence, Self-Command and Courage

In an extract from his lectures that I have used many times, Smith declared opulence and freedom to be twin blessings (*LJA* iii.112/185). Bestowing the accolade of 'blessing' on opulence is what is striking here (for a discussion of his views on freedom, see Chapter 21 and Berry 2013: Ch. 5) and it provides the entrée into what I earlier called Smith's recalibration of the virtues.[1] For Smith, one characteristic of a developed commercial society is the presence of a 'universal opulence which extends itself to the lowest ranks of the people' (*WN* I, i.10/22). A mark of this opulence is that these ranks are supplied 'abundantly' with what they have 'occasion for'. What this means is that members of a commercial society are able to enjoy a far better standard of living than those in earlier ages.

It is worth underlining, even at this preliminary stage, that this betterment is a mark of moral superiority; there is nothing commendable in the stratified, slave-based societies assumed by Aristotle and his heirs, where only a select few could enjoy an agreeable form of life. As Charles Griswold (1999: 13) neatly puts it, 'Smith is a devoted and resourceful defender of the standpoint of ordinary life'. In my terms, this 'standpoint' is that of a commercial society. In material terms, this 'life' comprises the basic needs of food, shelter and clothing, which are better and more adequately met by even 'the lowest' in that society (cf. respectively *WN* I, viii.24/89; I, i.11/24; V, ii.k.3/870). And, crucially important as this material betterment is, this enhancement also encompasses the less tangible aspects of life, such as being able to care for the vulnerable (see the Introduction to *The Wealth of Nations*). The obverse of the blessing of opulence is the misery of poverty, as Smith explicitly describes it in the Introduction (*WN* Intro, 4/10).

Smith firmly repudiates any notion that poverty is an 'ideal', that it is ennobling or redemptive (see Berry 2013: Ch. 3 for a fuller discussion). According to this idealised portrayal, 'poverty' and other similar expressions of simple living exemplify the virtue of temperance or continence. To live the simple life of poverty in this sense is to be in control of oneself and thus of one's actions; it is to know the true and proper value of things and thus to be in a position to reject or, at best, treat as indifferent what is of illusory value (like the quality of the flour in bread, to take an example from Seneca (1932: no. 119)). Thus understood, poverty is the exercise of judgement (Epictetus 1928: III, 17). As a product of choice or reason it is now possible to draw a conceptual distinction between poverty as a self-imposed voluntary state (see Seneca 1932: no. 17) and being impoverished (or necessitous, that is, having no choice).[2]

Cicero (1927: III, 8) linked frugality with the virtue of prudence. Smith also made that link but, for him, frugality is not a moralised synonym of 'poverty' but, as a key expression of his recalibration, is rather associated with industry (*WN* Intro, 4/10).[3] Smith associates frugality with prudence, because both are directed at the 'acquisition of fortune' (*TMS* IV, 2.8/190). That directed effort or industry is precisely not a corruption in the classical Aristotelian sense of placing a concern for one's own private interest above that for the public good. Opulence, the goal of that industry, is, we recall, a blessing.

Smith regards 'industry' itself as a virtue. However, he detaches it from its penitential moorings, as found in Christian doctrine.[4] In the typical eighteenth-century sense, by industry he means industriousness and he links it to that ceaseless desire of everyone to better their condition. This is, typically, manifest in seeking an 'augmentation of [their] fortune' (*WN* II, iii.28/341). It is important to note here that 'desire', along with its ceaselessness, is given a positive role, in contrast to its negative gloss prevalent in classical and Christian thought. What lies behind this is Smith's firm commitment to modernity, by which I mean (in shorthand terms) the broad movement in early-modern thought that displaced the Aristotelian teleological framework. While Galilean physics was a decisive development, this was accompanied by a fundamental re-evaluation of epistemology and ethics. Smith, like his fellow Scots, accepts, in an amended form, John Locke's empirical version of this, whereby reason as a motivating force is rejected in favour of passions or desires. Hence we find Smith commenting unequivocally that 'pleasure and pain are the great objects of desire and aversion', with the added observation that distinguishing these 'objects' is not the task of reason (*TMS* VII, iii.2.8/320).

Against this backdrop, how does Smith link frugality with prudence? He declares that of all the virtues prudence is the one most useful to ourselves (*TMS* IV, 2.8/189); its 'proper business' is care for one's health, fortune, rank and reputation (*TMS* VI, i.5/213). It is in 'the steadiness of his industry and frugality', in sacrificing present advantage (that is, incurring some pain now) for greater return (that is more pleasure) later, that the prudent man's conduct is approved of by Smith's moral benchmark, the Impartial Spectator or the internalised standard by which all conduct, including one's own, is judged (*TMS* V, i.i.11/215). Although prudence is not the 'most ennobling of virtues', it fits the circumstances of a society of merchants. The disposition or virtue of this prudent man of commerce is not to agitate or to involve himself in public service or in the pursuit of glory (*TMS* V, i.i.13/216).

When Cicero linked frugality with prudence, he linked it also to the virtue of moderation or self-command.[5] Just as Smith dismisses frugality as poverty, so he distances himself from prudence in the form of Stoic self-command. To appreciate this last point, we need to note, however briefly, Smith's relation to Stoicism. That Smith subscribes to Stoic tenets is a claim that is often made. It would not be surprising if he did subscribe, since that was a common stance. However, as I have argued elsewhere (for example Berry 2004) there are good grounds to question Smith's affiliation. Here I draw attention to just one relevant aspect that supports that questionability.

The basis of Smith's moral theory lies in the dynamics of social life. In a well-known analogy he likens society to a mirror, in which we see reflected the effect of our behaviour on others (*TMS* II, i.3/110). We learn how to behave by gauging these effects on others; for Smith, as stated at the head of this chapter, morality is a matter of socialisation. This is contrary to classical Stoicism.[6] For Epictetus, for example, the 'free man' is indifferent to his 'reputation' (*doxai*), that is to say, is indifferent to the opinions of others. In sharp contrast, Smith declares that 'respect for . . . the sentiments of other people is the *sole* principle which, upon most occasions, overawes all those mutinous and turbulent passions' (*TMS* VI, concl. 3/263; my emphasis). Note, additionally, that Smith's prudent individual cares about his reputation; indeed, a couple of paragraphs earlier he had remarked that the 'strongest of all our desires' was becoming the proper object of respect from our peers (*TMS* VI, i.3/213). In summary form, for the Stoics the virtue of self-command derives from the rational will; in Smith its source is social interaction.

Given this source, then, Smith can argue that the exercise of the virtue of self-command is enhanced by life in a commercial society. Most of the interactions in that environment occur with strangers (*TMS* 1, i.4.10/23) – the butcher is unlikely to be your bosom friend or kin. The enhancement is a consequence of Smith's account of sympathy. In the barest of outline terms, when confronted by the behaviour of another, we imagine how we would act in that situation. If we think the behaviour apt, we approve; and we disapprove if we think it inapt. Since, for Smith, actors want the approval of the spectators (it pleases), they adjust their behaviour accordingly. Compared to the interaction with the more forgiving family and friends, this adjustment requires greater effort in the relatively anonymous setting of the marketplace and that added effort serves to strengthen character. This enables an actor in a commercial society, in 'the bustle and business of the world' (*TMS* III, 3.25/146), to attain a greater degree of moderation and exhibit more consistently the virtue of self-command than is possible in more tribal or clannish times. In this way, individuals in a commercial society are (in general terms) able to act 'according to the dictates of prudence, justice and proper beneficence' (*TMS* VI, iii.11/241).

There is one more point to make about self-command that will lead us to consider another recalibration. Smith refers to these requirements of commercial living as 'gentler exertions of self-command', as giving 'lustre' to the distinctively commercial virtues of 'industry and frugality' (*TMS* VI, iii.13/242). In contrast to the severe demands of the Stoics, they are 'gentle' in two respects. He observes that the 'condition of human nature' would be 'peculiarly hard' if the affections (such as, say, those characteristic of family life), which naturally affect our conduct, could 'upon no occasion appear virtuous' (*TMS* VII, ii.3.18/305). It is, I think, clear that he has a severe Stoic like Epictetus in mind. To overall similar effect, he refers to those 'whining and melancholy moralists' who judge it wrong (impious even) to experience 'the natural joy of prosperity' when so many others are suffering poverty and disease (*TMS* III, 3.9/139).[7] One the main aims of *The Wealth of Nations* is to dispel that melancholy picture. In a properly organised commercial society the joy of prosperity is diffused; the poor share in its fruits. Prosperity or opulence, rather than a negative subject of moral disapproval, is positively joyous (a blessing) and, by extension, its provision through the activities of merchants is morally unwritten. The other respect in which Smith's use of 'gentle' is noteworthy is that it also shows his approach to the cardinal virtue of courage. Smith does not include courage in his dedicated section on virtue in the *Moral Sentiments* but the omission of this definitionally masculine virtue is not surprising. He does not question that command of fear is a virtue but, as an instance of the recalibration I am exploring, he effectively replaces it with the virtue of 'humanity'.

In a passage often commented upon, Smith refers to the decline in 'martial virtue' as a damaging effect of the division of labour (*WN* V, i.f.50/782, V.i.f.60/787). This could be reasonably read as Smith reaffirming the 'classical' perspective. In this passage he also refers to cowardice as a 'sort of mental mutilation, deformity and wretchedness' and to a coward as one who 'evidently wants [that is, lacks] one of the most essential parts of the character of a man'. These are forthright statements but two related observations are apt (see a more extended discussion in Berry 2013: 170–2). First, his context is 'modernist'. He is in this part of the book dealing with the expense of government. The 'martial spirit' is insufficient, a standing army is still needed, but its size (its cost to the public purse) would be reduced if that martial spirit could be diffused. However, that diffusion is limited by modern freedom: militias are unrealistic (*LJB* 337/543). Smith, in fact, leaves the whole question up in the air – government should attend to the etiolation of this spirit but how it should do so is never clearly spelt out. The second observation is that, despite these remarks on cowardice, the virtue of 'courage' is no longer so central to having an effective military capacity. Rather, what is more requisite is 'regularity, order and prompt obedience to command' (*WN* V, i.a.22/699). Indeed, as we will observe below, Smith is generally distrustful of 'heroes' (especially military ones – he makes an exception of Marlborough (*TMS* VI, ii.28/251)).

To return to the issue of recalibration in the context of the *Moral Sentiments*, Smith ties the expression of humane sentiments to a heightened sensitivity to the feelings of others. Significantly, this is subject to social and moral development. A 'humane and polished people', he says, have 'more sensibility to the passion of others' (*TMS* V, 2.10/207). This is demonstrated most dramatically when set against the infanticide practised by the Greeks (and condoned by its most eminent philosophers) but also when set against the 'hardiness demanded of savages', as manifest in their resistance to, and infliction of, torture. But, he says, this behaviour 'diminishes their humanity' (*TMS* V, 2.13/209). Being 'hard', bearing the pain of torture is not an exemplary exhibition of the virtue of self-command. Nor is the Stoic indifference to bodily travail any more commendable.[8] Even when Smith allows that command of fear and anger (as exhibited by the valorous) is 'great and noble', this is qualified because when not at the service of justice and benevolence it can be used to further injustice. In contrast, the 'gentler exertions of self-command' can 'seldom be directed to any bad end' (*TMS* VI, iii.13/242). Nor are these exertions to be judged inferior. The reverse is the case; it is in peaceable, civilised societies that they have their home and correspondingly it is there that both 'the most exquisite humanity' and also 'the highest degree of self-command' are to be found (*TMS* III, 3.36/152).

This recalibration, whereby courage is downplayed relative to humanity, where hard gives way to gentle, has another dimension. The savage is prone to 'falsehood and dissimulation' (*TMS* V, 2.11/208); the valorous are also liable to use their strength of mind to the same deceitful ends (*TMS* VI, iii.12/241) but a 'polished people' acquire habits that make them 'frank, open and sincere' (*TMS* V, 2.11/208). In his Glasgow lectures, and in direct contrast to Cicero's view mentioned earlier that merchants were liars, Smith observed that 'when the greater part of the people are merchants they always bring probity and punctuality into fashion' so that these are 'the principal virtues of a commercial nation' (*LJB* 326/538). Moreover, because, as we sketched out above, Smith's moral theory hinges on sympathetic responsiveness to others, these principal virtues will establish themselves and individuals will act accordingly. Given that the 'good opinion' of others is always desired, this, he says, will produce 'regular conduct' (*TMS* I, iii.5/63).

Justice, Benevolence and Self-Love

Smith's reference here to regular conduct is a direct reflection of the need for predictability and confidence in future-oriented 'market' dealings, and this need lies at the heart of his account of the virtue of justice. In addition to its indispensability (*TMS* II, ii.3.4/86), he stresses its regularity or rule-constitutiveness, qualities that are not apparent where the 'rudeness and barbarism of the people' obtain. In contrast, in 'more civilised nations' the 'natural sentiments of justice' arrive at 'accuracy and precision' (*TMS* VII, iv.36/341). He had earlier emphasised this point by declaring that 'the rules of justice are accurate in the highest degree and admit of no exceptions of modifications' (*TMS* III, 6.10/175). They are, he says, like the rules of grammar and, like the rules of grammar, the rules of justice can be taught, if less didactically, through the media of 'discipline, education and example'.

By being exposed to this range of instruction, which is in effect the process of socialisation, then, scarcely without exception, everyone can 'act upon almost every occasion with tolerable decency, and through the whole of his life to avoid any considerable degree of blame' (*TMS* III, 5.1/163). To all intents and purposes this instils a sense of justice and induces confidence in the reliability of conduct. It establishes the certainty and predictability necessary for a commercial society to function, for otherwise 'there is no man whose conduct can be much depended upon' (*TMS* III, 5.2/163). If the rules were not accurate (or strict) but were variable (or in, Hume's terminology (*T* III, 2.2), were 'flexible'), then that dependency would be compromised.

The premium to act justly in a commercial society, summarised in the negative injunction 'not to injure another' (*TMS* II, ii.3.3/86), constitutes the character of a 'perfectly innocent and just man'. And such a character, Smith continues, can 'scarce ever fail to be accompanied with many other virtues, with great feeling for other people, with great humanity and great benevolence' (*TMS* VI, 2.Intro 2/218).[9] As that quotation makes explicit, members of a commercial society can be both just and benevolent, even if 'beneficence is less essential to the existence of society than justice' (*TMS* II, ii.3.3/86). There is nothing startling here. It is another expression of a jurisprudential commonplace that the duty of benevolence is imperfect, or less strict, than the perfect obligation to be just; see, for example, Pufendorf (1934: I, 9 p. 69), Smith's teacher Hutcheson (*SMP* I, 258) and his mentor Kames (*PMNR* 37). In the commercial society of strangers mentioned above – that is, one where 'mutual love and affection' are absent (*TMS* II, ii.3.3/86) – what is necessary is keeping to the rules of justice, not sentimental ties.

Of course, Smith is denying neither the presence nor the virtuousness of benevolence. However, as he reads it, and contrary to the dominant tenor of the classical account,[10] the two virtues of justice and benevolence do have a different character and focus. While justice is accurate, like grammar, benevolence is 'loose, vague and indeterminate', like literary style (*TMS* VII, 4.1/327). While justice can be satisfied by inaction (not hurting) and abiding by rules, benevolence always consists in positive action. These actions are typically reserved for those known personally to us (the butcher is a stranger); they reflect what Smith calls 'habitual sympathy' developed by the persistent and iterative qualities of familial and amicable relationships (*TMS* VI, ii.i.8/220). The virtue of benevolence, as an imperfect obligation, is not enforceable and so is exercised at our discretion and in a necessarily partial fashion. Justice is not discretionary and is impartial. Our transaction with the butcher is payment for sausages; we do not in the normal course of events appeal to their benevolence or humanity but rather to their 'self-love' (*WN* I, ii.2/27). This, of course, is not to say that the butcher cannot exercise benevolence: she may give a beggar some sausages but that is at her discretion, whereas handing over sausages for the correct sum is not. Moreover, the 'reward' for acting justly, for keeping to the rules, is 'the confidence, the esteem and the love of those we live with' (*TMS* III, 5.8/166). In a mutually supportive manner, these three traits (confidence, esteem, love) will produce the rule-governed, predictable behaviour necessary to the functioning of a commercial society or, in other words, that 'regular conduct' referred to earlier (*TMS* I, iii.4.5/63).

Modern society, where the conjoined blessings of opulence and freedom are found, generates its own values and ideals (like humanity, probity and punctuality) and recalibrates the traditional stock (like prudence and justice). It is clearly not an 'ethics-free zone'. Nonetheless, if for no other reason than the still powerful presence of Christianised Stoic principles, Smith is aware that this society can be criticised because it relies on morally dubious premises.

Commercial Morality

What made Smith's position (and that others, of course) apparently vulnerable was that, having dismissed arguments that make morality a matter of objective rational judgement, it was by default left in the subjective realm of sentiment. This was an intellectually, or argumentatively, dangerous position because it seemed to be occupied by Hobbes, according to whom all human action was determined by the interests of the actor. This was the morally dubious premise that Smith had to counter. It was the common trait of the Scottish Enlightenment that they thought it necessary to put some conceptual distance between their position and that of Hobbes and that of its later, deliberately polemical, expression in Mandeville. The guiding thread in the Scots' moral philosophy is that, whatever their internal differences, they set themselves against Mandeville's 'licentious system', as Smith labelled it (*TMS* VII, ii.4/306–14).

Echoing Francis Hutcheson (1726, for example), Smith puts clear distance between himself and the licentious or selfish system. It is evident from everyday experience that it is false to reduce, in the manner of Hobbes or Mandeville, all human motivation to self-interest or self-love (there is no systematic difference between these two terms – but see Heath (2013) for discussion). Their account cannot accommodate the fact that the interactions of social life 'humble the arrogance of self-love' (*TMS* II, ii.2.1/83). However, once humbled – that is, subject to the constraints of social morality – self-love can still be seen to play a significant role in Smith's modern economy.[11]

Humans are social creatures (the key assumption of Smith's moral philosophy) and they lack self-sufficiency. This necessitates some mutual interaction, which for Smith is underwritten by the presence in human nature of a natural propensity or disposition to truck, barter and exchange. A 'propensity' is not of itself a motive. As we saw with the butcher, self-love is needed to activate it; as Smith succinctly and straightforwardly put it, 'give me that which I want [sausages] and you shall have this [payment] which you want' (*WN* I, ii.2/27). By giving a naturalistic foundation to exchange, exchange itself goes with the grain of human nature so that this interaction can reliably enough ensue. The way individual shortages can be most reliably met across a range of circumstances is by appeal to the 'self-love' of another.

The root of this reliability is the constancy of human nature (see Chapter 20 (Berry 2012)). In line with post-Aristotelian 'modernity', the material fact that all humans (whether male or female, slave or citizen, butcher or professor, Chinese or British) enjoy pleasure and avoid pain underwrites the predictability and certainty inherent in human behaviour. The most palpable evidence of such constancy is the 'fact' of the salience of self-interest in human nature; always noting, of course, that to say it is 'salient' is not to say it is all-encompassing. Accordingly, uncovering this trucking disposition is part of the science of human nature and can license the conclusion that market transactions are not a series of random contingencies but are, as 'constants', open, in principle, to causal analysis. Hence a science of political economy can proceed.

A significant consequence of this argument is that it deflects or counters the accusation that commercial transactions (and by extension a society found upon them) are ethically suspect. It is not the (Hobbesian) default that humans will naturally take the sausages unless 'terrorised' by Leviathan (Hobbes 1991: 120). What is natural – and what all the evidence of human experience reveals – is to engage in barter and exchange. Yet this is not a reprise of Aristotle. For the latter, properly undertaken, barter is indeed *kata phusin* but Smithian 'nature' eschews entelechy; it is a solidly empirical inductive generalisation from the evidence of human behaviour. This behavioural base, moreover, is underwritten by a range of experience far beyond the idealised city-state. And, of course, benevolence is equally solidly based, as the opening sentence of the *Moral Sentiments* states: 'How selfish soever a man may be supposed, there are evidently some principles in his nature, which interest him in the fortune of others ...' (*TMS* I, 1.i/9). Hence the butcher may indeed choose to present the 'beggar' with sausages. Yet if these three modes of interaction (force, gift, exchange) are examined, then the last has a definite advantage. It is more reliably anchored in human interaction than both the self-defeating arbitrariness of violence and the variable, contingent unpredictable humanity of the butcher as a commercial actor.[12] And, by extension, exchange is a more secure basis for dealing with those with whom we have no history (strangers) – we need know nothing more about them than that their self-interest can be appealed to. We can also add that this reinforces the link between commerce and peace (gentle virtue) and marks a key difference between modern and pre-commercial societies, where violence was endemic and where courage was the preeminent virtue.

Conclusion

Smith published *The Wealth of Nations* in 1776 but continued to work on the *Moral Sentiments* (the sixth, much altered, edition appeared in 1790, the year of his death) and this chronology should alert us to the fact that Smith never forsook his roots as a professor of moral philosophy at Glasgow University.[13] More significantly, it indicates that Smith's thought is a 'whole'. For Smith, 'economic' activity took place within society; its participants were socialised beings. This socialisation was also necessarily a moralisation. He rejected an Aristotelian version of a moralised economy based on the meeting of imputed finite needs and posited on a conception of a 'good life' devoted to transcending the essentially animalistic realm of appetite and desire. But that rejection does not mean that Smith (so to speak) 'de-moralised' the economy.

Just as Smith has no qualms about the butcher selling his meat on the basis of his own interest, so he has nothing against bankers, say, doing their proper business on the same basis. But it would be a mistake to see this as an abnegation of moral norms. Smith did think social well-being was best advanced by individuals making their own decisions and he was thus opposed to central attempts to direct 'the market'. However, what he really opposes is the attempt to direct individuals' activities, their 'natural liberty' to pursue their own ends in their own way, whether in choice of occupation, pastime, location, dress or food and so on (see Chapter 21 for an elaboration). This commitment to individual liberty is itself a 'moral' position. He is explicit: violations of natural liberty are unjust (WN IV, v.b.16/530). It follows from this that those private individuals who would distort the 'market' are morally culpable, as is evident in his language about merchants who complain about high wages, or traders who conspire to raise prices or those who seek to restrict competition (WN I, ix.24/115; I, x.c.27/145; I, xi.p.10/267). But, in the light of the opening section of this chapter, this is not be understood as a condemnation of merchants; rather, it re-emphasises that all individuals and all spheres of social activity are subject to moral norms, with none exempt.

It is not, indeed, the role of government to make people make pins. What government does properly, via the exact administration of justice, is enable the 'system of natural liberty' to function (WN IV, ix.51/687). While, as we have argued, it is morally wrong to use the power of the state to direct individual actions, so it is morally justified to ensure that this liberty does not damage the general welfare. Hence, consistently, Smith sees a proper role for government regulation. In the light of the recent financial crisis, a significant example of this is banking. He draws the enlightening parallel between the requirement to build firewalls (thus restricting the liberty of builders) and the restraints on bankers (WN II, ii.94/324). They should not issue notes below a certain sum and should be obliged to honour requests for payments as soon as they are made (WN II, ii.106/329). This is not an isolated case.[14] The basic message is clear. Regulation can be appropriately required and justified by the greater good of society.

Smith, we can say, shifted the basis of the valuation of that good and its constitutive virtues. This occurred on two fronts. Contrary to the Aristotelian (republican) emphasis on the virtues of active citizenship or deliberate pursuit of the public good, for Smith the true public good is the welfare of the public and that lay in the material well-being of a society's members. Abetted by the need to act with gentle moderation in a pluralistic environment, that well-being was best obtained via the prudent regard to self-interest and honest dealing of (say) the butcher, alongside the exercise of commercial virtues – the industrious business of (say) making pins and the punctual co-ordination required when (say) making coats. Opulence is a blessing.

Secondly, this endorsement of the materiality of well-being is a clear expression of Smith's rejection of the pre-modern perspective. Mutability, the ceaselessness of desire from womb to grave, was the way of the world – not the immutability of the First Cause or the eternal perfection of God – and that had to be the basis of judgement. By rejecting the normative superiority of the immutable, the worth of the mundanely mutable could be asserted. Desires are to be accommodated, not proscribed. Individuals should properly have the freedom to pursue those desires within the framework of the rule of law. Liberty is a blessing.

This is the view that comes to be called liberalism. In effect, liberalism valorises the mundane. As I have elsewhere labelled him, Smith is a mundane liberal (Berry 2010b). Smith's 'modern economy', with its attendant virtues, is 'moral', embodying as it does the blessings of opulence and liberty.

Postscript

This chapter is a much-amended version of a lecture I delivered in 2013 to the Seventh Congress of Modern Philosophy at Universidad de los Andes in Santiago. I am grateful to Professor Marita Elton for the invitation and for arranging support. The amendments draw on an earlier talk I gave in 2011 to the Faculty of Economics at Peking University chaired by Professor Qixiang Sun, to whom I also express my thanks. The chapter also incorporates some material previously published in Berry (2010b).

Notes

1. Compare Ryan Hanley's (2013: 221) reference to Smith's 'recovery' of ancient virtue. With my terminology I am indicating that I am less inclined than Hanley to treat Smith as a 'virtue theorist'.
2. See Chapter 13 for a discussion of this contrast in Hume.
3. For an elaboration, see Berry (forthcoming a). I draw on some of that discussion in what follows.
4. For example, in Puritan thought, industry (or diligence) was a Christian virtue acting as a bulwark against lasciviousness, as it inhibits those 'exuberant Spirits which are otherwise apt to break forth in unlawful flames' (Richard Steele 1684: 79. Cf. Luther, 1961: 68).
5. Cicero openly identified *frugalitas* with the Greek *sôphrosunê*, as especially manifested by control of (bodily) appetites and desires (*libidini*) (1927: II.8).
6. I am aware (as, of course, is Smith) that this is a generalisation but, for all the tempering of its original formulation in Zeno, by the middle (Roman) Stoics I think the point holds good. The late Stoic Epictetus represents a throwback to the earlier, more austere formulation.
7. I am grateful to Professor Hisashi Shinohara of Kwansei Gakuin University, Japan for a correction of an earlier formulation of this point (in Berry 2013).
8. See, for example, Epictetus, who says of a man who is disturbed when his leg is shackled that he is investing value in his leg (body) when a truly free man would not care (1926: I, 19).
9. Griswold (1999: 237) emphasises that for Smith there is more than simply rule-following involved in justice; it is also a character trait or disposition to revere those rules.
10. Smith explicitly differentiates his strict account of justice from a more expansive view that he associates with the Greeks. Following Grotius, he comments on Aristotle treating justice as, in part, 'comprehending all the social virtues' and proceeds, this time naming Plato, to identify a 'still more extensive' usage whereby justice comprehends 'the perfection of every sort of virtue' (*TMS* VII, ii.1.10/270). The clear implication (reminiscent of Hume) is that this loose, comprehensive sense of justice is too indeterminate, too prone to make exceptions in particular cases, and as such is unfit to uphold the edifice of a society that relies on the secure predictability of enforced rules.
11. The notion of self-love has a long and complicated history, which

cannot here be explored. I made some tentative remarks in that direction in Berry (2004, 2013) but see Brooke (2012) for a good discussion of its link with Stoicism.

12. While Smith allows that, in comparison to the nobility and generosity of giving gifts, barter is judged 'mean' but in a backhanded fashion that is precisely because, like hunger, thirst and sex, it is so 'strongly implanted' in human nature. Indeed, this very solidity explains its disparaging label; it requires no supplementary endorsement to act as an additional incentive, like 'honour' and similar socio-cultural epithets (*LJB* 302/527).

13. The title page of *The Wealth of Nations* identifies Smith as 'Formerly Professor of Moral Philosophy in the University of Glasgow'.

14. He is in favour of a legal rate of interest to inhibit those he labels 'prodigals and projectors' (*WN* II, iv.15/357). Also he favours discouraging the selling of 'futures' at least in part on moral grounds, in that it is the 'expedient of a spendthrift' (*WN* V, ii.c.12/831).

20

Adam Smith's 'Science of Human Nature'

According to Stuart Hampshire, 'it is possible to characterise philosophy itself as a search for a "definition of man" and to interpret the great philosophers of the past as each producing a different account of the powers essential to man' (1965: 232). This is merely one analyst's expression of a commonplace. But, of course, this claim is not the preserve of analysts: the philosophers themselves were often aware of the role played by their 'conception of human nature'. It follows from Hampshire's characterisation that this self-awareness is not the exclusive prerogative of any particular period but it did enjoy a programmatic salience during the Enlightenment.[1]

The following generalisations about that self-awareness seem defensible. There was a convergence on the idea that human nature is constant and uniform in its operating principles. Still in generalising mode, these referred to its determining motives (passions), source of knowledge (sense experience) and mode of operation (association of ideas). By virtue of this constancy, human nature was predictable, so that, once it was scientifically understood, social reform could be undertaken. Hume, for example, in his introduction to the *Treatise of Human Nature*, regarded his proposed 'science of man' as pioneering and fundamental because upon it depended not only logic, morals, criticism and politics but also even mathematics, natural philosophy and natural religion (*T* Intro, 5/4). He believed, employing Baconian imagery (cf. Bacon 1853: 150), that if science is conquered then a relatively easy victory over the others can be expected. While, as ever, Smith is more circumspect than his friend, he shares Hume's ambitions for the science of man, which Smith calls the 'science of human nature' and which he believes was, even in the seventeenth century, in its 'infancy' (*TMS* VI, iii.2.5/ 319). This chapter aims to explicate what Smith implies about this 'science'.

Smith's reference to the 'infancy' of the science of human nature occurs in Book 7 of *The Theory of Moral Sentiments*, in a chapter devoted to a critique of systems that invoke reason as the principle of approbation. The treatment, which remained unchanged through all six editions, is, however, cursory and the only rationalist discussed (and that briefly) is Cudworth. The rationalist perspective exemplified the historical fact that the 'distinct offices and powers of the different faculties of the human mind' had not yet been 'carefully examined and distinguished' (*TMS* VII, iii.2.5/319) – hence Smith's remark on the infancy of what is fully identified as 'the abstract science of human nature'. In his 'Letter to the Edinburgh Review', published three years previously in 1756, Smith comments that, in contrast to the French, it is the English who have led the way not only in natural philosophy but also in 'morals, metaphysics and part of the abstract sciences'. He then produces an illustrative list – Hobbes, Locke, Mandeville, Shaftesbury, Butler, Clarke and Hutcheson (*EPS* 249–50). Hume's list, in his introduction to the *Treatise* (1739), of those who have put the 'science of man on a new footing' (*T* 5n/*SBNT* xviin), contains five of these names (the two exceptions are Hobbes and Clarke, although Hume does append an 'et cetera'). The similarity of both context and content seems, at the very least, suggestive and in what follows it is an evanescent leitmotif.

Certainly, it is Hume who provides one of the century's clearest statements about the constancy and uniformity of human nature when he writes in the first *Enquiry* that 'it is universally acknowledged that there is a great uniformity among the actions of men, in all nations and ages, and that human nature remains still the same in its principles and operations' (*U* 150/*SBNU* 83).[2] These 'principles' and 'operations' are my concern in this chapter.

The 'Operations' of Human Nature

'Operations' can be reasonably taken to refer to the principle of the association of ideas. We know from Hume's own *Abstract* of the *Treatise* that he himself thought the most original element in the book was the use made of this principle. Starting from the Lockean premise that any inquiry into human nature must rely entirely on experience, these principles operate uniformly to enable humans to bind their discrete experiences together into a coherent whole. There is, accordingly, a 'general course' of nature with respect to 'natural evidence'. This 'generality' stems from the recurrent correlations between observed phenomena (the impressions of heat and flame, say) that are reproduced in the mind as an association of ideas. There is, similarly, a general course in human actions that links observed constancy in correlations between actions and motives (moral evidence) that are also associated in the mind (*T* 3.11.7/*SBNT* 401). Just as there has been great success in the understanding of natural phenomena, so Hume, along with many other thinkers, aimed to emulate that success in the moral sciences by adopting its 'experimental' procedures (as manifest in the *Treatise*'s subtitle).

Whether the implied reference here is to Boyle or Newton, it is the case that the latter's achievements were more generally paradigmatic.[3] We know that Smith was impressed by Newton.[4] To that end, it is revealing testimony that Smith's pupil, then colleague at Glasgow University, John Millar, called him the 'Newton of political economy' (*HV* II, 10/404n), meaning principally by that that he had reduced the complexity and seeming incoherence of market behaviour to a few simple, general explanatory principles. Hence early in *The Wealth of Nations*, Smith identifies the principle of the division of labour as the cause of labour's productiveness and then locates the source of this principle in a 'propensity in human nature ... to truck, barter and exchange one thing for another' (*WN* I, ii.1/25). Smith is not certain if this propensity – or 'disposition' in the records of his lectures at Glasgow (*LJA* vi.56/352; *LJB* 221/493) – is an 'original principle' which, as such, has simply to be accepted (a point Hume had stressed in his own endeavour to adhere to Newton's injunction 'not to frame hypotheses') or, as was more probable, is itself the consequence of the 'faculties of reason and speech' – or the 'natural inclination to persuade' in the lectures (*LJB* vi.56/352).

In the *Moral Sentiments*, Smith refers to speech as 'the characteristical faculty of human nature' (*TMS* VII, iv.25/356). Indeed, he appended an essay on language, which he first published in 1761, to the third edition of the *Moral Sentiments* (1767). In that essay ('Considerations concerning the First Formation of Languages') this connection with exchange is implied when he claims that language was formed as individuals ('savages') endeavoured to 'make their mutual wants intelligible to each other by uttering certain sounds whenever they meant to denote certain objects'

(*CL* 1/204). This essay, though, is more generally revealing about Smith's view of human nature.

In broadest outline, the argument of 'Considerations' is that the various elements in language (verbs, nouns, adjectives, prepositions, etc.) can be explained in developmental terms.[5] For example, for Smith, words that were originally the proper names of individuals 'insensibly become the common name of a multitude' (*CL* 1/204). The 'mechanism' at work here is resemblance, one of Hume's three principles of association. Smith gives two telling instances of this process: a child when just learning to speak calls everyone who comes to the house its papa or mama (*CL* 1/204) and, secondly, a savage 'naturally bestows' on each new object the 'same name' that had previously been given to a similar object when it was first encountered (*CL* 1/204).

What makes these two examples (of a child and of a savage) significant is that their conjunction reveals the presence of a particular (Lockean) model of human nature. Locke, in his *Essay on Human Understanding* (1690), argues that the mind by degrees advances to exercise its faculties of enlarging, compounding and abstracting ideas (1854: I, 222). It follows that the ability to think abstractly is a developmental capacity that children (along with 'idiots, savages and illiterate people') have to attain (1854: I, 153; cf. I, 140). Savages thus represent, in a favourite phrase in the Enlightenment (and in Scotland especially), 'the infancy of mankind'. Given that the capacity for mediation and abstraction is a later development, then both children and savages can be characterised as inhabiting a world of concrete immediacy. In Smith's essay we find these themes repeated. He says of prepositions, for example, that they express 'so very abstract and metaphysical idea [that they] would not easily or readily occur to the first formers of language' (*CL* 32/219).[6]

Smith's adoption of this model can, in the guise of this child/ savage parallel, also be found in his 'History of Astronomy' (*HA* III, 2/49). Just as Smith employs the assumptions of association in the 'Considerations', so, too, does he in this work; indeed, it provides one of the clearest occasions of Smith's open adoption of associationism (see also the essay 'Of the External Senses' in *EPS* 21/141). Smith's aim in his astronomy essay is to explain 'philosophical systems' as attempts 'to order chaos' by allaying the 'tumult of the imagination' (*HA* II, 12/45–6). It is his associationism that underlies his explanation. His account is heavily indebted to Hume's, not only because he follows his outline of its role but also, and significantly, because he adopts Hume's positive portrayal of the process. Hitherto, as employed by Locke (and others, including Hutcheson), associationism had been used principally to explain errors and deviations.[7]

In Smith's presentation, when objects are observed to have 'constantly presented themselves to the senses' in a particular order, they become associated, so that it is 'the habit of the imagination' to pass from one to the other (*HA* II, 7/40–1). Smith, it can aptly be interpolated, uses almost identical language in the *Moral Sentiments*: 'When two objects have frequently been seen together, the imagination acquires a habit of passing easily from one to the other' (*TMS* V, 1.2/194). In the astronomy essay, against this backcloth of imagined coherence, anything that disrupts the customary connections will produce initially 'surprise' and then 'wonder' at how the disruption occurred (*HA* II, 6 40). In the *Moral Sentiments* disruption is a source of 'disappointment', even 'impropriety' (*TMS* V, 1.2/194). Philosophy/science is the attempt to discover a 'connecting chain of intermediate events' such that the imagination can reassume its habits of association and in this way remove the wonder (*HA* II, 9/42). It is in line with this pattern of explanation that Smith accounts for polytheism as the first form of religious belief (*HA* II, 2/49).[8] That is to say, savages, due to their immersion in a world of concrete particularity, account for any irregularities in their experience by invoking, for example, Neptune's favour or displeasure to account for calm or stormy seas. Later, these superstitions are replaced as 'science' increasingly uncovers the true causes of the irregularities – an argument also found in the 'Ancient Physics' (*EPS* 9/112–13).[9] There is here a 'natural history of religion' and its outline recurs in the *Moral Sentiments* (see *TMS* III, 5.4 /164). Furthermore, though contestably I concede, this is one way to read those passages that talk of the 'consolation' offered by belief in an afterlife, a belief that is 'deeply rooted in human nature' (*TMS* III, 2.33/131–2).[10]

What underlies this move from superstition to science is that Lockean-derived model of human nature. Smith, like many of his compatriots, adopts this model and it is this, as intimated by the child/savage parallel, that underwrites the entire enterprise of a 'history of mankind', which was such a characteristic feature of the Scottish Enlightenment generally (see Berry 1997). An appropriate case in point is Dugald Stewart who, precisely in the context of discussing the essay on language, articulates, by way of retrospective summation, the guiding principles of 'conjectural' or 'natural history' (*Life* II, 48/293). For Stewart, this history rests on 'known principles of human nature' and on their basis, even in the absence of direct evidence, it is possible to construct a defensible account of the 'natural history of man' as a story of human progress. I do not think Stewart is here distorting Smith. For Smith himself, the science of human nature is primed to underwrite a naturalistic explanation of institutions, such as, to mention merely the two cases here noted, the development of language and religion. For these 'principles' of human nature to do the work required, they must have the property of constancy or uniformity.

The 'Principles' of Human Nature

There are two initial points to make about the 'constant' or 'unalterable' (as Smith at one point labels them [*TMS* III, 2.30/128]) 'principles' of human nature. The first concerns a consequential implication, the second pertains to its content. The implication is that it warrants a consistency or stable predictability in human conduct and this underwrote the ambitions for the establishment of the 'moral', that is, social, sciences. Viewed in this light and without parading its 'scientific' credentials, the *Moral Sentiments* relies upon there being a science of human nature (Raphael 2007: 5). Unless, for example, the death of a parent consistently caused distress (cf. *TMS* I, i.3.4/18), there would be no subject for a theory of moral sentiments. The example of 'distress' signals the second point. This constancy is rooted in mankind's material nature – all humans enjoy pleasure and avoid pain; they are, as such, creatures of passion and desire. Smith, too, focally locates this constancy in humans' affective or passionate states; they are, generically, creatures of desire. It has to be admitted that exploration of this issue is not helped by the fact that one looks in vain for a rigorous consistency in terminology or, indeed, for conceptual exactitude.

I start this exploration by returning to Smith's reference to 'trucking, etc.' as a 'propensity' in human nature and to the comment that he also leaves open: whether this is an 'original principle' or is consequent to speech (and reason) as a 'characteristical' faculty. Given that Smith says dogs don't barter over bones (*WN* I, ii.2/26) then, inferably, that is because they are unable to involve themselves in linguistic communication in the sense (following Aristotle) of persuasion (*logos*) rather than a bark (*phone*). Yet it would be a mistake to impose a Hegelian *Unterscheidung* here. For Smith, humans and animals still have much in common. All animals have an 'appetite' for self-preservation and propagation of their species (*TMS* II, i.5.10/77). This includes 'mankind', whom Smith depicts as endowed with desire for those ends and an aversion to the contrary. He then comments that securing those ends has not been left to the 'slow and uncertain determinations of reason'. Although these observations occur in a passage excised in later editions, they are echoed in retained material, as when he comments unequivocally that 'pleasure and pain are the great objects of desire and aversion', with the added observation that it is not reason that distinguishes those objects (*TMS* VII, iii.2.8/320). This last quotation occurs – and significantly so, as we shall see – just after his comment about the infancy of the science of human nature and it can be revealingly set against another passage, where he contests the views of 'some ancient philosophers'. These (unnamed) philosophers disparage passions based on the body on the grounds that, precisely because they are shared with animals, they cannot be 'characteristical qualities of human nature' but Smith, per contra, observes that there are 'many other passions' shared with brutes. He itemises 'resentment, natural affection, even gratitude' (*TMS* I, ii.1.3/28), all of which, of course, play a part in his own argument. And even when Smith distinguishes humans because they appreciate beauty and exhibit 'taste', this is prefaced by the phrase 'Man is the only animal' and even this difference is relative – humans have 'greater delicacey of mind' (*LJB* 209/488).[11]

Somewhat hesitantly, I interpose here reference to the place of 'instinct'. In that excised passage (*TMS* II, i.5.10/77–8) Smith, unremarkably, contrasts reason with 'original immediate instincts' – specified as hunger, thirst, sexual passion, love of pleasure and dread of pain. Elsewhere he refers to the natural desire of being believed as 'the instinct' on which the faculty of speech is founded (*TMS* VII, iv.25/336) but I do not think the word 'instinct' here is doing much work. Rather stronger claims have been about the significance of 'instinct' as it appears in his most sustained account of animal behaviour in 'Of the External Senses'. There, having stressed the endowment of 'instinctive perception' in other animals, Smith remarks that 'it seems difficult' to suppose humans are unique (*EPS* 74/163). This and attendant passages, with their reference to 'preconception', have seemed to some to break with strict empiricism. My own view is that Smith does not compromise his commitment to the evidential recourse to experience. It is, perhaps, worth recalling that Locke himself had carefully distinguished innate ideas from 'natural tendencies imprinted on the minds of men', while Hume happily allows that humans have instincts that 'nature has implanted for salutary purposes'.[12]

This rejection of a sharp human/other animal divide reflects the location of the constancy of human nature in man's material nature. To generalise sweepingly, we can detect here an expression of what may be called the early-modern consensus, namely that the world is matter in motion, itself part of what one historian has called 'the fundamental rethinkings of the age' (Rabb 2006: 145). It is, I want to claim, Smith's subscription to this consensus that helps explain why he can declare the science of human nature to be in its infancy. This entails that Smith also accepts the naturalisation of human nature on which, for all their differences, Descartes, Spinoza, Hobbes and others had embarked.[13] The consequence of this naturalisation is that the way to seek the truth about human nature is, in principle, no different from the way to seek the truth about nature in general. In both cases it is a search for causes. But the 'causes' in question reflect the 'modern' consensus, according to which when seeking explanations attention should be paid to efficient or material causes.[14] We explain human behaviour by identifying motives, that is, literally, what causes motion in us (cf. *LRBL* ii, 193/171).

In a generic sense, desires play this motivational role; there is no explanatory purchase to be gained from recourse to reason (recall that the context of the reference to the science of human nature is a critique of reason). This helps makes sense of Smith's otherwise bewildering, seemingly ad hoc, evocations of human desires and passions. On the one hand he recognises that we humans do desire bodily ease and security; on the other he is at pains to stress, against Epicureans like Hobbes, who treat these as primary, that it is the 'desire of becoming the proper objects of respect' which is 'perhaps the strongest of all our desires' (*TMS* VI, i.3/213). But clearly, Smith's demurral from the Hobbesian reading does not supplant or supersede the recourse to humans as creatures of desire.

Accordingly, even when a man 'acts from the most sublime and godlike motive which human nature is even capable of conceiving' this is attributable to the 'desire of becoming what is honourable and estimable' (*TMS* VII, ii.4.10/310–11). There is no motivational hierarchy. Despite Smith's language here, we do not with Aristotle (1894: 1177a-b) transcend desire as we 'put on immortality' and live the *bios theoretike* in line with the best part of us, our reason. Similarly, although I here perforce simplify a complex philosophical anthropology, for Aristotle, all humans properly aim at *eudaimonia,* which is a 'perfect and self-sufficient end' (1894: 1097b, 15–20), and those who attain that end are living life as it should be led; it is a complete life and, as such, one without 'desire'.[15] By contrast, for the 'modernist', humans as creatures of desire are always 'on the move'; they are in Locke's version 'uneasy' (a usage followed by Hutcheson).[16]

Smith's relation to Aristotle is the subject of debate[17] and, more broadly, it broaches one of the more deeply contended issues in some recent Smith scholarship. Does his commitment to 'a natural order' reveal or indicate an ultimately teleological or metaphysical cast to his thought or is it an empirical, inductively arrived at, generalisation?[18] The one clear place where Smith distinguishes efficient from final causes is not, it seems to me, clear cut – partly, though only partly, because the prose is especially convoluted (*TMS* II, ii.3.5/87). He says we are apt to confound these causal categories when dealing with the 'mind.' But, as I read it, this is another expression of Smith's critique of the reach of reason that mistakes the 'wisdom of man' for the 'wisdom of God'.[19] The latter is manifest in the 'natural principles' that support preservation and propagation. There is nothing here that precludes 'scientific' enquiry of those principles or sentiments and this enquiry can be, as Samuel Fleischacker (1999: 144) observes, 'agnostic' about final ends. Moreover, just as investigation of the efficient causes of digestion aids the alleviation of dyspepsia, so the science of human nature has the equally Baconian aim of the amelioration of human life.

This amelioration encompasses both moral and material welfare and depends on knowing the right causes in order to produce the desired effects (cf. *LRBL* ii, 17/90). The full title of *The Wealth of Nations* is, of course, that it is an inquiry into its 'Nature and Causes'. A recurrent pattern permits, for example, the identification of 'property and manners' as causes that produce the same effects, whether these be exemplified by 'remote antiquities' or by the case of Cameron of Locheil 'not thirty years ago' (*WN* III, iv.8/416). Thus the extension of the rule of law, markets and extended division of labour enjoyed by 'civilised' nations will effect the diffusion of abundance and the cessation of death from hunger experienced by 'savage nations' who remain 'miserably poor' (*WN* Intro, 4/10). [20]

Nor should we assume that this argument is absent from the *Moral Sentiments*. This is evident in Smith's critique of the Stoics. After having affirmed the presence of 'the necessary connection which Nature has established between causes and their effects', he proceeds immediately, in a striking passage, to apply this to human nature. He writes:

> The causes which naturally excite our desires and aversions, our hopes and fears, our joys and sorrows ... produce upon each individual, according to the degree of his actual sensibility, their proper and necessary effects. (*TMS* II, ii.1.47/293)

For example, resentment is a 'passion' of which the 'exciting cause' is pain (*TMS* II, iii.1.1.7/94, 96) and its '(human) natural consequence' is punishment (*TMS* II, ii.2.3/84). Since the integrity of society depends on justice (*TMS* II, ii.3.3/86), the social practice of punishment is needed to 'enforce' its observation. This enforcement relies on predictable human responses – on, indeed, 'the constitution of human nature' (*TMS* III, 3.29/148). Everyone exhibits 'dread of death' since that is 'one of the most important principles in human nature' (*TMS* I, i.1.13/13), hence the presence of a universal motivation to avoid 'dread and terror' (*TMS* I, ii.3.4/86; II, ii.2.3/85).[21] Thus, in line with the argument in *The Wealth of Nations*, the better this enforcement the better will be the society – as exhibited by the fact that 'natural sentiments of justice' attain an 'accuracy and precision' in 'civilised nations' that is missing where the people remain 'rude and barbarous' (*TMS* VII, iv.36/341).

The causality upon which this Baconianism relies expresses a truth about human nature that modern Galilean physics underwrites.[22] The universalism here undercuts any deep social or cultural differentiation and any recourse to 'essences'. Aristotle might claim that the final end (*telos*) of some is to be the natural slaves of others but, materially, prick any human and they bleed, as Shylock, the Jew, declared with powerful rhetorical force in Shakespeare's *Merchant of Venice*. In addition to this hard determinism of physical causation, there is also what we might call, to capture the explanatory thrust given to socialisation, the 'soft determinist' perspective of 'moral causation'.[23] In Smith this expresses itself in, for example, his comment that the difference between a philosopher and a porter arises 'not so much from nature as from habit, custom and education' (*WN* I, ii.4/29).[24] This 'softness' allows for qualification and can thus accommodate Smith's acknowledgement, as reported in his Rhetoric lectures, that there is no infallible link between human actions and their causes (*LRBL* ii, 192/171).

This 'modern' emphasis on material causality also required, especially in post-Lockean thought, that the facts about human nature had to be sought in experience. This was a decisive move because it deflated the accusation that this emphasis on desires and material causes necessarily gave a privileged role to self-interest. This explains the seriousness with which Mandeville's deliberately provocative coinages were taken. While he could severely criticise Shaftesbury's classicism for its hypocritical divergence from the evidence about how humans behaved, his own position was itself judged to diverge from those facts. It was experientially evident that humans naturally acted on more than purely self-interested grounds. This was the virtual obsession of Francis Hutcheson, Smith's teacher.

For Hutcheson, the undeniable fact of morality (both its actions and the very existence of a moral vocabulary) cannot be derived from the principle of self-interest. All humans, he argues, possess a 'moral sense' by means of which they perceive, independently of any personal benefit, the difference between actions motivated by self-interest and those motivated by 'an ultimate desire' for the happiness of others (*PW* 70–1). Smith accepts this affirmation of the reality of moral judgements and behaviour. However, he differs by rejecting Hutcheson's categorical separation of self-love from benevolence, since 'regard to our own private happiness and interest, too, may appear upon many occasions laudable principles of actions' (*TMS* VII, ii-3.16/304). Moreover, it would be a 'hard' view of the 'condition of human nature' if the 'affections, which by their very nature of our being' influence our conduct, could never appear virtuous (*TMS* VII, ii-3.18/305). Smith also rejects the need to invoke a distinct moral sense to justify the reality of moral judgement.

Rejection of moral sense theory does not mean a downgrading of the importance of human nature for a correct grasp of morality

– rather the reverse. While Smith as a literary stylist will sometimes employ the term 'human nature' as an emphatic device (see, for example, the set-piece account of my little finger versus hundreds of millions of Chinese being a trade-off at which 'human nature' would startle with horror (*TMS* III, 3.5/137)), I want here to note, without dismissing this rhetorical usage, that his theory does invoke 'human nature' substantively. Indeed, one need not look further than the opening sentence of the *Moral Sentiments*:

> How selfish soever a man may be supposed, there are evidently *some principles in his nature* which interest him in the fortune of others, and render their happiness necessary to him, though he derive nothing from it except the pleasure of seeing it. (*TMS* I, i.1.1/9; my emphasis)

Rather than rehearse the familiar contours of Smith's moral theory, I confine myself to noting some key elements of the theory where its reliance on certain further postulates about the operations and principles of human nature becomes evident. Although his key idea of 'sympathy' is declared to be an 'original passion of human nature' (*TMS* I, i.1.1/9), he adopts a more technical meaning as he develops his theory. In that theory he declares it to be a fact about human nature that 'nothing pleases more than to observe in other men a fellow-feeling with all the emotions of our own breast' (*TMS* I, i.2.1/12). We can make this observation only in, and from exposure to, society. I learn how to act so that the pleasure of concurrent emotions can be obtained. Humans are, as social creatures, educable. This sociality is decisive and effectively marks Smith's departure from Hutcheson's moral sense, which operates 'antecedent to instruction' (*PW* 199).

Smith illustrates the natural fact of human sociality (that it is human nature to belong to a group or to live in society) with his well-known mirror analogy (*TMS* III, 1.3/110). This whole passage exemplifies the operation of a Smithian science of human nature. By being the necessary subject of social gaze, 'a human creature' will observe that others approve of some of his actions and disapprove of others, with the consequence, for Smith, that he 'will be elevated in the one case, and cast down in the other; his desires and aversions, his joys and sorrows will now often become the causes of new desires and new aversions, new joys and new sorrows'. It is this responsiveness to others – pleasure in their approval, pain in their disapproval – that Smith used to explain why the rich parade their wealth while the poor hide their poverty. The rich value their possessions more for the esteem they bring than any utility and it is this 'ardent desire' for esteem that constitutes the key explanation of that incentive to better our condition (*TMS* I, iii.2.1/50–1). This 'desire of bettering our condition' paradigmatically exemplifies the characteristic restlessness of all desire because, as the well-known passage in *The Wealth of Nations* continues, this desire comes 'with us from the womb and never leaves us till we go into the grave' and 'there is scarce perhaps a single instant in which any man is so perfectly and completely satisfied with his situation as to be without any wish of alteration or improvement of any kind'. It is, of course, this particular expression of restless desire that creates the blessing of opulence, as he terms it in his *Lectures* (*LJA* iii, 111/185), because 'an augmentation of fortune is the means by which the greater part of men propose and wish to better their condition' (*WN* II, iii.28/341; cf. *TMS* VI, i.3/213).

Though presented in the universalistic language characteristic of human nature talk, the aptness of this for commercial society is apparent. A society of merchants does not operate on the principle of 'benevolence'; the butcher, the brewer and the baker will supply us with beef, beer and bread only if we appeal to their 'self-love', not to their 'humanity' (*WN* I, ii.2/26). This itself is 'laudable' but, of course, it is not that we do not act benevolently or with humanity in a commercial society; indeed, in the *Moral Sentiments* Smith is careful to say that a merchant society would be 'less happy and agreeable' than one where beneficence was practised (*TMS* II, ii.3.2/86). It is, rather, that in a commercial society the business of exchange is conducted between strangers; the butcher is unlikely to be also your friend.

Notwithstanding that each individual, whether in commercial society or not, has a 'natural preference . . . for his own happiness above that of other people' (*TMS* II, ii.3.2/ 86), it is a weakness of the Hobbesian/Mandevillean view, as revealed by the science of human nature, that it cannot take on board the fact that the interactions of social life 'humble the arrogance of self-love'. This socially induced humility enables Smith to identify how the 'perfection of human nature' is seen to lie in the restraint of the selfish, and in the indulgence of the benevolent, affections (*TMS* I, i.5.5/25). The agency that Smith comes to call upon here is the 'impartial spectator'. This figure hyperbolically represents the internalisation of behaviour learnt via the social mirror and, as such, its deliberations, too, build on the causal dynamics of human nature. Humans, Smith claims, have been endowed with an 'original desire to please and an original aversion to offend' (*TMS* III, 2.6/116) and it is yet another of the facts that Smith attributes to human nature that humans desire 'not only to be loved but to be lovely ... not only praise but praiseworthiness' (and, similarly, dread to be hated and to be blameworthy (*TMS* III, ii.1/113–14)). One consequence of this is that we are pleased with having acted in a praiseworthy manner even if nobody praises us, for we have 'a desire of being what ought to be approved of' (*TMS* III, 2.7/117) and, in line with modern psychology, we are 'anxious', that is, susceptible to Lockean 'unease', on that score.[25] The eventual result is that we do not rely on actual praise or blame but seek to act in such a way that an 'impartial spectator' would approve of our conduct (*TMS* III, 2.6/116).

This familiar account of moral judgement does not mean that there is no variation.[26] Smith devotes a whole section of the *Moral Sentiments* to exactly this issue. While he admits that virtues differ between 'rude and barbarous nations' and 'civilised nations' (*TMS* V, 2.8/204–5), the crucial point is his belief that the 'sentiments of moral approbation and disapprobation are founded on the strongest and most vigorous passions of human nature; and though they may be somewhat warpt, cannot be entirely perverted' (*TMS* V, 2.1/200). This statement, made in the context of a discussion of infanticide, makes explicit not only (once again) the commitment to the uniformity of human nature but also that this uniformity constitutes the foundation of moral sentiments. This means that there is a uniform or universal structure to morality; ethical relativism is false. Given this universality, particular practices may indeed be judged 'warpt': they are not all on a par; some deviate from an authoritative transcultural norm.

Diversity necessarily presupposes uniformity, since the ability to identify differences presupposes some basic common point of contact because without that commonality it is impossible to judge whether others do have beliefs or conceptual frameworks different from one's own.[27] But, this logical point aside, what is crucial for mainstream eighteenth-century thought is that the doctrine of human nature plays the role of providing this commonality. Yet, as Smith's account of infanticide reveals, this role is no mere formality; it carries a normative punch. That which is universal (in accord with human nature) carries, by virtue of that very trait, more moral weight than that which is 'merely' particular or local.

How successful, or ultimately cogent, an argument this is may be debated but it goes to the heart of the Enlightenment as 'the party of humanity'. The point is not simply theoretically to identify the 'warpt' but also practically to endeavour to straighten it – hence the humanitarian crusades against (inter alia) torture, slavery, disease, bigotry and superstition. While Smith's voice is not one of the most clamorous, since for the most part he eschews moralistic rhetoric – witness his 'economic' case against slavery (WN III, ii.9/387) – he does famously argue for education as a proper public expense to offset the 'stupidity and ignorance' occasioned by the division of labour (WN V, i.f.50/782). More generally, he exhibits an Enlightenment sentiment par excellence when he exclaims that 'science is the great antidote to enthusiasm and superstition' (WN V, i.g.14/796).

To attribute historicist or 'anthropological' sensitivities to Smith and the overwhelming bulk of his contemporaries is an error.[28] What changes, in what Smith calls the 'natural progress which men make in society' (LJA iv.19/207), are 'institutions'. These range across the gamut of social life from religion, to art, to governance, to the treatment of women, to forms of property and so on. All of these can be subject to a 'natural history', an enterprise made possible, as remarked upon earlier, by the underlying commitment to the constancy and universality of human nature: the evidentially apparent diversity of human experience is not random. Rather, the science of human nature enables us to see it as manifesting an 'order' or regularity. Human experience, because it is grounded in constant principles and operations, can thus be 'organised' as a progressive sequence, from the rude simplicity of concrete particulars to the civilised complexity of abstract rules. In the guise of the 'four stages', this natural history plots the diverse institutional structures that have emerged, more or less unintentionally, as humans have coped with the exigencies thrown up by their natural environment (such as population pressure on resources) and correlated shifts in the human environment (such as changes in property and manners).

Smith's Theory of Human Nature

What role does Smith's account of human nature play? Many years ago I advanced the argument that a theory of human nature establishes presuppositionally the area, field or conceptual space within which humans operate. The determination of this field realises two objectives, or ends (Berry 1986a: Ch. 10). Firstly, it procures for each theory a reading of the human world within which space prescriptions can be located. Secondly, and simultaneously, it provides each theory with an authoritative context (an ideal) in terms of which other prescriptions can be dismissed as unrealistic or not worth taking seriously. In telling 'how it is/this is the way the world goes', a theory of human nature is thus not only staking out the field within which normative issues can arise but it is, in doing this, also claiming that field as its own and applying it to other theories. An account of human nature thus aims to pre-empt the conceptual space and locate all accounts on its territory.

Smith's notion of a science of human nature fits this model. The propensity to truck, barter and exchange, for example, is a corollary of a conception of human nature that holds that wants are satisfied through mutual reciprocation based on convergent self-interest, as in our dealings with the butcher. This explanation of the relationship between a theory of human nature and economic activity, despite its pretensions to portray 'how it is', does not leave the world as found. The science of man's ambit is practical, not theoretical, wisdom. Here, in its account of an aspect of human behaviour, it also thereby establishes the normative parameters applicable to economic transactions. But precisely because economics (as an exemplification of the science of human nature) is a practical science, the 'facts' could be otherwise. Accordingly, a different account of what constitute the facts of human nature ('this is the way the world goes') would establish a different conceptual space and thus a different normative ground for action in the world. For Marx (1982), for example, it would be in accord with human nature for wants to be satisfied as a direct expression of man's communitarian nature without any need for reciprocation. The Smithian account would judge Marx's version as going so much against the grain of human nature as to be inoperable ('this is *not* how the world goes'), while the Marxian version would judge the Smithian version as not how it *is* but, rather, an ideological foreclosure that reifies, or naturalises, what are amendable historical practices.

This same argumentative pattern is present in the *Moral Sentiments*. An example of this is how Smith's account serves to undermine Hobbes' theory by virtue of its inability to explain, without unacceptable distortion, the reality of disinterested action and, equally, to undermine Hutcheson's recourse to a 'moral sense' as a redundancy. Neither thinker in fact takes seriously the social aspect of human nature and the corollary that morality is experientially acquired though human interaction. On his own 'territory', Smith is able to use the universally attested facts about 'human nature' to claim that humans universally make the same normative judgements, as infanticide falls foul of the love of parents for their children, a trait that 'Nature . . . has rendered so strong' (*TMS* III, 3.13/142). In this way I see Smith's 'commitment to normativity', to use Ryan Hanley's felicitous phrase (2007: 6, 93), as integral to his possession of a theory of human nature.

As a generalising conclusion, perhaps the historically most noteworthy aspect of Smith's science of human nature is its particular twin-track combination of positive and negative argumentation. On the one hand, positively, the natural human propensity to exchange enables the different products of separate individuals, each motivated by the natural desire to self-betterment, to combine to establish the foundations of a distinctively human form of social organisation. And, moreover, without any need to rely on the exercise of any far-seeing human wisdom, this combination has brought about, as in he says in the Introduction to *The Wealth of Nations*, the transition from miserable poverty to civilised opulence. This, on the other hand, negatively, enables him to dismiss, firstly, the cultivation of Stoic *apatheia* and the virtue of austerity as 'unnatural'; to dismiss, secondly, the pretensions of mercantilists to use human wisdom to advance social interests as unnecessary and an unnatural interference; and to dismiss, thirdly, the politics of neo-Aristotelean civic moralists, as, when not irrelevant, being – as he says of sumptuary laws – the 'highest impertinence' (*WN* I, iii.36/346). Through his adoption of these two strands, Smith exemplifies the claim of Stuart Hampshire cited at the start of this chapter. Smith, by means of his science of human nature, has provided a 'definition of man' that, in identifying 'essential powers', is engaged simultaneously in a descriptive and a prescriptive exercise.

Postscript

This chapter has gone through many versions over several years. This version was crucially shaped as a keynote lecture for a Smith Conference in Athens in 2009 and subsequently at a meeting of the HINT group of the Politics Department at Glasgow. Distant forerunners were delivered in Essen (European Science Foundation Workshop), Santiago (University de los Andes), Tokyo (Keio University), Kobe (Kansei Gwakuin University) and Fukuoka (Kyushu University). I am grateful to all, and latterly Eric Schliesser, for their invitations, comments and contributions.

While Smith scholars have not by and large engaged with the content of this chapter, it has been picked up in writings on environmental sustainability and international relations, as part of the wider use of Smith. My book *Human Nature* (1986: now available via Amazon as an ebook produced by Endeavour Press), which I utilise here, continues to be cited.

Notes

1. I deliberately sidestep debate about whether the definite article here is appropriate (see Chapter 1). Peter Gay's (1967: 4) Wittgensteinian-inspired notion of a 'family' is, I think, still helpful since it aptly permits generalisation while allowing for dispute.
2. This is echoed by many – see Berry (1982: Ch. 1) for a survey.
3. Eric Schliesser suggests that Boyle might be implied (2008). For Hume's exposure to Boyle while a student, see Barfoot (1990: 151–90).
4. For a combative exploration of the relation between Smith and Newton, see Montes (2004: Ch. 5) and Schliesser (2005).
5. For an analysis, see, for example, Land (1977), and for a comparative account, see Chapter 16 (Berry 1974).
6. In this, of course, he is not alone. A notable predecessor is Condillac (with whose writings Smith was familiar). It was a central feature of Condillac's attempt to make Locke more consistent that he paid much attention to the growth of language. One interesting aspect is that in his own argument that 'abstraction' is a late development, he cites LaCondamine's reports (1745) as to the absence of abstract terms in the languages of America. (Condillac 1947–53: Pt 2 sect.1, Ch. 10).
7. Locke (1854: I, 531ff.) allows that for some of our ideas there is a 'natural correspondence and connexion one with another' but the thrust of this added chapter is captured in his comment that association is the 'foundation of the greatest, I had almost said of all, the errors in the world' (1854: I, 534, 540). For Hutcheson, see *PW* 39. Malebranche is a significant precursor.
8. Smith is not alone – for a discussion, see Berry (2000: Ch. 6).

9. Smith (2006: 16) argues that it is a facet of Smith's view of human nature that there is a propensity to seek explanations that underline the 'gradual extension of the corpus of human knowledge'.

10. While acknowledging a Humean root in the 'hopes and fears of human nature', Smith declares that this belief in an afterlife is also derived from its 'noblest and best principles', the love of virtue and abhorrence of vice (*TMS* III, 5.10/169). The place of 'nobility' in Smith is emphasised by Hanley (2009: Ch. 5). Pack (1995) has made links between the 'Astronomy' and Hume's *Natural History of Religion*.

11. Note that this passage is prefaced with a reference to 'pleasure and pain' (*LJB* 209/488). For comment on the economic dimension to this, see Skinner (1996: Ch. 3).

12. Locke (1854: I, 58). In Hume these instincts include the 'usual' such as 'appetites' like hunger and thirst plus 'passions' like attachment to offspring but also 'resentment' (*M* 3.40/ 96/*SBNM* 201).

13. This is a theme in Cropsey (2001).

14. See Hobbes' revealing subtitle to *Leviathan* as 'The Matter, Forme and Power of a Commonwealth', with its allusion to Aristotle's four causes while pointedly excluding 'final'.

15. For Aristotle there are 'natural desires' (*phusikais epithumiais*) but these are naturally (*kata phusin*) limited (1894: 1118b15–18) and it is a hallmark of the *akratic* (and even more so of the *akolastic*) that they pursue bodily pleasures excessively and *para . . . orthon logon* (1894: 1151a10–12), whereas the *enkratic* man acts from choice (*proairesis*) not from 'desire' (*epithumia*) (1894: 1111b15). There is a more general category word (*orexis*) for a goal-directed activity, which Martha Nussbaum (1986: 274) claims Aristotle introduced.

16. Locke (1854: 337, 388) defines 'desire' as 'an uneasiness of the mind for want of an absent good' and remarks that 'we are seldom at ease and free enough from the solicitation of our natural and adopted desires, but a constant succession of uneasinesses out of that stock, which natural wants or acquired habits have heaped up, take the will in their turns: and no sooner is one action dispatched . . . but another uneasiness is ready to set us to work'. For Hutcheson, see *PW* 81.

17. For example, Calkins and Werhane (1998: 50) claim that on a practical level Smith's and Aristotle's notion of human flourishing differ 'very little', although they immediately say that 'Smith's scheme lacks Aristotle's focus on the telos or universal and final end of happiness'. Hanley (2007: 20, 19), for his part, while charting similarities in Smith's and Aristotle's substantive accounts as well as

their conceptions of methods and ends of ethics, admits that there are 'crucial differences' between Smith and Aristotle that 'may be insurmountable'. Fleischacker (1999: 120, 140) considers Smith as close to Aristotle while yet being crucially different.

18. See Evensky (2005), Hanley (2009), Otteson (2002) and Young (1997) – though he forbears from pursuing theological resonances – while Alvey (2003), in keeping with the theme of his book, regards him as ambivalent. The extreme converse that Smith is covertly atheistic is upheld by Minowitz (1993). For a subtle account of a duality between theological presupposition and secular empiricism in Smith, see Tanaka (2003). (See Oslington (ed.) (2011) for a collection of essays sympathetic to Smith as a theologian; for a robust argument that Smith did not express his true non-religious sentiments – largely in deference to the piety of his mother – see Kennedy (2013).)

19. Compare the non-dissenting discussion of this passage in Pack and Schliesser (2006). They contextualise it in terms of Smith's critique of Hume's utilitarian account of justice. Of course, Smith's reference here to the 'purposes of Nature' reflects the view put forward by, for example, Murphy (1993: 193ff.) that all of Smith's work combines recourse to efficient and final causes. Murphy, however, misinterprets the 'invisible hand' as a benign providentialist concept. For an instructively deflating account of that notion, see Rothschild (2006: Ch. 5).

20. For a full exploration of poverty in Smith see Berry (2013: Ch. 3).

21. The (Baconian) improvement of society via reform of punishment was a prominent theme in the Enlightenment. Both Beccaria (1965: 9) and Bentham (1948: 125), to name perhaps the two best known, premise their agenda on what the former calls 'un freddo esaminatore della natura umana' of which the basis, as expressed by the latter, is that all humans enjoy pleasure and avoid pain, such that they are their 'sovereign masters'.

22. See, helpfully, Cremaschi (1989: 198).

23. See Berry (2006a: Ch. 11). See Hume's definition of 'moral causes' as 'all circumstances which are fitted to work on the mind as motives or reasons and which render a peculiar set of manners habitual to us' (E-NC 198).

24. For an argument for a strongly egalitarian strain in Smith, see Fleischacker (2004; also 2013).

25. Inasmuch as men are always concerned to be praiseworthy, then this anxiety will remain. Smith, indeed, professed that 'man is an anxious animal' (LJB 231/497). While it is true that Smith does declare the

'natural and usual' state of mind to be 'tranquillity' (wherein lies happiness) (*TMS* III, 3.30/146) and the 'prudent man' will have 'no anxiety to change so comfortable a situation' (*TMS* VI, 1.12/215), in no way can this individual be presumed to be in a 'desire-less' state; indeed, we might impute that he averse to novelty and adventures.

26. For a discussion of this, see Forman-Barzilai (2007) and, now more fully, Forman-Barzilai (2010).

27. See Davidson (1984), Williams (2004: Ch. 3).

28. For a parallel argument regarding Hume, see Chapter 12 (Berry 2007). See, more generally, Smith (1995).

21

Adam Smith on Liberty 'in our present sense of the word'

[A] The important privileges above mentioned, that they might give away their own daughters in marriage, that their children should succeed to them, and that they might dispose of their own effects by will, were generally bestowed upon the burghers of the town to whom it was given. Whether such privileges had before been usually granted along with the freedom of trade to particular burghers, as individuals, I know not. I reckon it not improbable that they were, though I cannot produce any direct evidence of it. But however this may have been, the principal attributes of villanage and slavery being thus taken away from them, they now, at least, became really free in our present sense of the word Freedom.

[B] Nor was this all. They were generally at the same time erected into a commonalty or corporation, with the privilege of having magistrates and a town council of their own, of making by-laws for their own government, of building walls for their own defence, and of reducing all their inhabitants under a sort of military discipline by obliging them to watch and ward, that is, as anciently understood, to guard and defend those walls against all attacks and surprises by night as well as by day. In England they were generally exempted from suit to the hundred and county courts; and all such pleas as should arise among them, the pleas of the crown excepted, were left to the decision of their own magistrates. In other countries much greater and more extensive jurisdictions were frequently granted to them.

[C] It might, probably, be necessary to grant to such towns as were admitted to farm their own revenues some sort of compulsive jurisdiction to oblige their own citizens to make payment. In those disorderly times it might have been extremely inconvenient to have left them to seek this sort of justice from any other tribunal. But it must seem extraordinary that the sovereigns of all the different countries of Europe should have exchanged in this manner for a rent certain, never more to be augmented, that branch of the revenue which was, perhaps, of all others the most likely to be improved by the natural course of things, without either expence or attention of their own: and that they should, besides, have in this manner voluntarily erected a sort of independent republic in the heart of their own dominions.

The Wealth of Nations III, iii.4–6

Adam Smith, towards the middle of *The Wealth of Nations*, refers to freedom 'in our present sense of the word' (*WN* III, iii.5/400). In this chapter I explore what this self-consciousness reveals about Smith's understanding of his own time or, more grandly, of modernity. The reference itself implies not only that freedom can have different 'senses', or be understood differently, but also that this difference is temporal. More pointedly, the difference between modern freedom/liberty and earlier expressions is not a simple matter of chronology but has the further message that the contemporary sense is superior. A clue to where that superiority lies can be found in his lectures at Glasgow where he is recorded as professing that 'opulence and freedom' were the 'two greatest blessings men can possess' (*LJA* ii 111/185). It is in the implications of this linkage between these two blessings that indicates the distinctive, and superior, quality of modern liberty. Modern freedom goes hand in hand with opulence, whereas in pre-modern societies opulence was either identified as a threat or its expression was thwarted to societal disadvantage. Given Smith's argument in this particular passage, I here concentrate on the latter expression.[1]

I

Before looking at the wider context in which Smith makes the claim about 'our present sense' of freedom, I shall examine in some detail the three paragraphs above (for convenience, I have labelled them A, B and C). This examination needs to be prefaced with a word of caution: my argument is not straightforward. I will explicate what I judge to be implicit in Smith's position. Since Smith himself does not engage in any explication, my own endeavour is an imputation but, I think, consonant with the tenor (and polemical dimension) of Smith's overall argument. While the 'destination' may be familiar, the particular 'route' to it – my concern here – has not been subject to any extensive analysis.

The paragraphs in question appear in Book III in a chapter entitled 'Of the Rise and Progress of Cities after the Fall of the Roman Empire'. Paragraph A identifies three 'privileges': giving daughters away in marriage, having children 'succeed to' parental goods, and disposing of property ('effects') by will (cf, *WN* III, iii.1/397). Burghers, that is, town-dwellers, enjoyed these privileges in late medieval/early-modern Europe. In contrast to the leisured independent citizens of the 'antient republicks', these town-dwellers were 'chiefly tradesmen and mechanics'. Initially their status was servile but subsequently, as evidenced by 'antient charters', they were granted the aforementioned privileges either by the king or a 'great lord'. It is because these were granted that they are properly termed 'privileges', that is, derogations from the governance of some authority; a burgher no longer had to seek permission for his daughter to marry or for inheritance and bequests. It was because the effect of these privileges was to remove the 'principal attributes of villanage and slavery' that these individuals 'became really free in our present sense of the word'.[2] Given that the content of these privileges pertain to familial/property relations, they may be reasonably labelled exemplifications of private liberty, encompassing a sphere of life within which there is no requirement to obtain external permission before acting.

Paragraph B identifies further privileges. These burghers could form themselves into a 'corporation' with the privilege of having their own town council and magistrates who could make by-laws for their own government, including the imposition of 'a sort of military discipline' (*WN* III, iii.6/401). These we can reasonably label exemplifications of civic (or political) liberty. But I contend that there is a significant difference between these two exemplifications, between, that is, private and civic liberty. To anticipate, Smith widens the first category while he develops an argument that displaces the initial significance of the latter. My explication treats as indicative (nothing more) of Smith's overall argument the fact that he interposes the self-conscious reference to 'our present sense of the word Freedom' at the end of paragraph A, identifying private liberty and before paragraph B, which outlines civic liberty. However, first, the wider context of his chapter (the rise of cities) needs to be addressed.

The granting of these privileges to burghers was part of a gradual process but it was not uniform, since it produced different outcomes in Switzerland and Italy from those in France or England, where sovereign authority was never entirely lost (*WN*

III, iii.10–11/404–5). The process itself is embedded in Smith's broader narrative wherein he accounts for the development of 'order and good government' as the 'great proprietors' bartered away their power for 'the childish, the meanest and the most sordid of all vanities' (*WN* III, iv.10/419). The unintended consequence of this process – which he terms a 'revolution' (*WN* III, iv.17/422) – was the establishment of regular government and the rule of law. These are the benchmarks of modern liberty. They provide the framework for a 'properly commercial society', one based on exchange wherein everyone 'becomes in some measure a merchant' (*WN* I, iv.1/37) and one where a 'universal opulence . . . extends itself to the lowest ranks of the people' (*WN* I, i.10/22).

II

This modern liberty is superior to that of slave-owning ancient republics but – and this is central to the argument of this chapter – it is also superior to the 'civic liberty' of the late medieval/ early-modern European city-states or republics. To appreciate why this is the case, the burghers' privileges need to be further examined. As stated above, the privileges identified in paragraph A pertain to familial life (and the associated disposal of property). While, as initially depicted, these reflect the circumstances of a male head of a household, they in principle mark the discretionary liberty that individuals have to order their own affairs. It is the discretion here (the freedom from the need for external approval) that is the vital element. This becomes especially significant in a modern, commercial society because this private liberty has expanded to be a key component not only of that society's operation but also of its vindication. This progressive development is embodied in a number of Smith's best-known pronouncements. Hence, in his invocation of 'the obvious and simple system of natural liberty', he declares that 'everyman, as long as he does not violate the laws of justice is left perfectly free to pursue his own interest his own way'. This declaration prefaces his enumeration of the duties of government and it is in this context that Smith avers that the government is 'completely discharged from a duty . . . of superintending the industry of private people and of directing it towards the employments most suitable to the interest of society' (*WN* IV, ix.51/687). In line with this, it is a hallmark of this 'perfect', modern, liberty that everyone should be free to choose (and change) their occupation as they themselves deem advantageous (*WN* I, x.a.1/116, I.vii.6/73).

I will return to that context when I consider the civic privileges initially enjoyed by burghers. Here I want to note how it applies to private liberty because the principle of government non-involvement has a wider remit than commerce ('industry'). This is perhaps most apparent in Smith's scornful dismissal of sumptuary laws. He condemns this legislation for exhibiting 'the highest impertinence and presumption' as it 'pretend[s] to watch over the economy of private people and to restrain their expense' (*WN* II, iii.36/346).[3] These laws have been a persistent feature of social experience. They were developed iteratively by the Romans, where the focus was to address corruption (*ambitu*), typically by restricting the cost of banquets, and all medieval and early-modern societies in Europe (and beyond)[4] went into great detail to regulate apparel, especially of women. Importantly, the free cities of early-modern Europe were far from exempt. Smith himself refers in this general context to Italy and Switzerland. We know that Genoa, for example, issued eighteen sumptuary laws in the fifteenth century, and was not exceptional (Florence issued over thirty-three laws in the fourteenth century and Bologna issued eighty between the thirteenth and sixteenth centuries).[5] Swiss evidence is less substantial but Zurich, Bern and Basel all passed sumptuary legislation, which persisted into the eighteenth century. While a moralistic indictment of 'luxury' was a definite factor, the need to maintain or reinforce status differentials was perhaps the major concern, and a protectionist or 'mercantilist' element started to feature from the mid-fifteenth century (see Hughes (1983: 76) and Harte (1976: 138)).

Smith's dismissal of the aptness and legitimacy of sumptuary legislation is a clear marker of his conception of modernity. As implied by the notion of natural liberty, this conception encompasses a principle of equality. The principle is illustrated by his repeated example of the philosopher and a 'common street porter' to represent the 'most dissimilar characters' (*WN* I, ii.4/28–9; *LJA* iv.47/348; *ED* 26/572). While in his 1762–3 *Lectures* this dissimilarity is simply stated not to be an 'original difference', in the 1766 version (*LJB* 219/492) (as well as in two other citations in the *Early Draft* and in *The Wealth of Nations*) he is more specific, stating that it derives 'not so much from nature as from habit, custom and education'. Indeed, Smith reinforces this impact; the 'genius' that, in their maturity, distinguishes 'men of different professions' is 'not so much upon many occasions the cause as the effect of the division of labour'. Smith's strong implicitly egalitarian argument here (see Fleischacker 2013) consolidates his view that it is improper to use the law to maintain some form of social hierarchy. While sumptuary law gives some social groups freedom to dress in certain way, it denies that freedom to others; modern liberty, in contrast, is enjoyed by all, and what to wear (including 'style', fabric and ornamentation) is a matter of personal preference and means.

It is not that wanting to choose one's clothing (or diet or furnishings) is modern but that its expression in pre-modern eras is regulated. The tension here between the desire and its limitless expression in the form of the 'conveniencies and ornaments of building, dress, equipage [etc.]' (WN I, xi.c.7/181) is what made sumptuary legislation so unstable. In the Moral Sentiments Smith says the rich glory in their wealth because it 'naturally' draws upon them 'the attention of the world' (TMS I, iii.2.1/51). Others desire the social attention and the lifestyles of the rich and seek to emulate them and it is this sought-for emulation that produces the disruption to settled hierarchy that sumptuary laws were designed to suppress. But, as fashion (that is, the dress, etc. of those of 'high rank') exemplifies par excellence, this interaction cannot be effectively legislated against. Fashion is not a matter of law but of social perception and interaction. Modern liberty implicitly recognises this by confining law to matters of justice, not personal choice/preference/taste (see Smith 2013: 513).

This social process of emulation and the production of rank distinctions are anchored by Smith in human nature (the disposition of mankind) (see Chapter 20). One key reason for the failure of sumptuary laws is that they run counter to that disposition.[6] Smith's celebrated version of this trait of human nature is his attribution to everyone of a natural desire, from the womb to the grave, to better their condition (WN II, iii.28/341); he had used this same phrase in the Moral Sentiments in the context of rank distinctions (TMS I, iii.2.1/50). While sumptuary legislation attempted to control, thwart or neuter this desire, modern liberty allows it, within the constraints of justice, to express itself (I will return to that constraint). This expression finds its most common outlet in the desire of 'the greater part of men' to augment their 'fortune' and this is the source of public and private 'opulence' (WN II, iii.31/343).

Smith does acknowledge that modern liberty – in the guise of order, good government and security – originated in these free cities. The inhabitants were differentially able to better their condition. This betterment went beyond the acquisition of necessities to the acquisition of 'the conveniencies and elegancies of life' (*WN* III, iii.12/405; cf. *LJB* 209/488). But, and this reveals the pre-modern tenor of these civic privileges, it was precisely these 'elegancies' that were the subject of their sumptuary legislation. These laws indicate that the diffusion of this natural desire for betterment was constrained by these privileges, which, we can recall, included issuing by-laws, of which ordinances as to who could wear what were a persistent feature.[7] It was not until the 'revolution' established (especially in England) sufficient security and uniformity of circumstances that the broad populace was able to interact commercially – as, indeed, 'everyman became in some sense a merchant'.

III

From this vantage point we can begin to see how Smith's argument results in him overturning the political privileges originally granted to the burgher. The argument needs to be developed with care. The natural bent that produces opulence, as a consequence of the discretionary private liberty of individuals to seek their own fortune, also expresses itself to opposite effect in the conduct of 'politics'. As a first step, we return to Smith's account of the burghers' political privileges in paragraph B. The key here is his reference to the burghers making their own by-laws and engaging in military matters. Smith is here recognising the well-established association between cities, freedom and republics. While the roots of this association lie in Aristotle's (1978: 1279a20) declaration that the *polis* is 'a community of free men', it had a renaissance in the Italian cities.

At its heart is an idea of liberty as self-governance. Initially articulated by jurists, such as Baldus de Ubaldis and his teacher Bartolus of Sassoferrato, it was in making a case for the de facto independence of Italian cities from imperial rule that the link between liberty and self-government was forged.[8] Leonardo Bruni (1978: 170), for example, declared in his *Laudatio Florentinae Urbis* (early fifteenth century) that liberty flourished in Florence because what concerned many was decided by the action of the whole citizen body in accordance with the law. However, the most influential exponent of this argument was Machiavelli. He announces at the beginning of the *Discorsi* that he will deal only with those cities that are free from external rule and that govern themselves as they see fit.[9] Machiavelli's model (D I, 6/Op 70) was the early years of the Roman Republic as depicted by Livy. The crux is that citizens are active; they make law, they do not merely obey it. This activity, by encompassing contestation (paradigmatically between the plebians and the patricians), prevented one side dominating and thus oppressing the other and in this way kept liberty and the public good alive (D I, 4/Op 65). The activity also manifested itself in the duty to defend this liberty. He singled out the Swiss for being especially praiseworthy in this respect; indeed, they are *armatissimi e liberissimi* (P 12/Op 28; cf. D II, 10/Op 168; Op 295/AG). For Machiavelli, both the military and political dimensions of *libertà* required *virtù*. This was both an individual quality of audacity and initiative (P 25/Op 52) and a civic quality of commitment to the public good (as exemplified by the citizens of the 'German' republics who pay their due taxes willingly and who still exhibit the *antica bontà* of early Rome (D I, 55/Op 132)).

Alongside this account of the meaning of citizenship was an urgent concern with what threatened or corrupted it. As typically and influentially identified by Livy (1919: I paras 11–12), the Roman republic lost its greatness when riches, and with them avarice and a craving for luxury and licence, were imported. The implicit causality was that these imports promoted or facilitated the pursuit of private interests to the detriment of the public good. That subversion generically was the threat. An enduring manifestation of this threat was the effects of opulence or luxury; as tersely put by Machiavelli, princes who think of luxury (*delicatezze*) more than arms (*arme*) lose their state (*lo stato*) (P 14/Op 32). To live luxuriously is to wallow in self-indulgence. Men who live a life of luxury become effeminate. In an established idiom, they become 'soft', unable to endure hardship and act in a 'manly' fashion, where that means risking death and acting courageously; the virtues of a citizen were literally those expressive of virility (*virtù*).

A society where luxury is established will devote itself to private ends and men will be unwilling to act for the public good, including, crucially, in willingness to fight.[10] This society, it follows, will be militarily weak – a nation of cowards that will easily succumb. The only way a luxurious, soft nation could meet its military commitments was by hiring others to play that role. Hence there arose an important negative association between luxury, wealth (commerce) and mercenary armies. Machiavelli was emphatic that an army of citizens (a militia) was superior to one that fought for money (P 12/Op 27; cf. D I, 43/Op 118). Machiavelli also adumbrated what became a major preoccupation of later republicans when, in his *Arte della Guerra*, he warned against militia commanders having too much authority (*AG/Op 283*). The concern was that therein potentially lurked a threat to liberty. In later thinkers, especially in late seventeenth-century England, this was crystallised in the threat posed by the presence of standing armies. The nature of the threat is captured in the title of John Trenchard's influential pamphlet: 'A standing army is inconsistent with a free government' (1697). Such an army, paid for by the rulers, could be used not just to defend the 'state' but to be an 'instrument of tyranny'.[11]

It is these preoccupations with the virtues of active citizenship and militias and the corresponding distrust of luxury and opulence (that also stimulated sumptuary legislation) that Smith deems prejudicial to modern liberty. Those civic privileges originally granted to 'free cities' are no longer apt; modern liberty neither requires active citizenship nor participation in a militia. He develops an alternative positive argument, at the heart of which lies his classroom profession that 'opulence' is a 'blessing'. As we will observe later, the civic liberties of the burghers inhibit the diffusion and enjoyment of that blessing.

Opulence is produced by extensive division of labour and that extensiveness depends on the size of the market and that, in turn, relies on the confidence that follows from the establishment of the rule of law. This is the key attribute of 'order and good government' but in the free cities this is limited. Not only is their market constrained but, as we shall see, its operation is restricted.[12] For a commercial society, and hence universal opulence, to spread there had to be expansion and relaxation. How that occurred is part of the larger narrative that Smith goes on to provide in Book III of *The Wealth of Nations*. Here I want to pick out from that narrative how it bears on military organisation, a responsibility that, as we have seen, Smith attributes to the burghers.

IV

For Smith, the citizen militia is no longer needed as a bulwark of liberty. As he is reported as professing in his Glasgow classroom, militias are outmoded; standing armies 'must be introduced' (*LJB* 337/543). In a society where everyone participates in exchange (is in some sense a merchant), there is no incongruity in being paid to be a soldier. In 'modern armies', where artillery, itself the product of specialisation and technological advance, is a decisive factor, what matters is 'regularity, order and prompt obedience to command' (*WN* V, i.a.22/ 699). Going by these criteria, a standing army is superior to a militia. But in the present context two further features – one positive, one negative – are telling.

Negatively, he argues that if an 'industrious and wealthy nation' were to 'enforce the practice of military exercises', then it would require 'a very vigorous police' in the face of the 'interest, genius and inclinations of the people' (*WN* V, i.a.17/698; cf. *LJA* iv.83/231). And in a later context he refers again to the 'continual and painful attention of government' that in a modern society would be needed to maintain a militia (*WN* V, i.f.60/787). The clear implication is that this would be seen as an imposition, a resented restriction on individuals' personal liberty and the opulence-creating self-determined betterment of their circumstances. Positively, he claims that standing armies can 'in some cases be favourable to liberty'.[13] Here Smith is openly contesting the arguments of 'men of republican principles' or 'militia-men' for whom standing armies, he says, have been regarded as 'dangerous to liberty'. These 'cases' include toleration of private activity even when that 'approaches to licentiousness'. Again, this point is made in direct contrast to the 'troublesome jealousy' in (some) 'modern republicks' as they 'watch over the minutest actions and to be at all times ready to disturb the peace of every citizen' (*WN* V, i.a.41/706–7). [14]

That a modern commercial society has no need to call upon its citizens for military purposes – albeit that the complete atrophy of 'martial virtues' is to be guarded against (cf. *WN* V, i.f.50/782, V, i.f.60/787) – reflects Smith's view that the active citizenship enjoined by republicans, and seemingly exercised by the burghers, is no longer apt. His position is captured in the *Moral Sentiments* in a passage added to the sixth edition, that is, subsequent to *The Wealth of Nations*. In this passage Smith observes that the state is divided into different orders but that they are all subordinate to it. Although any particular order (he continues) may seek privileges, it is acknowledged by all that, from the perspective of the paramount importance of the 'prosperity and preservation of the state', it would be unjust to grant any such privileges (*TMS* VI, ii.2.10/231). As is true of the *Moral Sentiments* as a whole, it is the modern state (a commercial society) that is here assumed.

This assumption is evident in the next paragraph when Smith proceeds to characterise modern citizenship:

> He is not a citizen who is not disposed to respect the laws and to obey the civil magistrate; and he is certainly not a good citizen who does not wish to promote . . . the welfare of the whole society of his fellow citizens. In peaceable and quiet times [he goes on] these two principles coincide . . . the support of the established government seems evidently the best expedient for maintaining the safe, respectable and happy situation of our fellow citizens. (*TMS* VI, ii.2.11/ 231)

These requisite 'times' are, as a general rule, provided by a commercial society. To associate commerce with 'peace and quiet'[15] and to associate further the welfare of society with the pursuit of commerce within the framework of law-abidingness represents a recalibration of the virtues, including pre-eminently those classically (anciently) associated with the exercise of citizenship. Here, again, I merely highlight two aspects of recalibration.[16]

The first picks up the passing references to justice already made. A system of justice is an impersonal abstract order that operates through general rules, although it requires some personal commitment to that operation. Smith makes the strong claim that justice is the main pillar that upholds the whole social edifice (*TMS* II, ii.3.3/86). While this might be universally true, its expression has improved. In the conclusion of the *Moral Sentiments* he explicitly contrasts the circumstances where the 'rudeness and barbarism of the people' make the system of justice irregular to the circumstances of those in 'more civilized nations' where the 'natural sentiments of justice' arrive at 'accuracy and precision' (*TMS* VII, iv.37/341). Justice, that is to say, becomes 'regular'.

Since I have discussed this at length elsewhere (Berry 1997: 130–5; 2013: Ch. 4 and in Chapter 18 in this volume), I will here merely highlight the modernity of his view. It is only in 'commercial countries' that 'a regular administration of justice' or the rule of law is found. Not only does this protect 'the meanest man in the

state' (*TMS* VI, ii.i.13/223) but it also rules out discriminatory legislation, exemplified in sumptuary laws. Smith's modernity is also
detectable in his judgement that justice is a strict and a negative
virtue. It is strict because it is precise and accurate, admitting of
no exceptions (*TMS* III, 6.10/175). Exceptions would undermine
the 'edifice' that relies on the secure predictability of enforced rules
that enables commerce to flourish. The natural liberty to pursue
one's own interest occurs in the 'space' created by the observance
of justice and the restraints that observance imposes upon all
equally.

Justice requires forbearance; its rules can be adhered to by not
hurting another and by 'sitting still and doing nothing' (*TMS* II,
ii.1.9/82). This also describes the prudent man, who is steady in
his industry and frugality, and who does his duty and does not
meddle in other people's affairs. He is content for 'public business'
to be well managed by others to save him the trouble and 'glory'
holds no attraction (*TMS* VI, i.13/215–16). From that perspective,
it is an outmoded notion of the civic republicans that political
virtue requires action on the public stage (or the battlefield). Yet
commercial society is not lacking in virtue. The premium to act
justly in a commercial society, the concern 'not to hurt our neigh-
bour', constitutes the character of a 'perfectly innocent and just
man'. And such a character, he continues, can 'scarce ever fail to
be accompanied with many other virtues, with great feeling for
other people, with great humanity and great benevolence' (*TMS*
VI, ii.Intro 2/218).

The implications of Smith's use of 'humanity' here are the second
aspect of his recalibration that I want to highlight. His treatment
of humanity is indicative of his approach to the cardinal virtue of
courage. He does not include courage in his dedicated section on
virtue in the *Moral Sentiments* but the omission of this definitionally masculine virtue is not surprising. Originally the burghers did
need to exhibit Machievellian *virtù*, did need to be able to defend
themselves and their city, and the cultivation and the maintenance
of that ability constituted an important part of their 'liberty'. But
in the commercial era of 'peace and quiet' this facet of liberty loses
its purpose and cannot be seen as a key element of freedom 'in our
present sense'.

Smith does not question that command of fear is virtuous and,
as we have already noted, does refer to the decline in 'martial
virtue' as a damaging effect of the division of labour. He also

alludes to the possibility that civilised sensitivity is 'sometimes' at the cost of a 'masculine firmness of character'. But, more often, that 'cost' is offset by the greater diffusion of humanity. Smith, in effect, replaces courage with humanity – sensitivity to others. In contrast to the masculinity of courage, Smith defines humanity as 'the virtue of a woman'. Humanity, as a 'soft and gentle' feminine virtue, is appropriate to the peaceable, modern, commercial world. The contrast is reinforced by Smith's judgement that the bedrock commercial virtue of justice does not necessarily harmonise with that of courage because 'the most intrepid valour may be employed in the cause of the greatest injustice'; it may even be 'excessively dangerous'. Humanity, like justice, is a companion to 'probity and punctuality', which Smith regards as 'the principal virtues of a commercial nation'.

V

While the importance that courage held for the burghers has diminished, it can reasonably be supposed that probity and punctuality would have had their place in their environment and that these traits have carried through. Nevertheless, my argument requires that there be a difference such that the burghers do not exemplify freedom in our present sense of the word.

The crucial difference lies in the consequences attending the burghers' civic liberty. In line with Smith's depiction of the crafty insidiousness of 'politicians' (WN IV, ii.39/468), these burghers used their political privilege to govern themselves to uphold their economic 'rights'. Although Smith does not openly make the connection, in practice, in many of these towns the 'tradesmen and mechanics' became (selectively) the guild-masters, or, at least, those who attained the role of 'citizen' in an executive and legislator capacity were the leaders of branches of business or trade.[17]

This fusion of roles feeds into a major Smithian theme. The burghers, he declares, had an interest in 'restraining free competition'. It is the 'natural genius' of corporations to confine competition and subject trade to 'many burdensome regulations' (WN V, i.e.7/734). Contrary to Smith's delineation of the appropriate duties of (modern) government, these merchant/burghers 'superintended' industry. They imposed regulations that kept the market understocked and the branches of trade all agreed to buy from one another. This deliberate reduction of competition resulted in more expensive goods for consumers and had the added advantage that when dealing outside the city they were 'all great gainers' (*WN* II, x.c.17–18/140–1). In like vein they enacted by-laws to restrain the choice and flexibility of employment. They enforced regulations governing apprenticeships in order to reduce competition to the benefit of themselves as masters, but the outcome of this restriction was detrimental to the 'the publick' (*WN* II, x.c.6, 16/136, 140). Moreover, it was not as if this resulted in products superior to those produced by the piece-paid journeyman (*WN* II, x.c.14/139). We can add that the 'protectionist' element in sumptuary legislation was to restrict external competition in fabrics, jewellery and the like (in Genoa, for example, in the fifteenth century it was forbidden to import for resale any silk manufactured abroad).[18]

Smith, as is well known, vehemently opposed such anticompetitive practices. The source of these is the situation where politicians, who have a vested interest in maintaining restrictions, superintend economic activity. This not only works against public opulence but it is also unjust because it favours some over others (*WN* IV, viii.30/654). The privileges of the burghers, in their guise as guild-masters, privileged producers over consumers, when properly, according to Smith, the interest of the producer should be to promote that of the consumer (*WN* IV, viii.49/660).

The combination of political privilege and economic leadership in these burghs results in 'encroachments upon natural liberty' (*WN* IV, ii.42/470). This signals implicitly the difference between the 'private/economic' liberty in the 'present sense of the word' and civic liberty. Whereas the former developed or expanded to produce opulence to universal not partial benefit, civic liberty developed to produce 'a great hurt to the community' (*LJA* ii.35/84). Smith allows that originally the civic privileges were 'very convenient and *almost* necessary' but 'now' they are 'detrimentall to the community' (*LJA* ii.39/85; my emphasis; cf. ii.51/90, vi.88/363; *LJB* 175/472, 306/529). This reiterated attention to temporality – that however good or necessary possessing these privileges was at their formation, that no longer obtains – is a key plank in my argument that they are inconsistent with the 'present' understanding of liberty.

Historically, the 'great advantage which modern times have over antient' is the separation and independence of the judiciary (*LRBL* ii.203/176). This decisive, albeit accidental, development enabled the exact administration of justice to be established, which ensures, in principle, the impartiality that offers the security that enables opulence-generating activity to be sustained (*WN* V, i.b.25/723). The relevant point in the current context is that it is this separation of the judiciary that makes it 'scarce possible' that justice can be sacrificed (even without any corrupt intent) to 'what is vulgarly called politics' (*WN* V, i.b.25/723). But Smith is far from optimistic that even in a commercial society 'politics' will not intrude. For example, he remarks about his own scheme to deal with the crisis in the American colonies that it was fated to be a 'Utopia' because it ran counter to the 'private interests of many powerful individuals' (*WN* IV, ii.3/471; cf. V, iii.68/ 934).[19] This is representative of a wider truth; 'private interests' generally trump (they are 'unconquerable') those of the public. Smith here explicitly cites 'master manufacturers' who unanimously and zealously 'set themselves against every law that is likely to increase their rivals in the home market' (*WN* IV, ii.3/471).

If this is tendentiously true even where the law is supposedly independent, then in the era of mercantile 'free' cities where the merchants are the legislators (they possess the privilege of civic liberty) it obtains all the more forcefully. Modern liberty can be a source of countervailing power. Smith holds out some hope, at least, that the effort of individual self-betterment can surmount the 'impertinent obstructions with which the folly of human laws too often incumbers its operations' (*WN* IV, v.b.43/540; cf. *WN* II, iii.36/345). These efforts, as we have seen, will only be successful when there is confidence in the justice system.

VI

In sum, for Smith, the outcome of the privileges of the corporations as they developed to control who could buy or sell was to diminish 'public opulence' (*LJB* 232/498). In contrast, the outcome of the privileges of the private disposal of property has been the generation of opulence. Hence civic liberty cannot be 'freedom in our present sense of the word'. Liberty as now understood is the companion of opulence, as both embody the 'greatest blessing' that humans can possess. Of course, this is not uncontentious. For those whose chief aim is (say) anti-colonialism, freedom may be more important than opulence, while for those who seek ordered economic growth in order to induce opulence, liberty may need to be directed.

One final observation is that the 'our' in the key quotation is an act of complicity. Those excluded may take a different view, of which there are many, from non-domination to self-realisation to exercising capabilities and so on. But that is for another chapter.

Postscript

This chapter is an expanded version of a lecture I gave at a Smith Conference in Palermo in 2017; my thanks go to Fabrizio Simon for the invitation. An earlier version was given as a seminar paper at Okayama University. I am extremely grateful to Satoshi Niimura for the invitation and his comments. Its genesis lies in the curiosity that is a major motivation in my work, and I referred merely in passing to this passage in the course of a lecture on liberalism given at a small conference in Łodz in 1996. This short derivative piece was published in Berry (1998; and by chance in a Chinese translation 2002).

Notes

1. I have discussed the former elsewhere; see, for example, Berry (2013: Ch. 4) and Chapter 18 in this volume.
2. The context of Smith's reference to the blessings of opulence and freedom in *LJ* is slavery.
3. Hume is equally dismissive of such legislation (*HE* I, 535; cf. *HE* II, 231, 602). For him government has 'no other object or purpose but the distribution of justice' (E-OG 37). He also self-consciously refers to 'new' liberty (*HE* II, 602; *HE* III, 99) and labels it a 'revolution' (*HE* II, 603). I discuss Hume's version in Chapter 11. For a subtle account of 'modern liberty' in Smith and Hume, though from a different perspective than here, see Castiglione (2000).
4. This was not just a Western phenomenon but a characteristic also of Japan and China. See, for example, the 1,587 Ming Statutes, which, according to Craig Clunas (2004: 151), went into greater detail than any European legislation, and the Tokugawa era in Japan, which has been similarly described as the 'strictest ever seen' (Hurlock 1962).
5. Cf. Killerby (2000: 28) and Muzzarelli (2009: 609). For general discussion, see Hunt (1996). Muzzarelli and Campanini (2003) have edited a collection of studies of various national laws and there are, in addition, a number of studies of particular 'national' ordinances.
6. Compare Hume's phrase in 'Of Commerce', with reference to the

'restrictions on equipage and tables' that they run counter to the 'natural bent of the mind' (E-Com 263).

7. See Vincent (1969: 45) for explicit reference to the wives of guild members in Zurich in 1488 being permitted to wear silk when other women of a lower social status were prohibited from doing so. The Venetians instituted in 1514 a permanent *Magistrato alle Pompe* to ensure compliance with its sumptuary legislation (Fortini Brown 2004: 151). Not, of course, that these ordinance were the prerogative of republics. See, for example, the Act of Apparel of Edward III in 1363 (37 Edw III), which identified seven ranks, each with specific restrictions on what each rank could legally wear.

8. See, for example, Skinner (1978: I, 7). Baldus and Bartolus also decisively developed the idea of 'corporation' – the city-state as a *persona ficta* (as immortal) in terms of which a general assembly of mortals exercised governance; see, for a good brief treatment, Canning (1980). Note in the context of this chapter (paragraph B) Smith's reference to the burghers 'being erected into a commonality or corporation' (*WN* III.iii.6/400). Smith's own sources were Thomas Madox (1725) and Robert Brady (1711). While both of these books deal with English towns, they also refer not only to Scottish burghs but also to the experience in France and elsewhere in Europe.

9. I insert the following abbreviations of Machiavelli's works in the text: AG: *Arte della Guerra*; D: *Discorsi sopra la prima Deca di Tito Livio*, cited by book, chapter; P: *Il Principe*, cited by chapter. Op: *Tutte le Opere* (1998), cited by page. Hence here, D I, 2/Op 60.

10. I here summarise aspects of my argument in Berry (1994), partially reprised in Berry (2011: 16) on which this paragraph draws.

11. Trenchard (1698: 30). See also, for example, Henry Neville in 1681 (1969: 171, 180); Andrew Fletcher in 1698 (1979: 10/11). Smith owned a copy of Fletcher's pamphlet – see Mizuta (2000). For general context, see Schwoerer (1974).

12. The fact that Venice and Genoa, for example, were large-scale trading republics with colonies is not the issue here. It is their own self-governance, and its scale, that is pertinent. The population of Venice at the end of the fifteenth century was about 150,000, that of Britain in the early eighteenth century was about 7 million.

13. Typically, Smith qualifies this. It only applies in those circumstances where the chief officers in the army are drawn from the 'principal nobility and gentry', who have, in consequence, the 'greatest interest in the support of the civil authority' (*WN* V.i.a.41/706).

14. Notwithstanding these explicit remarks, Smith has been read

(unpersuasively to my mind) as sympathetic to 'republicanism'. For one of the more sensitive of such readings, see Montes (2009: 328). See Berry (2013) for further discussion; I have drawn on this in the preceding paragraphs.

15. This echoes Montesquieu (1961: II, 8), but the doctrine of *doux commerce* – as Albert Hirschman (1977: 60) termed it – was commonplace.

16. See, further, Chapter 19. I have covered further aspects in Berry (forthcoming a).

17. See Black (1984: 6) who, in his overview, remarks that 'in the thirteenth and fourteenth centuries craft-guilds assumed political power in a great number of towns'. See also Waley and Dean (2010: 157) on the political activity of guilds in Italy, and Vincent (1969: 2, 7) on the place of guilds in the city councils of Zurich and Basel, referring to the governance of these cities as a 'business aristocracy'. Smith's chief authorities also document the links between guilds and civic governance. Brady (1711: 20; cf. 23) records that the guilds comprised the wealthy who 'Superintended and Governed' the 'meaner sort of Burgesses', while Madox (1725: 29–30) records that 'being gildated and being corporated' are terms of the same import and that the position of alderman as the 'governor in a Secular Gild' came to refer to 'the Chief officer in a gildated City or Town'.

18. Killerby (2002: 49). That sumptuary laws atrophied in England before elsewhere in Europe is testament to the growth and entrenchment of commercial society as a definitive feature of a 'society' attendant upon the uniformity of jurisdiction. By contrast, in the still localised dispersed sites of power in the Italian peninsula, sumptuary laws persisted into the eighteenth century. Smith refers to restrictions on trade imposed by the Italian cities (*WN* III.iii.19/408).

19. See Muller (1995: 79), who judges that *The Wealth of Nations* contains a compendium of examples of how individuals and groups attempt to promote their interests at the expense of the public.

Bibliography

Cited Works by Christopher J. Berry

(1973a) 'James Dunbar and Ideas of Sociality in Eighteenth-Century Scotland', *Il Pensiero Politico*, 6: 188–201.

(1973b) 'Approaches to the Origin of Metaphor in the Eighteenth Century', *Neuphilologische Mitteilungen*, 74: 690–713.

(1974a) 'Adam Smith's "Considerations" on Language', *Journal of the History of Ideas*, 35: 130–8.

(1974b) 'James Dunbar and the American War of Independence', *Aberdeen University Review*, 45: 255–66.

(1974c) '"Climate" in the Eighteenth Century', *Texas Studies in Literature and Language*, 16: 281–92.

(1977a) 'On the Meaning of Progress and Providence in the Fourth Century AD', *Heythrop Journal*, 18: 257–70.

(1977b) 'From Hume to Hegel: the Case of the Social Contract', *Journal of the History of Ideas*, 38: 691–703.

(1980) 'Property and Possession: Two Replies to Locke', in J. Pennock and J. Chapman (eds), *Property* (*Nomos* XXII), New York: New York University Press, pp. 89–100.

(1982a) *Hume, Hegel and Human Nature*, The Hague: Martinus Nijhoff.

(1982b) 'Hume on Rationality in History and Social Life, *History and Theory*, 21: 234–47.

(1983) 'Conservatism and Human Nature', in I. Forbes and S. Smith (eds), *Human Nature and Politics*, London: F. Pinter, pp. 55–67.

(1986a) *Human Nature*, London: Macmillan.

(1986b) 'The Nature of Wealth and the Origins of Virtue: Recent Essays on the Scottish Enlightenment', *History of European Ideas*, 7: 85–99.

(1987a) 'James Dunbar and the Enlightenment Debate on Language', in J. Pittock and J. Carter (eds), *Aberdeen and the Enlightenment*, Aberdeen: Aberdeen University Press, pp. 241–50.

(1987b) 'Need and Egoism in Marx's Early Writings', *History of Political Thought*, VII: 461–73.

(1989a) 'Adam Smith: Commerce, Liberty and Modernity', in P. Gilmour (ed.), *Philosophers of the Enlightenment*, Edinburgh: Edinburgh University Press, pp. 113–32.

(1989b) *The Idea of Democratic Community*, Hemel Hempstead: Wheatsheaf Books.

(1992) 'Adam Smith and the Virtues of Commerce', in J. Chapman and W. Galston (eds), *Virtue (Nomos XXXIV)*, New York: New York University Press, pp. 69–88.

(1993) 'Shared Understanding and the Democratic Way of Life', in J. Chapman and I. Shapiro (eds), *Democratic Community (Nomos XXXV)*, New York: New York University Press, pp. 67–87.

(1994) *The Idea of Luxury: A Conceptual and Historical Investigation*, Cambridge: Cambridge University Press.

(1995) 'Introduction', in James Dunbar, *Essays on the History of Mankind in Rude and Cultivated Ages*, Bristol: Thoemmes Reprint, pp. v–xv

(1997) *Social Theory of the Scottish Enlightenment*, Edinburgh: Edinburgh University Press.

(1998) 'Liberty and Modernity', in K. Kujawinska-Courtney and R. Machnikowski (eds), *Liberalism Yesterday and Today*, Łodz: Omega Press, pp. 65–76.

(1999a) 'Austerity, Necessity and Luxury', in J. Hill and C. Lennon (eds), *Luxury and Austerity*, Dublin: University College Dublin Press, pp. 1–13.

(1999b) 'Human Nature and Political Conventions', *Critical Review of International Social and Political Philosophy*, 2: 95–111.

(2000a) 'Politics and the Unnatural Infirmity of Being Human', in N. Roughley (ed.), *Being Humans*, Berlin and New York: De Gruyter, pp. 317–33.

(2000b) 'Rude Religion: The Psychology of Polytheism in the Scottish Enlightenment', in P. Wood (ed.), *New Essays on the Scottish Enlightenment*, Rochester, NY: Rochester University Press, pp. 315–34.

(2003a) 'Sociality and Socialisation', in A. Broadie (ed.), *The Cambridge Companion to the Scottish Enlightenment*, Cambridge: Cambridge University Press, pp. 243–57.

(2003b) 'Lusty Women and Loose Imagination: Hume's Philosophical Anthropology of Chastity', *History of Political Thought*, 24: 415–32.

(2003c) 'Scottish Enlightenment and the Idea of Civil Society', in

A. Martins (ed.), *Sociedade Civil: Entre Miragem e Opportunidade*, Coimbra: Faculdade de Letras, pp. 99–115.

(2004) 'Smith under Strain', *European Journal of Political Theory*, 3: 455–63.

(2005) 'De la Vertu à l'Opulence: La Construction Libérale du Luxe' in O. Assouly (ed.), *Le Luxe: Essais sur la Fabrique de l'Ostentation*, Paris: Editions de l'Institut Français de la Mode/ Editions du Regard, pp. 85–99.

(2006a) 'Smith and Science', in K. Haakonssen (ed.), *The Cambridge Companion to Adam Smith*, New York: Cambridge University Press, pp. 112–35.

(2006b) 'Hume and the Customary Causes of Industry, Knowledge and Commerce', *History of Political Economy*, 38: 291–317.

(2006c) 'Aristotle, Hobbes and Chimpanzees', *Political Studies*, 54: 827–45.

(2007) 'Hume's Universalism: The Science of Man and the Anthropological Point of View', *British Journal for the History of Philosophy*, 15: 529–44.

(2008) 'Hume and Superfluous Value (or the problem with Epictetus' Slippers)', in C. Wennerlind and M. Schabas (eds), *David Hume's Political Economy*, Abingdon: Routledge, pp. 49–64.

(2009a) 'But Art Itself is Natural to Man: Ferguson and the Principle of Simultaneity', in E. Heath and V. Merolle (eds), *Adam Ferguson: Philosophy, Politics and Society*, London: Pickering & Chatto, pp. 143–53, 214–17.

(2009b) *David Hume*, New York and London: Continuum.

(2009c) 'Hume y la infleixibilidad de la justicia: propriedad, comercio y expectativas', *Anuario Filosofica*, 42: 65–88.

(2010a) 'Creating Space for Civil Society: Conceptual Cartography in the Scottish Enlightenment, *Giornale di Storia Costituzionale*, 20: 49–60.

(2010b) 'Adam Smith's Moral Economy', *Kyoto Economic Review*, 79: 2–15.

(2011) 'Science and Superstition: Hume and Conservatism', *European Journal of Political Theory*, 10: 141–55.

(2012) 'Adam Smith's Science of Human Nature', *History of Political Economy*, 44: 471–92.

(2013) *The Idea of Commercial Society in the Scottish Enlightenment*, Edinburgh: Edinburgh University Press.

(2015) 'The Rise of Human Sciences', in A. Garrett and J. Harris (eds), *Oxford History of Scottish Philosophy in the Eighteenth Century*, Oxford: Oxford University Press, pp. 283–322.

(2016a) 'Luxury: A Dialectic of Desire?' in J. Armitage and J. Roberts (eds), *Critical Luxury Studies: Art, Media, Design*, Edinburgh: Edinburgh University Press, pp. 47–66.

(2016b) 'Religion and Civil Society in the Thought of the Scottish Enlightenment', in R. Lazaro and J. Seoane (eds), *The Changing Faces of Religion in XVIIIth Century Scotland*, Hildesheim: Ohms, pp. 17–45.

(forthcoming a) 'From Poverty to Prosperity: the Recalibration of Frugality' in C. Viglietti (ed.), *Roman Frugality*, Cambridge: Cambridge University Press.

(forthcoming b) 'Hume on the Foundations of Politics' in A. Coventry and A. Sagar (eds), *The Humean Mind*, Abingdon: Routledge.

Primary Scottish References

Beattie, J. (1783), *Dissertations Moral, Critical and Literary*, London: W. Strahan, T. Cadell.

Beattie, J. (1787), *Scotticisms: Arranged in Alphabetical Order Designed to correct Improprieties of Speech and Writing*, Edinburgh: Creeech and Cadell.

Blackwell, T. [1735] (1972), *An Enquiry into the Life and Times of Homer*, Menston: Scolar Press reprint.

Blair, H. [1783] (1838), *Lectures on Rhetoric and Belles-Lettres*, London: C. Daly.

Blair, H. [1763] (1996), *A Critical Dissertation on the Poems of Ossian*, in H. Gaskill (ed.), *Poems of Ossian*, Edinburgh: Edinburgh University Press.

Dunbar, J. (1781), *Essays on the History of Mankind in Rude and Cultivated Ages*, 2nd edn, London.

Ferguson, A. (1756), *Reflections Previous to the Establishment of a Militia*, London.

Ferguson, A. (1766), *Analysis of Pneumatics and Moral Philosophy*, Edinburgh.

Ferguson, A. (1776), *Remarks on a Pamphlet lately published by Dr Price*, London.

Ferguson, A. [1783] (1813), *The History of the Progress and Termination of the Roman Republic*, 5 vols, new edn, Edinburgh.

Ferguson, A. [1767] (1966), *An Essay on the History of Civil Society*, ed. D. Forbes, Edinburgh: Edinburgh University Press.

Ferguson, A. [1769] (1994), *Institutes of Moral Philosophy*, 3rd edn, London: Thoemmes Reprint.

Ferguson, A. [1792] (1995), *Principles of Moral and Political Science*, 2 vols, Hildesheim: G. Olms.

Ferguson, A. (1995), *Correspondence*, ed. V. Merolle, 2 vols, London: Pickering.

Ferguson, A. (2006), *The Manuscripts of Adam Ferguson*, ed. V. Merolle, R. Dix and E. Heath, London: Pickering & Chatto.

Fletcher, A. [1698] (1979), 'A Discourse of Government with relation to Militias', in D. Daiches (ed.), *Fletcher of Saltoun: Selected Writings*, Edinburgh: Scottish Academic Press.

Gerard. A. (1774), *Essay on Taste*, 3rd edn, London.

Gregory J. [1765] (1788), 'A Comparative View of the State and Faculties of Man', in *Works of the Late John Gregory*, vol. 2, Edinburgh.

Hume, D. (1875), *Philosophical Works*, ed. T. Green and G. Grose, London: Longmans.

Hume, D. (1894), *The History of England*, 3 vols, London: George Routledge.

Hume, D. (1932), *The Letters of David Hume*, ed. J. Greig, 2 vols, Oxford: Clarendon Press.

Hume, D. (1970), *The History of Great Britain*, ed. D. Forbes, Harmondsworth: Penguin.

Hume, D. (1975), *Enquiries Concerning Human Understanding and Concerning the Principles of Morals*, ed. L. Selby-Bigge and P. Nidditch, Oxford: Clarendon Press.

Hume, D. [1739/40] (1978), *A Treatise of Human Nature*, ed. L. Selby-Bigge and P. Nidditch, rev. edn, Oxford: Clarendon Press.

Hume, D. (1985), *Essays: Moral, Political and Literary*, ed. E. Miller, Indianapolis: Liberty Press.

Hume, D. [1751] (1998), *An Enquiry Concerning the Principles of Morals*, ed. T. Beauchamp, Oxford: Oxford University Press.

Hume, D. [1748] (1999), *An Enquiry Concerning Human Understanding*, ed. T. Beauchamp, Oxford: Oxford University Press.

Hume, D. [1739/40] (2002), *A Treatise of Human Nature*, ed. D. and M. Norton, Oxford: Oxford University Press.

Hume, D. (2007), *A Dissertation on the Passions and The Natural History of Religion*, ed. T. Beauchamp, Oxford: Oxford University Press.

Hutcheson, F. [1726] (1989), *Observations on the Fable of the Bees*, Bristol: Thoemmes Reprint.

Hutcheson, F. (1994), *Philosophical Writings*, ed. R. Downie, London: Everyman.

Hutcheson, F. [1755] (2005), *A System of Moral Philosophy*, 2 vols, London: Continuum.

Hutcheson, F. [1757] (2007), *A Short Introduction to Moral Philosophy*, ed. L. Turco, Indianapolis: Liberty Press.

Irving, D. (1804), *The Lives of the Scottish Poets*, Edinburgh.

Kames, H. Home, Lord (1747), *Essays upon Several Subjects Concerning British Antiquities*, Edinburgh.

Kames, H. Home, Lord (1732), *Essays upon Several Subjects in Law*, Edinburgh.

Kames, H. Home, Lord (1774), *Sketches on the History of Man*, 3rd edn, 2 vols, Dublin.

Kames, H. Home, Lord (1777), *Elucidations Respecting the Common and Statute Law of Scotland*, Edinburgh.

Kames, H. Home, Lord (1779), *Historical Law Tracts*, 2nd edn, Edinburgh.

Kames, H. Home, Lord [1779] (2005), *Essays on the Principles of Morality and Natural Religion*, 3rd edn, Indianapolis: Liberty Press.

Kames, H. Home, Lord (1781), *Loose Hints on Education*, Edinburgh.

Kames, H. Home, Lord (1817), *The Elements of Criticism*, 9th edn, 2 vols, Edinburgh.

Keill, J. (1718), *Introductio ad Veram Astronomiam*, Oxford.

MacLaurin, C. (1750), *An Account of Sir Isaac Newton's Philosophical Discoveries*, 2nd edn, London.

Millar, J. [1771] (1773), *Observations Concerning the Distinction of Ranks of Society*, London: John Murray.

Millar, J. [1779] (1971), 'The Origin of the Distinction of Ranks', in W. Lehmann (ed.), *John Millar of Glasgow*, 3rd edn, Cambridge: Cambridge University Press.

Millar, J. [1787] (2006), *An Historical View of the English Government*, ed. M. Salber Phillips and D. Smith, Indianapolis: Liberty Press.

Monboddo (J. Burnett, Lord) [1773–93] (1779–99), *The Origin and Progress of Language*, Edinburgh.

Monboddo (J. Burnett, Lord) (1779–99), *Ancient Metaphysics,* vol. 3, Edinburgh: Balfour

Reid, T. (1846), *Works*, ed. W. Hamilton, 1 vol., Edinburgh: Maclachan Stewart.

Reid, T. (1990), *Practical Ethics*, ed. K. Haakonssen, Princeton: Princeton University Press.

Robertson, W. (1840), *Works*, ed. D. Stewart, 1 vol., Edinburgh.

Smith, A. [1795] (1982), *Essays on Philosophical Subjects*, ed. W. Wightman, J. Bryce and I. Ross, Indianapolis: Liberty Press.

Smith, A. (1982), *Lectures on Jurisprudence*, ed. R. Meek, D. Raphael and P. Stein, Indianapolis: Liberty Press.

Smith, A. [1759/1790] (1982), *The Theory of Moral Sentiments*, ed. A. MacFie and D. Raphael, Indianapolis: Liberty Press.

Smith, A. [1776] (1982), *An Inquiry into the Nature and Causes of the Wealth of Nations*, ed. R. Campbell and A. Skinner, Indianapolis: Liberty Press.

Smith, A. [1762–3] (1983), *Lectures on Rhetoric and Belles-Lettres*, ed. J. Bryce, Indianapolis: Liberty Press.

Smith, A. (1987), *The Correspondence of Adam Smith*, ed. E. Mossner and I. Ross, Indianapolis: Liberty Press.

Somerville, T. (1861), *My Own Life and Times 1741–1814*, Edinburgh: Edmonston.

Stewart, D. (1854), 'Dissertation: Exhibiting the Progress of Metaphysical, Ethical and Political Philosophy since the Revival of Letters in Europe', in W. Hamilton (ed.), *Works*, vol. 1, Edinburgh: Constable.

Steuart, J. [1767] (1966), *An Inquiry into the Principles of Political Economy*, 2 vols, ed. A. Skinner, London: Oliver & Boyd.

Stuart, G. (1768), *An Historical Dissertation Concerning the Antiquity of the English Constitution*, Edinburgh.

Stuart, G. (1779), *Observations Concerning the Public Law and the Constitutional History of Scotland*, Edinburgh.

Stuart, G. [1792] (1995), *A View of Society in Europe in its Progress from Rudeness to Refinement*, 2nd edn, Bristol: Thoemmes reprint.

Turnbull, G. (1740 [2003]), *Observations upon Liberal Education*, ed. T. Moore (Indianapolis: Liberty Press).

Turnbull, G. [1740] (2005), *The Principles of Moral Philosophy*, Indianapolis: Liberty Press.

Wallace, R. [1758] (1961), *Characteristics of the Present Political State of Great Britain*, New York: Kelley Reprints.

Wallace, R. [1809] (1969), *Dissertation on the Numbers of Mankind in Antient and Modern Times*, 2nd edn, enlarged, New York: Kelley Reprints.

Wallace, R. [1761] (2010), *Various Prospects of Mankind, Nature, and Providence*, Boston MA: Gale Ecco Print Editions.

Other Primary References

Adams, J. (1789), *Thoughts on the History of Man. Chiefly abridged or selected from the celebrated works of Lord Kames, Lord Monboddo, Dr. Dunbar and the immortal Montesquieu*, London.

Aquinas, T. (1932), *Summa Theologiae*, tr. English Dominican fathers, London: Burns and Oates.

Aristotle (1894), *Ethica Nicomachea*, ed. L. Bywater, Oxford: Classical Texts.

Aristotle (1944), *Politics*, ed. H. Rackham, London: Loeb Library.

Aristotle (1976), *Ethics*, tr. J. Thomson, Harmondsworth: Penguin.

Bacon, F. (1853), *The Advancement of Learning*, London: Bohn.

Beauzée, N. (1765), 'Langue' in *Encyclopédie*, IX, ed. D. Diderot, Neuchatel.

Beccaria, C. [1764] (1965), *Dei Delitti e delle Pene*, ed. F. Venturi, Torino: Einaudi.

Bentham, J. (1948), *Introduction to the Principles of Morals and Legislation*, ed. W. Harrison, Oxford: Blackwell.

Bentham, J. (1983), 'Deontology', in A. Goldworth (ed.), *Collected Works of J. Bentham*, Oxford: Clarendon Press.

Bodin, J. [1583] (1993), *Les Six Livres de la République*, ed. G. Mairet, Paris: Librairie Générale Français.

Bolingbroke (H. Lord) [1735] (1870), *Letters on the Study and Use of History*, London.

Brady, R. (1711), *An Historical Treatise of Cities and Burghs or Boroughs*, London.

Brosses, C. de (1801), *Traité de la Formation Méchanique des Langues*, Paris.

Brown, J. (1758), *An Estimate of the Manners and Principles of the Times*, 2 vols, London.

Bruni, L. (1978), 'Panegyric to the City of Florence', in B. Kohn and R. Witt (eds), *The Earthly Republic*, tr. B. Kohn, Manchester: Manchester University Press, pp. 135–75.

Buchanan, G. (1579), *De Jure Regni apud Scotos*, Edinburgh.

Buffon, C. (1812), *Natural History*, tr. W. Smellie, London.

Bullet, C. (1754), *Mémoires sur la Langue Celtique*, Besançon.

Burke, E. [1790] (1987), *Reflections on the Revolution in France*, ed. J. Pocock, Indianapolis: Hackett.

Butler, J. [1736] (1907), *Analogy of Religion*, ed. W. Gladstone, London: Oxford University Press.

Cicero (1913), *De Officiis*, ed. W. Miller, London: Loeb Library.

Cicero (1923), *De Divinatione*, ed. J. Babbitt, London: Loeb Library.

Cicero (1927), *Disputationes Tusculanae*, ed. J. King, London: Loeb Library.

Cicero (1928), *De Republica*, ed. C. Keyes, London: Loeb Library.

Cicero (1931) *De Finibus*, ed. H. Rackham, London: Loeb Library.

Condillac, E. (1947–53), *Oeuvres*, ed. G. LeRoy 3 vols, Paris: Presses Universitaire de France.

D'Alembert, J. [1751] (1963), *Preliminary Discourse to the Encyclopedia*, tr. R. Schwab, Indianapolis: Bobbs Merrill.

Diderot, D. (ed.) (1765), *Encyclopédie*, 17 vols, Neuchatel.

Dubos, J.-B. [1719] (1755), *Réflexions critiques sur la Poesie et sur la Peinture*, 6th edn, Paris.

Epictetus (1928), *The Manual and Discourses*, ed. W. Oldfather, London: Loeb Library.

Fénelon, F. [1699] (1962), *Les aventures de Télémaque*, ed. J. Goré, Firenze: Sansoni.

Filmer, R. [1640?] (1949), *Patriarcha*, ed. P. Laslett, Oxford: Blackwell.

Girard, G. (1747), *Les Vrais Principes de la Langue Françoise*, Paris.

Grotius, H. [1625] (2002), *On the Laws of War and Peace*, ed. R. Tuck, tr. J. Barbeyrac, Indianapolis: Liberty Press.

Hale, M. [1713] (1971), *History of the Common Law of England*, ed. C. Gray, Chicago: University of Chicago Press.

Harris, J. (1751), *Hermes*, London.

Hartley, D. [1749] (1810), *Observations on Man*, 2 vols, 5th edn, London.

Hegel, G. [1821] (1955), *Grundlinien der Philosophie des Rechts*, Hamburg: Meiner.

Hegel, G. [Heidelberg 1817–18] (1995), *Lectures on Natural Right and Political Science*, tr. P. Wannemann, Los Angeles: University of California Press.

Hegel, G. [1805/6] (1922), *Jenenser Realphilosophie in Werke*, vol. XX, ed. G. Lasson and J. Hoffmeister, Leipzig: Meiner.

Herder, G. (1891), 'Abhandlung über den Ursprung der Sprache' in B. Suphan (ed.), *Sammtliche Werke*, vol. 5, Berlin: Weidmann.

Herder, G. (1969), *Herder on Social and Political Culture*, ed. and tr. F. Barnard, Cambridge: Cambridge University Press.

Hobbes, T. [1651] (1991), *Leviathan*, ed. R. Tuck, Cambridge: Cambridge University Press.

Horace (1961), *Odes*, London: Everyman Library.

Johnson, S. [1755] (1792), *Dictionary of the English Language*, 10th edn, London.

Lipsius, J. (1583), *De Constantia*, Antwerp.

Livy (1914), *Ab Urbe Condita*, ed. B. Foster, London: Loeb Library.

Locke, J. [1689] (1965), *Two Treatises of Government*, ed. P. Laslett, New York: Mentor Books.

Locke, J. [1689] (1948), *A Letter concerning Toleration*, ed. J. Gough, Oxford: Blackwell.

Locke, J. [1690] (1854), 'An Essay Concerning Human Understanding', in H. St John (ed.), *Philosophical Works*, 2 vols, London: Bohn.

Luther, M. [1520] (1961), 'Freedom of a Christian', in J. Dillinger (ed.), *Martin Luther: Selections from his Writings*, Garden City, NY: Anchor Books, pp. 42–85.

Machiavelli, N. (1998), *Tutte le Opere*, Firenze: Newton.

Madox, T. (1725), *Firma Burgi*, London.

Malebranche, N. [1674] (n.d), 'De la recherche de la vérité' in J. Simon (ed.), *Oeuvres*, 4 vols, Paris: Charpentier.

Mandeville, B. [1714/35] (1988), *The Fable of the Bees*, ed. F. Kaye, Indianapolis: Liberty Press.

Mandeville, B. [1724] (1973), *A Modest Defence of Publick Stews*, Los Angeles: Clark Memorial Library.

Marsilius (of Padua) (1956), *The Defender of Peace*, ed. A. Gewirth, New York: Harper Torchbooks.

Marx, K. [1843] (1975), 'Critique of Hegel's Doctrine of the State', in Colletti, L. (ed.), *Marx's Early Writings*, Harmondsworth: Penguin.

Marx, K. (1982), 'James Mill' in K. Marx and F. Engels, *Gesamtausgabe* IV: 2, Berlin: Dietz, pp. 447–66.

Melon, J.-F. [1734] (1842), 'Essai politique sur le Commerce' in E. Daire (ed.), *Collection des Principaux Economistes*, vol. 1, Paris: Guillaumin, pp. 701–826.

Mill, J. S. [1861] (1910), *Utilitarianism*, ed. A. Lindsay, London: Everyman Library.

Mill, J. S. [1838–40] (1971), *On Bentham and Coleridge*, ed. F. Leavis, London: Chatto & Windus.

Montesquieu, C. (Baron de) [1734] (1951), *Considérations sur les causes de la grandeur des romains et de leur decadence*, ed. E. Faguet, Paris: Nelson.

Montesquieu, C. (Baron de) (1955), *Oeuvres*, Paris: Nagel.

Montesquieu, C. (Baron de) [1748] (1961), *De l'esprit des lois*, ed. G. Truc, Paris: Garnier.

Mornay (du Plessis-), P. [1579] (1924), *Vindiciae contra Tyrannos*, ed. H. Laski, London: Bell.

Neville, H. [1681] (1969), 'Plato Redivivus' in C. Robbins (ed.), *Two English Republican Tracts*, Cambridge: Cambridge University Press.

Newton. I. (1953), *Newton's Philosophy of Nature*, ed. H. Thayer, New York: Hafner.

Paley, W. [1785] (1845), 'The Principles of Moral and Political Philosophy' in *Works*, Edinburgh: Nelson.

Plato (1902), *Politeias*, ed. J. Burnet, Oxford: Clarendon Press.

Plutarch (2014), *Moralia,* ed. W. Falconer, vol. 2, London: Loeb Library.

Priestley, J. (1762), *Lectures on the Theory of Language*, Warrington.

Pufendorf, S. [1672] (1934), *On the Law of Nature and Nations*, tr. C. H. and W. A. Oldfather, Oxford: Classics of International Law.

Pufendorf, S. [1673] (1991), *On Duty of Man and Citizen*, ed. J. Tully, Cambridge: Cambridge University Press.

Rousseau, J.-J. [1755] (1962), *Discours sur l'origine de l'inégalité parmi les hommes*, Paris: Garnier.

Rousseau, J.-J. [1765] (1864a), 'Emile ou l'Education' in *Oeuvres Complètes*, Paris: Hachette.

Rousseau, J.-J. [1758] (1864b), 'Lettre à M D'Alembert', in *Oeuvres Complètes*, Paris: Hachette.

Sallust (1921), *The War with Catiline*, ed. J. Rolfe, London: Loeb Library.

Seneca (1928), *Moral Essays*, ed. J. Basore, 3 vols, London: Loeb Library.

Seneca (1932), *Epistulae Morales*, ed. R. Gummere, London: Loeb Library.

Sidney, A. [1698] (1990), *Discourse Concerning Government*, ed. T. West, Indianapolis: Liberty Press.

Smellie, W. (ed.) (1771), *Encyclopaedia Britannica*, Edinburgh.

Steele, R. (1684), *The Tradesman's Calling*, London.

Temple, W. [1673] (1680), 'Observations on the United Provinces of the Netherlands', in *Miscellanea*, London.

Tertullian (1951), *De Cultu Feminarum*, ed. J. Marra, Torino: Parania.

Trenchard, J. (1697), *A Standing Army is inconsistent with a Free Government*, London.

Trenchard, J. (1709), *The Natural History of Superstition*, London.

Turgot, A. (1913), *Oeuvres,* ed. G. Schelle, Paris: Alcan.

Vico, G. [1744] (1948), *New Science*, tr. T. Bergin and M. Fisch, Ithaca: Cornell University Press.

Voltaire, A. (1969), *Correspondance,* ed. T. Besterman, Oxford: Voltaire Foundation.

Voltaire, A. [1756] (2002), 'Essai sur les Moeurs et l'esprit des Nations', in *Les Oeuvres Complètes*, vols. 22–4, Oxford: Voltaire Foundation.

Voltaire, A. [1736] (2003), 'Le Mondain', in *Les Oeuvres Complètes*, vol. 16, Oxford: Voltaire Foundation.

Warburton, W. (1765), *Divine Legation of Moses Demonstrated,* 4th edn, 5 vols, London.

Ward, W. [1765] (1958), *An Essay on Grammar*, Menston: Scolar Press.

Xenophon (1923), *Oeconomicus*, tr. E. Marchant, London: Loeb Library.

Secondary References

Aarsleff, H. (1974), 'The Tradition of Condillac' in H. Hymes (ed.), *Studies on the History of Linguistics*, Bloomington: Indiana University Press, pp. 93–156.

Acton, H. (1959), 'Philosophies of Language in Revolutionary France,' *Proceedings of the British Academy*, 45: 204–19.

Adair, D. (1957), 'That Politics may be reduced to a science: David Hume, James Madison and the Tenth Federalist', *Huntingdon Library Quarterly*, 20: 343–60.

Allan, D. (1993), *Virtue, Learning and the Scottish Enlightenment*, Edinburgh: Edinburgh University Press.

Allen, D. (1981), 'Modern Conservatism: The problem of definition'. *Review of Politics*, 43: 582–603.

Alvey, J. (2003), *Adam Smith: Optimist or Pessimist?* Aldershot: Ashgate.

Anderson, R. (1966), *Hume's First Principles*, Lincoln: University of Nebraska Press.

Annas, J. (1993), *The Morality of Happiness*, Cambridge: Cambridge University Press.

Appleby, J. (1978), *Economic Thought and Ideology in Seventeenth-Century England*, Princeton: Princeton University Press.

Ardal, P. (1966), *Passion and Value in Hume's Treatise*, Edinburgh: Edinburgh University Press.

Baier, A. (1979), 'Good Men's Women: Hume on Chastity and Trust', *Hume Studies*, 5: 1–19.

Baier, A. (1988), 'Hume's Account of Social Artifice – Its Origins and Originality', *Ethics*, 98: 757–78.

Baier, A. (1989), 'Hume on Women's Complexion', in P. Jones (ed.), *The Science of Man in the Scottish Enlightenment*, Edinburgh: Edinburgh University Press, pp. 33–53.

Baier, A. (1991), *A Progress of Sentiments*, Cambridge, MA: Harvard University Press.

Baier, A. (1993), 'Hume: The Reflective Woman's Epistemologist', in L. Antony and C. Witt (eds), *A Mind of One's Own*, Boulder: Westview Press, pp. 33–48.

Barfoot, M. (1990), 'Hume and the culture of science in the early eighteenth century', in M. A. Stewart (ed.), *Studies in the Philosophy of the Scottish Enlightenment*, Oxford: Clarendon Press, pp 152–90.

Barry, B. (1989), *Theories of Justice*, London: Harvester Wheatsheaf.

Battersby, C. (1981), 'An Enquiry Concerning the Humean Woman', *Philosophy*, 56: 303–12.

Beauchamp, T. (2007), *Editorial Annotations (to Hume's 'Natural History of Religion')*, Oxford: Clarendon Press.

Beauchamp, T. and A. Rosenberg (1981), *Hume and the Problem of Causation*, Oxford: Oxford University Press.

Becker, J. (1961), 'Adam Smith's Theory of Social Science', *Southern Economic Journal*, 28: 13–21.

Benton, T. (1990),'Adam Ferguson and the Enterprise Culture' in P. Hulme and L. Jordanova (eds), *The Enlightenment and its Shadows*, London: Routledge, pp. 103–20.

Berg, E. and E. Eger (eds) (2003), *Luxury in the Eighteenth Century*, Basingstoke: Palgrave.

Berdell, J. (1996), 'Innovation and Trade: David Hume and the Case for Freer Trade', *History of Political Economy*, 28: 107–26.

Bevilacqua, M. (1965), 'Adam Smith's Lectures on Rhetoric & Belles Lettres', *Studies in Scottish Literature*, 3: 42–5.

Bitterman, H. [1940] (1984), 'Adam Smith's Empiricism and the Law of Nature', reprinted in J. Wood (ed.), *Adam Smith Critical Assessments*, vol. 1, London: Croom Helm, pp. 190–235.

Black, A. (1984), *Guilds and Civil Society*, London: Methuen.

Black, J. (1926), *The Art of History*, London: Methuen.

Bok, S. (2010), *Exploring Happiness: From Aristotle to Brain Science*, New Haven: Yale University Press.

Bonolas, P. (1987), 'Fénelon et le luxe dans le Télémaque', *Voltaire Studies*, 249: 81–90.

Bosanquet, B. [1899] (1958), *The Philosophical Theory of the State*, London: Macmillan.

Bourdieu, P. (1979), *La Distinction: Critique sociale du jugement*, Paris: Minuit.

Bowles, P. (1985), 'The Origin of Property and the Development of Scottish Historical Science', *Journal of the History of Ideas*, 46: 197–209.

Boyd, R. (2004), *Uncivil Society: The Perils of Pluralism and the Making of Modern Liberalism*, Lanham: Lexington Books.

Boyd, R. (2013),'Adam Smith and Civil Society', in C. Berry, M. Paganelli, C. Smith (eds), *The Oxford Handbook of Adam Smith*, Oxford: Oxford University Press, pp. 443–63.

Braddick, M. (2000), *State Formation in Early Modern England*, Cambridge: Cambridge University Press.

Brennan G. and A. Hamlin (2004), 'Analytical Conservatism', *British Journal of Political Science*, 34: 675–91.

Brewer, A. (1988), 'Luxury and Economic Development: David

Hume and Adam Smith', *Scottish Journal of Political Economy*, 45: 78–98.

Brewer, J. (1986), 'Adam Ferguson and the theme of Exploitation', *British Journal of Sociology*, 37: 461–78.

Brickman D. and D. Campbell (1971), 'Hedonic Relativism and Planning the Good Society' in M. Appley (ed.), *Adaptation-Level Theory*, New York: Academic Press, pp. 287–302.

Broadie, A. (1997), *The Scottish Enlightenment: An Anthology*, Edinburgh: Canongate.

Broadie, A. (2012), *Agreeable Connexions: Scottish Enlightenment links with France*, Edinburgh: Birlinn.

Broadie, A. (ed.) (2003), *The Cambridge Companion to the Scottish Enlightenment*, Cambridge: Cambridge University Press.

Brooke, C. (2012), *Philosophic Pride: Stoicism and Political Thought from Lipsius to Rousseau*, Princeton: Princeton University Press.

Brown, M. (1988), *Adam Smith's Economics*, London: Croom Helm.

Brown, S. (ed.) (1997), *William Robertson and the Expansion of Empire*, Cambridge: Cambridge University Press.

Brown, V. (1994), *Adam Smith's Discourse: Canonicity, Commerce and Conscience*, London: Routledge.

Brumfitt, J. (1958), *Voltaire Historian*, Oxford: Oxford University Press.

Bryson, G. [1945] (1968), *Man and Society – the Scottish Enquiry of the Eighteenth Century*, New York: Kelley reprint.

Buckle, S. (1991), *Natural Law and the Theory of Property*, Oxford: Clarendon Press.

Burke, J. Jr (1978), 'Hume's History of England', in R. Runte (ed.) *Studies in Eighteenth-Century Culture*, 7: 235–50.

Burns, S. (1976), 'The Humean Female', *Dialogue*, 15: 415–24.

Caffentzis, G. (2001), 'Hume, Money, and Civilization; or, Why Was Hume a Metallist?', *Hume Studies*, 27: 301–35.

Calkins, M. and P. Werhane (2001), 'Adam Smith, Aristotle and the Virtues of Commerce', *Journal of Value Inquiry*, 32: 43–60.

Campbell, R. and A. Skinner (eds) (1982), *The Origins and Nature of the Scottish Enlightenment*, Edinburgh: John Donald.

Campbell, T. (1971), *Adam Smith's Science of Morals*, London: G. Allen & Unwin.

Cannan, E. (ed.) (1896), *Adam Smith Lectures on Justice, Police, Revenue and Arms*, Oxford: Oxford University Press.

Cannan, E. (ed.) [1904] (1961), *Adam Smith's 'An Inquiry into the Nature and Causes of the Wealth of Nations'*, London: Methuen.

Canning, J. (1980), 'The Corporation in the Political Thought of the Italian Jurists of the Thirteenth and Fourteenth Centuries', *History of Political Thought*, 1: 9–32.

Capaldi, N. (1978), 'Hume as a Social Scientist', *Review of Metaphysics*, 38: 99–123.

Carr, R. (2013), *Gender and Enlightenment in Eighteenth-Century Scotland*, Edinburgh: Edinburgh University Press.

Carter, J. and J. Pittock (eds) (1987), *Aberdeen and the Enlightenment*, Aberdeen: Aberdeen University Press.

Cassirer, E. (1953), *The Philosophy of Symbolic Forms,* tr. R. Mannheim, New Haven: Yale University Press.

Cassirer, E. (1955), *The Philosophy of the Enlightenment*, tr. K. Koelln and J. Pettegrove, Boston: Beacon Press.

Castiglione, D. (2000), '"The Noble Disquiet": Meanings of Liberty in the Discourse of the North', in S. Collini, R. Whatmore and B. Young (eds), *Essays in British Intellectual History, 1750–1950*, Cambridge: Cambridge University Press, pp. 48–69.

Chamley, P. (1975), 'The Conflict between Montesquieu and Hume', in A. Skinner and T. Wilson (eds), *Essays on Adam Smith*, Oxford: Clarendon Press, pp. 274–305.

Charles, L. (2008), 'French "New Politics" and the dissemination of David Hume's Political Discourses on the Continent', in C. Wennerlind and M. Schabas (eds), *David Hume's Political Economy*, London; Routledge, pp. 81–202.

Chitnis, A. (1976), *The Scottish Enlightenment: A Social History*, London: Croom Helm.

Christensen, J. (1987), *Practicing Enlightenment: Hume and the Formation of a Literary Career*, Madison: University of Wisconsin Press.

Christie, J. (1987), 'The Culture of Science in Eighteenth-Century Scotland' in A. Hook (ed.), *The History of Scottish Literature*, vol. 2, Aberdeen: Aberdeen University Press, pp. 291–304.

Clark, H. (1993), 'Women and Humanity in Scottish Enlightenment Social Thought: The Case of Adam Smith', *Historical Reflections*, 19: 335–61.

Clark, I. (1970), 'From Protest to Reaction: the Moderate Regime in the Church of Scotland', in N. Phillipson and R. Mitchison (eds), *Scotland in the Age of Improvement*, Edinburgh: Edinburgh University Press, pp. 200–24.

Clive, J. and B. Bailyn (1954), 'England's Cultural Provinces: Scotland and America', *William and Mary Quarterly*, 11: 200–13.

Cloutier, D. (2012), 'The Problem of Luxury in the Christian Life', *Journal of the Society of Christian Ethics*, 32: 3–20.

Clunas, C. (2004), *Superfluous Things*, Honolulu: University of Hawaii Press.

Coats, A. (1958), 'Changing Attitudes to Labour in the Mid-Eighteenth Century', *Economic History Review*, 11: 35–51.

Coats, A. (1992), 'Economic Thought and Poor Law Policy in the Eighteenth Century', in A. Coats, *On the History of Economic Thought*, vol. 1, London: Routledge, pp. 85–100.

Cohen, A. (2000), 'The Notion of Moral Progress in Hume's Philosophy', *Hume Studies*, 26: 109–27.

Cohen, J. (2000), *If You're an Egalitarian, How Come You're so Rich?*, Cambridge, MA: Harvard University Press.

Cohen, J. and A. Arato (1992), *Civil Society and Political Theory*, Cambridge, MA: MIT Press.

Cohon, R. (2008), *Hume's Morality*, Oxford: Oxford University Press.

Cooper, J. (1975), *Reason and Human Good in Aristotle*, Cambridge, MA: Harvard University Press.

Cremaschi, S. (1989), 'Adam Smith: Skeptical Newtonianism, Disenchanted Republicanism and the Birth of Social Science' in M. Dascal and O. Gruengard (eds), *Knowledge and Politics*, Boulder: Westview Press, pp. 83–110.

Croce, B. (1955), *History as the Story of Liberty*, tr. S. Sprigge, New York: Meridian Books.

Cropsey, J. [1957] (2001), *Polity and Economy*, new edn, South Bend: St Augustine's Press.

Crowe, B. (2010), 'Religion and the "sensitive branch of human nature"', *Religious Studies*, 46: 251–63.

Cunningham, A. (2005), 'David Hume's Account of Luxury', *Journal of the History of Economic Thought*, 27: 231–50.

Daly, M. and M. Wilson (1978), *Sex, Evolution and Behavior*, N. Scituate, MA: Duxbury Press.

Danford, J. (1990), *David Hume and the Problem of Reason: Recovering the Human Sciences*, New Haven: Yale University Press.

Dascal, M. (2006), 'Adam Smith's Theory of Language' in K. Haakonssen (ed.), *The Cambridge Companion to Adam Smith*, Cambridge: Cambridge University Press, pp. 79–111.

Davidson, D. (1984), 'On the very idea of a Conceptual Scheme' in his *Inquiries into Truth and Interpretation*, Oxford: Clarendon Press, pp. 183–98.

Davie, G. (1961), *The Democratic Intellect*, Edinburgh: Edinburgh University Press.

Davie, G. (1981), *The Scottish Enlightenment*, Historical Association pamphlet No. 99, London.

Davie, G. (1994), *A Passion for Ideas,* vol. 2, Edinburgh: Polygon Books.

Davis, G. (2003), 'Philosophical Psychology and Economic Psychology in David Hume and Adam Smith', *History Of Political Economy*, 35: 269–304.

Dawson, D. and P. Morère (eds) (2004), *Scotland and France in the Enlightenment*, Lewisburg: Bucknell University Press.

Dedieu, J. (1909), *Montesquieu et la Tradition Politique Anglaise*, Paris: Gabalda.

Dees, R. (1992), 'Hume and the Contexts of Politics', *Journal of the History of Philosophy*, 30: 319–42.

Deleuze, G. [1953] (1991), *Empiricism and Subjectivity: An Essay on Hume's Theory of Human Nature*, tr. C. Boundas, New York: Columbia University Press.

Dickey, L. (1986), 'Historicizing the "Adam Smith Problem"', *Journal of Modern History*, 58: 579–609.

Diener, E. (2009), *The Science of Well-Being*, Dordrecht: Springer.

Donovan, A. (1975), *Philosophical Chemistry in the Scottish Enlightenment*, Edinburgh: Edinburgh University Press.

Dow, A. and S. Dow (2006), *A History of Scottish Economic Thought*, London: Routledge.

Droixhe, D. (1976),' Langage et société dans la grammaire philosophique de Du Marchais à Michaelis', *Études sur le XVIIIe siècle*, 3: 119–32.

Duke, M. (1979), 'David Hume and Monetary Adjustment', *History of Political Economy*, 11: 572–87.

Dunyach, J.-F. and A. Thomson (eds) (2015), *The Enlightenment in Scotland*, Oxford: Voltaire Foundation.

Durkheim, E. (1965), *Montesquieu and Rousseau: Forerunners of Sociology,* tr. R. Mannheim, Ann Arbor: University of Michigan Press.

Dwyer, J. (1987), *Virtuous Discourse*, Edinburgh: John Donald.

Dwyer, J. and R. Sher (eds) (1991), 'Sociability and Society in Eighteenth-Century Scotland', special issue of *Eighteenth-Century Life*, vol. 15, nos. 1 and 2.

Earl, D. (1961), *The Political Thought of Sallust*, Cambridge: Cambridge University Press.

Earl, D. (1967), *The Moral and Political Tradition of Rome*, London: Thames & Hudson.

Easterlin, R. (2001), 'Income and Happiness: Toward a Unified Theory', *Economic Journal*, 111: 35–47.

Eckstein, W. (ed.) (1926), *Adam Smith: Theorie der Ethischen Gefühle*, 2 vols, Leipzig: Meiner.

Edwards, C. (1993), *The Politics of Immorality in Ancient Rome*, Cambridge: Cambridge University Press.

Ehrenberg, J. (1999), *Civil Society: The Critical History of an Idea*, New York: New York University Press.

Ehrlich, J. (2013), 'William Robertson and Scientific Theism', *Modern Intellectual History*, 10: 519–42.

Emerson, R. (1973), 'The Social Composition of Enlightened Scotland: The Select Society of Edinburgh 1754–64', *Studies in Voltaire*, 114: 291–329.

Emerson, R. (1984), 'Conjectural history and the Scottish philosophers', *Historical Papers of the Canadian Historical Association*, pp. 63–90.

Emerson, R. (1986), 'Natural Philosophy and the problem of the Scottish Enlightenment', *Voltaire Studies*, 24: 243–88.

Emerson, R. (1988a), 'Science and the Origins of the Scottish Enlightenment', *History of Science*, 26: 333–66.

Emerson, R. (1988b), 'Sir Robert Sibbald, The Royal Society of Scotland and the Origins of the Scottish Enlightenment', *Annals of Science*, 46: 41–72.

Emerson, R. (1992), *Professors and Patronage: The Aberdeen Universities in the Eighteenth Century*, Aberdeen: Aberdeen University Press.

Emerson, R. (1995), 'Politics and the Glasgow Professors', in A. Hook and R. Sher (eds), *The Glasgow Enlightenment*, East Linton: Tuckwell Press, pp. 21–39.

Emerson, R. (2008a), 'The Scottish Contexts for David Hume's Political-Economic Thinking', in C. Wennerlind and M. Schabas (eds), *David Hume's Political Economy*, London: Routledge, pp. 10–30.

Emerson, R. (2008b), *Academic Patronage in the Scottish Enlightenment*, Edinburgh: Edinburgh University Press.

Emerson, R. (2015), 'The Moderate Enlightenment in Glasgow: The Glasgow Literary Society c.1752–c.1802' in R. Emerson, *Neglected Scots*, Edinburgh: Humming Earth, pp. 21–134.

Emerson, R. and P. Wood (2002), 'Science and Enlightenment in Glasgow, 1690–1802' in C. Withers and P. Wood (eds), *Science and Medicine in the Scottish Enlightenment*, East Linton: Tuckwell Press, pp. 79–142.

Evensky, S. (2005), *Adam Smith's Moral Philosophy*, Cambridge: Cambridge University Press.

Evnine, S. (1994), 'Hume, Conjectural History, and the Uniformity of Human Nature', *Journal of the History of Philosophy*, 31: 589–606.

Falkenstein, L. (2003), 'Hume's Project in "The Natural History of Religion"', *Religious Studies*, 39: 1–21.

Farr, J. (1978), 'Hume Hermeneutics and History', *History and Theory*, 17: 285–330.

Ferguson, W. (1968), *Scotland: 1689 to the Present Day*, Edinburgh: Edinburgh University Press.

Fielding, R. (2008), *Scotland and the Fictions of Geography*, Cambridge: Cambridge University Press.

Finlay, C. (2006), 'Rhetoric and Citizenship in Adam Ferguson's Essay on the History of Civil Society', *History of Political Thought*, 27: 27–49.

Finlay, C. (2007), *Hume's Social Philosophy*, London: Continuum.

Fitzgibbons, A. (1995), *Adam Smith's System of Liberty*, Oxford: Clarendon Press.

Fleischacker, S. (1999), *A Third Concept of Liberty: Judgment and Freedom in Kant and Adam Smith*, Princeton: Princeton University Press.

Fleischacker, S. (2004), *A Philosophical Companion to the Wealth of Nations*, Princeton: Princeton University Press.

Fleischacker, S. (2013), 'Smith and Equality' in C. Berry, M. Paganelli and C. Smith (eds), *The Oxford Handbook of Adam Smith*, Oxford: Oxford University Press, pp. 486–500.

Fletcher, F. (1939), *Montesquieu and English Politics 1750–1800*, London: E. Arnold.

Flew, A. (1961), *Hume's Philosophy of Belief*, London: Routledge.

Flynn, P. (ed.) (1992), *Enlightened Scotland: A Study and Selection of Scottish Philosophical Prose from the Eighteenth and Early Nineteenth Centuries*, Edinburgh: Scottish Academic Press.

Forbes, D. (1954), 'Scientific Whiggism: Adam Smith and John Millar', *Cambridge Journal*, 7: 643–70.

Forbes, D. (1966), Introduction to *Adam Ferguson, Essay on History of Civil Society*, Edinburgh: Edinburgh University Press, pp. xiii–vli.

Forbes, D. (1967), 'Adam Ferguson and the Idea of Community' in D. Young (ed.), *Edinburgh in the Age of Reason*, Edinburgh: Edinburgh University Press, pp. 40–7.

Forbes, D. (1970), Introduction to *David Hume: The History of Great Britain*, Harmondsworth: Penguin.

Forbes, D. (1975a), *Hume's Philosophical Politics*, Cambridge: Cambridge University Press.

Forbes, D. (1975b), 'Sceptical Whiggism, commerce and liberty' in A. Skinner and T. Wilson (eds), *Essays on Adam Smith*, Oxford: Oxford University Press, pp. 179–201.

Force, P. (2003), *Self-Interest before Smith*, Cambridge: Cambridge University Press.

Forman-Barzilai, F. (2007), 'Smith on "connexion" culture and judgment', in E. Schliesser and L. Montes (eds), *New Voices on Smith*, London: Routledge, pp. 89–114.

Forman-Barzilai, F. (2010), *Adam Smith and the Circles of Sympathy*, Cambridge: Cambridge University Press.

Fortini Brown, P. (2004), *Private Lives in Renaissance Venice*, New Haven: Yale University Press.

Foucault, M. (2010), *The Order of Things*, London: Tavistock.

Frank, R. (2000), *Luxury Fever: Money and Happiness in an Era of Excess*, Princeton: Princeton University Press.

Frankel, C. (1948), *Faith of Reason*, New York: Octagon Books.

Frazer, M. (2010), *The Enlightenment of Sympathy*, Oxford: Oxford University Press.

Funke, O. (1934), *Englische Sprachphilosophie im späteren 18, Jahrhundert*, Bern: Franke.

Furniss, E. (1920), *The Position of the Laborer in a System of Nationalism*, Boston: Houghton Mifflin.

Garrett, D. (1997), *Cognition and Commitment in Hume's Philosophy*, Oxford: Oxford University Press.

Gates, W. (1967), 'The Spread of Ibn Khaldun's Ideas on Climate and Culture', *Journal of the History of Ideas*, 28: 415–22.

Gatch, L. (1996), 'To Redeem Metal with Paper: David Hume's Philosophy of Money', *Hume Studies*, 22: 169–91.

Gautier, C. (ed.) (2001), *Hume et la concept de sociètè civile*, Paris: Presses Universitaires de France.

Gay, P (1966, 1969), *The Enlightenment*, 2 vols, London: Weidenfeld and Nicholson.

Geertz, C. (1975), 'The Impact of the Concept of Culture on the Concept of Man', in his *The Interpretation of Culture*, London: Hutcheson, pp. 33–54.

Geertz, C. (1983), *Local Knowledge: Further Essays in Interpretative Anthropology*, New York: Basic Books.

Gellner, E. (1994), *Conditions of Liberty: Civil Society and its Rivals*, Harmondsworth: Penguin.

Geuna, M. (2002), 'Republicanism and Commercial Society in the Scottish Enlightenment: The case of Adam Ferguson', in M. v. Gelderen and

Q. Skinner (eds), *Republicanism, a Shared European Heritage*, vol. II Cambridge: Cambridge University Press, pp. 177–95.

Giarrizzo G, (1962), *Hume politico e storico*, Torino: Einaudi.

Gierke, O. (1934), *Natural Law and the Theory of Society 1500–1800*, 2 vols, tr. E. Barker, Cambridge: Cambridge University Press.

Glacken, C. (1967), *Traces on the Rhodian Shore: Nature and Culture in Western Thought from Ancient Times to the End of the Eighteenth Century*, Berkeley: University of California Press.

Golinsky, J. (2007), *British Weather and the Climate of the Enlightenment*, Chicago: University of Chicago Press.

Gonzalez, A. (2013), *Sociedad Civil y Normatividad: La Teoría de David Hume*, Madrid: Universidad de Navarra, Instituto Cultura y Sociedad.

Graham, C. (2011), *In Pursuit of Happiness*, Washington: Brookings Institution Press.

Graham, G. (2014), 'Francis Hutcheson and Adam Ferguson on Sociability', *History of Philosophy Quarterly*, 31: 317–29.

Graham, H. (1901), *Scottish Men of Letters in the Eighteenth Century*, London: A. & C. Black.

Graham, H. (1906), *The Social Life of Scotland in the Eighteenth Century*, London: A. & C. Black.

Greco, L. (2017), 'A powerless conscience: passions, sympathy and society in Hume', *British Journal for the History of Philosophy*, 25: 1–18.

Gregoriev, S. (2015), 'Hume and the Historicity of Human Nature', *Journal of the Philosophy of History*, 9: 118–39.

Griffin, M. (1976), *Seneca: A Philosopher in Politics*, Oxford: Clarendon Press.

Griswold, C. (1999), *Adam Smith and the Virtues of Enlightenment*, Cambridge: Cambridge University Press.

Griswold, C. (2010), 'Smith and Rousseau in Dialogue', *Adam Smith Review*, 8: 59–84.

Griswold, C. (2017), *Jean-Jacques Rousseau and Adam Smith: A Philosophical Encounter*, Abingdon: Routledge.

Guthrie, D. (1950), 'William Cullen and his Times', in A. Kent (ed.), *An Eighteenth-Century Lectureship in Chemistry*, Glasgow: Jackson, pp. 49–65.

Haakonssen, K. (1981), *The Science of a Legislator: The Natural Jurisprudence of David Hume and Adam Smith*, Cambridge: Cambridge University Press.

Haakonssen, K. (1996), *Natural Law and Moral Philosophy*, Cambridge: Cambridge University Press.

Haakonssen, K. (ed.) (1998), *Adam Smith*, Aldershot: Ashgate Publishing.

Habermas, J. (1992), *The Structural Transformation of the Public Sphere*, tr. T. Burger, Cambridge, MA: MIT Press.

Hall, J. (ed.) (1995), *Civil Society: Theory, History, Comparison*, Cambridge: Polity Press.

Hamilton, H. (1963), *The Economic History of Scotland in the Eighteenth Century*, Oxford: Oxford University Press.

Hamowy, R. (1987), *The Scottish Enlightenment and the Theory of Spontaneous Order*, Carbondale: University of Southern Illinois Press.

Hampshire, S. (1965), *Thought and Action*, London: Chatto & Windus.

Hampson, N. (1968), *The Enlightenment*, Harmondsworth: Penguin.

Hanley, R. (2007), 'Adam Smith, Aristotle and virtue ethics', in E. Schliesser and L. Montes (eds), *New Voices on Smith*, London: Routledge, pp. 17–39.

Hanley, R. (2008a), 'Enlightened Nation Building: The "Science of the Legislator" in Adam Smith and Rousseau', *American Journal of Political Science*, 52: 219–34.

Hanley, R. (2008b), 'Commerce and Corruption: Rousseau's Diagnosis and Adam Smith's Cure', *European Journal of Political Theory*, 7: 137–58.

Hanley, R. (2009), *Adam Smith and the Character of Virtue*, Cambridge: Cambridge University Press.

Hanley, R. (2010), 'Scepticism and Naturalism in Adam Smith', *Adam Smith Review*, 5: 198–212.

Hanley, R. (2013), 'Adam Smith and Virtue' in C. Berry, M. Paganelli and C. Smith (eds), *The Oxford Handbook of Adam Smith*, Oxford: Oxford University Press, pp. 219–40.

Hardie, W. (1968), *Aristotle's Ethical Theory*, Oxford: Clarendon Press.

Hardin, R. (2007), *David Hume: Moral and Political Theory*, Oxford: Oxford University Press.

Harkin, M. (2013), 'Smith on Women' in C. Berry, M. Paganelli and C. Smith (eds), *The Oxford Handbook of Adam Smith*, Oxford: Oxford University Press, pp. 501–20.

Harpham, E. (1984), 'Liberalism, Civic Humanism and the Case of Adam Smith', *American Political Science Review*, 80: 764–74.

Harré, R. (1993), *Social Being*, 2nd edn, Oxford: Blackwell.

Harris, J. (2007), 'Hume's Four Essays on Happiness', in E. Mazza and E. Ronchetti (eds), *New Essays on Hume*, Milano: FrancoAngeli, pp. 23–35.

Harris, J. (2011), 'Reid and Hume on the possibility of character', in T. Ahnert and S. Manning (eds), *Character, Self and Sociability in the Scottish Enlightenment*, New York: Palgrave Macmillan, pp. 31–47.

Harris, J. (2015), *David Hume: An Intellectual Biography*, Cambridge: Cambridge University Press.

Harte, N. (1976), 'State control of Dress and Social Change in Pre-Industrial England', in D. Coleman and A. John (eds), *Trade, Government and Economy in Pre-Industrial England*, London: Weidenfeld & Nicolson, pp. 132–65.

Havel, V. (1990), *Disturbing the Peace*, tr. P. Wilson, London: Faber & Faber.

Hayek, F. (1967), *Studies in Philosophy, Politics and Economics*, London: Routledge.

Hayek, F. (1978), *New Studies in Philosophy, Politics and Economics*, London: Routledge.

Hazard, P. (1964), *The European Mind, 1680–1715*, tr. J. L. May, Harmondsworth: Penguin.

Hazard, P. (1965), *European Thought in the Eighteenth Century*, tr. J. L. May, Harmondsworth: Penguin.

Hearnshaw, F. (1933), *Conservatism in England*, London: Macmillan.

Heath, E. and V. Merolle (eds) (2008, 2009), *Adam Ferguson: A Reassessment*, 2 vols, London: Pickering & Chatto.

Henderson, W. (2010), *The Origins of David Hume's Economics*, London: Routledge.

Herdt, J. (1997), *Religion and Faction in Hume's Moral Philosophy*, Cambridge: Cambridge University Press.

Herdt, J. (2013), 'Artificial Lives, Providential History and the Apparent Limits of Sympathetic Understanding' in M. Spencer (ed.), *David Hume: Historical Thinker, Historical Writer*, University Park: Pennsylvania State University Press, pp. 37–59.

Hetherington, N. (1983), 'Isaac Newton's Influence on Adam Smith's Natural Laws in Economics', *Journal of the History of Ideas*, 44: 497–505.

Heydt, C. (2007), 'Relations of Literature and Philosophical Purpose in Hume's Four Essays on Happiness', *Hume Studies*, 33: 3–19.

Hexter, J. (1977), 'Review Essay of J. Pocock, "The Machiavellian moment"', *History and Theory*, 16: 306–37.

Hill, J. (2017), *Adam Ferguson and Ethical Integrity*, Lanham: Lexington Books.

Hill, L. (2006), *The Passionate Society: The Social, Political and Moral Thought of Adam Ferguson*, Dordrecht: Springer.

Hill, M. and W. Montag (2015), *The Other Adam Smith*, Stanford: Stanford University Press.

Himmelfarb, G. (1984), *The Idea of Poverty: England in the Early Industrial Age*, London: Faber & Faber.

Hirschman, A. (1977), *The Passions and the Interests*, Princeton: Princeton University Press.

Hirschman, N. (2000), 'Sympathy, Empathy and Obligation: A Feminist Rereading' in A. Jacobson (ed.), *Feminist Interpretations of David Hume*, University Park: Penn State Press, pp. 174–93.

Hollander, S. (1977), 'Adam Smith and the Self-Interest Axiom', *The Journal of Law and Economics*, 20: 133–52.

Homiak, M. (2000), 'Hume's Ethics: Ancient or Modern?', *Pacific Philosophical Quarterly*, 81: 215–36.

Hont, I. (1983), 'The "Rich country-Poor country" Debate in Scottish Classical Political Economy', in I. Hont and M. Ignatieff (eds), *Wealth and Virtue*, Cambridge: Cambridge University Press, pp. 271–316.

Hont, I. (2008), 'The "Rich country-Poor country" revisited', in C. Wennerlind and M. Schabas (eds), *David Hume's Political Economy*, London: Routledge, pp. 243–321.

Hont, I. (2015), *Politics in Commercial Society: Rousseau and Smith*, Cambridge, MA: Harvard University Press.

Hont, I. and M. Ignatieff (1983), 'Needs and Justice in the Wealth of Nations', in I. Hont and M. Ignatieff (eds), *Wealth and Virtue*, Cambridge: Cambridge University Press, pp. 1–44.

Hook, A. and R. Sher (eds) (1995), *The Glasgow Enlightenment*, East Linton: Tuckwell Press.

Hope, V. (1989), *Virtue by Consensus*, Oxford: Clarendon Press.

Hope, V. (ed.) (1984), *The Philosophers of the Scottish Enlightenment*, Edinburgh: Edinburgh University Press.

Höpfl, H. (1978), 'From Savage to Scotsman: Conjectural History in the Scottish Enlightenment', *Journal of British Studies*, 7: 20–40.

Howell, W. (1971), *Eighteenth-Century British Logic and Rhetoric*, Princeton: Princeton University Press.

Hrdy, S. (1999), *Mother Nature: Natural Selection and the Female of the Species*, London: Chatto & Windus.

Hubert, R. (1923), *Les Sciences Sociales dans l'Encyclopédie*, Paris: Alcan.

Hughes, D. (1983), 'Sumptuary Laws and Social Relations in Renaissance Italy' in J. Bossy (ed.), *Disputes and Settlements: Law and Human Relations in the West* Cambridge: Cambridge University Press, pp. 69–99.

Hundert, E. (1974), 'The Achievement Motive in Hume's Political Economy', *Journal of the History of Ideas*, 35: 139–43.

Hunt, A. (1996), *Governance of the Consuming Passions*, London: Macmillan.

Huntingdon, S. (1957), 'Conservatism as an Ideology', *American Political Science Review*, 51: 454–73.

Hurlock, E. (1962), 'Sumptuary Law', in M. Roach and J. Eicher (eds), *Dress, Adornment and the Social Order*, New York: Wiley, pp. 295–301.

Hursthouse, R. (1999), 'Virtue Ethics and Human Nature', *Hume Studies*, 25: 67–82.

Hutchinson, D. (1986), *The Virtues of Aristotle*, London: Routledge & Kegan Paul.

Hutchison, T. (1988), *Before Adam Smith: The Emergence of Political Economy, 1662–1776*, Oxford: Blackwell.

Ignatieff, M. (1983), 'John Millar and Individualism in the *Wealth of Nations*', in I. Hont and M. Ignatieff (eds), *Wealth and Virtue*, pp. 317–44.

Ignatieff, M. (1984), *The Needs of Strangers*, London: Chatto & Windus.

Immerwahr, J. (1989), 'Hume's Essays on Happiness', *Hume Studies*, 15: 307–24.

Israel, J. (2001), *Radical Enlightenment: Philosophy and the Making of Modernity, 1650–1750*, Oxford: Oxford University Press.

Jacobson, A. (ed.) (2000), *Feminist Interpretations of David Hume*, University Park: Penn State Press.

Janovic, V. (2010), *Confronting the Climate: British Airs and the Making of the Environment*, New York: Palgrave Macmillan.

Jespersen, O. (1922), *Language, its Origin, Nature & Development*, London: Allen & Unwin.

Jessop, T. (1966), 'Some Misunderstandings of Hume', in V.Chappell (ed.), *Hume*, London: Macmillan, pp. 35–52.

Jones, P. (ed.) (1988), *Philosophy and Science in the Scottish Enlightenment*, Edinburgh: John Donald.

Jones, P. (ed.) (1989), *The Science of Man in the Scottish Enlightenment*, Edinburgh: Edinburgh University Press.

Jost, J. (2009), 'Hume's Four Philosophers: Recreating the Treatise of Human Nature', *Modern Intellectual History*, 6: 1–25.

Juliard, P. (1970), *Philosophies of Language in Eighteenth-Century France*, The Hague: Mouton.

Kallich, M. (1970), *The Association of Ideas and Critical Theory in Eighteenth-Century England*, The Hague: Mouton.

Keane, J. (1988), 'Despotism and Democracy', in J. Keane (ed.), *Civil Society and the State: New European Perspectives*, London: Verso, pp. 35–71.

Kemp Smith, N. [1941] (1964), *The Philosophy of David Hume*, London: Macmillan.

Kennedy, G. (2013), 'Adam Smith on Religion', in C. Berry, M. Paganelli and C. Smith (eds), *The Oxford Handbook of Adam Smith*, Oxford: Oxford University Press, pp. 464–84.

Kettler, D. (1965), *The Social and Political Thought of Adam Ferguson*, Columbus: Ohio State University Press.

Kettler, D. (1977), 'History and Theory in Ferguson's Essay on the History of Civil Society', *Political Theory*, 5: 437–50.

Kidd, C. (1993), *Subverting Scotland's Past*, Cambridge: Cambridge University Press.

Kidd, C. (2005), 'Lord Dacre and the Politics of the Scottish Enlightenment', *The Scottish Historical Review*, 84: 202–20.

Kidd, C. (2014), 'The Phillipsonian Enlightenment', *Modern Intellectual History*, 11: 175–90.

Killerby, C. (2002), *Sumptuary Law in Italy 1200–1500*, Oxford: Clarendon Press.

Kim, K. (2012), 'Adam Smith's "History of Astronomy" and view of science', *Cambridge Journal of Economics*, 36: 798–820.

Kirk, R. (1960), *The Conservative Mind*, rev. edn, Chicago: Gateway.

Knight, I. (1968), *Geometric Spirit: The Abbé Condillac and the French Enlightenment,* New Haven: Yale University Press.

Knight, W. (1900), *Monboddo and some of his Contemporaries,* London: John Murray.

Knowles, D. (2000), 'Conservative Utilitarianism', *Utilitas*, 12: 155–75.

Kuhn, T. (1970), *The Structure of Scientific Revolutions*, 2nd edn, Chicago: University of Chicago Press.

Kuhn, T. (1977), *The Essential Tension*, Chicago: University of Chicago Press.

Labriolle-Rutherford, M. (1963), 'L'évolution de la notion Luxe jusqu'à la Révolution', *Voltaire Studies*, 26: 1025–36.

Lacoste, L. (1976), 'The Consistency of Hume's Position Concerning Women', *Dialogue,* 15: 425–40.

Land, S. (1976), 'Lord Monboddo and the Theory of Syntax in the Late Eighteenth Century', *Journal of the History of Ideas*, 37: 423–40.

Land, S. (1977), 'Adam Smith's "Considerations Concerning the First Formation of Languages"', *Journal of the History of Ideas*, 38: 677–90.

Lane, R. (2000), *The Loss of Happiness in Market Democracies*, New Haven: Yale University Press.

Laursen, C. (1992), *The Politics of Skepticism in the Ancients, Montaigne, Hume and Kant,* Leiden: Brill.

Layard, R. (2006), *Happiness*, London: Penguin.

LeFlamanc, A. (1934), *Les Utopies Prerévolutionnaires*, Paris: Le Grand.

Lehmann, W. (1930), *Adam Ferguson and the Beginnings of Modern Sociology*, New York: Columbia University Press.

Lehmann, W. (1952), 'John Millar – Historical Sociologist', *British Journal of Sociology*, 2: 30–46.

Lehmann, W. (1971), *Henry Home, Lord Kames and the Scottish Enlightenment*, The Hague: Nijhoff.

Levey, A. (1998), 'Under Constraint: Chastity and Modesty in Hume', *Hume Studies*, 23: 213–26.

Lindgren, R. (1969), 'Adam Smith's Theory of Inquiry', *Journal of Political Economy*, 77: 897–915.

Lindgren, R. (1973), *The Social Philosophy of Adam Smith*, The Hague: Nijhoff.

Livesey, J. (2009), *Civil Society and Empire: Ireland, Scotland and the Eighteenth-Century Atlantic World*, New Haven: Yale University Press.

Livingston, D. (1984), *Hume's Philosophy of Common Life*, Chicago: University of Chicago Press.

Livingston, D. (1988), *Philosophical Melancholy and Delirium*, Chicago: University of Chicago Press.

Livingston, D. (1995), 'On Hume's Conservatism', *Hume Studies*, 21: 151–64.

Longuet-Higgins, C. (1992), '"The History of Astronomy": a twentieth-century view', in P. Jones and A. Skinner (eds), *Adam Smith Reviewed*, Edinburgh: Edinburgh University Press, pp. 79–92.

Lothian, R. (1963), *Introduction to Adam Smith Lectures on Rhetoric and Belles-Lettres*, London: Nelson.

Lukes, S. (1971), 'Some Problems about Rationality', in B. Wilson (ed.), *Rationality*, New York: Harper Row, pp. 194–213.

Lukes, S. (1973), 'On the Social Determination of Truth', in R. Horton and R. Finnegan (eds), *Modes of Thought*, London: Faber & Faber, pp. 230–48.

McArthur, N. (2007), *David Hume's Political Theory*, Toronto: University of Toronto Press.

McClelland, J. (1989), *The Crowd and the Mob*, London: Unwin Hyman.

McCloskey, D. N. (2016), *Bourgeois Equality*, Chicago: University of Chicago Press.

McDaniel, I. (2013), *Adam Ferguson in the Scottish Enlightenment: The Roman Past and Europe's Future*, Cambridge, MA: Harvard University Press.

McDowell, G. (1983), 'Commerce, Virtue and Politics: Adam Ferguson's Constitutionalism', *Review of Politics*, 45: 536–52.

McElroy, D. (1969), *Scotland's Age of Improvement*, Washington: Washington State University Press.

Macfarlane, A. (2001), 'David Hume and the Political Economy of Agrarian Civilization', *History of European Ideas*, 27: 79–91

MacFie, A. (1967), *The Individual in Society*, London: G. Allen & Unwin.

MacIntyre, A. (1985), *After Virtue*, 2nd edn, London: Duckworth.

Mackie, J. (1980), *Hume's Moral Theory*, London: Routledge & Kegan Paul.

McMahon, D. (2006), *Happiness: A History*, New York: Grove Press.

MacRae, D. (1969), 'Adam Ferguson', in T. Raison (ed.), *Founding Fathers of Sociology*, Harmondsworth: Penguin, pp. 17–26.

Malherbe, M. (1995), 'Hume's "Natural History of Religion"', *Hume Studies*, 21: 255–74.

Mannheim, K. (1953), 'Conservative Thought' in P. Kecskemeti (ed.), *Essays on Sociology and Social Psychology*, London: Routledge, pp. 76–164.

Manuel, F. (1959), *The Eighteenth Century Confronts the Gods*, Cambridge, MA: Harvard University Press.

Markus, T. (1982), 'Buildings for the Sad, the Bad and the Mad in Urban Scotland, 1780–1830' in T. Markus (ed.), *Order in Space: Architectural Form and its Context in the Scottish Enlightenment*, Edinburgh: Mainstream, pp. 25–114.

Matson, E. (forthcoming), 'Smith's Humean Irony about Science', *Adam Smith Review*.

Maza, S. (1997), 'Luxury, Morality and Social Change', *Journal of Modern History*, 69: 199–229.

Medick, H. (1973), *Naturzustand und Naturgeschichte der bürgerlichen Gesellschaft*, Göttingen: Vandenhoeck & Ruprecht.

Medick, H. and A. Leppert-Fögen (1974), 'Frühe Sozialwissenschaft als Ideologie des kleines Bürgertums', in H.-U. Wehler (ed.), *Sozialgeschichte Heute*, Göttingen: Vandenhoeck & Ruprecht, pp. 122–48.

Medick, H. and A. Leppert-Fögen (1988), *Einleitung: A. Ferguson Versuch über die Geschichte der Bürgerlichen Gesellschaft*, Frankfurt-am-Main: Suhrkamp.

Meek, R. (1954), 'The Scottish Contribution to Marxist Sociology', in J. Saville (ed.), *Democracy and the Labour Movement*, London: Lawrence & Wishart, pp. 84–100

Meek, R. (1976), *Social Science and the Ignoble Savage,* Cambridge: Cambridge University Press.

Meek, R. (1977), *Smith, Marx and After,* London: Chapman and Hall.

Meinecke, F. (1946), *Die Entstehung des Historismus,* 2nd edn, Munich: Oldenbourg.

Merolle, V. (1994), *Saggio su Ferguson,* Rome: Gangemi Editore.

Merrill, T. (2015), *Hume and the Politics of Enlightenment,* Cambridge: Cambridge University Press.

Meyer, P. (1958), 'Hume and Voltaire as Historians', *Proceedings of Modern Language Association of America,* 73: 51–68.

Miller, D. (1991), *Philosophy and Ideology in Hume's Political Thought,* Oxford: Clarendon Press.

Miller, N. (2017), *John Millar and the Scottish Enlightenment: Family Life and World History,* Oxford: Voltaire Foundation.

Mills, R. (2016), 'Lord Kames's Analysis of the Natural Origins of Religion: The Essays on the Principles of Morality and Natural Religion (1751)', *Historical Research: The Bulletin of the Institute of Historical Research,* 89: 751–75.

Mills, R. (2018), 'William Falconer's Remarks on the Influence of Climate (1781) and the Study of Religion in Enlightenment England', *Intellectual History Review,* 28: 1–23.

Minowitz, P. (1993), *Profits, Priests and Princes: Adam Smith's Emancipation of Economics from Politics and Religion,* Stanford: Stanford University Press.

Mizuta, H. (1976), 'Moral Philosophy and Civil Society', in A. Skinner and T. Wilson (eds), *Essays on Adam Smith,* Oxford: Clarendon Press, pp. 114–31.

Mizuta, H. (2000), *Adam Smith's Library and Catalogue,* Oxford: Clarendon Press.

Montes, L. (2004), *Adam Smith in Context,* London: Palgrave.

Montes, L. (2009), 'Adam Smith on the Standing Army versus Militia Issue', in J. Young (ed.), *The Elgar Companion to Adam Smith,* Cheltenham: Elgar, pp. 315–34.

Montes, L. (2013), 'Newtonianism and Adam Smith', in C. Berry, M. Paganelli and C. Smith (eds), *The Oxford Handbook of Adam Smith,* Oxford: Oxford University Press, pp. 36–53.

Moore, J. (1979), 'The Social Background of Hume's Science of Human Nature', in D. Norton et al. (eds), *McGill Hume Studies,* San Diego: Austin Hill Press, pp. 23–41.

Moore, J. (1997), 'Hume's political science and the classical republican tradition', *Canadian Journal of Political Science*, 10: 809–39.

Moore, J. (2009), 'Montesquieu and the Scottish Enlightenment', in R. Kingston (ed.), *Montesquieu and his Legacy*, Albany: SUNY Press, pp. 179–95.

Moran, C. (2005), 'The Commerce of the Sexes: Gender and the Social Sphere in Scottish Enlightenment Accounts of Civil Society', in F. Trentmann (ed.), *Paradoxes of Civil Society*, rev. edn, New York: Berghahn, pp. 61–84.

Morrice, G. (ed.) (1977), *David Hume*, Edinburgh: Edinburgh University Press.

Mossner, E. (1954), *The Life of David Hume*, Austin: University of Texas Press.

Moscovici, S. (1956), 'À propos de quelques travaux d'Adam Smith sur l'histoire et la philosophie des sciences', *Revue d'Histoire des Sciences*, 9: 1–20.

Muller, J. (1995), *Adam Smith in his Time and Ours*, Princeton: Princeton University Press.

Muller, J. (ed.) (1997), *Conservatism: An Anthology of Social and Political Thought from David Hume to the Present*, Princeton: Princeton University Press.

Muller, M. (1875), *Lectures on the Science of Language*, 2 vols, 8th edn, London: Longmans Green.

Murdoch, A. (1980), *The People Above*, Edinburgh: John Donald.

Murphy, J. (1993), *The Moral Economy of Labor*, New Haven: Yale University Press.

Muzzarelli, M. and A. Campanini (eds) (2003), *Disciplinare il Lusso: La Legislazione Suntuaria in Italia e Europa tra Medioevo ed Eta Moderna*, Roma: Carocci.

Muzzarelli, M. (2009), 'Reconciling the Privilege of a Few with the Common Good: Sumptuary Laws in Medieval and Early Modern Europe', *Journal of Medieval and Early Modern Studies*, 39: 587–617.

Norton, D. et al. (eds) (1979), *McGill Hume Studies*, San Diego: Austin Hill Press.

Norton, D. (1982), *David Hume: Common-sense Moralist, Sceptical Metaphysician*, Princeton: Princeton University Press.

Noxon, J. (1973), *Hume's Philosophical Development*, Oxford: Oxford University Press.

Nussbaum, M. (1986), *The Fragility of Goodness*, Cambridge: Cambridge University Press.

Nyland, C. (2003), 'Smith, Stage Theory and the Status of Women', in

R. Dimand and C. Nyland (eds), *The Status of Women in Classical Economic Thought*, Aldershot: Elgar, pp. 86–107.

Oake, R. (1941), 'Montesquieu and Hume', *Modern Language Quarterly*, 2: 225–48.

Oakeshott, M. (1962), *Rationalism in Politics*, London: Methuen.

Oakeshott, M. (1975), *On Human Conduct*, Oxford: Clarendon Press.

Oakeshott, M. (1991), *Rationalism in Politics and Other Essays*, new and expanded edn, Indianapolis: Liberty Press.

O'Brien, M. (1981), *The Politics of Reproduction*, London: Routledge & Kegan Paul.

O'Brien, K. (1997), *Narratives of Enlightenment*, Cambridge: Cambridge University Press.

Okin, S. (1989), *Justice, Gender and the Family*, New York: Basic Books.

Olson, R. (1975), *Scottish Philosophy and British Physics 1750–1880*, Princeton: Princeton University Press.

Ophuls, W. (1996), 'Unsustainable Liberty, Sustainable Freedom', in D. Pirages (ed.), *Building Sustainable Societies*, New York: Sharpe, pp. 33–44.

Oslington, P. (ed.) (2011), *Adam Smith as a Theologian*, New York: Routledge.

O'Sullivan, N. (1976), *Conservatism*, London: Dent.

Otteson, J. (2002), *Adam's Smith's Marketplace of Morals*, Cambridge: Cambridge University Press.

Oswald, D. (1995), 'Metaphysical Beliefs and the Foundations of Smithian Political Economy', *History of Political Economy*, 27: 449–76.

Owen, D. (1999), *Hume's Reason*, Oxford: Oxford University Press.

Oz-Salzburger, F. (2001), 'Civil Society in the Scottish Enlightenment', in S. Kaviraj and S. Khilnani (eds), *Civil Society*, Cambridge: Cambridge University Press, pp. 58–83.

Pack, S. (1995), 'Theological (and Hence Economic) Implications of Adam Smith's "Principles which Lead and Direct Philosophical Enquiries"', *History of Political Economy*, 27: 289–307.

Pack, S. and E. Schliesser (2006), 'Smith's Humean critique of Hume's account of Justice', *Journal History of Philosophy*, 44: 47–63.

Pascal, R. (1938), 'Property and Society: The Scottish Historical School of the Eighteenth Century', *Modern Quarterly*, I: 167–79.

Pascal, R. (1953), *German Sturm und Drang*, Manchester: Manchester University Press.

Pearce, R. (1945), 'The Eighteenth Century Scottish Primitivists: Some Reconsiderations', *Journal of English Literary History*, 12: 203–20.

Phillips, M. Salber (2000), *Society and Sentiment: Genres of Historical*

Writing in Britain, 1740–1820, Princeton: Princeton University Press.

Phillipson, N. (1973a), 'Culture and Society in the Eighteenth-Century Province: The Case of Edinburgh and the Scottish Enlightenment', in L. Stone (ed.), *The University in Society*, Princeton: Princeton University Press, vol. 1, pp. 407–48.

Phillipson, N. (1973b), 'Towards a Definition of the Scottish Enlightenment' in P. Fritz and D. Williams (eds), *City and Society*, Toronto: Hakkert, pp. 125–47.

Phillipson, N. (1981), 'The Scottish Enlightenment' in R. Porter and M. Teich (eds), *The Enlightenment in National Context*, Cambridge: Cambridge University Press, pp. 19–40.

Phillipson, N. (1989), *Hume*, London: Weidenfeld & Nicolson.

Phillipson, N. (1997), 'Providence and progress: an introduction to the historical thought of William Robertson', in S. J. Brown (ed.), *William Robertson and the Expansion of Empire*, Cambridge: Cambridge University Press, pp. 55–73.

Phillipson, N. (2010), *Adam Smith: An Enlightened Life*, London: Allen Lane.

Phillipson, N. and R. Mitchison (eds) (1970), *Scotland in the Age of Improvement*, Edinburgh: Edinburgh University Press.

Pitson, A. (1993), 'The Nature of Humean Animals', *Hume Studies*, 19: 301–16.

Plank, F. (1992), 'Adam Smith: grammatical economist', in P. Jones and A. Skinner (eds), *Adam Smith Reviewed*, Edinburgh: Edinburgh University Press, pp. 21–55.

Pocock, J. (1957), *The Ancient Constitution and the Feudal Law*, Cambridge: Cambridge University Press.

Pocock, J. (1975), *The Machiavellian Moment*, Princeton: Princeton University Press.

Pocock, J. (1983), 'Cambridge paradigms and Scotch philosophers', in I. Hont and M. Ignatieff (eds), *Wealth and Virtue*, pp. 235–52.

Pocock, J. (1985), *Virtue, Commerce and History*, Cambridge: Cambridge University Press.

Pocock, J. (1999), *Narratives of Civil Government*, vol. 2 of *Barbarism and Religion*, Cambridge: Cambridge University Press.

Pocock, J. (2008), 'Historiography and Enlightenment: A View of their History', *Modern Intellectual History*, 5: 83–96.

Pollard, S. (1968), *The Idea of Progress*, London: Watts.

Pompa, L. (1990), *Human Nature and Historical Knowledge: Hume, Hegel and Vico*, Cambridge: Cambridge University Press.

Quinton, A. (1978), *The Politics of Imperfection*, London: Faber & Faber.

Rabb, T. (2006), *The Last Days of the Renaissance*, New York: Basic Books.

Rahmatian, A. (2015), *Lord Kames: Legal and Social Theorist*, Edinburgh: Edinburgh University Press.

Raphael, D. (1975), 'The Impartial Spectator', in A. Skinner and T. Wilson (eds), *Essays on Adam Smith*, Oxford: Clarendon Press, pp. 83–99.

Raphael, D. (1979), 'Adam Smith: Philosophy, Science and Social Science', in S. Brown (ed.), *Philosophers of the Enlightenment*, Brighton: Harvester Press, pp. 77–93.

Raphael, D. (1985), *Adam Smith*, Oxford: Oxford University Press.

Raphael, D. (1997), '"The True old Humean Philosophy" and its Influence on Adam Smith', in G. Morrice (ed.), *David Hume: Bicentenary Papers*, Edinburgh: Edinburgh University Press, pp. 23–38.

Raphael, D. (2007), *The Impartial Spectator*, Oxford: Oxford University Press.

Rasmussen, D. (2008), *The Problems and Promise of Commercial Society: Adam Smith's Response to Rousseau*, University Park: Pennsylvania State University Press.

Rasmussen, D. (2013), 'Adam Smith and Rousseau: Enlightenment and Counter- Enlightenment', in C. Berry, M. Paganelli and C. Smith (eds), *The Oxford Handbook of Adam Smith*, Oxford: Oxford University Press, pp. 54–76.

Rasmussen, D. (2014), *The Pragmatic Enlightenment*, Cambridge: Cambridge University Press.

Rawls, J. (1972), *A Theory of Justice*, Oxford: Oxford University Press.

Redman, D. (1995), 'Adam Smith and Isaac Newton', *Scottish Journal of Political Economy*, 40: 210–30.

Redman, D. (1997), *The Rise of Political Economy as a Science*, Cambridge, MA: MIT Press.

Redwood, J. (1976), *Reason, Ridicule and Religion*, London: Thames & Hudson.

Reisman, D. (1976), *Adam Smith's Sociological Economics*, London: Croom Helm.

Rendall, J. (ed.) (1978), *The Origins of the Scottish Enlightenment 1707–1776*, London: Macmillan.

Rendall, J. (1987), 'Virtue and Commerce: Women in the Making of Adam Smith's Political Economy', in E. Kennedy and S. Mendus (eds), *Women in Western Political Philosophy*, London: St Martin's Press, pp. 44–77.

Rendall, J. (1999), 'Clio, Mars and Minerva: The Scottish Enlightenment and the Writing of Women's History', in T. M. Devine and J. R. Young (eds), *Eighteenth-Century Scotland: New Perspectives*, East Linton: Tuckwell, pp. 134–51.

Riedel, M. (1962), 'Tradition und Revolution in Hegels "Philosophie des Rechts"', *Zeitschrift für Philosophische Forschung*, 16: 203–30.

Robbins, C. (1954), 'When it is that colonies may turn independent', *William and Mary Quarterly*, 11: 214–51.

Robertson, J. (1983), 'Scottish Political Economy Beyond the Civic Tradition: Government and Economic Development in the Wealth of Nations', *History of Political Thought*, 4: 451–82.

Robertson, J. (1985), *The Scottish Enlightenment and the Militia Issue*, Edinburgh: John Donald.

Robertson, J. (2005), *The Case for the Enlightenment*, Cambridge: Cambridge University Press.

Robins, R. (1967), *A Short History of Linguistics*, London: Longmans.

Roche, D. (1993), *La France des Lumières*, Paris: Fayard.

Rosen, F. (2003), *Classical Utilitarianism from Hume to Mill*, London: Routledge.

Ross, E. (1976), 'Mandeville, Melon and Voltaire: The origins of the luxury controversy in France', *Voltaire Studies*, 155: 1897–1912.

Ross, I. (1995), *The Life of Adam Smith*, 1st edn, Oxford: Clarendon Press.

Ross, I. (2010), ibid., 2nd edn.

Ross, I. (1972), *Lord Kames and the Scotland of his Day*, Oxford: Clarendon Press.

Ross, I. (2000), 'The Natural Theodicy of Lord Kames', in P. Wood (ed.), *New Essays on the Scottish Enlightenment*, Rochester: Rochester University Press, pp. 335–50.

Rothschild, E. (2006), *Economic Sentiments*, Cambridge, MA: Harvard University Press.

Rotwein, E. [1955] (1970), *David Hume Writings on Economics*, Madison: University of Wisconsin Press.

Rousseau, J.-J. (1960), *Politics and the Arts*, tr. A. Bloom, Ithaca: Cornell University Press.

Rousseau, J.-J. (1991), *Emile: or On Education*, tr. A. Bloom, Harmondsworth: Penguin.

Russell, D. (2012), *Happiness for Humans*, Oxford: Oxford University Press.

Rutherford, D. (2012), *In the Shadow of Adam Smith*, Basingstoke: Palgrave Macmillan.

Sabl, A. (2012), *Hume's Politics: Co-ordination and Crisis in the History of England*, Princeton: Princeton University Press.

Sakamoto, T. (2003), 'Hume's Political Economy as a System of Manners', in T. Sakamoto and H. Tanaka (eds), *The Rise of Political Economy in the Scottish Enlightenment*, London: Routledge, pp. 86–102.

Sakamoto, T. (2008), 'Hume's Economic Theory', in E. Radcliffe (ed.), *A Companion to Hume*, Oxford: Blackwell, pp. 373–87.

Salter, J. (1992), 'Adam Smith on Feudalism, Commerce and Slavery', *History of Political Thought*, 13: 219–42.

Sapir, T. (1907), 'Theological, Rational, Naturalist, in Herder's "Ursprung der Sprach"', *Modern Philology*, 5: 109–42.

Schabas, M. (2005), *The Natural Origins of Economics*, Chicago: University of Chicago Press.

Schabas, M. (2012), 'Hume on Economic Well-Being' in A. Bailey and D. O'Brien (eds), *The Continuum Companion to Hume*, London: Continuum, pp. 332–48.

Schliesser, E. (2008), 'Hume's Newtonianism and anti-Newtonianism', *The Stanford Encyclopedia of Philosophy*, winter 2008 edn, Edward N. Zalta (ed.). <https://plato.stanford.edu/archives/win2008/entries/hume-newton/>

Schliesser, E. (2005), 'Wonder in the Face of Scientific Revolutions: Adam Smith on Newton's "Proof" of Copernicanism', *British Journal for the History of Philosophy*, 13: 697–732.

Schmidt, C. (2003), *David Hume: Reason in History*, University Park: Pennsylvania State University Press.

Schmidt, C. (2013), 'Hume as a Philosopher of History', in M. Spencer (ed.), *David Hume: Historical Thinker, Historical Writer*, University Park: Pennsylvania State University Press, pp. 163–79.

Schmitz, R. (1948), *Hugh Blair*, New York: Twayne.

Schneider, L. (ed.) (1967), *The Scottish Moralists: On Human Nature and Society*, Chicago: University of Chicago Press.

Schor, J. (1998), *The Overspent American: Why We Want what We don't Need*, New York: Harper.

Schreyer, R. (1989), '"Pray what language did your wild couple speak, when first they met?" – Language and the Science of Man in the Scottish Enlightenment', in P. Jones (ed.), *The Science of Man in the Scottish Enlightenment*, Edinburgh: Edinburgh University Press, pp. 149–77.

Schumacher, E. (1971), *Small is Beautiful*, London: Blond & Briggs.

Schwoerer, L. (1974), *No Standing Armies: Anti-army Ideology in Seventeenth-century England*, Baltimore: Johns Hopkins University Press.

Scott, W. (1937), *Adam Smith as Student and Professor*, Glasgow: Jackson.

Sebastiani, S. (2013), *The Scottish Enlightenment: Race, Gender and the Limits of Progress*, Basingstoke: Palgrave Macmillan.

Seligman, A. (1992), *The Idea of Civil Society*, New York: Free Press.

Sen, A. (2010), 'Introduction', in R. Hanley (ed.), *The Theory of Moral Sentiments*, Harmondsworth: Penguin Classics, pp. vii–xxvi.

Shackleton, R. (1961), *Montesquieu: A Critical Biography*, Oxford: Oxford University. Press.

Shapiro, M. (1992), *Reading 'Adam Smith': Desire, History and Value*, London: Sage.

Shaw, J. (1983), *The Management of Scottish Society, 1707–64*, Edinburgh: John Donald.

Sheehan, B. (2010), *The Economics of Abundance*, Cheltenham: Elgar.

Shepherd, C. (1982),'Newtonianism in Scottish Universities in the Seventeenth Century', in R. Campbell and A.Skinner (eds), *The Origin and Nature of the Scottish Enlightenment*, Edinburgh: John Donald, pp. 65–85.

Sher, R. (1985), *Church and University in the Scottish Enlightenment*, Edinburgh: Edinburgh University Press.

Sher, R. (2015), ibid., 2nd edn with new preface, Edinburgh: Edinburgh University Press.

Sher, R. (1994), 'From Troglodytes to Americans: Montesquieu and the Scottish Enlightenment on Liberty, Virtue and Commerce', in D. Wootton (ed.), *Republicanism, Liberty and Commercial Society, 1649–1776*, Stanford: Stanford University Press, pp. 368–402.

Sher, R. (1995), 'Commerce, Religion in the Enlightenment in Eighteenth-Century Glasgow', in T. Devine and G. Jackson (eds), *Glasgow: Beginnings to 1830*, Manchester: Manchester University Press, pp. 312–59.

Shils, E (1997), *The Virtue of Civility: Selected Essays on Liberalism, Tradition and Civil Society*, ed. S. Grosby, Indianapolis: Liberty Press.

Shovlin, J. (2000), 'The Cultural Politics of Luxury in Eighteenth-Century France', *French Historical Studies*, 36: 577–606.

Shovlin, J. (2008), 'Hume's Political Discourses and the French Luxury Debate', in C. Wennerlind and M. Schabas (eds), *David Hume's Political Economy*, Abingdon: Routledge, pp. 203–22.

Siebert, D. (1990), *The Moral Animus of David Hume*, Newark: University of Delaware Press.

Skidelsky, R. and E. (2012), *How Much is Enough? Money and the Good Life*, London: Penguin.

Skinner, A. (1965), 'Economics and History – The Scottish Enlightenment', *Scottish Journal of Political Economy*, XII: 1–22.

Skinner, A. (1967), 'Natural History in the Age of Adam Smith', *Political Studies*, XIV: 32–48.

Skinner, A. (1974), 'Adam Smith: Science and the Role of the Imagination', in W. Todd (ed.), *Hume and the Enlightenment*, Edinburgh: Edinburgh University Press, pp. 164–88.

Skinner, A. (1975), 'Adam Smith: an Economic Interpretation of History', in T. Wilson and A. S. Skinner (eds), *Essays on Adam Smith*, Oxford: Clarendon Press, pp. 154–78.

Skinner, A. (1982), 'A Scottish Contribution to Marxist Sociology?', in I. Bradley and M. Howard (eds), *Classical and Marxian Political Economy*, London: Macmillan, pp. 79–114.

Skinner, A. (1993), ' David Hume: Principles of Political Economy' in D. Norton (ed.), *The Cambridge Companion to Hume*, Cambridge: Cambridge University Press, pp. 222–54.

Skinner, A. 1996), *A System of Social Science*, Oxford: Clarendon Press.

Skinner, Q. (1969), 'Meaning and Understanding in the History of Ideas', *History and Theory*, 9: 3–53.

Skinner, Q. (1978), *The Foundations of Modern Political Thought*, 2 vols, Cambridge: Cambridge University Press.

Slotkin, J. (ed.) (1965), *Readings in Early Anthropology*, London: Methuen.

Smith, C. (2006), *Adam Smith's Political Philosophy*, London: Routledge.

Smith, C. (2006b), 'Adam Ferguson and the Danger of Books', *Scottish Journal of Philosophy*, 4: 93–109.

Smith, C. (2008), 'Adam Ferguson and the Active Genius of Mankind', in E. Heath and V. Merolle (eds), *Adam Ferguson: A Reassessment*, vol.1, London: Pickering & Chatto, pp. 157–70, 217–22.

Smith, C. (2013), 'Adam Smith's "Collateral" Inquiry: Fashion and Morality in the Theory of Moral Sentiments and the Wealth of Nations', *History of Political Economy*, 45: 505–22.

Smith, C. (2016), 'Adam Smith's Views on Religion in Civil Society', in R. Lazaro and J. Seoane (eds), *The Changing Faces of Religion in XVIIIth Century Scotland*, Hildesheim: Ohms, pp. 47–71.

Smith, R. (1995), 'The Language of Human Nature', in C. Fox et al. (eds.), *Inventing Human Sciences*, Berkeley: University of California Press, pp. 88–111.

Smitten, J. (2017), *The Life of William Robertson*, Edinburgh: Edinburgh University Press.

Smout, T. C. (1969), *A History of the Scottish People 1560–1830*, London: Collins.

Snare, F. (1991), *Morals, Motivation and Convention: Hume's Influential Doctrines*, Cambridge: Cambridge University Press.

Sombart, W. (1913), *Luxus und Kapitalismus*, Munich: Duncker & Humblot.

Spadafora, D. (1990), *The Idea of Progress in Eighteenth-Century Britain*, New Haven: Yale University Press.

Stewart, J. (1963), *The Moral and Political Thought of David Hume*, New York: Columbia University Press.

Stewart, J. (1992), *Opinion and Reform in Hume's Political Philosophy*, Princeton: Princeton University Press.

Stewart, M. (ed.) (1990), *Studies in the Philosophy of the Scottish Enlightenment*, Oxford: Clarendon Press.

Stewart, M. 1996), 'The Scottish Enlightenment', in S. Brown (ed.), *British Philosophy in the Age of the Enlightenment*, London: Routledge, pp. 274–308.

Stockton, C. (1976), 'Economics and the Mechanism of Historical Progress in Hume's History', in D. Livingston and J. King (eds), *Hume: A Re-evaluation*, New York: Fordham University Press, pp. 296–330.

Strasser, H. (1976), *The Normative Structure of Sociology*, London: Routledge & Kegan Paul.

Struever, N. (ed.) (1995), *Language and the History of Thought*, Rochester: Rochester University Press.

Susato, R. (2015), *Hume's Sceptical Enlightenment*, Edinburgh: Edinburgh University Press.

Sutherland, S. (1977), 'Hume and the concept of pleasure' in G. Morrice (ed.), *David Hume*, Edinburgh: Edinburgh University Press, pp. 218–24.

Swingewood, A. (1970), 'Origins of Sociology: The Case of the Scottish Enlightenment', *British Journal of Sociology*, 21: 164–80.

Symons, D. (1979), *The Evolution of Human Sexuality*, Oxford: Oxford University Press.

Tanaka, S. (2003), 'The main themes of moral philosophy and the formation of political economy in Adam Smith', in T. Sakamoto and H. Tanaka (eds), *The Rise of Political Economy in the Scottish Enlightenment*, London: Routledge, pp. 134–49.

Taylor, C. (1989), *Sources of the Self*, Cambridge: Cambridge University Press.

Taylor, C. (1990), 'Modes of Civil Society', *Public Culture*, 3: 95–118.

Taylor, J. (2015), *Reflecting Subjects: Passion, Sympathy and Society in Hume's Philosophy*, Oxford: Oxford University Press.

Tegos, S. (2013), 'Adam Smith: Theorist of Corruption' in C. Berry, M. Paganelli and C. Smith (eds), *The Oxford Handbook of Adam Smith*, Oxford: Oxford University Press, pp. 353–71.

Teichgraeber, R. (1986), *'Free Trade' and Moral Philosophy*, Durham, NC: Duke University Press.

Thomson, H. (1965), 'Adam Smith's Philosophy of Science', *Quarterly Journal of Economics*, 79: 212–33.

Tolonen, M. (2013), *Mandeville and Hume: Anatomists of Civil Society*, Oxford: Voltaire Foundation.

Tooby, J. and L. Cosmides (1992), 'The Psychological Foundations of Culture', in J. Barkow, L. Cosmides and J. Tooby (eds), *The Adapted Mind: Evolutionary Psychology and the Generation of Culture*, New York: Oxford University Press, pp. 19–136.

Trevor-Roper, H. (1967), 'The Scottish Enlightenment', *Studies in Voltaire*, 58: 1635–58.

Trevor-Roper, H. (1977), 'The Scottish Enlightenment', *Blackwood's Magazine*, 322: 371–88.

Tribe, K. (1978), *Land, Labour and Economic Discourse*, London: Routledge & Kegan Paul.

Ulman, L. (1990), *The Minutes of the Aberdeen Philosophical Society 1758–1773*, Aberdeen: Aberdeen University Press.

Varty, J. (1997), 'Civic or Commercial? Adam Ferguson's concept of Civil Society', in R. Fine and S. Rai (eds), *Civil Society: Democratic Perspectives*, London: Frank Cass, pp. 29–48.

Veblen, T. (1909), 'The Limitations of Marginal Utility', *Journal of Political Economy*, 17: 620–36.

Veyne, P. (1976), *Le Pain et le Circque*, Paris: De Seuil.

Vickers, N. (2011), 'Aspects of Character and Sociability in Scottish Enlightenment Medicine' in T. Ahnert and S. Manning (eds), *Character, Self, and Sociability in the Scottish Enlightenment*, London: Palgrave, pp. 145–61.

Vincent, J. [1935] (1969), *Costume and Conduct in the Laws of Basel, Bern and Zurich 1370–1800*, New York: Greenwood Press.

Vlachos, G. (1955), *Essai sur la politique de Hume*, Paris: Institut Français Athènes.

Vogel, U. (1991), 'Political Philosophers and the Trouble with Polygamy: Patriarchal Reasoning in Modern Natural Law', *History of Political Thought*, 12: 229–51.

Waley, D. and T. Dean (2010), *The Italian City-Republics*, 4th edn, Harlow: Longman.

Walsh, W. (1975), 'The Constancy of Human Nature', in H. Lewis (ed.), *Contemporary British Philosophy*, London: Allen & Unwin.

Wellek, R. (1941), *Rise of English Literary History*, Chapel Hill: University of North Carolina Press.

Wences Simon, M. (2006), *Sociedad civil y virtud cívica en Adam Ferguson*, Madrid: Centro de Estudios Politicos y Constitucionales.

Wennerlind, C. (2001), 'The Link between David Hume's *A Treatise of Human Nature* and His Fiduciary Theory of Money', *History of Political Economy*, 33: 139–60.

Wennerlind, C. (2002), 'David Hume's Political Philosophy: A Theory of Commercial Modernization', *Hume Studies*, 28: 247–70.

Wennerlind, C. (2005), 'David Hume's Monetary Theory Revisited: Was He Really a Quantity Theorist and an Inflationist?', *Journal of Political Economy*, 113: 223–36.

Wennerlind, C. and M. Schabas (eds) (2008), *David Hume's Political Economy*, Abingdon: Routledge.

Wennerlind, C. and M. Schabas (2011), 'Hume on Money, Commerce and the Science of Economics', *Journal of Economic Perspectives*, 25: 217–29.

Werhane, P. (1991), *Adam Smith and his Legacy for Modern Capitalism*, New York: New York University Press.

Wertz, S. (1975), 'Hume, History and Human Nature', *Journal of the History of Ideas*, 36: 481–96.

West, E. (1969), 'The Political Economy of Alienation: Karl Marx and Adam Smith', *Oxford Economic Papers*, 21: 1–23.

Whelan, F. (1985), *Order and Artifice in Hume's Political Philosophy*, Princeton: Princeton University Press.

Williams, B. (1995), 'Evolution, Ethics and the Representation Problem', in his *Making Sense of Humanity*, Cambridge: Cambridge University Press, pp. 100–10.

Williams, B. (2004), *Truth and Truthfulness*, Princeton: Princeton University Press.

Wilson, E. (2014), *Seneca: A Life*, London: Allen Lane.

Wilson M. and M. Daly (1992), 'The Man who Mistook his Wife for a Chattel', in J. Barkow et al. (eds), *The Adapted Mind*, New York: Oxford University Press, pp. 289–322.

Wilson, T. and A. Skinner (eds) (1975), *Essays on Adam Smith*, Oxford: Clarendon Press.

Winch, D. (1978), *Adam Smith's Politics*, Cambridge: Cambridge University Press.

Winch, D. (1996), *Riches and Poverty*, Cambridge: Cambridge University Press.

Winch, P. (1958), *The Idea of Social Science*, London: Routledge.

Winch, P. (1970), 'On Understanding a Primitive Society', in B. Wilson (ed.), *Rationality*, New York: Harper & Row, pp. 78–111.

Wolin, S. (1954), 'Hume and Conservatism', *American Political Science Review*, 48: 999–1016.

Wokler, R. (1980), 'The ape debates in Enlightenment anthropology', *Voltaire Studies*, 192: 1164–75.

Wood, P. (1989), 'Natural History of Man', *History of Science*, 27: 89–123.

Wood, P. (1993), *The Aberdeen Enlightenment: The Arts Curriculum in the Eighteenth Century*, Aberdeen: Aberdeen University Press.

<Worlddatabaseofhappiness.eur.nl>

Wright, J. (1983), *The Sceptical Realism of David Hume*, Manchester: University of Manchester Press.

Yandell, K. (1990), *Hume's 'Inexplicable Mystery': His Views on Religion*, Philadelphia: Temple University Press.

Yeazell, R. (1991), *Fictions of Modesty*, Chicago: University of Chicago Press.

Young, D. (ed.) (1967), *Edinburgh in the Age of Reason*, Edinburgh: Edinburgh University Press.

Young, J. (1997), *Economics as a Moral Science: The Political Economy of Adam Smith*, Cheltenham: Edward Elgar.

Zachs, W. (1992), *Without Regard to Good Manners: A Biography of Gilbert Stuart*, Edinburgh: Edinburgh University Press.

Index

Note: pages in **bold** identify chapters which are the subject of the entry.